Places in Ontario

Mika Publishing Company gratefully acknowledge the assistance of the Canada Council and the Ontario Arts Council.

PLACES
in
ONTARIO

Their Name Origins
and History

Part II
F - M

by
Nick and Helma Mika

Mika Publishing Company
Belleville, Ontario
1981

IN PREPARATION

Vol. II Places in Ontario Part III N - Z

F
1056
.4
.M53
v. 2:2
F-M

244691

Places in Ontario
Copyright © Mika Publishing Company
ISBN 0-919303-48-X
FC3054.M54   917.13'003   C72-6372-3
F1050.4.M54

Printed and bound in Canada

INTRODUCTION

Part I of this ambitious undertaking, *Places in Ontario* (which began the second volume of Mika Publishing Company's even more ambitious *Encyclopedia of Ontario*) required four years of intensive investigation and correspondence to complete it. That volume covered places whose names begin with the letters A to E. Some material gathered then inevitably concerned places whose names put them later in the alphabet; but even so, it has taken almost another four years to compile the present work, covering F to M. After the success of the first Part, this Part II has been eagerly awaited. It has involved the labours of four persons handling correspondence, two special research assistants working in Belleville and other places, as well as the regular editorial work of the publishers. The result is the most thorough reference book in its field that has ever been produced in Canada, for any province.

Even so, many smaller places have had to be omitted. To those whose hometowns are missing, we understand their affectionate attachment and their disappointment. The publishers are regretful, and hope readers will understand that to include every village and hamlet in Ontario would have easily doubled the size of this already massive compilation.

For the scope of *Places in Ontario*, users are referred to the introductory matter in Part I. The present volume follows the same pattern, but opens up new worlds of fascination in toponymy and local history. It is remarkable, for example, how many places bear Old World names. Such, for example, is the Township of *Flanders* (Algoma District), named after the famous battlefield of two World Wars, in Belgium and France. Another is the Village of *Florence* (Lambton County), after the great Renaissance city in Italy, while *Hyde Park* (Middlesex County) is a community whose name recalls the famous park in London, England. Associations with North American Indians are enshrined in such names as *Hiawatha* (Algoma), a township named after Longfellow's epic poem and *Gogama* (Sudbury District), from an Indian word meaning 'jumping fish'. Even whimsy had a hand in the nomenclature of the province, as evidenced in such names as Honey Harbour (a Georgian Bay township), for the numerous bees encountered there by the early settlers, and the townships of Tiny, Tay, and Flos, all in Simcoe County, and all named in remembrance of the three pet dogs of Lady Sarah Maitland, wife of the Lieutenant-Governor of Upper Canada (1818-1828).

It will be seen that this is not only a standard work of reference, but also of such captivating interest for the local history buff that it makes excellent bedside reading as well!

William F.E. Morley

* * *

After more than four years of intensive research and writing to many places for information and verification of names, dates and events, Mika Publishing Company proudly presents Part Two of *Places in Ontario* covering localities starting with the letters F to M. As in Part One, maps and pictures of landmarks have been included to enhance the value of the book.

We are very grateful for the help which we received during those years of gathering information from numerous organizations, Mayors of Ontario towns and cities, Reeves of townships, and individual people throughout the Province who took the time to answer our letters, and who lent us books, pamphlets, old maps and old city directories. A sincere thank you to all.

Our research would not have been possible had it not been for the assistance received from the staff of the Public Archives of Canada. In particular, we wish to thank Lise Perron-Croteau who provided us with many of the books used as the sources for our historical sketches; Lise Gobeil, Denise L. Wagern who searched for and supplied us with pictures; and Betty Kidd who provided us with many of the maps shown in the book.

We like to say thank you also to the staff of the Ontario Geographic Names Board and the Ministry of Natural Resources for permitting us to obtain information regarding the origin of place names. And we would like to express our appreciation to Louise Roy of the Archives of the City of Ottawa; to Allen R. Kaiser of Parks Canada; to George A. Neville, Canadian Publications; and to James Anderson, Perth County Historical Board.

As usual, a great deal of our research was carried out at Special Collections, Douglas Library, Queen's University. The Curator of Special Collections, Mr. William F.E. Morley, and his staff provided us with valuable information and often gave us practical advice.

And last but not least we wish to thank our own Research Assistants, Elizabeth Ewan, Katie Revington-Olechowski, Paula Scott, Olive Maeers, Patricia Hunter and Carol Thompson.

F

FABBRO, geographic township, Algoma District
Position 46° 51' 82° 31'

The township, formerly designated as Township 5, was named in 1973 after J.J. Fabbro, the Mayor of the City of Sudbury. Situated in the southwest is large Rocky Island Lake and to the east is the Mississagi Wild River Provincial Park.

FACTOR, geographic township, Kenora District
Position 49° 56' 91° 25'

The township, established in 1945, was named after Samuel Factor, Member of Parliament for Toronto-Spadina. There are a few lakes in the township, the largest being Lake of Bays. A railway station, Umfreville, on the Canadian National Railway is located in the extreme southwest corner of this township.

FAIRBAIRN, geographic township, Sudbury District
Position 47° 02' 81° 31'

The southern boundary of the township was surveyed in 1888, the northern, eastern and western boundaries in 1911. The township was named after R.R. Fairbairn, former Deputy Minister of Public Works. Highway 144, just west of the township, links the area with the city of Sudbury to the southeast, and with Highway 101 and the town of Timmins to the north.

FAIRBANK, geographic township, Sudbury District
Position 46° 30' 81° 22'

Named for J.H. Fairbank, former MP for East Lambton, part of the area was annexed to the Township of Dowling in 1969, and in 1973 a portion was annexed to the Town of Walden.

Vermilion Lake covers most of the township's northern section. Fairbank Provincial Park with Fairbank Lake are located in the southwestern corner.

FAIRBANK PROVINCIAL PARK, Fairbank Township, Sudbury District
Position 46° 29' 81° 25'

This park, located 13 miles north of Highway 17 at Whitefish, is a 260-acre Provincial Recreation Park and provides facilities for

7

camping and daytime use.

Well-wooded with maple and white and yellow birch, southern deciduous forest trees unusual in the district north of Sudbury, the park is situated in an area where the main forest production is for pulp and paper industries.

Ontario Ministry of Natural Resources, Brochure.

FAIRLIE, geographic township, Kenora District, Patricia Portion
Position 51° 04′ 93° 59′

The township was named after a mining engineer of the Mining Corporation of Canada. Red Lake covers a large part of this township. The nearest communities are Balmertown, Red Lake and Couchenour to the east.

FAIRVIEW, community, West Zorra Township, Oxford County
Position 43° 17′ 80° 57′

Formerly in the Gore of Downie in Perth County before the reconstitution of Oxford County in 1975, this dispersed rural community was the site of a number of small local industries in the late nineteenth century. Picturesquely situated on the north branch of the Thames River 7 miles from Stratford, it is today mainly residential.

Among the first settlers in the area were John Thistle who emigrated from Ireland in 1830 and his countryman Samuel Monteith who arrived in 1834. Other early residents included William Bell, J.W. Monteith, and George Reincker.

By 1871 there was a flourishing cheese factory operated by Hugh Dempsy & Co. Richard A. Forrest was the community's postmaster and also ran the grocery store, while Roland Thompson served the 75 residents as blacksmith.

Fairview's population was approaching 100 by the turn of the century. By 1895 the community had a store, a cider mill, a cheese and butter factory, and a Presbyterian church. However, the early years of the twentieth century saw a decline in the settlement's prosperity and by 1908 the population had dropped to 30. Fairview has remained a small community.

H. Belden & Co.: *Historical Atlas of Perth County*, 1879.

FALCONBRIDGE, geographic township, Sudbury District
Position 46° 35′ 80° 45′

Named after William Glenholme Falconbridge, Justice of the High Court of Ontario and Chief Justice of the King's Bench, from 1900 to 1920, Falconbridge was erected into a municipal Township on January 1, 1958. On January 1, 1973 the township amalgamated with the Town of Coniston and the geographic township of Maclennan, as the Town of Nickel Centre. The area is located a few miles south of Wanapitei Lake, is served by the Canadian National Railways and is linked by roads to the nearby city of Sudbury.

FALCONER, geographic township, Nipissing District
Position 46° 09′ 80° 16′

Surveyed in the 1890's, the township was named after Professor Falconer, former President of the University of Toronto. The township lies a few miles south of Lake Nipissing's West Bay. Highway 64 passes along its northwestern boundary and links the area with major highways to Sudbury and North Bay.

FALLIS, geographic township, Thunder Bay District
Position 48° 54′ 90° 05′

This township may have been named after any one of the following Members of the Provincial Parliament: Wm. A. Fallis, MPP for Durham East in the 1890's; James R. Fallis, MPP for Peel in 1914; or Albert J. Fallis, MPP for Durham East in 1923. Trans-Canada Highway 17 and the CNR crosses this township at the northeast corner.

FALLON, geographic township, Timiskaming District
Position 48° 14′ 81° 00′

Situated southeast of Timmins, the township was named in honour of the late Bishop Fallon. Night Hawk River crosses the eastern part of this township. A dry weather road passing through the western section links the area with centres to the north and south.

FALLOWFIELD, community, Nepean Township, Regional Municipality of
Ottawa-Carleton
Position 45° 16′ 75° 50′

Situated about 15 miles southwest of Ottawa, this dispersed rural community of 296 (1971) was named in 1870 when the residents petitioned for a post office. A meeting was held to decide on a name and as Robert Wallace, a leading farmer in the district, had come to the meeting after a day spent summer fallowing the field behind his home, the name Fallowfield was suggested.

Fallowfield was first settled in the early nineteenth century. An old stone manor on Piety Hill near the community was built in 1827 by James Smith and is now one of the oldest houses in the township. Other early settlers included the Tierneys, O'Gradys, Wallaces, Fosters, O'Mearas, and Houlahans, most of them being from Ireland.

Following the establishment of a post office in Fallowfield in 1872 with F. O'Meara as postmaster, Paddy O'Meara opened a store and Mr. McNamara built a hotel to accommodate travellers on the Richmond Road. By 1881 the population of the community was about 100. Four churches, and two stores served the 120 residents by 1895.

Today this pretty community is largely residential. The post office has been closed and Richmond, six miles south, serves as the nearest business centre.

Near Fallowfield stands an escarpment known as Piety Hill on which the residents built their churches in the nineteenth century.

The first Roman Catholic service in the area was held in the house of Denis Tierney. In 1866 St. Patrick's Church was erected on Piety Hill by the community's large Roman Catholic population. A Methodist church was opened in 1870 and serves today as a United Church. Two more churches were built in the 1880's, a Presbyterian one in 1885 and a Methodist one in 1886.

One of Fallowfield's best-known residents was Rev. Dr. Aneas Macdonell Dawson, organizer of a Christian crusade and a religious and political leader in the nineteenth century. A red granite monument stands in his memory in St. Patrick's churchyard.

H. Belden & Co.: *Historical Atlas of Carleton County*, 1879.

Harry and Olive Walker, *Carleton Saga*, 1968.

FARADAY, township, Hastings County
Position 45° 00′ 77° 56′

The township, noted for its mineral wealth and scenic beauty, was named in honour of Professor Michael Faraday, a distinguished British scientist of the 1800's who developed the first dynamo and discovered electro-magnetic induction.

Faraday was one of twelve northern townships created by the

government in 1858 and attached to Hastings County. At that time the Hastings Colonization Road was being constructed northward from Madoc to attract settlers to the rugged northern parts of the county. Quintin Johnston had surveyed the area west of the road in 1857 and had reported that the site of present-day Bancroft was best suited for settlement in Faraday Township. He noted that the southern section was "rough, ridgy, stony, rocky and swampy", but that he had found iron ore deposits throughout the township and marble in the L'Amable Lake area.

The earliest settlements developed in the immediate vicinity of Bancroft and at L'Amable Lake. The latter was first known as Lamb's Lake, and here a grist and sawmill were in operation by the mid-1860's.

Among the township's pioneer settlers along the Hastings Road were Alfred Barker, James Cleak, Michael Gaffney, Philip Harding, Patrick Kelly, the Kennedy, Moore, O'Neil and Vance families. A number of families settled on the township's southern boundary forming the hamlet of Faraday. Here Henry Johnston operated an early mill. Another small settlement sprang up in the Paudash Lake area where a school was opened around 1878.

The settlement at Bancroft, situated as it was at the junction of the Hastings and Monck Colonization Roads and blessed with abundant water power from the falls in the York River, soon became the township's main centre. Known in the early days as York Mills, it was called York River when a post office was opened here in 1861. In the 1870's Senator Billa Flint, a Belleville merchant and one of the county's leading businessmen, erected a planing mill and a woollen mill at York River and succeeded in having the village's name changed to Bancroft after his wife, the former Phoebe Bancroft.

For a number of years Faraday was united with the neighbouring township of Dungannon. John Robertson Tait, a Scotsman who had settled at L'Amable, was the first reeve of the united townships. Faraday became an independent township in 1891 with Chester Davy as the first reeve.

The discovery in the 1940's of rich uranium deposits in the area led to a mining boom and accelerated growth. Arthur H. Shore who had staked a number of claims in the township formed a company known as the Faraday Uranium Mines. The first uranium precipitate was produced at the company's mill in the spring of 1957. One mining company active in Faraday erected two hundred homes for its workers on the township's western border at Cardiff. A declining world market, however, forced the closing of all of the township's uranium mines in the early 1960's. During the 1970's renewed interest in uranium saw the re-opening of Faraday Uranium Mines under the name of Madawaska Mines Ltd., which is part of an American-based firm (Federal Resources Ltd.) and currently employs approximately 400 people.

The township's 1,476 residents (1978) depend for their livelihood mostly on farming, lumbering and tourism. Some are employed at the village of Bancroft.

Gerald E. Boyce: *Historic Hastings*, 1967.

FARQUHAR, geographic township, Algoma District
Position 49° 15′ 84° 24′

Named after the late Col. Farquhar, Commanding Officer in the Canadian Forces. The Canadian National Railway with the railway point of Penhurst, crosses the southern part of the township. The nearest community is Hornpayne, about 20 miles to the west.

FARQUHAR, community, Usborne Township, Huron County
Position 43° 22′ 81° 22′

A dispersed rural community about 30 miles west of London, Farquhar was a flourishing settlement in the late nineteenth century. In the early 1860's most of the officials of Usborne Township, including the reeve, treasurer, and clerk had their homes here. A post office was opened in 1862 and William Edmond became postmaster.

By 1871 the community's population had increased to 150. Among Farquhar's early businessmen were C.J. Clark, merchant; John Ewen, weaver; James Davis, hotelkeeper; Thomas Friendship, wagonmaker; James Gullett, shoemaker; Mrs. Kay, storekeeper; and Robert Monteith, blacksmith and wagonmaker.

In 1895 the community had two churches, Methodist and Presbyterian, two stores, one hotel, and a blacksmith shop.

FARR, geographic township, Timiskaming District
Position 47° 49′ 80° 28′

Subdivided in 1907, the township commemorates the name of C.C. Farr of Haileybury. Farr, a Hudson Bay Co. factor at Fort Timiskaming, was the first to establish a business at Haileybury and it was he who gave the town its name. Highway 65 passing through the northeastern part of this township provides access to New Liskeard in the southeast, and in the north it connects with Highway 66 which, in turn, links the area with Kirkland Lake.

FARRINGTON, geographic township, Rainy River District
Position 48° 44′ 92° 51′

Surveyed in 1894, this township appears to have been named for a village in Devonshire, England. On the south the township is bordered by Rainy Lake with Seine Bay. Trans-Canada Highway 11 crosses the township with the CNR passing through the northeastern part.

FASKEN, geographic township, Timiskaming District
Position 48° 14′ 80° 52′

The township is located southeast of Timmins and bears the name of a Toronto family. Whitefish River crosses the township from south to north emptying into Night Hawk Lake.

FATHOM FIVE PROVINCIAL PARK, Georgian Bay, Bruce County
Position 45° 17' 81° 42'

This provincial park, unlike Ontario's many provincial parks, is the first underwater park, geared to an aquatic environment for visitors. This water-based park comprises an area of 11,655 hectares and includes several islands, mostly privately owned, except Flowerpot Island, part of Georgian Bay Islands National Park.

Off the tip of the Bruce Peninsula, it is reached by Highway 6 and at Tobermory is the Fathom Five Visitor Centre. This Natural Environment Park has much to offer. Glass-bottomed boats, boat tours, sea caves, and, because Fathom Five is essentially a day use park only, nearby Cyprus Lake Provincial Park offers camping, swimming, picnicking, and visitor services also. The Bruce Trail, beginning at Queenston, finishes at the Bruce Peninsula near Fathom Five Visitor Centre.

Ontario Ministry of Natural Resources, Brochure.

FAUQUIER, township, Cochrane District
Position 49° 23' 82° 10'

The township was named for a railroad contractor who built part of the transcontinental railway in the Cochrane District.

A large portion of this township is occupied by Remi Lake, with Remi Lake Provincial Park in the north. The CNR with Moonbeam Station and Trans-Canada Highway 11 crosses this township in the southern part.

FAUST, geographic township, Sudbury District
Position 47° 22' 82° 32'

The name of this township appears to have been taken from Gounod's opera *Faust*. Frechette and Shannon are the largest lakes in the area, and the Spanish River flows through the central part of the township. Faust is accessible only by waterways and a short stretch of dry weather road.

FAUTEUX, geographic township, Thunder Bay District
Position 50° 03' 86° 37'

Named in 1945 after the Hon. Gaspard Fauteux, Speaker of the House of Commons, the township is situated northeast of Geraldton. The Canadian National Railways' Longlac-Nakina branch runs along the western boundary of the township.

FAWCETT, geographic township, Sudbury District
Position 47° 31' 81° 06'

Named after surveyor and explorer Thomas Fawcett, the township is accessible by an unimproved road from Highway 560. The nearest community is Shining Tree in the neighbouring township to the west.

FAWN, geographic township, Sudbury District
Position 47° 38′ 82° 32′

The name origin of this township is not known, but it appears to have been inspired by an abundance of deer in the area. Secondary roads link the township with the surrounding lake districts. The nearest railway point is Sultan on the Canadian Pacific's route between Sudbury and Chapleau.

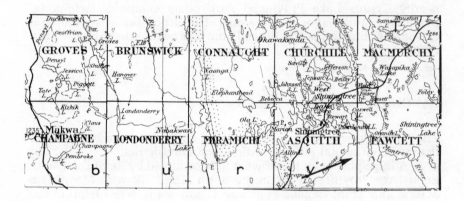

FAWN BAY, community, Rama and Mara Townships, Simcoe County
Position 44° 38′ 79° 21′

Lying on the eastern shore of Lake Couchiching above Lake Simcoe, this dispersed rural community was known as Fawn in the nineteenth century and was part of the old County of Ontario.

A post office was opened in Fawn in 1874 and Leonard Wilson, a storekeeper and carpenter was among the early residents. The Northern Railway was built through Rama and Mara Townships, to the east of Fawn Bay, in the late nineteenth century.

By 1895 Fawn had three stores and a Methodist church and its population had reached 300. Today it is mainly a residential community.

J.H. Beers & Co.: *Historical Atlas of Ontario County,* 1877.

FELL, geographic township, Nipissing District
Position 46° 35′ 79° 49′

This township was named after John Fell, MPP for Victoria North and East in the 1880's. Located north of Sturgeon Falls, the area is accessible by road. Tomiko Lake occupies much of the township's central southern section.

FENAGHVALE, community, Caledonia Township, Prescott County
Position 45° 28' 74° 49'

Formerly known as Caledonia Flats, the community was renamed after the Irish estate of the ancestors of the wife of John Downing, an early inhabitant of the settlement.

John Chesser, the first settler in Caledonia Township, arrived here about 1824, attracted by the rich pine forests in the area. However, he and most of his family died in the cholera plague of 1832. Other early settlers in 1836 were John Stephens, Robert Nicholson, William Bradley, and James Proudfoot, postmaster.

A school had been built by the 1870's and the first church services were held here. St. Paul's Church was erected in 1874 with Rev. Arthur Phillips as minister. A town hall was constructed in 1857.

Today Fenaghvale is a dispersed rural community.

C. Thomas: *History of the Counties of Argenteuil, Que. and Prescott, Ont.,* 1896.

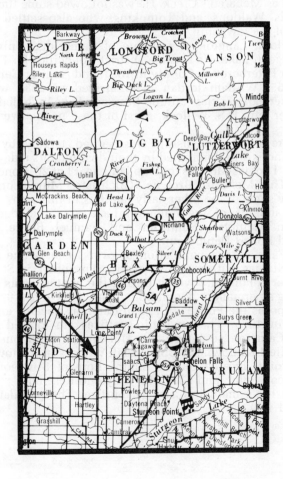

FENELON, township, Victoria County
Position 44° 30′ 78° 47′

Situated in the central part of Victoria County, about 25 miles northwest of Peterborough, Fenelon Township is named after Father Fenelon, a Sulpician missionary and explorer who founded a mission on the Bay of Quinte in 1668.

A large part of Fenelon's 54,995 acres is taken up by three lakes, Sturgeon, Cameron, and Balsam, and the area is known as a tourist's paradise. The land is hilly in the northern section, but in the south it is well suited for agricultural use. Highway 121 and the CN railway run through the eastern part of the township.

Evidence has been found of at least 16 Indian villages which once existed in what is now Fenelon Township. Although surveyed in 1822 there was little immigration into Fenelon until the 1830's. One of the earliest settlers was Angus McLaren, who took up land at what became known as McLaren's Creek. He was followed some time later by the Edwards, Waldons, and Tompkins, who also settled in the southern part of the township.

In 1833, John Langton, a graduate of Cambridge University, settled on Sturgeon Lake. He became District Councillor for Fenelon in 1842, MP for Peterborough County in 1851, and Auditor-General of Canada in 1855. William Jordan, who arrived in 1834 was his neighbour. Other early settlers around Sturgeon Lake included James Cook, E. Palmer, and D.S. Willock. Most of these people were Irish Protestants.

The centre of the township was settled largely by Scots Presbyterians and is still dominated by their descendants today. Isaac G. Moynes and Thomas Moynes took up land near Lot 20, Concession 5, in 1840. The McNabs, Browns, Gilchrists, Murchisons and McNevins were some of the other early families in this area.

Early inhabitants of the Cameron Lake area included John Bellsford, John McIntyre, Hamilton and Samuel Boyce, James Humphrey, and Robert Dennistoun.

Fenelon Falls with a population of over 1,600 is one of two incorporated villages within the township. The other is Sturgeon Point, a summer community which during the winter seems all but deserted having a permanent population of only forty-five (1979). For municipal purposes the Police Village of Cambray became a part of the township in 1975. The township's offices are located in the community of Cameron, so named after Duncan Cameron, one of the township's earliest landowners. Other small villages in the township are Pleasant Point, located on the south shore of Sturgeon Lake opposite Sturgeon Point, and Glenarm, Islay and Rosedale.

The township's main industry is tourism. The population in 1979 numbered 4,242.

Watson Kirkconnell: *County of Victoria Centennial History*, 1967.

Lower Wharf, Fenelon Falls, c. 1925

FENELON FALLS, village, Fenelon Township, Victoria County
Position 44° 32' 78° 45'

Located about 30 miles northwest of Peterborough on Cameron and Sturgeon Lakes, this village of some 1,600 people was named after Father Fenelon, a Sulpician missionary and explorer who founded a mission on the Bay of Quinte in 1668. He was the brother of Francis Fenelon, the famous 17th-century Archbishop of Cambrai, France.

James Wallis, an immigrant from Ireland, was the founder of the village. In 1834, in partnership with Robert Jamieson, he erected a sawmill at the waterfall which thunders down over a twenty-three foot cliff at the southeast end of Cameron Lake into a rocky gorge that half a mile distant opens up into Sturgeon Lake. The mill site was to form the nucleus of a settlement, at first known as Cameron Falls after Duncan Cameron, a Toronto banker who had once owned the land. In 1837 Wallis built a house for his family near the mill. He named it "Maryboro" after his home in Ireland. This historic old home is now the Fenelon Falls Museum. He is also commemorated by a historical plaque for his philanthropic deeds and his business ability in the establishment of the community.

By 1838, Wallis had opened a post office and added a grist mill and a community had begun to grow on the north bank of the river. Lumbering in those days was the settlement's main industry, and at one time there were three large sawmills in operation with an annual output of 18 million feet of cut white pine. The mills closed down when the huge pine forests of the area were depleted.

It was Wallis who donated the land for the settlement's first church in 1835, and he himself conducted the services until the first Anglican clergyman came in 1838.

The first steamboat of the Kawartha Lakes, the *Woodman*, arrived at Fenelon Falls in 1851. A year later James Wallis launched the *Ogemah*, built at Fenelon Falls to carry the lumber from his mill to Port Perry from whence it was teamed to the Lake Ontario port of Whitby. The entire village turned out to celebrate the launching and Mr. Wallis provided a free banquet for everyone.

Another pioneer settler on Sturgeon Lake for whom a historical plaque was raised, was John Langton. An MA of Cambridge University and noted author, he held several civic offices and became Auditor-General of Canada in 1855.

Fenelon Falls was incorporated as a village in 1875 and J.D. Smith became the first reeve. Village councillors were J.W. Fitzgerald, Joseph McArthur, William Jordan and Richard Jackson.

The 1870's brought the railway to the village greatly stimulating its further growth. A weekly newspaper, the *Fenelon Falls Gazette*, began publication in 1873. Founded by E.D. Hand, the paper still publishes to this day. By the 1880's the village had several stores, as well as a bank, library and hotel. The latter had been established in 1854 by William Martin as the Clifton House. Situated on a hill overlooking the Fenelon River, it was later known to tourists as the Kawartha House and eventually as the Alpine Inn.

In 1882 work was begun on the local section of the Trent Canal and four years later the Fenelon Falls locks were opened. In 1965 these old locks were replaced by modern hydraulic lift locks.

By the turn of the nineteenth century, the village had become an industrial centre. A former paper mill had been taken over by a chemical company producing alcohol and charcoal. There was a carriage works and a stave factory, and Sanderson's employed fifty men to manufacture chairs, tables, sashes, and doors. In later years the old grist mill which had stood beside the waterfall since the early days of the settlement was converted into a spinning mill.

Today, Allen Wood Products, manufacturers of the popular "Tinkertoy" is Fenelon Falls largest employer next to the tourist industry which remains the area's mainstay. The village population more than doubles each summer as tourists flock to this scenic part of Ontario and summer cottages in the vicinity are opened. The picturesque village of Fenelon Falls itself is often called the "Jewel of the Kawarthas".

Watson Kirkconnell: *County of Victoria Centennial History*, 1967.

FENTON, geographic township, Cochrane District
Position 49° 01′ 82° 32′

The township's boundaries were surveyed in 1919-20, and it appears that it was named for Wm. H. Fenton, the MPP for Bruce North at that time. The Saganash Lake is the largest body of water in the township, covering much of the central part. Keenoa Lake is situated in the southeast corner. Fenton is linked by road to all neighbouring townships.

FENWICK, geographic township, Algoma District
Position 46° 45′ 84° 25′

Surveyed in 1860, the township covers an area of over 18,400 acres of Indian lands on the shore of Goulais Bay, an inlet of Whitefish Bay, Lake Superior. Here the Goulais River empties into the Bay.

Communities within the township are Goulais Bay and Goulais River. The area is linked by Highway 17 to the city of Sault Ste. Marie, some 20 miles to the south.

FENWICK, part of the Town of Pelham, Regional Municipality of Niagara
Position 43° 01′ 79° 22′

Situated on the historic Canboro Road, Fenwick was originally a police village in Pelham Township, Welland County. In 1970 Lincoln and Welland Counties were amalgamated to form the Regional Municipality of Niagara, and Fenwick was joined to the village of Fonthill and the Township of Pelham and became a part of the newly created Town of Pelham. The town is situated in a rich market-gardening and fruit-producing area. Prior to annexation, the population of Fenwick was 737.

Fenwick was first settled in the early 1800's and then it was known as Diffin's Corners. In 1853 a post office opened in the settlement and the name officially changed to Fenwick — likely in honour of a British nobleman. Some time in the 1860's the settlement was incorporated as a police village.

Many of the original settlers in the area were United Empire Loyalists and Quakers who had emigrated from Pennsylvania and New Jersey. The Haney family appears to have been the first to settle in the Fenwick area in 1808. George Garner, an Englishman, also arrived in the settlement at an early date.

The early churches of Fenwick included the Episcopalian Methodist and the New Connexion Methodist. Today there are three churches in Fenwick, the United Church, whose history began in 1835, with the present building erected in 1900, the Church of Christ, and St. Ann's Roman Catholic Church. In 1955 the Polish congregation built the latter church and services were conducted in Polish.

Fenwick had two hotels, the usual small businesses necessary to serve a pioneering community, and later, an Oddfellow's Hall, and the Lion's Club, which, in more recent times officially opened Centennial Park.

Memorial School was named for the much respected Ed. Farr, an early school teacher.

Fenwick Fall Fair, under the auspices of Pelham Township Agricultural Society, was held in Fenwick in the middle 1850's. Excursion trains brought people from Fort Erie, Hamilton and Toronto.

Early industries in Fenwick included an apple-drying factory, a spinning mill, a sawmill, a cooperage and several blacksmith shops.

Hamilton Spectator, 1962.

FERGUS, geographic township, Cochrane District
Position 49° 15′ 83° 09′

The township bears the name of an ancient Irish king and warrior. It is linked by secondary road to Highway 11 and thus to the towns of Hearst and Kapuskasing.

Fergus, Ontario, Main Street looking south, c. 1906

Public Archives Canada, PA 16650

FERGUS, town, Nichol Township, Wellington County
Position 43° 42′ 80° 22′

The small but prosperous town of Fergus is situated on the banks of the Grand River in the heart of Wellington County. The town was named after Adam Fergusson, a Scottish lawyer who had come to Canada in 1831 to explore colonization possibilities for the Highland Society of Scotland. His journey led him to Niagara Falls and then north to the Guelph area. He was so impressed with the scenic beauty of the countryside that upon his return to Scotland he persuaded James Webster, a fellow lawyer, to emigrate with him to Canada.

The two men, accompanied by six of Fergusson's seven sons, arrived in Nichol Township in 1833, purchased some 7,300 acres of land and set out to develop a settlement. Four streets were laid out on the first small clearance, log houses were erected, and within a few short months Fergus had 70 inhabitants. In 1834 Adam Fergusson built the first primitive bridge across the Grand, and the following year Hugh Black opened a tavern in the settlement. Fergusson did not remain permanently in the town he founded, but went to live in

Waterdown near Burlington. However, James Webster continued to make Fergus his home as did two of Fergusson's sons.

The settlement's first industry was a grist mill, erected on the Grand River in 1835. It burned down the following year but was soon rebuilt. Other early business establishments included Tom Webster's store and blacksmithy, and James Walker's bakery. A post office was opened in 1836, with Thomas Young as postmaster.

All of Fergus' pioneer settlers were of Scottish origin, most of them well-educated men. Early log houses were soon replaced by fine limestone buildings by the Scottish masons among the settlers. Those stone houses that still survive include "Belsyde" built by A.D. Ferrier, and "Craighead", once owned by Hugh Black.

Education of their children being of prime concern to the Scottish settlers, the first school, a one-room log building, was opened soon after their arrival in 1836 with James McQueen as the teacher. McQueen later became postmaster and served as township clerk and eventually as Fergus' first librarian. A second school was constructed in 1846 and several private schools were established about the same time. The Fergus Grammar School was built in 1865. It became Fergus High School in 1871. A new high school was opened in 1878 and served until 1928, when it was replaced by a new building. In 1875 a separate school began to teach the Roman Catholic pupils of Fergus.

Rev. Alexander Gardiner was the first minister serving the community's early Presbyterian church, built by Charles Allan in 1835. This building was replaced by St. Andrew's Presbyterian in 1865. A second church, "Melville" was erected in 1846, followed by the Methodist Wesley Church in 1852, the Roman Catholic St. Joseph's in 1857, and the Anglican Church in 1858.

Fergus was incorporated as a village in 1858, when its population had reached about 1,000. Alexander Wilkie served as the first reeve. In 1870, new impetus was given to the town's development when the Wellington, Grey and Bruce Railway was built. This was followed by the construction of the Credit Valley Railway (CPR) in 1880.

At one time or another there were sawmills, flax, and woollen mills, distilleries, breweries, tanneries, foundries, and a stave factory giving employment to the inhabitants.

A sewing-machine factory was one of the busiest local industries in the early 1870's. The Templin Carriage and Wagon Works, founded in 1869, began to manufacture sleighs and eventually developed into an automobile sales outlet.

In 1874 George and Mathew Beatty founded Beatty Bros., and for many years thereafter, the growth of Fergus was closely tied to the growth of this company. As it prospered, so did the village. Today it is still an important employer, making washing-machines and other household appliances as the Beatty Division of General Steel Wares Limited. Fergus now has some twenty industries including Moore Business Forms, Noranda Metal Industries, and the Savage Shoe Company.

The *Fergus News-Record* which is still being published today, traces its origin back to 1854, when George Pirie founded the weekly

Fergus Freeholder.

A hospital, the Royal Alexandra, was opened in 1902 by Dr. Abraham Groves, who became famous as the first man to perform an appendectomy in North America. Dr. Groves also established a training school for nurses. Today's Groves Memorial Hospital has replaced the older building.

Fergus' Scottish heritage is expressed in its Highland Games, established in 1946 by Alex Robertson. The town also has a Highland pipe band, as well as a brass band. The oldest curling club west of Kingston was founded in Fergus in 1832 by Hugh Black, and lacrosse was first played in Fergus in the 1860's. The Wellington County Fair, which was begun in Fergus in 1837, is probably one of the oldest established fall fairs in Ontario.

George Clephane a Fergus resident who died in 1851, was immortalized in the well-known hymn, "The Ninety and Nine". Another famous resident of Fergus was Patrick Bell, the inventor of the reaping machine. Fergus which now has a population of about 6,000, was incorporated as a town in 1953.

A.C. Byerley: "Pioneers and Pioneer Days in Fergus" in *Ontario Historical Society*, 1933.

Fergus Chamber of Commerce: *History of the Town of Fergus.*

FERGUSON, geographic township, Parry Sound District
Position 45° 30' 80° 03'

The township was established in 1869 and appears to have been named after Major Thomas Robert Ferguson, a Member of Parliament for South Simcoe just prior to that time. The area is served by Highways 69 and 124. Canadian National Railways' Parry Sound to Sudbury route passes through the eastern section of the township.

Among the largest of Ferguson's numerous lakes are Round, Marsh, Nine Mile and Lorimer Lakes.

FERGUSON'S FALLS, community, Drummond Township, Lanark County
Position 45° 03' 76° 17'

Situated on County Road 10 in the northern part of Drummond Township, this community was originally known as Millford because of the number of mills in the area. It was renamed after Captain George Ferguson who claimed 70 acres of land along the Mississippi River in the 1820's.

Thomas McCaffrey was the first settler at Ferguson's Falls, arriving about 1815. He was soon followed by other colonists, mostly Irish Catholics, and by 1823 a small community had developed near the present bridge. Among these early residents were Thomas Rathwell, John Cullen, and Patrick and John Quinn. Father Lamothe arrived to minister to them in 1823, although a church was not built until 1856.

A dam was built across the river by Robert Blair in the 1850's to provide power for the saw and grist mills which he erected. A post office was opened in 1853 and Robert Hicks, owner of the general store, became the first postmaster. Hotels were later opened by Charles Hollinger and John Boyle. Hollinger also ran a beef and pork packing business.

The first school was opened in 1872, with James Ferguson as teacher. A second school was constructed later, but was closed in 1965. Today no schools remain in this dispersed rural community.

Jean S. McGill: *A Pioneer History of the County of Lanark*, 1968.

Claire Thompson: *Township of Lanark, 1820-1970*, 1970.

FERNDALE, community, Eastnor Township, Bruce County
Position 44° 58' 81° 17'

The rural community of about 70 inhabitants derives its name from the abundance of fern which was once found in the vicinity. The hamlet is situated in the Bruce Peninsula on Highway 6, about 20 miles northwest of Wiarton.

A school was built in 1891 at the settlement with Miss A. Watt as the first teacher. It was converted into a community centre when a new Central School was opened in the township in 1964. Until 1909 Mennonites and Methodists of the area used to hold services on alternate Sundays in the Ferndale school. That year the Methodists erected what was eventually to become the Centreville United Church. A year later the Mennonites built a church at Ferndale, but in 1947 this edifice was moved to Lion's Head, a couple of miles to the northeast.

Agriculture and tourism are the community's mainstay.

Norman McLeod: *The History of the County of Bruce, 1907-1969*, 1969.

FERNOW, geographic township, Thunder Bay District
Position 49° 55' 86° 03'

This township, located northeast of Longlac, was named in honour of Prof. B.E. Fernow. There are several lakes, the two largest of which are Fernow in the centre and Proctor in the south. Secondary roads link the township with Highway 11 and the community of Longlac.

FERRIE, geographic township, Parry Sound District
Position 45° 47' 79° 47'

Established in the 1860's, the township was first surveyed in 1877 by J.W. Fitzgerald. It was named after the Hon. Adam Ferrie (1777-1868). The area is watered by numerous rivers, streams and lakes. A road through the eastern section of the township gives access to Highway 520 and the community of Maple Island in the southeast. In the north this same road links the area with Highway 522.

FERRIER, geographic township, Algoma District
Position 47° 11' 83° 24'

The township, originally designated as 7F, was named for the Rev. W.

Ferrier, once MPP for Cochrane South.

The area is not accessible by road, but Highway 129 (Thessalon to Chapleau) passes a few miles to the east.

FERRIS PROVINCIAL PARK, Trent River, Northumberland County
Position 44° 18′ 77° 48′

A rural park located along the Trent River, a short distance from the town of Campbellford, the park area is situated on a series of drumlin hills, those elongated hills caused by glacial drift. Part of the park was once the farm of the Ferris family of Campbellford, generously donated to the province in 1962. Hiking, fishing, and boating on the Trent Waterway are some of the attractions the park provides.

Ontario Ministry of Natural Resources, Brochure.

FESSERTON, community, Tay Township, Simcoe County
Position 44° 44′ 79° 41′

A community of over 200 people, Fesserton is situated on Matchedash Bay (part of Georgian Bay), 2 miles southeast of Waubaushene.

The locality was once known as Bush's Point after a pioneer settler of the area. When the Midland Railway of Canada extended its line to Midland on Georgian Bay in the 1870's, a station was built at this point and the developing settlement was named Fesserton by the president of the railway for one of his close friends. Benjamin Dusong, who came around 1840, is considered one of the earliest settlers in the immediate vicinity of Fesserton.

Andrew F. Hunter: *A History of Simcoe County, Part II*, 1948.

FEVERSHAM, community, Osprey Township, Grey County
Position 44° 20′ 80° 22′

The village of Feversham about 16 miles southeast of Thornbury had its beginnings in the early 1850's when Edward Horton built a dam on the headwaters of the picturesque Beaver River and erected a saw and flour mill. He laid out his property into village lots and his sawmill soon began to supply lumber to settlers coming to the area. Another sawmill was built in 1855 by Richard Heron near the village, and later his son, William, constructed a woollen mill on the Heron property.

Feversham had developed into a community of some 180 residents by the 1880's with two stores, a carriage maker, two blacksmiths, a shoemaker and a tailor. The village had a post office, a school, an Orange Lodge, a well patronised Temple of the Independent Order of Good Templars, and two churches: Canada Presbyterian and Episcopal Methodist. Around the turn of the century township farmers formed a co-operative milling company and purchased the Horton mill. The old mill burned to the ground in 1904, but a new stone structure was erected the following year on the site.

E.L. Marsh: *A History of the County of Grey*, 1931.

T. Arthur Davidson: *A New History of the County of Grey*, 1972.

FIDDLER, geographic township, Algoma District
Position 48° 03' 84° 28'

The township, until 1974 known as No. 27, Range 24, was named after Chief Jacob Fiddler of Deer Lake and is part of the Algoma Central & Hudson Bay Railway land grant.

Whitefish Lake occupies much of the township's western section. A hydro-electric generating station is located at the southern end of this lake.

Highway 101 links the area with the nearby town of Wawa.

FIELD, township, Nipissing District
Position 46° 30' 79° 58'

The township is located on the banks of the Sturgeon River, some 50 miles northwest of the city of North Bay. Its population (741 in 1978) is concentrated mainly in the community of Field, named after C.C. Field, MPP for Northumberland West 1886-90, by surveyors who laid out the township in the 1880's.

The area with its vast stands of forests had been opened up for logging operations by Barnet and Mackay in the mid-1800's. The company was bought out by Ottawa lumber baron J.R. Booth in 1866 and it was under his leadership that the community of Field began to develop. Booth owned all the logging rights in the area and his permission was required before a settler could build a house here. So far as is known this permission was never refused.

As the lumbering industry expanded, so did the population of Field and settlement was spreading out in the shape of a fan on the banks of the Sturgeon River. Mrs. John Deschamps became the township's first postmistress in 1899. The first store was opened in 1903 by J.Z. Vinet as settlers arrived from Ontario, Quebec, and the United States. In 1905 a sawmill was erected by Louis Parent. It was purchased by Joseph Vezina in 1907 and moved to the centre of the community, where Field Lumber Ltd. now stands.

Construction of the railway in 1914 made it possible to expand milling operations and in the same year, the Field Lumber Company was formed by Vezina, Zotique Mageau, and Ubald Lamarre. The new company purchased all logging rights in the area and became the main employer of township residents.

In 1915 Field township was incorporated. Ubald Lamarre, Felix Legault, Magloire Major, and Avila Lafantaisie served on the first town council led by Mayor Edgar Gagne.

A fire destroyed the mill in 1922, but a new building was erected in the same year and production soon increased dramatically from 2 million to 10 million feet of lumber per year. The population of Field rose from thirty families to over one hundred. Over the years, fires and floods damaged the mill on several occasions but it continued in operation, and in 1956 the company was bought by Jack Hope.

Meanwhile, in 1948 a bridge had been built across the Sturgeon linking the settlements on either side of the river. Two years later, electricity was brought to Field.

By 1971 the population had reached 655. Plans to expand the industrial base of the community got underway with the formation of the Field Industrial Commission in 1974 under Garfield Morrison, the first president. First on the list was the construction of a new wood plant as a subsidiary to West Nipissing Enterprises.

Today Field's main industry is still lumbering but some arable land is being farmed, and the community has a reputation as an outdoor sports centre. Voyageur Park, one of the largest public beaches in the area, was opened in 1970. Other facilities include a skating rink, a baseball field, and a community hall. Several stores, a Roman Catholic church, an elementary school, and a public library serve the largely bilingual population of French and English Canadian origins.

Ministry of Industry and Tourism: *Traveller's Encyclopaedia of Ontario/Canada*, 1979.

FINAN, geographic township, Algoma District
Position 48° 20′ 84° 29′

The name of the township commemorates Canadian Army Sergeant Elvin M. Finan of the Thunder Bay District who was killed in World War Two. Prior to 1974 the township, located southeast of the community of White River, was designated as No. 49.

The Algoma Central Railway passes along the western boundary with the railway point of Dubreuilville located in the northwestern corner of the township. A secondary road links the area with the railway point of Goudreau on the Algoma Central and the station of Lochalsh on the Canadian Pacific.

FINCH, township, Stormont County
Position 45° 11′ 75° 07′

Situated in the northern half of Stormont County, Finch is bounded on the northeast by Roxborough Township, on the southeast by Osnabruck, on the southwest by Dundas County, and on the northwest by Russell County. The South Nation River on its way north to the Ottawa River, enters the western portion of Finch Township and two of its tributaries flow through the township. A family by the name of Finch, related by marriage to David Murray, 7th Viscount Stormont, who named Stormont County, in turn gave their name to Finch Township and to Finch village.

Finch was settled in the first years of the nineteenth century mainly by Scottish immigrants. In the year 1802, Allan McMillan, living on Lochaber Bay in the County of Invernesshire, Scotland, saw a map of Finch Township. In that same year he chartered a boat, the cost being met by each of the McMillan and Cameron families paying ten pounds for passage fare. After a crossing of thirteen weeks, the entire boatload of McMillans and Camerons landed at Montreal in the autumn of 1802. From Montreal to Lancaster, the families travelled by portage up the St. Lawrence and thence walked through the bush, carrying their belongings. They spent their first winter with friends in

26

the settlements of Kirkhill and Laggan, Lochiel Township. The next spring four of each of the McMillan and Cameron families walked to Finch, selected their lots, built their log homes, obtained their patents, and in 1803 brought their families to their wilderness homes. Unlike the settlers along the St. Lawrence, they received no rations and supplies for three years. Their group had no half-pay officers receiving a little ready cash. Their only sources of revenue were potash and oak barrel staves.

The first white child born in Finch was Harriet, daughter of Alexander McMillan. In 1805 other settlers including Hugh and John McMillan, Lachlin McLean, and more Camerons, joined them. The clearing of the land was by their own labour, as the first horse was not brought into the area until 1820.

By 1846 the township had a grist mill and three sawmills to serve its 756 inhabitants. Much of the land was covered by dense forests of pine, later greatly removed by lumbering and agriculture.

Although no large communities have developed in Finch, the population of the township increased to 2,305 by 1978.

H. Belden & Co.: *Historical Atlas of Stormont, Dundas and Glengarry Counties*, 1881.

FINDLAY, geographic township, Cochrane District
Position 49° 00' 80° 20'

Named after the Hon. Findlay G. Macdiarmid, a former Minister in the Ontario Government, the township is located some thirty miles east of Cochrane. It is traversed by several streams and by dry weather roads.

FINGAL, geographic township, Sudbury District
Position 47° 33' 82° 17'

The township appears to have been named after a place in Ireland. It is linked by several roads to the surrounding areas. The closest railway point is Ramsey on the Canadian Pacific's Sudbury-Chapleau route.

FINGAL, village, Southwold Township, Elgin County
Position 42° 43' 81° 19'

Situated just a few miles north of Lake Erie not far from the city of St. Thomas, Fingal is the oldest village in Southwold Township. Col. Thomas Talbot, the colonizer of the area, named the settlement after Fingal's Cave in Scotland.

The first settler was Titus Cowle, who sold his land to Levi Fowler in the 1820's. Other early settlers included William McDonald and Samuel Burwell. In 1830 Levi Fowler laid out part of his land into village lots, and soon after he opened a general store. He later went into partnership with Amasa Wood, who, because of his habits of rising early and talking loudly, was commonly known as the "Town Bell". Wood who also ran a tavern, loaned money, and bought mortgages, became one of Fingal's wealthy and influential citizens.

The first church in the village was built in 1837 by the

Presbyterians. Eventually a Methodist Church was erected to be followed in the 1850's by a Baptist house of worship. A Mr. Hanna was the first school teacher in Fingal. A town hall was built in 1852 and Levi Fowler became the first reeve of Fingal. The lively council meetings of those early days which used to be the scene of much quarreling and fighting led to the village being nicknamed the "Devil's half-acre".

In 1844 George Metcalfe and J. Conrad started a cabinet, chair-making, and undertaking business. Capt. Alex Pollock erected the first grist mill in 1850. A cheese factory was opened in the settlement and William Doyle set up a marble works. The Fulton Bros. sawmill, Messrs. Culver and Barber's brickyard, and Charles Edmond's ashery were all in operation before the 1890's. The most important industry of that era was the foundry of Harvey, Glasgow, and McPherson, which manufactured separators, engines, reapers, and mowers.

The year of 1889 was a tragic one for the village, as a smallpox epidemic struck down many of its inhabitants. The population which at one time reached 1,000, had declined to about 500 by 1890. Prospects for renewed growth were dim because of the proximity of St. Thomas, a rapidly growing centre which attracted industries and settlers. Fingal's dwindling business establishments towards the end of the nineteenth century included three general stores, a bakery, three butcher shops, two hotels, a shoe store, a foundry and a cheese factory. Fingal's population continued to decline and the 1971 census lists a population of 322.

Just outside the village is the site of a unique archeological find, a double-walled aboriginal earthwork which shows no trace of European contact by its builders. The fort's origin and antiquity remain a mystery.

James S. Brierly: *A Pioneer History, Elgin County*, 1896.

H.R. Page & Co.: *Historical Atlas of Elgin County*, 1877.

FINGERBOARD, community, Mariposa Township, Victoria County
Position 44° 14' 78° 55'

Situated about 15 miles from Midland on the shore of Lake Scugog, this dispersed rural community was a prosperous industrial settlement in the late nineteenth century. It was formerly known as Port Hoover after an early settler, Thomas Hoover. Its name was changed to Fingerboard when a post office by that name was established here in 1881.

Fingerboard was settled in the first half of the nineteenth century. George Shell was the local blacksmith, Tiers & Yerex were dealers in dry goods, and the Steamboat Hotel, managed by Edward Vetch, accommodated Lake Scugog travellers. Two weavers and a carpenter plied their trades by the 1870's and a number of residents were employed in the steam, saw, and shingle mills and general manufacturing establishment of D. Hoover & Co. During the early twentieth century, the steamer traffic on the lake decreased and gradually Fingerboard lost its importance and became the small community it is today.

FINLAYSON, geographic township, Nipissing District
Position 45° 29' 78° 53'

Situated in the southwest corner of Algonquin Provincial Park, the township was established in 1878 when it was surveyed by Ontario Land Surveyor James Dickson. It was named after Hugh Finlayson, MPP for North Brant in the 1860's and 1870's. The area is served by Highway 60 which passes the northern tip of beautiful Smoke Lake and runs southeastward along the scenic Oxtongue River. The nearest town is Huntsville.

FINLAYSON POINT PROVINCIAL PARK, Strathcona Township, Nipissing District
Position 47° 03' 79° 48'

Finlayson Point is a 74-acre Provincial Recreation Park situated on a point of land jutting into Lake Temagami. It is one mile south of Temagami and 60 miles north of North Bay on Highway 11. Lake Temagami, itself, with more than 1,200 islands and 370 miles of shoreline, offers sailing, canoeing, boating and superb scenery. A plaque in memory of Grey Owl, the naturalist who made extensive studies of the habits of the beaver, has been erected in the park.

Ontario Ministry of Natural Resources, Brochure.

FINTRY, geographic township, Cochrane District
Position 49° 54' 84° 35'

The township was named after the English birthplace of H. Anderson, Legislative Reporter of Toronto.

The Pitopiko River, a tributary of the Nagagami, which enters Fintry for a short stretch in the southwest, winds its way in a northerly direction through the township. The Canadian National Railway skirts the township's southwestern corner.

FIRSTBROOK, geographic township, Timiskaming District
Position 47° 27' 79° 49'

Surveyed in 1901 by McCubbin, the township was named after T. Firstbrook of Hamilton. It is situated a few miles west of the town of Haileybury and is linked by Highway 558 and other roads to Highway 11 and the nearby towns.

FISHER, geographic township, Algoma District
Position 46° 56' 84° 32'

Located north of Batchawana Bay (Lake Superior), the mainland of this township is Indian lands. The township which covers over 12,200 acres was established and surveyed in 1865. It is named in honour of Charles Fisher, a judge and the Premier of New Brunswick in the 1850's and 1860's. A delegate to the Quebec Conference of 1864, he was thus one of the Fathers of Confederation.

Highway 17 passes through Batchawana Provincial Park in the southern part. A large island is located a short distance offshore.

FISHERVILLE, community, part of the Town of Haldimand, Regional Municipality of Haldimand-Norfolk
Position 42° 52′ 79° 54′

Formerly in Rainham Township, Haldimand County, Fisherville is a compact rural community, which was once a police village. On April 1, 1974, it became part of the Town of Haldimand. The community is situated about 4 miles south of Highway 3, and approximately 3 miles from the north shore of Lake Erie. Population: 232 (1971).

Fisherville and the surrounding area were settled in the early 1800's. Most of the original settlers came from the United States and were of German or French origin. Among the area's pioneers were Frederick Albert, George Held, George Nablo, Nicholas Raicheld, Jacob Rohrbach, and Christian Snell.

A post office was opened in 1863, and by the late 1870's there were two general stores, a hotel, a harness shop, a wagon shop, and a blacksmith shop in the settlement. Also by this time there was a handsome brick church built by the Lutherans of Fisherville.

H.R. Page & Co.: *Historical Atlas of the County of Haldimand,* 1879.

FITZGERALD, geographic township, Nipissing District
Position 46° 03′ 78° 12′

The township was named after J.W. FitzGerald of Peterborough, Ontario, who surveyed the area in 1886. Being part of the vast wilderness of Algonquin Provincial Park, roads are to be found only in the southern section linking the Radiant Lake area with the Petawawa River.

FITZROY, part of West Carleton Township, Regional Municipality of Ottawa-Carleton
Position 45° 27′ 76° 15′

Until 1969, Fitzroy, formerly a township, was the most northwesterly portion of the County of Carleton.

On January 1, 1969 Carleton County became part of the Regional Municipality of Ottawa-Carleton. Fitzroy amalgamated January 1, 1974 with the Township of Huntley and the Township of Torbolton as the Township of West Carleton.

Charles Shirreff and his sons Robert and Alexander, were the pioneers of Fitzroy Township. Shirreff, a Scottish immigrant, had first purchased land near the present town of Port Hope in 1817. However, he was persuaded to come to the Ottawa Valley which was to be part of a proposed waterway known as the "Huron Route". A grant of 3,000 acres of land was offered to him if he would settle at "The Chats" and develop the area. He accepted the offer and during the winter of 1818-19 moved to Fitzroy Township with his family. He cleared land and laid the foundation of the village formerly called "The Chats" after the rapids in the Ottawa River and now known as Fitzroy Harbour.

The township was surveyed in 1821 by Colonel Sherwood and opened for settlement in 1823. It was named in honour of Sir Charles Augustus Fitzroy, Governor of New South Wales. The first patent, dated March 4, 1823, was granted to Billa Flint; the second, to Charles, Robert and Alexander Shirreff.

Alexander Shirreff undertook an exploratory expedition at his own expense to bring the "Huron Route" of the waterway to reality, but due to political pressure, the route of the Rideau Canal was chosen instead.

The first sawmill in the township was built in 1825 by Alex. McMillen and Donald Dingwall, two of the earliest settlers of Fitzroy, who also operated one of the first stores in the township. The first grist mill, and for some years the only one in the township, was built in 1824 on the Carp River by Herman Laudon, son of a United Empire Loyalist who had settled in the Township of Augusta after the American Revolution. Laudon, a captain in the Provincial Dragoons during the War of 1812-15, drew a grant of land for his military services. One of the leading men in the community, he became the oldest magistrate in the township. At the time he settled in Fitzroy there were only four other settlers there: Charles Shirreff, Alex. McMillen, Donald Dingwall and Richard McArthur. Other early settlers to follow included: Thomas McCormick, Edward Owens, John Grant, Thomas Fraser, Cornelius Gleeson, Henry Willis and John Marshall. James Keating settled on the Mississippi in 1825; the Lowerys and Hamiltons came in 1826. In later years G. Learmonth, another leading member of the district, built a grist and sawmill on the site of the first sawmill of McMillen and Dingwall on the Mississippi River.

In 1832 Mr. Shirreff erected at The Chats a log building to be used as a school during weekdays and as a house of worship on the Sabbath. The first teacher was a Mr. Ramsay. Another school, also a log building, was erected by Mr. Forbes in 1827 with a Miss Clarke assuming post of teacher.

The Reverend Playfair of Perth was the first Methodist preacher in the township, and the Reverend Alex Mann the first Presbyterian minister. The latter church was a frame building on the 9th line. The Roman Catholics of the township built their first church at Fitzroy Harbour in 1858. This was St. Michael's, built of wood, it was burned and replaced by a stone church in 1861. Rev. Bernard McFeely was the first resident priest.

The first, and for a long time the only, post office in the township was opened at The Chats (Fitzroy Harbour) in 1832.

When the municipality of Fitzroy was created by the Municipal Act of 1850, Mr. Steene who previously had been representative in the

District Council at Perth, became Fitzroy Township's first reeve. William Dean, James Howe, Robert Carss, and W.P. Taylor were the first councillors. Thomas Elliott served as clerk.

Fred Sadler: *Fitzroy Township*, 1967.

H. Belden & Co.: *Historical Atlas of the County of Carleton*, 1879.

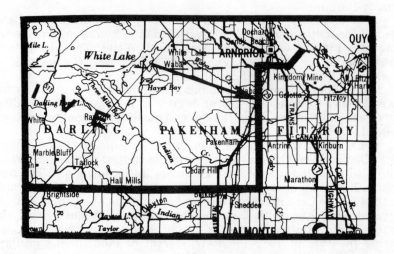

FITZROY HARBOUR, community, West Carleton Township, Regional Municipality of Ottawa-Carleton
Position 45° 28' 76° 13'

Fitzroy Harbour is situated about 35 miles northwest of Ottawa and about 12 miles northeast of Arnprior. Population 317 (1974).

It was first known as "The Chats" after the Ottawa River rapids at whose foot it is located. Charles Shirreff established his home here in 1818 in anticipation that the "Huron Route", a waterway connecting East and West, would be built via the Ottawa Valley. He cleared land on Lot 25, Concession 10 and erected his house. No other homesteaders came until 1823 when Alex. McMillen, Donald Dingwall, and Herman Laudon arrived. When boats began to ply between Aylmer and the Upper Ottawa, the community at The Chats became known as Fitzroy Harbour.

In 1832 Charles Shirreff erected a log building used as a school during the week and as a house of worship on Sunday. A post office was established in 1832, with William Gillespie as the first postmaster. Mr. Laudon acted as the first magistrate. The village site was surveyed and laid out by John Robertson for Robert Shirreff, Charles Shirreff's son, in 1836.

By the 1860's Fitzroy Harbour had five general stores, two grist mills, one sawmill, a tannery and three hotels and several blacksmith shops. There were three churches, the Church of England, the Presbyterian church and the Roman Catholic church, as well as a two-room school.

One by one, these early businesses closed, and only the general stores continue to serve the community.

Fitzroy Harbour's tourist attraction once provided by the sight of Chats Falls, no longer exists. The Chats Falls Generating Station and Power Dam built in the early 1930's, silenced the mighty rapids.

In 1960 a Provincial Park was established which again attracts visitors to the Fitzroy Harbour area.

Fred Sadler: *Fitzroy Township*, 1967.

H. Belden & Co.: *Historical Atlas of the County of Carleton*, 1879.

FITZROY PROVINCIAL PARK, Fitzroy Township, Carleton County
Position 45° 29' 76° 13'

Situated on the south shore of the Ottawa River and 20 kilometres east of town of Arnprior, this Recreation Park was once part of the 5,000 acres bought by Charles Shirreff, Scottish merchant and early settler of the area in 1819. It was opposite Fitzroy that Chats Falls and the dangerous "Les Chats" were located before being submerged as a result of the completion of the Chats Falls Hydro Dam in 1933. The rapids were a favourite ambush site for the Iroquois as fur-traders negotiated the treacherous waters on their way to Montreal.

Ontario Ministry of Natural Resources, Brochure.

FITZSIMMONS, geographic township, Sudbury District
Position 47° 31' 83° 47'

Formerly known as No. 22, Range 18, the township was named in 1974 after G.J. Fitzsimmons, Reeve of South River. It is connected by partially improved roads to Highway 101 and the Chapleau area, and to the community of Pineal Lake in the neighbouring township to the east.

FIVE MILE LAKE PROVINCIAL PARK, Townships 11D and 11E, Sudbury District
Position 47° 34' 83° 14'

This park is located twenty-three miles south of Chapleau on Highway 129 and stretches between Five Mile Lake and Unegam Lake. It includes two small lakes (White Bark and Red Bark Lakes) and is 1700 feet above sea level. Its forests abound with wildlife and the Northern pike is found in its waters.

At Chapleau may be seen the monument erected in memory of Louis Hemon, author of *Marie Chapdelaine*, classic story of French-Canadian rural life. In Sultan, about 30 miles east of Highway 129, John Ceredigion Jones, Welsh-Canadian poet is buried.

Ontario Ministry of Natural Resources, Brochure.

FLAMBORO CENTRE, community, Flamborough Township, Regional Municipality of Hamilton-Wentworth
Position 43° 22′ 79° 56′

This dispersed rural community is situated about 7 miles north of Hamilton in the centre of Flamborough Township, hence its name.

In the mid-nineteenth century the locality was an important stopping place on the Hamilton Road and a station on the Great Western Railway. Its population was about 150 and its businesses included four stores, a tavern, a foundry, four blacksmith shops, one wagonmaker shop, and tailor, saddler, and shoemaking establishments.

The population of the community decreased with the closing of the railway station in the late nineteenth century and the early twentieth century, and by 1903 only 50 people lived in Flamboro Centre. However, in recent years the population has been rising once more and by 1971 the community had 106 inhabitants.

H.R. Page: *Historical Atlas of Wentworth County*, 1875.

FLAMBOROUGH, township, Regional Municipality of Hamilton-Wentworth
Position 43° 22′ 79° 56′

Prior to the formation of the Regional Municipality of Hamilton-Wentworth, the township was part of Wentworth County and was divided into East and West Flamborough. On January 1, 1974 East Flamborough amalgamated with the village of Waterdown to form the Township of Flamborough; part of West Flamborough was annexed to the Town of Dundas and the remainder to the newly formed Township of Flamborough.

In 1793 Augustus Jones surveyed a line through the area for the Dundas Road, which was to run from Dundas to York, but the township itself was not surveyed until 1797 when John Stegmann began the work. Land grants had been made by 1796 in an attempt to establish settlements along the Dundas Road, but few pioneers took up their land at that time. John Green, the first settler, arrived in 1797 and built a grist mill. He was followed by the Markle family and then by the Mordens, United Empire Loyalists who settled in the vicinity of Dundas and along Crooks' Hollow. Other early settlers included the Mornings and Alexander MacDonnell. Alexander Brown, an agent of the North West Company, also took up his grant and had built two sawmills by 1804.

The township, named for the famed Flamborough Head in the Heights of Yorkshire, developed slowly at first. By 1817 there were only 360 people. In 1824 George Baker began clearing the land in East Flamborough on the site which became Bakersville. In 1827 Ebenezer Culver Griffin built a flour mill and a sawmill. A paper mill was constructed at Crooks' Hollow where the Hon. James Crooks, a noted personality of the day, had secured 300 acres suitable for mill sites along Spencer Creek.

Plans were made to make Crooks' Hollow the county town and a canal from Burlington Bay to Crooks' Hollow was proposed. These plans, although not carried out for the time being, encouraged settlement in the area. Greensville began to grow around a number of mills and eventually Waterdown became the major community.

By 1850 the population had reached 2,428 and the township had a grist mill, sawmills, a distillery, a paper mill, a woollen factory, and a tannery. The Great Western Railway was built through the area with a station at Flamboro village. The removal of this station in the 1870's resulted in a decline in the community's prosperity.

The first school was built on the property of Mr. Manary. Beechgrove School was opened in 1864. The High School was once housed in the Baptist Church but students now go to Hamilton, Waterdown, or Galt for secondary school education.

Early township churches included the Baptist Church, erected in 1866, the United Church, opened in 1899, and the Roman Catholic Church, Our Lady of Carmel.

The population of Flamborough Township, now part of a prosperous industrial region, is 23,747.

Hamilton Spectator, 1947.

H.R. Page: Wentworth County Illustrated Atlas, 1875.

FLANDERS, geographic township, Algoma District
Position 49° 23′ 85° 12′

The township's name commemorates the World War One battlefield of Flanders, a region in Western Belgium and Northern France. Canadian National Railways' Hornepayne-Longlac route passes through the centre of the township. The scenic Foch River with numerous rapids winds its way across the northeast corner where it empties into Nagagami Lake.

FLAVELLE, geographic township, Timiskaming District
Postion 47° 59′ 80° 28′

First surveyed in 1905 by Ontario Land Surveyor Abrey, the township was named after the Flavelle family of Peterborough and Toronto. Sir Joseph Wesley Flavelle, a great industrialist and financier of the early 1900's was a member of this family. Highway 66 which passes through the northern section of the township links it with nearby Kirkland Lake.

FLECK, geographic township, Cochrane District
Position 49° 46′ 82° 58′

The township, originally surveyed in 1908, appears to have been named after Robert Fleck, a Lambton County farmer and County Council member for thirty years. A secondary road links the southern part of the township with Highway 11 to the south.

FLEETWOOD, community, Manvers Township, Victoria County
Position 44° 13' 78° 37'

Located a short distance southeast of the town of Lindsay, the dispersed rural community of Fleetwood is believed to have been named after a village in Ireland by its pioneer settlers, most of whom had come from Ireland or England. Another version traces the name origin to Chief Fleetwood, chief of one of the area's Indian tribes. At one time the community was known as Brick Corners, probably because of the schoolhouse built of brick in the 1850's.

Among the early settlers in the immediate vicinity were the Staples family, William Mitchell, William Stinson, H. Wiley, James Bushell, Joseph Touchburn, James Dean, James Jones, John Porter, T. Laidley, William Ingram, Thomas Howes, Joseph Lee, and Henry Stewart. A general store was opened by James Morrow, while the Staples, Argue and Gardiner families were the early mill owners at Fleetwood. The original village site was planned on land owned by members of several Staples families. Located in the midst of good farmland, Fleetwood developed into a flourishing community from where large quantities of lumber, cattle, hogs and sheep were shipped via a Canadian Pacific Railway siding in the early 1900's. A cheese factory, established by James Albertus Wood, operated in Fleetwood from 1891 to the late 1920's.

Today the village as such exists in name only. The last store was closed in the 1930's, and a decade later, in 1947, the last service was held in the Fleetwood Church which had its beginnings in a red brick building used by the early Methodists as well as the Bible Christians of the area. Followers of the latter group erected the Fleetwood Church in 1875.

Mrs. Ross N. Carr: *The Rolling Hills,* 1967.

FLEMING, geographic township, Rainy River District
Position 48° 52' 93° 46'

It is believed that this township, northwest of Fort Frances, was named after Sir Sandford Fleming, noted civil engineer and Canadian railway builder. An area in the northeastern part is designated as Indian Lands and here is situated the community of Manomin.

FLESHERTON, village, Artemesia Township, Grey County
Position 44° 16' 80° 33'

Flesherton is situated about 30 miles southeast of Owen Sound at the intersection of the Owen Sound-Toronto and the Collingwood-Durham Roads (now Highways 10 and 4). The village owes its existence to W.K. Flesher, an English-born settler who acquired land at the crossroads in 1853. He built a dam on the rushing Boyne River, a tributary of the Beaver, erected a large saw and grist mill and laid out a portion of his property into village lots.

The first permanent settler on the village site was Aaron Munshaw who opened a tavern for stagecoach travellers in 1849 across from the present cemetery. Just to the north of it he built another hotel in the 1860's which still remains one of the historic landmarks in the village.

A post office, the first in the township, was established at the crossroads in 1851 under the name of Artemesia. It was a great help to the pioneer settlers of the area who previously had to travel thirty miles to Orangeville to post a letter.

Among the village's early settlers were Alfred Down, T.H. Heard, Roger Lever, Henry Meldrum, John McKee, George Stewart, James Beecroft, the Campbells, T.W. Henderson, John Porteous, the Spaffords, Smiths and Taylors. R.T. Sproule, another pioneer, kept a general store and ran a law office. He also was postmaster.

Mr. Flesher's mills attracted a number of other business enterprises, among them a woollen mill and a pump factory in addition to various shops and stores. The settlement was first known as Flesher's Corners, but as it soon expanded well beyond the "corners", the more suitable name of Flesherton was adopted in honour of the founder. Flesher, who established the first Masonic Lodge in the hamlet and organized a militia company, was a member of parliament, a warden of the county, and for many years reeve of Artemesia Township.

At one time Flesherton could boast of a carriage shop, two carriage factories, a tannery and a cheese factory. On the north bank of the Boyne River was the Boyne Water Hotel operated by Arthur John Jones. Opposite the hotel stood the predecessor of the present school.

Flesherton continued to progress until the railway built its line a mile and a half west of the village, thus causing a decline in local industries. Today the village has a population of just under 600 people.

E.L. Marsh: *A History of the County of Grey*, 1931.

FLETCHER, geographic township, Thunder Bay District
Position 50° 22′ 90° 13′

The township was named after Charles G. Fletcher, MPP for Essex South in the 1920's and again in the 1930's. The area is covered with lakes and rivers and is not accessible by road. Highway 599 passes some 20 miles to the west.

FLETCHER, community, Tilbury East Township, Kent County
Position 42° 18′ 82° 18′

This dispersed rural community of 100 people (1971) is situated about 12 miles from Chatham, on the old Canada Southern Railway. It was probably named after David Fletcher, one of the early settlers in the area.

The community developed around the railway station that was opened in the late 1800's when the Canada Southern Railway was built through the area. A post office was established in 1875 and a telegraph station opened about the same time. By 1881 the population was about 200 and the community had two stores and a sawmill. A large warehouse was built in the 1890's.

By 1908 Fletcher's population had fallen to 100 but many of the businesses remained open. Residents were employed in the telegraph office, express office, 2 stores, a branch bank, 2 blacksmith shops, and a wagon shop. There was also a Presbyterian church to serve the community.

H. Belden & Co.: *Historical Atlas of Essex and Kent Counties*, 1881.

FLETT, geographic township, Nipissing District
Position 46° 51′ 79° 34′

Located north of Nipissing Lake, the township was named after William Flett, MPP for St. Andrews (Toronto) in 1926. Boyce, Fanny and Mackenzie Lakes occupy a major part of the township's central section. The Ontario Northland Railway passes through the southeastern part where the communities of Kenney and Bushnell are located.

FLINTON, community, Kaladar Township, Lennox and Addington County
Position 44° 41′ 77° 13′

This compact rural community of about 150 inhabitants is situated on the Skootamatta River in the Land O'Lakes Tourist region, about 16 miles northeast of the village of Tweed.

Prior to 1855 the place was known as Flint's Mills, being the site of a sawmill constructed by Billa Flint. Flint, a Senator, was a wealthy Belleville merchant who owned large tracts of timber in Kaladar Township. Aside from his lumber camps there were no permanent settlements in the vicinity of Flinton at that time. By 1855, however, the Addington Road, constructed by the government under the supervision of Ebenezer Perry to open up the northern part of the county, was nearing completion, and settlers began to take up land around Flint's Mills. Perry was appointed land agent and set up his headquarters at the village which became known as Flinton when a post office was opened in 1858.

Walter S. Herrington: *History of the County of Lennox and Addington*, 1913.

FLOOD, geographic township, Thunder Bay District
Position 48° 45′ 85° 23′

Flood is named after Nicholas Flood Davin, a noted lawyer and brilliant journalist of the 19th century who founded the Regina *Leader* and served for 13 years as a Member of the Canadian Parliament. The township is linked by secondary roads to Highway 17 which passes a few miles to the south. Flood Lake and a large portion of Kwinkwaga Lake occupy the northeastern corner of the township.

FLORADALE, community, Regional Municipality of Waterloo
Position 43° 37' 80° 35'

Originally known only as Flora, Floradale is a small rural community about 16 miles north of the city of Waterloo.

The Canacagigue Creek which flows past the settlement provided power for small industries in the nineteenth century and by 1873 Flora had a grist and sawmill. A post office was opened in 1876 and soon the community also boasted a store and a hotel.

By 1895 the settlement was known as Floradale. It had grown substantially and now had a population of 250. Industries included a gristmill, two sawmills, a flax mill, and a pump factory. There were three churches to serve the residents.

Floradale retained its industrial character into the early twentieth century. Gradually, however, these local establishments disappeared, and today Floradale is a largely residential community of just over 200.

FLORANNA, geographic township, Sudbury District
Position 48° 09' 83° 18'

The name origin of this township which remains unsurveyed is not known. The area is linked by dry weather roads to points north, and to the town of Chapleau some thirty miles to the south. The Swanson River flows through the centre of the township, and Floranna Lake occupies most of the central section in the southern part.

FLORENCE, police village, Euphemia Township, Lambton County
Position 42° 39' 82° 00'

Situated on the banks of the Sydenham River, the small village of Florence lies on the border of Dawn and Euphemia Townships in the southeast corner of Lambton County. At one time, Florence was one of the more prominent settlements in southwestern Ontario; population in 1880 was 400. In 1971, the population of the village was 196.

The first settler in Florence was Job Hall, who arrived in 1820. A mill was erected at the village site in 1827. This mill was not only the first in the township but it was likely the first in Lambton County. At that time the township of Euphemia was known as Zone Township, and the settlement became known as Zone Mills. Among settlers who arrived in the 1830's were William Hutchinson, William Granger, the Boyce family, and the Kerby family.

A post office opened in 1840 under the name of Zone Mills. Later the name was changed to Victoria, in honour of the new Queen who had just ascended the British throne. The name, however, proved confusing; mail was frequently being mixed up with mail for Vittoria in Norfolk County. George Kerby, postmaster in 1856, solved the problem by naming the community Florence, after the city of the same name in Italy.

In 1859 the village was incorporated. It was the centre of a thriving pearl ash trade in the early days and the hardwood forests of the area were the basis of a lucrative lumbering operation. By the 1880's, however, these forests were beginning to dwindle. A fire swept through the village and destroyed most of the businesses. When the railway by-passed the village, the decline of the settlement became inevitable.

Victor Lauriston: Lambton County's Hundred Years 1849-1949, 1949.

H. Belden & Co.: Historical Atlas of the County of Lambton, 1880.

FLOS, township, Simcoe County
Position 44° 33' 79° 52'

The Township of Flos covering an area of nearly 64,000 acres, is located in the northern portion of Simcoe County. It borders in the west on Nottawasaga Bay (Georgian Bay) with its numerous beach resorts, Wasaga Provincial Park and the favorite tourist attraction of Wasaga Beach. The population of the township is just over 2,400.

Flos Township was named after one of the two lapdogs of Elizabeth Simcoe, wife of Upper Canada's first Lieutenant Governor, John Graves Simcoe. Because of its dense forests, the area was settled somewhat later than other parts of the county. The township was surveyed in 1822 and it fronted on the old Penetanguishene Road, a military road constructed from Kempenfeldt Bay to the garrison at Penetanguishene in 1814. Land along the road was to be settled under a free-grant system, but the first permanent settler in Flos was a black man named Davenport who chose to settle in a more remote region of the township, rather than on land offered by the government along the road.

Most of the early settlers arrived in the township during the 1830's, among them the McAvoys, Barnards and Coughlins. Hugh Marlow moved into Flos from neighboring Medonte Township in 1834 taking up Lot 65 on the Penetang Road. Here he opened a store and later, a tavern. He also kept the Penetanguishene Road post office, and early Petty Court sessions were held at his house. By 1842 the total population of the township had barely reached 200 as most settlers preferred to take up land in less timbered areas of the county.

John Cumming settled in the Fergusonvale area around 1843 as did Gideon Richardson. James Harvey was the first pioneer in the vicinity of Elmvale; William Wood and Thomas Allen settled on the site of the future hamlet of Allenwood.

The Roman Catholics built the first church in the township. It was located on the Vespra townline, west of Craighurst. One of the first schools was opened not far from Hillsdale with a Mr. Moorhead as the first teacher. Another early school was established in the Elmvale area, then known as the Elm Flat settlement, and here the Presbyterians were the first to erect a church. The Reverend George Craw served as their first minister.

The hamlet of Vanvlack bears the name of the first settler in that part of the township. Near the mouth of the Nottawasaga River which winds its way through parts of the township stood the sawmill of John Hunter; and in the Vigo area Henry Gribbin was the pioneer settler.

The first representative from Flos Township to become a member of the Simcoe District Council in 1844 was James Richardson. From 1850, when municipal government was first established in the Province of Ontario, to 1854, the Township of Flos was united for municipal purposes with its neighbours, Vespra and Sunnidale. The first township meeting was held at Hamilton's Inn, Lot 60, on the Penetang Road. Peter Cleland was named reeve; and the first councillors were John Cumming, John Graham, Patrick McAvoy and William Swan. George McKay was appointed as the clerk-treasurer.

Farming and lumbering were the main industries in those days in the township with products being shipped to markets in Barrie and Stayner. The hamlet of Phelpston gained importance when a line of the North Simcoe Branch of the Northern Railway opened up in 1879 and the settlement became a station. The railway also ran through Elmvale, today the only incorporated village in the township.

Andrew F. Hunter: *The History of Simcoe County*, 1909.

H. Belden & Co.: *Illustrated Atlas of the County of Simcoe*, 1881.

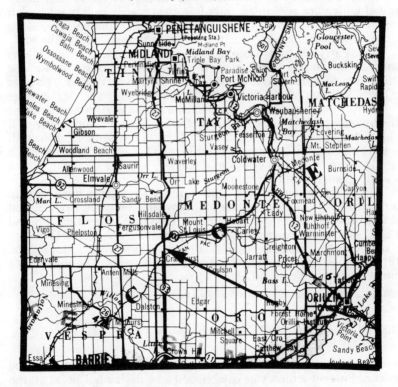

FOCH, geographic township, Algoma District
Position 49° 15′ 85° 12′

The township commemorates the name of Marshal Ferdinand Foch, a

41

distinguished French army officer who became commander-in-chief of all Allied Forces in World War One.

Foch, less than 20 miles west of Hornepayne, is accessible only by waterways; although the railway point of Tondern on the Canadian National is located only a few miles to the east of the township's northern boundary.

FOLEY, township, Parry Sound District
Position 45° 48′ 79° 56′

Situated south of the town of Parry Sound, the township was established in 1866 and surveyed that year by Ontario Land Surveyor G.A. Stewart. Stewart reported strong indications of iron ore, which was later discovered at Otter Lake. The township, named after the Hon. Michael Hamilton Foley, former MP for Waterloo is bounded by McDougall Township to the north, Christie and Humphrey Townships to the east, Conger Township to the south, and Cowper Township to the west.

Foley Township is hilly and has numerous rivers and lakes, many of which are very deep and offer great scenic beauty with their steep, rocky shores and picturesque islands. The principal river is the Seguin which enters the township with two branches from the east.

The Parry Sound Colonization Road passed through the township facilitating settlement in the area. Among the earliest settlers to come to the township were William Wilcox, Thomas McGown, William McPhillmay and William Scott.

At the mouth of the Seguin, touching on the northwestern corner of the township, developed the town of Parry Sound around a sawmill set up by James and William Gibson in 1857. A few years later the mill was acquired by William Beatty and his sons James and William Jr. To this mill were floated saw-logs and timber from the township down the south branch of the Seguin.

In the latter part of the 19th century, township residents in summer still travelled by steamer plying weekly between Parry Sound and Collingwood and thence by rail to Toronto. Today the CPR and the CNR service the township, as do Highways 69 and 518. There are six communities within Foley's borders: Black Road, Duckmure, Falding, James Bay, Rosseau Road and South Parry. The township's population in 1978 was 1,070.

H.R. Page & Co.: *Guide Book and Atlas of Muskoka and Parry Sound Districts,* 1879.

FOLEYET, geographic township, Sudbury District
Position 48° 16′ 82° 30′

The township originally surveyed in 1916, takes its name from the hamlet of Foleyet which was established as a divisional point on the Canadian Northern Railway around 1912. The story is that railway builder Sir Donald Mann wanted to name the station Foley after railway contractor Timothy Foley. When told by the superintendent that the name Foley had already been given to another station on the line, Sir Donald angrily replied: "I'll name that place Foley yet!" "Foleyet will be fine, Sir," said the superintendent.

Today the railway which runs through the scenic northeastern section of the township is known as the Canadian National. Highway 101 linking the centres of Timmins and Chapleau, passes through the southeastern part of Foleyet.

FOLEYET, community, Foleyet Township, District of Sudbury
Position 48° 15′ 82° 27′

This small community is located some sixty miles southwest of Timmins on Highway 101 and on the mainline of the Canadian National Railway. The settlement grew up when the Canadian Northern Railway established a divisional point at that location around 1912. Timothy Foley was a railway contractor on the Canadian Northern Railway and Sir Donald Mann, a builder of railways, wished to name the new station Foley. But this name had already been applied to another station. However, Mann stubbornly held to his wish and by ingenious compromise the station was named Foleyet.

Railway shops, a roundtable and freight yards were constructed and the families of railroad workers moved into the area. The railway, plus a thriving lumber company, provided employment for the budding community. When diesel engines came into use, however, the importance of the settlement declined because the refuelling facilities were no longer required.

Two floods, one in 1918 and one in 1960, caused much devastation in the community. This was rectified with the building of a concrete dam in 1962 nearby in the Ivanhoe River.

Foleyet has one public school and one separate school. High School students are bused to Timmins.

Today Foleyet benefits from a busy tourist trade. Hunting and fishing have made the area a sportsman's paradise. The population of Foleyet in 1975 was 800.

Ministry of Natural Resources: *Directory of Statutes and Data for Unincorporated Communities in the Northern Region*, 1975.

FONTAINE, geographic township, Algoma District
Position 46° 51′ 82° 23′

The township formerly designated "O", was named in 1974 after R. Fontaine, the Mayor of the town of Hearst at that time. Accessible only by waterways, the township is located about 40 miles northeast of Elliot Lake.

FONTHILL, part of the Town of Pelham, Regional Municipality of Niagara
Position 43° 02′ 79° 17′

The village of Fonthill, situated on the boundary between Pelham and Thorold Townships was first named Osborne's Corners when it was settled in 1842. Later this name was changed to Temperanceville, and finally English immigrants named the village Fonthill, after Fonthill Abbey in England. In 1922 Fonthill was incorporated as a village and in 1970 the village officially became part of the town of Pelham.

Many of the first settlers in the area had emigrated from England and they included the Giles, Oxley, Hobson, Willett and Robertshaw families. Another group of settlers arrived from United Empire Loyalist settlements in Nova Scotia. They included the Kinsman, Randall and Gore families. Possibly the most influential settler in the area was Dexter D'Everardo; he was responsible for persuading many families to move up from Nova Scotia, and he retained an important role in the development of the village.

In 1841 the first post office in the area was established under the name of Pelham, with John Price as the first postmaster. Dexter D'Everardo was appointed the first county registrar in 1851.

The first church in Fonthill was the Baptist Church, built in 1846. It was replaced by the present structure in 1909. The Fonthill United Church (formerly the Methodist Church) was originally built in 1850 by the Universalists. The Methodists purchased it in 1856 and the church was remodeled in 1912. It is said that the church bell is the same one that was originally brought from Buffalo in 1863. The Church of God (also known as Second Advent Church) was built in 1908. The Anglican Church, built in 1862, was replaced by the present building in 1915. In 1960 the convent of the Vicentian Sisters of Charity, Pittsburgh, Pa., U.S.A. was dedicated. Located on Highway 20, just outside of Fonthill, it was the first such convent to be erected in Canada.

In 1856 the Fonthill Grammar School was established, but twenty years later grants for the school were withdrawn and the school was abandoned. Over the years three different public school buildings have stood on the site of Fonthill Public School. The A.K. Wigg School was opened in 1955 and in 1958 Saint Alexander's Separate School was established. In the same year the Thorold-Fonthill High School first opened its doors to students.

The Fonthill Nurseries, founded in 1837 by Samuel Taylor, achieved a nationwide reputation. In 1912 Canadian Canners established a factory in Fonthill with Mr. R.W. Reid as manager. The plant primarily processed the local tomato crop, but soon encouraged the planting of fruit trees, especially peaches, in the area. At the peak canning season this factory gave employment to several hundred residents. Owing to the centralization of the canning industry, the factory closed in 1958. The Kinsman General Store in Fonthill opened in 1850 and has been operated by three successive generations of the Kinsman family. The *Welland Tribune* which is the oldest publication in the County of Welland, originally started in Fonthill in 1854 as the *Welland Herald*.

A public library was established in Fonthill as early as the 1850's. It was located in the Concert Hall which was destroyed by fire in 1888. The Fonthill Mechanics Institute, the immediate forerunner of the present library, was organized in 1890. The present Fonthill Public Library was built in 1897.

Electricity came to Fonthill in 1909; gas service arrived in 1916. The village had no train service, but a trolley line was built from St. Catharines to Fonthill in 1907.

The village of Fonthill is surrounded by good farmland, and orchards planted since the turn of the century have made this an important fruit-producing area.

Fonthill Women's Institute: *History of the Village of Fonthill*, 1963.

FOOTE, geographic township, Thunder Bay District
Position 49° 11' 85° 23'

The township, located northeast of the community of Manitouwadge, bears the name of Major (Rev.) John W. Foote, V.C., MPP for Durham 1948-1955.

A Hydro-Electric Transmission Line crosses the southern part of the township.

FOOTES BAY, community, District Municipality of Muskoka
Position 45° 08' 79° 45'

Footes Bay is a small community near the junction of Highways 69 and 118 in the scenic lake region of Muskoka. Its name was derived from the bay on which it is situated. The bay, part of Lake Joseph, had been named after William Edward Foot who came from Ireland with his family in 1871 and acquired land along the bay shore. Foot later moved to Bracebridge and then to Manitoba, finally returning to Parry Sound where he became Deputy Registrar and Justice of the Peace.

The inhabitants of Footes Bay today cater to the summer cottagers who considerably swell the community's population each year. There is a large concrete government dock, a grocery store, a post office and a boat service centre.

Geraldine Coombe: *Muskoka: Past and Present*, 1976.

FORBES, geographic township, Thunder Bay District
Position 48° 37' 89° 39'

This subdivided township which was surveyed in 1915, was named after the former long-time MLA, MPP for York West, the Hon. Dr. Forbes E. Godfrey. The township is situated just northwest of the city of Thunder Bay and is linked by roads to the Trans-Canada Highway.

FORD, geographic township, Cochrane District
Position 49° 01' 81° 57'

The township, located southwest of Smooth Rock Falls, was most likely named after John Ford, MPP for Halton in 1919, when its northern, southern and western boundaries were surveyed. There are no roads within the township's borders.

FORDWICH, police village, Howick Township, Huron County
Position 43° 52' 81° 02'

Fordwich, named for a village in Kent County, England, is situated in the centre of Howick Township, about 35 miles north of Stratford, and was the first village to be inhabited in Howick Township.

On the original survey Fordwich is described as the town plot of Howick and it was designated as the future site of a city. This ambitious plan, however, was not realized, but the settlement did progress rapidly. Arthur Mitchell, Joel Rogers and W.G. Walker were the first settlers, arriving in 1854. The first post office, known as Lisadel, was opened about 1855 with Arthur Mitchell as postmaster.

By the 1870's Fordwich had a large steam planing mill, two sawmills, a flouring mill and a cheese and butter factory. In its business section, which was situated between three hills, were three general stores, a grocery store, two carriage shops, a harness shop, three blacksmith shops and two hotels. In 1873 a new post office was opened in Fordwich. The building of the southern extension of the Toronto, Grey and Bruce Railway further encouraged the village's development.

Until School Section 17 was established in 1872, students of Fordwich attended Gough's School, a mile from the village, and which was the first school built in Howick Township. The present school was built in 1900 and a Continuation School added later.

The first church was the Anglican Trinity Church, built in 1861 with the Rev. C.H. Drinkwater as minister. The Presbyterians built in 1865 and Methodist church was erected in 1875. The village also has a Good Templar Lodge, a Loyal Orange Lodge, and a Masonic Lodge.

H. Belden & Co.: *Historical Atlas of Huron County*, 1879.

R.W.N. Wade: *Early History of Howick Township in Huron County*, 1952.

FOREST, town, Warwick Township, Lambton County
Position 43° 06' 82° 00'

The town of Forest is located in the northeast portion of Lambton County, about twenty-three miles northeast of the town of Sarnia on Highway 21 and the CNR.

The beginning of Forest dates from 1859, when the Grand Trunk Railway line from Stratford to Sarnia was completed. A small pumping station, nicknamed Forest because of the heavy forests that covered the area, was built at the Junction of the townships of Bosanquet, Warwick, and Plympton. The railway station became the nucleus for the growth of the community. Some settlers had arrived in the area as early as the 1840's and 50's, including George West, Lachlan McFadyen, the McPhersons, Bradleys, Pettits, Holdsworths, Brodies, Haynes, Bayleys, Diers, Karrs and Carscaddens. In 1858 Timothy Resseuie laid out the first village lots.

That year a post office was opened with Robert Dier as the first postmaster. About the same time, John Woodroff started a general store and Philip Smith opened a tavern. In the late 1850's the first town hall was built. The Forest Mechanic's Institute was formed in 1871, and in 1897 it became the Forest Free Public Library.

The community was incorporated as a village in 1872. The village council of 1873 included George West, reeve; and George Coultis, John Coultis, Robert Dier and John Mason, councillors. In 1888, villagers expressed the desire to become incorporated as a town, but Forest did not quite have the required population of 2,000. To circumvent the problem, it was arranged to have one of the Grand Trunk Railway passenger cars remain at the station for an hour — just long enough to register the passengers and crew as Forest citizens! Alvin Rawlings was the town's first mayor in 1889.

The first school in the community opened in 1867. It was a private school for girls operated by a Miss McConough. A brick four-room school built in 1874 was replaced in 1911 when Central School was erected. Forest High School opened its doors in 1890. Destroyed by fire in 1940 it was rebuilt, and in 1960 the name was changed to North Lambton Secondary School.

The Anglicans were the first to erect a church in Forest in 1861. It stood on the site of the present-day Anglican Church. A Congregational church was built in 1863; a Roman Catholic church followed in 1865; and St. James Presbyterian Church was built in 1868. The Forest Baptist Church was constructed in 1871, the Gospel Hall in 1872, and the Salvation Army Citadel and the Pentecostal Hall were both built in 1937. Forest United Church opened in 1926. The Forest Christian Reformed Church was built in 1953, and in 1956 the Jehovah's Witnesses opened a Hall.

Forest has always benefited by being the centre of a thriving agricultural region. Over the years a number of industries have contributed to Forest's growth, including the Forest Basket Company, Huctwith Produce, the Hopper Foundry, Forest Co-operative Creamery, Hillside Feeds, and others. As well, Forest has a busy tourist season because of its proximity to Lake Huron.

The Forest-Lambton Museum opened in Forest in 1964. The population of the town in 1978 was 2,679.

Forest Centennial 1859-1959, 1959.

Sarnia Observer, 1967.

FOREST HILL, part of City of Toronto, Municipality of Metropolitan Toronto
Position 43° 42′ 79° 25′

Although it lies in the centre of a city, Forest Hill has maintained its traditional identity as a separate community. Noted for its wealth and its excellent education system, this urban community has a long history as a village separate from the large municipality which surrounds it.

It began when Forest Hill was part of North York, a large municipality running north from Lake Ontario to Vaughan and Markham Townships, and extending from the Scarborough boundary on the east to the Humber River on the west. From the forested ridge centred in the area now known as Forest Hill, early settlers could look across the intervening open country to the Town of York as it steadily grew towards the stature of the city of Toronto it became in 1834. The Indians hunting through the local forest in search of deer must have heard the sounds of the War of 1812 as the Americans advanced on Fort York. One of the earliest families to settle in the area were the Baldwins who came in 1830. They played an important part in the development of the village. Lawrence Baldwin, first reeve of the newly incorporated village of Forest Hill in 1923, was a nephew of Robert Baldwin, premier of Upper Canada in 1834.

John Wickson, a settler of the middle 1860's built a summer residence at Eglinton Avenue and Old Forest Hill Road. He called it Forest Hill, thus unwittingly providing the future name of the village. In 1909, with a population of 500, it became known as Spadina Heights, attracting monied Toronto families eagerly seeking a location away from the city. In 1923, by petition of ratepayers' signatures presented to York County Council, a request was granted incorporating Spadina Heights as a village to be known as Forest Hill. Forest Hill, at that time, had a population of 2,100 and was to become the privileged reserve of affluent and powerful Torontorians and the site of their fabulous, estate-like homes. The first council to sit in 1923 effected zoning bylaws making Forest Hill a restricted residential area coming under the scrutiny of a Board of Architects.

In 1910, because the two nearest schools were difficult for the children to reach, Forest Hill petitioned for and was granted School Section 30. Misses McKee and Rutherford became the first teachers of School Section 30. By 1950 the village had three elementary schools, a junior high school and a collegiate. The Village has long since been the site of Upper Canada College, a private school which was moved to the area from Toronto in 1891.

In 1911 the village received its first house of worship when Christ Church of Toronto moved its old church to the community and became Grace Church-on-the-Hill, on the boundary between Forest Hill and the city.

In 1967 Forest Hill finally became part of the city of Toronto. Today it consists of 940 acres bounded by Avenue Road, Bathurst Street, Eglinton Avenue and St. Clair Avenue West. It still retains its separate identity and continues to be regarded as the exclusive territory of wealthy industrialists, civic leaders, and professional men.

William French: *A Most unlikely Village*, 1964.

FOREST MILLS, community, Richmond Township, Lennox and Addington County
Position 44° 20′ 77° 03′

To the early pioneers of Richmond Township the site of the present community of Forest Mills on the Salmon River, northwest of Napanee, was known as "The Falls". Here was the only bridge across the river and all traffic to and from the northern part of the township crossed at this point. At certain seasons salmon which used to come up the stream in great numbers would congregate at the foot of the falls unable to leap over the high barrier, and settlers could scoop up a cart-load of salmon in a matter of minutes. No salmon was found above The Falls.

The first house was erected at The Falls by Chauncey Windover in the late 1830's. Other early settlers in the vicinity were the McConnels, Calvin Dafoe, Aaron Oliver and Peter Bumhour. Archie McNeil built a saw and grist mill and the settlement took on the name of McNeil's Mills. When a post office was opened in 1868 the name was changed to Forest Mills.

Walter S. Herrington: *History of the County of Lennox and Addington*, 1913.

FORFAR, community, Bastard Township, Leeds County
Position 44° 40' 76° 13'

This dispersed rural community lies about 55 miles west of Brockville where Highway 42 meets the Canadian National Railway line. During the late nineteenth century it was a busy little settlement, with its trade stimulated by the railway.

A post office was opened in 1854 with William Young, a local storekeeper, as postmaster. By 1857 the community's population was about 50. Residents included the blacksmith Elijah Mattice, the innkeeper Henry Morris, and Gilbert S. Auslin, a teacher. The Rev. James Hales ministered to the New Connection Methodist Congregation.

By 1871 Forfar's population had doubled in size. Two blacksmiths, a carpenter, a storekeeper, and the postmaster were among the businessmen of the community. Forfar grew little after this time, although around the turn of the century a second store, a cheese factory, and a telephone office were opened.

FORGIE, geographic township, Kenora District
Position 49° 43' 94° 57'

Named after John Forgie of Stayner, Ontario, the township is dotted with lakes and streams. Highway 17, which is part of the Trans-Canada Highway, links the area with Keewatin and Kenora some twenty miles to the east.

FORKS OF THE CREDIT, part of the town of Caledon, Regional Municipality of Peel
Position 43° 48' 80° 00'

This picturesque dispersed rural community received its unusual name because it is here that two branches of the Credit River meet, forming a fork. It was the river, itself, that attracted economy because the terrain, with the steep valley walls, could not be used agriculturally. The settlement was originally known as Credit Forks, but with the arrival of the Credit Valley Railway in 1879 the name Forks of the Credit was more frequently used and this was made official in 1976. The junction of the Credit River branches gave rise to industry during the 1870's. Price's dam and sawmill located just below the present CPR trestle, was the first such operation.

The excellence of the limestone, sandstone and freestone existing at the Forks gave employment to several hundred men, both unskilled quarrymen and skilled stonecutters, during the 1880's. The local quarries supplied stonework for the Ontario Parliament begun during 1886, and also for the Toronto City Hall, many University of Toronto buildings and Knox Presbyterian Church, Toronto. There were three groups of quarries. One was located near Brimstone, where an overhead tramway transported the immense blocks of stone to waiting flatcars on a siding above the Forks of the Credit Station. This operation was owned first by K. Chisholm and later by John McKnight. Another, the Forks Quarries, extending along the main wall of the valley, near the CPR tracks, also had a tramway track constructed up the face of the incline. The third, the "Crow's Nest" quarries were situated on the Belfountain branch of the Credit River. With the introduction of cement for building use, the quarries declined in the 1900's. With Toronto producing and shipping by rail, the station at the Forks of the Credit was closed in 1932.

Another industry, albeit unsuccessful, was the Credit Forks Tile and Brick Company, formed to make use of large clay deposits. The Caledon Ski Club now occupies the site of this early company which planned to build a china and plate factory using the local clay, but the quality of the clay proved too inferior. A dam built for this factory remains today and forms a lake, an excellent spot for picnickers. A lime-kiln located near the Forks Quarries was also in operation for a time.

Gradually the industrial economy waned and the area reverted to a rural state and became a popular nature spot for outings. The Bruce Trail passes nearby on its way through the beautiful Caledon section. The Caledon Mountain Trout Club was formed in 1901 just east of the Forks of the Credit.

Ralph Beaumont: *Cataract and the Forks of the Credit*, 1973.

Pauline J. Roulston: *Place Names of Peel: Past and Present*, 1978.

FORMOSA, community, Culross Township, Bruce County
Position 44° 02′ 81° 16′

Situated 8 miles southwest of the town of Walkerton on the county road separating Culross and Carrick Townships, Formosa is a thriving community with a population of nearly four hundred.

The village's early settlers were almost all of German or Alsation descent and of the Roman Catholic faith. John B. Kroetsch built the first sawmill at Formosa in the 1850's and the village has had a sawmill in operation ever since. As befitting a German settlement, a brewery was established at an early date. It was opened in 1869 by Andrew Rau and became known in more recent years as the Formosa Springs Brewery.

The first store in the village was kept by Mr. A. Schick, while

John Kartes operated the first hotel. A post office was established in 1862 with Francis X. Messner as postmaster. By the 1880's Formosa counted among its numerous prospering business establishments three blacksmiths and two wagon shops, a grist mill, a carding mill, a cigar factory, two cooperages, two cabinet and two harness shops, five shoe shops, a tin and hardware store, five general stores and several hotels. Francis X. Messner and his brother Anthony originated several successful business enterprises, encouraged new settlers to come to the village, acted as private bankers and liberally assisted charities throughout Canada. To help promote Catholic education they built two Convents, one at Formosa in 1872, the other at Walkerton.

Roman Catholic church services were held in a little log schoolhouse until in 1857 a frame church was completed. Reverend Father Stier was the first priest to reside at the village. Some twenty years later the congregation built a large stone church. Workmen carried on construction around the old church until at last it was all but hidden from view. The magnificent new church which still serves Formosa and the surrounding area, was opened on December 9, 1883. When in 1901 attempts were made to drill for oil at Formosa, a column of water gushed up to a height of 16 feet above ground from a depth of 945 feet. The clear sparkling water still flows from the Formosa well. Surrounded by lovely gardens known as the Palace Gardens, it has become a major tourist attraction of the area.

H. Belden & Co.: *Historical Atlas of the County of Bruce*, 1880.

Norman Robertson: *The History of the County of Bruce*, 1906.

Norman McLeod: *The History of the County of Bruce, 1907-1969*, 1969.

Fort Erie

FORT ERIE, town, Regional Municipality of Niagara
Position 42° 54′ 78° 56′

Situated at the junction of the Niagara River and Lake Erie, the town is 55 miles southeast of Hamilton, on the Queen Elizabeth Way. Two international bridges leading to Buffalo, in neighbouring New York State have made Fort Erie an important and prosperous centre, with a 1978 population of 23,808.

A trading post and stockade were built here by the French about 1750, but were destroyed in the 1760's at the end of the Seven Years War. In 1764 Capt. Montresor was commissioned to establish a British trading post at the site. It was named Fort Erie by his superior officer, Col. Bradstreet. A community connected with the garrison began to grow up around the fort and a survey of the site was made in 1781. In 1800 the first regular ferry service with Black Rock, New York was begun. In 1807 about twenty-five houses were occupied by such families as the Baxters, Hirrots, Hersheys, Pounds, and Sherks.

The garrison at Fort Erie saw considerable action in the War of 1812-14. The American ships *Ohio* and *Somers* were captured by the British near here, in the last naval action of the war. The fort itself manned by a force of only 150 defenders, was seized in July of 1814 by the American General Winfield Scott, who turned it into a formidable strong point. A British attempt to recapture the fort in August 1814 was unsuccessful. The American forces having made a sortie in September, fell back on Fort Erie after their defeat at Lundy's Lane and on November 5th, they blew up the fortifications before withdrawing to the United States. The fort was restored in the 1930's and is now a museum.

There was, after the war, an influx of new immigrants to the area. Most of them were United Empire Loyalists and disbanded soldiers of Butler's Rangers. Fort Erie's situation on a major waterway contributed greatly to the community's early development and during the first quarter of the nineteenth century it was more important than Buffalo, its U.S. neighbour to the south. The Canadian village was the shopping centre for the inhabitants of Buffalo and the distribution point for manufactured goods and imports for the surrounding area.

However, the construction of the Erie Canal in 1825 and later the Welland Canal, led to a decline in prosperity as the new water routes bypassed the community. Not until the Erie and Niagara Railway extended its line to Fort Erie in the 1860's did a new period of growth begin. In 1857 the community had been incorporated as the Village of Waterloo, with Alexander Douglas as the first reeve. Prior to this, the settlement had been known variously as Fort Erie Mills, Fort Erie Rapids, and Sandy Town. In the year of its incorporation the village stretched for two and a half miles along the waterfront and boasted four taverns, ten stores, four churches, a blacksmith shop and a drill shed.

The 1860's were troubled years. A great fire in 1862 destroyed much of the village. In 1866 the Fenians, Irish nationalists from the United States, determined to "free Canada from British domination", crossed the Niagara Bridge and then fell back on Fort Erie in their retreat. They caused widespread destruction to the property of the village's 1,200 residents and the American government's refusal to pay compensation caused much bitterness at the time.

In 1872 the village suffered yet another setback when the Grand Trunk Railway opened a line a mile away from the nearest ferry and the ferries were moved to Windsor. However, prosperity returned following the building of the International Railway Bridge in 1873 by Colonel Sir Casimir Stanislaus Gzowski. Today this is the only bridge built across the Niagara River before 1900 that is still in use.

The construction of the bridge resulted in the creation of a whole new community. Originally called Victoria, the name of the community was changed to "International Bridge" when a post office was opened. It surpassed Fort Erie in population and commerce by the 1890's. Boardinghouses, stores, taverns, a school and a church, rapidly went up and in 1895, with a population of 895, the community became the incorporated village of Bridgeburg. John T. James was the first reeve. Incorporated as the Town of Bridgeburg in 1915, it amalgamated with Waterloo in 1932 to form the Town of Fort Erie. The first mayor of this new town of 7,000 was W.J. Hawley.

On August 11, 1927, Fort Erie residents and a throng of visitors witnessed the historic opening by the Prince of Wales of the Peace Bridge, an international road bridge connecting the town to Buffalo.

In the early twentieth century a number of industries were established in Fort Erie, including Williams Gold Refining, one of Canada's largest refiners. By 1930 Fort Erie had a chemical plant, a steel plant and Irvin Air Chute Ltd. Fleet Manufacturing, producing aircraft, was also set up in 1930. The year 1947 saw the opening of Gould Batteries and Strong, Cobb, Arner Co., one of Canada's largest suppliers of pharmaceutical products.

Today Fort Erie bustles with tourists passing over the International Bridge, the largest point of entry into Canada. With its sizeable work force the bridge is one of the town's major employers. The town also has one of the largest horse-racing tracks in the country.

A Historical and Descriptive Sketch of the County of Welland, 1866.

Evening Review, Centennial Edition, 1967.

FORT FRANCES, town, Rainy River District
Position 48° 36' 93° 24'

Situated on the north bank of the Rainy River, the town is 141 miles southeast of Kenora and 230 miles west of Thunder Bay. Named after the wife of Sir George Simpson, a governor of the Hudson's Bay Company, who visited the fort in 1830, Fort Frances is the oldest continuous settlement west of Lake Superior and also the largest community in the Rainy River District.

The first explorer in the area was Jacques de Noyon, who opened a canoe route for the fur trade in 1688. In 1731 Pierre Gaultier de Verennes, Sieur de la Vérendrye, established Fort St. Pierre, two miles east of the present town, at Pithers Point, to serve as a fur-trading post. The post became a very important one, as it marked the farthest point to which canoes could travel from Montreal and still return before freeze-up. Here traders who travelled farther west into the Athabaska area received their supplies. Six different companies occupied the post until finally the Hudson's Bay Company took it over in 1821.

Following the decline of the fur trade, lumbering became the principal industry of the community. In 1873 H.S. Fowler built one of the earliest sawmills. The Fort Frances Canal from Rainy Lake to Lake of the Woods, built in 1878 to improve communication with the West, aided the development of trade, commercial fishing, and logging. A canal was also begun from Rainy Lake to Rainy River but was not completed because of the coming of the railway in 1902. Steamships played an important role in transportation until 1908 when the Fort Frances Canal became part of a dam and power project. The hydro-electric developments on the Seine and Rainy Rivers have contributed much to industrial expansion. Today the Ontario-Minnesota Pulp and Paper Co. Ltd., which took over many of the smaller firms, is the largest employer in Fort Frances and produces insulating board and paper. Other industries include Herrem Woodworkers Ltd., Fort Frances Steel and Welding, and International Block Company Ltd.

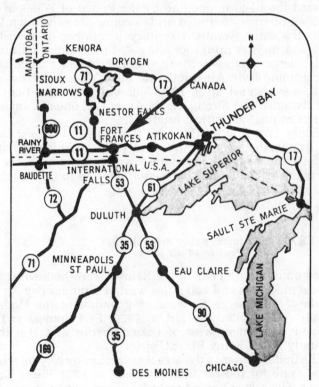

A post office was established in 1876. The community gained municipal government in 1891 when the municipality of Alberton was formed consisting of Fort Frances and the townships of McIrvine, Raddick, and Crozier. However, Fort Frances withdrew from the union in 1898 and in 1903 became an incorporated village.

Today, Fort Frances, with a population of 9,088 (1978), is the judicial and economic centre of the district. Much of the town's importance stems from its position on the international border. Across the river is its twin town, International Falls, Minnesota. The two towns are joined by a busy international bridge and Fort Frances has become the point where most of the traffic from the American Midwest enters Canada. The town is served by train, bus and air. Canadian Voyageur Airlines operates from the Fort Frances airport. As a result, tourism has become a very important industry. The annual "Fun in the Sun" jamboree held in the first week of July, attracts many summer visitors.

Fort Frances has six primary, two secondary, and three separate schools, as well as two libraries and a weekly newspaper, the *Fort Frances Times*. Several government offices are located here. Twelve churches and the LaVérendrye Hospital also serve the townspeople and there are now twelve hotels and motels to meet the demands of the ever-expanding tourist trade.

Department of Lands and Forests: *History of the Fort Frances Forest District*, 1963.

Ministry of Natural Resources: *Directory of Statistics and Data*, 1976.

Fort George, 1913. Old Stone Magazine

Public Archives Canada, PA 51871

FORT GEORGE, near Niagara-on-the-Lake, Regional Municipality of Niagara
Position 43° 15′ 79° 04′

Fort George, located at Niagara-on-the-Lake, was reconstructed following an agreement in the mid-1930's between the federal and provincial governments to share the cost of the project. Begun in 1937, the Fort was completed in 1940 but the official opening did not take place until after World War II. In June 1950, in a ceremony attended by both Canadian and American military forces, the site was formally declared open to the public. Today it depicts Fort George as it existed during the British occupation of 1796-1813.

The first Fort George was built between 1796 and 1799. Situated on the west bank of the Niagara River, approximately one mile from Lake Ontario, the post was constructed to replace Fort Niagara, which the British were forced to evacuate in 1796 by the terms of Jay's Treaty. Far from being an imposing work this first Fort George consisted of six small bastions connected by a line of cedar picketing and surrounded by a shallow dry ditch.

The fort was originally intended to command the Lake Ontario entrance to the Niagara River and protect the town of Niagara-on-the-Lake (at that time called Newark), but it was too far away from the entrance of the river to be effective. Sir George Prevost, Captain-General and Governor-in-Chief of British North America, reported in May of 1812 that Fort George was undergoing repairs but that in its most improved state it could not make much resistance against an enemy force, or withstand the cannonading of heavy guns.

Despite this announcement Fort George continued its role as the military headquarters for His Majesty's Forces in Upper Canada, and on the outbreak of war with the United States, assumed a position of considerable importance.

On May 27, 1813, the Americans launched a major bombardment and assault against Fort George. As Prevost had predicted the British post was levelled completely by the fire from Fort Niagara and the American contingent of 6,000 men embarked upon the defenders under cover of the morning mist, and after a gallant fight the British, under Brigadier-General John Vincent, evacuated the fort.

The Americans, now in command of the fort, set about to construct a new and better fort on the site with trenches leading to the river bank and to St. Mark's Anglican Church.

Throughout the summer and autumn of 1813 the British and their Indian allies bottled up the Americans behind their new entrenched fort. By December 1813 the American commanding officer, General McClure, had only 100 men to continue the defense of the fort. The British then advanced on the fort and McClure evacuated Fort George and retired to the American side of the river.

For the duration of the war the British retained the control of the mouth of the Niagara River. By the end of the war Fort George, the scene of so much military activity, was again in decay. In August, 1815, Sir Gordon Drummond, Commander-in-Chief of His Majesty's Forces in Upper Canada, gave orders that Fort George be abandoned.

However, it was not until 1826 that the military headquarters of Upper Canada was transferred to York.

In 1812 a red-hot cannon ball fired from Fort Niagara had penetrated the roof of the powder magazine and set fire to the wooden supports. With 800 barrels of gunpowder in storage, there was immediate risk of a disastrous explosion. While most of the garrison left to escape what appeared to be certain death, a small party of men led by an officer of the Royal Engineers stayed behind and they were able to climb onto the roof and extinguish the fire before it reached the gunpowder.

The bodies of General Isaac Brock, hero of the battle of Queenston Heights, and his aide-de-camp, John MacDonell, were originally buried at Fort George. But in 1824 they were removed to a vault beneath the newly constructed memorial on the Queenston Heights, overlooking where the battle was fought and Brock was killed. A stone now marks the site of their original graves.

The decision made in the 1930's to reconstruct the fort as it was in the beginning of the last century, resulted in a museum, three blockhouses, a sawpit, guardhouse, officers' quarters, kitchen and powder magazine within the gates of this historic Fort.

National Historic Parks Branch, Ministry of Indian Affairs and Northern Development: *Fort George: National Historic Park.*

Fort Henry

FORT HENRY, Kingston, Frontenac County
Position 44° 14′ 76° 30′

In 1936 Fort Henry, Kingston, was little more than a great mass of crumbling limestone with grass and weeds growing out of the chinks between the carefully hand-cut stone. The work of reconstruction, sponsored by the federal and provincial governments, began in the summer of that year. The object was to restore the fort to its condition one hundred years before.

Careful research and painstaking workmanship succeeded in making it as accurate as any similar achievement in North America. Completed on August 1, 1938 Fort Henry is not only well restored but alive with the sounds of the past as the famous "Fort Henry Guard" perform their military drills to the delight of thousands of visitors.

When the War of 1812 was declared Kingston was undefended. Fort Henry was built to protect the Naval Dockyards situated there. Under the direction of Captain Benjamin Marlowe of the Royal Engineers construction began in May 1813. By 1820 it was the strongest point west of Quebec.

The fear of future invasion following the War of 1812-14 was so strong that in 1826 the Rideau Canal was undertaken from Kingston to Ottawa to ensure a safe route to Montreal should the Americans gain control of the St. Lawrence and Lake Ontario. It was deemed that Fort Henry was not strong enough to protect the Rideau Canal so in 1829 approval was given to plans to improve the Fort.

It was not until 1832, following the completion of the Rideau Canal, that Lt. Col. Wright was authorized to proceed with the demolition of the existing Fort Henry and begin the construction of the new fort. The stone for the Fort was quarried on both sides of the road leading from Kingston to Gananoque. Considering the limitations of equipment the Fort was a considerable feat of engineering which continued despite the cholera epidemic 1832-34 that wiped out one-tenth of the population of Kingston. By 1836 the main portion of the present fort was completed and two batteries of Royal Garrison Artillery and one regiment of the line took possession.

In military language the Fort is a casemated redoubt, the main portion consisting of a pentagonal figure, the three-sided front of which faces inland towards the north and completely covers the Rideau entrance and the site of the naval establishment against attack from that direction.

Although never attacked by an enemy, the history of Fort Henry has not been lacking in colourful incidents. When it was first garrisoned, Upper Canada was seething in the unrest that culminated in the Rebellion of 1837. A plan by the American Rensellaer Van Rensellaer, who was in sympathy with the Canadian rebels, to capture the Fort while the regular forces were absent in Lower Canada failed when 1,600 militiamen manned the Fort. The rebels did not attempt to take the Fort.

Following the Rebellion it held rebel prisoners and was the scene of the daring escape of John Montgomery and his companions. In 1908 the Fort was used as a quarantine for victims of Kingston's smallpox epidemic. And during the two World Wars German prisoners were interned there.

The gradual improvement of relations with the United States, combined with military developments of the late nineteenth century, slowly decreased and finally nullified the importance of Kingston's defenses. At the time of the Northwest Rebellion in 1885, Fort Henry was considered to be of little value and was soon afterwards abandoned as obsolete. Thus it fell into the mass of rubble which was once more brought to life with its restoration in 1938.

Ronald L. Way: "Old Fort Henry: The Citadel of Upper Canada" in the *Canadian Geographical Journal* April 1950.

FORT HENRY HEIGHTS, suburban community, Pittsburgh Township, Frontenac County
Position 44° 14′ 76° 27′

Situated just east of Kingston, overlooking the St. Lawrence River, the community was founded to provide accommodation for married personnel of the armed forces. It was named after the historic fort which stands beside it.

The postwar expansion of military installations in the area was the main cause of the Fort Henry Heights development. The first families moved there in 1949 and the community began to grow at an astonishing pace. By 1953 the population had reached 2,455, making Fort Henry Heights the largest suburban development of its kind in Canada.

A school was built in 1952. In 1957 Batoche Avenue Public School became the community's third school. There were no stores by 1952 but space was allocated for a future shopping centre.

A distinctive feature of the community is the naming of most of its streets after events and places in military history.

Kingston Whig-Standard, 1953; 1960.

FORT LA CLOCHE, community, Victoria Township, Algoma District
Position 46° 07′ 82° 05′

This dispersed rural community is located on a historic site on Great La Cloche Island in the North Channel of Lake Huron. Here on the island, the North West Company set up a fur trading post and a vessel repair station around 1790. The fort consisted of a couple of large log buildings, and a cluster of huts nearby made up a small village.

FORT MALDEN, Amherstburg, Essex County
Position 42° 06′ 83° 06′

Fort Malden, Amherstburg, is located on the east bank of the Detroit River, 18 miles north of the city of Windsor. It was built in 1797-99 by the Second Battalion of the Royal Canadian Volunteers, under Captain Hector McLean, to replace Fort Lernoult at Detroit, one of the posts evacuated by the British under the terms of the Jay Treaty. The town of Amherstburg came into existence at the same time, a portion of the Military Reserve being laid out for a Town Site.

When the War of 1812-14 broke out Major-General Sir Isaac Brock reinforced Fort Malden with regulars and militia from the east. Upon his arrival at the fort he consulted with Colonel Procter, commander at Fort Malden, and with Tecumseh, chief of a vast Indian confederacy who opposed the influx of American settlers into their hunting grounds. These consultations resulted in the formulation of a plan which led to the capture of Detroit in August, 1812.

At the same time ships were being built in the Navy Yard near Fort Malden and the heavy guns were stripped from the fort to arm these vessels. Despite British efforts to reinforce their squadron on the Great Lakes they were defeated on September 10, 1813 in the decisive Battle of Lake Erie, thus leaving Canada open to invasion. General Procter felt that no effective resistance could be offered to an advance by the Americans under Major-General Harrison, so fell back towards Burlington after burning the public buildings at Fort Malden and Detroit.

The American Cavalry pursued the retreating column and on October 5, 1813, at Moraviantown, the British and their Indian allies were defeated and dispersed. The great Tecumseh met his death in this action.

The Americans rehabilitated Ford Malden and, apart from minor foraging raids to the east along the Thames Valley and to the north shore of Lake Erie, the countryside was not disturbed. When the Treaty of Ghent brought an end to the war on July 1, 1815, Fort Malden was restored to the British.

Following the conclusion of the war there was a long unbroken era of peaceful relations with the United States, thus in 1851 British troops were withdrawn and replaced with "enrolled pensioners" who stood guard until 1859, when the fort was converted for civil use.

The tranquility of the border was interrupted only once. That was during the outbreak of the Mackenzie Rebellion of 1837 when the local militia were called out to augment the detachment of Regulars at Fort Malden. American filibusters known as Patriots hoped to capture the fort and succeeded in occupying Bois Blanc Island near the fort opposite Amherstburg. They then bombarded the fort and the town of Amherstburg for two days from the decks of the schooner *Anne*. There were no large guns at the fort with which to shell the *Anne* but the helmsman was shot and the ship ran aground. Members of the militia waded out, boarded the ship and overpowered the crew.

Later when the Patriots crossed the ice of Lake Erie and seized Pelee Island, 30 miles from Fort Malden, militiamen from the fort advanced in sleighs routing the Patriots in a battle fought on the ice. The final Patriot assault came in December, 1838. Advancing from Detroit they burnt the barracks at Windsor but with the help of militiamen from Fort Malden they were dispersed. Among the defenders of the Canadian frontier during the Patriot invasion were several scores of Negroes. Many were formerly slaves in the southern United States who had escaped to freedom in the British province. A black company at Fort Malden was headed by Josiah Henson.

Fort Malden is now part of a historic park. Only the earthworks of the fort remains but a museum which contains much early memorabilia stands nearby to tell the story of this historic Fort.

Fort Malden National Historic Park, National and Historic Parks Branch, Ministry of Indian Affairs and Northern Development.

FORT ST. JOSEPH, St. Joseph Island, Lake Huron, Algoma District
Position 46° 13′ 83° 57′

Fort St. Joseph is located approximately 30 miles southeast of Sault St. Marie, off Highway 17, on a small headland at the southwest tip of St. Joseph Island. This site was chosen by the British in 1796 to be their post in the Upper Great Lakes region after they were forced by the Jay Treaty to their outpost at Michilimackinac.

As the headquarters of the British Indian Department and the meeting place of hundreds of warriors from the Upper Great Lakes Indian Nations, Fort St. Joseph was considered a formidable base for operations in the old northwest.

In 1812 the British at Fort St. Joseph heard from the Indians that the Americans had declared war on Great Britain before the Americans at Michilimakinac knew of the outbreak of hostilities. A force of regular soldiers, Canadian volunteers and Indians, captured the American fort.

Only a small guard was left at Fort St. Joseph after the capture of Michilimackinac and the fort was eventually abandoned altogether. In 1814 an American force on its way to attack Michilimackinac burned Fort St. Joseph. Over the years all but the stone powder magazine and chimney have disappeared under a blanket of earth.

Archaeological excavations at the site have revealed the outlines of palisades and the foundations of several buildings including a blockhouse, guardhouse, two bakeries and some traders' huts.

A visitor reception centre has been constructed to house displays of artifacts and other information.

Parks Canada: *Historic Guide to the National Historic Parks and Sites of Canada*, 1978.

FORT STEWART, community, Carlow Township, Hastings County
Position 45° 10′ 77° 37′

This compact rural community a few miles north of Highway 500 is situated near the southern tip of Fraser Lake, just west of the Little Mississippi River. Like the other communities in the eastern section of the township, it was settled with the opening of the Carlow Colonization Road which ran from Mayo Township to Combermere.

A post office was opened in 1891, and the place was named for a pioneer tavernkeeper by the name of John Stewart. The hamlet never was the site of a fort, but as the tavern stood on a height of land from where travellers could see for miles around, calling the place "Fort" Stewart seemed appropriate.

Gerald E. Boyce: *Historic Hastings*, 1967.

FORTUNE, geographic township, Cochrane District
Position 48° 39′ 81° 58′

This township, northwest of the city of Timmins, is named after William Fortune, Deputy Surveyor in the 1780's. The Nat River flows through the centre of Fortune, which is accessible only by waterways.

61

Fort Wellington

Public Archives Canada, C 79319

FORT WELLINGTON, Prescott, Grenville County
Position 44° 43′ 75° 31′

Fort Wellington, located in Prescott, overlooks the St. Lawrence River. In addition to housing a garrison during extended periods, the Fort was called upon for national service on several occasions from the date of its first construction in 1812 until its final abandonment in 1886. The Fort was named after the Duke of Wellington, the most renowned British soldier of the day.

On the outbreak of the War of 1812-14 British authorities decided to fortify Prescott as it was one of the most vulnerable points of attack, and a main base for the defence of communications between Kingston and Montreal. Another reason for building the Fort here was the fact that an American military post lay directly across the river at Ogdensburg, New York.

The Fort's construction was directed by Frederic, Baron de Gaugreben, Lieutenant of the King's German Engineers, and it was built by a corps of the King's German Legion, a regiment serving the British Crown at that time. The Fort consisted of a wooden blockhouse surrounded by earthen ramparts on which were mounted 24-pounder cannons. It was designed to both shelter the men who patrolled the border and to command all navigation in the river opposite.

During the War of 1812-14 two attacks were made by the garrison against Ogdensburg: the first was unsuccessful but the second attack, under Lt.-Col. Macdonell, resulted in the capture of the town and command of the river.

During the Rebellion of 1837, the fort again became the scene of activity for it was here that Lt. Col. Plomer Young assembled his forces to repel the invasion at Windmill Point by Canadian rebels and American sympathizers.

The fort was in a dilapidated state by 1838, so local contractors, supervised by the Royal Engineers, began to build a new blockhouse which was completed in 1839.

For several years following the Battle of Windmill Point, Fort Wellington remained strongly garrisoned in case further troubles ensued. None did and it became a quiet border post garrisoned by the Royal Canadian Rifles from 1843 to 1854.

The Fort was empty for a few years but with the threat of invasion by the Fenians, an Irish-American society violently opposed to British rule, it was reoccupied in the 1860's. During the Northwest Rebellion of 1885 a few troops were stationed briefly at the Fort but the next year it was permanently abandoned by the military.

In 1923 the site was transferred to the Department of the Interior. Fort Wellington was declared a National Historic Park in 1940 and is now administered by Parks Canada.

Ministry of Indian and Northern Affairs: *Fort Wellington: National Historic Park.*

FOSTER, geographic township, Sudbury District
Position 46° 14' 81° 38'

Situated southwest of the city of Sudbury, the township is thought to have been named after Sir George Foster, MP for King's County, New Brunswick from the 1880's to the early 1900's. The township is dotted with lakes, some of them accessible by dry weather roads. The Trans-Canada Highway (17) passes a few miles to the north. Espanola located in the neighbouring township to the west is the nearest town.

FOUCAULT, geographic township, Algoma District
Position 46° 51' 82° 16'

Previously designated "K", the township was named in 1974 after L.A. Foucault, Mayor of Espanola at that time. The township, located northeast of Elliot Lake, is traversed by several streams and is not accessible by road.

FOULDS, geographic township, Algoma District
Position 47° 11' 83° 16'

Known as Township 7E until 1974, Foulds was named after Harry Foulds Sr., a pioneer resident of Port Arthur and the grandfather of James F. Foulds, MPP. Highway 129 which links Thessalon in the south with the community of Chapleau in the north, passes immediately to the east of the township.

FOURNIER, geographic township, Cochrane District
Position 49° 00′ 81° 08′

Located just southeast of the town of Cochrane, the township is believed to have been named after the Hon. Telesphore Fournier, MP in the 1870's. Fournier is traversed by numerous roads with Highway 11 passing along its northern border. The Frederick House River flows through the township.

FOURNIER, police village, South Plantagenet Township, United Counties of Prescott and Russell
Position 45° 26′ 74° 54′

This small village is located close to the centre of the United Counties in the eastern part of South Plantagenet Township. It is on Paxton Creek, a branch of the South Nation River, about fifty miles east of Ottawa. In 1971 the population of the village was 252. About seventy percent of the population is of French origin.

The first settler in Fournier was Bernard Lemieux, who arrived from Quebec in 1855. He erected a sawmill and a grist mill on the stream. In 1856 Cajetan Fournier opened a store in the settlement. He also became the first postmaster when the post office opened in 1856, and it is after him that the village is named. The date of the incorporation of the settlement as a police village is unknown.

In 1859 a Catholic chapel was built, and replaced in 1877 by a larger stone church. A Methodist church was built in 1873. In 1881 the settlement included a cheese factory, two hotels, a school, two stores, a tannery and a mechanics' shop.

Fournier is situated in a dairying district and hops are an important crop in the area.

H. Belden & Co.: *Illustrated Historical Atlas of Prescott and Russell Counties*, 1881.

C. Thomas: *History of the Counties of Argenteuil, Quebec and Prescott, Ontario*, 1896.

FOWLER, geographic township, Thunder Bay District
Position 48° 41′ 89° 31′

Located north of the city of Thunder Bay, the township was subdivided and named after R.A. Fowler, MPP for Lennox in the early 1900's. Dog Lake, accessible by road, covers much of the northeastern part, while smaller lakes dot the western portion of the township.

FOX, geographic township, Cochrane District
Position 49° 00′ 80° 45′

The township was surveyed in 1905 by Ontario Land Surveyor Dobie and was probably named for Samuel J. Fox, MPP for West Victoria at that time. It is situated just southeast of the town of Cochrane and is traversed by the Canadian National Railway's transcontinental line.

FOXBORO, community, Thurlow Township, Hastings County
Position 44° 15' 77° 26'

This community of some 300 people on the Moira River is situated on Highway 62, 6 miles north of the city of Belleville.

William Reed and Richard Smith were among a group of Loyalist settlers to come to the area in 1789. The compact settlement which formed at the site of Foxboro was known for many years as Smithville, presumably after the family of pioneer settler Richard Smith. Some claim that the village might have been named for Smith Demorest, a local blacksmith who, being able to make nails, built the first clapboard house in the neighbourhood around 1800. The name Foxboro was not adopted until the 1860's.

One of Smithville's most prominent early residents was William Ashley who, in 1835, established a carriage and wagon factory that was to contribute greatly to the village economy for many years to come. Ashley served as the first postmaster and donated the land on which a new school was built in 1854 to replace the first log school dating back to the 1820's. The property adjoining the school was given by Mr. Ashley for a church, and here a brick edifice was erected in 1870 which still remains in use today as a church hall. The Wesleyan Methodists had built a church on Lot 37, Concession 6, in 1869, and another Methodist church was built in the village in 1877.

By the late 1800's Foxboro had a population of 200, and aside from Ashley's carriage works there were several stores and a thriving cheese factory.

Gerald E. Boyce: Historic Hastings, 1967.

Luella Sills and Margaret Smith: Foxboro, A Portrait of a Village, 1975.

FOXMEAD, community, Orillia Township, Simcoe County
Position 44° 42' 79° 33'

Situated northwest of the City of Orillia, this dispersed rural community was at one time known as Satterthwaite. Among its early settlers were James Hadden, a farmer and lumber merchant who arrived from Scotland in 1872, William Stark, Bones Addison, William Black, Enoch Bradley, William Dodd, George May, John Fox, and J. Mead. The combination of the latter two gentlemen's names resulted in the present name of Foxmead.

When the Midland Railway was built in the late 1870's, Foxmead became a station. A post office was opened in 1879 and by 1881 the community had a population of 120. A store and a sawmill served the inhabitants of the surrounding area.

A second sawmill had been built by 1895 and the population of Foxmead had increased to 200. A Methodist church was erected in the late 1800's.

David Williams: The Origin of the Names of the Post Offices of Simcoe County, 1906.

FOY, geographic township, Sudbury District
Position 46° 46' 81° 16'

Named after the Hon. James J. Foy, MPP for South Toronto in the early 1900's, the township is located 30 miles northwest of Sudbury. It is linked by a secondary road to Highway 144.

FRALECK, geographic township, Sudbury District
Position 46° 51' 80° 52'

This township was named after a mining engineer by the name of Fraleck and is located less than 20 miles north of the town of Capreol. The Wanapitei River flows through the area in a southerly direction.

FRALEIGH, geographic township, Thunder Bay District
Position 48° 11' 89° 49'

This township was first surveyed between 1908 and 1914 and is believed to have been named after Thomas H. Fraleigh, MPP for Lambton East in the late 1920's. Highway 593 skirting the western border links the area with the city of Thunder Bay and other centres.

FRANCES, geographic township, Algoma District
Position 49° 39' 85° 12'

The name origin of this township is unknown. It is situated immediately northwest of Nagagami Lake, one of the largest bodies of water in the area. There are a few dry weather roads in the southwestern part leading to the railway point of Hillsport on the Canadian National.

FRANCHÈRE, geographic township, Algoma District
Position 47° 59' 85° 07'

The township, designated as No. 32, Range 23 until 1974, was named to commemorate Gabriel Franchère, a noted fur trader and merchant of the early 1800's. In 1820 Franchère, who lived for a time in Montreal, published the recollections of his voyage along the northwest coast of North America.
    The township borders in the south on Lake Superior.

FRANKFORD, village, Sidney Township, Hastings County
Position 44° 12' 77° 36'

Nestled among the Murray hills, Frankford is situated on the Trent River at the mouth of Cold Creek, some 8 miles north of the town of Trenton, on Highway 33.
    In the 1820's Abel Scott built a grist mill and a sawmill on this site which is at the head of what was then known as the Nine Mile Rapids, a treacherous section in the Trent River that descends one

hundred feet to Lake Ontario from here to Port Trent (Trenton). Scott's mill attracted other settlers, among them W.R. Bowen, a magistrate and merchant from the Napanee area. Both Scott and Bowen played leading roles in the rapid development of the settlement of the mid-1830's. A covered wooden bridge across the Trent River near Cold Creek, built by subscriptions in 1836, was a great convenience to the inhabitants who previously had had to ford the river at low water. A post office was established about that time and the settlement which had been known as Scott's Mills, or sometimes as Cold Creek, was officially named Frankford, probably in honour of Lieutenant-Governor Francis Bond Head. The village was granted the right to have its own market and hold semi-annual fairs and the first Frankford fair was staged in 1838.

During the 1840's the head office for the construction of the lower part of the Trent Canal was located at Frankford, and the village was a bustling place with five blacksmith shops and five hotels, the Clarke House, the McDonald House, McCambridge's, Brennan's, and Sweetman's. The latter hotel, destroyed by fire around 1912, was a three-storey building which contained at one time the town hall. A gravel road was constructed in the early 1850's between Frankford and Trenton and a toll road opened between the village and the town of Belleville. Lumbering flourished in the area with thousands of logs being rafted just north of the village to be sent down the Trent River to Lake Ontario each spring.

In 1853 Frankford was incorporated as a police village. By the 1860's the prosperous community of about 700 people could boast of two sawmills, a large woollen factory, carriage shops, general stores, a distillery, a tannery, a foundry and a pump factory. There were two Methodist churches, a Roman Catholic church and a commodious schoolhouse built from stone, which stood on the site of the present community hall. A new bridge was built across the Trent in 1869. It was destroyed by ice in the spring of 1904. With lumbering declining, the latter part of the nineteenth century brought a substantial drop in Frankford's population. The E.G. Sills paper mill then was the largest employer in the immediate area. It remained in operation until forced to close down during the Great Depression of the 1930's.

The local section of the Trent Canal was under construction from 1906 to 1914, bringing renewed activity to the community. In 1920 Frankford was incorporated as a village with Walter Windover serving as the first reeve from 1921 to 1923.

On the site of Emmanuel Church, which was completed in 1958, once stood an opera house and later a grist mill. When a new Continuation School was built in the early 1920's the old stone school was converted into municipal offices and town hall. The structure, however, was destroyed by fire in 1942, and three years later a community hall was erected on the site.

A. McAllister, Frankford's first fire chief, built the village's first fire hall in his spare time along with the equipment used to fight fires in the early 1920's. A new fire hall was constructed in 1962.

Electricity was first supplied to a few Frankford residents by the Canadian Paperboard Co. which had its factory at the north end of the village. A water turbine installed by the company operated an electric generator. Later a powerhouse was built at the plant where two generators produced the power to supply the entire village.

In 1939 the Bata Shoe Company established a factory just south of the village, setting up temporary quarters in the former paper mill and bringing a large number of new families to the area. Since then the population of Frankford has increased gradually. Many new homes were built and by the late 1950's a new water system and sewage disposal plant became operational.

Today Frankford has a population of 1,872 (1978).

Gerald E. Boyce: *Historic Hastings*, 1967.

H. Belden & Co.: *Historical Atlas of Hastings & Prince Edward Counties*, 1878.

FRANKLIN TOWNSHIP, part of the Township of Lake of Bays, Muskoka District
Position 45° 18' 79° 00'

This township is located in the northern portion of the Muskoka District. It was named after Sir John Franklin, the famous Arctic explorer. The northern townships of the Muskoka District were settled after the passing of the Free Grant Act in 1868. The eastern boundary of the township was the line of the old Bobcaygeon Colonization Road. Franklin Township was not placed on the market for settlers until 1877.

One of the first settlers in the area was Rev. Rowland Hill, a Methodist minister who arrived from York County in 1869. He gave his name to the settlement of Hillside and established the Vernon Mission. In 1893 the Hillside Church was erected. Another early pioneer was G.F. Marsh, who built a sawmill on the Oxtongue River. The settlement that developed there was known as Marsh's Falls. The Cunnington family were the first to settle at a spot known later as Port Cunnington. The principal community in the township, Dwight, was named for H.P. Dwight, president of the Great North West Telegraph Company, who visited the area often to hunt and fish.

In 1888 a canal opened up the lakes for navigation and a road was built to connect South Portage to North Portage, the head navigation point. In 1903 a railway was constructed between North and South Portage and had the distinction of being the shortest railway in the world.

Other communities in the township include Birkendale, Point Ideal and Sea Breeze. The area is popular with tourists and sportsmen alike.

In 1971 Franklin Township was amalgamated with the Township of Ridout and the geographic township of Sinclair as the Township of Lake of Bays.

George W. Boyer: *Early Days in Muskoka*, 1970.

FRANKLIN, community, Manvers Township, Victoria County
Position 44° 14' 78° 35'

Franklin is a dispersed rural community on the town line between

68

Manvers Township and Peterborough County. It is situated in the heart of the Bethany Ski Hills.

Franklin is supposed to have derived its name from the owner of the first sawmill in that location — Frank (Francis) Lynn. The sawmill and a school were in existence as early as the 1850's. In 1856-57 the Midland Railway (later the Grand Trunk Railway), was constructed and a station was opened at Franklin. The railroad brought prosperity to the settlement. In 1858 Franklin consisted of a school, two churches, a grist mill, a sawmill, grain elevators, cattle yards, hotels, a blacksmith shop and two general stores. One of the churches was a Bible Christian Church, eventually torn down, and the other was the Wesleyan Methodist Church, now closed. A post office served the settlement by 1863.

In 1912 the CPR built a line through the area but missed the settlement by several miles. By 1928 the Grand Trunk Railway in that area had ceased to operate and the community declined.

Mrs. Ross N. Carr: *The Rolling Hills*, 1967.

FRANKLIN'S CORNERS, community, South Plantagenet Township, Prescott County
Position 45° 26′ 74° 56′

At one time an important centre in Prescott County, Franklin's Corners is today a small dispersed rural community. It was named after one of its earliest settlers, Henry Franklin.

Benjamin Franklin and his family had come to Canada from England in 1830 and settled near the present-day community. The eldest son, Henry, became involved in the lumber business when he was 16 and soon prospered. In 1869 he opened a store at the site of Franklin's Corners and around this store a community developed. William Franklin opened a second store in 1884.

Other early residents of that area included Samuel Hunter who emigrated from Ireland in 1822 and William John Reid. A Methodist Church was built by the settlers in 1849.

C. Thomas: *History of the Counties of Argenteuil, Quebec, and Prescott, Ontario*, 1896.

FRANKTOWN, community, Beckwith Township, Lanark County
Position 45° 02′ 76° 04′

The hamlet of Franktown is located on the River Jock in the southern portion of the township, northeast of the town of Smiths Falls. In 1971 the population of the settlement was 142.

In the period from approximately 1816 to 1822, an officer named Colonel Francis (Frank) Cockburn was making plans for the settlement of discharged soldiers and Irish immigrants. It is from him that Franktown received its name. Colonel Cockburn wanted a government storehouse built close to the centre of the township and on the road that had been built to connect the military depots of Perth and Richmond. (This road is now the highway linking Franktown and Richmond.) The storehouse encouraged many new settlers to move into the territory.

The lots for the village of Franktown were laid out in 1821. Stephen Redmond and Josiah Moss were the first to receive town lots. In 1820 Patrick Nowland and Thomas Wickham each opened an inn at the village site. Among the first settlers at Franktown included Dr. George Nesbitt, Owen Quinn, John Conboy, John Nesbitt, Andrew Houghton, and Owen and Charles McCarthy. A post office opened in Franktown in 1832.

In 1822 Reverend William Bell, a Presbyterian minister, arrived in the county to conduct religious services. The Anglicans of the area erected St. James Church in 1827. Not only is this church the oldest church in continued use in Lanark County, but it is also one of the oldest in eastern Ontario. Some time later, the Scottish Baronial Church was built in Franktown. A school was opened in the village as early as 1824 with a Mr. Kent as the teacher. Franktown began to decline when the railway by-passed it.

Jean S. McGill: *A Pioneer History of the County of Lanark*, 1968.

FRANKVILLE, community, Kitley Township, Leeds County
Position 44° 43′ 75° 58′

Frankville is a small community situated on Highway 29 in the southeast area of Kitley Township, close to the centre of the United Counties of Leeds and Grenville. The population of the settlement in 1971 was 143.

The first settler at the site where Frankville stands today, was Levi Soper. The land was sold several times after that and, consequently, the settlement bore different names for each successive landowner. At various times it was known as Willson's Corners, Brennan's Corners, Brennanville, and Brandenburgh. When the post office opened in 1852, the inhabitants decided to choose the name "Frankville". However, no one seems to know why they picked this name, or if it bears any relation to any one person.

By 1800 a man named Duncan Livingston had erected a grist mill at the village. When the Perth Road was built in 1826, Frankville began to grow. In 1834, the village town sites were surveyed by John Booth. By the 1840's Frankville had a public school, high school, and model school (a teacher-training institution). St. Thomas Church was built in 1859 and it is the oldest used church structure in Kitley Township. The famous Canadian painter, A.Y. Jackson, sketched the church in 1932 and the sketch hangs in the gallery at Kleinburg today.

An historical plaque in Frankville commemorates the birth of Louise C. McKinney (1868-1931). Mrs. McKinney and her husband moved to Alberta in 1903. In 1917 she became the first woman in the British Empire to gain a parliamentary seat.

Glenn J. Lockwood: *Kitley 1795-1975*, 1974.

FRANZ, geographic township, Algoma District
Position 49° 07′ 84° 07′

Partially surveyed in 1914, the township was named after W.G. Franz who was the General Superintendent of Algoma Steel, Sault Ste. Marie in the early 1900's.

The Algoma Central & Hudson Bay Railway crossing the Canadian National line at Oba passes through the central part of Franz. The town of Hearst lies less than 50 miles to the northeast.

FRASER, township, Renfrew County
Position 45° 43' 77° 24'

Situated southwest of Pembroke, Fraser is bordered on the north by McKay Township, on the east by Alice, on the south by North Algona, and on the west by Richards. Both Highway 62 and the CN Railway pass through the township.

Incorporated in 1854, Fraser was probably named after Alexander Fraser (1785-1853), who was appointed to the Legislative Council of Canada in 1841. There are few farms in the area and no settlements. Indian, on the Indian River, is a railway point in the northern part of the township.

The land is rugged and covered mostly by bush. There are a number of small lakes, including Middle Long, Kelly, Colby, and Flat Iron. A range of hills is known as the "Gardez Pieds" mountains, meaning literally "watch your feet".

For municipal purposes, Fraser and Alice Townships are united. The combined population of both townships is 3,193 (1979).

Mrs. Carl Price and Clyde Kennedy: *Notes on the History of Renfrew County*, 1961.

A. Rayburn: *Geographical Names of Renfrew County*.

FRATER, geographic township, Sudbury District
Position 47° 43' 82° 04'

Boundaries of this township were surveyed in 1914 by surveyors Lang and Ross. The township was named after T. Frater, former President of Algoma Eastern Railway Co., a line opened from Sudbury to Little Current, Ontario in 1914.

Most of the central part of the township is covered by the waters of Pebonishewi Lake. A portion of Rice Lake takes up a considerable area in the southwest.

FRECHETTE, geographic township, Sudbury District
Position 47° 07' 81° 17'

The township is named after the Fréchette family of Quebec. One member of this family, Louis Honoré Fréchette, lawyer, journalist, poet and politician, represented the riding of Levis in the House of Commons in the 1870's. The Canadian National with railway points of Old Thor Lake and Thor Lake passes through the township.

FREEBORN, geographic township, Rainy River District
Position 48° 49' 91° 42'

The township is located northwest of the community of Atikokan.

Steep Rock Lake is situated in the western part of the township. The name origin is not known.

FREELE, geographic township, Cochrane District
Position 49° 07' 80° 23'

This township east of Cochrane is named after William L. Freele, MLA, MPP for Middlesex West in the late 1920's. Dry weather roads in the southern part link the area with neighbouring townships.

FREELTON, community, Regional Municipality of Hamilton-Wentworth
Position 43° 24' 80° 02'

Situated midway between Hamilton and Guelph, on Highway 6, the community was named after its founder, Patrick Freel, who built a hotel here in the 1840's. Before the present regional government was introduced, Freelton was in the unique position of standing where the townships of East Flamborough, West Flamborough, and Beverly all met.

A post office was established in 1854. Thomas Campbell, Freel's brother-in-law, built the Central Hotel, said to be so-named because it was equidistant from Galt, Hamilton, and Guelph. The first store was opened by Edward Hunt and George Currie became the first blacksmith. Other early settlers included the Suttons, Grays, Manarys, Logans, Farrishes, and Archibald and William Stuart.

By the late nineteenth century, the community had two general stores, two blacksmiths, a grist mill, and a carriage works, which made wagons, sleighs, and buggies. The Freelton fair was begun in 1888 and continued to 1925. In 1907 Freelton was incorporated as a police village. Today it is a compact rural community with a population of 319 (1971).

The first school was built on Mr. Manary's property. It was replaced by the Beechgrove School in 1864. A new school was built in the 1950's. At one time, a continuation school was held in the Baptist church, but this has now ended and pupils go to schools outside the village to receive their secondary education.

Freelton has four churches. The Baptists erected their building in 1866. The Roman Catholic, Our Lady of Mount Carmel, was dedicated in 1899 as was the United Church (formerly Methodist). The Jehovah Witnesses' Hall was built in the twentieth century.

Hamilton Spectator, 1946, 1960.

FREEMAN, part of Georgian Bay Township, Muskoka District
Position 45° 06' 79° 52'

Situated in the northwest corner of Muskoka District, the former geographic township of Freeman is bordered on the north by Parry Sound District, on the west by Georgian Bay, on the south by Gibson Township, and on the east by Melora Township. It was named after John Bailey Freeman, Liberal MLA for North Norfolk, Ontario, who became government whip in 1883.

The northern boundary of the township was surveyed in 1865, the eastern boundary in 1869, and the southern boundary in 1880. The township was formed in 1881, but the interior was not surveyed until 1895-96. David Beatty, the surveyor, reported that the land was rocky and rolling with good pine forests. He considered the southeast portion to be the best agricultural land in the township.

Beatty, at the time of the survey, found only one white settler, Myers, and four Indian settlers: King, Isaac, William and Mekesemonge. In the 1890's the Tadenac Club of Toronto acquired a large part of the township as a summer camping-ground because there seemed to be no prospect of the area being developed. Some settlement took place in the eastern part after a CPR track was built through the west Muskoka District in 1906 and a small settlement grew up at Muskoka Station (now MacTier).

Freeman was incorporated as a township municipality in 1919. The first reeve was a railway conductor and his councillors consisted of a railway car inspector, a locomotive fireman, a locomotive engineer, and a trainman. In 1971, with its population at about 850, Freeman was amalgamated with the geographic townships of Gibson and Baxter to form Georgian Bay Township. In 1978 the population of the combined townships was 2,006.

Today, the shores of Twelve Mile Bay are dotted with cottages, and sections of west Freeman, along Georgian Bay, have been designated as an Indian Reserve. An airport has been proposed at the site of a landing strip, established by a construction company during the building of a highway. A road has also been built from Twelve Mile Bay to Highway 103 to allow children to attend school at MacTier.

Healey Lake, off Highway 69 and about three miles north of MacTier, is the site of annual boat races.

George W. Boyer: *Early Days in Muskoka*, 1970.

Geraldine Coombe: *Muskoka Past and Present*, 1976.

FREEPORT, station, Regional Municipality of Waterloo
Position 43° 25′ 80° 25′

Situated near Cambridge in the southern part of the former Township of Waterloo, the site was named Freeport by Henry Lutz and his brother who were early settlers in the community.

Freeport played an important role in the early history of the township because it was here that a toll bridge across the Grand River accommodated traffic. The community was originally called Toll Bridge. The name was changed to Freeport in 1863 when a post office was established and at that time the toll was abolished.

Most of the early settlers in the area were of Pennsylvania Dutch origin. They were later followed by groups of German immigrants. A school was opened in an old hotel building in 1867 and became the Freeport Academy; George Scott was principal. However, the Academy had a short life, closing in 1874. In 1873 the United

Brethren Church was the only house of worship in the community. Its minister was the Reverend George Plowman. A Sanatorium was also in existence in the village in the late nineteenth century.

By 1873 the community had a number of craftsmen including a shoe cobbler, Henry Hilker; a carpenter, and a weaver. Christopher Kress ran a stage line from the settlement. The population was about 100 in 1881, but has since declined and the community has all but disappeared.

H. Parsell & Co. Walker & Miles: *Historical Atlas of Waterloo and Wellington Counties*, 1881

M.G. Sherk: "Reminiscences of Freeport, Waterloo County" in *Waterloo Historical Society*, 1924.

FRENCH, geographic township, Nipissing District
Position 46° 30′ 79° 11′

The township was first surveyed in 1886. It was named for Fred F. French, MPP for Grenville South in the late 19th century. It is located a short distance northeast of the city of North Bay to which it is linked by Highway 63.

FRESWICK, geographic township, Nipissing District
Position 45° 51′ 78° 30′

Established in 1885, the township was named after a village in Scotland. It is located in the centre of Algonquin Provincial Park. There are several stretches of road within the township much of which is covered with large lakes, among them Hogan, Big Crow and Lake La Muir.

FREY, geographic township, Sudbury District
Position 48° 22′ 81° 57′

This township is named after Phillip Frey, Deputy Surveyor in 1784, when Upper Canada along the St. Lawrence River was being settled by United Empire Loyalists. The northwest corner is occupied by Bromley Lake, the largest lake in the township. A road leading south from the shore of the Crawford River connects with Highway 101.

FRIPP, geographic township, Timiskaming District
Position 48° 14′ 81° 25′

The township's boundaries were surveyed in 1910 and it was named after A.E. Fripp, MPP for Ottawa West about that time. A road passing near the township's eastern border gives access to Timmins about 30 miles north.

FRONT OF ESCOTT, township, Leeds County
Position 44° 26′ 75° 57′

Originally part of Yonge Township, Escott was known as the Gore of Yonge because of its shape. It separated from Yonge Township in

1794, but did not officially become a township in its own right until 1844. The name Escott, however, originated back in the days of Lieutenant Governor Simcoe whose friend, Sir George Yonge, resided at "Escott" in Devonshire, England. Yonge was British Secretary of War from 1782-1794.

Among the first to take up land in Escott was Enoch Mallory whose family name is perpetuated in the nearby community of Mallorytown.

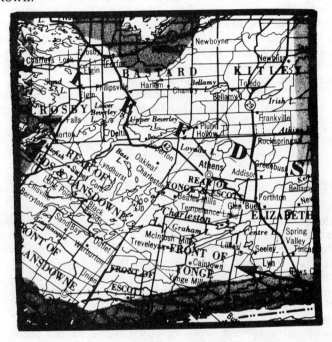

William LaRue, a United Empire Loyalist, was one of the most enterprising of the pioneers to settle in the township. In the late 1790's he built dams on a creek flowing down to the St. Lawrence River, and here, on LaRue Creek, just west of Mallorytown Landing, he erected saw and grist mills. The latter supplied British troops stationed on the LaRue property during the War of 1812. LaRue became a wealthy man, and after his death in 1832, people began searching at night for gold on his property where he supposedly had buried a fortune. No gold was ever found. Today his mansion built of squared logs still stands. Now clapboarded over, its semi-circular doorstep consists of two half millstones placed one on top of the other and taken from LaRue's old mill.

Henry Trickey was another early township settler. He arrived before 1800 and built the first grist mill at the site of Waterton. James Thomson was one of the first residents of the community of Escott. His land was granted to him as a reward for military service. He was to become well-known in the area, being the father of twenty-two children.

A post office was opened in the township in 1851. Both the post office and the store in which it was housed were run by Mr. Hutchison.

Early industries in the Front of Escott consisted mainly of grist mills and lumber mills. Today tourism is an important source of income for the township residents. The township is situated just east of the Ivy Lea International Bridge, and south of its boundary in the St. Lawrence lie the renowned Thousand Islands which attract large numbers of tourists from Canada and the U.S. each summer. Charleston Provincial Park is located in a neighboring township a few miles to the northwest. The area is accessible by rail and road, with the CNR, Hwy. 2, and Hwy. 401 all traversing the southern part of the township. Hotels, campgrounds, and marinas provide facilities for the many tourists that visit the area.

During recent years more people have come to live in this beautiful township on the St. Lawrence. From 954 in 1973, the population has increased to 1,078 in 1979.

South Leeds Planning Board: South Leeds Planning Area Background Study #2.

Mika Publishing Co.: Historical Atlas of Leeds and Grenville, 1973.

FRONT OF LEEDS AND LANSDOWNE, township, Leeds County
Position 44° 25' 76° 06'

Situated in the heart of the beautiful Thousand Islands region, the township is bounded on the west by Frontenac county, on the north by Rear of Leeds and Lansdowne Township, on the east by Front of Escott Township, and on the south by the St. Lawrence River. It was named Lansdowne in honour of The Marquis of Lansdowne, Major-General William Fitzmaurice, a soldier-statesman and personal friend of Governor Haldimand; and Leeds after the county of which it is a part.

The early settlers were mostly United Empire Loyalists who moved into the area from the neighbouring townships. Col. Joel Stone was the first to take up his land grant in the Gananoque area in 1792 and he was to become the founder of that town. It was Charles McDonald, Stone's son-in-law, however, who laid the industrial foundation of Gananoque which in later years came to be called the "Birmingham of Eastern Ontario" because of its numerous foundries, machine shops and factories which produced nails, bolts, screws, shovels, stoves, pumps and farm machinery.

In the Lansdowne area Oliver Landon, like Stone, a Loyalist from Connecticut, was the first settler. He arrived with his wife and six sons just after the western part of Leeds County had been opened for settlement and the Front of Leeds and Lansdowne had been surveyed in 1788.

Although large land grants were made at that time, many lots remained unoccupied until the early 1800's. Among other early settlers in the area were the Crosses, the Armstrongs, and the Percivals, the latter coming from Ireland in the late 1700's. They were followed by a group of other Irish immigrants who settled in the township between 1814 and 1827.

Today tourism is one of the most important industries in the two townships which are amalgamated for municipal purposes. The resort town of Gananoque attracts thousands of visitors each year. Many of these tourists come across the Ivy Lea International Bridge from the United States. Others reach the area by the CNR, Hwy. 2, and Hwy. 401. The beautiful forest scenery and the lovely Thousand Islands make the Front of Leeds and Lansdowne a natural resort area well worth a visit.

Mika Publishing Co.: *Historical Atlas of Leeds & Grenville*, 1973. Township Clerk.

FRONT OF YONGE, township, Leeds County
Position 44° 32′ 75° 53′

This township, covering over 32,000 acres, stretches along the St. Lawrence River, just southwest of the City of Brockville. Highways 2 and 401 and the CNR cross the front of the township, bringing tourists to enjoy the beautiful scenery of the Thousand Islands.

The name of the township commemorates Sir George Yonge, the British Secretary of War from 1782 to 1794, and a friend of Upper Canada's first Lieutenant Governor, Lord Simcoe.

The township was surveyed in 1794 and was settled by United Empire Loyalists. Prominent in the early history of the township were the numerous members of the Mallory family. Nathaniel Mallory, who came to Canada in 1790, became the founder of Mallorytown. He had thirteen children. His son, Andrew, operated a glass factory west of Mallorytown for a short time in the late 1830's producing beautiful blue-green pitchers, bowls and flasks. The site of this factory, the first such glassworks known to have been established in Canada, was excavated in the 1950's.

Mallory's eldest son, Daniel, owned land along the lake front as did another son, Lemuel. David Mallory, yet another one of his sons, ran a brickyard on the outskirts of Mallorytown as well as a store in the village.

Among the other early settlers in the township was Captain Peter Purvis, a Scotsman who had fought in the Revolutionary War with the British Army. For his services he received a land grant in Elizabethtown, but in 1801 he moved to the Front of Yonge where he built his house near the site of Yonge Mills. Since he had never lived in the American colonies, Purvis was not granted the status of a "Loyalist", but the family was noted in the area for their faithful support of the Presbyterian Church in Elizabethtown (Brockville) which Purvis had helped to establish.

Mika Publishing Co.: *Historical Atlas of Leeds and Grenville*, 1973.

FRONTENAC, county
Position 44° 40′ 76° 45′

Frontenac, a county of a thousand lakes, and areas of great scenic beauty, lies on the northern shore of Lake Ontario where the waters of that lake empty into the St. Lawrence River. Long and narrow in shape, it is bounded on the west by Lennox and Addington County, on the north by Renfrew, and on the east by Lanark and Leeds Counties.

Frontenac is a county steeped in history. It takes its name from Count Frontenac, the Governor of New France, who, more than three centuries ago, in the summer of 1673, accompanied by 120 war canoes, sailed from Quebec up the St. Lawrence River to the mouth of Lake Ontario. Here at a place called Cataraqui by the Indians, he built a crude fort which he named after himself. The site had been recommended earlier by Sieur de La Salle, a French adventurer and explorer who had visited the area. For his services, La Salle was given as a seigniory Fort Frontenac and the adjacent land, now the site of Kingston, as well as two islands later named Wolfe Island and Amherst Island. La Salle soon replaced the original primitive fort with a larger structure and induced some fifty French labourers and artisans to start a settlement along the waterfront. Thus Frontenac County can claim to have been the site of the first settlement by white men in what is now the Province of Ontario since the missionary settlement in Huronia in the 1640's. However, the French were mainly interested in the area as a hunting ground and missionary field, and the development of other settlements was not encouraged.

In 1758, during the Seven Years War fought between the English and French for the control of North America, Col. Bradstreet and his English forces captured Fort Frontenac. Its walls were battered down, and the era of French rule at Cataraqui had come to an end.

For a quarter of a century after that the place remained deserted. Not until the American Revolutionary War brought an influx of Loyalists into Upper Canada in the 1780's were settlements again established along the county's lakefront. Captain Michael Grass with a party of Loyalists were the first to arrive at Cataraqui in the spring of 1784. The land along the St. Lawrence and the Bay of Quinte at that time was being surveyed and divided into townships. What is now Kingston Township was designated as No. One. Today a stone cairn in City Park, Kingston, commemorates the planting of the first survey post under Civil Authority in Ontario, on October 27, 1783 by John Collins, Deputy Surveyor General. Michael Grass and his party settled in Kingston Township.

The Reverend John Stuart, the first Anglican clergyman in the province, also received a grant of land in the area. Stuart established what was to be the first Anglican church in the province. It was built in Kingston in 1792. Stuart was also responsible for founding the first school in the county and in Upper Canada. This "Select Classical School" opened in Kingston in 1785. A grammar school established in 1792 later became Kingston Collegiate and Vocational Institute, now the oldest secondary school in Ontario.

A grist mill, the first in Upper Canada, was built by the government near the present site of Kingston. The settlers were given some implements and supplies and soon a small community developed on the shore of Lake Ontario, destined to become the county seat and for a while the capital of Canada.

Bedford Mills

In 1788 the region which now comprises Frontenac County was proclaimed part of the judicial district of Mecklenburgh which in 1792 became the Midland District. The County of Frontenac came into existence on July 16 of that year when it was created for parliamentary representation and militia organization. The county finally became also a judicial and municipal unit in 1849.

Frontenac County covers just under 1,600 square miles of territory and comprises fifteen townships: Barrie, Bedford, Clarendon and Miller, Hinchinbrooke, Howe Island, Kennebec, Kingston, Loughborough, Olden, Oso, Palmerston and North and South Canonto, Pittsburgh, Portland, Storrington, and Wolfe Island. Howe Island lies in the St. Lawrence River opposite the Township of Pittsburgh and the larger Wolfe Island, with Simcoe Island nearby, also lies in the St. Lawrence River, opposite Kingston.

In 1792 the settlement of Kingston briefly became the capital of Upper Canada when Governor John Graves Simcoe held the first session of Parliament here on July 17th, inaugurating representative government in the province and choosing the first Legislative Council. The capital was shortly thereafter moved to Newark (Niagara-on-the-Lake) but Kingston continued to grow and other communities began to develop in the southern part of the county.

Once again, in 1841, this time for a period of three years, the Frontenac County seat of Kingston was elevated to the status of "capital" when it was declared the capital of United Canada. The first

Parliament of United Canada convened here on June 14 of that year.

In 1798 construction began on the Danforth Road, one of the first roads in the province, between Kingston and Bath. The War of 1812 demonstrated the need for an inland water route in the event of an American attack, and in 1826 the Rideau Canal linking Kingston and Ottawa was begun. The southern stretch of the canal follows the Cataraqui River through the county to Lake Ontario. Early roads to serve settlements in the county included a stretch of the Addington Road; the Frontenac Road running northerly through the centre of the county; the Perth Road joining Kingston and Perth; and the Mississippi Road from Palmerston across the county to connect with the Vennacher Road in Lennox and Addington.

The construction of the Grand Trunk Railway in the mid-nineteenth century through the southern part of Frontenac County encouraged the development of industry and agriculture in that area by providing excellent shipping facilities.

The northern townships were more remote. Their rocky soil was not suited to agriculture. However, as the southern areas filled up settlement gradually extended northwards and by 1900 there were a number of flourishing communities in that part of the county. The Kingston and Pembroke Railway, built in the 1870's, had provided impetus to potential settlers in the northern areas. Passing through Oso Township, it greatly stimulated lumbering activities in this region. Once many small sawmills clustered along streams and rivers which facilitated the rafting of the timbers throughout the county. Little trace of the extensive lumber operations remains today in Oso Township. At Sharbot Lake the largest of the early lumbering operations was that of the Thomson and Avery Lumbering Company. It continued for sixty years with five sawmills, and some one hundred and fifty employees. Another large lumbering camp was that of Egan's at White Lake.

With the deep rock formation forming much of the county's terrain, a flurry of mining activity at one time occupied Oso and other townships. Apatite (a superphosphate used in fertilizers) and feldspar, lime and mica were mined both in Oso and Bedford Townships. In Palmerston, the Robertsville Iron Mining Company shipped their iron products to Sault Ste. Marie, and in Loughborough Township there were several small mines, chiefly of the lead and graphite group.

The community of Godfrey on Highway 38 in the Township of Hinchinbrooke, first settled in the early 1800's, was once called Iron Ore Junction. Godfrey was the headquarters for the Feldspar Mines opened up by H. Richardson of Kingston. There was also a mica mine on Chester Godfrey's property; he was the man who donated the land on which the village stands.

Frontenac county, or at least the county seat of Kingston, can lay claim to yet another first. Its weekly paper, the *British Whig* was the first newspaper west of Montreal to change into a daily beginning January 1, 1849. Kingston, too, was the place where in 1859 Canada's first association of newspaper publishers was formed. Known as the

Canadian Press Association, it represented at the time 23 papers from Ontario and Quebec.

Today, the majority of Frontenac County's population is still concentrated in the south. Of the 114,219 people (1978) who live in this region, 61,088 reside in Kingston, the county seat, site of Queen's University and the Royal Military College. Another 25,820 live in Kingston Township, which has become almost completely urban. Frontenac County has never been highly industrialized and what industries there are today are mainly concentrated in the south.

Tourism has long since become one of the county's major sources of income. The beautiful lakes and forests of the northern part and the scenery along Lake Ontario make the region a favourite place for summer visitors. Excellent roads, among them Highway 401, provide easy access to the district. Summer cottages abound in the region north of Kingston and hunters and fishermen are catered to by resorts throughout the county. Sharbot Lake Provincial Park in the northeast attracts many visitors as does the Rideau Trail, a nature walk which starts in Kingston and wends its way through the county on its route to Ottawa, the nation's capital. Old Fort Henry, just outside of Kingston, is another major tourist attraction in the county, and here the visitor gets a glimpse into Canada's past.

Helen Arthur: Our Historic Community Latimer 1787-1973, 1973.

Directory of Frontenac County, 1864.

Government of Ontario: British Farmer's Guide to Ontario, 1880.

Alice E. Hogeboom: Your County Has a Past, 1961.

Nick and Helma Mika: Mosaic of Kingston, 1969.

FROOMFIELD, community, Moore Township, Lambton County
Position 42° 54′ 82° 27′

Froomfield, a community of just under 200 residents, is a summer resort on the St. Clair River, about 5 miles south of Sarnia.

The early settlement clustered around a grist mill erected in 1823 by two brothers, Froom and Field Talfourd. Like most of the area's pioneers, the brothers were Englishmen. Their earnest attempts to develop a town at the site failed, but their combined Christian names gave the settlement its name. The little stream which powered the mill was known as Talfourd Creek.

Among Froomfield's early settlers were Admiral Vidal and Captain Wright of the British Navy, and John Wheatley who opened a general store.

Froom Talfourd was responsible for the building of an Anglican church at the village in 1840. When steamers began plying the St. Clair River, the Talfourd brothers, together with Messrs. Baxter, Bertrand and Stone, built a dock on the river bank and offered cordwood for sale to passing vessels.

Nowadays freighters stop at this site to take on diesel fuel.

Jean Turnbull Elford: History of Lambton County, 1967.

H. Belden & Co.: Historical Atlas of Lambton County, 1880.

FROST, geographic township, Algoma District
Position 49° 30' 84° 47'

Located west of the town of Hearst, the township was established and named in 1943 after L.M. Frost, MPP for Victoria at that time. The nearest community is Hornepayne, some 20 miles to the south and accessible by Highway 631. The Nagagami River winds its way in a northerly direction through the township. A portion of Nagagamisis Provincial Park occupies the southeastern corner.

FRYATT, geographic township, Cochrane
Position 50° 02' 82° 45'

The township's name commemorates an English sea captain shot by the Germans in Belgium on July 27, 1916. He had defended his ship against a German submarine in a battle of World War One. Fryatt, located northwest of Kapuskasing, is traversed by numerous streams. There are no roads within the township.

FULFORD, geographic township, Thunder Bay District
Position 49° 47' 87° 01'

Named for G.T. Fulford, MPP for Leeds in 1934, the township is located just north of the community of Geraldton, accessible by Highway 584. The township has numerous streams and lakes, the largest of which are Fulford, Grenville, Hutchison and Dionne Lakes.

FULLARTON, township, Perth County
Position 43° 24' 81° 13'

Named for a director of the Canada Company, Fullarton is one of the smallest but also one of the most fertile townships in Perth County. It covers an area of about 41,516 acres and has a population of just over 1,600.

Part of the Huron Road opened by the Canada Company in the late 1820's from Goderich to Guelph to promote the sale of its lands in the Huron Tract, ran through the northern part of the township. Lots were surveyed along the road on the Fullarton side in 1829, while other sections of the township were opened for settlement in 1832 and 1835.

The township's first settler was Hugh Kennedy Junck who located on Lot 20 in the first Concession in the fall of 1832. He built a sawmill on Whorl Creek in the vicinity of present-day Mitchell. Although Mr. Junck's mill was a great convenience to the settlers arriving in the township, to his immediate neighbours it was a source of constant annoyance, as the mill pond frequently overflowed flooding the surrounding countryside. Complaints were voiced for nearly a quarter century to no avail until circumstances and time removed the cause of the problem.

Soon after Mr. Junck, Daniel Kerr and his wife settled in the township on land that is now part of the Town Site of Mitchell. The

Kerrs' son Daniel was the first settler's child born within the township's limits. Other early settlers included a number of Alsatians, among them Valentine Rohfreitsch, Jacob Kramer, Jacob Schelleberger and George Paulin. They took up land several miles to the east of Junck's property, in the vicinity of Andrew Sebach's tavern on the Huron Road. Later arrivals were spreading south and westward from here.

The southern and central part of Fullarton was not settled until the mid-1840's. James Wansley and Andrew Tinning each located in the 8th Concession during 1843. The next couple of years saw an influx of Scottish settlers from Lanark County. The Andersons, Watsons, Rogers, Browns, McIntoshes and Youngs were among those who settled along the Thames River which flows through a beautiful valley southward through the central part of the township. Along the Mitchell Road, chopped out of the wilderness by Canada Company men, settled the Heals, Moores, Beers and Pridhams. By 1844 the township had a population of 419.

The Woodleys and Bakers were the pioneers in the vicinity of the present-day hamlet of Fullarton, about 6 miles south of Mitchell. James Woodley who came in 1853 laid out the village site on his land in 1864 naming it Summervale, but the place was usually called Fullarton Corners. When a post office had been opened here in 1854 it had been named Fullarton after the township. The township hall was erected at this village which, by 1880, had a school with two teachers, three churches, a first class hotel, and a number of shops and stores.

Carlingford situated on Black Creek, a few miles to the east of Fullarton, was laid out into village lots by Abraham Davidson who had settled here in 1844. A school was opened at Carlingford in 1850 by a Mr. Reilly, described by one historian as "an odd character, not very prepossessing in appearance but a fairly good teacher, blessed with a goodly portion of commonsense". In the 1850's Abraham Davidson erected a general store where he also kept the post office.

Another early postal village was Motherwell in the Thames River valley, near the southern border of the township. It was founded by James Brown who named it for his ancestral town in Scotland. Mr. Brown who became the village's first postmaster in 1863, had been the teacher in the township's first school, a log building put up in 1847 on Lot 25 just west of the Thames River on the Mitchell Road.

The municipal history of the township had its beginning in 1842 when the first town meeting was held. At first the township was united with Blanshard and Downie, but in 1844 it became a separate municipality. There are no town records until 1847 but it is known that during the year of 1845 Hugh Kennedy Junck served as the first district councillor. Thomas Boyle was the first town clerk, and Duncan Campbell the first assessor. Town meetings at that time were held in Small's mill at Mitchell. The first township council elected in 1850 after the Municipal Act took effect in the province, was composed of James Hill, reeve; Robert Porteous, Robert Rogers, George Leversage, John Arbogast, councillors; John McIntyre was clerk and James Brown treasurer.

H. Belden & Co.: *Historical Atlas of Perth County*, 1879.

William Johnston: *History of Perth County 1825-1902*, 1903.

FULLARTON, community, Fullarton Township, Perth County
Position 43° 23′ 81° 14′

The pioneers of this small community, nestled in the Thames River valley near the centre of the township, were the Bakers and the Woodleys.

James Woodley, who came in 1853, laid out the village site on his property in 1864 and named it Summervale. The vicinity, however, was generally known as Fullarton Corners, and a post office had been established in 1854 under the name of Fullarton after the township. So Fullarton eventually became the official name and the little village which clustered around a hotel built in 1855, was chosen as the township seat.

A town hall was erected and local industries, at one time, included a cheese factory, a sawmill, a chopping mill and a cider mill. There was a school with two teachers. The Methodists as well as the Baptists, established congregations and built their respective churches in the village.

H. Belden & Co.: *Historical Atlas of Perth county*, 1879.

William Johnston: *History of Perth County 1825-1902*, 1903.

FULLER, community, Huntingdon Township, Hastings County
Position 44° 24′ 77° 25′

The hamlet located about 2 miles east of Ivanhoe and Highway 62 was named after pioneer settler John Fuller. Martin Mills who arrived around 1830 is believed to have been the first white settler in the vicinity. A stone school was built at Fuller around 1850, and the Bible Christians of the area erected a church at the settlement. Fuller's main industry for a number of years was a sand and gravel company which closed its operation in the early 1950's.

Gerald E. Boyce: *Historic Hastings*, 1967.

FULTON, geographic township, Sudbury District
Position 47° 07′ 82° 32′

This township appears to have been named after a former Member of Parliament. The western portion is occupied by part of the Mississagi Wild River Provincial Park.

FURLONGE, geographic township, Thunder Bay District
Position 50° 17′ 90° 13′

The township was named after Ontario Land Surveyor W.H. Furlonge. The Canadian National's main line with the railway point of Allanwater passes along the southern boundary of the township. The area is covered with numerous lakes and is not accessible by road.

FURNISS, geographic township, Kenora District
Position 49° 20′ 91° 10′

In September, 1945, the township formerly designated as No. 18, was named after S.J. Furniss, M.P. for Muskoka Riding at the time. Furniss is located just north of the Trans-Canada Highway (No. 17). The Canadian Pacific Railway passes through the southwestern corner of the township on its route towards Dryden some 100 miles to the northwest.

FUSHIMI, geographic township, Cochrane District
Position 49° 54′ 83° 59′

The township's southern, eastern and western boundaries were surveyed in 1907 and it was named in honour of Prince Fushimi, Japanese Envoy to the British Court, who had visited Canada in the early 1900's. The Kabinakagami River, with a series of rapids, flows through the central part. In the southeastern corner lies Fushimi Provincial Park.

FUSHIMI LAKE PROVINCIAL PARK, Stoddart, Hanlon and Bannerman
Townships, Cochrane District
Position 49° 50′ 83° 54′

Fushimi Lake Provincial Park is located about 25 miles north and west of Hearst, which is, itself, situated on the CNR and Highway 11. It is a recreation park and lies within the zone called the Boreal Forest. As well as small forest animals there is also the opportunity to see moose and bear. During the summer of 1907 when the area was surveyed, His Imperial Majesty Prince Fushimi of Japan paid a state visit to Canada and the nearby township of Fushimi was named to commemorate his visit.

Ontario Ministry of Natural Resources, Brochure.

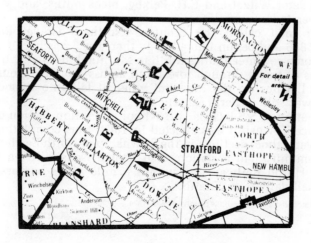

G

GABY, geographic township, Cochrane District
Position 51° 12′ 81° 11′

This northern township, situated less than twenty miles west of Moosonee, bears the name of the late Dr. F.A. Gaby of the Hydro-Electric Power Commission of Ontario. Several rivers rise in the area and the Kwataboahegan River, a tributary of the mighty Moose River, flows in a southwesterly direction through the township.

GADS HILL, dispersed rural community, North Easthope Township, Perth County
Position 43° 26′ 80° 55′

Gads Hill is a small community located on highway 19 six miles east of the city of Stratford. In earlier days it assumed some importance because of its proximity to Stratford, a larger and more bustling centre. There is no explanation for the name Gads Hill, but it is used by Shakespeare in his works and it may be that a person of literary discernment chose it.

Located on the boundary between Ellice Township and North Easthope Township, its population at the turn of the 19th century was 125.

First settled by Henry Ratz who built a mill there, other settlers opening businesses and plying their trades were: Wm. Miller, who kept a hotel; Thomas O'Donnel and J.W. Wettlaufer, who each ran a general store; Peter Witzel and E.H. Pelkey, blacksmiths; and Wm. Smith who operated a sawmill.

A gravel road called the Stratford Northern Gravel Road organized in 1856 and begun immediately thereafter, was built from Stratford for some seventeen miles north to Mornington Township to afford a means of travel through forest and across swampy ground. There were toll gates on the road but when it fell into financial difficulties it was sold to Perth County.

The formation of S S 8 Gads Hill school in a union section of a portion of Ellice Township was effected in 1864, thus completing a division of seven school sections in the Township of North Easthope.

The community had a station, also named Gads Hill, on the Stratford and Huron Railway line within a mile of its borders. It received its mail daily from Stratford.

H. Belden & Co.: *Illustrated Historical Atlas of the County of Perth*, 1879.

GAIASHK, goegraphic township, Algoma District
Position 46° 25′ 82° 23′

Formerly known as Township 137, the township was named in commemoration of Canadian Army Private Alphonse F. Gaiashk of the Manitoulin District, who was killed in action in World War Two. The township, located east of the town of Elliot Lake, is not subdivided and was detached from the Elliot Lake Improvement District as of January 1, 1959. There are no roads within the township.

GAINSBOROUGH, part of the Township of West Lincoln, Regional
Municipality of Niagara
Position 43° 03′ 79° 30′

Prior to the formation of the Regional Municipality of Niagara in 1970, the geographic township of Gainsborough (formerly a part of Lincoln County), amalgamated with the Township of Caistor and the Township of South Grimsby as part of the Township of West Lincoln. Gainsborough Township was named after the town of Gainsborough in Lincoln County, England.

The township is well watered by the Welland River in the south and Twenty Mile Creek, once known as the Jordan, to the north. The Welland River was formerly called the Chippawa, because of the Indians of that tribe who lived along its shore. Several other streams traverse Gainsborough, including Fifteen Mile and Sixteen Mile Creeks. These are so named for their distance from the mouth of the Niagara River. The area is a rich farming district, having clay loam soil.

The first settlers in the southern part of the township chose the sites along the Welland River. John Dochstader arrived in 1782 to be shortly followed by the Dils, Hodges, McDowells, Barkers, Henrys, Robins and Heaslips. In the north, along Twenty Mile Creek, came the Snyders, Deans, Felkers, Roys, Rozells, Wrongs, Johnsons, Comforts, Lanes, Gees, Kennedys and Glendenings. They arrived from New Jersey, New York and Pennsylvania in 1793. The interior of the township was settled by German immigrants. This area, not so well favoured as that to the south or to the north, was considered fairly worthless. However, within a short span of years the new immigrants had converted their holdings into some of the best farms in the township.

In 1788-9, the end of the three years during which the government provided the settlers with their first provisions, there occurred the period known as the "Hungry year". Ammunition was scarce and so was money. Many settlers were forced to subsist on roots, buds and bark of trees, with what occasional game could be snared. Another dismaying occurrence that befell the early Gainsborough settlers was a tornado, referred to as "The Hurricane", that tore through the entire province cutting a swath of one to two miles of devastation.

Adam Snyder began a grist and sawmill on Twenty Mile Creek in 1794 and the spot became known as Snyder's Mills. This is now St.

Anns and according to the story told, Adam's wife, Ann, a busy mother of eight children, was a good friend to the Indians who came to her door and they looked upon her as a saintly person and named her place "St. Ann's". Adam Mingle built an inn at St. Anns in 1816 which was a stage coach stop. Across the road he erected a trading post, the main part of which was still standing in the middle 1950's. Today St. Anns is the centre of a dairy and beef farming area and there is considerable poultry raising. The Toronto, Hamilton & Buffalo Railway (T.H. & B.) has a station at St. Anns which handles a busy freight in livestock.

Bismarck and Wellandport are two other villages in Gainsborough Township. Bismarck, situated at the intersection of Highways 20 and 57, is also the site of the Gainsborough Township Hall. Centrally placed, Bismarck was once a busy shopping centre with several stores and cheese factories.

Wellandport, on the bank of the Welland River, at the junction of Highway 57 and the Canborough Road, was settled in the beginning of 1795 and soon had grist and sawmills operating to handle the quantity of lumber and logs rafted down the river. Once there were four hotels that were kept busy in Wellandport. Today Wellandport is a busy centre serving the surrounding agricultural country.

The early schoolhouses were one near the Gee bridge in the north part of the township in 1798, one at Snyder's Mills, and one on William Dils' land, the latter about one mile west of the village of Wellandport. The first church in Gainsborough, north, was built by the Presbyterians in 1799. A Methodist church followed in 1818. The first church in the south of the township was one sometimes curiously referred to as the "Log Jail". Another 1835 church, Methodist, was erected on the Heaslip property. None of the original church buildings or schoolhouses remain today.

By the 1870's six post offices had been established in the township. They were at St. Anns, Bismarck, Rosedene, Elcho, Wellandport and Candaceville. By this time a line of the Toronto, Hamilton and Buffalo Railway (T.H. & B.) had been built across the northern part of the township with stations at St. Anns and the community of Silverdale. A branch of this same railway ran through the township and was known as the Dunnville branch, with stations that included Vaughan and Port Davidson.

H.R. Page: *Historical Atlas of Lincoln and Welland*, 1876.

George A. Carefoot: *History and Geography of Lincoln County*

GALBRAITH, geographic township, Algoma District
Position 46° 29′ 83° 39′

Located northwest of the town of Thessalon, the township was established and subdivided in 1877. It appears to have been named for Daniel Galbraith, MPP for Lanark in the late 1860's. The small communities of Havilah and Dunns Valley are located in the township.

GALBRAITH, community, Ramsay Township, Lanark County
Position 45° 10′ 76° 14′

Situated on the border of Ramsay and Lanark Townships, this dispersed rural community was named after Mr. Galbraith, who represented this riding in the Parliament of Upper Canada in the nineteenth century.

A number of settlers took up land here in 1825. They were: Thomas Thompson, James Kidney, James Wright, John Watt, Daniel Coleman and William and Robert Penman. In the early days settlers were ministered to by the Methodist, Mr. Clark, who held outdoor services for them. As the community grew, the different denominations began to attend church in nearby villages; Galbraith itself had no house of worship.

One of the best-known features of the community was its "Floating Bridge" across Clayton Lake. The contract for this bridge was given in 1877. Each time the bridge began to be submerged, a new layer of timber was added until, eventually, there were five layers. The bridge was finally closed in 1944.

A school was built in Galbraith before 1863. It closed in 1965 along with other small schools in the area. Since the 1960's the area around Galbraith has become mainly a cottage development.

Claire Thompson: *Township of Lanark 1820-1970*, 1970.

GALETTA, village, West Carleton Township, Regional Municipality of
Ottawa-Carleton
Position 45° 25′ 76° 15′

Located on the Mississippi River at its falls, about four miles east of Arnprior, Galetta's population by the 1971 census was 142. The settlement began when Andrew Forbes arrived in 1823 and established on the 6th Concession, about one mile east of the present community.

Originally the place was named Hubbell's Falls after James Hubbell who leased in 1823, from the Clergy Reserve, the lot on which the water privileges at the falls were situated. He did not develop the property, and in 1832 sold the mill rights to James Steen, who at once built a mill. The hamlet then became known as Steen's Falls and soon was a thriving little settlement. James Steen sold his mill to J.G. Whyte and purchased property a little farther down the stream, where he built another grist and sawmill. Mr. Whyte named the place Galetta after his own middle name.

A post office was established in Galetta in 1878. At this time the village had two grist and two sawmills, a shingle mill, a carding and spinning mill, a telegraph, and general stores.

The village economy benefitted greatly when the Ottawa, Arnprior and Parry Sound Railway came through in 1892.

In 1902 the Anglican church was built, and in 1907 the Galetta Electric Light Company was formed to harness the falls.

Until 1969 Galetta was part of Fitzroy Township in Carleton County. On January 1 of that year, Carleton County was dissolved and became the Regional Municipality of Ottawa-Carleton. Fitzroy Township, in 1974, became part of the Township of West Carleton.

Fred Sadler: *Fitzroy Township*, 1967.

GALLAGHER, geographic township, Sudbury District
Position 47° 48′ 83° 18′

The township immediately east of the town of Chapleau, was first surveyed in 1907 and was named for J.L. Gallagher, MPP for Frontenac at the time. Highway 101 crosses the northwest corner where several Indian Reserves are located. Borden Lake takes up a portion of the central section.

GALNA, geographic township, Cochrane District
Position 48° 50′ 80° 13′

This township, east of Iroquois Falls, was originally subdivided in 1905 (annulled in 1963) and was named after John Galna, MPP for Parry Sound at that time.

Part of Lake Abitibi, one of northwestern Ontario's great bodies of water, its western shoreline indented by numerous bays and inlets, covers the southeastern corner and much of the eastern part of the township.

GALT, part of the City of Cambridge, Regional Municipality of Waterloo
Position 43° 22′ 80° 19′

Galt, once a city in its own right with a population of close to 38,000 is the largest of the municipalities which comprise the city of Cambridge created on January 1, 1973 with the amalgamation of Galt and the nearby towns of Hespeler and Preston.

Galt is situated on the Grand River, on the CNR, the CPR, and the intersection of several major highways, less than 60 miles southwest of Metro Toronto and 11 miles southeast of the city of Kitchener.

It had its beginnings in 1816 when William Dickson, a Scottish merchant and member of the Legislative Council from Niagara, bought here some 92,000 acres of land, including the area at the confluence of Mill Creek and the Grand River. He commissioned Absalom Shade, a carpenter by trade from Pennsylvania, to develop a settlement at the site. Shade erected a two-storey log building at what later became the corner of Main and Water Streets and opened a store and set up headquarters for his operation. He then proceeded to build a grist mill and a sawmill in 1818. Settlers were soon attracted by the news that excellent land was being offered for sale in the newly surveyed township of Dumfries and at Shade's Mill, as the small village clustered around the mill was being called. By 1820 the settlement had already numerous buildings, including a distillery and a blacksmith shop.

A bridge had been built across the Grand River in 1819. Morgan L. Hermonts opened the settlement's first tavern in 1821. The first frame building in the hamlet, it stood near the Main and Water Streets corner. By 1827 a road was opened from Shade's Mill to Guelph. That year a post office was established and the settlement was renamed Galt in honour of John Galt, a Scottish novelist and friend of William Dickson. As commissioner of the Canada Company, John Galt opened up the country between Lakes Huron and Erie for settlement, and founded the city of Guelph.

The first wooden church was built in Galt in 1828. The first regular preacher is said to have been the Rev. William Stewart who arrived in 1831. St. Andrew's Presbyterian Church was commenced in 1833. A schoolhouse had been erected the previous year at the head of Main Street with James Milroy as the first teacher. A subscription library was opened in Galt as early as 1836.

Galt, Presbyterian Church

A large number of Scottish immigrants had settled in Galt by the late 1830's. Absalom Shade built a fleet of boats which carried flour downriver to Dunnville. Numerous business enterprises flourished in the hamlet and the first macadamized road in Upper Canada was opened between Galt and Dundas.

The year of 1834 went down in Galt's history as the year of the Cholera Epidemic. The disease appeared to have been brought to the village by a company of travelling entertainers. Dr. Robert Miller, the only local physician, went on horseback from house to house ministering to the many victims who lay dying.

Galt's first newspaper, the *Dumfries Courier*, made its appearance in 1844. Trinity Anglican Church, the oldest church in Galt still in use, was dedicated that same year.

In 1850 Galt was incorporated as a village. Andrew Elliott was elected as the first reeve, and the council consisted of Morris C. Lutz, Sidney Smith, William Ferguson and John Davidson. Tassie Grammar School, later to become the Galt Collegiate Institute, opened its doors in 1853 under William Tassie.

The Great Western Railway came to Galt in 1856 adding further impetus to the growing village. Galt's industries at that time included two foundries, two flouring mills, a woollen mill, an axe factory, a distillery, a furniture factory, a brewery, a carriage factory, and a planing shop.

In 1857 Galt was incorporated as a town and M.G. Lutz was elected mayor. Council consisted of John McNaughton, D. Ramore, Wm. Robinson, James Kay, Samuel Richardson, John Young, Thomas Armstrong, Thomas Sparrow, Ed. L. Cutten, Francis Lowell, Richard Blain, Robt. Scott and Benj. Hobson.

A new town hall was erected in 1858. It became later the city hall. Renovated in 1965, it has since been declared an historic site. The first post office building at Galt opened in 1861. The second post office which eventually became the customs building was constructed in 1885. The Galt Hospital, in later years converted to the Eventide Home, opened in 1891. A new hospital, the South Waterloo Memorial Hospital, opened its doors in 1953. In 1900 the Carnegie Library was established, and in 1909 the first movies were shown in Scott's Opera House which had been built in 1899. Electric street lights were turned on for the first time in 1911.

Galt, which long since had become one of western Ontario's foremost manufacturing centres, was incorporated as a city in 1915. It continued to flourish with new and varied industries being established during the next several decades; with a daily newspaper, the *Recorder*; a radio station serving the citizens; and new schools, churches and modern recreational facilities being opened.

Galt's identity as a municipality may have ceased, but its heart continues to beat as vigorously as ever within the larger framework of the new city.

Waterloo Historical Society Papers.

London Free Press, 1949.

The Evening Reporter, Galt, 1967.

GALWAY, township, Peterborough County
Position 44° 44' 78° 31'

Situated in the northwest corner of the county, Galway is bordered on the east by Cavendish Township, on the south by Harvey, on the west by Victoria County, and on the north by Haliburton County. It was named after the County of Galway in Ireland.

The township was surveyed in 1857 by M. Dean who travelled through the western and northern portions. He reported that the area was well watered but the stony nature of the soil and the rock ridges made the land more suitable for pastoral than arable farming. W. Drennan completed the survey in 1860 and noted the extensive pine forests in the area.

The Bobcaygeon Road, a colonization road which formed the western boundary of the township, was only partially completed when the first settlers arrived in the late 1850's. Lumberman-farmer William Leeson and tavernkeeper Thomas White took up land in southwest Galway in 1856. From 1857 to 1859 there was a large influx of settlers, including such men as James Lyle, John Coulter, Thomas McGahey, Duncan Molyneux, and Michael, George and John O'Brien. Most of these men were farmers and they settled mainly along the Bobcaygeon Road. Catholic and Protestant Irish predominated, but there were also Scots, English and German immigrants.

Lumbering was once an important industry in the township's economy. The first settlers were attracted by the extensive pine forests in the area and many farmers supplemented their income by lumbering. In the 1860's William Leeson operated a lumber shanty and employed many Irish-Canadian lumberjacks from Lower Canada. Large tracts of land were leased by various lumber companies, including the Gilmour Company of Trenton, A.H. Campbell and Company of Nassau Mills, and Boyd, Smith & Co. of Bobcaygeon. The presence of iron and graphite deposits encouraged mining activity in the area and much land was bought by Henry Calcutt of Ashburnham.

Thomas Probert opened the first store in the township in 1858. In 1860 he became postmaster and then reeve in 1862. By 1884, Kinmount, the largest community in Galway, had six stores, two blacksmiths, four sawmills, and a grist mill. A post office had also been established at Mount Irwin.

By 1875, there were two churches in the township, one Episcopal and one Roman Catholic. A second Episcopal church had been built by 1885. Among the first clergymen in the area were the Methodists, Rev. John A. Dowler and Rev. George H. Kenny; the Presbyterian, Rev. Mr. Clark; and the Anglican minister, Rev. John Vicars. Four schools were in operation by the 1880's.

Galway has been united with Cavendish Township for municipal purposes since the two townships were first formed. Galway, however, has always been the more populous of the two. Of the 521 people making up the population of the combined townships in 1871, over 400 lived in Galway. The combined population had risen to 787 by 1881, but it has since declined to 342 (1978). However, it is swelled in the summer when cottagers take up residence along the shores of Swamp Lake and the other lakes found in the area.

Historical Atlas Foundation Inc.. *Historical Atlas of Peterborough County 1825-1875*, 1975.

C. Blackett Robinson: *History of the County of Peterborough*, 1884.

GAMBLE, geographic township, Timiskaming District
Position 47° 22′ 80° 35′

The boundaries of this township were surveyed in 1908 and it was named after surveyor Killaby Gamble. A road passing just outside the eastern border of the township connects the area with Highway 65.

GAMEY, geographic township, Sudbury District
Position 47° 54' 83° 03'

The township which is subdivided, was surveyed in 1905 and was named after Robert Roswell Gamey, the MPP for Manitoulin from 1902 to 1914. Highway 101, skirting the northwestern corner of the township, links the area with the nearby town of Chapleau.

GANANOQUE, separated town, Front of Leeds and Lansdowne Townships
Leeds County
Position 44° 20' 76° 16'

Situated 18 miles east of Kingston on Highways 2 and 401 in the extreme southwest corner of Leeds Township, Gananoque is known as the "Canadian Gateway to the Thousand Islands". Its name is an Indian word which means both "land which slopes toward the water and disappears under it" and "place of good health".

The region was known to early French explorers and missionaries. Members of Samuel de Champlain's company may have visited here in 1615. Frontenac, the Governor of New France, referred to the site as Onnondakoui in 1673. In the late eighteenth century the Mississaugas sold the land to the British Government which intended to settle there the Loyalists who had fled to Canada after the American Revolution. One of the first to claim land in the area was Loyalist Joel Stone who had gone to England in 1783 to petition for compensation for his losses in the Revolution. Stone spelled the name of the area Cadanoryhqua and Ganenoquay. In all, there are 52 variations of the spelling of Gananoque. The present spelling first appeared in the 1820's.

Stone first saw the site in 1787. Impressed by the potential for millpower of the two falls on the Gananoque River, he asked for a grant on both sides of the river. However, a conflict arose when Sir John Johnson, leader of a group of Loyalists from the Mohawk Valley and member of the Executive Council, also petitioned for the land. A compromise was reached in 1789. Johnson was granted 1,000 acres on the east side of the Gananoque River and Stone 700 acres on the west side.

Joel Stone, who settled on his land in 1792, is considered the founder of Gananoque. He opened the first store, built a grist mill, and, with a Frenchman named Carey, erected a tavern for river travellers. He also rafted logs to Montreal, Quebec and Kingston. A Customs House was opened on his property in 1801 and he became the first collector. On the east side of the river, a small mill had been built in 1792, but nothing more was done to develop the site for many years.

By 1803 there were three houses in Gananoque, those of Stone, Captain Bradish, and Seth Downs. A bridge was built across the

Gananoque River in 1806. In 1812 Charles McDonald opened a store, and a sawmill and grist mill were built at this time.

One of the first skirmishes of the War of 1812 between Canada and the United States took place at Gananoque. An American contingent under Captain Benjamin Forsyth, having forced the retreat of the Canadian militia, attacked the hamlet, seized the government stores and burned the depot. Stone's house was ransacked and Mrs. Stone, alone in the house, was wounded by a random shot. In 1813 a blockhouse was built on the east bank of the Gananoque River by Charles McDonald to guard against future American raids.

Gananoque, St. John's Church

Stone's daughter, Mary, married McDonald, who was Stone's business partner and who later founded the firm of C. and J. McDonald and Bro., a company involved in lumbering, sawing, grinding and merchandising. If Joel Stone was the actual founder of Gananoque, the enterprising McDonald was the man largely responsible for the early growth of the settlement.

By 1818 there were 46 dwellings at the site of Gananoque and 319 inhabitants. In 1824 C. and J. McDonald bought Sir John Johnson's property, surveyed it, and laid out the village site of Gananoque. Soon settlers began to arrive in increasing numbers. Most were United Empire Loyalists and British immigrants.

In 1826 the McDonalds built the largest flour mill in the province. Grain was shipped here by lake schooner from various farms in the western regions of the province. It was estimated that at one time one quarter of all the flour sent to Montreal came from the Gananoque mill. The mill continued to prosper until the 1840's when it became more profitable to export wheat, rather than milled flour.

Richard P. Colton, in 1830, started the metal industry which in later years was to become the mainstay of Gananoque's economy. He manufactured rakes and forks, first by hand and later by machine. Other industries were established and by 1848 the village had a custom mill, a stove factory, a tannery, a pail factory, a carding and cloth dressing works, a turning shop, a shoe and boot last and tack factory, and a nail factory. As the lumber trade decreased due to the depletion of forests, Gananoque became increasingly industrialized. By the mid-nineteenth century it produced wheels, springs and axles for carriages, barrel hoops, rivets, nuts and bolts, rakes, and shovels. It was known as the "Birmingham of Canada" because of the variety of metal products manufactured by its industries. In 1863 Gananoque, its population 1,700, was incorporated as a village.

Gananoque's first school was built in 1816 on part of Joel Stone's land. John S. McDonald was one of the first teachers. This schoolhouse also served as the first house of worship for the Methodists of the community. There were a number of private schools in the community for young ladies, and the Roman Catholic children were taught by a Mr. McNamara. A stone schoolhouse was built in 1849. In 1859 the Grammar and Common schools were united and J.D. Platt became principal of the new Academy. The Macdonald School began classes in 1896. A County Model School was opened in 1888 to train teachers. It remained in operation until 1907. The High School was erected in 1896, with R.E. Graham as principal. A modern Secondary School was built in 1949 and R.E. Lewis was principal. A separate school for the Roman Catholic children, who had hitherto attended the public schools, was built in 1921. The teachers came from the order of the Sisters of Providence. In 1962 a modern separate school was constructed.

The early Methodists used the 1816 schoolhouse for their services and by 1836 had their own Grace Methodist Church. Rev. Stephen Miles arrived in 1841 as the first resident Methodist minister. Still later in 1873 a new Methodist church was dedicated. A Presbyterian church erected in 1836 had the Rev. Henry Gordon as its first minister. John Carroll, Gananoque's first Anglican minister, supervised the building of Christ Church in 1857. A Roman Catholic church was erected in 1846 with Rev. John O'Dowde as the first priest, and again in 1891 a new church was dedicated.

Joel Stone had built a town hall in the 1830's and here the first library was housed. But it was not until 1892 that the Mechanics' Institute, forerunner of the present Public Library, was founded. In 1911 the fine Georgian residence of the late Hon. John McDonald was deeded to the town with the stipulation that it was to be used for Town Offices, Council Chamber and Public Library.

In present-day Gananoque there are many historic attractions for the visitor. They include the clock tower of the Market Square which has been a landmark since the early 1900's. The Victoria Hotel, built in 1840, is now the Gananoque Historic Museum and houses a collection of military artifacts. An old bandstand is the scene of concerts by the town's Citizens' Band, in existence for over 125 years.

The town also has a wax museum. Just outside of Gananoque is Half Moon Bay where for over 80 years non-denominational services have been held with the congregation in boats and the pulpit placed on a rock.

By the late nineteenth century Gananoque, which had become a town when its population reached 3,500 in 1890, had developed into a tourist resort. Excursion boat lines, such as the Great White Squadron of the Folger Company, were established by the Rathbun Lumber Company. The Thousand Islands Railway, built in 1889, brought an increasing amount of visitors to the area. The railway offered special excursions to Gananoque linking up with boat tours of the Thousand Islands. Due to the advent of cars and buses, the railways' passenger traffic has long since diminished, but the famed Thousand Islands attract a continuous stream of visitors who enjoy the boat tours conducted from Gananoque. Today triple-deck aluminum vessels replace the old fifty-passenger tour boats. Gananoque is also the boarding point for plane tours of the Islands. Thus Gananoque, a town of about 5,000 people, rightly takes its place as a major resort centre catering to hundreds of tourists who crowd its streets during the summer months.

Frank Eames: "Gananoque Block House 1813-1859", in Ontario Historical Society, 1937.

Frank Eames: "Gananoque's First Public School 1816", in Ontario Historical Society, 1919.

Gananoque Historical Society: The Story of Gananoque, 1970.

H. William Hawke: Historic Gananoque, 1974.

GANONG, geographic township, Cochrane District
Position 50° 09' 81° 10'

The township located northwest of Smooth Rock Falls is not subdivided. Its name origin is not known. Although the area is well watered, there is only one small lake near the southern boundary. The township is not accessible by road.

GAPP, geographic township, Algoma District
Position 47° 07' 83° 54'

Formerly known as No. 23, Range 13, the township was named in 1974 after Douglas E. Gapp, W.O. 2, RCAF, of the Algoma District, who lost his life in World War Two.

Gapp is located a few miles to the east of the Algoma Central Railway point of Megatina. A secondary road links the township with roads to the east and ultimately with Highway 129.

GARDEN, geographic township, Cochrane District
Position 50° 09' 82° 45'

The township, situated northwest of Kapuskasing, was named after A.C. Garden, MPP for Hamilton West in the 1920's. Friday Creek, with its tributaries, waters the southeast corner of Garden.

GARDEN HILL, community, Hope Township, County of Northumberland
Position 44° 03' 78° 24'

The small settlement of Garden Hill is situated in the northern half of Hope Township, about ten miles north of Port Hope. Prior to 1870 the hamlet was known as Adam's Corner's, or, later, Waterford. To avoid confusion with several other post offices of the same name, the settlers renamed the hamlet Garden Hill.

The first settlers in the area arrived in the 1830's and 40's and included the Kilpatricks, Leiths, Corbetts, Hammills and Seatons. In 1861 Frank Beamish built a mill at the settlement and leased it to a United States firm to manufacture hats, etc. The mill was destroyed by fire, but Beamish had it rebuilt and fitted with machinery to manufacture lumber, shingles, etc. In 1869 James Dyer of Orono purchased Mr. Beamish's mill in the village and erected large woollen mills in Garden Hill. In 1870 a post office was established in the village and Mr. Dyer opened a general store and served as first postmaster.

By the 1870's Garden Hill had become a flourishing community. John McElroy, Jr. opened a flour mill in 1872. John Martin of North Canton, the subsequent owner, equipped the mill for sawing and planing. In 1879 the Garden Hill Methodist Church was erected and in 1880 a Presbyterian church was built. Only the Presbyterian Church is in use today, having become Garden Hill United Church. The Methodist Church was taken down shortly after church union in 1925.

In 1880 the population of Garden Hill was between 400 and 500 people, but in 1886 disaster struck and fire destroyed the woollen mills, the general store, a stable, the Telephone Exchange and several homes. The mill was re-established at a new location and the settlement began to decline.

In 1890 Dyer returned to Garden Hill and built a new mill. It operated successfully for a number of years, but was struck by lightning and burned down in 1911. The old Dyer dam was rebuilt by the Ganaraska Conservation Authority in 1960.

According to the 1971 census, the population of Garden Hill had dwindled to 78.

Harold Reeve: *The History of the Township of Hope*, 1967.

GARDEN ISLAND, settlement, Wolfe Island Township, Frontenac County
Position 44° 12' 76° 28'

Garden Island is situated about 2 miles south of the city of Kingston and is one of the most westerly of the Thousand Islands. Today most of its 65 acres are occupied by summer cottages.

The history of the island is closely linked with that of the Calvin Company, a forwarding business which specialized in the shipping of timber to Quebec City. Dileno D. Calvin established his company on Wolfe Island in 1826 but later expanded his business to Garden Island. The most economical way to ship timber down the St. Lawrence in those days was by raft, and Garden Island developed into an important transshipment point as here the cargo was transferred from Great Lakes ships to the rafts of the Calvin Company.

The company grew into a vast operation. By 1865 it was the largest timber concern shipping to Quebec City, and one of the six largest timber firms in Canada. It also provided tugboats and wrecking outfits. The company's enterprises on the island included shipyards, sawmills, pattern shops, planing mills, and machine and boiler shops.

At the height of its prosperity, between the years 1860 and 1885, Garden Island had a population of about 750. All its inhabitants were connected in some manner with the Calvin Company. Labourers worked in the company shipyards, farmers cultivated company land, and everyone lived in company-owned houses. D.D. Calvin, known as "the Governor", dominated island society, but his rule was beneficial to the community. The company's general store sold goods at fair prices, the school was subsidized and achieved a high reputation, and the island was able to boast of one of the finest Mechanics' Institutes in Canada.

Garden Island was incorporated as a village in 1866 and Calvin served as the first reeve. A post office was opened in 1868. By the late nineteenth century the village had a school, department store, bakery, slaughterhouse, public library and church. However, the decline in lumber markets after the turn of the century ended the Calvin Company's prosperity and it went out of business in 1914. The island's population decreased and today its inhabitants are mainly summer residents who return to the mainland in the winter. Reminders of the community's past connection with the shipping industry can still be found all over the island in the form of stray boat parts, winches, anchors, etc., and in the sunken ships to the southeast.

Dictionary of Frontenac County, 1865.

Kingston News, 1894.

Kingston Whig-Standard, 1963, 1979.

GARDHOUSE, geographic township, Sudbury District
Position 47° 54′ 82° 04′

The township, south of Highway 101 some fifty miles east of Timmins, was established in 1934 and named after William J. Gardhouse, then the MPP for York West. Arbeesee and Scraggy Lakes are two of the largest bodies of water in the western part of the township. There are no roads within the township's boundaries.

GARDINER, geographic township, Cochrane District
Position 50° 41′ 81° 35′

The township, located about 100 miles north of Smooth Rock Falls, was most likely named after Chris Gardiner, MPP for Kent East in 1926.

The Mattagami River and its tributaries flow through the western part of the township and is joined in the northwest corner by the Missinaibi, which courses across the northern section of the township. The confluence of these two great rivers marks the beginning of the mighty Moose River.

GARIBALDI, geographic township, Sudbury District
Position 47° 27′ 81° 25′

The boundaries of this township were surveyed between 1910 and 1911, and it was later named after Guiseppe Garibaldi, famed Italian nationalist revolutionist of the 1850's who fought for the freedom and unification of the Italian people.

Located southwest of the Gowganda mining district, the township is linked with major highways by Highway 560. The township's main river is the Opikinimika.

GARRISON, geographic township, Cochrane District
Position 48° 30′ 79° 57′

The township, east of the town of Matheson, was named for F. Lynwood Garrison, a mining engineer of Philadelphia, Pennsylvania. Highway 101 links the area with the Quebec border and points west.

GARROW, geographic township, Nipissing District
Position 46° 41′ 79° 19′

The township was named after Judge James T. Garrow, who was the MPP for Huron in the 1890's and early 1900's. There are no roads within the township, but a number of waterways, the Jocko River being the largest.

GARSON, part of the towns of Nickel Centre and Valley East, Regional Municipality of Sudbury
Position 46° 55′ 80° 52′

Garson is situated on Highway 541, a few miles northeast of Sudbury and is one of the fastest growing areas in the Sudbury Region. An Orkney Islander immigrating in 1887 gave his name to Garson. He was William Garson, MPP for Lincoln.

Emery Lumber Company was the first to begin lumbering operations here in the early 1880's, holding timber rights in Garson, Falconbridge, Cleland, Capreol and Lumsden townships. Because there was no waterway to transport felled timber, the logs had to be hauled by horse-drawn vehicles to Wahnapitae where they were milled. A narrow gauge railway, the Wahnapitae and North Western, then carried the lumber to a site near the present-day Sudbury Airport.

In Garson, settlement began near the lumber headquarters and along one of the early roads. Goodwill, after whom the road was named, was the first to arrive with his family in the township. Other homesteaders followed and at the end of the road a small community formed known as Happy Valley. The Ruff and Moore families were among those who settled there to farm. Other early settlers were the Wrights, Carrs, Bradys and Scagnettis. Ben Scagnetti immigrated to Canada in 1915. A hardworking businessman, he ran a general store with a horse-drawn delivery service. Civic-minded, he served as a public school trustee for 20 years, was on the Council and became reeve in 1945.

John Cryderman had staked a mineral claim in Garson which he sold in the early 1900's to Ludwig Mond, an English chemist who had discovered a method to refine nickel ore in 1892. In 1900 the Mond Nickel Co. was incorporated to develop mining properties in Garson and thus Garson Mine began operations in 1907.

Mond built company houses, and new businesses sprang up. Former farmers and loggers now became miners. During the 1930's when the Depression hit mining activities, the Garson Mine closed. Some of the men went to work for Falconbridge Mine, which continued operations. The Garson Mine opened up again in 1936 and in 1939 constructed a new shaft. The mine is in operation today, producing some of the richest ore of the Inco Mines in the Sudbury Basin.

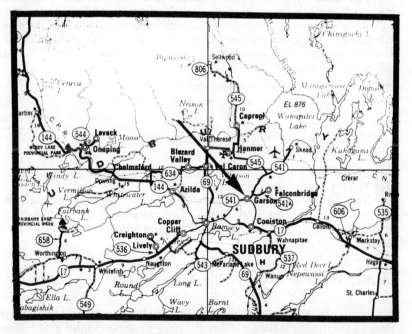

The first school in Garson was a one-room school built in 1907 by loans subscribed by the Mond Nickel Co. and the government. Protestants and Catholics united to form the first school section. Miss Clara Morceau was the first teacher. Secondary School students travelled to Sudbury to continue their education. Roman Catholic students shared a school with Protestant students until 1945 when St. John's Parish Hall was available to them. In 1946 a four-room separate school was opened. In 1963 the Garson Falconbridge Secondary School opened under the principalship of William R. Roman.

The Garson Volunteer Fire Brigade was first organized through a section in the War Measures Act. The equipment was kept in Pacquette's garage until a fire hall was built on Church Street. The civic-minded merchants of Garson donated the furniture for it.

Until the 1930's log houses could still be found in Garson, roads were gravelled and in poor condition. Today Falconbridge Highway (Hwy. 541) runs its four-lane course through Garson to Sudbury.

In 1967, Canada's Centennial Year, Garson opened a new library known as the Neelon and Garson Municipal Library. This replaced the library previously housed in a small building in the downtown business section of the community of Garson. The latter originally built by the mining company, was known locally as "Inco Town". In the 1970's, with the advent of shopping plazas and the opening of a large shopping centre in the Sudbury area, businesses in Garson closed and moved to the plazas. In 1974 a fire destroyed a number of the old buildings in the downtown section.

For municipal purposes, Garson had been united with neighbouring Neelon Township in its early history. With the institution of regional government in the Sudbury area, the township of Garson was annexed by the newly created towns of Nickel Centre and Valley East, effective January 1, 1973. Garson now is the seat of the Municipal offices of the town of Nickel Centre.

Trent Block, et al: *Nickel Centre Yesterdays*, Northern Heritage, 1974.

Charles Dorian: *The First 75 Years: A Headline History of Sudbury, Canada.*

GARVEY, geographic township, Sudbury District
Position 47° 27' 81° 31'

The township's boundaries were surveyed in 1911 and it was named after W.H. Garvey, a Toronto barrister.

The Canadian National Railway passes through the southwestern corner of the township where the railway point of Westree is located. The nearest community is Gogama some twenty miles to the north.

GAUDETTE, geographic township, Algoma District
Position 46° 50' 84° 02'

The township, east of Batchawana Bay (Lake Superior), is part of the Algoma Central and Hudson Bay Railway Company land grant. It was named after a northern Ontario pioneer settler. The area is linked by road with the Trans-Canada Highway.

GAUDRY, geographic township, Algoma District
Position 47° 07' 83° 47'

The township, known earlier as No. 22, Range 13, was named after C. Gaudry, former Chairman of the Sioux Narrows Improvement District.

The Goulais River flows westward through the southern part of the township which is accessible by road from Highway 129.

GAUNT, geographic township, Algoma District
Position 47° 11' 83° 09'

The township, first designated on maps as 7D, is named after Murray Gaunt, MPP for Huron-Bruce. It is located north of Rocky Island Lake and borders on the Sudbury District. Highway 129 (Thessalon to Chapleau) passes through the centre.

GAUTHIER, geographic township, Timiskaming District
Position 48° 09' 79° 49'

The township was named after the Most Reverend C.H. Gauthier, D.D., Archbishop of Kingston. Gauthier which has a population of about 150 (1979) was designated as an Improvement District in 1945.

Highway 66 passing through the township links it with the town of Kirkland Lake about ten miles to the west.

GEARY, geographic township, Cochrane District
Position 48° 50' 81° 40'

The township's boundaries were surveyed in 1905 and 1911, and its name commemorates that of G.R. Geary, mayor of Toronto from 1910 to 1912. Geary is located northwest of Timmins and is not accessible by road.

GEIKIE, geographic township, Timiskaming District
Position 48° 09' 81° 06'

The township bears the name of Professor Walter B. Geikie, 19th century pioneer in medical education and one-time Dean of Trinity College.

Geikie is located some 40 miles south of Timmins and is accessible by dry weather road only to its western border. The Redstone River flows northward through the township.

GEMMELL, geographic township, Thunder Bay District
Position 49° 10' 85° 48'

The township, located just north of Manitouwadge, was named after the late Hon. Welland Steward Gemmell, MPP for Sudbury who served as Minister of Lands and Forests and as Minister of Mines. The Canadian National Railway's Hillsport-Manitouwadge branch passes through the centre of the township.

GENIER, geographic township, Sudbury District
Position 47° 32' 83° 39'

Formerly designated as Township 11H, it was later named after R. Genier, reeve of the township of Glackmeyer in the Cochrane District.

The community of Pineal Lake is located in the southeast corner of the township, which is linked by dry weather roads to Highway 101 and the Chapleau area.

GENOA, geographic township, Sudbury District
Position 47° 48′ 82° 10′

The township is named after the Italian city of Genoa, an important Mediterranean port since ancient days.

Located south of Highway 101, about midway between Timmins and Chapleau, more than a quarter of the township is covered by Rush Lake. There are no roads within the township's boundaries.

GENTLES, geographic township, Cochrane District
Position 50° 33′ 82° 00′

The township, northeast of Kapuskasing, bears the maiden name of the wife of the Hon. W.H. Price, Attorney General for Ontario in the 1930's. The Missinaibi River flows in a north-westerly course through the area.

GEORGETOWN, part of the town of Halton Hills, Regional Municipality of Halton
Position 43° 39′ 79° 55′

Georgetown is situated in the rolling hills of the Credit River Valley on the banks of the Credit River. It is accessible by Highway 7 and is also on the CNR rail-line. Georgetown is located twenty-nine miles west of Toronto and thirty-three miles northwest of Hamilton.

The first settler on the land where Georgetown stands today was George Kennedy, who came to the area in 1821. Some believe that the town was named after him, while others claim that the name honours the British monarch, George III. In any case, the settlement was first known as Hungry Hollow. Marquis Goodenow and Sylvester Garrison were also early pioneers in the area.

George Kennedy built a grist mill on the banks of the Credit and later erected a sawmill and a foundry. In 1837 William and Robert Barber moved to the area and purchased one of Kennedy's mills. This was the beginning of the renowned Barber Woollen Mills and a long and profitable alliance between Georgetown and the Barber family. In 1840 two more Barber brothers, James and Joseph, established a sawmill and a foundry in the locality. By 1869, one Barber brother only remained in Georgetown, James, with his family, continued his prominence in that town's economic structure. His paper-making mill, a new industry he took over in 1854 produced until 1948 when it was sold to the Provincial Paper Limited.

In 1840 John Sumpter opened the first general store, and he became Georgetown's first postmaster when a post office was established in 1851. That year, supposedly, the first church in the settlement was built by the Wesleyan Methodists.

In 1864 Georgetown was incorporated as a village. Many of the municipal facilities and institutions had been in operation before this date, however, because the size of the settlement had given it the potential of a village. In 1865 a town hall was constructed on Guelph Street.

Isaac Hunter, founding editor, formed the Georgetown *Herald* in 1866. Published bi-weekly, it was Georgetown's newspaper and continued, through various changes of ownership, over the next hundred and more years.

Georgetown, Post Office

In 1871 the Hamilton and Northwestern Railway was opened making Georgetown the junction of two important railways, the Grand Trunk Railway having been completed in 1856.

During the 1870's many new industries were established in Georgetown. The Dayfoot Company, originally a tannery in 1843, reformed in 1892 as the C.B. Dayfoot and Company, manufacturers of heavy work boots until 1944. Other businesses included Creelman Brothers knitting machinery, 1876; J.H. Day Paint Company, Hillock's Tannery, Crawford Brothers, sash, door and planing factory, and the Georgetown Carriage Factory, which had burned in 1866, was rebuilt in 1876. Georgetown's thriving commercial and industrial enterprises have been an economic mainstay for that community for many years. William Bradley, an energetic businessman of the early 1900's, began a small seed trade on a mail order business, and by 1928 he had established the Dominion Seed House, a large mail order service in garden seeds attaining world-wide custom.

The first school in the early settlement was held in a private home until 1858 when classes opened in the old Town Hall. There were two private schools in the 1850's, one under the tutelage of a

Miss McMaster and the other operated by Reverend Charles Dade, an Anglican minister. From 1860 to 1868 the "Town Hall School" was taught by James Beckenridge. A year later the school moved into a new building on Chapel Street, known as the Chapel Street School. Here began the first high school tuition. Mr. M.S. Clark and Mr. E. Longman taught seventy students in classes in the Chapel Street School. The high school was built in 1889 on Guelph Street, the site of the present Georgetown District High School. Today there are five junior public schools, two senior public schools, two schools for the Trainable Retarded and three Separate Schools in the Georgetown area.

The Baptist Church of 1869 today serves the Pentecostal religion and is known as the Georgetown Alliance Church. The Methodist Church built in 1880 on Guelph Street is now St. John's United Church. First ministering to its congregation in 1845, the present Knox Presbyterian Church, aided in its cost by the Barber family, was built at the corner of Main and Church Streets. The establishment of St. George's Anglican Church in Georgetown was begun by land donated by George and Elizabeth Kennedy in 1852. The Reverend Charles Dade was the first pastor. Today this church is located on Guelph Street near Queen. A wooden building on Main Street served Georgetown's early residents of the Roman Catholic faith. In 1885 it was replaced by a stone church on Main Street, now the Church of the Sacred Heart. By 1960 the Church of the Holy Cross with the nearby Separate School of Holy Cross was erected on Maple Avenue.

Henry Pratt Lawson's water-powered generator produced the first electric power for Georgetown. In 1890-1 a water system was constructed to serve the village. Telephone service was provided in 1917 and in 1921 Georgetown officially became a town.

From the early 1950's on, Georgetown experienced a population and building boom. Its location made it a favoured residential area for workers commuting to nearby Toronto, Hamilton and Oakville. With easily accessible transportation facilities, many industries chose Georgetown as promising sites.

On January 1, 1974 the town of Georgetown amalgamated with the town of Acton to become the town of Halton Hills in the Regional Municipality of Halton.

Kathleen Saunders: Saunders' History of Georgetown, 1976.

Walker and Miles: The Historical Atlas of Halton County, 1877.

GEORGIAN BAY, township, District of Muskoka
Position 45° 00' 79° 50'

The township of Georgian Bay was formed following the creation of the District Municipality of Muskoka on October 19, 1970, and is the result of an amalgamation of the former township of Freeman and the geographical townships of Gibson and Baxter. All three of these townships border on Georgian Bay, hence the name of the new municipality. Port Severn is the seat of the municipal offices which were opened in 1974.

The township comprises a total area of 150,310.4 acres. It has a permanent population of 2,006, but this number is swelled each summer as tourists and cottagers invade the area.

The area, once a wilderness paradise, much of which was inaccessible by road, has been opened up since the construction of Highway 103 in 1957.

Georgian Bay has an extremely irregular shoreline, dotted with 30,000 islands, including fifty-five within the Georgian Bay Islands National Park. Many of these islands lie within the District of Muskoka. The waters along this coast are frequently rough since the shore is exposed to prevailing west winds and storms from the north. The islands offer some protection and thanks to marine weather reports and up-to-date charts, the danger to small boats is reduced.

Explorer Etienne Brûlé is said to have been the first white man to visit the shores of Georgian Bay in 1610. Samuel de Champlain, somewhat later, travelled through Georgian Bay with the Huron Indians during an attack against the Iroquois. The bay is 120 miles long and 50 miles wide, connecting at its northwestern end with the North Channel. It was charted by Captain Henry W. Bayfield, Royal Navy, in 1822 and named after King George IV.

During the War of 1812-14 American and British forces battled for control of the bay. The Americans attacked a small post at the mouth of the Severn River, which was an important part of the British trade route used to transport supplies to Mackinac and western trading posts. The uncharted rocks and islands shrouded in a dense fog successfully foiled the assault. Georgian Bay remained in British hands during most of the war.

About one-quarter of all the land in the District of Muskoka still belongs to the Crown, much of this land being located in the township of Georgian Bay.

Muskoka Mills, one of the township's communities, was located at the mouth of the Musquosh River and had a population of some 400 in its heyday when it was a centre of tanbark production. The mill was dismantled and moved considerably farther north in 1882 when all the merchantable timber was used up. The settlement became a ghost town and gradually disappeared.

Georgian Bay's history is recalled by Brébeuf Lighthouse, a lake freighter guide, named after one of the early Jesuit martyrs in the Midland area. The Watcher Islands are known to have once been a lookout point for the Huron Indians.

Orville Wright, who flew the first powered plane at Kitty Hawk in 1903 bought Lambert Island in Georgian Bay in 1916 and built a cottage on its highest point. Wright designed and constructed an escalator to haul supplies from the shore to his cottage.

Honey Harbour, near Port Severn, is typical of a Georgian Bay community with hundreds of boats tied up at the many marinas waiting for their island owners. Didace Grisé built a hotel in Honey Harbour in 1870. Although it has since disappeared the family has continued in the innkeeping business operating the well-known Delawana Inn.

The township contains the Gibson Indian Reserve which was

established in 1881 to accommodate 30 families of the Iroquois tribe who were moved from the province of Quebec. Today the band has 246 members; however, only about 90 live on the Reserve property. The residents of Gibson in the late 1960's formed an association known as the "Iroquois Cranberry Growers", thus developing a natural local resource into a thriving business.

In winter Georgian Bay freezes to a depth of 22 to 30 inches. The bay becomes a rendezvous for snowmobilers and provides a means of transportation to those who live in isolated spots along the shore.

Geraldine Coombe: *Muskoka: Past and Present*, 1976.

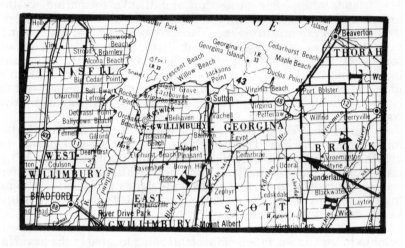

GEORGINA, township, Regional Municipality of York
Position 44° 17' 81° 56'

The township is situated in the northeast corner of the former County of York. It borders in the north on Lake Simcoe and now covers an area of 70,739 acres with a population of 18,476 (1978). Prior to 1971, Georgina was a much smaller township with less than 3,700 inhabitants. But at the time the Regional Municipality of York was formed, Georgina amalgamated with the village of Sutton and the Township of North Gwillimbury, including Fox and Snake Islands, to form the new and enlarged Township of Georgina.

Named in honour of King George III, Georgina was laid out later than the other townships in the county, although some settlement preceded the 1817 survey by Duncan McDonald. Two of these earlier settlers were disbanded half-pay officers, Captain James O'Brien Bouchier and John Comer. Captain Bouchier had commanded Fort Penetanguishene during the War of 1812-13. Owning considerable land and of an energetic and shrewd nature, he founded Sutton, the principal village in the township, establishing a flouring mill and other business enterprises. John Comer was the first assessor and collector for some years following the early township meeting, around

1827. His eldest daughter was the first white child born in the township.

Good agricultural land encouraged rapid settlement and the population grew steadily from 586 in 1842 to 1,987 in 1871. In the next decade, when the population of most of the other townships decreased, the number of inhabitants in Georgina increased to 2,482. Of these, 2,039 were native Canadians. By 1885 two-thirds of the land was occupied with over half of it improved. Spring and fall wheat utilized thirty percent of the farm land, and pasture land another thirty percent. Thoroughbred stock was also raised. The remaining land was mostly in forests of hemlock and hardwood.

The township was united with North Gwillimbury until 1826. The 1827 council meeting, the first for Georgina as a separate township, elected Alexander Craig Lawson as the first clerk. In 1850 when the Ontario Municipal Act took effect, Charles H. Howard became the township's first reeve.

The village of Sutton, by that time, had a grist and sawmill, a carding and fulling mill, a tannery, and a cloth factory. The first Anglican and Presbyterian churches were located here. Jackson's Point, north of Sutton at the terminus of the Toronto and Nipissing Railway, became a popular resort for boaters, fishermen and picnickers even in the early days. Other communities in Georgina include Pefferlaw, Virginia, Baldwin, Udora, Cedarbrae and Vachell.

Sibbald Point Provincial Park is now located a few miles to the east, along the shoreline there are a number of beach resorts catering to tourists.

Snake and Fox Islands are both Indian Reserves, and so is the larger Georgina Island in Lake Simcoe, a few miles offshore from the Provincial Park.

Jesse Edgar Middleton and Fred Landon: *The Province of Ontario — A History 1615-1927 Vol. II*, 1927.

Miles and Co.: *Historical Atlas of York County*, 1878.

C. Blackett Robinson: *History of Toronto and County of York, Vol. I*, 1885.

GERALDTON, town, Ashmore Township, Thunder Bay District
Position 49° 44′ 86° 57′

This town of approximately 3000 people is situated on the CNR, just north of Highway 11, some 170 miles northeast of the city of Thunder Bay. Its name is a combination of the names of E.J. Fitzgerald and Joseph Errington, two mining promoters largely responsible for financing the first gold mines in the area.

Geraldton's history began in 1931 when "Hardrock" Bill Smith discovered gold in the southern arm of Little Long Lac. In 1932, Smith, Tony Oklend and Tom Johnson staked the first claims in the area. News of the strike travelled fast, first to the nearby Hudson's Bay Company post at Longlac, and from there to the rest of the country. Soon a number of mines were opened up at the site of the strike and a community began to grow around the mines. Among the first to start operations was the Hard Rock Mine in 1935. By the 1940's twelve mines employed most of the town's 3,500 people. Geraldton had been incorporated as a town in 1937.

As the gold became exhausted, the mines went out of business, with the last mine closing in 1970. Some of the town's people moved away, but others found employment in the forest industries of Kimberly Clark of Canada and Weldwood Canada. Today lumbering is Geraldton's most important industry, situated as it is in the middle of the largest pulp-cutting districts in Ontario. A woodworking plant, opened in 1973, manufactures lumber components for furniture. Other local industries include The Geraldton Millworks, Loudon Bros., Domtar, and The Geraldton Bottling Works.

The town, today, has an elementary school, B.A. Parker Public School opened in 1973; and a separate school, as well as a high school built in 1957. Hope Haven School for the trainable retarded was established in 1966.

Eight churches serve the town's French and English population. There is a public library, and the *Geraldton Times-Star* publishes weekly. A TV station is also in operation.

Several government offices are located in Geraldton, including the district offices of the Ministry of Natural Resources and the Northern Affairs Department. In 1973 the government built an Upper Atmosphere forecasting station just outside the town. There is a hospital as well as medical and dental clinics.

Seven hotels and motels serve the area's growing tourist trade. Two provincial parks, located near Geraldton are major attractions. The town has been accessible by air since 1973, when an airport was built.

Geraldton Profile, 1973.

Ministry of Natural Resources: *Directory of Statistics and Data*, 1975.

GERMAN, geographic township, Cochrane District
Position 48° 35' 80° 53'

Since 1973, a part of the city of Timmins, the area was subdivided in 1904 by O.L.S. Fairchild and was named after Wm. M. German, MPP for Welland in the 1890's.

Kettle Lakes Provincial Park is situated in the southwest of the township. Barbers Bay, a southern arm of Frederick House Lake, lies in the north. The area is served by Highways 67 and 101.

GEROW, geographic township, Algoma District
Position 46° 25' 82° 16'

This township, east of Elliot Lake, was named after George Gerow who, together with William Boon, pioneered commercial fishing in Ontario by starting to ship salted fish to Toronto in the 1870's. It was formerly designated as No. 130. Highway 553 runs along Gerow's eastern border.

GERTRUDE, geographic township, Thunder Bay District
Position 49° 06′ 85° 48′

The township was established in 1955 and named after the wife of former Ontario Premier Leslie Frost. Her name was Gertrude Jane Carew.

The mining community of Manitouwadge lies in the northwest corner of the township. There is a hospital at Manitouwadge, and the town is served by the Struthers branch of the Canadian Pacific Railway as well as the Hillsport branch of the Canadian National Railway.

GERVAIS, geographic township, Algoma District
Position 46° 51′ 82° 09′

The township, known as Township G until 1974, was named after A.A. Gervais, the mayor of the town of Iroquois Falls. It is located north of the town of Massey and is accessible by secondary road. In the centre lies Airport Lake.

GIBBARD, geographic township, Thunder Bay District
Position 48° 59′ 90° 05′

The township, located northwest of Thunder Bay, is believed to have been named after David Gibbard, a pioneer surveyor of Ontario. Muskeg Lake takes up much of the township's northeastern corner. The Canadian National Railways crosses the central section while the Canadian Pacific Railway and the Trans-Canada Highway skirt the southwestern edge of the township.

GIBBONS, geographic township, Nipissing District
Position 46° 35′ 80° 06′

The township is believed to have been named after Sir George Gibbons, a London lawyer, and the Chairman of the Canadian section of the International Waterways Commission in the early 1900's.

Highway 539 and the Canadian National Railways cross the southwestern section of the township following the Sturgeon River which winds its way through the area in a southeasterly direction.

GIBSON, geographic township, District of Muskoka
Position 45° 00′ 79° 48′

Part of this township is Indian Lands. The name commemorates Sir John Morison Gibson who served as Lieutenant Governor of Ontario from 1908-1914.

Accessible by Highway 103, the area abounds in lakes and rivers and is a tourist's paradise.

Effective January 1, 1971, Gibson became a part of the newly formed municipality of Georgian Bay Township in the District of Muskoka.

GIBSON, Indian Reserve, East shore Gibson Lake, Muskoka District
Position 45° 00′ 79° 42′

The Gibson Reserve is located in the geographic townships of Freeman and Gibson, since 1971 part of the municipality of Georgian Bay Township. The name of the reserve is taken from Gibson Township, which was formed in 1880 and named after Thomas Gibson, MPP for a Huron County riding 1867-1898.

The residents of Gibson are descended from Quebec Iroquois who moved to Gibson in 1881. In 1717 those Indians which had been converted to Christianity were moved from the Island of Montreal to Lake of Two Mountains, where the settlement of Oka grew up on land held by the religious order of the Sulpicians. The Indians frequently found their land grants insufficient and made use of other lands as well, causing disputes with the Sulpicians. In the early 1870's renewed tension arose when Protestant missionaries converted the Iroquois to their faith and a Wesleyan Methodist chapel was built in the area. The Sulpicians took court action, claiming the land to be theirs, and when a decision was handed down in their favour, a mob of French Canadians destroyed the chapel. The issue escalated into a nationwide religious controversy. There was much unrest at Oka where eight arrests were made in 1877 and the Roman Catholic church was destroyed. The Methodist church urged government intervention, but no action was taken until 1881, when the Indians were given their choice of new reserve lands. They chose Gibson.

The first families, about 30 of them, arrived at Gibson in cold winter weather. Led by Chief Fleecy Lowi Sahanatien, these pioneers included the families of Commandant, Decaine, Montour, Rivers and Thompson. Conditions were harsh but the abundance of fish and deer helped the settlers survive their first winter. Aid was also sent by the Sulpicians, and French carpenters helped construct permanent buildings. When a post office was established, the inhabitants of Gibson called it Sahanatien in honour of their chief.

In 1882 a school was opened in a building left behind by the French carpenters. A new one was constructed in the following year. It served until 1952 when a new modern building was erected. The first church was a log structure. Services were given first by a missionary, then by a school teacher. A new church was built in 1906 with Rev. William Kendall as minister.

The people of Gibson worked in the lumber camps in the winter and farmed and raised livestock in the summer. In 1969 Sid Commandant formed the Iroquois Cranberry Growers to help stimulate the economy of the community.

Today, tourism is an important industry on the reserve. The Gibson Reserve Trailer Park is situated on Webster Lake, at the junction of Highways 103 and 660. Another attraction is the experimental "Arctic" houses, inflated polyethylene domes sprayed with materials which harden into a weatherproof veneer, completely insulated and almost indestructible. There is also a monument raised to the memory of the chiefs of Gibson in 1931, marking the golden anniversary of the reserve. Philip La Force, a native of Gibson, who wrote *History of Gibson Reserve*, was chosen by the Ontario Weekly Newspaper Association in 1959 as the best country correspondent.

Geraldine Coombe: *Muskoka Past and Present*, 1976.

GIDLEY, geographic township, Kenora District
Position 49° 48′ 94° 50′

The township was named after H. Gidley of Midland, Ontario. Much of the township is covered by lakes with Pickerel and Rosina Lakes in the northern part being the largest.

The area is accessible by road from the nearby centres of Kenora and Keewatin. The Canadian Pacific Railway, with the railway points of Busteed and Sherwood Lake, passes through the southern section.

GILBERT, geographic township, Sudbury District
Position 46° 51′ 81° 53′

Situated north of Espanola, and on the Algoma District border, the township appears to have been named after Marwood Gilbert, a local patentee. Dry weather and secondary roads provide access to the interior of the township.

GILBERTSON, geographic township, Algoma District
Position 47° 11′ 83° 01′

The township, known as No. 7C until 1974, was named after Brent Gilbertson, MPP for Algoma District at that time. Gilbertson is located north of Rocky Island Lake and a few miles to the east of Highway 129.

GILES, geographic township, Algoma District
Position 47° 28′ 84° 46′

The township, formerly designated No. 30, Range 17, was named after M.D. Giles, then the reeve of James Township in the Timiskaming District.

Triangular in shape, this small township fronts on Lake Superior. Offshore lie several islands, among them Rowe Island and the Lizard Islands.

GILL, geographic township, Cochrane District
Position 49° 46′ 84° 21′

The township was subdivided in 1912 by Griffin and was named after J.S. Gill, a Sudbury merchant. It is located some thirty miles west of the town of Hearst, to which it is linked by Highway 11. The Canadian National Railways main line passes through the northern part of the township.

The picturesque Shekak River which enters the township in the south cascades with numerous rapids in a northwesterly direction through most of Gill before joining the Nagagami, just outside the township's western border.

GILL, part of the Town of Haldimand, Regional Municipality of Haldimand-Norfolk
Position 42° 56′ 79° 59′

This dispersed rural community is situated in what was formerly Oneida Township, Haldimand County. It was named after Squire Matthew Gill, who owned the land on which the settlement was built, and who had established himself there before 1860.

Other early settlers included the families of Hall, Fleming, Calvert, Irving and Rountree. The farm house of James Mitchell, built in 1862, still stands today. Robert Fleming was probably the community's first blacksmith. A sawmill operated in the early years and a post office was opened in 1878 with Mr. Brounridges as postmaster. Squire Gill donated the land for the building of a Wesleyan Methodist Church at Gill. He also gave the land for the cemetery.

Cayuga-North Cayuga Centennial History, 1967.

GILLIES, township, Thunder Bay District
Position 48° 16′ 89° 42′

Situated less than 20 miles southwest of Thunder Bay, the township was named after Alexander Gillies, an early lumberman. It was surveyed in 1885 and subdivided. Communities in the township include Hymers, Sellers and South Gillies. The first township council meeting was held at Hymers in 1921.

Today Gillies has a population of 408 (1978). Recreational facilities include two community halls and an outdoor rink. The township has a Roman Catholic church and a public school. All other public services are available in the nearby city of Thunder Bay.

Ministry of Natural Resources: *Directory of Statistics and Data, 1975.*

GILLIES LIMIT, geographic township, Timiskaming District
Position 47° 17′ 79° 44′

This township, a few miles west of Lake Timiskaming, is named after the Gillies Bros. who were owners of the timber limits in the area. It became a part of the Timagami Provincial Forest in 1931.

Highway 11 passes through the township linking it with the towns of Cobalt and Haileybury, a short distance to the north.

GILLILAND, geographic township, Sudbury District
Position 47° 54′ 83° 41′

Formerly designated as Township No. 35, it was named after Thomas B. Gilliland, a surveyor in northern and northwestern Ontario during the 1880's. The township is located a few miles to the west of the town of Chapleau.

GILLMOR, geographic township, Algoma District
Position 46° 39' 83° 47'

The township was established in 1878. It is named after the late Col. Gillmor who served as Clerk of the Legislative Assembly of Ontario. It is located east of Sault Ste. Marie and is not accessible by road.

GILMOUR, community, Tudor Township, Hastings County
Position 44° 49' 77° 37'

Named after the Gilmour Lumber Company of Trenton, the community of Gilmour is situated fifty miles north of Belleville and east of Highway 62. In 1974 the population was 70.

The settlement developed after the Central Ontario Railway was built from Trenton to Coe Hill in 1881. A post office opened in 1887.

Among the early settlers were Philip Dafoe, Holmes Lidster and Thomas Ricketts. The North American Telegraph Company operated its district telephone exchange from 1905 to 1910 in the general store of W.A. McMurray. By 1911 the exchange had become part of the Bell system and the first Gilmour directory was published in that year.

Gilmour's first school, a frame building, was erected in 1891 on land purchased from the Crown for five dollars. A new area school was opened in the community in 1950.

Gerald E. Boyce: *Historic Hastings,* 1967.

GISBORN, geographic township, Algoma District
Position 47° 11' 82° 53'

The township which was designated as No. 7B, was named in 1974 after R. Gisborn, then the Member of the Provincial Parliament for Hamilton East. It is located north of Rocky Island Lake and west of the Mississagi Wild River Provincial Park.

GLACKMEYER, township, Cochrane District
Position 49° 07' 80° 58'

This township north of the town of Cochrane was surveyed in 1907 by A.S. Cade and named after F.J. Glackmeyer, a former Sergeant-at-Arms in the Ontario government at Toronto.

The first settler in Glackmeyer was Fidel Bradette who built his home on Lot 21, Concession 6. A sawmill and a cheese factory were the earliest industries in the township. Today the major industry is milk-production.

In recent years, parts of Glackmeyer have been annexed by the town of Cochrane. There have been four such annexations in the last decade. In 1978 the population of the remaining township was 1,137.

The Abitibi River flows in a northerly course through the eastern half of the township. The Ontario Northland Railway passes through the western section.

GLADMAN, geographic township, Nipissing District
Position 46° 41' 79° 41'

The township which is located north of Lake Nipissing, was subdivided in 1890. It was named after George Gladman, an early fur trader and explorer who was placed in charge of a Canadian government expedition to explore the country between Lake Superior and the Red River Settlement in 1857-58.

Highway 11 passes through the township linking it with the city of North Bay.

The main body of Marten Lake occupies much of the township's northern section.

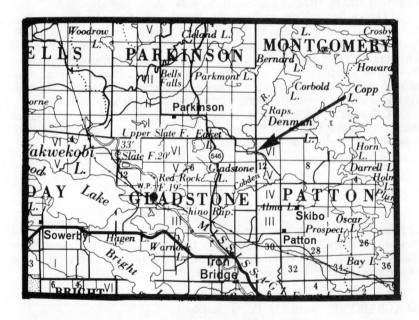

GLADSTONE, geographic township, Algoma District
Position 46° 19' 83° 16'

Surveyed in 1879, the township was known first as WO 179 and eventually was named after the Hon. W.E. Gladstone, noted prime minister for Great Britain around the 1850's.

The southern half was designated as an Improvement District in 1957 and it became a part of the village of Iron Bridge in 1960.

The Mississagi River flows southward through the township on the last stretch of its journey before emptying into Lake Huron's North Channel west of the town of Blind River.

GLADSTONE, community, North Dorchester Township, Middlesex County
Position 42° 55′ 81° 03′

The hamlet of Gladstone is located in the southeast corner of Middlesex County, not far from the city of London. The settlement was first known as Hares Corners, after Arthur Hare, who farmed on the site. He also built the first brick house in the community. In 1875 the name of the settlement was changed to Gladstone, presumably after the famous British statesman, elected four times to the office of Prime Minister, William Ewart Gladstone. Among the early settlers who moved into the area after Hare were the Marshes, Hills, and Smiths.

The first school for Gladstone's children was built on the north side of the 5th Concession and opened in 1845. In 1874 the present school grounds were purchased and a new school built. This was destroyed by fire in 1886 and another school built on the same site and used until June 1966.

A post office opened in Gladstone in 1864 with Charles Shain as the first postmaster. A general store was also opened in the settlement. Both the general store and the small adjoining post office were destroyed by fire in 1929.

As early as 1842 Baptist meetings were held in the area and in 1848 the Gladstone Baptist Church was organized with the Reverend John Williams as the first pastor. A fine brick church was built by the congregation in 1895.

When the CPR put a line through the county, a small station for Gladstone was built about a half-mile from the hamlet. High School students from Gladstone used the train to commute to the high school in Ingersoll, and local farmers shipped their milk by train to Toronto. The Gladstone Cheese Factory opened in 1922 and was in operation until 1947, when, for a while, it was converted into a pork packing plant. Gladstone is set in a prosperous farming district.

Mrs. Harold Ross: *North Dorchester — A Century Past to Present,* 1967.

GLADWIN, geographic township, Sudbury District
Position 47° 07′ 82° 24′

The name origin of this township is not known. It is situated immediately to the east of the Mississagi Wild River Provincial Park and is accessible only by waterways.

GLAMMIS, community, Kincardine Township, Bruce County
Position 44° 12′ 81° 23′

This dispersed rural community extends its territory into three townships: Greenock, Kincardine and Bruce. While the largest area of the settlement lies in Greenock Township, the largest portion of the population live on the Kincardine Township side. Glammis is situated approximately some thirty miles northeast of the town of Goderich. The early Scottish settlers probably named the site after Glamis Castle in Scotland.

There was no village on the site when Allan Ross and Duncan Campbell arrived about 1858, but a Presbyterian congregation had been formed by the settlers in the district and a church had been built. In 1860 a post office was established with James Crawford as postmaster. The first sawmill in the settlement was erected by John Fraser.

In addition to the early Presbyterian church, Glammis once had a Baptist church and a Methodist church. The Glammis school was in use from 1899 to 1964.

By the 1880's Glammis was a small but bustling post village containing four stores, two hotels and steam mills. Today the population of Glammis numbers less than 80.

Norman McLeod: *The history of the County of Bruce*, 1969.

H. Belden & Co.: *Historical Atlas of Grey and Bruce Counties*, 1880.

GLAMORGAN, township, Provisional County of Haliburton
Position 44° 55' 78° 28'

Glamorgan Township, surveyed in 1862, derives its name from an ancient Welsh prince, Gwald Morgan. Wooded, rolling hills and plains make up the countryside, with Greens Mountain rising to a height of 1,466 feet above sea level in the southeast corner of the township. On top of the mountain stands the township's fire watch tower. The mountain, supposedly, was named for a lumberman of the firm of Green and Ellis, which once operated a camp in the immediate vicinity. Lumbering companies were the first to come into the township followed by settlers in the 1870's who, once established, supplied the camps with provisions.

The earliest settlements developed along the Burnt River and the Monck and Buckhorn Colonization Roads, which were the main traffic arteries in the township in those days. Gooderham village grew up near Greens Mountain between Pine Lake and the Burnt River, at the intersection of the two roads. The settlement, originally known as Pine Lake, was christened Gooderham one fine evening when a travelling salesman from the noted Toronto distillery of Gooderham's generously treated the inhabitants to samples of his firm's whiskey in the local tavern.

J.M. Pickens, one of the township's earliest pioneers arrived in 1870 and settled two miles from Gooderham on the Monck Road. He was followed by Samuel Wiley who took up land on the Bobcaygeon Road. The first post office in the township was kept by Charles Way, operator of a hotel just west of Gooderham. Two other early township settlers, Charles and Anthony Hall, ran a portable shingle and sawmill.

Gooderham's pioneers included the Deweys, the McColls and the McConnels. Isaac and J.J. Hunter who came to the area around 1876, built a saw and grist mill on the bank of the Burnt River.

Glamorgan, for municipal purposes, was once united with Cardiff and Monmouth. In June 1874 the first county council met in session at Minden, then awarded the honour of being county town, and Reeve Philip Harding attended representing Glamorgan, Monmouth and Cardiff. Beginning 1881 the first reeve to be elected for Glamorgan was Richard Sidley. The first election for council was held at the residence of Sam Whittaker, located at the Monck and Buckhorn Roads. Whittaker had been the first hotelkeeper in the village of Gooderham.

Forest fires struck the township of Glamorgan on more than one occasion. So disastrous were two of these fires that forty percent of the township land was laid to waste. Just prior to the start of World War One, less than ten percent of Glamorgan's land was under cultivation, some of it unfit for agriculture. A number of farmers, unable to pay their taxes, had lost their farms and municipal coffers were empty. But Glamorgan's inhabitants, now numbering some 520, weathered the hard times. The beautiful lakes and rivers in the township attract fishermen and tourists in ever-increasing numbers to the area. There are eight principal lakes, the largest of which is Koshlong Lake covering an area of 770 acres.

Highway 503 serves the area. Over half of the township's population is concentrated in the community of Gooderham.

Nila Reynolds: In Quest of Yesterday, 1967.

GLANBROOK, township, Regional Municipality of Hamilton-Wentworth
Position 43° 09′ 79° 55′

Originally the smallest township in Wentworth County, Glanford Township was situated between the townships of Ancaster and Binbrook. On January 1, 1974, for municipal reasons, the townships of Binbrook and Glanford were amalgamated to create the new Township of Glanbrook. It has an area of 50,099 acres and a population of 9,934 (1979).

The early township of Glanford had, by 1815, 50 ratepayers. Jacob Smith, United Empire Loyalist, arrived from Sussex, New Jersey around 1788. Jabez Clark took up land in 1818, and his land was successively farmed by Isaac, David, Irvin and Arnold Clark. Maggie Clark was immortalized in the popular song written by her husband, George Johnson, "When You and I were Young, Maggie". From Northumberland, England, in 1832, came George Bell, and in 1846, John and Samuel Weylie, of Irish stock. Others were the Jeromes, Coates, Hannons and Longs.

Glanford and Binbrook both had large blocks of land, ranging from 1,000 acres up, set aside as Clergy Reserves, chiefly for the benefit of the Church of England. Blocks were also granted to favoured friends of the Family Compact. The holders of this land were absentees and held the land for speculation purposes. No taxes were paid on the land, nor was there any attempt toward road building. The land blocks were an obstruction to the farmers wedged in between, as they had to bypass them to get their produce to market. Appeals to the government for redress were ignored and, ultimately, this kind of practice flared into the resentment that fired the Rebellion of 1837. James Reed, who came from England around 1850, took up about 200

119

acres of a block of this land that had been set aside in the name of King's College (University of Toronto).

Today's Highway 6 follows the first road attempted in Glanford Township. Leading south to Long Point and other Lake Erie settlements, it was planked through Mount Hope, about 1839. The early Hamilton and Lake Erie Railway was later taken over by the Grand Trunk Railway, and the line now is part of the Canadian National Railways' system which bisects Glanbrook Township.

In 1849 there was one sawmill only in the township, but though industry did not flourish, the land produced abundant crops. Mount Hope was the only village of importance in Glanford, located mid-way between Hamilton and Caledonia on what is now Highway 6. There were two churches in this village, the Church of England and the Wesleyan Methodists. A church near the village of Binbrook became a notable landmark. Case United Church, formerly Methodist Episcopal and named after the noted circuit-rider, Elder William Case, was erected in 1894 on the farm of William Case Smith.

The first Municipal Council of Glanford was organized in 1850, its reeve was Joseph Hannon. Councillors were: Aley Binkley, Henry McSherry, James O'Loane and James S. Wetenhall.

The first settler in the township of Binbrook is said to have been Brian Condon, who took up residence on the first concession in the early 1800's. Two early settlements of importance were Binbrook (first called Hall's Corners), located on present-day Highway 56, and Woodburn in the southeast corner of the township, where the first sawmill was built in 1835. Six sawmills were kept busy in the township, well supplied with dense pine forests.

Binbrook Township was named after a village in Lincolnshire, England and when the post office came to the village of Hall's Corners in 1848, its name, too, became Binbrook.

In 1850 the first municipal council of the township was held with Henry Hall chosen reeve. Councillors were: James Sliptel, Dr. Kennedy, John Sidey, A.B. Sweezey, and James Duff was clerk.

The Welland River and Twenty Mile Creek course through the township of Glanbrook. Highways 6 and 56, and the Canadian National Railways provide transportation services.

Page and Smith: *Illustrated Historical Atlas of the County of Wentworth*, 1875.

GLANMIRE, community, Lake and Tudor Townships, Hastings County
Position 44° 45′ 77° 41′

This dispersed rural community is situated six miles north of Millbridge on the Old Hastings Road. Formerly called Jelly's Rapids, after pioneer settler and early reeve Andrew Jelly, it was renamed Glanmire but was known for many years also as Beaver Creek.

Early settlers of this English settlement included the families of Lavender, Breen and Lummis. A post office was established in 1858 and a school opened in 1860.

In 1887 John Ray gave land for the building of St. Margaret's Anglican Church. By 1963 the church was no longer used for services as there was no one living within four miles of it. However, a meeting held in that year proposed that it be repaired and used as a cemetery chapel and memorial to the early settlers of the area.

Today Glanmire is the site of cottage settlements which greatly swell the population of the townships in the summer.

Alma Blackburn, et al: *Pilgrimage of Faith 1824-1974*, 1974.
Gerald E. Boyce: *Historic Hastings*, 1967.

GLANWORTH, community, Westminster Township, Middlesex County
Position 42° 52' 81° 12'

The rural community of Glanworth is located in the southern portion of Middlesex County, a few miles southeast of the city of London. In the 1971 census, the population of Glanworth was 109.

The land where Glanworth stands today was originally cleared for the farm of Richard Rose in 1834. As other settlers moved to the area, a post office opened in 1857 and a Mr. Webb was the first postmaster. A station was built for Glanworth when the London and Port Stanley Railway constructed a route through the township. By 1887 Glanworth had a population of 160 and the businesses there included a general merchant, hotel, carriage-maker, and a blacksmith.

In 1888 a cheese factory was added to the hamlet's establishments and Mr. L. Smith was the first manager. The Borden Milk Company was the last to own the factory and when they moved the business to the neighbouring village of Belmont, the old building was torn down. In 1927 a new cheese factory was opened in Glanworth.

Today, Glanworth is almost engulfed by the suburbs of the neighbouring city of London.

London Free Press, 1949.

GLASGOW, geographic township, Algoma District
Position 48° 23' 84° 12'

The western half of this township which is named after Glasgow, Scotland, was formerly a part of the Algoma Central & Hudson Bay Co. Land Grant.

The Canadian Pacific Railway skirts the township's southern boundary. Much of the township is covered by the southern portion of Wabatongushi Lake.

GLASS, geographic township, Kenora District
Position 49° 37' 94° 57'

The township is situated southwest of the town of Kenora and was named for J.J. Glass, MPP for St. Andrew (Toronto riding) 1934-37.

Shoal Lake, with its several islands, covers most of the township. Clytie Bay in the northern part of Glass is accessible by road from the Trans-Canada Highway (No. 17). A large Indian Reserve is located to the west of the township boundary.

GLEN, geographic township, Thunder Bay District
Position 48° 53′ 88° 38′

The township, located northeast of the city of Thunder Bay, was established in 1945 and was named after the Hon. James A. Glen, federal Minister of Mines and Resources at that time.

Wolf Lake takes up a portion of the township, and at the southern tip where it empties into the Wolf River, a dam is located. The area is linked by road to the Trans-Canada Highway.

GLEN ALLAN, community, Peel Township, Wellington County
Position 43° 39′ 80° 42′

This compact rural community is situated 28 miles northwest of Guelph. It was named after George Allan who laid out the village lots.

In the late 1800's the community had several stores, a blacksmith shop, a wagon shop, a mill, a hotel, and two churches. In the late nineteenth and early twentieth centuries, Glen Allan was a thriving settlement with a population of about 800. In 1903 Joseph Coote ran the local hotel while W.C. Quickfall operated the sawmill. Two general stores, a hardware store, two wagon shops, a harness shop, a jewellery store, and a blacksmith shop served the residents.

During the twentieth century Glen Allan's population decreased greatly. However, recently the number of inhabitants has begun to rise again, almost doubling from 68 in 1966 to 126 in 1971.

Historical Atlas Publishing Co.: *Historical Atlas of Wellington County*, 1906.

GLENBURNIE, community, Kingston Township, Frontenac County
Position 44° 19′ 76° 29′

Although today Glenburnie is a dispersed rural community, in the nineteenth century it was a post village of some importance.

By the time a log school, known as the "Cole Hill" school, was built in 1835 on the Worden farm, the area was thickly settled by immigrants from Scotland and Ireland. In 1845 land for a stone school was deeded by Archibald McMillan. In 1878 the stone school was replaced by a brick building, at which Annie Slavin was the first teacher. A separate school was built on Patrick Black's farm.

This early stone school was also used for Presbyterian services by a minister who travelled from St. Andrew's church, Kingston. Later the congregation built a small brick church on ground donated by W.J. Blacklock. With church union in 1925, the church was closed and sold to the United Farmers' Society of Glenburnie for a hall. Later still, it was enlarged and used as a community hall.

The first church built by Methodists in 1856 was of stone and stood on land donated by Reuben Spooner, Sr. Members of the Roman Catholic religion worshipped at the church of St. Mary's, Kingston, travelling by wagon and oxen over trails and through bush. Often a priest would arrive at the log house of a Mr. Hickey and hold services. The Holy Name Church is now located at nearby Cushendall.

At one time Glenburnie was the site of a cheese factory, now closed. Hydro was introduced to the community in 1937.

Frontenac County Directory, 1865.

Kingston *Whig-Standard*, 1952.

GLENCAIRN, community, Tosorontio Township, Simcoe County
Position 44° 18′ 80° 01′

The community of Glencairn on the Mad River is situated in the northwestern corner of Tosorontio Township, less than twenty miles southeast of the town of Collingwood. It was named after James, Earl of Glencairn, a patron of the Scottish poet, Robert Burns.

Marshall N. Stephens built the first mill at Glencairn about 1853. Later, 1878, Mr. Stephens also supported the construction of the Hamilton and North Western Railway through Glencairn. A post office opened in 1867 and by the 1880's Glencairn had several hotels and shops, a grist mill, a sawmill, a general store, and a Dominion Telegraph Office. The population of the settlement in 1881 was 200.

Today Glencairn is a small rural community that serves as a centre for the surrounding farming district.

H. Belden & Co.: *Illustrated Atlas of the County of Simcoe*, 1881.

Andrew F. Hunter: *The History of Simcoe County*, 1909.

GLENCOE, village, Mosa and Ekfrid Townships, Middlesex County
Position 42° 45′ 81° 43′

The largest village in Middlesex County with a population of 1,743 in 1978, Glencoe is situated about 30 miles southwest of London on Highway 80, the CNR, and the CPR. It was named after Glencoe in Scotland by surveyor A.P. Macdonald.

The area was first settled by William Sutherland who began farming here in 1853. At this time the site of the future village was little more than a swamp but soon more settlers arrived and a community began to develop. The village was laid out in 1860 and incorporated in 1873. James Dykes served as the first clerk.

Glencoe grew into an industrial centre in the late nineteenth century. In 1882 the Glencoe Manufacturing Company was established, becoming the first large industry in the village. About the same time Robert and Frederick Aldred invented a rake-harvester with binding attachment which enjoyed a large market. By 1903 there were several small factories employing Glencoe's 1200 residents. These included R.J.F. Alfred's factory, which manufactured bakers' and confectioners' machinery; Graham Bros., makers of agricultural implements; the R.C. Vause woollen mill and the flour mills of Cameron & Sons, and the Woodburn Milling Co. Ltd. Two carriage makers, four blacksmiths, five grocers, and two shoemakers served the community while visitors were accommodated in any one of three hotels.

Glencoe has maintained its industrial character during the

twentieth century. In 1959 its industries included a creamery, two grist mills, a sash-and-door factory, a textile plant, and a copper-tubing plant. Today manufactured products from the village include ornamental metal, concrete, and house slippers.

The proximity of Glencoe to two major railroads led to the village becoming a shipping-point for the surrounding agricultural area. Today freight services handle a wide variety of produce, including fruits, tobacco, corn, soybeans, beets, and cattle.

A district high school and a public library serve modern Glencoe's 1,743 inhabitants. The village also has a weekly paper, the *Glencoe-Alvinston Transcript and Free Press*, founded by William Sutherland in 1870.

William B. Hamilton: *Macmillan Book of Canadian Place Names*, 1978.

London Free Press, 1949.

Ontario Gazetteer, 1903.

GLENELG, township, County of Grey
Position 44° 15' 80° 45'

The township was named after either the Scottish hometown of the first settler, John Jessiman, or Lord Glenelg, the British Colonial Secretary under Lord Grey. It is situated in central Grey County and is bordered to the north by Holland Township, to the east by Artemesia, to the south by Egremont, and to the west by Bentinck and the Garafraxa Road.

The township comprises 70,350 acres much of which is thin, porous soil, not suitable for agriculture. The Glenelg Gravelly Hills in the south and east are mostly forest or pasture land. The more rolling land around Markland is largely agricultural with wheat and flax the important crops. The northeast includes the highest land in south-western Ontario and is the watershed for the area. There are many beautiful lakes, including Bell's Lake. The Saugeen River flows through the township.

The Garafraxa Road, surveyed in 1837, provided access to the area for John Jessiman, a retired officer of the Black Watch, who arrived in 1838 and settled on lot 3, concession 1. He was followed in 1841 by James Bolton and Thomas Laybourne who also settled on the free lots along the Garafraxa Road. Archibald Hunter arrived in 1842, and with his family, began the settlement of Durham. He later opened the first hotel in the township.

Many of the settlers were from Ireland and the Highlands of Scotland. Early sermons were often given in both English and Gaelic. A large number of settlers also came from Lower Canada. Pioneer families included the McFarlanes, Camerons, Ledinghams, Barbers, Duncans, and Kerrs. After 1848, when the Durham Road was laid out as a "colonization" road, many more families arrived, including the McNallys, Weirs, and Tophams. The population peaked in the 1880's, with 4,060 people in 1880.

Glenelg was organized as a municipality in 1850. A.B. McNab

was the first reeve. On the Council were James Ledingham, Allen Cameron, Donald McCormack, and Duncan Smith. In 1879 Glenelg township hall was built on Lot 10, Concession 4. It was replaced by a new hall in 1969.

A school for both Glenelg and Bentinck was established prior to 1850. A second school was built north of the Rocky Saugeen about 1850. Andrew Muir was the first teacher at the school which was replaced by a new building in 1873. A third school at Latona was established in the 1850's. Here the first teacher was Archibald McLellan. In 1852, School section 1, the first school completely within the township, was organized. Archibald Black taught here for the first nine years. Several other schools, including a number of separate schools, were established by 1870. One of these, School Section 10, was reputed to be haunted. A strange humming noise, for which no explanation could be found, finally caused the school to be abandoned in 1894.

The first Presbyterian church in the township was built in 1856. The church was replaced by a stone building in 1878. St. Paul's Roman Catholic Church was constructed in 1858, with Father Bardon as the first pastor. St. Peters, erected about 1860, was used until 1893 when St. John's was built at Glenelg Centre. A flour mill near Glenroadin was the site for services by a Baptist circuit rider. The North Glenelg Baptist Church grew out of this congregation in 1876. Alex Warren was the first minister.

In 1847 the Dunsmore flour mill was built on the Rocky Saugeen. This was followed in 1848 by the Edge flour and chopping mill on the main Saugeen. In 1855 a four-storey flour and sawmill was established near Markdale by Matthew Irving. Other early mills included Travers' flour and sawmill at Traverston, George Roswell's sawmill and ashery at Hayward's Falls, Purdy's flour mill near Priceville, Barrhead's sawmill near Markdale and Sim's Woollen mill.

The first store in the township was opened in the 1840's by H. Schofield. Jacob Griffin set up the first store in Dornoch. Isaac Elder was the first blacksmith in the township.

Latona was established as a post office in 1853 with Mark Appleby as postmaster. Post offices were later also set up at Glascott, at Traverston (later Waverly), and at Bunessan. In 1881 Edge Hill became a post office with James Edge as Postmaster, followed by Rocky Saugeen in 1885 with Postmaster Donald McKecknie.

Glenelg grew rapidly until the 1880's but the population has declined since then. In 1978, 1,416 people lived in the township.

H. Belden and Co., *Illustrated Atlas of the County of Grey*, 1880.

T. Arthur Davidson, *A New History of Grey County*, 1972.

E.L. Marsh, *A History of the County of Grey*, 1931.

Audrey M. Rutherford, *Grey County Centennial 1852-1952*, 1952.

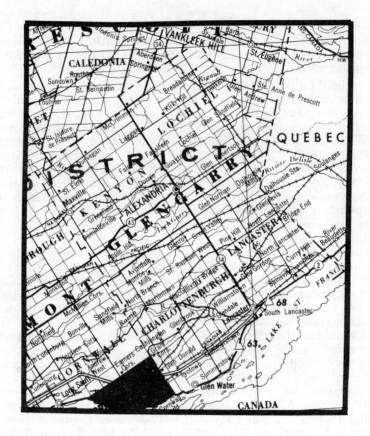

GLENGARRY, county
Position 45° 15′ 74° 46′

Glengarry, the most easterly county of Ontario, is one of the United Counties of Stormont, Dundas and Glengarry. Fronting on the St. Lawrence River and Lake St. Francis, it has the Quebec counties of Solanges and Vaudreuil bordering to the east, Prescott County to the north and Stormont County to the west. Its 478 square miles comprise the townships of Charlottenburgh and Lancaster in the south and Kenyon and Lochiel in the north. The Canadian Pacific Railway and the Canadian National Railways, as well as Highways 34, 43 and 2 provide excellent transportation facilities for the county.

Glengarry is one of the original counties into which the district of Lunenburg was divided in 1792 by proclamation of Lord Dorchester, then officiating Governor of Canada. Many of the early settlers came from Glengarry, Scotland and held to the memory of their Scottish homes in choosing Glengarry for the name of their new homes.

Early pioneers were mainly United Empire Loyalists from the Mohawk Valley in New York. When they were forced to move to Canada, about 1784, they were fairly well experienced in pioneering.

They included the names of Macdonell, the McLennans, Charles Rose, John Hay and Benjamin Glassford. They chose Charlottenburgh, the most westerly and largest of Glengarry's four townships. In 1794 forty families from Scotland, the McLeods, McGillivrays, McCuaigs, McIntoshes, Campbells, Cains and Frasers among them, arrived in Lochiel and settled near Kirkfield.

From Knoydart, a part of Glengarry, Scotland, there arrived about 500 Scottish Highlanders. Families dispossessed by landlords wanting their lands for sheep grazing, they were under the superintendence of a Roman Catholic priest, the Reverend Alexander Macdonell. They settled, in 1786, in St. Raphaels, the first settlers in Glengarry County to be away from a river highway. Of necessity they pioneered a road from St. Raphaels to Coteau, the nearest grist mill. These people, the Grants, McLeods, McCrimmons, McDonalds and McMillans among them, knew little about pioneering agriculture, but with the aid of earlier settlers they survived and gradually improved their holdings. A number of them took up land in Lochiel Township, in northeast Glengarry, included are the names of John Dewar, John McPhee, Donald and Archibald McGillivray, and Roderick and Alexander McLeod. The Reverend Alexander MacDonell built the first Roman Catholic church in the county at St. Raphaels around 1789. Constructed of wood, it was called the Blue Chapel, because of its blue ceiling. In 1802 St. Raphaels was erected officially into a parish and from this focal point missions in the Roman Catholic religion spread across the county. The Reverend Alexander Macdonell died in 1803.

Yet another Alexander Macdonell, of the Greenfield branch of the family, brought members of his clan to Canada in 1792. His son, Lt. Col. John Macdonell (Greenfield) was aide-de-camp to General Brock and with Brock was killed at the Battle of Queenston Heights in 1812. At that time he was Attorney-General of the province and member of the Legislative Assembly for Glengarry.

Again, in 1804, a namesake of the first priest, Alexander Macdonell, arrived in St. Raphaels. He was the Reverend Alexander Macdonell, chaplain of the Glengarry Fencibles, who brought a party of that disbanded militia regiment to settle at St. Raphaels. Zealously he discharged his pastoral duties. Travelling by horseback, by birch canoe, living with the Indians en route, he covered hundreds of miles each year and soon St. Raphaels became the centre of the Roman Catholic religion in Upper Canada. Reverend Alexander Macdonell began the erection of a fine stone church in 1819; the doors opened in 1826. In 1970 a fire burned the church, leaving a stone shell as a fascinating memorial. He also erected a stone presbytery and a seminary, not only for the training of priests, but also for use as a boys' school. Reverend Alexander Macdonell was appointed bishop in 1819, and in 1826 he became the first Bishop in Upper Canada. He died while on a visit to Scotland and later was buried in Kingston. Alexandria, Lochiel Township, was named in his honour. From the days of the early Glengarry Fencibles, a fine military tradition has come down to the present Glengarry Highlanders.

Glengarrians involved in the North West Company were: Hon.

William McGillivray, chief director of that company; Angus Bethune, son of Reverend John Bethune, who brought organized Presbyterianism to Glengarry in 1787 — Angus Bethune was great-grandfather of Dr. Norman Bethune, famous for his medical work in China.

The lives of the three greatest explorers associated with the North West Company, David Thompson, Sir Alexander MacKenzie and Simon Fraser, briefly touched the County of Glengarry. David Thompson lived for a time in Williamstown and with his sons ran a general store. Sir Alexander MacKenzie, whose uncle settled in Glengarry in 1784, gave a bell to the Presbyterian Church at Williamstown and maintained a pew there, though he, himself, spent little actual time in the county. Simon Fraser lived for many years at St. Andrews, close by in Stormont County.

Farming was the main occupation of Glengarry families and although the county is well watered by the Raisin, the Baudette and the Delisle Rivers, as well as several branches of the Rigaud River, the land did not produce too many rich farms and it became customary for the young men to winter in the lumber shanties to supplement their income. Tales of log drives and shantymen belong to Glengarry's cultural heritage. The men also left for parts of the United States and the western provinces seeking a more lucrative way of life.

By the early nineteenth century Glengarry's population was almost exclusively Scottish. Gradually this began to change. A shortage of land in the populated areas of the neighbouring Quebec townships induced French Canadians to move into Glengarry. Some of the Scots, in turn, moved to settle elsewhere. Today the population of the county is about half French and half English. Because of this trend, many of the Protestant churches fell into disuse while the Roman Catholic churches flourished. In 1978 there were 2 Anglican, 5 Presbyterian and 11 United churches, with one each of Seventh Day Adventist and the Covenanters. There were 15 Roman Catholic Churches in that same year.

In 1789 the first post office of Glengarry was opened at Charlottenburgh. It served an area of almost 500 square miles, although most of the people were concentrated along the river front and a few miles inland. Mail couriers on foot or horseback ran the mail to various destinations. Canoe, river steamer, stage coach and railway were also used at various times. In 1869 the mail came up the north shore of the St. Lawrence via the Grand Trunk Railway. From the first post office of 1789 to the last opened in Williamstown in 1833, Glengarry numbered 58 post offices. In the late 1800's many were, for various reasons, closed and the coming of rural mail in the early 1900's caused the closing of others.

The Montreal Telegraph Company built a telegraph line across Glengarry in 1847 to provide communication between Toronto and Montreal. They located a station at Lancaster and one in Cornwall. This was the first of such telegraph lines that were built in Glengarry. The telephone first came to Cornwall in 1880 and was soon followed by this service in other centres, and by 1911 the telephone was available to anyone in Glengarry who wished to have it.

The Grand Trunk Railway opened in 1855 between Montreal and Brockville with a station at Lancaster. In 1856 the line continued to Toronto. In 1882 the Canada Atlantic line was completed in Glengarry County greatly benefitting the county. In particular, Maxville quickly thrived as a principal intermediate station on the line, with new stores and hotels built for the welcome commerce. In 1904 the Grand Trunk bought the Canada Atlantic. In 1914 Glengarry's final railway was the Stormont and Glengarry line connecting Cornwall with the CPR main line and five more railway stations were opened in Glengarry making a total of 19 altogether.

Alexandria, founded as Priest's Mills in 1819, became the county seat and principal shopping area for the district. Today it is still the most important centre in Glengarry. By 1903 Alexandria's industries included Munro and McIntosh, carriagemakers, the Schell Factory and Foundry, and the Canadian Bond Hanger Company. The Graham Creamery opened in 1922, the Carnation Plant in 1952 and Brown's Shoe Company in 1960. Alexandria is no longer the county seat. Glengarry was one of the original counties of the District of Lunenburg until the Municipal Act of 1850 when it was united with the counties of Stormont and Dundas. Cornwall then became the county seat of the United Counties.

The first newspaper, the *Glengarry Times*, under its editor, J.C. McNeil printed a first issue in December 1880 in Lancaster. The paper foundered and was followed in three or four years by the *Glengarry Review*, a Conservative-slanted paper which changed its name in 1888 to the *Glengarrian*. The Liberals then established the *Glengarry News* in 1892 and today it is the sole newspaper in Glengarry.

Glengarrians of Scottish descent retain an active interest in their culture and are proud of the Gaelic language which is zealously preserved. The Glengarry Highland Games, held annually in Maxville, are the largest of their kind in North America. The Nor'Westers Museum, opened in an old brick school in Williamstown in 1967, and the Glengarry Pioneer Inn and Museum in Dunvegan, both tell the early history of the county. The Glengarry Historical Society was organized in 1959. Historic sites are in evidence all over Glengarry.

For such a small county (population about 30,000 in 1976), Glengarry has produced a large number of well-known figures. The most famous of these is Ralph Connors, born Charles Gordon, whose two books, *Man from Glengarry* and *Glengarry School Days*, sold more copies than any other Canadian book at the time. Three other authors, Carrie Holmes MacGillivray, Grace Campbell, and Dorothy Dumbrille, have also written novels set in the county. Sir Edward Peacock (1871-1962), born at St. Elmo, was a schoolmaster in Canada before leaving for England where he became a prominent financier and director of the Bank of England. Near St. Raphaels lived John Sandfield Macdonald, who became the first Premier of Ontario, 1867-71.

While there is a number of manufacturing industries located in the various centres of the county, much of Glengarry remains rural and farmers are engaged in dairy and poultry farming and hog raising.

In addition, the bustling city of Cornwall with its large paper industry and its factories and service industries, also provides employment for county residents.

Royce MacGillivray and Ewan Ross: *A History of Glengarry*, 1979.

John Graham Harkness: *Stormont, Dundas and Glengarry, A History*, 1946.

GLEN HURON, community, Nottawasaga Township, Simcoe County
Position 44° 21' 80° 11'

The hamlet of Glen Huron is located on the banks of the Mad River, approximately fifteen miles south of the town of Collingwood. Glen Huron is named for the glen in which the settlement is situated, and in recognition of the Huron Indian tribe who first inhabited this territory.

James Cooper was the first to build a sawmill on the spot where Glen Huron stands today. In 1852 he either sold or abandoned this mill and moved to another village. Another early settler, James D. Stephens (nicknamed "Tally-Ho" Stephens), arrived in 1845. He built a carding mill and operated the Green Bush Hotel. Mr. Stephens became prominent in local township politics, and he developed business interests in Hurontario, as well. Other settlers who arrived at this time were the Robertsons and the Campbells. A post office was opened in the settlement in 1869 and the name Glen Huron was bestowed on the community by the first postmaster, Mr. Frame.

In 1873 James Hamilton moved to Glen Huron and bought out Stephens' mill. He cleared out the carding machinery and modified the mill for grist and feed grinding purposes. In 1884 he built a new mill for flour production. The firm of James Hamilton and Sons prospered and became renowned for quality flour and cereals. In 1894, after James Hamilton's death, the firm became known as Hamilton Brothers. Other early industries in Glen Huron included the Gosnell lime industry and a cooperative cheese factory.

A Methodist church was built in 1865 and the present church was built in 1906.

Today Glen Huron is a farming settlement in the heart of a mixed farming district. In 1971 the population of the settlement was 54.

Andrew F. Hunter: *The History of Simcoe County*, 1909.

J. Allan Blair: *Introduction to Nottawasaga*, 1967.

GLEN MEYER, community, Norfolk Township, Regional Municipality of Haldimand-Norfolk

Prior to 1974, the dispersed rural community of Glen Meyer was part of Houghton and North Walsingham Townships, Norfolk County. It is situated approximately 20 miles southwest of the town of Simcoe.

In 1854, one of the settlers in the area was George Edward Meyer, who bought 50 acres of the prime farm land, part of Lot 1 in the 14th Concession of Walsingham. When the post office was established in

1865, the community was called Glen Meyer.

Others who settled this area in the first half of the 19th century, were Benjamin Birdsill, James Boyd, Enoch Harvey, and John Meharg. Jehu Mosher operated a mill in 1851, while in 1875, Thomas Matthews had a grist mill.

H.R. Page & Co.: *Historical Atlas of the County of Norfolk*, 1877.

Bruce M. Pearce: *Historical Highlights of Norfolk County*, Ontario, 1877.

GLEN MORRIS, community, South Dumfries Township, Brant County
Position 43° 16' 80° 21'

The small community of Glen Morris is situated on the banks of the Grand River, about ten miles northwest of the city of Brantford and six miles south of the city of Galt. According to the 1971 census the population of Glen Morris was 279.

The site of Glen Morris was settled as early as 1823 by pioneers from Scotland and New York State. In 1831 John Dawson built a sawmill at this spot. In that same year, Mr. Dawson constructed a bridge across the Grand River and the settlement became known as Dawson's Bridge. A general store was opened in 1845 by Robert Shiel. During this later period Glen Morris was known as Middleton because it was situated in the centre of a ring of villages formed by Ayr, Paris and St. George.

In 1848, Samuel Latshaw, whose father, Joseph, had been one of the first settlers in the area, laid out the village for settlement. A town hall was erected in 1850 (torn down in 1938). In 1851, when a post office was opened with Robert Shiel as postmaster, the community was christened Glen Morris; the name Morris was bestowed in honour of the postmaster-general of that time.

In 1854 George Herbert built the first grist mill in the hamlet. Robert Wallace established a distillery in 1857. Other early businessmen in the settlement were Gavin Fleming, who operated a mercantile business until 1925, and Thomas Scott, who opened a store in 1882. Industries in the Glen Morris area included German's Woollen Mills, and the Hannah Varnish Factory, manufacturers of Grand River Paint Products, which was established in 1921 and transferred to Galt in 1946.

The Grand Valley Electric Railroad ran a line through Glen Morris in 1905 providing direct rail service to Galt. The line was replaced with the Lake Erie and Northern Railroad in 1915 and later became the CPR route.

A Presbyterian church was built in 1849 on land donated by Samuel Latshaw. After church union in 1925, the Presbyterian Church became the Glen Morris United Church. A Methodist church had also been erected in the settlement and after church union it became a lodge hall; later the Women's Institute took over the building.

In 1868 a village school was built. Although the building is no longer a school today, it continues to exist as the headquarters for Preston Girl Guides and Brownies and is known as Paxglen. For several years Glen Morris had a library in connection with the local

Mechanic's Institute. In 1910 a public library was formed.

Today Glen Morris is a charming, quiet rural community that appeals to many city dwellers as a weekend retreat.

Hamilton Spectator, 1963.

Centennial Committee: *The Township of South Dumfries-Centennial*, 1952.

GLENORA, community, North Marysburgh Township, Price Edward County
Position 44° 02' 77° 03'

Known today to motorists on Highway 33 as the site of the ferry which takes them from Prince Edward County to Adolphustown across the Adolphus Reach of Lake Ontario, the dispersed rural community of Glenora was a busy industrial centre in the late nineteenth century. The origin of the name is obscure, but it may have been bestowed on the settlement by a daughter of J.C. Wilson, a prominent local industrialist. Nearby Glen Island, also may have inspired the name.

Glenora was originally two hamlets, Mountain Mills and Stone Mills. In 1786 Major Peter Van Alstine, who had arrived in Prince Edward County two years earlier with a group of disbanded soldiers and United Empire Loyalists, was given a grant of land on the shore of Lake of the Mountain. Van Alstine built a grist mill by the lake and soon a small settlement known as Mountain Mills grew up. A store was later opened by the family.

About 1813 Van Alstine erected a second mill at the foot of the cliff. Stone Mills, which developed around the new mill, became a commercial centre while Mountain Mills remained largely residential. In the 1820's and 30's the mill was operated by J. Hugh

Macdonald, whose son John A. Macdonald became the first Prime Minister of Canada. Macdonald expanded the business to include the carding and dyeing of wool but the venture was not very successful and in 1839 the mills were bought by David Lake who closed the Mountain Mills operation. Lake later built a plaster mill beside the grist mill.

In 1877 James C. Wilson opened a "little giant turbine water-wheel works" at Stone Mills. The water wheels produced here became world-renowned. By this time the community had become an industrial centre with three mills, an iron foundry, and a nail factory. The water-wheel works was active until World War One when it was converted into a munitions factory. It was sold to the Ontario Government in 1922 and from then on was used as a fish hatchery. Today it is the site of the Fisheries Research Station and is a major tourist attraction.

Glenora's importance was based not only upon its industrial activities, but also on its geographical position. At one time it was a key link on the old Danforth Road (now Highway 33), built between Kingston and Toronto from 1798 to 1801. Stone Mills then was the second stop on the stage run between the two centres, and later became a port for steamers plying the waters of the Bay of Quinte. The Glen House Hotel, built in the 1880's, provided accommodation for travellers. The first known ferry operator at Glenora was Joe Thurston. In 1905 a steam-powered ferry was put into service and in 1928 it was replaced by the diesel engine *Nahomis*. In 1936 the Ontario Provincial Government took over the ferry and provided free service. Today two ferries, *M.V. Glenora-Picton* and *M.V. Quinte Loyalist*, carry travellers the scant mile across the water to Glenora free of charge.

Intelligencer, 1969.

Aleda O'Connor: *Glenora, Community Spotlight*, 1974.

GLENN ORCHARD, community, District Municipality of Muskoka
Position 45° 05′ 79° 39′

Glen Orchard is situated between Ada Lake on the west and Butterfly Lake on the east, at the junction of Highways 69 and 118. It was named after a pioneering family by the name of Orchard.

Another early name having a close association with Glen Orchard is that of Lambert Love, blacksmith and carriage builder, who first settled with his wife in the late 1800's on Lake St. Joseph where he operated a shingle and sawmill. Active in Glen Orchard community and church, he helped to develop the tourist industry by the building of Elgin House. This, with its additional lodges and golf course, became a thriving resort which was carried on by his sons and grandsons until 1971, when it was sold. On the south side of Lake St. Joseph he also built Glen Home for tourists, close to the Glen Orchard community.

Today, Glen Orchard is the hub of the surrounding district. Here is located the Central School, as well as the Community Centre, which was formerly a school. Several small businesses in Glen Orchard manufacture a variety of goods from candleholders to circular staircases to cobblers' benches. The population as reported in the 1971 census was 104.

Geraldine Coombes: Muskoka: Past and Present, 1976.

GLEN TAY, community, Bathurst Township, Lanark County
Position 44° 53' 76° 18'

Glen Tay is located on the river of the same name, some two miles west of the town of Perth. Because of its superior water privileges, it was at one time a bustling manufacturing village.

Among its many industries was an extensive woollen factory which employed 80 people, manufacturing from 65,000 to 100,000 yards of fine tweeds a year. The tweeds from this mill were of good quality taking first prize at the first Industrial Exhibition at Toronto and at the Dominion Exhibition at Ottawa in 1879.

There was also a large grist mill, an oatmeal mill, a tannery, and stores, blacksmith and waggon shops.

Glen Tay was once called Adamsville, after Captain Joshua Adams, who built there the first mill within the settlements forming on the Rideau.

H. Belden & Co.: Illustrated Atlas of Lanark and Renfrew Counties, 1880-1881.

GLENVILLE, community, King Township, Regional Municipality of York
Position 44° 03' 79° 31'

Situated in northern King Township, about 4 miles west of Newmarket on Highway 9, this dispersed rural community was the site of a number of industries in the nineteenth century. It was probably given its name because of its location hemmed in by hills.

Early settlers included the families of Bolton, Webster, Brodie, Wray, Sommerville, and Graham. In 1807 William Lloyd built a sawmill by the south pond, and in 1836 a large flour mill was erected on the north pond by William Cawthra. In the 1840's William Roe opened a distillery to produce whiskey. Christopher Scott established a blanket and carpet-making business, and one of the community's stores became the site of a felt hat manufactory. Two hotels were opened, the Sand Bank Hotel by John Hare, and the Central Hotel by Charles Brodie, who was also one of the first blacksmiths. Samuel Waldock, a miller, became the first postmaster in 1900. Today there are no industries left and Glenville is a quiet residential area.

The first church in the village was built by Methodists. Its congregation became part of the United Church of Canada in 1925. Dwindling attendance and lack of a steady minister caused services to be discontinued in 1952. The church building is now used for recreational purposes when required.

The original Glenville public school was erected on the Rogers farm in 1839. The building was later moved to another site. A new school, constructed in 1885 taught pupils until 1953. Students now attend the nearby Kettleby School.

Elizabeth McClure Gilham: Early Settlements of King Township Ontario, 1975.

GLEN WILLIAMS part of town of Halton Hills, Regional Municipality of Halton
Position 43° 40' 79° 55'

In the northern section of the town of Halton Hills, in what was formerly the township of Esquesing, lies the compact rural community of Glen Williams. Originally known as Williamsburg after its founder Charles Williams, its name was changed to Glen Williams when a post office was opened in 1852.

The land on which Glen Williams stands was owned by a Mr. Muirhead of Niagara in the early nineteenth century. In 1824 the property was purchased by Charles Williams who settled here with his family. The Credit River provided an excellent source of power and the sawmill built by Williams in 1825 soon attracted more settlers to the area. Among these early residents were Archibald Cooper, John Leslie, James Reid, and Robert Sloan.

The Williams family continued to contribute to the development of the community. A general store was opened by Charles Williams in the late 1830's and in 1839 Jacob Williams erected a woollen mill, which by the late 1870's, had become Glen Williams' largest industry. Joseph Williams operated a flour mill and the Bobbin Spool and Turning Factory in the 1870's.

By 1877, Glen Williams had a population of about 500. Among its industries were a steam shingle mill, a grist mill, a pump and cistern manufactory, the woollen mill, the bobbin factory, and a brickyard. W. Tost ran a blacksmith and carriage shop, W. Watkins owned a general store, and Mr. McCrea was proprietor of a general dry-goods and grocery store. A Methodist Episcopal church and a public school served the residents.

The first hydro power in nearby Georgetown was supplied from a power plant in Glen Williams. The old plant in more recent times became the site of Apple Products.

The Glen Hotel was a popular community meeting-place in the early twentieth century. The hotel's stables were used by Seagram Distillers to house their horses during their training for the Queen's Plate.

Most of the industry has disappeared from Glen Williams and today it is a pleasant residential community of 656 (1971).

John McDonald: *Halton Sketches*, 1976.

Walker & Miles: *Historical Atlas of Halton County*, 1877.

GLOUCESTER, township, Regional Municipality of Ottawa-Carleton
Position 45° 21' 75° 34'

Situated in the northeast part of the municipality, Gloucester is bounded on the east by Russell County, on the south by Russell Township, on the west by the Rideau River, and on the north by the Ottawa River. It was named after William Frederick, the second Duke of Gloucester and nephew of George III.

Gloucester was the second township in Carleton County to be settled. Bradish Billings arrived from New England in 1809 and took up land on the south shore of the Ottawa. In 1812 he built a log shanty here with the help of three earlier settlers, William Blakely, Elkanah Stowell, and William Marr. A barn erected by Billings in 1814 was the first frame building in the township.

No other permanent settlers appear to have lived in the township until 1819 when the Doxeys, the Ottersons, and Andrew Wilson arrived. Captain Wilson's house "Ossian Hall" became a stopping-place for many travellers and for settlers on their way to claim their land.

Although the boundaries of the township had been laid out earlier by Steadman, the interior was not surveyed until 1820. Initial lots were laid out along the banks of the Rideau and Ottawa Rivers. Among the first to settle on these lots were Hugh McKenna and Capt. William Smyth who arrived in 1821. The Johnstons took up land on a site which was named "Hardscrabble" by Captain Wilson, after he heard Mr. Johnston's description of his first days in the bush. Other early settlers included Daniel O'Connor, who later became Treasurer of Carleton County; and the Hon. Thomas McKay, the first indus-trialist on the Ottawa River and the builder of Rideau Hall, the residence of the Governors-General.

Other Gloucester men to achieve distinction were Capt. William Smyth, an early settler, who was one of the leaders of the Loyalist expedition from the Mohawk Valley to Cornwall; James Siveright's son became Baron d'Everton in return for distinguished service in India. The American inventor, Lee De Forest, chose Gloucester to try out the commercial potential of the wireless. William Ogilvie, a resident of the township, became an explorer, surveyor, and administrator in the Yukon Territory and in 1887 laid out the boundary line between the Yukon and Alaska. Members of the Hurdman family introduced the practice of treating swill to sterilize it before it was fed to hogs in order to reduce cholera. This practice was made mandatory by the Government.

The development of Bytown (now Ottawa) on the opposite side of the Rideau led to the construction of a bridge across the river to Billing's Bridge in 1829. The settlement there became the gateway into Gloucester with all roads and trails in the township radiating from it. Its importance declined when more bridges were built across the Rideau in the later nineteenth century.

Settlement in the township increased rapidly after completion of the Rideau Canal in 1832. A number of communities grew up. Long Island Village developed from the building of the Long Island Locks when the canal hands settled here. A line of villages established along the Montreal Road, included Janesville (now Eastview), Cyrville, Rockcliffe, and St. Joseph.

The township was organized in 1832. The first town meeting was held in the home of John Cunningham. Formerly part of the District of Johnstown, then part of the District of Bathurst, Gloucester became part of the District of Dalhousie in 1842. In 1850 James Siveright became the first reeve. The first township hall was erected at Billings Bridge in 1874.

Settlers continued to arrive in large numbers as industries

developed and transportation improved. In 1837 the first public road was built and in 1854 the first railway, the Bytown and Prescott, went into operation. Steamers sailed along the Rideau, providing both luxury cruises and a freight trade. By 1879 Gloucester had become the most populous township in the county, with 7,815 inhabitants. Although the majority were of British descent, there was also a large French element. The inhabitants of Cyrville and St. Joseph were almost all French-Canadians.

Lumbering and farming were the most important industries in the township in the nineteenth century. An early industrialist was M.K. Dickinson, who, with J.M. Currier, was the first to manufacture sawn lumber for the American market. The Hurdman brothers, became one of the chief timber operators in the Quebec market. It was to connect their lumber and storage yards with Bytown that a third bridge was constructed across the Rideau in 1867. (A second bridge had been built at New Edinburgh before this.) The Queensway Bridge was opened beside it in 1955.

The late nineteenth century saw the development of Carlsbad Springs as a popular holiday-place. Legend has it that an Indian chief, "Donnaconna", recommended its mineral waters to Jacques Cartier and his crew. From the 1860's to the early 1900's the site was a major resort. The Dominion Trotting Park, a steeple chase course built at Carlsbad Springs in the 1880's, was a popular attraction and the opening of the Canada Atlantic Railway in 1883 made the site easily accessible.

During the twentieth century, much farmland in the township has been converted to the use of one of the most important military and civilian airports in the country. During the Second World War, the British Commonwealth Air Training Plan was developed at Uplands and led to large scale land expropriations in 1950-51. The old village of Bowesville was demolished to make room for airport expansion. Recently more land has been taken over and used for the construction of the Rideau Carleton Raceway and the group of Federal Government buildings at Confederation Heights. Many farms in the area have been purchased for future housing developments.

Its location beside the national capital has often made it difficult for Gloucester to maintain its autonomy as large areas have been broken off and annexed by Ottawa. New Edinburgh, Ottawa East, and Stewarton have all become part of the capital. A large-scale annexation in 1949-50 reduced the population of the township from 13,051 to 5,131. All of the Junction Gore and large areas of the Rideau Front and Ottawa Front were lost. However, with the upsurge of industrial development and the growth of new communities, the township's population has increased rapidly. New subdivisions include Blossom Park, Uplands, Orleans, and Cardinal Heights. Today Gloucester's population is 65,050 (1978). The Federal Government is the area's largest employer.

H. Belden & Co.: *Historical Atlas of Carleton County*, 1879.

Harry and Olive Walker: *Carleton Saga*, 1968.

GOBLES, community, Blandford-Blenheim Townships, Oxford County
Position 43° 09′ 80° 34′

This small rural community is located near the border of the township and the County of Brant, on Highway 2, east of Woodstock.

The settlement was named after William L. Goble, whose father, Rev. Jacob Goble, came from New York State and settled on the site in 1823. William Goble opened a general store at the corners and when a post office was established in 1855, he became the first postmaster.

The Great Western Railway ran its line through Gobles, but for some reason the station was called Arnold, after the owner of a steam sawmill, T.H. Arnold.

In the past two decades the population of Gobles has declined sharply. In 1966 the number of residents was 102; in 1971 they numbered only 48.

Ontario Historical Society: *Place and Stream Names of Oxford County, Ontario.*

Walker and Miles: *Historical Atlas of Oxford County,* 1876.

GODERICH, township, Huron County
Position 43° 38′ 81° 38′

The township of Goderich is bounded on the north and northeast by the Maitland River, which divides it from Colborne Township, and on the east by Hullett Township. The Bayfield River in the south divides it from Stanley Township, to the west is Lake Huron. The township comprises 56,666 acres. In 1978 the population was 2,365.

John Galt named the township after Viscount Goderich, then Secretary of State in Britain, at the time John Galt was in Canada. He arrived in 1825 and initiated the founding of Canada Company, a colonization scheme to open the country between Lakes Huron and Erie to settlement. The Canada Company purchased some million acres, including the Huron Tract, for resale to settlers on easy terms. In 1828 a trail was blazed from a point near present-day Stratford, continuing across Goderich Township to its western terminus of Goderich on Lake Huron. Col. Van Egmond then contracted to build the Huron Road (Highway 8) following along this trail. It was at the terminal point of the Huron Road that Galt and his men began clearing a town site which was to be today's town of Goderich.

Between 1831 and 1837 early settlers located along the Huron Road. They included Thomas Ginn, Samuel Rathwell, Hugh Sturdy and a Mr. Taylor. In 1831 the nearest mill was in London, then a small village. In the following year Canada Company had a mill built at the Goderich site. To the southeast of this site where Holmesville village is located now, there came James Johnson, and John and Samuel Holmes around 1831 and 1832. Four brothers: James, Thomas, John and George Ford and Robert Proctor settled nearby. These early settlers were employed by the Canada Company in the building of roads and so were fortunate to be able to pay off the land purchased from the company. Other major settlements in Goderich Township were Clinton, 1831, and Bayfield, 1832.

The earliest records of township government date from 1835. In that year George Gordan was township clerk and George Elliot, W.F. Gooding and Robert Shaw were township commissioners.

The first school in the township was opened at Goderich as early as 1830. St. George's Anglican Church, erected in 1834, was also at Goderich and it was the first church built in the township.

Besides the old Huron Road (Highway 8) and the Blue Water Highway (Highway 21), the CNR runs a line through the township. As well, the township has two natural harbours — one at Bayfield and one at the town of Goderich.

Goderich harbour, in the beginning of its development a fine natural harbour, fell into severe disrepair for a number of years so that by 1850 it was hardly usable. Today ships winter at Goderich, in summer many freighters use the harbour, and adding to its elevator capacity are new storage facilities for grain.

The beautiful Blue Water Highway follows the east shore of Lake Huron for many miles, from Southampton, its northern point, to Ipperwash Provincial Park, its southern point. As well as the latter park there are Point Farms Provincial Park and Pinery Provincial Park along this highway giving much pleasure to vacationers.

Bayfield, with its good harbour, south of Goderich on the Blue Water Highway (Highway 21) became a thriving village by 1840. The incorporation of the village came in January, 1876.

Goderich Township enjoys a singular location on the shore of Lake Huron whose blue waters attract vacationers and summer trade.

James Scott: *Huron County*, 1966.

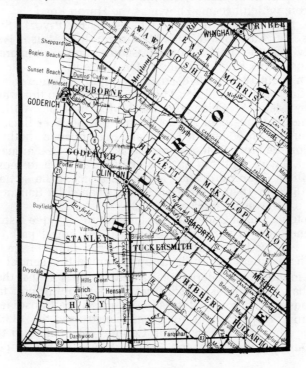

GODERICH, town, Goderich Township, Huron County
Position 43° 45′ 81° 43′

This town which is often called "The Prettiest Town in Canada", is located on Lake Huron at the mouth of the Maitland River. It is at the junction of Highway 8 (the old Huron Road) and Highway 21 (the Blue Water Highway), and is served by CNR and CPR lines. Goderich is some sixty miles northwest of London.

The history of Goderich is tied very closely to the history of the Canada Company, chartered in 1826 as a colonizing company to purchase Crown lands and open up the uncivilized western portions of Upper Canada for settlers. The lands acquired by the Canada Company became known as the Huron Tract. John Galt, superintendent of the Canada Company, is considered the father of the Huron Tract and the founder of Huron County. He founded the city of Galt (now part of Cambridge), the city of Guelph, and with his friend, "Tiger" Dunlop, he founded and developed the town of Goderich.

In 1828 Dr. William "Tiger" Dunlop and a group of men made their way through the Huron Tract until they reached Lake Huron. They came upon a group of Indians camped on a high bluff overlooking the lake. Dunlop was much taken with the site and later when John Galt joined him there, the two men decided to build a town on this spot and name it Goderich, in honour of Viscount Goderich, then Secretary of State in Britain. That same year, Galt sent out a group of men to survey and clear the town site for settlement. Galt also made Goderich the western terminus of a road built from Guelph to Lake Huron, which became known as the Huron Road.

The first settlers in Goderich were the Pryors, Brewsters, Goodings, Mac MacDonald, Alex MacGregor, John Wilson (who built a tannery on the flats), Ronald Goode, Louis Belmore, Frank Deschamps, Frank Kneeshaw and Peter Andrews.

From about 1828 to 1838, any building in Goderich was done on the river flats below the bluffs. The only exception to this was a cabin erected by Major Strickland on the bluffs. In 1830 William Reed opened the first tavern in Huron County on the river flats. He later sold the business to Valentine Fisher and Reed opened another tavern, this time on the bluff. Reed also served as the official mailman for the settlement. Twice monthly he made trips to Guelph to pick up the mail. William Gooding opened a general store in the settlement as early as 1828. In 1830 another store was opened by Benjamin Hale. The post office was established in 1835.

The town site of Goderich was laid out in a unique fashion. The plan of the town is perfectly geometrical. A central park, or town "square", is actually octagonal and eight streets radiate from the eight angles. The business section is grouped around this central park.

The founders of Goderich realized from the start that the town's location had tremendous possibilities for developing port facilities. Today Goderich harbour is the largest port on the Canadian side of Lake Huron. A permanent pier was constructed in 1835 and a lighthouse (the only one in Huron County) established in the early 1850's. During the 1850's and 1860's, Henry Marlton operated a successful shipbuilding industry out of Goderich harbour. In later years, large grain elevators were erected at the harbour.

The first school in Huron County was a common school built in Goderich by the Canada Company on the site where the Church of Scotland building was later erected. This school was in existence as early as 1830. Another school was built on East Street in 1840 and in 1844, a grammar school was opened. In the 1860's, Goderich Central School was built on North Street. Before, 1876, a high school was established. Today, Goderich has many old and new schools and is the site of a district high school.

St. George's Anglican Church was the first church to be erected in Goderich. Built in 1834, it was destroyed by fire in 1879, and the present church building dates from 1881. The Presbyterian Church was built in 1843. The Church of Scotland, St. Andrew's, was built in 1846. The New Connection Methodist Church opened in 1856, The Episcopal Methodist Church was erected in 1857, and the Wesleyan Methodist Church was built in 1860. A second Presbyterian church, Knox Church, was constructed in 1861.

In 1848 Goderich had its first newspaper, the *Signal*, with Thomas McQueen as editor. In the late 1850's Thomas McClenehan started a rival paper, the *Canadian Empire*, this later became the *Star*. The Goderich *Signal-Star* is the town's official newspaper today.

In 1842 when Huron was officially recognized as a county, Goderich became the county town. Although Goderich was never incorporated as a village, it was officially incorporated as a town in 1850. The first mayor was Benjamin Parsons. A jail and Court House had been erected in 1840. The Court House burned in 1953 and has since been replaced.

Railway service has been a determining factor in the growth of the town. The arrival of the Brantford, Buffalo and Goderich Railway (later the Buffalo and Lake Huron Railway) in 1858 promoted both settlement and trade. The railway was taken over later by the Grand Trunk which, in turn, was eventually absorbed into the Canadian National Railways. In 1907 a Canadian Pacific route was put through to Goderich.

During the 1850's and 1860's, there were many small industries operating in and around Goderich, the biggest being Henry Marlton's shipbuilding yards, and the Huron Foundry, operated by Robert Runciman and Matthew M. Weatherald. However, the year of 1866 marked the beginning of the town's most important industry. While drilling for oil near the harbour, a man named Samuel Platt made a surprising discovery. After drilling to a depth of 960 feet, Platt discovered not oil — but salt. Soon afterwards the Goderich Salt Company was formed. Today, the salt mine is known as Sifto Salt, a division of Domtar Chemicals Limited. At the Evaporator Plant, table salt is produced by pumping up brine and letting the water evaporate off the salt. At the mine located at the harbour, two shafts have been sunk in the salt bed to produce rock salt. Approximately 1,500,000 tons of rock salt are produced annually.

From the 1870's on, Goderich has been known as a favoured lakeside resort and its popularity with vacationers and tourists continues today. Modern Goderich has the appearance of a prosperous town; it is the site of many industries, including the Canadian Salt Company Limited, Dominion Road Machinery Company, Goderich Manufacturing Company, Shaeffer Pen Company, Sifto Salt Limited, and Upper Lakes Shipping Limited. The Huron County Pioneer Museum is located in Goderich providing a fascinating glimpse into the daily lives of the early Huron County settlers.

John Galt's dream town, his favoured Goderich, has grown to be a charming and thriving community. The population of Goderich in 1978 was 7,298.

James Scott: *The Settlement of Huron County*, 1966.

The Signal-Star, 1967.

GODFREY, geographic township, Cochrane District
Position 48° 39' 81° 31'

Subdivided in 1908, this township west of Timmins became part of the city of Timmins in 1973. It is named after the late Hon. Dr. Forbes E. Godfrey, MPP for York from 1908 to 1929. The Mattagami River courses through the northwest corner of the township. The area is served by Highway 576.

GODFREY, community, Hinchinbrooke Township, Frontenac County
Position 44° 32' 76° 41'

Situated on Highway 38, about 25 miles north of Kingston, this picturesque rural community was known to the early settlers in the area as Iron Ore Junction. When a post office was opened in 1854, it was given the official name of Deniston, but in 1878 the name was changed to Godfrey in honour of Chester Godfrey who had donated the land on which the village stands.

Among the first to settle in the neighbourhood of present-day Godfrey were James Hickey, John McKnight, Michael Judge, James Hill, James Kennedy and Terry Nefcey. Early industries in the village included a sawmill and potash kilns, and there was a casket maker as well as a cabinetmaker.

In the 1870's the Kingston and Pembroke Railway was built, opening up the northern part of the countryside. The station at Godfrey was first known as Bedford, but became Godfrey in 1906. Construction work on the line provided an extra source of income for local farmers.

The railway gave access to markets across Ontario and Montreal, and Godfrey area farmers started to ship large quantities of eggs and butter by rail to other centres. Cheese produced in two Godfrey factories was sent by rail to Montreal.

Around 1900 Godfrey experienced a mining boom in felspar. H. Richardson's Feldspar Mines established its headquarters in the village. A mica mine was also opened around that time. The importance of felspar has since decreased and the Richardson mine, having had a succession of different owners, is now closed.

Businesses in Godfrey today, include a machine shop, which sells chain saws, power lawnmowers, and snowmobiles, and is possibly the largest of its kind north of Kingston. A large Hydro switching station is located just outside the community.

Godfrey's first school, known as Hill's School, was built in 1840. A new school constructed to replace it in 1901 is now closed. Bethel Church was built by the Methodists in 1872. Its congregation joined the United Church of Canada in 1925. Closed in 1968, the old church building was torn down a short time later.

Reg Whitty: *Godfrey, Community Spotlight*, 1974.

GODSON, geographic township, Kenora District
Position 49° 09′ 93° 51′

The township is located east of Sabaskong Bay (Lake of the Woods). It was named in 1939 after Judge Godson of the Mining Court of Ontario.

The southern portion of Kakagi Lake extends across the northern section of the township. An Indian Reserve is located on the lakeshore along Highway 71. The small community of Nestor Falls lies in the southwestern corner of the township.

GOGAMA, community, Jack and Noble Townships, Sudbury District
Position 47° 40′ 81° 43′

Situated 70 miles south of Timmins, just south of Highway 144 and the Canadian National Railways, this dispersed rural community's name comes from an Indian word meaning "the fish leap up over the surface of the water", or, in short, "Jumping fish".

Gogama's position on Minisinakwa Lake and the Minisinakwa River accounts for the descriptive name. These waterways were part of the early fur traders' routes and the first white inhabitant of the area was probably James Miller, a factor of the Hudson's Bay Company post at Mattagami to the north. The post was moved to Gogama after the Canadian Northern Railway had completed its line from Sudbury northward and Gogama had become a railway point on what was to be the railway's transcontinental line (now Canadian National Railways). Prior to this, when the Canadian Pacific had constructed its transcontinental line farther to the west, supplies were freighted to the Hudson's Bay post at Mattagami from Biscotasing on the CPR and freighting parties used to camp at a point near Gogama before continuing northward on the waterways.

Arthur L'Abbe settled in the little village in 1917 and became postmaster and general merchant. In his poolroom the first religious services were held in 1922 by the Roman Catholic priest, Msgr. A. Cournoyer. The building was later renovated and used as a church until a new house of worship was erected in 1947. The community also has an Anglican church, although no resident minister. The bell of this church came from England to Hudson Bay and thence via canoe to the Mattagami post in the mid-1800's. Fifty years later it was brought to Gogama to call worshippers of this community to service in their new church.

Extensive lumbering operations in the area contributed to Gogama's growth during the first half of the twentieth century. The population now stands at approximately 700. Today Gogama has a separate school and a public school. Secondary school students receive their education in Timmins. Tourism is important to the economy of Gogama and the community offers excellent facilities for hunters and fishermen.

Ministry of Natural Resources: *Directory of Statistics and Data*, 1975.

W.F. Moore: *Indian Place Names in Ontario*, 1930.

GOLDEN LAKE, community, North Algona Township, Renfrew County
Position 45° 35′ 77° 14′

Golden Lake separates North and South Algona Townships, giving its name to the community of Golden Lake which lies at its foot.

The lake takes its name from John Golden, said to be the first settler on its shores, and not, as may be inferred, from the lake's fine yellow sand beaches.

Golden Lake was an outpost of the Hudson's Bay Company in the early 1800's when one of the company's best traders, John McLean, raced on snowshoes up the frozen Bonnechère River to establish contact with the Indians ahead of the independent traders.

Located on Highway 60, Golden Lake is, today, a haven for tourists seeking to experience the atmosphere of a north that once was the domain of trappers and lumbermen.

Renfrew, 1943.

GOLDIE, geographic township, Thunder Bay District
Position 48° 37′ 89° 49′

The township is subdivided and was named after the Hon. Lincoln Goldie, MPP for Wellington South and the Provincial Secretary for Ontario during the 1920's.

It is located northwest of the city of Thunder Bay. The Trans-Canada Highway passes through the southern and western part, while the Canadian National Railways and the Canadian Pacific Railway run side by side through the eastern sector of the township.

GOLDING, geographic township, Thunder Bay District
Position 48° 49′ 89° 57′

Originally part of the Grand Trunk Pacific Land Block, the township was named in 1945 after Wm. H. Golding, Member of Parliament for Huron-Bruce at that time.

Across the northeastern corner of the township where the mountains reach a height of 1,580 feet, travel side by side the Canadian Pacific and the Canadian National Railways, as well as the Trans-Canada Highway.

GOLDSMITH, community, Mersea Township, Essex County
Position 42° 07' 82° 32'

Situated in the eastern part of Essex County, a few miles northeast of Leamington, this dispersed rural community was named after the English author and poet Oliver Goldsmith, by John Ogle, an early settler.

Most of the early inhabitants of the community came from near Huntingdon in Quebec about 1860. By 1870 an Orange Lodge had been organized and in 1880 an Orange Hall was built by the settlers. There was a Methodist Church as well as a Presbyterian Church in the settlement which became a post village in 1877.

A.W. Marsh "Place Names of Essex County" in *Ontario Historical Society*, 1913.

GOLDWIN, geographic township, Cochrane District
Position 49° 54' 83° 10'

The southern boundary of the township was surveyed in 1907. The name origin is not known. The Missinaibi River, with Isabell and Alice Islands in the south, flows northward through the centre of the township. Dry weather roads link the southwestern part with secondary roads and ultimately with Highway 11 and the nearby town of Hearst.

GOODALL, geographic township, Kenora District, Patricia Portion
Position 51° 15' 92° 45'

The township was named after James Goodall Dickenson who was the manager of the O'Brien Mines, Cobalt, Ontario. The area is covered by lakes, chiefly Woman Lake and Washagomis Lake. The tiny communities of Narrow Lake and Swain Post are located in Goodall Township.

GOODERHAM, geographic township, Nipissing District
Position 46° 46' 79° 34'

The township which is located north of Lake Nipissing, is named after the late George Gooderham of Toronto, who served as MPP for Toronto South-West between 1908 and 1914. The Ontario Northland Railway traverses the eastern part of the township.

GOODERHAM, community, Glamorgan Township, Haliburton County
Position 44° 54' 78° 23'

Situated on Highway 503 in southern Haliburton County, this compact rural community was formerly known as Pine Lake. Local legend says that the name was changed when a visiting salesman from the famous Gooderham distilleries in Toronto gave a barrel of whiskey to each of the three hotels at Pine Lake. The whiskey was to be sampled by the woodsmen and farmers of the area. Consequently, a giant party was held and so grateful were the local men that they renamed their community Gooderham.

The first post office of Pine Lake was opened just west of the present site of Gooderham by Charles Way. Gooderham Post Office was established in 1873. William Ritchie built the first house in the community and Sam Whitaker and Charles Way operated the first hotels. S.S. Hadley and Richard Hadley were the community's pioneer storekeepers. A sawmill dating back to those early days can claim the distinction of being the last mill in Ontario to have remained in operation, regularly using only water power.

Today Gooderham, with a population of 233 (1971) is a busy tourist centre and the shopping centre for the district. The rugged and picturesque scenery of the Haliburton Highlands is a major attraction.

History of the Provisional County of Haliburton, 1931.

GOODFELLOW, geographic township, Thunder Bay District
Position 48° 54′ 90° 14′

Established in 1945, the township was named after Wm. A. Goodfellow, MPP for Northumberland at that time.

The township lies south of the Trans-Canada Highway about 70 miles northwest of Thunder Bay. In the west it borders on an arm of Lac des Mille Lacs (Lake of a Thousand Lakes).

GOODWILLIE, geographic township, Algoma District
Position 47° 27′ 84° 41′

Designated formerly as Township 29, Range 17, it was named in 1974 after J. Goodwillie, Reeve of the Township of Red Lake in the District of Kenora at the time. The Trans-Canada Highway passes along the picturesque shore line of Lake Superior on which the township borders.

GOODWIN, geographic township, Cochrane District
Position 50° 02′ 86° 03′

The northern and western boundaries of this township were surveyed in 1908. The name chosen appears to be in honour of Dr. Goodwin of Queen's University, Kingston, Ontario. The township is located just south of the Canadian National Railways' transcontinental line, some twenty miles east of the railway point of Nakina.

GOODWOOD, community, Uxbridge Township, Regional Municipality of Durham
Position 44° 02′ 79° 12′

By 1836 there were two villages in the Township of Uxbridge, one of the first townships to be settled in the area. One was Uxbridge and the other Goodwood. This compact rural community of 356 people (1971 census) is situated about 25 miles northwest of Whitby on Highway 47. Among the pioneers to arrive in the early nineteenth century were

T. Robinson, arriving in 1825, and Henry Stapleton, machinist and lumberman, in 1833, both of whom emigrated from England.

A post office was established in 1852. By 1877 Goodwood had gained importance as a station on the Toronto and Nipissing Railway. A shingle and lumber mill erected by R. Nesbitt about 1870 was one of the community's main industries. Businessmen included D. McCarty and Gregg Albert, general merchants; James Percy, an insurance agency; and James Todd, proprietor of the Victoria Hotel. A mason, a blacksmith, and a carpenter also served the residents.

Expanding, by 1903 a second hotel had been built and other businesses included a loan company, grain dealer, an express office and a telegraph office. The population was 375.

Commuters from nearby busy centres, especially with the advantage of excellent highways, have made their homes in this pleasant rural community.

J.H. Beers & Co.: *Historical Atlas of Ontario County*, 1877.

Ontario Gazetteer, 1903.

GORDON, township, Manitoulin District
Position 45° 53' 82° 30'

Surveyed by Edgar Bray in 1871, the township was first given the name of Sherborne by the then Indian Department of Ontario in August of that year. Only a month later, however, the name was changed to Gordon as it was discovered that a Sherborne Township already existed, albeit in the Haliburton area. The name of Gordon is believed to have been chosen to commemorate the Hon. James Gordon of Toronto, a member of the Legislative Council of Canada from 1845 until his death in 1865.

Gordon Township, less than a hundred years ago, was a stretch of endless forest, home to a number of Indians who hunted and fished. Today the area, still Indian Land, supports a population of over 400 on well kept farms, and the township counts itself among the best agricultural regions in the district.

In the north this Manitoulin Island township borders on the North Channel of Lake Huron. Here on the shore of Gore Bay, the town of Gore Bay is located, providing school and library service for township residents, as well as police and fire protection. There are no industries within the township itself, and the only commercial enterprise of note is a furniture outlet. Recreational facilities include a race track, two community halls and an old schoolhouse used for meetings. The only church in the township is that of the Jehovah Witnesses. Highways 540, 540A and 542 serve the area.

Ministry of Natural Resources: *Directory of Statistics & Data*, 1975.

GORDON LAKE, community, Johnson Township, Algoma District
Position 46° 25' 83° 52'

This dispersed rural community of about 100 people, situated on

Gordon Lake northwest of Bruce Mines, has existed since the early twentieth century and was once known as Desert. The name Gordon, probably refers to an early settler.

GORE BAY, town, Gordon Township, Manitoulin District
Position 45° 55′ 82° 28′

Situated on the north shore of Manitoulin Island, on Highway 540, Gore Bay is the district town and government centre of the island. The Indians originally called the site Pushk-dinang, meaning "barren hill". The area surrounding the town is anything but barren, however; Gore Bay is situated in the midst of beautiful pine and hardwood stands. The Indian name referred to a sheer wall of grey limestone on the east side of the bay. The bay itself was named Gore Bay after a steamship, the Gore, which had frozen in the ice in the North Channel in the 1850's, and subsequently the settlement on the bay took the same name.

The first settler on the site was Williard Hall. He was followed by the Frasers, Clarks, Thorburns, Kinneys and Bickells. These early inhabitants made their living from fishing and lumbering. A number of sawmills were established. In 1860 the community received a post office and in 1890 it was incorporated as a town.

Today Gore Bay has a population of 783 (1978) and serves as the supply centre for the area as well as the home of Federal and Provincial Government offices. The town's sheltered harbour attracts much water traffic and Gore Bay is the Canadian Port of Entry for many U.S. boats. Yachtsmen on the North Channel find excellent docking services at Gore Bay and tourists can enjoy the town's recreational facilities.

The town has one public school and a school for retarded children. A public library serves the townspeople, as do five churches of various denominations. The Gore Bay Museum, which is housed in an old jail, is a major tourist attraction.

Ministry of Natural Resources: *Directory of Statistics and Data,* 1975.

Traveller's Encyclopaedia of Ontario / Canada, 1978.

GORE'S LANDING, community, Hamilton Township, Northumberland County
Position 44° 07′ 78° 14′

Situated on the south shore of Rice Lake and north of Cobourg, this dispersed rural community was named after Thomas S. Gore, a British navy captain who owned land here in 1845.

The site had been visited long before settlers began to build their homes. Charles Fothergill came to this area around 1820 to gather information for his *Natural History of the British Empire.* Permanent settlement began in the 1840's. Among the pioneers were Judge Falkner, Capt. Hayward, Col. Robert Brown, Capt. Gore, George Ley and Lt. Traill.

The community prospered when it became the terminal point of the plank road from Cobourg to Rice Lake, built in 1847-8. A private boarding school, F.W. Barron Boys' School, was opened by a former headmaster of Upper Canada College. There were also a hotel and a few small industries. An Anglican church was dedicated in 1848, with Rev. Alexander MacNab, as first rector. A post office was established in the same year.

Gore's Landing did not grow much in the years to come. A port of call for Rice Lake steamers in the early 1900's, it is now a quiet summer resort of camps and marinas, with a population of 204 (1971). One of its most interesting possessions is a battle flag used at Nelson's victory at Trafalgar in 1805. It is kept in St. George's Anglican Church, which replaced the earlier church in 1908.

Many of the Gore's Landing residents have become well-known Canadian figures. Archibald Lampman, the famous nature poet, attended the private school here in the 1860's. Derwyn T. Owen (1876-1947) became Anglican Primate of All Canada, 1934-47. J.D. Kelly (1862-1958), historical artist, had his home in the community, as did Gerald S. Hayward (1843-1926), a painter of miniatures who won acclaim in both the United States and Britain.

N. & H. Mika: *Historic Sites of Ontario*, 1974.

St. George's Church.

GORHAM, geographic township, Thunder Bay District
Position 48° 34′ 89° 18′

The township was surveyed in 1891 and 1914 and it was named after the Hon. Thomas A. Gorham, a County Court Judge and the Mayor of Port Arthur around the turn of the nineteenth century. Gorham is situated immediately to the north of the city of Thunder Bay.

GORRIE, police village, Howick Township, Huron County
Position 43° 52′ 81° 06′

Situated in northern Huron County, about 50 miles northwest of Stratford, on Highway 87 and the Teeswater branch of the CNR, Gorrie was named by the Leech brothers, who developed the community, after a place near their parents' home in Ireland.

The first settlers on the site were the Creer brothers who arrived in 1854 but it was the Leeches who were responsible for the growth of the community. In 1856 James and Nathaniel Leech purchased mill sites here. The Leech Bros. Grist and Flour Mill, built in the same year, soon became one of the most important mills in the area.

In 1857 the Leeches laid out the village site. The name on the plans was "Howick Village", but everyone knew the community as Leechville. The post office established in the same year was called Gorrie. James Hanna was the first postmaster.

The village grew very rapidly. By 1861 its population had reached 400. Much of its growth was due to the industrial enterprises of the Leeches. Two brothers of Nathaniel and James established a tannery, while two more brothers set up a foundry. The family remodelled their original grist mill in 1867 and also built a sawmill and lathe machine. Several of the business blocks built by the Leech brothers still remain today.

By 1879 Gorrie equalled in importance its neighbour, Wroxeter. Its businesses included: R. Cluterham's tin and stove store, J.C. Passmore's drugstore, Sam Gilmore's and John Haskett's hotels, three general stores, a bookstore, shoe, tailor, and barber shops, a carriage shop, and a weekly newspaper. Among the industries were Richard James' foundry, a cheese factory, two lime-burning establishments, and a pork-packing establishment. The People's Cheese Factory was opened in the 1880's.

The first school was built in 1857. G. Deacon and a Mr. Patterson were early teachers. A new school was erected in 1899. The first service in Howick Township was held in the house of Hugh Hollinshead, who lived near Gorrie. The Methodist Henry Smith was the preacher. Rev. J.A. Dowler became the regular Methodist minister in 1856. A church was built in 1859 and Rev. D. Connelly began to preach there. Another congregation, the New Connection Methodists, was organized in 1857 by Rev. Thomas Jackson. They erected their own church in 1866, but then joined the other Methodists in 1874. Their old church was used first by the Baptists, then by the Presbyterians under Rev. Thomas Muir. Anglican services were first held by Rev. C.H. Drinkwater in 1858. Rev. Edward Newman became minister of the Anglican church when it was built in 1870.

Gorrie became a police village in 1895 but its early rapid development has not continued. Its population according to the 1971 census has decreased to 380. Present industries include the "Farmatic" Factory which manufactures automatic farm equipment. The village also has three general stores, a hardware store, a furniture store, two garages, a bank, and an implement business.

H. Belden & Co.: *Historical Atlas of Huron County*, 1879.

James Scott: *The Settlement of Huron County*, 1966.

Norman Wade: *Early History of Howick Township*, 1952.

GOSCHEN, geographic township, Sudbury District
Position 46° 09′ 81° 16′

The township's boundaries were surveyed in 1870 and 1892 and it was named after an Edward Goschen. The southwestern part is occupied by a section of Killarney Provincial Park and here David Lake is situated. The area is accessible only by waterways. The city of Sudbury lies less than thirty miles to the northeast.

GOSFIELD, township, Essex County
Position 42° 04′ 82° 45′

Divided into the Townships of Gosfield North and Gosfield South in the late nineteenth century, Gosfield is situated in the southern part of Essex County and is bordered on the east by Mersea Township, on the north by Maidstone and Rochester, on the west by Colchester North and South, and on the south by Lake Erie. It was named after a village in Essex, England.

The first influx of settlers, mostly United Empire Loyalists, arrived before 1788 but the hostility of the Indians in the area drove them back to the United States. However, in 1792 many of them returned. By this time the borders of the township had been surveyed by Patrick McNiff and Abraham Treadwell and lots were laid out along the lakeshore. Among these settlers of 1788 who returned was Leonard Kratz, a German immigrant to America, who settled on Lot 9. His name became anglicized to Scratch. John Wendel Wigle and Philip Fox who came to the township, were also Germans. They too had settled in America, but were forced to move to Canada after the American Revolution. The Malottes were another early family arriving in the township. There was little immigration for some years after this first influx, until the settlement at Ruthven, known as the "Back Settlement" was formed. The Toffelmeyer and Brunner families, and John and Thomas Little were among the pioneers in this area. Another early settler was Mr. Stewart, a Baptist elder, who was the second person to hold religious services in the township. The first minister was the Methodist, Mr. Case.

The land around Talbot Street, which ran from the centre and through the northwest part of Gosfield, was not occupied until 1818 when there was another general influx of settlers. Among the first inhabitants in that section were George and Frank Nevil, Thomas Williams, and John Clarke.

Kingsville, the main centre in the township, was founded in the 1840's by James King, who opened an office for conveyancing on the site. The community grew rapidly and provided a market for the farmers of the area. Previously Detroit had been the nearest market town.

An early mill was built just west of Kingsville. Peter Scratch erected a windmill, but this did not prove very successful until he replaced the source of power with horsepowered machinery. In later years he also constructed a steam mill east of Kingsville. Near Kingsville, in 1904, the noted naturalist John Thomas Miner founded his now world-famous bird sanctuary for the conservation of migrating Canada geese and ducks. Miner lectured throughout North America on the conservation of wildlife, wrote two books on bird life, and was awarded the O.B.E. "for the greatest achievement in conservation in the British Empire" in 1943.

The first teacher in the Gosfield area was Robert McMurray who arrived in the township about 1800. He kept a private school. The education received by his pupils was not of a very high quality, but for some time his was the only school in the township.

When District Council government was introduced in 1842, Prideau Girty was the first man elected to represent Gosfield. Joseph Malotte became the first reeve in 1850 when the new Ontario Municipal Act took effect. In 1887 ratepayers requested the government to divide Gosfield into two parts so that the southern part could vote separately on the proposal of a bonus to the Lake Erie and Detroit

River Railway scheme which had been defeated by the whole township. The request was granted and Gosfield South became the Junior Township. Today it is the more populated of the two townships. In 1978 7,260 people lived in Gosfield South and 3,705 in Gosfield North. The area is linked by Highway 3 with the city of Windsor to the northwest, and the town of Leamington near the southeastern border.

Essex County has the climate and soils favourable to various orchard fruit and early vegetables, which reach the market several weeks earlier than those from any other area in Canada. Kingsville, itself, has a number of industries that include tobacco curing and packing, fruit and vegetable canning, and extensive fisheries. A provincial government fish hatchery is located here.

H. Belden & Co.: *Historical Atlas of Essex and Kent Counties*, 1881.

A.W. Marsh: "Place Names of Essex County" in *Essex Historical Society*, 1913.

GOUGH, geographic township, Sudbury District
Position 46° 20' 82° 00'

Named after Lord Gough, the township was first subdivided in 1892. It is situated a few miles west of the town of Espanola, and secondary roads link the area with the Trans-Canada Highway. Gough Lake takes up most of the southeastern section of the township.

GOUIN, geographic township, Sudbury District
Position 47° 59' 81° 31'

Situated south of Timmins, the township was named after Sir Jean Lomer Gouin, Lieutenant Governor of Quebec in 1929. The northern portion of Mattagami Lake, a body of water that extends over several townships, is situated along the western border of Gouin. Highway 144 travels across the northwestern corner of the township.

GOULAIS RIVER, community, Fenwick Township, Algoma District
Position 46° 43' 84° 23'

The community of Goulais River is located near the mouth of the Goulais River in a farming area which was settled in 1882. Descendants of the early pioneers still remain on the same farms.

The first bridge built over the Goulais River at this locality was a timber span completed in 1890, a few miles west of the present steel bridge on Highway 17. The new bridge spans 180 feet of the Goulais River.

Eighteen miles along Highway 522 to the west is the Goulais Indian Reserve where the Indians have lived since the 1850's. The first Roman Catholic bishop of the area, Bishop Baraga, built a church there in 1862 and it is still used today by permanent as well as summer residents of Goulais River and the Goulais Bay area.

Algoma Regional Tourist Council: *Algoma Vacationland Visitors Guide.*

GOULBOURN, township, Regional Municipality of Ottawa-Carleton
Position 45° 10′ 75° 56′

Situated in the western part of Ottawa-Carleton on the Lanark County border, Goulbourn was named after Henry Goulbourn, British Under-Secretary of State in 1810 and Secretary for the Colonies in 1812.

Part of the township was surveyed in 1794 by John McNaughton but no settlement took place until after the War of 1812-14. The British government decided to settle the area with British emigrants, preferably militiamen, in order to protect the border of the country and to counteract the growing influence of American settlers attracted to the area by generous land grants. In 1816 the Government purchased land from the Chippewa and Mississauga Indians and a rough survey was made from 1816 to 1818. A few pioneers had taken up land in the Ashton area as early as 1815, but the great tide of settlement came with the government-assisted emigrations of 1818-24. Among these first families were the Grants, McCabes, Dwyers, Ryans, and O'Connors. Ex-soldiers and civilians combined made Goulbourn the most populous township in the county by 1842.

Many small villages grew up in the township during the first half of the nineteenth century. Ashton developed as ex-soldiers took up land along the Jack River around 1818. George Argue's tannery, Lindsay's mill, and Donald McFarlane's establishment for manufacturing small ploughs were among the early industries of the community. Richmond, which was founded about the same time, grew rapidly as well, but separated from the township in the 1850's. Jackon Stitt settled near what is now Stittsville, in 1818. Hazeldean, the site of some of the best agricultural land in the county, developed from a settlement of Scottish and Irish immigrants who arrived in 1818-19. Other villages in the township included Dwyer's Hill, Munster, Rothwell's Corners and Shillington.

The sons of Thomas Herron, an early settler in Goulbourn, became famous in the history of the Canadian West in the 1870's. Both John and James Herron were members of the North West Mounted Police and it was Sergeant John Herron who persuaded Chief Crowfoot, head chief of the Blackfoot tribe, not to join the Sioux in their attack on the white men.

In 1842 William Mackey and Robert Grant represented Goulbourn on the new District Council. Thomas Garland became the first reeve in 1850. James Henderson, James Shillington, Thomas McCaffrey, and William Hodgins were on the Council. A township hall was built in 1853 and replaced in 1872 after it was destroyed by fire.

A Methodist chapel in Shillington settlement was among the first of Goulbourn's houses of worship. A Methodist log church was built in the centre of the township with Rev. Mr. Horner as minister. He later became the Bishop of the Hornerite sect. Anglicans, who were in the majority by 1864, at first held services in William McFadden's house. Christ Church was erected by the Anglicans in 1845. The Presbyterians were led by Rev. John L. Gourlay, who wrote the first history of the Ottawa Valley.

Schools were established in most of the settlements by an early date. Among the first teachers were Charlie McGee and M.G. Barry in the Munster School. Farsighted trustees in the nineteenth century set up an educational trust fund from the proceeds of the sale of the Clergy Reserves. In 1966 part of this fund was used to erect a school at Stanley's Corners. In 1947 Stittsville built the first modern rural school in Ontario.

By 1864 the population of the township had reached 2,914, although by 1879 Goulbourn had lost its position as the county's most populous township and stood only sixth. However, the number of inhabitants continued to increase, especially after the Second World War when people began to move out from Ottawa. By 1968 the population was about 3,500 and in 1971 it was 5,333. The "Glen Cairn" development at the western end of the Queensway, in which farm land has been converted into suburbia, added about 1,500 residents in 1968. In 1974 the township annexed the villages of Richmond and Stittsville (which had separated in 1961), and the population jumped to 14,350 in 1976. In 1978 part of Goulbourn amalgamated with the township of March and part of the township of Nepean as the city of Hazeldean-March. At the end of 1978 the city of Kanata was formed by annexation of the township of March and the Glen Cairn Hazeldean portion of the Township of Goulbourn. Goulbourn's population is now 9,327 (1978).

H. Belden & Co.: *Historical Atlas of the County of Carleton*, 1879.

Andrew Haydon: *Pioneer Sketches in the District of Bathurst*, 1925.

Harry and Olive Walker: *Carleton Saga*, 1968.

GOULD, geographic township, Algoma District
Position 46° 29′ 83° 24′

Gould is located north of the town of Thessalon to which the area is linked by Highway 129. The southern half and parts of the northern section are covered with lakes. The township, which was surveyed in 1885, was named after Isaac J. Gould, MPP for Ontario North at that time.

GOULET, geographic township, Thunder Bay District
Position 49° 58′ 86° 37′

Located north of the community of Longlac on the Canadian National Railways' transcontinental line, the township was established in 1945 and named after A. Goulet, at that time the Member of Parliament for Russell. The Canadian National Railways' branch line from Longlac into northwestern Ontario passes along Manitounamaig Lake through the western section of the township.

GOUR, geographic township, Kenora District
Position 49° 30′ 91° 40′

Located southeast of the town of Dryden, the township was named after Joseph D. Gour, former MP for Russell. The Trans-Canada Highway and the Canadian Pacific Railway pass to the south of the area. The southern half of Indian Lake takes up much of the township's central section, while Sandbar Lake Provincial Park occupies the southeast.

GOURLAY, geographic township, Algoma District
Position 48° 52' 84° 54'

Located northeast of the community of White River, in season one of the coldest places in Ontario, the area is linked by Highway 631 to the Trans-Canada Highway. Gourlay Lake lies in the centre of the township. The name origin is unknown.

GOWAN, geographic township, Cochrane District
Position 48° 40' 81° 08'

This township, northeast of Timmins, was first subdivided in 1904 by O.L.S. Fairchild. Along with a number of other townships, Gowan amalgamated with the Town of Timmins and part of the Town of Iroquois Falls to form the newly incorporated City of Timmins. It is believed to have been named after J.R. Gowan, C.M.G., K.C.M.G., a member of the Canadian Senate from 1885 to 1907. For most of this time he served as chairman of the Senate Divorce Committee.

GOWGANDA, community, Nicol Township, Timiskaming District
Position 47° 39' 80° 46'

Situated on the northeast shore of Lake Gowganda, about 70 miles west of New Liskeard, this dispersed rural community is known for its beautiful natural surroundings which attract thousands of visitors each year. Gowganda is an Indian word meaning "place of the porcupine".

In the early years of the twentieth century, lumbering operations were carried out in this area. The logs were shipped to mills on the Ottawa River as there were no local sawmills. Gowganda itself developed after the discovery of silver deposits in the region in 1907. Further exploration in 1908 revealed rich silver veins at Miller and Gowganda Lakes and soon a silver rush began. A road was built from Elk Lake in 1909 and mining machinery and equipment brought in. By 1910, seven mines were in operation.

A business and residential centre developed at the site of modern Gowganda and the population rose rapidly until there were over 5,000 people in the area. However, the period of prosperity was short-lived. A disastrous fire in 1911 destroyed much of the business section and many residents left. The discovery of gold at Kirkland Lake drew more people away and by the 1920's only serious prospectors and miners were left.

The mines continued to operate until the Depression of the 1930's when several were forced to close. Renewed demand for silver during World War Two resulted in the reopening of the mines, but many closed in the 1950's and 60's. By 1959 only three mines remained in production and in 1972, the last mine, Siscoe Silver, closed.

In the early 1900's lumbering also had become important in Gowganda's economy. The local lumber industry developed as a result of the mining discoveries. Sawmills were built to meet the demand for lumber by the mines and the community. The industry flourished after World War One but again the Depression put sawmills out of business. A new sawmill was opened at Gowganda in the 1940's but closed in 1955 when the local timber supply was exhausted.

Today tourism is the main industry in Gowganda. Excellent hunting and fishing opportunities draw many visitors who stay in the tourist camps on the shores of the surrounding lakes. The area is one of the few regions where the rare Aurora trout can be found. A museum in the community depicts the early history of Gowganda and also features a mining display. Built in 1912 by the Western Federation of Mines, the structure is one of the oldest union halls in North America.

Gowganda's approximately 290 residents (1975) are mostly involved in tourism-related activities. Recreational facilities include a picnic ground, a baseball field, a hockey rink, and a curling rink. A public school serves the children of the community.

Micheline Boucher et al: Our Timiskaming, 1977.

Ministry of Natural Resources: Directory of Statistics and Data, 1975.

GRAFTON, community, Haldimand Township, Northumberland County
Position 44° 00′ 78° 01′

This historic community of about 350 near the north shore of Lake Ontario is situated approximately eighty miles east of Toronto on Highway 2 and the CNR. The hamlet was settled round 1798 by United Empire Loyalists, mostly from Vermont and Massachusetts. Later, British and Irish immigrants arrived.

United Empire Loyalist, Eliakim Barnum, came from Vermont to Grafton in 1808. He erected a log cabin and established a profitable milling and distilling business. During the War of 1812 Barnum's house was accidentally burned by British troops. Barnum rebuilt a home on the same site and today Barnum House (or "The Poplars", as it is also known), is one of Ontario's finest remaining examples of the Loyalist-style architecture. Barnum House is marked by an historic plaque and is now a museum open to the public.

Prior to 1832 the settlement was known as Haldimand. In 1832 the name was changed to Grafton, after Grafton in Massachusetts. A post office was established in the village in 1858. Grafton's fine natural harbour made the settlement a shipping point as early as the 1830's when a company was incorporated and wharves were built. By the 1870's one hundred thousand bushels of grain were exported from Grafton.

The Great Pine Ridge Tourist Council: Great Pine Ridge, Travel Guide, 1974.

156

Grafton, Barnum House, erected c. 1814

Public Archives Canada, PA 26873

GRAHAM, geographic township, Sudbury District
Position 46° 25′ 81° 16′

The township lies immediately to the southwest of the city of Sudbury. The southern portion, which is covered with lakes, is taken up by a large Indian Reserve. Both the Canadian National Railways and the Trans-Canada Highway travel through the centre of Graham.

The township is believed to have been named after the Hon. Geo. P. Graham, MPP for Brockville in the late 1800's and early 1900's, or after Peter Graham, once MLA for East Lambton.

For municipal purposes, Graham was united with the neighbouring townships of Drury and Denison until January 1, 1973 when the municipality amalgamated with the Town of Lively and other municipal and geographic townships to form the new Town of Walden.

GRAIN, geographic township, Thunder Bay District
Position 48° 51′ 86° 34′

Located northwest of the community of Marathon, and just to the north of Highway 17 (Trans-Canada) and the Canadian Pacific Railway transcontinental line, the township was named after Dr. Orton I. Grain, medical assistant to Dr. Smellie, who was the medical supervisor during construction of the CPR along the north shore of Lake Superior in the 1880's. Immediately to the south lies the Coldwell Peninsula, site of Neys Provincial Park.

GRAND BEND, village, Bosanquet Township, Lambton County
Position 43° 19′ 81° 45′

This popular summer resort village is located on Lake Huron at the mouth of the Ausable River and at the junction of Highways 21 and 81.

The history of Grand Bend is inextricably tied up with the story of the meandering course of the Ausable River. The river has not always flowed into Lake Huron at Grand Bend. In fact, the river originally flowed to a point within 200 yards of the lake, then took an abrupt bend and coursed thirteen miles parallel to the lakeshore before it finally emptied into Lake Huron at Port Franks. In 1832 a man named Brewster built a mill at the point of the "grand bend" in the river. The settlement that grew up around the mill was known as Brewster's Mills.

In 1845 a group of French Canadians who had fled from a famine in Quebec settled in the area. They referred to the spot as "Aux Croches", meaning "crooked tongs", a name which suggested the crooked course of the river. The Desjardins, Masson, Ravelle and Charrow families are descendants of this group of French Canadians.

Because of Brewster's mill and the skill of these French Canadian axemen, the settlement thrived on a lumbering business. Later, when the lumber was used up, the settlement became a fishing village. Names associated with this phase in Grand Bend's history are Gill, Kennedy and Green.

J. Brenner built a hotel in the settlement and the first two stores were opened by J. Ironside and a Mrs. Bradshaw. A school was built in 1857. The post office was established in 1872 and in 1874 a Presbyterian church was built. It was the first church in the community.

From the time that Brewster's mill was first built, settlers had complained that the mill dam caused the river to flood their farm land. During the 1840's and 50's the settlers even tried legal action, but to no avail. Brewster was determined that his milling operation would remain intact. In 1860 a group of angry settlers had had enough and they attacked the mill dam and destroyed it. The mill itself was swept away in the subsequent flood. Brewster's Mills was no more; the settlement was renamed Grand Bend.

Ironically, the destruction of the mill did not end the flooding. The fault seemed to lie in the course of the river and the terrain of the land itself. The Canada Company, who held the land as part of the Huron Tract, decided that they could solve the problem by altering the course of the river. They built a straight channel, cutting across the series of loops in the river course, from the village of Port Franks to the loop of the river at Grand Bend. The project was not a success. The natural harbour at Port Franks was destroyed and the Ausable itself almost stopped flowing completely. In 1891 the course of the river was changed again. A channel was cut through from the river to the lake and after this point, Grand Bend began to develop as a popular summer resort.

Originally, Grand Bend was part of Huron County, but a dispute over liquor laws caused the village to secede. For many years after the general repeal of the Canada Temperance Act in Ontario, Huron County had continued to be "dry". Grand Bend businessmen felt that temperance would hurt their tourist trade and so Grand Bend seceded to Lambton County.

Today, Grand Bend attracts tourists and vacationers from all over the province. Its population swings from about 750 people in winter (1978) to 15,000 people in the summer. The Pinery Provincial Park is located about five miles south of Grand Bend on Highway 21. It has fine sand beaches and excellent camping facilities. The Eisenbach Museum containing pioneer artifacts is also located in Grand Bend.

Andrew Dixon: *What Most People Don't See at Grand Bend,* 1963.

James Scott: *The Settlement of Huron County,* 1966.

GRAND VALLEY, village, East Luther Township, Dufferin County
Position 43° 54' 80° 19'

This picturesque village, through which the Grand River flows, is located on Highway 104, about 12 miles west of Orangeville. Situated in the south of the township of East Luther, in the heart of one of the most fertile agricultural districts of Ontario, it is the largest village in the township, and has a population of 1,160 (1978). The Grand River, itself, beginning north of Dundalk and coursing for 125 miles through five counties to its final outlet, Lake Erie, was prominent in the lives of the early settlers, providing waterpower for innumerable small industries along its riverbanks and was used as a shipping and navigation route until the advent of the railway in the latter 1800's. About 15 miles to the northwest of Grand Valley in the Monticello district, the Grand River Conservation Authority has constructed a control and storage dam.

The area surrounding Grand Valley was first settled about 1836 with the arrival of Richard Joice, Samuel Stuckey and Richard Ponsford, among others. Wm. McPherson brought his family from Kingston in 1851 and settled on the banks of the Grand Valley River at a spot where the War Memorial now stands in Grand Valley. He sold medicines and so was referred to as "Dr." McPherson. He later began the erection of a building which, though never fully completed, he used as a hotel. In 1854 Mrs. George Joyce and her sons, George and Richard, arrived. They built a house and barn of logs and later a log tavern at Amaranth and Main Streets. Robert Erskine and three brothers by the name of King followed next. Settlement was slow and by 1869 fifteen persons only were living there.

When the first post office was established in 1860, Sam Stuckey acted as first postmaster.

Towards the end of the eighteenth century education was of excellent quality. Mr. Campbell, a principal highly esteemed, was assisted by Mr. Mosley and the Misses Reid and Munro.

The first storekeepers, Wm. Dawson and W.R. Scott, came from Toronto in 1869 and set up a well-stocked general store. This was a great boon to the settlers who had been obliged to walk to Fergus and other larger centres for supplies. The first sawmill, placed west of the village, was operated by Steven Beals. Because there was little money among the settlers, he took his payment in lumber. With an accumulation of lumber he built houses in the village and erected the first Disciple Church. He also built the first schoolhouse on what is now the corner of Main and Amaranth Streets. The early days saw such small industries as weaving, shoemaking, carriage building, woodworking, a cooperage, harnessmaking and planing mills.

Settlement was slow but with the surveying of 50-acre parcels of land into town lots it increased, and with the coming of a branch of the Canadian Pacific Railway and the establishment of a station in 1875, Grand Valley's serious development began. Two grain elevators were built at the railway point and a busy centre for livestock, farm produce, and the buying of grain boomed. Now the villagers felt that Luther, the name by which the settlement was hitherto known, was not entirely to their liking. At an 1883 meeting the name Grand Valley was chosen.

Alex Richardson's grist mill produced a fine flour that became famous under the brand name of Grand Valley Flour. Butter and cheesemaking added to the prosperity and when the creameries took over, ice-cutting on the Grand River became a side business. From primitive harvesting methods through to the mechanized farm machinery, and from carriages and buggies through to motor cars, Grand Valley has kept pace.

By 1896 Grand Valley was established as a market town serving the surrounding agricultural area, having several flour and planing mills and a sawmill. New stores: furniture, jewellery, hardware, drygoods, as well as business blocks to accommodate professional services were evidence of new prosperity. There were two physicians, a dentist, a veterinary surgeon, and two newspapers, *The Tribune* and *The Star*. In 1897 Grand Valley became an incorporated village.

Stephen Sawden: *History of Dufferin County*.

Dept. of Municipal Affairs, *Grand Valley Centennial*, 1961.

GRANT, geographic township, Nipissing District
Position 46° 30′ 79° 49′

The township is located north of Lake Nipissing. It was subdivided in 1884 by S. James and was probably named after the Rev. G.M. Grant, Principal of Queen's University from 1877 until his death in 1902.

The northwestern section is occupied by Tomiko Lake and Chebogomog Lake, and the lake shores are linked by secondary and dry weather roads to Highways 64 and 11.

GRANTHAM, geographic township, Regional Municipality of Niagara
Position 43° 11′ 79° 13′

Situated in the former County of Lincoln, Grantham was named by Governor Simcoe after the town of Grantham in Lincoln County, England.

The township was settled in 1784 when soldiers from the disbanded Butler's Rangers were given land grants in the area. Many of the men, however, did not take up their grants but instead bartered them away for next to nothing. It was not until the early nineteenth century that settlers began to arrive in any great numbers. Among these pioneers were the families of Bessey, Secord, O'Brien, Emmett, Durham and Goring. From this time on the township grew rapidly and it eventually became the most heavily populated area in Lincoln County.

The first official meeting of the township's inhabitants took place at Paul Shipman's Inn in 1818. William Chisholm at that time was elected clerk. Future township meetings were held in various places. After Grantham was incorporated as a township in 1850, Caver's Inn served as the regular meeting-place. In 1884 the Grand Jury Room of the Lincoln County Buildings in St. Catharines became the home of township council and remained so until 1942.

Among the settlements which grew up within the township's boundary, Shipman's Corners was the most important. It developed into a thriving centre in Lincoln County, and long since has become the bustling City of St. Catharines. The so-called "Upper Ten" settlement developed on the bank of Ten Mile Creek and was named Homer when a post office was opened in 1859. This picturesque community was cut in two when the new Welland Canal was built. De Cew Falls on Beaver Dam Creek grew up around a grist mill. It was to DeCew Falls that Laura Secord travelled from Queenston to warn General FitzGibbon of an intended American attack in the War of 1812-14. Port Weller, originally known as the "Lower Ten", in more recent years has developed into an important shipbuilding centre. Two small early hamlets, Reynoldsville and McNab, have since disappeared. A church was built east of Ten Mile Creek as early as 1795. Christ Church, erected at McNab in 1853, served parishioners for over 100 years.

Grantham's many waterways contributed greatly to the early industrial development of the township, the biggest spur being the construction of the Welland Canal from Lake Erie to Lake Ontario, 1824-29.

In 1961 the municipality of Grantham Township was dissolved, part of it being amalgamated with the City of St. Catharines, and part being annexed by the Township of Niagara. In 1970 Lincoln County itself became part of the Regional Municipality of Niagara for municipal purposes.

George A. Carefoot: History and Geography of Lincoln County.

Lincoln County Council: Lincoln County 1856-1956, 1956.

H.R. Page & Co.: Historical Atlas of Lincoln and Welland, 1876.

GRANTON, police village, Biddulph Township, Middlesex County
Position 43° 13' 81° 18'

This small rural community of approximately 350 people is situated about sixteen miles north of the city of London.

The site of the present-day village was settled around 1842 by three brothers, Alexander, William, and James Grant. William Grant later donated some of his land to be used as a Presbyterian cemetery. Two other early settlers in the immediate vicinity of Granton were William Levitt and George Foreman. But the story of Granton village does not begin until the Grand Trunk Railway built its line through the area in the 1860's. At that time Alexander and James Grant, William Levitt and George Foreman got together to lay out a village at the point where the Grand Trunk had established a flag-station. Trains stopped here for passengers only when flagged down. The four farmers had the fronts of their lots surveyed, and land was offered for sale.

There was serious disagreement, however, over the naming of the village. The Grant brothers suggested that it be named "Granton"; Levitt and Foreman felt that this name would cast too much glory on the Grant family, and they favoured the name "Awmik", the Indian word for "beaver". At an open meeting the inhabitants drew lots out of a hat to make the final decision. The name "Awmik" was drawn, but neither railroad nor post office officials would accept the name. Mr. Christie, the local superintendent of the railway, had come from a village named Granton in Scotland. Thus the Grant brothers got their wish and the community became known as Granton. Residents of the settlement remained divided on the issue for many years to come and the north side of the railroad track was referred to as Granton, while the south side was known as Awmik.

The GTR proceeded to erect a station, freight sheds, and switch yards in the settlement. The first settlers in Granton proper were Mr. and Mrs. Hugh Cameron; James Harrison opened the first store; and the first hotel — the Ontario House — was opened by Samuel Hodgins. Hugh McFee operated the first mill. A post office had opened in the settlement in 1864 with James Harrison as first postmaster.

In the early days of Granton, school was held in an empty log house on the farm of William Levitt on the south side of the railway track. Later a log school was constructed which eventually was replaced by a brick school. In 1896 the old brick school, in turn, made way for a new two-room school.

The Presbyterian church was organized in 1860 and a brick church erected in 1861. This building was replaced by a new church in 1902 and after the union of churches in 1925, the Presbyterian church became Granton United Church. The Methodists built a frame church in the village in 1870; it was replaced by a new brick church in 1894 and the frame building was then used as a concert hall. With church union in 1925 the Methodist congregation joined the Presbyterian congregation and in 1928 the Methodist church was sold to the Anglican congregation which had built a little frame church in 1883.

In 1907 Granton was designated as a police village. The Granton Library was organized in 1922 and the Granton community Centre opened its doors in 1947. In 1957, because of a decline in passenger, mail, and freight service, the Canadian National Railways, successor of the Grand Trunk, decided to close down the old GTR station at Granton.

Today Granton is surrounded by a prosperous mix-farming district. The village serves as a social and business centre for the local farmers.

Jennie Raycraft Lewis: *Sure An' This is Biddulph*, 1964.

GRASETT, geographic township, Algoma District
Position 46° 29' 83° 16'

The township was first surveyed in 1886 and was named after former Chief Constable Lt. Col. H.J. Grasett of Toronto. It lies immediately to the east of Highway 129, about twenty miles northeast of the town of Thessalon. The community of Kynoch is situated in the southern part of the township.

GRASSIE, community, Regional Municipality of Niagara
Position 43° 09' 79° 37'

Situated about 6 miles west of Grimsby, Grassie is on the dividing line between the two former townships of North and South Grimsby. Lincoln County Road No. 15 is its main east-west road. The community was originally known as Muir Settlement after a pioneer family who settled on the site in the early 1800's. It was later named Grassie after the first blacksmith in the vicinity.

Among the earliest settlers were Curtis Lymburn and Thomas Hopkins; the latter was given a land grant as a reward for his service in the British army. A post office was established and also named Grassie, although when the Toronto, Hamilton, and Buffalo Railway was built, the station was called Grassies. At one time there were two passenger trains a day from the community, and shipments of cattle were an important part of the station's freight business. The station house no longer stands.

Today, many of the inhabitants of this dispersed rural community are commuters, working in nearby industries. Some are engaged in dairy farming. Exploratory drilling rights in the area were given to Imperial Oil Enterprises Ltd. in the 1960's.

Hamilton Spectator, 1963.

GRATTAN, township, Renfrew County
Position 45° 28' 77° 02'

This township is located in the south central part of Renfrew County. It was organized as a township in 1851 and was settled mainly by Irish immigrants. It was named after Irish statesman Henry Grattan (1746-1820), who supported Irish emancipation and opposed the slave trade.

The township borders in the north on Wilberforce Township, from which it is separated by the Bonnchère River, a tributary of the Ottawa. The Bonnechère River was the travel route of the fur traders in the 1820's when a Hudson Bay Company Post was operating at nearby Golden Lake.

Here, on either side of the Bonnechère, lies the picturesque village of Eganville. Straddling the border between two townships, Eganville was administered by both Grattan and Wilberforce Townships until 1891 when it was incorporated as a village. It is named after John Egan, a native of Ireland and one of the pioneers who arrived in the area in the 1830's, together with Robert Mills, John Coyne, William Jessup, Robert Turner, Roger Foy and Abraham Boland.

Egan purchased the farm of James Wadsworth who, in 1826, had bought the property from the first temporary settler, Gregoire Belang and had cleared some land and established a lumber business. Continuing the lumber business, Egan added a sawmill and opened a store. Later he built a stone grist mill on the south bank of the Bonnechère, and around this mill soon clustered a small settlement. A post office was opened in 1852, and the following year Egan had the village laid out into lots. There were, by then, some 170 residents, and the community was the supply and marketing centre for the surrounding farming area, as well as a bustling lumber town.

Near the settlement of Knightington at the Fourth Chute on the Bonnechère River, are the Bonnechère Caves, a great tourist attraction since 1955 when they were developed and made accessible. A variety of fossils are found in the limestone deposits of the area.

The Opeongo Colonization Road, constructed in the 1850's by the government from the Ottawa River to the western border of Renfrew County, ran through Grattan Township, bringing settlers in its wake. Along this road developed the settlement of Esmonde.

In the southeastern corner of the township lies Constant Lake with the small settlement of Balaclava. The township is served by Highways 41 and 513. Both the Canadian National Railways and the Canadian Pacific Railway travel through the northeastern section.

Mrs. Carle Price and Clyde C. Kennedy: *Notes on the History of Renfrew County*, 1961.

GRAVENHURST, town, District Municipality of Muskoka
Position 44° 55' 79° 22'

Situated at the south end of Lake Muskoka, 106 miles north of Toronto and 11 miles south of Bracebridge, Gravenhurst is the gateway to the Muskoka Lakes resort area. The town was named by a Canadian postmaster-general in 1861, after a fictional place in either Washington Irving's *Bracebridge Hall* or William Smith's *Gravenhurst*.

The first explorers in the area were those led by Lieut. Henry Briscoe in 1826, but there was little settlement until the completion of the Muskoka Road in 1858-1859. The first settler of Gravenhurst is considered to have been James McCabe who built a tavern at the site in 1859. The building was expanded into a hotel and housed the first post office that opened in 1862, with McCabe as postmaster. The hotel was named the "Free Masons Arms" Hotel. McCabe was known as

"Mickey", and his wife was called "Mother" by the early settlers of the area who had stayed at the hotel before taking up their land grants in the district. Among these pioneers were the Symingtons, David Leith, James Jackson, Joseph Brock and David Wright.

The settlement at Gravenhurst grew quickly. Its early development was largely due to Messrs. Peter Cockburn and Son, who began a lumbering business in 1865-66. The lumber trade gave impetus to other industries, as well as providing employment for the settlers in the winter months. Alexander Cockburn, Peter's son, made Gravenhurst a lake port when he launched the *Wenonah*, the first steamer on Lake Muskoka, in 1866. The *Wenonah* was soon followed by other boats as steamboats substituted for settlement roads and brought people north. Already prosperous by 1867, the community grew even more rapidly after the Free Grants Act of 1868 was passed and settlers flocked to the area to take advantage of the offer of land.

Lumbering became increasingly important in the 1870's and the community could boast of being the mill capital of Northern Ontario, having at one time a total of seventeen mills. The Cockburn Mill was one of the earliest of these and later expanded to include a planing mill and sash and door factory. The proliferation of mills led to Gravenhurst being dubbed "Sawdust City" in those days.

In 1875 the Northern Railway was extended into the area and a station was built at Gravenhurst. A spur line was laid to Muskoka Wharf and there trains were met by the Cockburn company's two steamers. Four more boats were purchased by the Cockburns during the next two decades and in 1881 the company became part of the Muskoka and Nipissing Navigation Company, later to be taken over in 1889 by the Muskoka and Georgian Bay Navigation Company.

A number of other industries were established in Gravenhurst in the 1870's. Dougald Brown, who built the Steamboat and Stage House Hotel in 1867, founded Brown's Beverages in 1873. It has become the oldest continuing industry in the community. Clipsham Carriage Works, pioneered by James Everett Clipsham, the first such business north of Orillia, went into operation in 1877. Lambert Love became a manufacturer of wagons and sleighs.

Gravenhurst was incorporated as a village in 1875. It became a town in 1887 with J.T. Harvie as mayor. By this time the population of Gravenhurst was about 2,200. A disastrous fire hit the new town a few months after its incorporation and destroyed the entire business district. However, an ambitious program of rebuilding was begun and Gravenhurst soon regained its former prosperity.

The 1880's saw the beginning of the Library Association (1883), the formation of the Town Band (1881), and the opening of the first Agricultural Fair (1886). In 1882 the Gravenhurst Electric Light Company, for the first time, provided electric lighting for the town.

In 1897 the Town Hall burned down and in 1901 the beautiful Opera House was built in its place. The Muskoka Cottage Sanatorium was opened in the immediate vicinity by Sir William James Gage in 1897 for patients suffering from Tuberculosis. A fee-paying hospital, it was followed in 1902 by the Muskoka Free Hospital for

Consumptives. The Calydor, a private sanatorium, was established in 1916.

As the lumber trade decreased many of Gravenhurst's mills closed in the early nineteen hundreds. By the 1920's the mill of Mickle-Dyment and Son was the only one left. A number of new industries were established in Gravenhurst around that time, but most survived only a few years. Among them were the Canadian Steel Specialty Company, the National Potash Corporation, and the Gravenhurst Crushed Granite Company. The Silver Black Fox Farm, begun in 1922, remained in business until 1932.

Arch at Gravenhurst, c. 1926

Public Archives Canada, PA 87448

As the town developed into a popular tourist resort, lake traffic increased and the Navigation Company expanded. The Ditchburn Company which had begun by manufacturing rowboats for tourists in the 1870's, brought out a new line of speedboats as well as building boats for the Navy during the Second World War. The Clark Manufacturing Company, established in 1903 to manufacture barber and dental chairs, was not successful, but in 1920 it was bought by the Rubberset Company which produced wooden handles and it became one of the town's most prosperous industries. Greavette Boat Works, builders of the "Streamliner" boat, was founded by Tom Greavette in 1930 and remains in operation today.

In 1919 a new railway station was opened at Gravenhurst to replace the earlier one which had been destroyed by fire. An airport was built near the town in the 1930's. In 1932 "Little Norway", a training centre for Norwegian pilots, was constructed at the airport. Doherty Air Services of Muskoka Ltd. began operation in 1946 and continued service until 1954.

In 1959 Highway 11 from Toronto was widened to four lanes to accommodate the increasing flow of tourists into the Muskoka region. With the development of these alternative forms of transportation, the steamship business declined rapidly and in 1958 the last steamboat was taken out of service. The *Seguin* was bought by the town in 1962 and turned into a floating museum. Today the *Miss Muskoka* and her sister ship, *Lady Muskoka*, take tourists on a four-hour cruise of Lake Muskoka.

In the 1920's the Free Hospital and the Sanatorium merged into the Muskoka Hospital. This became an annex to the Ontario Hospital in Orillia in 1960 and served as a school for retarded girls. Detached from Orillia since 1973, it is now the "Muskoka Centre". Over the years a number of institutions were established near the town. In 1940 an Internment Camp was built and about 400 German officers were imprisoned there. The Camp closed in 1946. The Ontario Fire College, the first residential fire college in the province, was constructed in 1958. In 1960 the Federal Government bought the buildings south of the airport and established Beaver Creek Correctional Camp, a minimum security camp for prisoner rehabilitation training.

Since the Second World War, Gravenhurst has seen a renewed increase in industrial activities. The Livingston Wood Manufacturing Company operated here from 1953 to 1962. The year 1967 saw the opening of Marlyn Superior Products Ltd., producing moulded and curved plywood furniture components; and the Oliver-MacLeod Company, manufacturing light metal products; and Corning Glass. Other modern industries in this town of 8,046 (1978) include Northern Plastics, Baxter Publishing Limited, and Pioneer Handicraft Ltd.

The Anglicans built the first church in Gravenhurst near McCabe's Tavern in the 1860's. St. James Anglican Church was dedicated in 1887. Rev. John Pepper became the first minister of the Methodist church in 1877, and Rev. John Garnett organized the Primitive Methodists in 1882. Calvary Baptist Church was erected in 1884 and a Salvation Army Hall was constructed two years later. St. Paul's Roman Catholic Church first opened its doors to worshippers in 1878.

The community's first schoolhouse was built in the 1860's. It was replaced in 1872 and again in 1877. A new public school was constructed in 1889. In 1896 a high school was erected with William Hawthorne as first principal. A new public school opened in 1924.

The *Lumberman*, which was published for one year in 1876, was Gravenhurst's first newspaper. The *Banner* began publication in 1880. In 1961 it became The *Muskoka News and Gravenhurst Banner*. The *Muskoka News* replaced the old newspaper in 1966, but was not successful. Today the town has one weekly paper, the *Gravenhurst News*.

The Lyceum Theatre which opened in 1911 was the town's first movie theatre. Entertainment was also presented in the Opera House. In the 1940's and 1950's the "Straw Hat Company" was an active theatre group in Gravenhurst and included such performers as Kate

Reid and Donald Sutherland. The present-day attraction of "Music on the Barge" had its beginning in 1949.

Gravenhurst's most famous son was Dr. Norman Bethune, a medical missionary to China, who was born in the town in 1890. His house is preserved as a historic site. Charlie Barnes, an outstanding athlete and a champion walker from the 1920's to the 1940's, was also once a resident of the town.

George W. Boyer: *Early Days in Muskoka,* 1970.

Geraldine Coombe: *Muskoka Past and Present,* 1976.

George F. Hutcheson: *Head and Tales,* 1972.

GRAVES, geographic township, Kenora District
Position 51° 10′ 93° 59′

Situated immediately northwest of Red Lake and the Balmertown mining district, the township was named after Edwin C. Graves, MPP for St. Catharines in the 1920's. There are no roads within the township.

GRAYDON, geographic township, Thunder Bay District
Position 49° 17′ 88° 38′

The township lies south of Lake Nipigon. Unimproved roads link the area ultimately with Highways 11 and 17. Graydon was established and named in 1945 by the Department of Lands and Forests after Gordon Graydon, MP for Peel at the time.

GREENBUSH, community, Elizabethtown Township, United Counties of Leeds and Grenville
Position 44° 41′ 75° 51′

This small rural community, located in the central part of Elizabethtown Township, approximately eight miles north of Brockville, is, today, a quiet farming community.

The first settlers in the Greenbush area were the Loverin, Blanchard, Haskins, Williams, Olds, Keeler, and Kerr families. James Olds built the first sawmill in 1834. In 1835 Hiram Herrick opened a tavern in the settlement. Other early businessmen in Greenbush were Truelove Manhard, who operated a tannery in 1834; Alpheus Hamlin, who opened a furniture-making business in 1844; and H.W. Blanchard, who operated a store by 1836. A post office was established in 1852 with Mr. Blanchard as the first postmaster. In 1863 a cheese factory, owned by Daniel Blanchard, went into production.

The first school in the settlement opened as early as the 1830's. In 1845 the schoolhouse burned and for a period of three years the school was held in various locations around the village. In 1848 a stone school was constructed.

168

The Greenbush Methodist Church built in 1837 was renovated in 1887.

Richard Kerr: *History of Greenbush*, 1908.

GREENLAW, geographic township, Sudbury District
Position 47° 43' 82° 48'

The township, situated north of the Canadian Pacific Railway point of Sultan, was named after Frank H. Greenlaw, MPP for St. Catharines in 1919. Dry weather roads link the area with Highway 129 and the town of Chapleau to the northwest.

GREENOCK, township, Bruce County
Position 44° 10' 81° 20'

This irregularly-shaped township is located in the middle of Bruce County, and is completely landlocked by other townships in the county. The Teeswater River cuts through the area from Riversdale in the south to just beyond the township boundary in the north, where it empties into the Saugeen River. The township covers nearly 66,890 acres and has a population of 1,953. (1978)

Greenock, named after a seaport at the mouth of the Clyde River in Scotland, was the last of the county's townships south of the Bruce Peninsula to be surveyed in 1852. Settlement began along the Durham Colonization Road. The first to decide to settle in Greenock was John Caskanette, a French Canadian. He had selected a lot in 1849 when he was a member of the surveying party who laid out the Durham Road. A little later he returned to Quebec to collect his family and when he arrived in Greenock in 1850, he brought with him the families of Raphael, Luke, John and Peter Chartreau. All settled close to the present-day hamlet of Riversdale.

The township at first was slow to develop because of the Greenock Swamp that prevented the construction of roads. The swamp did, however, prove of some value to the early settlers. In the 1870's the Cargill family purchased the swamp area and began a lucrative lumbering business using the pine, cedar, maple and elm trees growing within the swamp. The community of Cargill was named after this enterprising family. Three of the township's churches are located at Cargill: an Anglican, a Roman Catholic, and a United Church.

The settlement of Glammis lies on the township borders of Greenock, Kincardine, and Bruce. The Glammis Presbyterian Church was built in 1858. For a time the community also had a Baptist and a Methodist church. Glammis School operated from 1899 to 1964.

Other communities in Greenock Township include Chepstow, Narva, Portal, Pinkerton, Bradley, and the small hamlet of Greenock (formerly Enniskillen).

The earliest township records date from 1858 and John Valentine was reeve of Greenock Township in that year.

During the 1920's several tile yards operated in the township.

Today Greenock Township thrives mainly on farming and a small lumbering industry.

Norman McLeod: *The History of Bruce County*, 1969.

H. Belden & Co.: *Historical Atlas of Grey and Bruce County*, 1880.

GREEN RIVER, Part of the Town of Pickering, Regional Municipality of Durham
Position 43° 53′ 79° 11′

Green River, now part of the town of Pickering, is located on Duffin Creek, about twenty miles northeast of the city of Toronto.

One of the first settlers at the spot where Green River stands today was Benjamin Doten, who arrived in 1849. He established a wagon and blacksmith shop known as Dotenville Carriage Works. Other early settlers were the Osburn, Rice, Runnals, Vardon, Ferrier, Turner, McIntyre, Poucher, and Winter families. In 1857 William Barnes built a sawmill and in 1870 he added a factory to turn out tubs, pails, fork handles, brush handles, and baskets. In the early 1870's two brothers, Edward and John Smith, bought one of the old sawmills in the area and put it back in working order. The Smith brothers played a large role in the history of Green River, erecting a grist mill, a store, and a public hall in the village. They also were instrumental in getting a post office established in the community in 1870, and it is the Smith brothers who are credited with the naming of the settlement.

Green River was originally part of Pickering Township in the former County of Ontario. In 1974 the community, along with part of Pickering Township was incorporated in the newly created town of Pickering in the Regional Municipality of Durham.

William R. Wood: *Past Years in Pickering*, 1911.

GREENSVILLE, community, Regional Municipality of Hamilton-Wentworth
Position 43° 17′ 80° 00′

This dispersed rural community is situated on the banks of Spencer Creek, about two miles northwest of Dundas on Highway 8. According to the 1971 census the population of Greensville was 237.

The settlement's early history is closely linked with an industrial development located by the 1820's about half a mile west of present-day Greensville. The area was known then as Crook's Hollow, so named for James Crook, who had built several mills here and had thus created one of the pioneer era's largest concentration of industries in the province. Crook's Hollow at that time was also the location of Upper Canada's first paper mill. The enterprises at Crook's Hollow provided the financial impetus for the growth of several communities in the area, among them Greensville, named for the Green family.

William Green had arrived here in 1799; his father came in 1801. Originally, the site on which they had settled was known as Franklin Corners and later the name was changed to Joyce's Corner. In 1846 the name was officially changed to Greensville. A post office was established and James Joyce became the first postmaster.

In 1884 a community school (SS No. 5) was built to replace a two-room frame schoolhouse erected in 1848. Today modern facilities are available for Greensville students.

By 1860 Greensville was the site of the largest distillery in Ontario. In 1870 the distillery was converted into a malt house, and in 1907 it was adapted to become an apple evaporating factory. In later years the old building became part of the Tip Top Canners' facilities.

Thomas M. Thomson: *The Spencer Story*, 1965.

The Hamilton Spectator, 1963.

GREENWATER PROVINCIAL PARK, Colquhoun Township
Position 49° 12′ 81° 17′

Greenwater Provincial Park, a natural environment park, is located just off Highway 11, with Cochrane 32 km to the southeast on Highway 11 and Smooth Rock Falls to the northwest on Highway 11.

The park is in the Boreal, or northern forest, area. However, much of it has been logged or burned over by forest fires. There are 26 lakes, the largest are Blue Lake, Green Lake, Sandbar Lake and Horshoe Lake to provide summer activities for visitors. As well as boating, fishing, and hiking trails, the park has another unusual treat, the fascinating spectacle Aurora Borealis (northern lights), flickering streamers of coloured light spanning the night horizon.

During the period from 1909 to 1931 the Great Clay Belt in the Cochrane district attracted many settlers to farm the fertile soil. The distance to markets, however, was too costly and many settlers left abandoning their farms within the park boundaries.

Ontario Ministry of Natural Resources.

GREENWOOD, geographic township, Algoma District
Position 47° 27′ 84° 32′

Bordering to the west and south on Lake Superior Provincial Park, the township was part of the Algoma Central and Hudson Bay Railway land grant. The Algoma Central Railway, with the railway point of Canyon, passes along the township's eastern border. Formerly designated as Township 28, Range 17, the township was named after A.H. Greenwood, at one time reeve of the township of Hudson in the Timiskaming District.

GREENWOOD, part of the Town of Pickering, Regional Municipality of Durham
Position 43° 56′ 79° 03′

This rural community is located about twelve miles northeast of the city of Oshawa, near Highway 7. The area was settled in the 1830's and was first known as Norwood. Among the first influx of British and Irish settlers were Andrew McKittrick, Andrew Byers, William Sadler,

Frederick Green, John Adamson, William Clark, George Wilson and William Gibson.

In 1840 Matthew Cockerline erected a mill on property he had bought from Benjamin Hallowell. It was known as the Lower Mill and in 1843 it was sold to Frederick Green. Mr. Green was to acquire another mill, erected by the Howell family, who had moved into the area from a neighbouring village in 1847. As well, Mr. Green operated a profitable distillery. The importance of the Green family in the development of the community led to the settlement being renamed Greenwood. Lower Mill was one of the first mills in the county and farmers came long distances to have their grain ground into flour. Surplus grain from the area was shipped to warehouses on Lake Ontario for export.

In 1843 Lennon and Shea, both of Irish descent, opened a cooperage in Greenwood, assisted by Michael Carey. Samuel Boyer, who had come from Pennsylvania in 1830, ran a flour, grist and sawmill. His son Abe, carried on in the milling business until Thomas Bayles took over in 1905. Benjamin Boyer, Samuel's brother, started a carding mill in 1845. John Adamson operated a brickyard until his death in the 1850's, at which time his son, Samuel, took over the business.

Until 1876 church services in Greenwood were held at the Orange Hall. The Greenwood Methodist congregation established in 1863, erected a church in 1876, and in 1927 a new brick church, Greenwood United Church, was built on the same site.

The first school for the area was located at nearby Salem, with George Gamble as teacher. He also held religious services on Sundays. In 1860 the present school was constructed on the site of the first village school. One notable former student was John George Diefenbaker, who became the thirteenth prime minister of Canada, and whose father, W.T. Diefenbaker, at one time taught school in Greenwood.

Greenwood Farm Forum: *Greenwood Through the Years*, 1960.

GREER, geographic township, Cochrane District
Position 51° 20′ 80° 58′

Named after a Crown Attorney Greer of Cochrane, the township lies immediately to the west of Moosonee. It is watered by numerous rivers, all flowing in a southwesterly direction through Greer on their way to join the Moose River.

GRENFELL, geographic township, Timiskaming District
Position 48° 09′ 80° 13′

Located a few miles west of Kirkland Lake, the township bears the name of world-renowned medical missionary, explorer and writer, Sir Wilfred Thomason Grenfell. Grenfell founded numerous hospitals, nursing stations, orphanages, stores and industrial centres along the northern Newfoundland and Labrador coasts in the early twentieth century.

The township is traversed by Highway 11 and the Ontario Northland Railway.

GRENOBLE, geographic township, Algoma District
Position 47° 01' 84° 10'

Named after an explorer who accompanied Etienne Brûlé to the Sault Ste Marie area in the 1600's, the township was formerly part of the Algoma Central and Hudson Bay Railway land grant. It is still shown on recent maps as Township 25, Range 12. The Algoma Central traverses the township which lies north of Sault Ste Marie.

GRENVILLE, county
Position 44° 50' 75° 40'

Situated in the southeastern part of the province, the county fronts on Lake Ontario. In the northwest it borders on the Regional Municipality of Ottawa-Carleton and on Lanark County, in the northeast on Dundas County, and in the southwest on Leeds County. For administrative purposes, Grenville and Leeds are united, with Brockville in Leeds being the county seat. Surveyed in 1784, Grenville was named after William Wyndham Grenville, British Secretary-of-State for Foreign Affairs, 1791-1801.

The area was first visited by the Surveyor-General in 1783 to assess its potential for the settlement of United Empire Loyalists and disbanded soldiers from the American Revolutionary War. His report was favourable and lots were marked out in 1784. The first settlers arrived a few months later. Among these pioneers were Dr. Solomon Jones, Ephraim Jones, Major Edward Jessup, Capt. Justus Sherwood, and Capt. Peter Drummond. By the end of the year the population was 394.

Barbara and Paul Heck, Loyalists from New York, were among Grenville's earliest settlers. This husband and wife, who arrived in 1785 in Augusta Township, were to play a leading role in the development of Methodism in Upper Canada, joining other families in 1790 to establish the interdenominational "Blue Church". In the early nineteenth century Wilson's Inn, at the southern end of South Gower Township, served as the Methodist meeting-place in the county. Barbara Heck, known as the "Mother of Methodism in North America", died in 1804 and is buried in the graveyard of the Little Blue Church, today a historic site along Highway 2.

Communities grew up first along the St. Lawrence River, Johnstown being one of the earliest. A French-Canadian, Guillaume de Lorimier, had already built a house there when the Loyalists arrived in 1784. The community was laid out in 1789-90 and its inhabitants expected it to become the leading centre of the Eastern District which was formed in 1791. However, their hopes were not to be fulfilled, as Johnstown ceased to be the geographical centre when the county became part of the new District of Johnstown in 1798, and

Brockville gained prominence instead.

Captain Hugh Munro built a grist mill and sawmill and later a carding and spinning mill at Munro's Point. This was the beginning of the community of Cardinal. Spencerville was founded in 1812 when David Spencer built a dam and sawmill at the site. Maitland developed on the site of an old French fort, Pointe au Baril, erected in 1758. A house on the grounds of the fort became the county's first school. Prescott was surveyed by Major Edward Jessup on his land in 1810. The settlement developed into an important transfer point for shipping on the St. Lawrence River and is, today, Grenville's largest town. Fort Wellington became the main base for defence between Kingston and Montreal. During the War of 1812 an attack on Ogdensburg was launched from here in 1813.

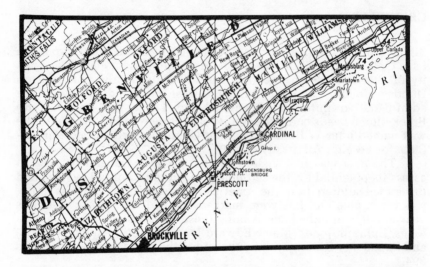

Grenville County's northern townships of Wolford, Oxford, and South Gower were settled later than the lakefront townships of Augusta and Edwardsburg. Settlement was impeded, at least to a degree, by land speculators. Much of the land in Oxford, which was surveyed as early as 1791, had been granted to settlers already established in the lakefront townships and who, according to recent new government regulations, were entitled to additional land grants. By 1801 there were only 14 settlers in Oxford, all members of the Harris family. The first permanent settler on the Rideau, which flows along the northern border of the county, was Stephen Burritt, who founded Burritt's Rapids. Other early families in that area included the Hurds and the Olmsteds. Kemptville, the county's second town and today the home of an Agricultural College, was founded in 1813 when Lyman Clothier built a dam and grist mill here on the south branch of the Rideau River.

The township of Wolford was surveyed in 1796. Its early settlers included Joseph Easton, who opened the first tannery in the

174

township; Joseph Haskins and Richard Olmsted, sawmill owners; and Samuel Dow, the first blacksmith. William Merrick laid the foundations of Merrickville when he built a dam and sawmill on the site in 1800.

After the War of 1812, the British Government embarked on a policy of giving free land grants to disbanded British soldiers in order to counterbalance the number of American settlers in the area. This encouraged people to move into the northern townships of the county. South Gower, Grenville's smallest township, received many of its first inhabitants from the southern part of the county. Peter McAlpine Grant built one of the first sawmills in this township and David Beach constructed a dam and sawmill. Thomas and Joseph McCargar were early settlers of the area.

Meanwhile, by 1812 the population of Augusta and Edwardsburg had reached 2700. The construction of the Rideau Canal in 1832 along the northern border gave impetus to further development in that area. Railway fever gripped the county in the 1850's. The Bytown and Prescott Railway was built in 1854, the Grand Trunk Railway in 1856. The Canadian Pacific Railway followed in 1881. Today motorists gain access to the county by Highways 2 and 401 and by the Prescott-Ogdensburg Bridge built in 1960.

A lighthouse west of Johnstown on the St. Lawrence River was originally a windmill built in 1822 by a man named Hughes. Here the famous Battle of the Windmill was fought in 1838 when, as an aftermath of the 1837 Rebellion, a force of Americans invaded Canada and took over the windmill. One hundred and fifty invaders were taken prisoner, and Colonel Von Schultz, their leader, was sentenced to death.

Although Grenville is primarily a rural area with over half of its 25,000 people living in small villages or on farms, a number of industries have flourished in the area. Brickyards were a common sight in the nineteenth century. In 1858 the first starch factory in Canada, which later became the Canada Starch Company, was opened in the county by W.T. Benson and Thomas Aspden. A.J. Bissell built the first cheese factory in the county in 1867.

Today there are about 50 manufacturing plants in Grenville, including DuPont of Canada (1953), Maitland Charts Ltd., manufacturers of roll charts for recording instruments, and the Oxford-on-Rideau Co-operative, a fertilizer and feed manufacturing plant.

The *Grenville Gazette*, founded in 1832 in Prescott by Stephen Miles, was the county's first newspaper. CFLC Prescott, which began broadcasting in 1926, was one of the earliest community radio stations in Canada. It is now CFJR Brockville.

Among the county's better known residents have been the Hon. G. Howard Ferguson, Premier of Ontario 1923-30; and Dr. Walter Thomas Connell, a pioneer in the fields of pathology and bacteriology and one of the founders of the Royal College of Physicians and Surgeons of Canada.

Mrs. Burritt: "The Settlement of the County of Grenville" in *Ontario Historical Society*, 1901.

C. Blackett Robinson: *British Farmers Guide to Ontario*, 1880.

Mika Publishing Company: *Historical Atlas of Leeds & Grenville*, 1973.

GRENVILLE, geographic township, Thunder Bay District
Position 49° 06′ 86° 03′

Grenville is located to the west of the town of Manitouwadge, to which the area is linked by a secondary road. The township's name origin is unknown.

GREY, county
Position 44° 20′ 80° 45′

The county of Grey borders on Georgian Bay and its inlets, Colpoys Bay, the Owen Sound, and Nottawasaga Bay, in the north. Wellington County lies to the south, Simcoe and Dufferin Counties border the east, and Bruce County is situated to the west. Grey is comprised of sixteen townships covering an area 1,113,107.2 acres. The population of the county numbers 72,596 (1978).

The countryside is rolling and hilly with the Niagara escarpment traversing the northern townships of the county fronting on Georgian Bay. The Beaver, Bighead and Sydenham Rivers, the county's main rivers, drain into Georgian Bay, while the Saugeen River and its tributaries drain into Lake Huron. Grey County was named after Earl Grey who was the British Colonial Secretary from 1846 to 1852.

The original inhabitants of Grey County were Algonkian, Petun, and Cheveux Relevés Indians. In 1640 invading Iroquois bands wiped out these tribes. However, the Algonkian Ojibwa Indians took control of the area later, and were living in the territory when the first white settlers arrived.

Champlain was probably the first white man to explore the region. Shortly after, Jesuit and Recollet priests arrived to set up missions among the Indians. The Indians signed a series of treaties between 1817 and 1857 giving up their land rights, and subsequently they withdrew to the Saugeen and Cape Croker reserves.

The county was surveyed between 1833 and 1857; Collingwood Township was the first to be surveyed and Sarawak Township was the last. The first settler in Grey County was Charles Rankin, a surveyor, who took up land in St. Vincent Township in 1834. Later that year several retired army officers settled in the area, including Captain Workman, "Squire" Corley, John Londry, and two men named Waddell and Beebe. Most of the pioneers were Canadian-born. Later a group of immigrants from the British Isles, and a small number of German immigrants (in Normanby Township) joined the settlers. One of the earliest mills in the county was the Edge mill at Durham, erected in 1847.

Prior to the Municipal Institutions Act of 1849, Grey was part of the District of Waterloo. In 1852 Grey became a provisional county. The boundaries of the county were adjusted at this time, and several of Grey County townships were traded with those of Simcoe County. In 1854 Grey became an independent municipal county. Richard Carney was elected as the first Warden. The last major municipal change occurred in 1881 when Melancthon Township was transferred to the newly formed Dufferin County.

Several colonization roads helped to open up the county for settlement. The Garafraxa Road was surveyed in 1837 by Charles Rankin; later it was altered extensively by John McDonald. It ran from Fergus to the mouth of the Sydenham River, where Owen Sound stands today. Today the Garafraxa Road is Highway 6. The Durham Road was surveyed 1848-49 and it ran from east to west, crossing both Grey and Bruce Counties. The Old Mail (or Government) Road ran from Barrie to Owen Sound via Meaford. It was laid out in 1849. The Sydenham Road, surveyed in 1850, ran from Toronto to Owen Sound via Orangeville.

Railways did not arrive in Grey County until the 1870's. The Grey and Bruce Railroad was built in 1873 and it linked Toronto, Orangeville and Owen Sound. Later this railroad became part of the CPR. The Wellington and Georgian Bay Railway was built from Palmerston to Durham in 1882. The Stratford and Huron Railway linking Palmerston and Wiarton was built in 1882 and later was extended to Owen Sound in 1894. These railroads eventually became part of the Grand Trunk Railway, which was itself absorbed by the CNR some years later.

Grey County contains one city, four towns, and six incorporated villages. Owen Sound, a city of 19,697 (1978), is the county seat. The town plot was surveyed in 1840 as the terminus of the Garafraxa Road. A government agent named John Telfer was the first settler in that locality in 1840. The settlement was first known as "Sydenham" because of its location at the mouth of the Sydenham River. It was incorporated as a town in 1857 under the name of Owen Sound. The city was named after Admiral William Fitzwilliam Owen, who undertook the first Admiralty survey of Lake Ontario and Georgian Bay from 1814 to 1816.

The four towns of Grey County are Durham, Hanover, Meaford, and Thornbury. The incorporated villages are Chatsworth, Dundalk, Flesherton, Markdale, Neustadt, and Shallow Lake.

Grey County has several native sons and daughters of whom she can be justly proud. Owen Sound was the birthplace of "Billy" Bishop (1894-1956), the famous World War I flying ace. Novelist Margaret Marshall Saunders (1861-1947), author of the well-loved children's story *Beautiful Joe*, was born in Meaford. The first Canadian to win the world heavyweight championship was born near Hanover in 1881. "Tommy Burns" (Noah Brusso) won the title in 1906. The small community of Leith was the home of Tom Thomson, one of the important artists in the history of Canadian art, and a member of the famous "Group of Seven". Though not born in Leith, he lived there with his family from the age of two months to twenty-one years. Grey County is also the birthplace of two outstanding Canadian feminists. Nellie McClung, lecturer, legislator, teacher, writer and ardent advocate of Women's Rights, was born in Chatsworth in 1873. Agnes Macphail, born in 1890 in Hopeville (Proton Township) was the first woman elected to the parliament of Canada in 1921.

Because of its vicinity to Georgian Bay, Grey County has a busy tourist industry. The Bruce Trail, a favourite hiking route of nature lovers, meanders through Grey County on its way to Tobermory on the

Bruce Peninsula. A fine provincial park is established at Craigleith. Grey County also possesses some excellent skiing country.

Economically, this area is primarily a mixed farming district. The Beaver and Bighead River Valleys are particularly well-known for their apple orchards. Perhaps the most important manufacturing industry in the county is that of household furniture.

Ontario Department of Economics and Development: *Georgian Bay Region, Economic Survey*, 1963.

H. Belden & Co.: *Historical Atlas of Grey & Bruce Counties*, 1880.

E.L. Marsh: *A History of the County of Grey*, 1931.

GREY, geographic township, Huron County
Position 43° 43′ 81° 10′

The township of Grey is located in the northeast sector of Huron County. It covers an area of 66,464 acres and is the third largest township in the county.

The township was originally part of the Queen's Bush, a portion of land north of the Canada Company Huron Tract. Until 1836 the area was still in the possession of the Ojibway and Saugeen Indians. That year the British Crown gained the title to the land and it became known as the Queen's Bush. Later this "new Crown Land" was sold off to settlers. The township was named for Charles, the second Earl of Grey, best remembered for the passing of the Reform Bill (1832), two years after he had become Prime Minister of Great Britain.

The first settlers in Grey Township were mostly Scottish and English, but there were some Irish and German immigrants. The earliest settler was a French Canadian named Beauchamp, who had squatted on the land before it was put up for sale. Originally he settled near the border of Perth County; later he moved to a spot close to the present-day community of Cranbrook. John Mitchell, the second settler, arrived in 1852 and settled on the site of the present-day community of Molesworth. Other early township settlers included John, Peter, and Duncan Ferguson, Robert and Ronald McNaughton, Peter McDonald, Thomas Blackie, James J. Ford, William Douglas, John Stewart, John Blair, Donald Allen, and the Lamonts, Sellars, Hyslop and McFadzean families.

The first post office was opened in 1854 in Cranbrook with Andrew Govenlock as first postmaster. The Wellington, Grey and Bruce Railway, constructed in the early 1870's between Guelph and Kincardine, passed through the township of Grey and established stations at the settlements of Henfryn and Ethel.

Grey did not become a separate municipality until 1856. Peter McDonald was the first reeve, and John Stewart the first township clerk. The only village in the township is Brussels, incorporated in 1872. Other settlements in Grey are Walton, Molesworth, Jamestown and Morrisbank. Grey Township is primarily a mixed farming area. In 1978 the population of the township was 2,036.

James Scott: *The Settlement of Huron County*, 1966.

GRIESINGER, geographic township, Rainy River District
Position 48° 47′ 93° 29′

Located north of Fort Frances, the township was established in 1945 and named after William Griesinger, elected as MPP for Windsor-Sandwich in that year. The township, to a large extent, is covered by the waters and numerous islands of Rainy Lake.

GRIFFIN, geographic township, Cochrane District
Position 48° 55′ 82° 20′

Located west of the Groundhog River, the township was presumably named after W.A. Griffin, an official of the Temiskaming and Northern Ontario Railway. A secondary road from the north shore of Griffin Lake links the area with Kapuskasing to the north.

GRIFFITH, township, Renfrew County
Position 45° 18′ 77° 10′

Situated in the southern part of Renfrew County, Griffith is bordered on the south by Matawatchan Township, and both these townships are united for municipal purposes. Griffith Township was surveyed in the 1850's at the same time as its neighbours, and is believed to have been named after Colonel Griffith, commander of the Greys at the Battle of Balaclava in the Crimean War.

Griffith is sparsely populated, except for the summertime, when tourists come to the township's lake areas by Highway 41, which passes through the southern part of the township. The dispersed rural communities of Griffith and Khartum are located along this road. The picturesque Madawaska River flows across the southwestern corner of the township.

The combined permanent population of the municipality of Griffith and Matawatchan is 351 (1979).

Mrs. Carl Price and Clyde C. Kennedy: *Notes on the History of Renfrew County*, 1961.

GRIGG, geographic township, Sudbury District
Position 47° 02′ 80° 52′

The township is located less than twenty miles north of the town of Capreol and is accessible from there by road. The Wanapitei River flows southward through the centre of the township on its way to Wanapitei Lake, a large body of water just east of Capreol.

The township was named after Albert Grigg, MPP for Algoma prior to World War One.

GRIMSBY, town, Regional Municipality of Niagara
Position 43° 12′ 79° 34′

Situated between a mountain and the south shore of Lake Ontario, 11 miles southeast of Hamilton, Grimsby is a town with a long history.

Originally, the site on which the town stands was called "The Forty" because of its location at the mouth of Forty Mile Creek. It was renamed Grimsby in 1816 after the city of Grimsby in Lincolnshire, England.

The first settlers in the area were United Empire Loyalists who had been forced to leave the United States after the American Revolution. Colonel Robert Nelles, a Loyalist from the Mohawk Valley, New York, built his home at The Forty in 1788. This fine colonial manor, completed in 1798, is now a historic site. Nelles, his father, Henry, and his younger brothers had been among the first to settle at the mouth of The Forty. Robert later served as a justice of the peace, a township warden, and a member of the legislative assembly, and became commanding officer of the 4th Lincoln Militia.

From 1784 to 1790, Loyalist settlers flocked in great numbers into the Niagara Peninsula. Finding the land along the Niagara River already taken up, a group of about 400 Loyalists pushed westward. Many of these people settled around The Forty. Among the early families were the Pettits, the Carpenters, the Muirs, the Nixons, and the Smiths. Unfortunately for some of the pioneers, they had arrived at their new home at the beginning of the "Hungry Year", 1787-88. Drought and heat ruined the crops, and the people were forced to depend on the lake for water and fish.

John Green built the first sawmill at The Forty in 1788 and a year later he erected a grist mill. Two more sawmills, owned by Nelles and John Beamer, were in operation by 1792.

On April 5, 1790, the inhabitants of The Forty made history by holding a town meeting, the earliest known session of municipal government in Ontario. Two years later the community became part of the new District of Nassau. Nathaniel Pettit was chosen to represent The Forty. The settlement later became part of Lincoln County. Much crop and property damage was suffered by the settlers during the War of 1812. In Grimsby's Waterworks Park stands a historic sites plaque commemorating the Battle of The Forty, which took place here on June 8, 1813. American forces, having retreated to The Forty from the Battle of Stoney Creek, were bombarded by a British flotilla under Sir James Lucas Yeo. Indians and militiamen joined in the attack and forced the Americans to retreat to Fort George.

In 1816 a post office was opened at The Forty and at that time the settlement took on the name of Grimsby. William Crooks was the first postmaster. By 1824 streets had been laid out and the actual village had begun to take shape. A cholera epidemic hit the community in 1834, but it rallied and expanded. By 1852 the population had reached 300 and businesses included those of Allison and Vandyke, coachmakers; Seth Dean, miller and lumber merchant; and Morris Udell, brewer and distiller.

In 1854 the Great Western Railway (now the CNR) was constructing its line from the suspension bridge over the Niagara River to Windsor via Grimsby, opening up markets in Western Ontario and ushering in a period of prosperity for the village.

Located in the centre of one of Canada's major fruit-growing areas, Grimsby became the home of an early canning factory, opened in 1856 by W.W. Kitchen. John H. Grout established the Grimsby Agricultural Works. Charles Woolverton and A.M. Smith began the first commercial peach orchards in the area. In 1859 the first Lincoln County Agricultural Show was held in the community. By the end of the 1860's, Grimsby had become known as the "Garden of Canada", but entrepreneurs of the community also branched out into other fields. The Grimsby Petroleum and Saline Co. had been formed in 1860 to undertake oil exploration. Robert Gibson established a stone quarrying industry. Daniel Marsh had begun a construction industry which became the forerunner of Penn Building Centers. A basket factory was another of Grimsby's industries.

Grimsby, St. Andrew's Anglican Church

Public Archives Canada, PA 20785

Grimsby Park, originally known as the Ontario Methodist Camp Meeting Grounds, was once the site of huge temperance meetings. Such meetings had been held on the property of John Beamer

Bowslaugh as early as 1846, but the first official meeting took place in 1859 after Bowslaugh had donated his land specifically for that purpose. Soon after, about seventy cottages were built on the site, a small Grand Trunk Railway Station was opened, and Grimsby Park became a popular vacation spot. Accessible by road and by rail, it could also be reached by water, and there was a daily steamer which carried passengers the 27 miles across Lake Ontario from Toronto. The Park was a miniature community with its own post office, barber, butcher, ice-cream parlour, book store, grocery, drugstore and two hotels. Recreational activities, excursions and competitions abounded and educational and inspirational meetings were held in the large auditorium in the centre of the Park. A new auditorium, "the Temple", was built in 1888 and remained a landmark until it was dismantled in 1922.

In 1876, Grimsby was incorporated as a village, with John Grout as the first reeve. By this time the population had reached about 600. There were five churches, one each for the Anglicans, Baptists, Methodists, Presbyterians and Roman Catholics. Three doctors served the community which had a high school, a public school, a Mechanics' Institute with over 1000 volumes in its library, a Grange, and a Lodge of Good Templars. There were three merchants, two butchers, three blacksmiths, two carriage makers, and a harness maker among the businesses of the community.

Grimsby's first church had been housed in a school erected in 1794 on land given by Robert Nelles. The building was replaced by St. Andrew's Anglican Church in 1804. A stone church was built in 1825. Methodist services were held as early as 1817, although the congregation had no house of worship until 1864. The Presbyterian church was erected in 1837 under Rev. J.G. Murray. The Roman Catholics built their house of worship in 1880 and the Baptist church opened its doors in 1880.

The first schoolhouse, a log structure, was built in 1794 and John Oakley served as the first teacher. By 1812 there were two schools in the area and in 1857 a Grammar School was opened with pupils under the instruction of David Campbell.

Since the turn of the century, Grimsby has developed into an industrial centre. It was incorporated as a town in 1922 with Charles T. Farrell as the first mayor. In the following years many new industries were established. Niagara Packers Ltd., which made Grimsby its headquarters in 1932, and Grimsby Stove and Furnace Ltd., which began in 1933, were among the first. More industries were set up in the 1940's, including Arkell Foods Ltd., which produces canned fruits, vegetables, and meats. The 1950's saw the establishment of John Bakker and Sons, manufacturers of furniture; Robertson-Gordon Appliances, which produces heating appliances and components; Canadian Westinghouse Co. Ltd.; Jason Enterprises, producer of garden benches and ornaments; Williamson Printing Materials; two egg factories, and a winery. Two printers, a foundry, and Reyco of Canada, arrived in the 1960's. More recently, Avco

Limited, Andres Wines, and Rieder Distillery Ltd. have opened in the town.

In 1968 Grimsby's population was 3,088. A sharp increase, however, occurred in 1970 when the town was amalgamated with the township of North Grimsby in the new Regional Municipality of Niagara. In 1978 Grimsby had 15,265 inhabitants.

The town's newspaper is the weekly *Independent*, founded in 1885 by James A. Livingston. Grimsby also has an active Historical Society, which from 1950 to 1959 put out one book a year on the town's history. The Stone Shop Museum, opened in 1963 in a shop built by Allan Nixon about 1800, and the Village Depot, a restored 1900 railway station, are reminders of Grimsby's past.

A.E. Coombs: *Niagara Peninsula and the New Welland Canal*, 1930.

Grimsby Historical Society: *Annals of The Forty*, 1950-59.

Grimsby Independent, Image 67, 1967.

H.R. Page: *Historical Atlas of Lincoln and Welland*, 1876.

GRIMSTHORPE, township, Hastings County
Position 44° 48' 77° 28'

Grimsthorpe and its southern neighbour Elzevir Township, united for municipal purposes, are part of the Highlands of Hastings, a favourite district for tourists. Tudor Township lies to the west of Grimsthorpe, Cashel to the north, and Anglesea Township in Lennox and Addington County to the east. The township was named in the 1820's by Lieutenant Governor Sir Peregrine Maitland, after Grimsthorpe Castle in Lincolnshire, England. The combined population of the municipality of Grimsthorpe and Elzevir is 661 (1978); nearly all of the inhabitants reside in Elzevir.

A survey of Grimsthorpe was begun in 1823 under surveyor Samuel Ryckman. After surveying two concessions he was forced to give up in the face of swamps, streams and mountains that hindered his progress and discouraged his assistants. Not until 1867 was another attempt made to survey the rest of the township. Surveyor William Murdoch and his party arrived in the spring of that year and had to travel by canoe because of widespread flooding from Job Lingham's dam to Lingham Lake. In June, flies and mosquitoes put a temporary halt to their work. When the job was completed two months later, surveyors had come to the conclusion that the township had very little to offer prospective settlers. Consequently, Grimsthorpe remained largely without permanent residents. But the area, well forested and rich in natural beauty, offers good fishing in season and attracts hunters from near and far. There are a number of old mine pits which still show traces of gold and other minerals, a fact well known to rock and mineral collectors.

Lingham Lake is the township's largest lake. In the 1960's a dam was built at the lake by the Moira River Conservation Authority to regulate the flow of water on the Black River, a tributary of the Moira.

Gerald E. Boyce: *Historic Hastings*, 1967.

183

GROOTENBOER, geographic township, Algoma District
Position 47° 27' 84° 25'

Located east of Lake Superior Provincial Park, the township was formerly known as No. 27, Range 17. It was named after J.A. Grootenboer, once the reeve of Oliver Township in the Thunder Bay District.

GROSEILLIERS, geographic township, Algoma District
Position 47° 59' 85° 15'

This small township west of the town of Wawa and on the border of Thunder Bay District, fronts on Lake Superior. It is still shown on recent maps as Township 33, Range 23, but it has since been named after the noted French Explorer and fur trader, Sieur Médart Chouart des Groseilliers, who came to Canada in the mid-seventeenth century. On one of his expeditions, supported by a group of English gentlemen, he reached Hudson Bay in the ketch, *Nonsuch*, and his report formed the basis for the Royal Charter granted to Hudson's Bay Company in 1670.

GROSS, geographic township, Timiskaming district
Position 47° 59' 80° 20'

The township was subdivided in 1902 and named at that time after John Franklin Gross, MPP for Welland. Gross lies less than 20 miles southwest of Kirkland Lake, to which it is linked by Highway 66.

GROSSMAN, geographic township, Algoma District
Position 47° 11' 82° 46'

Named in 1974 after the Hon. Allen Grossman, MPP for the St. Andrews-St. Patrick riding of Toronto, the township had formerly been designated as 7A. It is located on the Sudbury District border, northwest of the Mississagi Wild River Provincial Park. The township is accessible only by waterways.

GROVES, geographic township, Sudbury District
Position 47° 38' 81° 37'

Situated immediately to the southeast of the mining district of Gogama, the township was named after a George H. Groves, probably at the time its boundaries were surveyed in 1911 and 1912. The Canadian National Railways passes through the western sector of the township.

GROVETON, community, Edwardsburgh Township, Grenville County
Position 44° 53' 75° 34'

Groveton is situated just off Highway 16, about 12 miles north of

Prescott. It was named by Rev. Philander Smith, a Methodist missionary, who held religious services in the woods here in the 1850's. These camp meetings continued to be held annually until a small church was built.

One of the first settlers was Isaac Wilson who bought the land on Lot 23, Concession 9, in 1835. His property included a ridge of the highest level of land between the St. Lawrence and Ottawa Rivers. In 1905, a geological survey party from Ottawa erected a balloon tower about eighty feet high here, as well as a concrete marker in case it fell down. During a November gale, a few years later, the tower did collapse, but the concrete marker still stands.

Most of the settlers of the area came from Mayo County in Ireland in 1849 after the Irish famine. They made good pioneers as they were used to small rocky farms such as they found in their new home. Among these early farmers were Michael Derrig and his brother-in-law John Collins, George Baker, and John Wilson. A log schoolhouse was built on the Derrig farm.

Many of these early inhabitants pursued other trades as well as farming their land. The Wilsons, Cliffords, Gibsons and Ingrams were known for their weaving. Moses Grue and Michael Derrig were shoemakers and David Gamble and John Jarvis were tinsmiths. John Kingston and Hugh B. Ingram did carpentry work. There were several blacksmiths, including Hamilton Moorehead and five Carmichael brothers. John Jennings made harnesses and there was also a carriage-making business.

The area was mainly rural, although there was some industry in the early twentieth century. Lemuel Grue built a threshing mill in 1905. A cheese factory was also in operation at this time. By the mid-1900's, most of the old farms had disappeared or had been converted into summer homes. Farmers who remain often have part-time employment elsewhere to supplement their income.

Edwardsburgh Centennial Committee: *History of Edwardsburgh Township*, 1967.

GRUMMETT, geographic township, Kenora District
Position 49° 15' 91° 26'

Grummett was established in 1945 and named after W.J. Grummett, elected MPP for Cochrane South that year. The township, covered with lakes in the southern section, lies north of the town of Atikokan.

GRUNDY LAKE PROVINCIAL PARK, Mowat Township, Parry Sound District
Position 45° 56' 80° 32'

Grundy Lake Provincial Park, a natural environment park, is situated at the conjunction of Highways 522 and 69, south of the French River district, a connecting waterway for the voyageur routes followed by Samuel de Champlain, Etienne Brûlé and Alexander MacKenzie. The CPR line cuts across the eastern boundary, running north.

Located on the southern portion of the Canadian Shield, its

landscape is typical of the rugged, lake-dotted terrain. Grundy Lake, with much of its shoreline comprised of sloping Canadian Shield rock, Gut Lake, Clear Lake, Beaver Lake and Pakeshkag Lake are inter-connecting providing an extensive network of waterways for canoeists. No powerboats are allowed on the lakes.

For vacationers there are thousands of acres of forest and bog to be explored abounding with wildlife and birdlife. There are five marked trails with beaver dams and nesting places of the Great Blue Heron.

Ontario Ministry of Natural Resources.

GRZELA, geographic township, Algoma District
Position 47° 27' 84° 27'

Formerly known as Township 26, Range 17, the township was named after R.G. Grzela, reeve of Shackleton and Machim Township in Cochrane District.

The township is located east of Lake Superior Provincial Park and north of the Montreal River.

GUELPH, township, Wellington County
Position 43° 34' 80° 18'

Named after the Royal House of Brunswick, the family of the English monarch, George IV, Guelph township was surveyed in 1830 by John McDonald. The land had been bought by the Canada Company, a company consisting of a group of British speculators who acquired more than two million acres of land in Upper Canada for colonization purposes. A large number of the township's early inhabitants had already arrived before the survey was undertaken. The first settler was Samuel Rife, who squatted near the westerly limits of the township about 1825. He lived on what became the Waterloo Road, about five miles from the city of Guelph. His daughter, Sarah, was the first white child to be born in the township. The Hind and Ryan families also settled in this area in 1825.

The Waterloo Road, then known as the Broad Road, was built by Absalom Shade and was finished about 1827, the year that the settlement of Guelph in the southern part of the township was founded. Many more settlers arrived in that year and took up land in different parts of the township. William Darby, Hugh McDonald, Martin Tobin, Archibald McFee, and Alex McCrae were among the pioneers on the Elora Road. The future site of the Agricultural College of Guelph was settled by James Thompson, James McQuillan, Andrew McCrae, and William Patterson. On the east side of the township, George Davis, William Bilby, Alexander McConachie, and Richard Oliver were among those who arrived in the years 1827-1830.

A group of Scottish immigrants, known as the La Guayra Settlers, also arrived in 1827. Originally they had emigrated to Carracas, Venezuela, but conditions there had been so bad that they moved on to Philadelphia. In 1827, with the help of John Galt,

Superintendent of the Canada Company, they settled in Guelph Township in the "Scotch Block". Galt's generosity was criticized by the Company and was one of the reasons for his recall to England in 1829. Among the La Guayran settlers were Joseph McDonald, Hugh Kennedy, Donald Gillies, and Alex McTavish.

The Paisley area, known as the "Paisley Block", was settled by families from Paisley, Scotland, who bought the land from the Company in 1829. The first immigrants to take up land here were John McCorkindale, William Alexander, Nathan Ferguson, and James Craig. They were followed by many more families in the 1830's. These early inhabitants helped build the old Guelph and Goderich Road.

Division B of the township, excluding the Paisley Block, was first settled in 1832 by Alex McIntosh. Other early residents were John Fyfe, George Henderson, John Spiers, William Hearn, and Edward Vance. The West End was inhabited by George Bruce, John Gregory, Capt. Sutherland, William Whitelaw, and others.

Among the early businessmen of the township were Mr. Griffin and Mr. Blyth, hotelkeepers, Evan MacDonald who founded the firm of MacDonald Bros., and F.W. Stone, an importer of thoroughbred stock. Stone's farm was later sold to the Agricultural College and his house became its first building. Township resident, John "Quaker" Howitt is said to have been the largest landowner in the county and James Laidlaw, owner of the largest farm. Mrs. Caldwell opened one of the first stores in the community of Marden, and Benjamin Taylor, also of Marden, was one of that area's earliest blacksmiths.

John Howitt and Benjamin Thurtell represented Guelph Township at the first District Council in 1842. In 1850 when the Municipal Act took effect, Thurtell became the first reeve.

The first school in the township was opened in the Paisley Block in 1832 in a house owned by Robert Laidlaw. John Craw was the first teacher. A new school was erected on Laidlaw's land in 1833, with James Key as teacher. William Hiscock became the teacher when a school was built on the Spiers farm. William Cowan was the first to teach in the frame building constructed in 1853. This was replaced by a new school in 1872.

Guelph Township has been the home of a number of literary figures. Thomas Laidlaw, poet and author of *Old Concession Road*, was born here. John Taylor was another poet born in the township. Mary Leslie wrote the first book-length novel in this part of Ontario, *The Cromaboo Mail Carrier*.

Because of repeated annexations by the city of Guelph, the township's area has decreased from 42,338 acres in the late nineteenth century to 29,171 acres in 1976. The population of Guelph Township in 1978 was 2,918.

A.E. Byerley: *The Beginning of Things*, 1935.

Historical Atlas Publishing Company: *Historical Atlas of Wellington County*, 1906.

GUELPH, city, Guelph Township, Wellington County
Position 43° 33′ 80° 15′

Guelph, a city of over 71,000 and the seat of Wellington County, is situated at the confluence of the Speed and Eramosa Rivers, about 28 miles northwest of Hamilton and 60 miles west of Toronto, and at the junction of Highways 6, 7 and 24. The "Royal City" as it is often called, was named in 1827 by its founder, John Galt, after the family name of George III of England. No other place in the Commonwealth bears the royal name of Guelph.

Guelph is unusual in that its founding can be given an exact date. On April 23, 1827, St. George's Day, John Galt, administrator of affairs for the Canada Company, struck the first tree on the site of the future city. Guelph's development was planned from its very beginning. To indicate the street pattern of the new settlement, Galt spread out the fingers of his hand and Guelph's radial street pattern has not been substantially altered since.

The early growth of the community was aided to a great extent by the Canada Company, an organization interested in the settlement of immigrants on its lands. Galt brought in workmen and mechanics, including a blacksmith, shoemaker, baker, wagon maker, and carpenter, by offering good wages. These men and their families, among the first settlers of Guelph, included Joseph Croft, Samuel Wright, and Joseph MacDonald.

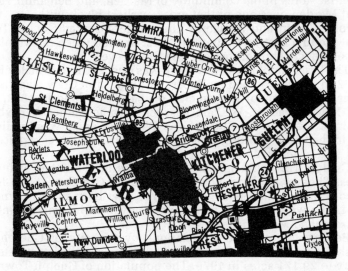

Unfortunately, relations between the city's founder and the Company were not always cordial. When the Company ordered Galt to change the name of the community to Goderich, he refused. Galt was criticized for concentrating too much on the future of Guelph and not enough on profits for the Company. Disheartened by the Company's hostility towards his plans, Galt returned to England just a few years after the founding of Guelph.

Guelph's first store was opened in 1827 by David Gilkinson, who also built a sawmill in 1828. John Galt had proposed the construction of a mill on the west bank of the river in 1827. It was erected by Horace Perry in 1830. Included in the mill's buildings were a cooper shop, a blacksmith and metal working shop, a planing mill, and a woodworking shop.

In the early 1830's immigration to Canada increased greatly and a large local market was created. Guelph became the main centre of the surrounding agricultural area. By 1832 it had a grist mill, sawmill, distillery, brewery, tannery, five inns, four merchant shops, a drugstore, four blacksmith shops, and three churches. The flour trade became increasingly important and Guelph developed into one of the largest grain markets in Upper Canada. In 1838, with its increasing population, Guelph became the seat of Wellington County.

By 1840, Guelph, with 699 inhabitants, had become the leader in the settlements of the Canada Company. It now had two tanneries, three breweries, and a distillery. More flour mills were built, including the Victoria Mill by Joseph Pratt, and the Wellington Mill by D. Gilkinson & Co. The Priory, Guelph's first residence which had been built by John Galt, served as the Canada Company's offices. The growth of settlement in the area north of Guelph resulted in further expansion of the town, and in 1847 the community's population had reached 1,480. The Brock Road was built between 1848 and 1850 from Dundas to Guelph in order to encourage trade. By this time, Guelph had three printers, four lawyers, four surgeons, two druggists, seven blacksmiths, four distillers, and four tanners, all living in the community. Robert Armstrong made carriages and James Mays ran a tanning mill. A. Robertson and Son opened Guelph's first foundry. Dr. Welsh, one of the first medical men in Guelph, was commonly known as the "mad doctor". He built himself a log house with no door. The entrance was a square hole about six feet from the ground.

In 1851 Guelph was incorporated as a village. Samuel Smith served as the first reeve. In 1852 the first train of the Toronto and Guelph Railway arrived at the new village station. The Grand Trunk Railway was built through the village in 1856. That year, with its population approaching 5,000, Guelph became a town. John Smith was chosen head of the town council. A combined town hall and market building was also built in that same year.

The 1860's saw the opening of McCrae & Co., knitting and weaving, Bell Organ Company, James Goldie Company Ltd., and Raymond Sewing Machine Company. Industries established in the 1870's included Guelph Carpet Mills Co. Ltd., and Guelph Spring and Axle Co. Ltd.

By 1879 Guelph's population had reached 9,890. It was incorporated as a city and Mr. Howard became the first mayor. Guelph, in the years to follow, developed into a major manufacturing centre. The Guelph Soap Co., the Royal Knitting Co., owners of one of Canada's largest knitting mills, and James Steele Ltd., makers of carriage springs, valve springs, etc., were only a few of the industries established in the city during the 1880's.

In 1887 the city built the Guelph Junction Railway, a 16-mile connecting link with the CPR. This railway gives Guelph the distinction of being the only city in Canada to own its own railroad. Known locally as the "Toonerville Trolley", the railroad's profits have been used throughout the years to reduce municipal taxes.

By the early 1900's the city's industries included the Guelph Furniture Manufacturing Ltd., which at the time owned and operated more furniture factories than any other furniture firm in the world; Colonial Whitewear Co. Ltd., the largest manufacturer of ladies' quality dresses and shirtwaists in Canada; Guelph Oiled Clothing Co. Ltd., which first made rainproof outdoor clothing available in Canada; Aspinwall Manufacturing Co., the largest makers of potato machinery in the world; and Gibson Manufacturing Co. Ltd., then the largest manufacturer of gasoline engines for farm use in the Commonwealth.

Between 1971 and 1978 Guelph's population increased from 58,606 to 71,349. The city has expanded in area as well, annexing parts of the Township of Puslinch and parts of Guelph Township in the sixties and early seventies. An Industrial Park was established in 1957 and today Guelph has over 120 industries with products ranging from electrical and radio supplies to leather goods and textiles. It serves as a shipping centre for Windsor-Detroit, North Bay, Montreal, and Western New York. The many intersecting provincial highways have led to the city being nicknamed the "Main Street of Ontario".

Guelph has long had a reputation as an educational centre. Its earliest schoolhouse was one of its first buildings. David Matthews was the settlement's first teacher. In 1854 Arthur Cole Verner became principal of Guelph's first grammar school. Rev. John Holzer founded the boys' college of St. Ignatius in the mid-nineteenth century and by 1883 had opened two separate schools, St. Stanislaus for boys and St. Agnes for girls. By 1906 the city had 8 public schools and a high school. More schools were built in the twentieth century and by 1963 twenty-five schools were giving instruction to the children of the city, including John F. Ross Vocational Institute, Guelph College and Vocational Institute, and two other high schools. St. Stanislaus Novitiate is an English-speaking Jesuit novitiate. A school for handicapped children is held in the Crippled Children's Centre and a special school is held for retarded children.

The University of Guelph has a long history. It began as three separate colleges. The Ontario Veterinary College, founded in Toronto in 1862, was the first institute in Canada to offer courses in veterinary medicine. It moved to Guelph in 1922. In 1874 the Ontario Agricultural College was opened with William Johnston as principal. By the 1950's it was the largest agricultural school in the Commonwealth. The Macdonald Institute was established in the early 1900's. In the 1960's the three colleges known as the "Federated Colleges", applied for university status. This was granted and in 1964 the University of Guelph was formed. Today the university carries out the majority of Ontario's agricultural research.

The Guelph Business College was in existence at the turn of the century. Over the years a number of training schools have been established in Guelph, including a wireless training school, a pilot training centre, and an annual police school of instruction, started in the 1960's. Guelph is also the site of the Ontario Reformatory, built in 1908, and used as a boys' training school.

Guelph's first library was started in 1832 by Thomas Sandilands. It became a Mechanics' Institute in 1850 and the first free library in Canada in 1883. The library moved into a new building in 1905.

The city's first newspaper was the weekly *Advertiser*, founded in 1845. The *Herald* began publication in 1847 and in 1854 G.M. Keeling started to print the *Mercury*. By 1867 the *Guelph Evening Mercury* was the largest country paper in Canada. In 1873 the *Advertiser* amalgamated with the *Daily Mercury* to form today's *Mercury*. Among the editors was Thomas B. Costain, noted Canadian author, who edited the paper from 1907-1910. The city is the headquarters of the Wellington Historical Society, founded in 1928, which since then has put out several volumes of historical *Records*.

Music and theatre have been noteworthy in the city's life for most of its history. Noah Sunley organized Guelph's first band in the 1840's. In 1898 the Guelph Musical Society was founded and the Guelph Pipe Band was formed in 1922. A music festival, the Guelph Spring Festival, became an annual event. Both the Guelph Concert Singers and the Guelph Little Theatre are active in entertainment.

From 1871 to 1915 the city was the site of the Guelph Central Exhibition. The Guelph Horticultural Society, founded in 1900, is the largest of its kind in Ontario.

When he founded Guelph, John Galt reserved three sites on the hills of the future city for churches. The churches to be erected on these sites were the Roman Catholic Church; St. Andrew's Presbyterian, constructed in 1832; and the Episcopal Church. In 1876 the Church of Our Lady of the Immaculate Conception was built by the Roman Catholic congregation. It was styled after that magnificent Gothic cathedral in West Germany, Cologne Cathedral, and is today a landmark in the city of Guelph.

The pioneer missionary in the settlement was the Roman Catholic Father Campion, who ministered to the people in 1827. The Jesuit Fathers came to Guelph in 1852. Rev. John Holzer was the first Superior. James Smith, who arrived in 1832, was the first Protestant clergyman in Guelph. He oversaw the building of St. Andrew's, first church in the community. The Congregational Church was formed in 1834 and worshipped in the house of Samuel Wright. A meetinghouse was constructed in 1840 under Rev. W.P. Wastell. This became Trinity United Church in 1925.

In 1834 the Anglican church, St. George's, was erected and in 1836 the Methodist congregation was organized by Rev. Mr. Fear. The organization of the Baptist church took place in 1853. In 1868 Rev. Dr. Wardrope began preaching at the Presbyterian Chalmers' Church. Today there are over 35 churches in the city.

Guelph has two main hospitals and a mental hospital. Rev. John Holzer founded St. Joseph's Hospital in the second half of the nineteenth century. The General Hospital opened in 1872. In 1883 Homewood Sanatorium began to receive patients.

Sports have always been an important part of Guelph residents' lives. In 1864 the fourth Queen's Plate was run here. In 1874 the "Maple Leafs" of Guelph became the World Amateur Baseball Champions. Today the Thanksgiving Day Roadraces are held every year in the city and are the largest such races in Canada.

Besides contributing a number of well-known players, such as Lou Fontinato, to the National Hockey League, Guelph has also produced champions in other sports. These include Jack Purcell, world champion at badminton; Jack Taylor, Canadian badminton champion; Fred Meadows, one of Canada's best middle-distance runners; and George Orton, who held the Canadian record for the mile.

Guelph also has been the home of many distinguished Canadians in arts, finance, and politics. Lieut.-Col. John McCrae, physician, soldier, poet, and the author of "In Flanders Fields" lived here, as did the poets Thomas Laidlaw and James Gay, that self-proclaimed "Poet Laureate of Canada". John McLean, a noted nineteenth century explorer and author of a valuable book on the fur trade, lived in Guelph for ten years. Major Samuel Strickland, early Canadian author, came to the community in 1829. Frank Coffee produced the Commonwealth's first atlas and geography. F. Boyce Waters, Eddie Smith, and Evan MacDonald are among the city's artists. Edward Johnson (1878-1959), one of the world's leading operatic tenors and a principal member of the New York Metropolitan Opera, is another of Guelph's sons. Edward C. Cutten, a spectacular grain market manipulator, became known as "King of the Chicago Wheat Pit". James J. Hill was a pioneer railroad builder in the northwest United States. Lester B. Pearson, former Prime Minister of Canada and winner of the Nobel Peace Prize, lived in Guelph when he was young, and Olive Diefenbaker, wife of another former Prime Minister, John Diefenbaker, taught at Guelph Collegiate.

The 100-foot wide Main Street of Guelph is bordered on each side by limestone edifices. A special law decrees that all buildings erected on Main Street must be constructed out of the local grey limestone. In one of the city parks a mechanical floral clock adds beauty as well as telling the hours of the day. Tourist attractions include the John McCrae Home, the Streetcar and Electrical Railway Museum, and the Kortright Waterfowl Park, a wildlife area and waterfowl research centre.

Jim and June Cameron: The Early Days in Guelph, 1967.

Guelph Chamber of Commerce: Guide to Guelph, 1972.

Guelph, The Royal City, 1958.

Leo. A. Johnson: History of Guelph 1827-1927, 1969.

Mercury Centennial Edition, 1954.

Ontario Historical Society Papers, Sept. 2, 1962.

Carol Priamo: Mills of Canada, 1976.

Wellington Historical Society Papers, 1933.

Frank Wood: "Guelph, Its Founding and Its Growth" in "Canadian Geographical Journal", 1964.

GUIBORD, geographic township, Cochrane District
Position 48° 30′ 80° 13′

Located to the southwest of the town of Matheson, the township was subdivided in 1905 and was named after Onesime Guibord, MPP for Russell around the turn of the century. Highway 572 passes along the western border, while Highway 101 skirts the northern boundary linking the area with all major centres to the west, north and south.

GUILFORD, township, Provisional County of Haliburton
Position 45° 00′ 78° 34′

Guilford was surveyed in 1862. Of all the townships in Haliburton, Guilford has the largest water surface. Redstone Lake alone, covers 2,500 acres.

The first settlers who came around 1869 were George Kelso, William Overton, and Francis Coates. They took Lots 25, 26 and 30 on the 2nd Concession. William Edward, Samuel Lane, Robert McCormick and John Masselas followed and settled on the 1st and 2nd Concessions. Around Eagle Lake the early homesteaders were Thomas Agnew, Robert Groom, William Haskins, Thomas Merry and Edward Ward. The post office at Eagle Lake, established in 1873, was operated by Charles Wensley.

The first lot in the western part of the township was purchased in 1872 by Stephen Benson. The W.W. Roberts family were early residents in the Pine Lake area. James Stevens purchased land in Guilford Township in 1875.

The nearest post office to the West Guilford settlement was at Maple Lake. Nelson Barnum became the first postmaster when an office was opened at his home. He was followed as postmaster by his son-in-law, Mark Sisson, who also kept Guilford's first general store.

The first school in Guilford, S.S. No. 2 and 3, was built in the early 1880's from squared pine timber. A larger brick building was erected in 1895. The latest school building was built in 1948. One of the first teachers at the log school was a Miss Gregan. Miss Addy Smith was the first to teach at the brick schoolhouse.

The first church in the township was erected by the Baptists in 1906. Saint Andrew's Anglican Church was built in 1931. Gospel Chapel, a brick structure, was completed in 1956.

A large cooperage mill which operated at the foot of Eagle Lake from 1933 to the 1950's, was twice destroyed by fires, once in 1935 and again in 1940.

Guilford was at one time noted for its horse races. George Barry, proprietor of the Minden Hotel in the 1890's, organized the first races.

Guilford Township is part of the municipal unit of Dysart, Bruton, Clyde, Dudley, Eyre, Guilford, Harburn, Harcourt and Havelock Townships. The combined population of these townships is 3,379 (1978).

Nila Reynolds: *In Quest of Yesterday*, 1967.

GUILFOYLE, geographic township, Cochrane District
Position 49° 46′ 82° 22′

The name origin of this township is unknown. Located north of Kapuskasing, the township's southern part is traversed by railway lines of the Spruce Falls Power & Paper Co. In the centre lies Guilfoyle Lake, accessible by road from Kapuskasing.

GUINDON, geographic township, Algoma District
Position 47° 11′ 82° 38′

Shown on recent maps as Township 7Z, Guindon was since named after the Hon. Fernand Guindon, MPP for Stormont. In the north and west the township borders on Sudbury District and to the south lies the Mississagi Wild River Provincial Park.

    White Owl Lake in the southeast corner is linked by portages to the lakes in the northwestern section. There are no other roads in the township.

GUNDY, geographic township, Kenora District
Position 49° 48′ 95° 05′

Bordering in the west on the Province of Manitoba, this township west of Kenora was named after a prominent Toronto family. James Henry Gundy was a financier and a partner in the noted investment firm of Wood, Gundy & Co.

GUNTER, community, Cashel Township, Hastings County
Position 44° 53′ 77° 33′

The community of Gunter is located in the southwest corner of Cashel Township. It developed on the Old Madawaska Road, a rough lumbering road at best in the early days. It took a surveyor by the name of Henry A. Macleod eleven days to reach the township from Belleville in 1806, using this route.

    Gunter was at that time the chief settlement of the township. It was named after four Gunter brothers who arrived from Murray Township: Abraham, Ephriam, John Harvey and Hiram. Among the other early settlers were the Trumbles, Kemps, Weeses and Kellys.

    The first water-powered mill in the vicinity was put into operation by James Cunningham around 1865. The same year a small school, containing only log seats without desks, was built. This building became the woodshed for a larger schoolhouse erected ten years later. A frame building eventually replaced it but in 1951 it was closed, students being transported to Gilmour.

    One of the pioneering Gunter brothers, John Harvey, became the community's first postmaster (1883-1901). It is said that he kept a rooster in his kitchen to assist him in meeting his obligation to be in Gilmour at 7 a.m. each morning to pick up the mail. His nephew, Abram Gunter, was responsible for the erection of the Free Methodist

Church in 1894.

Agriculture and timber have been the main occupations of the area residents during the present century. Unfortunately some people have, as a result of soil exhaustion and agricultural competition, been forced to leave the area, thus decreasing the trade in small centres such as Gunter. Lumbering remains as the most important source of livelihood in this northern community of Hastings County.

An abundance of lakes just north of Gunter offer excellent fishing; and the area is frequented by rock and mineral hunters who find treasures for their collections in the abandoned mines.

Gerald E. Boyce: *Historic Hastings*, 1967.

GUNTERMAN, geographic township, Algoma District
Position 46° 25′ 82° 38′

Originally designated as Township 149, it now commemorates the name of Karl Gunterman, a Sault Ste Marie prospector who first discovered the evidence of radio-activity south of the Elliot Lake area that resulted in the discovery and mining of uranium and put the town of Elliot Lake on the map. This mining town, which came into existence in 1954, forms the hub of the township.

GURNEY, geographic township, Cochrane District
Position 49° 30′ 82° 10′

Gurney is located a few miles northeast of Kapuskasing. Its boundaries were surveyed in 1900 and 1906, and it was named after Edward Gurney, President of the Gurney Foundry Co. of Canada. A large portion of Remi Lake Provincial Park occupies the south central part of the township.

GUTHRIE, geographic township, Nipissing District
Position 45° 45′ 77° 50′

Guthrie Township, established and surveyed in 1890 and believed to have been named after Donald Guthrie, Q.C., MPP for Wellington South 1886-90, is part of the vast Algonquin Provincial Park.

It is located in the southeastern part of the park and is linked by secondary road to the Bonnechère Provincial Park on Highway 62 about 20 miles to the southeast.

GUTHRIE, community, Oro Township, Simcoe County
Position 44° 28′ 79° 33′

This small rural community is situated on Highway 11, approximately eight miles northeast of Barrie. The early settlers in the area came before 1840 and among them were the McCuaig, Cameron, Reid, Gilchrist, Morrison, Campbell, Sinclair, Graham, McCulloch, and MacDougald families.

The settlement was named after two men who happened to have the same surname. In 1867 Thomas Guthrie, a local settler, wrote to friends in Scotland requesting help in the way of funds for the completion of the settlement's church. Money was sent to Canada with the stipulation that the church be called Guthrie, after the great Scottish minister, Dr. Thomas Guthrie. Thus both church and settlement became known as Guthrie, after the Scottish minister and the local family.

The first school in the Guthrie area was built in 1843. Later another school was erected in 1866. Increased settlement made another school necessary and thus a third schoolhouse was built in 1887. In 1958 the third school was replaced by a new two-room building. Finally, in 1965, this structure was replaced by a new central school.

In 1862 the first Presbyterian Church was opened on the site of the present United Church. This frame building was replaced by a brick structure in 1892. In 1925, at the time of church union, the church became known as Guthrie United Church.

At the turn of the century, Guthrie had a sawmill, grist mill, chopping mill, two blacksmith shops, a wheelwright shop and several general stores. A cheese factory opened in 1890 but was closed down in the early 1900's. A post office was established in the community in 1876 and it was first operated by the Guthrie family. In 1971 the population of Guthrie was 188.

Oro Historical Committee: *The Story of Oro*, 1972.

GZOWSKI, geographic township, Thunder Bay District
Position 50° 18′ 87° 30′

This township, traversed by the Canadian National Railways north-western Ontario branch line, bears the name of one of Canada's noted railway builders. Sir Casimir Stanislaus Gzowski came to Canada in 1842, and his name is associated with the construction of the St. Lawrence and Atlantic Railway, portions of the Grand Trunk Railway, and it was he who built the International Bridge across the Niagara and planned the extensive parks system along the river on the Canadian bank.

The township is located east of the northern tip of Lake Nipigon. Its western boundary was surveyed in 1916, its southern boundary in 1925. Both the northern and eastern borders remain unsurveyed.

H

HABEL, geographic township, Cochrane District
Position 50° 25' 82° 34'

Named after Joseph A. Habel, MPP for Cochrane North in 1934-37, this township is watered by the Missinaibi and various other smaller rivers. It is located some 50 miles, as the crow flies, northwest of the town of Kapuskasing.

The nearest known settlement is that of Smoky Falls, some 20 miles to the southeast.

HADDO, geographic township, Sudbury District
Position 46° 14' 80° 22'

Situated west of Lake Nipissing, this township was subdivided in 1897 and it was named after Haddo House, seat of the Earl of Aberdeen, in Aberdeenshire, Scotland. Its boundaries were surveyed in the years 1882-1896. It is bordered to the east by the District of Nipissing and Highway 64 runs parallel with its eastern boundary line.

HADLEY, geographic township, Algoma District
Position 47° 27' 84° 10'

Formerly designated as Township 25, Range 17, this township was named in 1914 after B.L. Hadley, Reeve of Chapple Township, Rainy River District, at that time. The area lies about 10 miles to the north of the Montreal River and was part of the Algoma Central and Hudson Bay Railway Land Grant.

HAENTSCHEL, geographic township, Sudbury District
Position 47° 11' 80° 52'

The township is situated about 30 miles directly north of Capreol. Its boundaries were surveyed in 1909 and it was named after Dr. C. W. Haentschel of Haileybury. A dry-weather road links the area with Wanapitei Lake to the south. The Wanapitei River waters the southwestern part of the township.

HAGAR, township, Sudbury District
Position 46° 30' 80° 29'

Situated less than twenty miles east of the city of Sudbury, the township was named after Albert Hagar, MPP for Prescott, 1882-83. It was subdivided by Ontario Land Surveyor Purvis in 1892.

There is little industry in Hagar, as most of the residents work in nearby Sudbury. Eighteen commercial buildings, two churches, and two elementary schools serve the 1,081 (1978) inhabitants of the township, many of whom live in mobile-home parks. Recreational facilities include an arena, a recreation hall, and an outdoor rink, while two hotels provide accommodation for visitors. Markstay is a small community situated on the Veuve River near the western border.

Highway 17 passes through the southern section of Hagar, as does the Canadian Pacific Railway.

Ministry of Natural Resources: *Directory of Statistics and Data for Incorporated Communities in Northeastern Region,* 1975.

HAGARTY, geographic township, Renfrew County
Position 43° 33' 77° 29'

Hagarty Township, located south of the Bonnechère Provincial Park, was formed in 1868 and has been in municipal union with Richards Township since that time.

It lies between and to the west of Round and Golden Lakes reputed to be two of the most beautiful lakes in Eastern Canada, and a popular spot for tourists.

The township was named in honour of the Honourable J.H. Hagarty, who was appointed Chief Justice of Ontario in 1868.

Hagarty and Richards combined have an acreage of 70,796.8 and a population of 1,284.

Highways 60 and 62 serve the area and link it with Barry's Bay to the west and Pembroke to the northeast. Killaloe Station west of Golden Lake, and on the CNR, is the site of a weather station.

Mrs. Carl Price and Clyde C. Kennedy: *Notes on the History of Renfrew County,* 1961.

HAGERMAN, township, Parry Sound District
Position 45° 37' 79° 54'

This township was established in 1869 and subdivided that same year by T. Byrne. It was named in honour of Judge Christopher Alex Hagerman.

Located north of Parry Sound, the area is linked to that town by Highway 124. The township has a population of 400 (1979) with most of the inhabitants living at Dunchurch or Fairholme.

George Kelcey, a painter and contractor from Rugby, England, was the first to settle at the site of Dunchurch which by the late 1870's had developed into the principal village of the township. Beautifully located at a narrow channel that connects the southern and northern

198

part of Whitestone Lake, the settlement had a post office, a steam sawmill, a wagon maker's shop and a blacksmith shop, a schoolhouse, a union meeting house and a Methodist church. Dunchurch is situated on what was known in the pioneering days as the North Road, the main artery of travel from Parry Sound into the interior of the District.

The early settlers in the township depended on lumbering and farming for their livelihood. Their farms were productive and, although neighbouring townships to the south were longer settled, Hagerman's farmers were the first in the northern part of the district to send grain to market in Parry Sound; no produce was marketed, however, in the year 1872 when grasshoppers ate all the crops. Mr. Kelcey is said to have raised such fine potatoes in other years, that the government agent sent some to Paris, France, at the time of the Exhibition.

Today the township with its many lakes and streams attracts tourists and fishermen in increasing numbers.

HAGERSVILLE, part of the Town of Haldimand, Regional Municipality of Haldimand-Norfolk
Position 42° 58′ 80° 03′

This community, now part of the town of Haldimand, is located on Highway 6 approximately twenty-three miles southwest of Hamilton.

The settlement was named after an early pioneer, David Hager, who built a hotel on the site in 1842. For many years the place was little more than a stopover for the daily stage between Hamilton and Port Dover. Eventually, James Haskett established a store there and a settlement began to grow. Among the first to make their homes here were U.B. Almas, David Almas, J.H. Porter, and David Hager's brother, Charles Hager. In 1852 a post office was established and the settlement was named Hagersville.

The Canada Southern Railway building a line between Windsor and Niagara Falls in the 1870's, passed through Hagersville, and the Hamilton and Lake Erie Railway arrived about the same time, greatly stimulating the economy of the settlement. In 1870 Charles Hager, David Almas, and John H. Porter had laid out town lots, but their plans for immediate growth were hampered somewhat because the boundaries of an Oneida Indian Reservation extended to the centre of the village. Nevertheless, by 1875 Hagersville was incorporated as a police village, with Dr. R. McDonald as the first reeve. For some reason, however, this incorporation was set aside and two years later the village was incorporated once again. This time P.R. Howard was elected as reeve.

A Methodist church was erected in Hagersville in 1869. Following the formation of the United Church of Canada in 1925, it became the Hagersville United Church. The Hagersville Presbyterian congregation used various buildings for its services over the years until a new stone church was built in 1883. St. Mary's Roman Catholic Church was erected in 1914 and Hagersville Baptist Church opened in 1883. All Saints' Anglican Church was built in 1870 and the

Pentecostal Church in 1933.

The Hagersville Public Library was first organized as a Mechanics' Institute in 1894. In 1897 a Free Library was established and in 1972 the library was re-organized and rebuilt as the Davison Centre.

In 1974 Hagersville village amalgamated with the Town of Caledonia, the Village of Cayuga, the Township of North Cayuga, the Township of Oneida, the Township of Seneca and the Township of South Cayuga, to result in the Town of Haldimand within the newly-formed Regional Municipality of Haldimand-Norfolk.

Russell Harper: *The Early History of Haldimand County*, 1950.

Mabel Burkholder: *The Hagersville Story*, 1950.

HAGEY, geographic township, Thunder Bay District
Position 48° 37' 90° 14'

Lying in the Shebandowan Lakes area this township is largely covered with water. The Canadian National Railways passes through the northern half, with a station point at Kabaigon at the northwestern tip of the township. The southern, eastern and western boundaries of Hagey were surveyed in 1938, and it was named after H. Louis Hagey, MPP for Brantford around that time.

HAGGART, geographic township, Cochrane District
Position 49° 15' 81° 46'

Situated just to the west of the town of Smooth Rock Falls, the township was named for Sir John Haggart, MP for Lanark and Cabinet Minister from 1889-1892.

Both the Canadian National Railways and Highway 11 pass through the northern half of this area, linking it to Kapuskasing, farther northwest, and Cochrane to the southeast.

Various small lakes dot the landscape, and the Muskego River meanders through the southeastern corner.

HAIG, geographic township, Algoma District
Position 49° 15' 84° 35'

The township is located approximately 10 miles to the south of Nagagamisis Provincial Park. It is dotted with various lakes and was named after Field Marshall Haig, Commander in Chief of the British Forces in the Great War of 1914.

The Canadian National Railways crosses the southern part of the township and secondary roads link the area to Hornepayne, six miles to the west.

HAIGHT, geographic township, Cochrane District
Position 50° 48' 81° 48'

Located just north of the Missinaibi River, the Cheepash River bisects the township, and numerous other rivers and creeks flow westward through the area.

The township was named after W.L. Haight, K.C., of Parry Sound.

HAILEYBURY, town, Bucke Township, Timiskaming District
Position 47° 27′ 79° 38′

This town on the west shore of Lake Timiskaming, is located five miles northeast of Cobalt and five miles south of New Liskeard, on Highway 11. The Ontario Northland Railway also serves Haileybury.

A man named Humphrey had cleared some land by 1883 at the site where Haileybury stands and he sold hay to lumbering companies operating in the area. However, he was only a squatter on the land. Settlement at Haileybury did not begin until the arrival of Charles C. Farr in 1889.

Farr had attended the exclusive public school of Haileybury in England. Here boys were trained for imperial service with the East India Company and the Hudson's Bay Company. He became an employee of the latter and in Canada was involved in the survey of the Ontario-Quebec boundary. On a visit to Lake Timiskaming his imagination was captured by the natural beauty along the shore and he dreamed of establishing a thriving town there. In 1887 he purchased the rights to Humphrey's holding from a man named Louis Sirouin, who had acquired the title to the land in 1884. That same year Farr built a log house halfway up the hillside above the spot where the Haileybury Wharf now stands. In 1889 Farr moved his family to the new wilderness home and several other settlers followed, including P.T. Lawlor. Previously, the spot had been known as Matabanick, an Indian name meaning "the place where the trail comes out". Mr. Farr renamed the settlement "Haileybury" in remembrance of the college of his English school days.

Farr felt settlement at Haileybury was slow because of the misconception that the north was too cold for agricultural purposes. Inadequate transportation facilities were also a drawback. The community was accessible only by water. Settlers coming in by water had to transfer from steamboat to small boats, their farm animals swimming ashore. While Farr's settlement was a trading centre for the pioneers, farmers bypassed Haileybury seeking out pockets of the rich clay belt soil in the area.

Wishing to encourage immigrants to settle the area, Farr wrote several pamphlets on colonization that were distributed by British steamship companies. Attracted by the pamphlets, English pioneers set up businesses. In 1889 Haileybury was named as a post office, the first on the west shore of the lake. Paul Cobbold became the first postmaster and also ran a general store. When Indian mothers shopped here, they hung their babies in their Indian cradles on a tree outside the store. Siegfried Atkinson, with his brother, operated another general store; John Westron ran a hardware business. Stuart Blackwell and S. Norfolk were other newcomers. Dr. H.R. Codd was the first resident doctor in Haileybury. A police department with

Charles Philips as first chief began in 1903. By this time construction of a railway, as planned, was assured. The first railway station in Haileybury was simply a boxcar.

In 1903 news of the discovery of silver in Cobalt marked a turning point for Haileybury. The Matabanic Hotel, already built, expanded and three other hotels were built: the Vendome, the Attorney and the Maple Leaf. Here in 1904 the first of many mining deals were made. With the silver boom, Haileybury's commerce expanded. Four banks opened, the first being the Union. The Haileyburian, owned by Charles C. Farr, began publication under Vic Oliver, editor. It is the oldest weekly newspaper in northern Ontario. A mining Recorder's office was established to handle mining claims and lawyers came in to handle mining litigation. Other services, such as a newly built Government Dock, a public library, a curling club, a Horticultural Society were organized, and a Freemasons and Oddfellows were instituted. The facilities for lake travel and shipping made Haileybury a communications centre for the surrounding areas. Cobalt was a camp of tents and the wealthy mine owners made their residence in Haileybury.

Haileybury, Cathedrale Couvent Srs de l'Assomption, c. 1914

Public Archives Canada PA 30216

Population figures climbed for the next eight years to peak at 4000, which was maintained until 1922. In 1904 Haileybury was incorporated as a town and P.T. Lawlor was the first mayor. In 1912 Haileybury became the District Seat of Timiskaming.

In 1905 the Nipissing Central Railway linked Kerr Lake with Haileybury and New Liskeard and this, as well as the Cobalt silver mines, promoted several new industries: the Haileybury Brick Company, the Energite Explosive Company, the Dominion Express Company (carriage manufacturers), and a cigar factory, producer of the famous "Northern Lights" cigars.

The first school, a one-room school, was opened in 1894 under a Mrs. Clifford. This was followed in 1909 by a new public school and yet another in 1910. In 1910 the first high school north of North Bay was built and in that same year a separate school opened. The Sisters of Assumption also operated a school and novitiate known as St. Mary's Academy. The Provincial Institute of Mining, a school of mining, was established in 1909.

Early religious services were held in the home of Charles C. Farr, and the first proper church building, Anglican, was constructed in 1896. St. Andrew's Presbyterian Church was erected in 1898 and the Central Methodist Church followed shortly afterwards. From 1910 to 1912 both congregations rebuilt their churches. In the holocaust of the 1922 fire both churches were destroyed. Because of church union in 1925 only St. Andrew's Church was rebuilt; it was renamed St. Andrew's United Church. Haileybury is also the seat of the Roman Catholic Diocese and a Roman Catholic Cathedral was erected in 1909.

Throughout its history, Haileybury has been plagued by fires. In 1889 Farr's early settlement was threatened by a conflagration in the area. In 1906 fire swept through the community and destroyed the centre of the town. Haileybury rebuilt. In 1922 a disastrous fire overcame Haileybury and many of the surrounding communities leaving these towns and villages in ashes. Over 200,000 acres were destroyed, $6,000,000 worth of property was lost and 43 lives were claimed. Haileybury, its heyday as a boom town over, settled into a quieter existence.

Tourism is a thriving industry today. Hunting and fishing are popular with sportsmen, and vacationers can enjoy the cool waters and sandy beaches of Lake Timiskaming. In 1978 the population of Haileybury was 4,997.

North Bay Nugget, 1967.

S. John Mason: Haileybury, 1974.

Terence D. Tait: Haileybury: The Early Years, 1963.

G.L. Cassidy: Arrow North — The Story of Temiskaming, 1976.

HAINES, geographic township, Thunder Bay District
Position 48° 57' 90° 21'

Situated in the Shebandowan Lakes area, the township is named after J. Haines, MPP for Lincoln, 1937. Its southern and eastern boundaries were surveyed in 1938. A large portion of the township is occupied by parts of the Middle Shebandowan Lake and of Greenwater Lake. Canadian National Railways passes through the northern section of the township with a station point at Postans. Highway 11 runs almost parallel with the railway line.

HALCROW, geographic township, Sudbury District
Position 47° 48' 82° 56'

Named after George C. Halcrow, MPP for Hamilton East in 1919, this township is situated approximately 20 miles north of Wakami Lake Provincial Park. The Ivanhoe River flows through the northwest corner, and several small unnamed lakes and rivers are also in the area.

HALDIMAND, geographic county
Position 42° 57' 79° 50'

The geographic county of Haldimand encompasses a portion of the fertile southwestern Ontario farmlands that lie along the northern shore of Lake Erie. The county is bounded on the west by Brant County and the geographic county of Norfolk; on the east by Lincoln and Welland counties (now the Regional Municipality of Niagara); on the north by Wentworth County (now the Regional Municipality of Hamilton-Wentworth); and on the south by Lake Erie. The county was named after Sir Frederick Haldimand, Governor-in-Chief of Canada 1778-1786, and the man who planned the settlement of thousands of United Empire Loyalists in the wilderness of Upper Canada after the American Revolution.

The county contains part of a grant made in 1784 to the Six Nation Indians who were led by Loyalist Chief Joseph Brant. The land was given to the Indians by the government in grateful recognition of their support of the British cause during the American Revolution. Under the terms of the land grant, the Indians received a strip of land, twelve miles wide, lying on each side of the Grand River. The boundaries were two imaginary parallel lines running from the north shore of Lake Erie to where the city of Brantford stands today. In 1784 this grant comprised 310,391 acres.

Chief Brant was appointed Agent of the Nations and at his invitation many of the white officers who had fought for the British during the Revolution came north to settle on the Indian Lands. Among these pioneers were veterans of Butler's Rangers, a corps which, under Major John Butler, had valiantly fought to maintain the unity of the Empire during the Revolutionary War. John Huff, John Dochstader, the Sheehan brothers, and the Nelles and Young families were among those who arrived to settle in 1784. Other settlers also filtered into the area, including Perry Gifford, David Thompson, Richard Martin, the Hoover family, Jacob Fite, Peter Culver, Charles Anderson, Nicholas Cook, Thomas Runchy, Michael Sprangle, Edward Evans, and the Doans.

Many of the Indians were being cheated out of their land by white speculators and in 1832 a treaty was signed surrendering the Indian Lands again to the government.

New transportation facilities opened up the county for increased settlement. In 1833 the Grand River Navigation Company started construction on eight locks and dams. A plank road was built in 1839 from Hamilton to Port Dover. Today the "Plank Road" has become the route of Highway 6. In 1840 the Talbot Road (now Highway 3) was opened for traffic. Settlements that sprang up along the route included Jarvis, Hagersville and Caledonia. The pioneers also settled on the banks of the Grand River and Oswego Creek because these sites were accessible by boat and canoe.

Haldimand County was officially established in 1850. The new county included ten townships: Canborough, Cayuga North, Cayuga South, Dunn, Moulton, Oneida, Rainham, Seneca, Sherbrooke and, Walpole. The village of Cayuga became the county seat and Edmund Decew became the county's first Warden. The first newspaper in the County, the *Independent*, began publication in Cayuga in 1851. Cayuga was incorporated as a village in 1859.

In 1852 the Buffalo, Brantford and Goderich Railroad (later the Grand Trunk Railroad) built a line through the county. In 1870 the Great Western Loop Line and the Canadian Southern Railway was completed, and the Hamilton and Lake Erie Railroad was pushed through in 1878.

In its early days, Haldimand County was an important supplier of pine and oak timber. When most of the forests were depleted, the county developed a prosperous farming industry. Market gardening and dairying remain popular while several canning companies established in the area help to utilize the abundant farm produce. Gypsum mining is also an important industry. The mines are located on the extensive gypsum reserves situated near the village of Cayuga.

Prior to its formation as a regional municipality, the county's population was approximately 31,000 and contained two towns, Caledonia and Dunnville, and three villages, Cayuga, Hagersville and Jarvis. As a municipality, the county was dissolved effective April 1, 1974, as was the county of Norfolk, and both counties joined to become the Regional Municipality of Haldimand-Norfolk, having now a total population of about 86,668 (1979).

Dunnville retained its status as a town. The village of Jarvis became part of the newly created city of Nanticoke and a new town known as Haldimand was formed out of the former town of Caledonia and the former villages of Cayuga and Hagersville.

H.R. Page: *Historical Atlas of Haldimand and Norfolk Counties*, 1877.

Russell Harper: *The Early History of Haldimand County*, 1950.

HALDIMAND, geographic township, Northumberland County
Position 44° 05′ 78° 03′

This township, bordered on the south by Lake Ontario, is the largest township in terms of area in Northumberland County, comprising 80,710 acres. Highways 2 and 401 run through the southern portion of the township; Highway 45 runs through to the north. In 1978 the population of Haldimand Township was 3,364.

The township was surveyed in part in 1792 and was finally completed in 1822. It was named after Sir Frederick Haldimand, Governor-in-Chief of Canada 1778-1786.

Most of the original settlers were United Empire Loyalists. Joseph Keeler, David Rogers, Patrick Moore, and Benjamin Ewing were among the township's early pioneers. Soon mills were established all along Shelter Valley Creek and two busy harbours were in operation at Grafton and Lakeport. Both settlements had thriving milling, distilling and shipbuilding industries.

The Haldimand Township Council met in the present township hall for the first time in 1860. Until that time, meetings had been held in Grover's Tavern beginning as early as 1835.

In the early days of the township, most of the hills and fields were stripped of their timber by lumber companies until only a dry wasteland remained and the area was deemed unsuitable for cultivation. In 1924 the Northumberland County Forest Reserve was planted to repair these ravages. The Forest Reserve now covers an area along Highway 45 between Baltimore and Fenella.

There are several historic buildings located in Haldimand Township. The Barnum House in Grafton is an early example of domestic Georgian (or Canadian Loyalist) architecture. Colonel Eliakim Barnum, a United Empire Loyalist, built the house in 1817. Today it is a museum open to the public.

At the small settlement of Wicklow, about three miles east of Grafton, stands the oldest Baptist Church in Ontario. Erected in 1824, it, too, is a museum today.

Haldimand Township is a prosperous agricultural region. The area specializes in dairy farming, and apple and tobacco growing. In summer vacationers are attracted to the shores and harbours of Lake Ontario; in winter, they enjoy the ski hills in the Northumberland Forest Reserve.

Settlements in Haldimand Township include Fenella, Burnley, Oak Heights, Mill Valley, Centreton, Carmel, Eddystone, Vernonville, Brookside and The Gully.

United Counties Centennial Book Committee: *United Counties of Northumberland and Durham*, 1967.

The Great Pine Ridge Tourist Council: *Pine Ridge Travel Guide and Directory*, 1972-73.

HALDIMAND, town, Regional Municipality of Haldimand-Norfolk
Position 43° 00' 79° 50'

The town of Haldimand came into existence on April 1, 1974 with the formation of the new Regional Municipality of Haldimand-Norfolk. As a municipality, the town is composed of the former town of Caledonia, the former villages of Cayuga and Hagersville, and the former townships of North Cayuga, Oneida, Seneca, and South Cayuga. As well, Haldimand town annexed the former police villages of Canfield and Fisherville and parts of Rainham and Walpole Townships. The town is named after Sir Frederick Haldimand, Governor-in-Chief of Canada from 1778 to 1786.

In the early days the community of Caledonia grew side by side with the settlement of Seneca until the Hamilton and Port Dover Plank Road came through Caledonia and a bridge was built across the Grand River, both advancing its importance. In 1840 the community was laid out and the town plot took in the village of Seneca and was then known by that name. Among the first settlers in the community was Ronald McKinnon who changed the name to Caledonia, built a sawmill and a store, built a dam and lock for the Grand River

Navigation Company, erected a grist mill in 1844 and a woollen factory in 1848. When Caledonia was incorporated as a village in 1853, Ronald McKinnon became the first reeve.

Now part of the town of Haldimand, Hagersville is located on Highway 6 approximately 23 miles southwest of Hamilton. David Hager, an early pioneer, gave Hagersville its name when the post office was established in 1852. Other early settlers were U.B. Almas, David Almas, J.H. Porter and Charles Hager, brother to David.

A stopover for the daily stage between Hamilton and Port Dover, Hagersville was given an economic lift when the Canada Southern Railway ran a line between Windsor and Niagara Falls through the community in 1870. About this same time the Hamilton and Lake Erie Railway also arrived. In 1875 Hagersville was incorporated as a police village with D.R. McDonald as first reeve. This, however, was set aside for another two years, when it was incorporated once again with P.R. Howard elected as reeve.

Situated on Highway 3, 10 miles north of Lake Erie, Cayuga is named for the Cayugas of the Six Nations Indians, grantees of land here in 1784 by Sir Frederick Haldimand, then Governor of Upper Canada. The Indians were given permission by Indian Treaty to sell off their lands for settlement and the first settlers arrived in 1833. Among them were John Welch, Michael Finlan, John Waters, Duncan Campbell, and Joe Hursell, later first reeve of the village. In 1851 a post office was established and eight years later Cayuga was incorporated as a town. With the Grand River providing water transportation, lumbering was the chief industry of the village. Centrally located, Cayuga was the county seat of Haldimand County before regional government was established in the area.

Fisherville, 4 miles south of Highway 3 and about 3 miles from the north shore of Lake Erie, was settled in the early 1800's, the pioneers being mostly of German or French stock and arriving from the United States. It became the centre of a German settlement, the Lutheran faith predominating. Benjamin Ullman, Frederick Albert, George Held, George Nablo, Nicholas Raicheld, Jacob Rohrback and Christian Snell were among the early pioneers.

About 9 miles northwest of Dunnville, Canfield, located on Highway 3 and the Canadian National Railways, developed at a point where the survey for a branch of the Grand Trunk Railway from Goderich to Buffalo crossed the Talbot Road. First called Azoff, after a Russian village prominent during the Crimean War, the railway station was named Canfield, after Albert Canfield, local builder and contractor, when the railway was completed in 1859. A busy supply centre and stopover for travellers in the 1850's, Canfield had several stores, hotels, blacksmith shops and sawmills. Early settlers in the 1840's were William Haynes, W.G. Murphy, Stephan Street, G.A. Weaver and Peter Schram. Prior to April 1, 1974 when it became part of the new Regional Municipality of Haldimand-Norfolk, Canfield, a pleasant rural community, was a police village in North Cayuga Township.

The combined resources of three thriving communities have

made Haldimand a prosperous town. Local industries include a stone quarry, gas wells, a wood flour factory and seed cleaning plant, and gypsum mines.

In 1978 the population of Haldimand was 16,427.

N. & H. Mika: *Places in Ontario*, 1977.

Mabel Burkholder: *The Hagersville Story*, 1950.

HALDIMAND-NORFOLK, regional municipality
Position 42° 49' 80° 05'

The Regional Municipality of Haldimand-Norfolk was incorporated on January 1, 1974 and consists of the city of Nanticoke, the town of Dunnville, the town of Haldimand, the town of Simcoe, the township of Delhi, and the township of Norfolk. Both the counties of Haldimand and Norfolk were dissolved to create the new municipality.

The town of Haldimand was created out of the former town of Caledonia, the former villages of Cayuga and Hagersville, and the former townships of North Cayuga, Oneida, Seneca, and South Cayuga. The town also annexed part of the townships of Rainham and Walpole.

Nanticoke, formerly an unincorporated settlement, was erected into a city on April 1, 1974. The new municipality is made up of the former towns of Port Dover and Waterford and the former village of Jarvis. Nanticoke also annexed part of the former townships of Rainham, Townsend, Walpole, and Woodhouse.

The town of Dunnville amalgamated with the former townships of Canborough, Dunn, Moulton and Sherbrooke in 1974. It retained its status as a town after the regional municipality was formed.

The town of Simcoe also retained its status as a town after the municipal changes. In 1974 it annexed parts of the former townships of Charlotteville, Townsend, Windham and Woodhouse.

The former town of Delhi lost its status and, with parts of the former townships of Charlotteville, Middleton, South Walsingham, and Windham, became a township municipality bearing the name of the Township of Delhi on April 1, 1974.

The new township of Norfolk was also formed on April 1, 1974 out of the former village of Port Rowan and the former townships of Houghton, and North Walsingham. Norfolk Township also annexed part of the former townships of Middleton, and South Walsingham.

The population of the Regional Municipality of Haldimand-Norfolk stood at 87,262 in 1979, with the city of Nanticoke accounting for more than 19,000. Haldimand is the largest town with a population of 16,426, followed by the town of Simcoe with 14,149 and the town of Dunnville with 11,470.

The region covers nearly 711,000 acres and is a prosperous farming district.

Municipal Directories 1974-1979.

HALFWAY LAKE PROVINCIAL PARK

Adjacent to Highway 144, 55 miles north of the city of Sudbury, itself on Highway 144, this Provincial Recreation Park of 3,840 acres provides campsites, beach facilities, fishing and nature trails.

A lumbering area in former years it is possible to canoe south on waterways to the end of Bailey Lake, a distance of some four miles, and see relics of an old wooden dam remaining from the early logging days.

Cartier to the south on Highway 144 is the nearest supply centre, while Levack, farther south on Highway 544, has shopping plazas, and a medical centre and ambulance service.

HALIBURTON, provisional county
Position 44° 10' 78° 31'

Haliburton, a tourist's paradise, is located in the central region of Ontario. It is bounded on the south by Victoria and Peterborough counties, on the west by the Muskoka District, on the east by Hastings County, and on the north by Nipissing District. Haliburton County is both rugged and beautiful; about 555 named lakes dot the countryside. The county also encompasses some of the highest land in the province, which accounts for the descriptive name for the area — The Haliburton Highlands. Haliburton County covers an area of 1,030,118 acres.

The county was named in honour of Judge Thomas Chandler Haliburton (1796-1865), noted Canadian historian and humorist, and first Chairman of the Canadian Land and Emigration Company. The company had bought several wilderness townships in the 1860's and developed settlements and industries for the new immigrants.

Originally, Haliburton County consisted of parts of Peterborough and Victoria counties. The townships of Galway, Snowdon and Minden from Peterborough County, and the townships of Lutterworth and Anson from Victoria County joined together to form an Independent Union of Townships, for municipal purposes, in 1859. In 1861 the township of Stanhope was attached to these and Galway became a separate municipality (eventually reuniting with Peterborough County). In that same year, Lutterworth and Anson townships separated from Snowdon, Minden, and Stanhope, and each became a separate municipality. The county of Haliburton, itself, was finally formed when these townships requested permission from Peterborough County to increase taxes and provide a bonus to encourage the construction of the Victoria Railway from Lindsay to Haliburton Village. Peterborough County denied permission for the plans, so the townships demanded separation. In 1874 the new county of Haliburton was created comprising twenty townships from Peterborough County and three from Victoria County. It is called a "Provisional" county because the full privileges and powers of a county were not granted at that time. The judicial system of the county is administered by the County of Victoria.

Today, Haliburton County consists of the independent townships of Cardiff, Glamorgan, Lutterworth, Monmouth, Snowdon and Stanhope; and the three united townships of (1) Anson, Hindon and Minden; (2) Sherborne, McClintock and Livingston; (3) Dysart, Bruton, Clyde, Dudley, Eyre, Guilford, Harburn, Harcourt and Havelock.

The first Haliburton county council met in 1874. A. Niven was the first county warden and S.S. Peck became the first county clerk and treasurer. Both the communities of Minden and Haliburton Village vied for the honour of county seat and Haliburton Village eventually won out.

The settlement of Haliburton County began when government colonization roads were constructed through the district. The Bobcaygeon Road was built from Port Hope north in 1856; the Peterson Road was built from the Ottawa Valley to Penetanguishene in 1859. The Canadian Land and Emigration Company, in the 1860's, opened up other parts of the territory for settlement.

The community of Minden is the oldest settlement in the county. Here settlers were found as early as 1859. A group of settlers homesteaded at the point where the Bobcaygeon Road crossed Gull River. By 1864 Minden already had a hotel, a blacksmith shop, several stores and a sawmill.

The settlement of Haliburton Village dates back to 1864 when the Canadian Land and Emigration Company surveyed a town site and built a sawmill there.

The county from the beginning thrived on the lumber industry. Several lumber companies have operated out of Haliburton Village through the years, including the Lucas and Ritchie Company, the William Laking Lumber Company, the W.O. Bailey and Son Company, the Malloy and Bryans Lumber Company, and the Austin and Roberts Lumber Company. The Donald Wood Products company was established in the settlement of Donald in 1908. The company which manufactured charcoal and chemicals, was later purchased by the Standard Chemical Company Limited, who operated until 1945. Later the holdings were sold to Canadian industrialist E.P. Taylor. Some uranium mining is carried out in the district.

In 1878 the long awaited Victoria Railway arrived and Haliburton Village became its northern terminus. Today, the railway is part of the Canadian National Railways system.

Haliburton County has many attractions for the tourist, vacationer and sportsman. In fact, Haliburton has been referred to as the "summer suburb of Toronto". Hunting and fishing abound and the Haliburton lakes are perfect for swimming and boating. The Haliburton School of Fine Arts is located in Haliburton Village and offers courses in photography, ceramics, weaving, jewellery, enamelling, sculpture, and creative writing. The Haliburton Highlands Museum is also located in the village and it offers displays on lumbering, mining, and pioneer life. Lawrence, Nightingale, Clyde and Bruton townships lie within the borders of the Algonquin Provincial Park, one of Canada's best known and best loved parklands.

There are no incorporated cities, towns or villages in Haliburton County. Besides Minden and Haliburton Village, other county communities are Gelert, Irondale, Gooderham and Wilberforce.

In 1978 the population of Haliburton County was 10,681.

Haliburton Highlands Chamber of Commerce: *Haliburton Highlands*, 1974.

History of the Provisional County of Haliburton, 1931.

Rotary Club of Haliburton: *Haliburton, 100 Years*, 1975.

HALIBURTON, community, Dysart Township, Haliburton County
Position 45° 03′ 78° 31′

This small community is situated at the head of Lake Kashagawigamog, at the junction of Highways 121, 519, and 530, approximately forty-five miles northeast of the town of Gravenhurst.

The village which is not incorporated but remains part of the township for municipal purposes, was founded by the Canadian Land and Emigration Company of London, England. The company had purchased several wilderness townships in the area for the purpose of settlement in the early 1860's. A town plot was surveyed by 1864 and Charles R. Stewart was appointed the first resident land agent. He thus became the first settler in the community.

The settlement was named in honour of Judge Thomas Chandler Haliburton (1796-1865), first Chairman of the Canadian Land and Emigration Company and noted Canadian historian and humorist.

Among the first settlers in the community were Captain John Lucas, Steve Thompson, James Erskine, David Sawyer, William Murray, William Gainforth, and James Holland.

In 1864 a sawmill was built by Messrs. Lucas and Ritchie on the town site. The Canadian Land and Emigration Company opened a store and a post office in the settlement that same year, with Charles Stewart as the first postmaster. A grist mill was added to the settlement's enterprises in 1865 and also in that year the first school and church were built.

St. George's Anglican Church, as the church was called by the tiny congregation, was nothing more than a small wooden cabin. A short while later it was rebuilt and Mrs. Haliburton, widow of the late Judge Haliburton, donated an organ to St. George's in memory of her husband. On January 25, 1920 this church burned to the ground, but a new brick church was erected to replace it. The new St. George's Church was dedicated by Bishop Sweeney of Toronto on October 24, 1923.

In 1875 the Presbyterians built their church in Haliburton and in the late 1870's the Methodists erected their house of worship. In 1904 a Baptist church was opened in the settlement.

The Victoria branch of the Midland Railway made Haliburton its terminus in 1875, ushering in a new era of prosperity. Today this railway is part of the Canadian National Railways system.

The lumber industry has always played an important part in the development of Haliburton village. Enterprising lumbermen, such as Mossom Boyd, operated large lumber camps in the area. Other companies who have operated sawmills in Haliburton village include the William Laking Lumber Company; W.O. Bailey and Son; the Malloy and Bryans Lumber Company; and the Austin and Roberts Lumber Company.

Haliburton village, today, is the home of the Haliburton School of Fine Arts, a branch of the Sir Sandford Fleming Community College. The school was established in 1967 and offers courses in photography, ceramics, weaving, jewellery, enamelling, sculpture, and creative writing.

The Haliburton Highlands Pioneer Museum opened in 1968 and here the visitor finds displays on lumbering, mining and pioneer life.

The community's location among the picturesque hills and lakes of the Haliburton Highland region has made it a favourite spot for tourists, vacationers and sportsmen.

According to the 1971 census the population of Haliburton village was 899.

Rotary Club of Haliburton: *Haliburton*, 1975.

HALIFAX, geographic township, Sudbury District
    Position 46° 14' 81° 01'

Situated south of the city of Sudbury, this township houses Lower White Oak Lake, W. Tanner Lake, and Halifax Lake.

It was named in 1945 after Lord Halifax of England. The Township's boundaries had been surveyed in 1873 and 1898. The area is linked by secondary and dry weather roads to Highway 69 to the east.

HALKIRK, geographic township, Rainy River District
Position 48° 44' 93° 00'

Subdivided in 1894, this township northeast of Fort Frances is named after a village in Caithnesshire, Scotland.

The township borders in the south on Swell Bay (Rainy Lake). Redgut Bay takes up much of the southeastern section of Halkirk. Highway 11 and the Canadian National Railways travel through the southern part.

HALL, geographic township, Sudbury District
Position 47° 22' 82° 24'

Partly subdivided, but completely annulled in 1962, the first survey was made in 1915. The township was named either after Zachariah A. Hall, MPP for Waterloo South in 1914, or Francis W. Hall, MPP for Lanark South in 1914.

The Mississagi Wild River Provincial Park encroaches in the southeastern corner of the township, and Tassie Lake and Macle Lake straddle the eastern boundary. Turf Lake, the largest in the vicinity, is more centrally located.

Secondary roads connect the area with Highway 17.

HALLAM, geographic township, Sudbury District
Position 46° 14' 81° 53'

Subdivided in 1883 and re-surveyed in 1934, this township, formerly a municipality in its own right, is named after John Hallam of Toronto. Since 1975 the area is part of the municipal township of Spanish River. Within Hallam's boundaries lies the community of Webbwood, a station point of the Canadian Pacific Railway.

The Spanish River flows through the northern half of the township emptying into the North Channel of Lake Huron. Highway 17 connects the township with Sudbury, to the northeast.

HALLEBOURG, community, Kendall Township, Cochrane District
Position 49° 40' 83° 31'

This hamlet of about 400 people is situated a few miles southeast of the town of Hearst, on Highway 11 and the Canadian National Railways.

Locally the place was called Holleywood by the early settlers who came to the area around the first decade of the 20th century. The community has a church and school.

HALLETT, geographic township, Algoma District
Position 47° 27' 84° 02'

Formerly known as township 24, Range 17, this township lies to the east of Lake Superior Provincial Park, and borders on the District of

Sudbury. It has a lake in the north named Convey Lake and Indian River meanders through the area to the Montreal River. There are no known roads in the township.

It is named after N.J. Hallett, former Reeve of Harris.

HALLIDAY, geographic township, Sudbury District
Position 47° 54' 81° 06'

Probably named after the Halliday family of Bruce County, this township borders on the east with the District of Timiskaming. Halliday Lake straddles the western boundary and the area encompasses Campbell Lake, Dumbell Lake and Relic Lake.

HALLOWELL, township, Prince Edward County
Position 44° 00' 77° 14'

Hallowell Township is located in the centre of picturesque and historic Prince Edward County. Settled mainly by United Empire Loyalists after the American Revolution, the county was originally divided into three townships which were named for the daughters of King George III, Mary, Sophia and Amelia. Hallowell Township was not formed until 1797 when an Act of Parliament was passed. Its territory was to take in the western part of Marysburgh and the southern part of Sophiasburgh. The result was an extremely irregular outline of the township's borders, with Picton Bay and West Lake forming the natural boundaries to the east and west respectively.

The name of the township is taken from Benjamin Hallowell, a Loyalist from Boston who fled to Canada and was given a grant of 1200 acres at the head of Picton Bay to compensate for his confiscated land holdings in the United States. The name Hallowell was first applied to a bridge that crossed a stream emptying into Picton Bay. Later the name was also attached to a small community which sprang up here and, eventually, the name was applied to the newly created township.

First settlers in the township are believed to have been the Stinsons who came about 1775. Ebenezer Washburn is believed to have been the first to settle at Hallowell Bridge. Other early township settlers included the Conger, McFaul, Spencer, Johnston, Bowerman, Bull, Dorland, Hubb, Haight and Garrett families.

During the 1790's a former British army officer, Lt. Moore Wolvennde Hovenden, erected an inn just above the Hallowell bridge. Hovenden House, as it was called, had become the centre for social gatherings by the early 1800's and Hallowell Bridge had developed into the shipping and distribution centre of the county. Meanwhile, across the bridge on the east side of the creek, another village was spreading out, known as Picton. The two thriving villages vied for the honour of becoming the district capital when Prince Edward County was declared a separate District in 1831. The rivalry did not come to an end until 1837 when the two villages were amalgamated, henceforth to be known as the town of Picton.

The Congers, Loyalists from New Jersey, who settled in 1787, erected the first sawmill and grist mill in the township. The mills were operated by waterpower from Hallowell Falls. Stephen Conger donated the land for the first Methodist church built in Prince Edward County. Erected in 1809 and known as Conger Church or the White Chapel, this church which resembles the meetinghouses built in New England in the 18th century, has been maintained as a house of worship for a longer period of time than any other Methodist church in Ontario. The township also attracted a large Quaker community and they erected their church at Bowerman's Hill in 1800. Schools were operating in the township as early as 1834 and a Quaker Friends' school was erected in 1841.

The seat of the municipality is the village of Bloomfield. A town hall was built there in 1858. Bloomfield, incorporated as a village in 1909, was once known as Bull's Mill after its pioneer settler, John Bull, who built a grist mill near the site. The settlement which grew up around the mill was the heart of early Quakerism in Prince Edward County, and at one time three different Quaker meetinghouses were located here.

The township is primarily an agricultural and dairying district. Several large canning factories have operated in the district; the first fruit and vegetable canning factory in Eastern Canada was established in Picton in 1881. A cheese factory was located in Bloomfield in 1867. Shipbuilding yards flourished in Hallowell, as they did in most other townships in the county. At the turn of the century, many farmers were growing hops and shipping facilities and wharves were located along the shore to accommodate the shipping of the product. In 1878, the railway came to the county and a station was erected close to Picton. Highway 33 (part of the old Danforth Road) is another major transportation route through the township.

Hallowell Township, like most of Prince Edward County, is a desirable vacation area due to its proximity to Lake Ontario. In particular, the fine white sand of the Sandbanks has made Hallowell's beaches among the most popular in the county. Population (1978) 4,444.

The Historical and Centennial Committee: *Picton's 100 Years*, 1937.

H. Belden & Co. *Historical Atlas of Hastings & Prince Edward Counties*, 1879.

HALSEY, geographic township, Sudbury District
Position 47° 43' 83° 41'

Lying southeast of Chapleau, Halsey was named after Admiral William Frederick Halsey of the U.S. Pacific Fleet, who played a major role in the Pacific campaigns of World War II. The township is watered by the Nemegosenda River. The main lakes in the area are Halsey and Nemegos Lakes.

The Canadian Pacific Railway travels through the area, with a station point at Nemegos. Secondary roads link the township with Highway 129.

HALTON, regional municipality
Position 43° 30' 79° 53'

The Regional Municipality of Halton was formed on January 1, 1974 out of the former County of Halton.

Located between the regional municipalities of Peel and Hamilton-Wentworth the region fronts on Lake Ontario.

While the former county was comprised of five towns and two townships, the new municipality now contains one city and three towns.

The urban centre of Burlington with a population of well over 111,000 was elevated to the status of a city, excluding a portion which was annexed by the town of Milton. Milton and Oakville retained their status as towns under the new municipal government. The third town, Halton Hills, was created on January 1, 1974 out of the former towns of Acton and Georgetown. As well, Halton Hills annexed part of the township of Esquesing and part of the town of Oakville. The former township of Nassagaweya was dissolved and a part was annexed by the town of Milton while another part was annexed by the township of Eramosa in Wellington County, the region's neighbour to the northwest.

The Regional Municipality covers an area of close to 236,900 acres and includes some of the most prosperous industrial and commercial areas in the province. The total population of the Region numbers some 240,000.

Municipal Directories 1974-1979.

HALTON, geographic county
Position 43° 30' 79° 53'

The county, fronting on Lake Ontario, lies between two of Ontario's largest centres, Metropolitan Toronto to the east and the city of Hamilton to the west. Although the county is one of the smallest in the province, it is also one of the most densely populated. It was named after Major William Halton, secretary to Francis Gore, Lieutenant-Governor of Upper Canada from 1806-1817.

The province of Ontario was originally divided into four districts: Lunenburgh, Mecklenburgh, Nassau and Hesse. The Provisional Act of 1792 continued these four divisions, but called them Eastern, Midland, Home and Western Districts respectively. Halton formed part of the Home District. A short while later, Halton County together with adjoining Wentworth County formed the Gore District. At that time Halton contained the townships of Beverly, Dumfries, Esquesing, Flamborough West and East, Nassagaweya, Nelson and Trafalgar.

Settlement in the area dates back to the 1780's when United Empire Loyalists, refugees from the American Revolution, took up land. The Gore District was well populated by 1817. At that time there were 6,684 inhabitants, four churches, eighteen grist mills, forty-one sawmills, and three doctors in the District. Around that time, some townships were annexed to new counties and Wentworth and Halton were reduced in size. Halton county then consisted of the townships of Esquesing, Trafalgar, Nelson and Nassagaweya. Wentworth and Halton remained united until 1853, when they became separate municipalities. That year the first provisional Halton County Council met and James Young was elected as the first Provisional Warden. Milton became the county seat because of its central position.

Among the pioneer families in the Trafalgar Township area were the Sovereigns, Proudfoots, Kattings, Freemans, Posts, Chisholms, and Hagars. Nelson Township was settled as early as 1800 by the Davis, Ghent, Kerns, and Bates families. The township of Esquesing was settled somewhat later. The Humes, McDonalds, McPhersons, McColls, Standishes, Watkins, Reeds, Nuckells, Frazers, Stewarts, Laidlaws, Dobbies, Neilsons, Campbells, Barbours, Kennedys, Robertsons and Swackhammers were among the pioneers there. The oldest community in Halton County is Stewarttown in the northeastern part of the county, just south of Highway 7.

The town site of Milton was first settled in 1822 by the Foster and Martin families. In that year Jasper Martin built a mill, ashery, store, tavern, and blacksmith shop. Milton was incorporated in 1857. About two and a half miles from Milton is a rocky ridge which is a continuation of Hamilton Mountain. At one time the oldest brick company in Canada operated at this site, known as Milton Heights. Early Milton industries included Robertson's steam Sash Door and Blind Factory, Rodler and Huff's Tannery, Socrates Center's Ashery, Ramshaw's Quality Buggies, and MacKenzie's Blacksmith and Carriage Works.

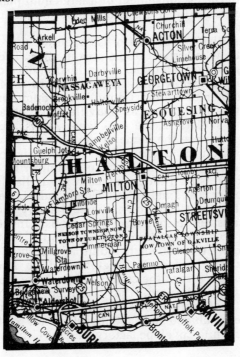

Halton County can also boast of being the home of Joseph Brant, the famous Mohawk Indian Chief, who was decorated for his bravery and loyalty while fighting for the British cause during the American Revolution. In 1798 Brant was given a Crown grant of 3,450 acres including the area on the Lake Ontario shore, where the city of Burlington stands today. James Gage purchased land from the Brant tract in 1810 and he laid out a town site that became known as Wellington Square. In 1873 Wellington Square and a neighbouring hamlet, Port Nelson, were amalgamated and incorporated as the village of Burlington. In 1914 the village was elevated to the status of a town. With the amalgamation of Burlington, Nelson Township and a part of East Flamborough Township in 1958, Burlington was greatly enlarged. That year the Burlington Bay Skyway was opened and at the time it was the largest bridge constructed by the Ontario Department of Highways. The centre span of the bridge is 120 feet above the harbour entrance, and the length of the bridge is 4.37 miles. At one time Burlington was primarily a centre for marketing farm products. Early industries were flour mills and shipbuilding. A city since 1974, Burlington today is a manufacturing centre of major importance.

The town of Oakville, situated on Highway 2 and the shore of Lake Ontario, had its beginnings in 1825 when Colonel William Chisholm of Burlington selected the site for the establishment of an oak barrel stave industry. Oakville, which was incorporated as a town in 1857, became famous for its woodworking industries in the early days. Since World War Two the town's population has greatly increased due to the establishment of a large auto plant by the Ford Motor Company. Oakville also is a long-time summer resort for some Toronto families.

The first settler on the site of Georgetown was a man named George Kennedy, who arrived in the area in 1821. The settlement in later years began to flourish under the industrial developments of the Barber brothers. Georgetown was incorporated in 1864.

Acton, another of Halton County's communities, was settled about 1820. It was first known as Danville and then as Adamsville. Among the first settlers in the area were Zenas, Rufas, and Ezra Adams. Acton was once the home of the Canada Glove Works, and today it possesses one of Ontario's largest leather factories.

During the early days of the county, lumbering was the most important local industry. There were many sawmills along the Credit River, and its branches, Twelve Mile Creek and Sixteen Mile Creek. The Barber brothers of Georgetown operated a very successful paper mill. Other industries also chose to establish in Halton County because of its central location and proximity to transportation facilities. There were excellent harbours at the small settlement of Bronte, at Oakville, and at Burlington, and no fewer than four railways at one time served the county. These were the Grand Trunk Railway, the Great Western, the Hamilton and North-Western Railway, and the Credit Valley Railway. Early industries in the Georgetown area included the Creelman Brothers knitting machine factory, the E.C. White Envelope factory, and the Georgetown Carriage Factory.

Among the smaller communities in Halton are Glen Williams, Norval, Limehouse, Ashgrove, Hornby, Speyside, Eden Mills, Brookville, Haltonville, Moffat, Milton Heights, Campbellville, Kilbride, Sheridan Park, Omagh and Palermo.

In 1974 the municipality of Halton County ceased to exist and the Regional Municipality of Halton was created. The town of Burlington was elevated to the status of a city, Milton and Oakville retained their status as towns, and Acton and Georgetown were amalgamated to form the new town of Halton Hills. Esquesing Township was annexed in part to the town of Milton and in part to Wellington County.

In 1978 the population of the Regional Municipality of Halton was 234,872.

Walker & Miles: *The Historical Atlas of Halton County*, 1877.

Hamilton Spectator, 1946.

HALTON HILLS, town, within the Regional Municipality of Halton
Position 43° 37′ 79° 56′

The town of Halton Hills did not come into existence until January 1, 1974. Effective that date the town of Acton amalgamated with the town of Georgetown as the new town of Halton Hills. The municipality is situated approximately twenty-eight miles west of Toronto.

Acton was settled about 1820 and was known at first as Danville, but later named Adamsville after the first settlers Zenas, Rufas, and Ezra Adams. In 1844 the first postmaster, Robert Swann, named the village Acton after his native place in Northumberland, England. The first store was kept by Miller Hemstreet, and in 1835 a Mr. McCullum built a small grist mill. In 1842 Abraham Nelles erected a tannery on the site now occupied by one of the largest manufacturers of leather in Ontario. In 1868 W.H. Storey commenced the manufacture of gloves. The company was known as the "Canada Glove Works".

Acton was incorporated as a village in 1873. The first council was composed of W.H. Storey, reeve; John Speight, Asa Hall, C.T. Hill, and Dr. McGavin, councillors.

The first settler on the site of Georgetown was a man of United Empire Loyalist origin, George Kennedy. He arrived there in 1821. The settlement was first known as Hungry Hollow; later it became known as Georgetown, either after George Kennedy or after King George III of England.

George Kennedy built a grist mill and later he erected a sawmill and a foundry in the settlement. In 1837 William and Robert Barber moved to the area and purchased one of Kennedy's mills. This was the beginning of the renowned Barber Woollen Mills and also marked the beginning of a long and profitable alliance between Georgetown and the Barber family. Later they would establish a sawmill, a foundry, and a paper mill.

In 1840 Mr. John Sumpter opened the first general store in the settlement and he later became Georgetown's first postmaster in 1851.

Mr. A.M. Bush opened a hotel in 1842.

Other early industries in Georgetown included the C.B. Dayfoot Company (manufacturers of heavy work boots), the Creelman Brothers knitting machine factory, the E.C. White Envelope factory, the J.H. Day Paint Company, and the Georgetown Carriage Factory.

These two industrial towns have amalgamated to create an even larger industrial centre. Today local factories manufacture everything from leather and knitted goods to plastics, electrical apparatus, tools and ceramics. In 1978 the population of Halton Hills was 34,051.

Acton Free Press, 1967.

Walker and Miles: The Historical Atlas of Halton County, 1877.

Kathleen Saunders: Saunders' History of Georgetown, 1976.

HAMBLETON, geographic township, Algoma District
Position 48° 52' 85° 06'

Twenty miles northeast of the town of White River, the township has many small lakes. One dry weather road exists in the western half of the area.

Established in 1943 by the Ministry of Lands and Forests, the township is named after J. Hamblet, Director of Ontario Publicity and Travel Bureau, 1934-38.

HAMBLY, geographic township, Cochrane District
Position 50° 17' 82° 34'

This township, located to the east of the Opasatika River, was named either after Wm. Hambly, pioneer surveyor, or Chas. W. Hambly, MPP for Lennox 1924 and MPP for Frontenac and Lennox 1929. The Missinaibi River flows through the northwestern corner of the area. The nearest major community is the town of Kapuskasing, some 50 miles to the southeast of the township.

HAMILTON, township, Northumberland County
Position 44° 03' 78° 13'

Hamilton Township was settled by United Empire Loyalists and immigrants from England and Scotland. Amongst the earliest grantees of land in the broken front of Hamilton and along the shore of Lake Ontario (which forms its southern border) were: Liberty White, Thos. Fleming, Jos. Purdy, John Benson, Richard Benson, Asahel Jerome, Ronner Pevney, Geo. Ash, Sr. and Jr., Stanborough Stanchcliff, Jas. McColl, Eluid Nickerson, Nathaniel Herriman, Nathan Williams and Elias James.

Nickerson is credited to have been the first settler on the site of present-day Cobourg. He arrived in 1798 and built a log cabin. Elias James followed sometime later and opened the first store in the vicinity.

Cobourg soon became the main centre in the township and when a harbour was built at the foot of Division Street in 1832, it expanded even more rapidly. Lumber was the chief export commodity in those days, followed closely in importance by flour and wheat. Other products shipped from Cobourg's harbour included potash, barley, oatmeal and potatoes. Cobourg also was a regular port of call for Durham boats and early steamers on Lake Ontario. Located on the York (Toronto) to Kingston Road, it was a stopover for stages and Cobourg's inns and hotels prospered. William Weller (1788-1863) one of Ontario's noted pioneer stagecoach operators, made his home in Cobourg. The village remained a part of the township until 1837 when it was incorporated under a Board of Police.

Situated between Lake Ontario and Rice Lake, the landscape of Hamilton is a mixture of small hills, winding valleys, wooded areas, and spreading farm fields. Primarily an agricultural area, the township today is also a very popular vacation spot. The shores of Rice Lake abound with summer residents.

Several small communities sprang up along the north-south pioneering roads. Among these are the villages of Baltimore, Camborne, Coldsprings, Plainville, Gore's Landing, Harwood and Bewdley.

Hamilton covers an area of over 65,300 acres and has a population close to 9,000.

H. Belden & Company: *Illustrated Historical Atlas of the Counties of Northumberland and Durham*, 1878.

Cobourg *Centennial Review*, 1967.

HAMILTON, city, Regional Municipality of Hamilton-Wentworth
Position 43° 15' 79° 51'

Situated at the western end of Lake Ontario, about 40 miles southwest of Toronto, Hamilton has the second largest population of any city in Ontario and the sixth largest in all of Canada. It is Canada's most industrialized city, known today as "Steel City" because it is the largest steel producer in the country. Hamilton was named after George Hamilton who bought land here in 1813. The city is situated on the south side of Hamilton Bay, a triangular-shaped landlocked harbour bounded on the lake side by a sandbar known as Burlington Beach. The Queen Elizabeth Way from Toronto crosses this sandbar. The city is also accessible by CNR, CPR and the Toronto, Hamilton and Buffalo Railway.

The site is believed to have been once the scene of an Indian battle, and formerly there was a burial mound for Indian chiefs located there. The first white man in the area was probably Etienne Brûlé, explorer Samuel de Champlain's interpreter, who visited the district in 1615. The first recorded visit to the locality was that of French explorer René Robert de la Salle in 1669.

In 1784 the British government bought the land from the Mississauga Indians in order to provide homes for United Empire Loyalists who had been forced to leave the United States after the American Revolution. Robert Land, the first settler in the area, had already arrived by 1778 and had taken up land in the valley at the foot of the Niagara Escarpment. However, it was some time before he had any near neighbours, as most of the incoming settlers preferred the higher land to the south and west. Among these pioneers were John Aikman, Nathaniel Hughson, and Peter Ferguson.

However, gradually the population in the valley also began to increase and the small settlement that resulted became a centre for surrounding communities. By 1795 Freemasons held their meetings at Smith's tavern, the first tavern in the area. More settlers arrived after 1796 and another wave came after the War of 1812.

In 1813, one George Hamilton moved to the community because he thought it would be safer there during the war than at his home in Niagara-on-the-Lake. Events proved him right. Although the Battle of Stoney Creek, which repelled the American invaders, took place only a short distance away, the settlement was not harmed during the war.

George Hamilton became a prominent man in his new home. In 1813 he subdivided his farm and laid out the streets of the future city, named after him. Most of the streets he named after members of his family, and later he donated Gore Park, which is still the centre of the city.

Christ Church Cathedral, Hamilton, Ont., Canada

Hamilton, Christ Church Cathedral

Among the businessmen who established themselves in Hamilton shortly after the war, were Knight and Shute, cabinetmakers; Edward Jackson, tinsmith; and John Aikman, wagonmaker. Messrs. McQuesten and Fisher opened the first foundry.

The community was incorporated as a village in 1816 and became the court centre for the new District of Gore in the same year. In the 1820's its development was, to some extent, overshadowed by that of Dundas, as the latter was connected with the bay (Lake Ontario) by the Desjardins Canal. However, the construction of the Burlington Canal in 1830 made Hamilton a much more convenient port and the resulting growth of the village soon outstripped that of its rival. Many of the men involved in building the canal had settled in Hamilton and the new warehouses and wharves which were erected attracted many more workers to the community.

Despite a fire which destroyed many businesses in 1832, and the cholera plague of that same year which devastated Upper Canada, Hamilton continued to expand and in 1833 it became a town. Its first government was carried out by a "Board of Police". By 1845 the town had 6,478 residents and in the following year was incorporated as a city.

With the advent of railways in the 1850's, Hamilton developed into an industrial centre of great importance. The Great Western Railway, constructed in 1854, carried trade past Dundas to Hamilton. As the city was the only place where the railway touched navigable water, it became a port for the importation of railway stock and pig iron. Railway repair shops established here were the beginning of Hamilton's steel industry. It was here at Hamilton that in 1854 the first Canadian-built locomotives, passenger and freight cars originated, as did the world's first sleeping car. Hamilton was among Canada's leading wholesale import centres in the 1850's. The peak years of its expansion were 1854 to 1856, when the population reached 21,855. Encouraged by the city's rapid growth and its prosperity, the municipal government built expensive sewers and gas works and invested large sums of money in stock in the Hamilton and Port Dover Railway. This over-investment resulted in a financial crisis in 1857 and growth came almost to a standstill for the next decade. Buchanan, Harris & Co., Hamilton's largest wholesale house was seriously affected by the financial collapse, and the city bank closed its doors in the 1860's. Trade with the United States was disrupted by the Civil War. The Grand Trunk Railway gave many of the city's former customers in the hinterland easy access to Toronto, and for the time being Hamilton lost much of its appeal as a market for the rich agricultural land which surrounded it.

However, Hamilton was back on the road to prosperity soon after Confederation in 1867. Spreading railway fever, and the rapid growth of industries in the United States contributed to the expansion of Hamilton's steel industry. The Hamilton and Lake Erie Railway opened in the early 1870's. A new wave of immigrants came from continental Europe to work in newly-established industries such as Charlton's Vinegar Works, the marble trade, the largest foundry in Canada, sewing machines, agricultural implement and glass factories. By 1877 the city's population had risen to about 32,000.

The opening of the Welland Canal in 1887 gave another boost to the city's economy. The hub of Canada's steel industry moved to Hamilton from Montreal, as manufacturers could now ship their goods on the Great Lakes as far as Fort William on Lake Superior. In the 1890's a blast furnace started operations in Hamilton. Ontario

Rolling Mills, founded by Charles Wilcox in 1879, merged with the Hamilton Blast Furnace in 1899 to form the Hamilton Steel and Iron Company, the first fully integrated steel company in Canada. In 1910, largely due to the efforts of Max Aitken, later Lord Beaverbrook, the leading steel companies in Ontario and Montreal merged in order to block American takeover of the market. The result was the Steel Company of Canada (Stelco). Canadian Westinghouse, located in Hamilton by this time, helped electrify the industrial plants in the area, and in 1913 Stelco opened its first electrically-powered rod and bar mill.

Two other important industries were also established about this time. Dominion Foundries, producing wheels and undercarriages for railway cars, began operations in 1912. In 1955 it became known as Dofasco (Dominion Foundries and Steel Ltd). Dofasco became the first Canadian producer of floor plate, continuously galvanized steel and electrical steels, and also pioneered North American oxygen steel-making. The second industry, Canada Steel Company, later known as Burlington Steel Co. Ltd. founded around that time, started out rolling bar products from used railroad rails. In 1962 this company became a division of Slater Steel Industries Ltd.

The late nineteenth century saw the development of Hamilton's electric railways. Three were built in the 1890's, the Hamilton, Grimsby, and Beamsville Electric Railway, the Brantford and Hamilton Electric Railway, and the Hamilton and Dundas Electric Railway.

Hamilton can boast of many firsts, a number of them in the automotive industry. One of the first automobiles made in Canada was manufactured in the city. The Studebaker, a Canadian car, was a Hamilton product. Pete Smith of Hamilton invented the idea of the white centre line used for vehicle control on roadways, and John S. Kendall invented the flashing turn signal. In 1903 the first Automobile Club in Canada was formed in the city of Hamilton.

In 1878 Hamilton became the site of the first telephone exchange in the British Empire and the second in the world. In 1879 the first long distance lines in Canada were put up between Hamilton and Dundas. The city also had the first pay phones in the country. In 1849 the Canada Life Assurance Company based in Hamilton became the country's first life insurance company. The city's manufacturers produced Canada's first sulphur matches, threshing machines, sewing machines, coal-oil lamp burners, and cloth-covered funeral caskets; also the first iron steamboat to sail on fresh water in America, and the first long-distance power transmission line in the world. Hamilton, too, was the site of the first experiments in lighting by electricity attempted in Canada.

The city had been a major centre for trade union activity since the 1800's. A railway workers' strike in 1856 was the first notable strike in Upper Canada. A printers' trade union had been formed in the early part of the 19th century and the first assembly of the Knights of Labor in Canada had been organized in the city in 1881. Hamilton labour unions played a leading role in the movement for shorter working hours. The first organization of the Co-operative Union of

Canada took place here in 1909. During the Depression years a number of powerful unions were established, including the Steelworkers' Union in 1936. The Reconstruction Party had its beginnings in Depression-era Hamilton.

Like all major Canadian centres, Hamilton was hit hard by the Great Depression of the Thirties. But advent of the Second World War with its resultant demands on iron and steel foundries soon lifted Hamilton out of its Depression doldrums. By 1940 Hamilton had tripled its population and the value of its property since 1900. This city of 155,000 people now had over 450 manufacturers and had attracted more U.S. industries than any other Canadian city. It had 60 branch factories of American firms, including Westinghouse, Firestone, International Harvester, Hoover and Aylmers. Products ranged from iron and steel to foods to tobacco to hosiery and knitted goods. Railways and three steamship lines provided transportation facilities.

It was during this period that the present layout of the city began to develop. Almost all heavy industries were grouped together in the northeast, while most retail and professional businesses were grouped around Gore Park in the centre of the city. New residential areas were developed on the Mountain, that part of the Niagara Escarpment which cuts through Hamilton, although today two-thirds of the population still live on the lower level of the city. Waterfront land began to be reclaimed to provide room for industrial expansion. Today a large industrial area is the result.

In the last 30 years the boundaries of the city have continually expanded. In 1956 Hamilton annexed Burlington Beach and part of Halton County. In 1960 Barton Township and parts of Glanford, Saltfleet and Ancaster Townships were added to the city. Today Hamilton is 11 miles long and 9 miles wide and has a population of 308,365. (1978)

Modern Hamilton is the largest inland port in the country and its waterfront is the most impressive industrial concentration in Canada. The city produces over half of Canada's steel output. Almost 50% of the labour force work in the more than 500 manufacturing plants, and 40% of the industry is primarily engaged in steel manufacture. Other products include chewing gum, thread, clothing, tires and jewellery.

In the past decade Hamilton has been the site of Canada's largest urban-renewal project. The city has been divided into 118 neighbourhoods to encourage citizen participation in urban redevelopment. Hamilton Place, a modern cultural centre, was built and successful efforts are being made to revitalize the downtown core. Proposals included the construction of a theatre-auditorium, art gallery, hotel, trade and convention centre, underground shops, pedestrian malls and restaurants. Hesse Village, an area of restaurants and shops in restored Victorian houses is one of the results.

One of Hamilton's earliest schools was the Gore District School opened in 1821. Egerton Ryerson, who played a leading role in the development of Ontario's educational system, was a pupil there. By 1846 there were 6 common schools in the town, and 28 private schools by the 1850's. In 1861 Wesleyan Female College, Ontario's first private school for girls opened in Hamilton. Hamilton Collegiate

Institute, the city's first high school, was built in 1866. Westdale Secondary School, constructed in 1929, was probably the largest secondary school in the Empire at the time. Today Hamilton has ten secondary schools, three junior vocational schools, and seventy-six public schools.

The first separate school classes were held in 1852 in the Sisters of St. Joseph Convent. There were two separate schools by 1856. Bishop Ryan, a Roman Catholic high school, was opened in 1959. There are now thirty separate schools in the city.

The County Model School was established in 1877 to provide training for teachers. In 1885 a training school for teachers of secondary schools was opened. The Hamilton Normal School, which became Hamilton Teachers' College was built in 1908. S.A. Morgan was the first principal. From 1923 to 1946 the city was the site of the Ontario Training College for Technical Teachers.

In 1897 Dr. C.L. Harris founded the Royal Hamilton College of Music. A Technical Institute was opened in 1908.

In 1887 the Hon. William McMaster established a Baptist University in Toronto. McMaster University moved to Hamilton in 1930. It was the first university in Canada to have a nuclear reactor built for research purposes and McMaster is today very involved in scientific research. Hamilton is the centre of the South Central Regional Library System which was established in 1965. The city has three public libraries.

The *Gore Balance*, published in 1829 was the community's first newspaper. The present *Hamilton Spectator*, the ninth largest English language newspaper in Canada, was founded in 1846. By 1875 there were two daily papers, the *Times* and the *Spectator*, and the weekly *Christian Advocate*. By 1858 the *Spectator* was the only daily. The *Review* was published weekly.

Hamilton has two radio stations and one television station. CKOC began broadcasting in 1922 and CHCH-TV went on the air in 1954.

The city has long been the home of societies wishing to preserve its history and culture. The Wentworth Historical Society was founded in 1889 and published papers between 1892 and 1924. The Head-of-the-Lake Historical Society replaced this society in 1944. The Hamilton Association for the Advancement of Literature, Science, and Art, founded in 1857, is the oldest cultural society in Canada. The Hamilton Club established in 1873, is one of the oldest social clubs in Ontario.

In 1845 the Gentlemen Amateurs of the Theatre Royal became Hamilton's first theatre group. In 1880 the Grand Opera House was opened in the city. The Savoy Theatre showed the first moving pictures in 1906. In 1908 a Summer Stock Company first performed their repertoire on the "Mountain". Today the Hamilton Theatre Inc., the Opera Company, and the Hamilton Philharmonic perform in the city's new cultural centre, built in 1973.

Hamilton has taken an active role in sports since the first softball rules were drafted here in the 1820's. A curling club was founded in

1852 and a golf club in 1894. The sixth running of the Queen's Plate was held in Hamilton in 1866 and the Canadian Golf Open in 1919 and 1930. Local track enthusiasts, including M.M. Robinson and Sam Manson, who founded the Hamilton Olympic Club, conceived the idea of the British Empire Games, which were first held in 1930. Many Olympic and Empire Games team members came from Hamilton, including swimmer Timmy Thompson, and runner Billy Sherring, who won the Olympic Marathon in Greece in 1906. A football team, the "Hamilton Tiger Cats", was formed in 1950 and had an excellent athletic stadium for the game. In 1964 the Chedoke Winter Sports Pack was opened. Hamilton is also the home of the "Football Hall of Fame".

The Methodists were the first to organize a congregation in Hamilton, in 1800. In 1863 the first Jewish Reform Temple in Canada was built at Hamilton. By 1875 the city had 23 churches and 2 cathedrals and was the seat of the Sees of the Anglican Bishop of Niagara and the Roman Catholic Bishop of Hamilton. The Salvation Army was established in 1882. By 1940 there were 119 churches of various denominations in the city.

In 1848 the House of Industry was built for the sick and the destitute. It was buried in a landslide in 1852, and in 1853 army barracks dating back to 1830 became the City Hospital. A new hospital was erected in 1882 and the old hospital was converted into a home for the aged. It has long since been replaced by Macassa Lodge. St. Joseph's Hospital was opened in 1890, as was St. Peter's Infirmary, which became St. Peter's Home for the Incurables in 1893, the second of its type in Ontario. The Asylum for Inebriates, founded in 1875 became a mental asylum in 1876. It is now the Ontario Hospital.

The twentieth century has been a period of rapidly expanding medical facilities in the city. The Mountain Sanatorium built in 1906, became the largest tuberculosis sanitorium in the Empire. The first section of Mount Hamilton Hospital was constructed during World War One and the City Hospital became Hamilton General shortly after the War. In 1922 the McGregor Clinic opened and in 1930 the Medical Arts Building was completed. Grace Haven opened its doors in 1950 as a home and hospital for unmarried mothers. The Nora-Frances Henderson Hospital was built in 1954, followed a few years later by the Brow Infirmary, a chronic and convalescent hospital.

In more recent years the General and Children's Hospital was added to the city's medical facilities. Hamilton and District Rehabilitation Hospital went into operation in the Sixties, as did a children's psychiatric diagnostic and treatment centre. The Nora-Frances Henderson and Mount Hamilton Hospitals merged in the 1960's and are now known as the Henderson General Hospital.

One of Hamilton's most famous sons was Sir Allen Napier MacNab (1798-1862), Prime Minister of Canada 1854-56. The Hon. Isaac Buchanan of Hamilton was President of the Executive Council in 1864. Another Hamiltonian, T.B. McQuesten, was the father of the Ontario northern highways system, the restorer of Fort Erie, Fort George, and Fort Henry, the developer of the Niagara Parks system, and the builder of three international bridges. The discoverer of acetylene gas, Charles Willson, lived in the city, as did William Southam (1843-1932), owner of a large chain of newspapers. Hamilton was also the home of artist William Blair Bruce (1859-1906), and the poet George Washington Johnson, who wrote *When you and I were Young, Maggie*.

Among the many attractions Hamilton offers to the visitor are Dundurn Castle and the Royal Botanical Gardens. Built by Allan Napier MacNab in the nineteenth century, Dundurn Castle is the largest house ever erected in Upper Canada. The Royal Botanical Gardens include a beautiful rock garden opened in 1941, and a wildlife sanctuary.

Page & Smith: *Wentworth County Illustrated*; 1875.

Hamilton Spectator Centennial Edition: 1967.

Charles Paul Hay: *Great Cities of Canada*, 1968.

Head of the Lake Historical Society: *Wentworth Bygones*, 1960.

Ontario Historical Society: *Profiles of a Province*, 1967.

Ontario Historical Society Papers: 1907, 1916, 1973.

Wentworth Historical Society; 1892.

Wentworth Historical Society Transactions: 1902.

HAMILTON-WENTWORTH, regional municipality
Position 43° 15′ 80° 00′

The Regional Municipality of Hamilton-Wentworth was incorporated on October 15, 1973 and consists of the City of Hamilton, the Town of Ancaster, the Town of Dundas, the Town of Stoney Creek, the Township of Flamborough and the Township of Glanbrook. The new region includes all of the former County of Wentworth.

The former Townships of Beverly and Flamborough East, and the former Village of Waterdown, prior to the formation of the region, were amalgamated as the new Township of Flamborough. The former Township of Flamborough West was annexed in part to the town of Dundas, and in part to the Township of Flamborough. The former Township of Binbrook was amalgamated with the former Township of Glanford as the new Township of Glanbrook. The former Township of Saltfleet was amalgamated with the Town of Stoney Creek, as the Town of Stoney Creek. Ancaster Township and Ancaster Police Village were amalgamated and erected from a township into a town.

The population of the Regional Municipality of Wentworth stood at 407,486 in 1978, with the city of Hamilton accounting for 308,365. Stoney Creek is the largest town with a population of 32,628, followed by the town of Dundas with 19,129 and the town of Ancaster with 14,073.

The region covers an area of 275,020 acres and includes a prosperous industrial belt around the west end of Lake Ontario.

Municipal Directories 1973-1977.

HAMLET, geographic township, Cochrane District
Position 50° 09′ 81° 45′

Situated east of the Mattagami River, the township was probably named after the well known Shakespearean character.

The Ontario Northland Railway point of Coral is located on the northeastern boundary.

HAMMELL, geographic township, Nipissing District
Position 46° 41′ 79° 34′

Located north of Lake Nipissing, this township was first subdivided in 1899 and appears to have been named after Jack Hammell, a prominent mining financier of Toronto. Main lakes in the area are North Spruce Lake, Poplar Lake and Kaotisinimigo Lake. Martin River Provincial Park lies to the northwest of Hammell and a dry weather road links the area to Highway 11.

HAMMERTOWN, community, Regional Municipality of York
Position 43° 56′ 79° 45′

Situated in the 12th concession of King Township, Hammertown was so named because of a smithy located there in the early days of settlement. At one time a busy and prosperous village, today all that remains is a dispersed rural community.

The first settlers who arrived in the second quarter of the nineteenth century were mainly Scottish families. They included the Crawfords, McKinleys, Jacksons, Irwins, Thompsons, Halls, Stuarts and Watsons. Thomas Elmer was the first blacksmith in the settlement, and the first carpenter was Tom Bowes. In 1842 Duncan Anderson, a leatherworker, started to make shoes. A post office was opened in 1912 with Robert Barry as postmaster. It closed in 1947.

The first school in Hammertown was known as the Crawford School, as it was built on the farm of William Crawford. It was replaced by a new building in 1926, which served the community until 1966.

At one time there were two churches at the hamlet, one a Baptist, the other a Methodist house of worship. Fire destroyed one and the other has since been demolished.

Elizabeth McClure Gillham: *Early Settlements of King Township, Ontario*, 1975.

HAMMOND, geographic township, Sudbury District
Position 47° 27′ 83° 54′

Formerly known as Township 23, Range 17, the township was named after D. Hammond, Reeve of Alberton Township, Rainy River District. It borders in the west on the District of Algoma. Straddling its western boundary, the Tikamaganda River courses through, interspersed by numerous rapids and falls.

HANCOCK, geographic township, Sudbury District
Position 47° 27' 83° 47'

Formerly designated as Township 22, Range 17, Hancock was named in 1974 after S.G. Hancock, Reeve of Atikokan Township, Rainy River District at that time. The area lies just northeast of the Montreal River.

A dry weather road links the township with the small community of Pineal Lake and ultimately with the town of Chapleau to the northeast.

HANDLEMAN, geographic township, Algoma District
Position 47° 07' 83° 31'

The township, located northeast of Sault Ste. Marie, and previously designated as No. 6G, was named in 1974 after S.B. Handleman, MPP for Carleton.

Gong Lake and Anvil Lake occupy the southern section of the township which is linked by secondary road to Highway 129 to the east.

HANEY, geographic township, Cochrane District
Position 50° 02' 82° 34'

Named after Wilfred S. Haney, MPP for Lambton West 1923-26, this area lies north of Kapuskasing. The township's main river is the Opasatika, dotted with numerous rapids and flowing along the eastern boundary.

The township is not accessible by road.

HANLAN, geographic township, Cochrane District
Position 49° 46' 83° 46'

The township is named after Edward Hanlan, a noted oarsman of Toronto, 1855-1908.

The Fushimi Provincial Park encroaches into the northwestern corner of the township and Lake Fushimi occupies the greater portion of the northern half of the area.

Close to the town of Hearst, the Canadian National Railways passes through the southwest corner, with a station point at Ryland. Highway 11 runs parallel with the railway line.

HANMER, part of town of Valley East, Regional Municipality of Sudbury
Position 46° 39' 80° 56'

Situated a few miles north of Sudbury, this compact rural community was named after Gilbert Hanmer, a farmer from Brant County.

The first settlers in the area were French Canadians, and they were Jacob Proulx, Henry Beaulieu, Napoleon Labelle, and Joseph Chartrand. All of them arrived in April of 1898. All had families except Chartrand, and they were all farmers. Their prized possessions between them were two horses, one of them old and infirm, and one cow. They struggled to make a meagre living from the soil, but they put down roots and were soon followed by other settlers.

A hotel was opened in 1903 by Monsieur Lalonde. It was later taken over by Onesime Tremblay. In 1904 Hanmer became a post office and Napoleon Nemard was appointed as the first postmaster. Soon the community had a blacksmith and several stores. A school was built in 1904.

Most of the early settlers were Roman Catholics. The first missionary in the area was a Jesuit priest, Father Chartier. In 1905 M. Stephane Coté became the first missionary to hold regular services. A church was erected in 1906 with Father Roy as the community's first resident priest. A new church was built in the 1920's.

By the 1960's Hanmer had over 3,600 residents. In 1969 Hanmer became part of the township of Valley East and in 1973 the township was made part of the new Town of Valley East.

Sudbury Star, June 1923.

HANNA, geographic township, Cochrane District
Position 48° 56′ 81° 00′

This township houses the tiny community of Berylvale, and is located just south of the town of Cochrane. Highway 11 passes through the heart of the township. Fletchers Lake is situated in the northeastern section.

Hanna was subdivided in 1907, but the subdivision was partly annulled in 1964. It is named after William G. Hanna, Provincial Secretary 1905-14.

HANNIWELL, geographic township, Thunder Bay District
Position 49° 04′ 90° 53′

Located in the Shebandowan Lakes area, the township borders the District of Kenora on the western side. It houses the northern half of an Indian Reservation. Dry weather and secondary roads link the area with Highway 17.

Established in 1945 by the Ministry of Lands and Forests, it was named after Carl D. Hanniwell, MPP for Niagara Falls in 1945.

HANOVER, town, Bentinck Township, Grey County
Position 44° 09′ 81° 12′

This town is situated on the county line between Grey and Bruce on Highway 4. It was apparently named after Hannover, Germany, the hometown of one of the early settlers. However, according to another source, the story is that a Mr. Hahn wished the new community to be named Hahnover.

The town's history began in 1849 when Abraham Buck, the first innkeeper, and a Mr. Jasper blazed a trail for eleven miles west of Durham. They settled by the Saugeen River, near the site of the future

CPR station and the early name of the settlement was Buck's Crossing, or Buck's Bridge. Christian Hassenjaeger, whose daughter, Hannah, was the first white child born in this area, arrived shortly after and was soon followed by a number of German settlers from Waterloo County. By 1854 a grist and sawmill had been constructed and proposals were made to form a village. In 1856 a post office was opened and given the name of Hanover. A.Z. Gottwals, the first storekeeper was also the first postmaster.

The industrial character of the community was established about 1860, with the opening of a tannery by James Crispen, a furniture factory by Thomas Crispen and G.W. Black, and a foundry by Duncan Campbell. In 1866, with the town's population reaching 400, Daniel Knechtel opened a furniture factory which was to contribute much to the town's prosperity. He formed a partnership with his brother, Peter, in 1873 and bought a building to expand the business. Peter sold out to Daniel in 1882 and in 1884 a new brick structure was erected. A disastrous fire at the turn of the century destroyed the factory and resulted in heavy financial losses, but with the town's assistance, a new building was constructed and the business continued to prosper.

Other furniture manufacturing companies were also established in the early years of the town's history, including Peppler Bros. and Ball Furniture. The large number of Hanover's sawmills, grist, woollen and lumber mills which supplied the furniture industry resulted in the community being nicknamed "Slab Town". By 1880 the Hanover Woollen Mills, the Britannia Metal Work, and a shingle factory, were employing much of the growing population which had reached about 1,200.

With the building of the Grand Trunk Railway in 1882, Hanover became an important railway station. By 1898, with the population now at 1,612, there was a growing demand that the community be incorporated as a village. This occurred in 1899 with Daniel Knechtel becoming the first reeve. In 1904 Hanover became a town. Dr. W.A. Mearns was the first mayor. In 1967 the town annexed part of the Township of Bentinck.

Aware that too much dependence on one industry was not wise, the businessmen of the town decided in the early 1900's to build a large factory for other types of manufacturing. A hosiery company has made use of it. Swift Canadian Packing Co. also has a large plant here. However, it is still its furniture for which Hanover is best known and which provides employment for many of the town's 5,786 people (1978).

The first school was a private one held in the home of the teacher, Mrs. Campbell, in 1864. In 1868 or '69, a brick school was built but soon proved to be too small. A new school was erected in 1875 with William Coles as principal. In 1912, another school was opened under Principal James Magee, and the first separate school began classes with Father Lenhard in charge. A high school was established in 1924, and also another new separate school.

The first church service by an ordained minister was held in Hassenjaeger's home, the minister being from the Church of England. This was the start of St. James Anglican congregation for which a log church was built in 1858. It was replaced by the present brick building in 1876. The first Baptist church was erected in 1860, the first Presbyterian church in 1862. By 1866, Hanover had six churches. A.Z. Gottwals provided a frame structure which was used by the different denominations until they had their own church.

Hanover has always been active in the arts, especially music. The first local concert was held in 1881 and a choral group was organized under Herbert James in 1896. The Hanover Band has been in existence since 1872. Carl Schaefer, a well-known Canadian artist is a native of the town.

H. Belden and Co.: *Illustrated Atlas of the County of Grey*, 1880.

T. Arthur Davidson: *A New History of the County of Grey*, 1972.

E.L. Marsh: *A History of the County of Grey*, 1931.

Audrey M. Rutherford: *Grey County Centennial, 1852-1952*, 1952.

HARBURN, township, Provisional County of Haliburton
Position 45° 12′ 78° 24′

This township was named either for the town of Harburn in Edinburgh County, Scotland, or for the River Harburn in England. It was surveyed in 1862 by John James Francis.

For municipal purposes, Harburn is united with the Townships of Dysart, Bruton, Clyde, Dudley, Eyre, Guilford, Harburn, Harcourt and Havelock. The combined population of these townships is 3,379 (1978).

The early settlers of the Harburn area were Thomas Peever, William Eady, George Thompson, John Irwin, Jeshua Paul, Thomas and James Roberts, John and William Wilson, Albert Curry and Daniel Bowen. The latter built a sawmill at Moose Lake.

On the largest lake in the township, Haliburton Lake, C.W. Hodgson once operated a sawmill. The shore of this lake now is lined with summer cottages.

Harburn in the early days had a large Orange Lodge membership. An Orange Hall which was used as a church on Sundays, once stood across the Peterson Road that separates Harburn from Dudley Township. Here also was the site of an early public school. Both buildings have long since been destroyed by fire.

International Cooperage Company of Canada Ltd., a Canadian subsidiary of a large American barrel manufacturing firm, purchased extensive tracts of timber in Harburn in 1932 and in 1933 the new cooperage mill at the foot of Eagle Lake was in operation. The mill, once the largest in the county, gave employment to many township residents and handled an immense quota of lumber. It was closed in the 1950's and the mill buildings were dismantled.

Nila Reynolds: *In Quest of Yesterday*, 1967.

HARCOURT, township, Haliburton County
Position 45° 08′ 78° 12′

Situated in the eastern part of Haliburton County, Harcourt is part of the municipality of Dysart, Bruton, Clyde, Dudley, Eyre, Guilford, Harburn, Harcourt and Havelock. The combined population in these townships is 3,379 (1978). Harcourt was named after either a village in Shropshire, England, or the family of Martha Harcourt, sister of the Earl of Harcourt.

The township was first surveyed by James W. Fitzgerald in 1860. He reported that there were good agricultural lands in the north and west and extensive pine woods in the east. In 1861, Harcourt and the other eight townships, which now form one municipal unit, were bought by the Canadian Land and Emigration Company from the government to be opened up for settlers.

By 1869 Harcourt's inhabitants included H. Beanord, George Cole, Thomas Peever, Thomas and James Scott, Archie Williams, and Donald Watt. But settlement remained slow at first due to the lack of roads. About 1864 the Burleigh Road was constructed by the Land Company along Harcourt's southern boundary in order to encourage colonization. The Company also built a sawmill and a grist mill in the 1860's. By 1871 the township's population stood at 61.

Lumbering was the mainstay of the early settlers and a sawmill was built at the site of Kennaway. Many small mills came on the scene in the following years and their owners included "Black Archie" Scott, Mr. Brownridge, and Bill McLaren. Extensive logging was carried out by the Standard Chemical Co., Erie Flooring Co., and the Martin Lumber Co.

Kennaway, named after a baronet who had visited the area in 1869, was the first community which developed in the township. Originally planned as an agricultural centre, this was delayed due to indifferent soil and bad or non-existing roads. The Kennaway Road, built in 1872, improved the situation by enabling farmers to market their produce to lumbermen in the northern townships.

The Irondale, Bancroft & Ottawa Railway (I.B. & O.) was built through Harcourt in the 1890's. A railway station named Harcourt was constructed in the southern part of the township in 1911. A store and post office were also opened here.

The school in Kennaway built in 1870 burned down in 1908 and was replaced in 1915. In the 1960's a new school was built.

One of the largest tourists resorts in the area opened its doors in the 1930's. Run by Catherine and Russell Schickler in those days, it was known as Elephant Lake Lodge and has remained a popular recreation spot over the years.

History of the Provisional County of Haliburton, 1951.

Florence B. Murray, ed.: *Muskoka and Haliburton 1615-1875*, 1963.

Nila Reynolds: *In Quest of Yesterday*, 1967.

HARDIMAN, geographic township, Sudbury District
Position 48° 00′ 82° 06′

Named in 1912 by the Ministry of Lands and Forests, the name origin is unknown. Mostly occupied by lakes, the largest being Hardiman Lake, the area is connected by secondary and dry weather roads to Highway 101, and thus to Timmins in the northeast.

HARDWICK, geographic township, Thunder Bay District
Position 48° 12′ 90° 05′

This township lies a few miles north of the United States Border and the State of Minnesota. It houses large areas of Whitefish Lake and Arrow Lake, and there are some smaller lakes in the centre. Highway 588 and various dry weather and secondary roads link the vicinity with Middle Falls Provincial Park and Highway 61.

It was named after either the Earl of Hardwick or one of the Duke of Devonshire's estates.

HARDY, geographic township, Parry Sound District
Position 46° 00′ 79° 56′

Located south of the French River and housing a considerable part of an Indian Reservation, this township was subdivided in 1877 and 1881. It was named after Hon. Arthur Sturgis Hardy, Premier of Ontario, 1896-99.

Secondary roads link the area to Highway 11. Restoule Provincial Park lies just to the east.

HAREWOOD, geographic township, Cochrane District
Position 50° 01′ 81° 10′

The French River straddles the eastern boundary of this township, ultimately emptying into James Bay to the north. Lying in the central area is Lake Harewood. Some 16 miles to the east, the Ontario Northland Railway links the area with Cochrane to the southeast.

The township is probably named after Princess Victoria Alexandra Alice Mary, Countess of Harewood.

HARKER, geographic township, Cochrane District
Position 48° 30′ 79° 49′

The township is located approximately 8 miles north of Esker Lakes Provincial Park. Ghost River flows through the western half of the township. Highway 101 passes through the northern section, linking the area with the town of Matheson, about 35 miles to the west.

The name commemorates Dr. Harker, a past president of the Geological Society of London.

HARLEY, township, Timiskaming District

Position 47° 38′ 79° 42′

This township is located north of the town of New Liskeard. It was subdivided in 1887 by D. Beattie. Being part of the "Little Clay Belt" a fertile stretch of land between New Liskeard and Englehart, the area attracted settlers soon after. They came by way of the Ottawa River and Lake Timiskaming to take up farming and lumbering. Around 1904 the township was incorporated. Its name is believed to commemorate Archibald Harley, once the MP for South Oxford.

Highway 11, travelling through the centre of the township, links the area with New Liskeard to the south and Englehart to the north. The Ontario Northland Railway passes along the township's western border.

The township has a population of approximately 600 (1979). The community of Hanbury is situated on Highway 11.

HARLOWE, community, Barrie Township, Frontenac County
Position 44° 48′ 77° 05′

Today a dispersed rural community, Harlowe was at one time an important crossroads in Barrie Township with five roads leading out from the village.

Harlowe, situated a short distance west of Big Gull Lake, grew with the lumber trade carried on by firms such as Rathbun's. Farming and a wool industry were other mainstays of the area.

Among the early settlers were the Thompsons who arrived in the early 1860's, and the Neals, who took up land in 1865. Other pioneer families included the Cliffords, Whitemans, Delyeas and Van Alstynes.

The first store owner was probably John Hillier. Mr. Critchley set up a second store in which the post office was housed. Will Black was the first blacksmith in the settlement. At the peak of its prosperity, Harlowe had three cheese factories.

A Methodist church was built on the land of Elizabeth Van Alstyne in the late nineteenth century.

Gene Brown and Nadine Brumell, eds.: *The Oxen and the Axe*, 1955.

HARMON, geographic township, Cochrane District
Position 50° 02′ 82° 10′

Situated approximately 35 miles northeast of the Town of Kapuskasing, the township's south and west boundaries were surveyed in 1923. The Spruce Falls Power and Paper Company Railway with the station point of Smoky Falls links the area with Kapuskasing. The Mattagami River widens at the base of the township as it flows through the area.

The origin of the township's name is not known.

HARPURHEY, community, Tuckersmith Township, Huron County
Position 43° 33′ 81° 25′

Situated about 20 miles southeast of Goderich on the CNR and Highway 8, the community was named after the residence of its first settler.

Dr. William Chalk, the founder of Harpurhey, arrived in the area in 1834. At first he lived in a house which had previously belonged to a Roman Catholic missionary, but after buying land from the Canada Company he built the first brick house in the township and named it "Harpurhey". Chalk was Tuckersmith Township's first doctor, first collector of taxes, and first reeve in 1850. He was also involved in the promotion of the Buffalo, Brantford and Goderich Railway.

In 1843 Dr. Chalk laid out the site for Harpurhey village. The community grew quickly with new businesses being established in quick succession. Among the early settlers were Francis Scott, Joseph Brown, George Gouinlock, and Malcolm McDermid. The Meyer brothers, who had arrived in the late 1830's, played a large part in the community's business life. Adolph Meyer became postmaster; Ludwig, Division Court Clerk and builder of Thornton Hall; Franz, a harness maker; and Jacob, the owner of a cabinet shop. Thomas Knox opened the Harpurhey Hotel in the 1840's. In the 1850's Andrew Maulhters built Union House and James McBride erected McBride Hotel. James Dill and Billie Fowler were early tavernkeepers.

Edward Cash opened a general store in 1851 and Joseph Brown established a dairy a few years later. In 1856 Hugh Robb with Frank Case began their successful pork-packing plant business which eventually carried on after the turn of the century under the name of T.R.F. Case & Co. By the 1860's the community had a shoemaker, carpenter, tailor, carriage and wagon factory, and cabinet factory. Its population peaked at just under 500.

When the Buffalo, Brantford and Goderich Railway was built through the township in 1858, a station was established at nearby Seaforth, thus depriving Harpurhey of direct rail service. The result was loss of business which became even more evident when a post office was opened at Seaforth, rather than Harpurhey in 1859. An improved road was built from Egmondville to Wroxeter in the early 1860's, but bypassed Harpurhey. Soon the merchants of Harpurhey, one by one, moved to Seaforth. By 1876 Harpurhey had declined so much that it was not even mentioned in the Huron County Directory for that year.

A building boom in the 1950's resulted in an increase in the population of the community. Many new houses were erected along Huron Road. By 1971 Harpurhey had 141 inhabitants. Huron Concrete Pipe Co., a sewer tile plant begun by Peter Christensen in 1955, is the only industry in the community today. In 1965, on land donated by Mrs. Robert Scott, Jr., the Interdenominational Pioneer Mausoleum, a red brick structure, was dedicated to the memory of Robert Scott Sr., and his wife, Margaret Elliott, and all other pioneers.

The first church at Harpurhey was built in 1847 by the Presbyterians and their minister, Rev. Alexander McKenzie. The Anglicans first held services in the Harpurhey Hotel under Rev. William Cresswell. A school built on the land of Francis Fowler in 1855 was closed in the 1880's.

Isabelle Campbell: *From Forest to Thriving Hamlets*, 1968.

HARRIETSVILLE, community, North Dorchester Township, Middlesex County
Position 42° 55′ 81° 00′

Situated 10 miles north of Aylmer on Highway 73, this dispersed rural community was named in 1847 by Captain McMillen, an early settler, after his wife Harriet.

The first settlers arrived in the 1830's, although land grants had been made as early as 1816-18. A post office was established in 1856 with Capt. McMillen as postmaster. J.J. Jelly, another early homesteader, opened a hotel about this time. In the 1860's Harrietsville became known as the military centre of North Dorchester. McMillen had formed the Harrietsville Militia in 1863 and commanded them against the Fenian invasions of nationalistic Irishmen from the United States. The Government erected a drill shed and armory in the village soon after this.

A cheese factory was established at Harrietsville by the Facey family in the second half of the nineteenth century. By 1867 it had become a sizeable plant. The Faceys continued to operate it until the 1940's when it was sold to the Borden Company, and eventually became a milk receiving station.

By 1878 Harrietsville's population was approximately 100. Residents included J.J. Jelly, John McMillen, D.F. Jelly and H. Shane. The community's population has remained fairly stable over the years. According to the 1971 census, Harrietsville had 114 residents.

H.R. Page & Co.: *Illustrated Historical Atlas of Middlesex County*, 1878.

Elizabeth Ross, ed.: *North Dorchester, 1867-1967*, 1967.

HARRINGTON WEST, community, West Zorra Township, Oxford County
Position 43° 14′ 81° 00′

This small rural community of under 100 people is located in the northwest area of the township, on the banks of the Thames River.

The settlement was first named Springville, but when a post office was opened at the locality in 1854, the name Harrington was chosen by Sir Francis Hincks, then the Postmaster General of Canada. The name honoured a friend of Sir Hincks, John Harrington, a local politician and warden of Oxford County.

By the 1870's Harrington West was a bustling community with several general stores, churches, hotels and mills. Today it is little more than a quiet rural hamlet.

Ontario Historical Society: *Place and Stream Names of Oxford County, Ontario*.

Walker & Miles: *Historical Atlas of Oxford County*, 1876.

HARRIS, township, Timiskaming District
Position 47° 33′ 79° 34′

This township is located at the north end of Lake Temiskaming, on the Upper Ottawa River. It was first surveyed in 1887 by H.B. Proudfoot and was probably named after the Harris family of Toronto. W.R. Harris was the Assistant Treasurer of Ontario at one time.

The first settlers to arrive in Harris Township were: J. Dawson, in 1888; G. Bateson, in 1890; and C.W. Tucker and R.J. Phillips, both coming in 1895.

The first school in the township was located on a spot known as

Dawson's Point. Another school was built in the centre of the township in 1904. It was known as the Ball School.

The township was incorporated in 1911. The first township council was made up of Charles W. Tucker, as reeve; Thomas Waugh, George Delury, Barry Huggins, and George B. Smith as councillors; and Fred Wilson as township clerk.

Harris Township covers an area of 12,314 acres and has a population of approximately 500. A secondary highway and dry weather roads link the area to Highway 46 in the Province of Quebec.

Harris Township Municipal Office.

G.L. Cassidy: *Arrow North: The Story of Temiskaming,* 1976.

HARRISBURG, community, South Dumfries Township, Brant County
Position 43° 14′ 80° 13′

This dispersed rural community is situated approximately eight miles northeast of the city of Brantford. The 1971 census lists the population of Harrisburg as 143.

Once Harrisburg was a shipping point on the Great Western Railway for the surrounding area. The station being located in a deep cut and there being no road leading to it, freight had to be lowered down on a slide to be loaded. When a branch line was built to Galt in the early 1850's as part of a larger network serving Western Ontario, Harrisburg became a busy junction. A town site was laid out and it was thought that the village would become a major railway point. But when it became apparent that not enough water was available to serve both a growing town population and the needs of the steam locomotives of the railway, the terminal was moved to Hamilton. The Grand Trunk took over the line in 1882 and built a new station at Harrisburg, and this time a driveway was constructed to accommodate traffic to the station. Once again Harrisburg was a busy railway centre.

The settlement was first known as Vroomenia, after the first settler, A.N. Vrooman, who arrived in 1855. Later it was called Carstairs, and finally it became Harrisburg, after the Harris family, one of which was the village blacksmith.

Early industries in Harrisburg included two brickyards, one of which operated up until 1912. At one time the community had two churches, Methodist and Baptist, and a school. Today, one church is closed and the other no longer exists. Harrisburg students attend township schools or commute to Brantford. The railway no longer plays a major role in the lives of villagers. Nowadays all main line traffic is routed via Brantford and Harrisburg is a quiet rural hamlet.

The Township of South Dumfries, 1952.

The Hamilton Spectator, 1962.

HARRISON, geographic township, Parry Sound District
Position 45° 26′ 80° 15′

Located on the shores of picturesque Georgian Bay, the township was established and surveyed in 1876. It was named after Chief Justice Harrison of Ontario 1833-78. The early subdivision was partly annulled in 1955.

There are many lakes, the largest of which is Six-Mile Lake.

A small Indian Reservation encroaches on the northern boundary of the township. The Canadian Pacific Railway travels through the area, with a station point at Point au Baril. Highway 69 also passes in the vicinity.

HARRISTON, town, Minto Township, Wellington County
Position 43° 54' 80° 53'

Located on Highway 9 about forty-five miles northwest of the city of Guelph, Harriston grew up on the banks of the Maitland River. It was named after Archibald Harrison, the first to settle in the area. He erected a sawmill in 1854, laid out town lots a few years later, and with James Stark opened the first hotels in the growing settlement.

Joshua Harrison built the first grist mill in 1856; Alexander McCrea opened a general store in 1859, and in that same year Andrew Montgomery started to operate a blacksmith shop. When a post office was established in the settlement, Archibald Harrison became the first postmaster.

Harriston's first church, a frame structure, was the Knox Presbyterian Church erected in 1860. Its first pastor was Reverend George McLennan. A public library was opened in 1867 and in 1872 the Harriston High School was erected.

The arrival of the Wellington, Grey and Bruce Railway, a line built between Guelph and Kincardine on Lake Huron in the 1870's, stimulated Harriston's growth. Prior to this time all goods offered for sale in Harriston had to be carted in from Guelph by teams, and as many as fifty farmers' teams could be seen before market days taking their produce from Harriston to Guelph over poorly built roads. In 1873 the settlement was incorporated as a village with A. Meiklejohn as reeve. One year later Harriston achieved the status of a town, and Meiklejohn became the first mayor.

By the early 1900's Harriston had two Presbyterian churches, one Methodist church, and one Anglican church. There were two foundries, a grist mill, a sawmill, two planing mills and sash and door factories, a pork packing plant, a furniture factory and a carriage factory.

The town's newspaper, the *Review*, was established in 1896. Harriston, with a population of just under 2000 in 1979, is situated in a mixed-farming district. Several industries provide employment to residents.

Historical Atlas Co.: *Historical Atlas of Wellington County*, 1906.

HARROW, geographic township, Sudbury District
Position 46° 09' 82° 00'

Located on the north shore of the North Channel of Lake Huron,

Harrow lies just south of the community of Massey. La Cloche Lake occupies a considerable part of the southwestern corner of the township.

Named after a famous college in England, this area was subdivided in 1896 by Jack Dickson. Various secondary roads link the township with Highway 17.

HARROW, town, Colchester South Township, Essex County
Position 42° 02′ 82° 55′

The town of Harrow is located on Highway 18 about 24 miles southeast of Windsor, near the resort centres of Colchester and Oxley on Lake Erie.

The early name of Harrow was Munger's Corners, probably after a pioneer settler. The name, Harrow, which came into use about 1860 appears to have been chosen to commemorate a famous English institution for secondary and higher education. Today's industries and the prosperity of Harrow's inhabitants are closely tied to the agriculture of its surrounding countryside. The southern portion of Essex County, in which it is located, has light, high, well-drained soils suited to intensive farming practices.

Prior to the 1840's, when the small agricultural settlement first began to take form, Harrow was a primeval forest. Being situated inland before the advent of highways and railways, Harrow did not enjoy rapid growth in its early years. By 1880 it had a population of only 150. But it was the municipal centre of Colchester Township, and here the Town Hall had been built. The community had two sawmills, a hub and spoke factory, a carriage and wagon manufacturer, two flour and grist mills and a cheese factory. These industries, of course, have long since disappeared along with a boot and shoe factory, a harness repair shop and the blacksmithies that once operated at Harrow.

It was not until the late 1880's that a railway from Walkerville was put through to Harrow, Kingsville and Leamington. This meant the end of isolation for Harrow's inhabitants and by the middle 1890's Harrow had become an important shipping centre for corn and other grains, dressed and live hogs. This came at an opportune time as the surrounding forests had been depleted and were no longer able to provide farmers with winter work and extra money.

By the close of the nineteenth century Harrow had been incorporated as a police village.

The twentieth century brought Harrow into its own. The light soil of South Essex combined with high prices for tobacco stimulated tobacco production. In 1909 the Harrow Tobacco Station was opened by the Government of Canada. In 1923 it became the Dominion Experimental Station which eventually began to concentrate its research on the growing of peaches, pears and apricots; early and late vegetables, particularly greenhouse and processing types; and field crops, with emphasis on hybrid corn, soybeans, tobacco and white beans.

Increased urban population and improved transportation has greatly expanded markets for early crops which the Harrow-Kingsville-Leamington section with its early season and quick-warming soils is particularly able to provide.

Harrow which was incorporated as a town in 1930, is an important shopping centre for both its prosperous farming community and a growing resort industry.

Essex County Tourist Association: *Essex County Sketches*, 1947.

Department of Agriculture: *Research Station Harrow.*

HARROWSMITH, community, Portland Township, Frontenac County
Position 44° 26' 76° 40'

Situated on Highway 38, 20 miles north of Kingston, this compact rural community of some 500 inhabitants was originally known as Spike's Corners. Its name was changed to Harrowsmith in 1840 to honour Sir Henry (Harry) Smith of Kingston, one of the original members of the Legislative Assembly of Ontario.

The first settler appears to have been Brian Spike, who arrived in 1811. Other early inhabitants included Absalom Day, John Cowdy, Richard Ellerbeck, Robert Patterson, and James Hughes. In 1825 Robert Freeman established a carriage manufactory and G.W. VanLuven started to make harnesses. John Herchimer, in 1828, built a sawmill.

The village was laid out in 1840. Unlike many nineteenth century rural communities, Harrowsmith was not laid out in one long street, but in blocks. By the mid-nineteenth century it had added to its establishments a grist mill, a potash business, a tannery, a cooperage, and a paint shop. William Russell and D.E. Buck were the village blacksmiths. Among the early shopkeepers were Samuel Stewart and George and William Griffith, and two doctors, three hotelkeepers, a milliner, a tailor, and an undertaker offered their services.

A prominent industrialist in nineteenth-century Harrowsmith was John S. Gallagher, who was a Member of the Legislative Assembly for Frontenac County for 14 years. Gallagher was involved in the livestock business and eventually became one of the largest shippers of live hogs in eastern Ontario.

In recent years Harrowsmith became known for its heritage furniture factory which reproduces pioneer furniture.

HART, geographic township, Sudbury District
Position 46° 41' 81° 38'

Hart is situated northwest of the city of Sudbury. Named after J.I. Hart, MPP for Prince Edward in 1883, this township was originally subdivided in 1885, but the subdivision was partly annulled in the 1930's.

Secondary roads link the area to Highway 144, which passes through the far northeastern corner.

HARTFORD, community, part of the city of Nanticoke, Regional Municipality of Haldimand-Norfolk
Position 43° 00′ 80° 10′

Hartford, formerly part of Townsend Township in Norfolk County,
was once known as Circularville because here one of the first circular
saws in Upper Canada was used in a mill owned and operated by John
Wilcox. The name was changed to Hartford in 1852 when the post
office was established. At that time, an American school teacher
suggested that the settlement be named after the capital of Connecticut.

A Baptist church, the first house of worship in the settlement,
was built in 1834. Some time later, a Methodist church was erected.
This church was replaced by a brick building in 1885. The original
schoolhouse of Hartford was located on the northeast corner of the
Hartford-Bealton Road.

In 1974 when regional government came to the area, the hamlet
of Hartford, along with part of Townsend Township, was annexed by
the newly formed city of Nanticoke.

Christopher Blythe, et al: Townsend and Waterford — *A Double Portrait,* 1977.

HARTINGTON, geographic township, Thunder Bay District
Position 48° 06′ 89° 57′

Partially subdivided but annulled in 1963, this township lies just
north of Lake Superior, and borders on the State of Minnesota in the
United States of America. It is watered by North Fowl Lake and South
Fowl Lake. Arrow River flows through the northern half and Pigeon
River flows through the southern half of the Township. The two rivers
join farther west to drain into Lake Superior.

Secondary roads connect the area to Highway 61.

The township was named after either the Marquis of Hartington
or one of the Duke of Devonshire's Estates.

HARTINGTON, community, Portland Township, Frontenac County
Position 44° 26′ 76° 40′

Situated less than 20 miles north of Kingston, on Highway 38,
Hartington was a prosperous village before 1900. Today it is a
dispersed rural community of a little over 100 people. Descendants of
the first settlers still occupy many of the farms which are some of the
best in the county.

Among the early settlers were Thomas Beford Sigsworth, who
arrived in 1825, Joseph Leonard, Benjamin Campsall, the Babcocks,
Matthew Trousdale, and Joseph Watson. Hartington is believed to
have been so named because it is located in the heart of the township.

By the late nineteenth century, the settlement had three stores,
two sawmills, two blacksmiths, a cheese factory, a church and a
school. It had the distinction of having two railway stations which
few other communities of its size can claim. One station was located
in the village, the other a short distance to the south. The latter was

named after the Sigsworth family, which was large in numbers and obviously influential in those days. The post office was located in Freeman's General Store.

Hartington is the seat of the township of Portland. The old schoolhouse has since become the home of the Frontenac County Branch Library and a new school has been built. In 1970 a new church was dedicated. Known as the Portland Community Church, it replaced the original Methodist Church which had become a United Church in 1925 but was closed in the 1960's. A number of new homes have been constructed on the outskirts of the community in recent years.

Reg. Whitty: *Community Spotlight*, 1974.

HARTLE, geographic township, Nipissing District
Position 46° 56′ 79° 34′

This township is situated east of Lake Temagami. Its northern, southern and eastern boundaries were surveyed in 1928 by E.W. Neelands. The western boundary was surveyed in 1885 by A. Niven.

The township is believed to have been named after W. Hartle, Crown Land Inspector. Dry weather roads link the area to Highway 11 and North Bay in the south.

HARTMAN, geographic township, Kenora District
Position 49° 46′ 92° 29′

Surveyed in 1904 and lying to the east of Wabigoon Lake and Aaron Provincial Park, the township was named after Joseph Hartman, MPP for North York in the 4th, 5th and 6th Parliaments of Canada.

Hartman Lake occupies a large area in the central part of the township. Highway 72 passes through the district linking it to Highway 17 directly to the south.

HARTY, geographic township, Sudbury District
Position 46° 46′ 81° 22′

The township lies to the northwest of Sudbury. The Onaping River, interspersed with numerous rapids, cascades through the western half of the township. Its northern boundaries were surveyed in 1899 and it was named after Hon. Wm. Harty, Commissioner of Public Works for Ontario 1894-99 and MPP for Kingston 1892-98.

HARVEY, township, Peterborough County
Position 44° 37′ 78° 23′

Harvey Township, located north of the city of Peterborough, was named after Sir John Harvey, commander of the British forces at the Battle of Stoney Creek, and later Governor of New Brunswick, Nova Scotia, and Newfoundland. Twelve miles in length and fourteen miles in breadth, it is covered with many lakes and streams, a fisherman's paradise. About half of the township is rolling land, more fit for dairying and cattle raising than growing crops.

The area was originally inhabited by the Mississauga Indians. A 20-foot high rock at Buckhorn, known as Council Rock, is believed to have been the site of Indian council meetings. Sandy Lake, to the Indians, was the "Lake of Spirits" a sacred place because of the unique green colour of its waters and the shimmering silvery colour of its fish. A heart-shaped rock formation which lies on the bottom of the lake in the shallow south bay was called the Giant's Heart because on sunny days it has a purplish hue. There, relics have been found of an Indian battle near the lake. In 1825 the Chemong Lake Indian Reserve was established near here.

The township was first surveyed by John Huston in 1826 and resurveyed in 1864-65 by Theodore Clementi. John Hall, the first settler, arrived in 1827. He bought the government mill on the Buckhorn River, in partnership with Moore Lee. In 1828 he built a dam across the river and in 1830 a saw and grist mill at Buckhorn Falls. The name Buckhorn came from Hall's practice of mounting the horns of deer he had shot on the side of his mill.

In 1832 a group of English gentlemen, mostly Napoleonic War veterans and naval officers, attempted to establish a settlement in the southwest corner of the township. Robert Dennistoun, Captain Wallis, Matthew Warner and their fellow officers, however, were ill-equipped to make a living as pioneer farmers. The distance from markets and bad roads, combined with their lack of agricultural knowledge, resulted in the failure of the settlement and within ten years all the original inhabitants had left.

Growth remained slow for many years. In 1839 Harvey's population was 50, a year later it had risen to 69. Lumbering was the chief industry and much of the land was owned by non-resident lumber merchants. In the 1850's a number of mills were built including William Henry's sawmill on Buck Lake in 1858. The Buckhorn sawmill made squared timbers, ship's masts, shingles and barrels.

With the building of mills and roads, including the Bobcaygeon Road along the western boundary and the Buckhorn Road to the northern townships of the Canada Land and Emigration Company in 1864, Harvey became much more attractive to potential settlers. A new wave of settlers arrived in the 1860's, with many moving in from the adjacent townships. By 1867 the population had risen to 438 and the township had three shinglemakers, three lumbermen, a seamstress, a merchant, a tavernkeeper, a plasterer, and a civil engineer. By 1875 there were 817 inhabitants.

B.M.N. Shaw erected a mill at Buckhorn in 1872 and William Parse Chase erected a mill at Gannon Narrows. Chase also operated the ferry which crossed the Narrows. In 1863 W.A. Scott and Son bought the mill constructed on Mississauga Creek in 1858 by William Henry. Scott was one of the lumber barons of the time. His firm built the steamboat *Sampson No. 2* to haul lumber barges and log booms.

In the 1860's Mossom Boyd kept buffalo on Boyd Island in Pigeon Lake. He tried unsuccessfully to crossbreed them with Hereford cattle.

The site of John Hall's mill became known as Hall's Bridge after the mill owner built a bridge across the river. In 1867 it became a post office. At this time S. Purser operated a general store here; Tom Eastwood was the proprietor of Eastwood House, and Edward Shaver ran a tavern beside Council Rock.

The deserted English settlement in the southwest of the township gradually attracted other settlers and developed into the village of Lakehurst. John Tarlington became the first postmaster here in 1869. By 1875 Lakehurst had a town hall, general store, cheese factory and Orange Hall.

A third community grew up at Nogie's Creek, on the north shore of Pigeon Lake, named after Old Nogie, an Indian hunter and trapper. The first, and for many years the only, white settler was John B. Crowe, who took up land here in 1836. Henry H. Humphries arrived in 1856 and Thomas Gordon and William Tate in 1864. Many more settlers came to the area in the late 1860's.

For many years Harvey was united with Smith Township for municipal purposes. It became independent in 1865 and W.A. Scott served as the first reeve.

The first school to serve the township's children was School Section No. 10, built in 1860 to educate the children of both Smith and Harvey Townships. Barbara Ryan was the first teacher. By 1866 a school had been erected at Buckhorn and by 1867 three new schools were opened. By the late nineteenth century Harvey had eight schools.

Early church services were held in the schoolhouses. Rev. Vincent Clementi preached in John Hall's house from 1863 to 1873. In 1867 "The Little White Church" was erected in Smith Township and served Harvey Township residents.

The township has a population of just over 1900 (1979). The area is served by Highway 36.

C. Blackett Robinson: *History of the County of Peterborough*, 1884.

Peterborough Historical Atlas Foundation Inc.: *Historical Atlas of Peterborough County 1825-1875*, 1975.

HARWICH, township, Kent County
Position 42° 23′ 82° 02′

Situated in the southern part of Kent County, Harwich is bounded in the south by Lake Erie. The topography is fairly flat but in the southern part of the township there is a high stretch of land known as the Ridge. The township was named after the town of Harwich in Essex, England.

When the area was first surveyed, surveys were carried out from three different directions. Thus the same lot and concession numbers appear three times. A partial survey was carried out in 1795 by Abraham Iredell and a road was laid out between Chatham and Little Lake but construction was not completed until 1844.

The first settler was probably Thomas Clark who took up land near Chatham in 1792. East of his land the Traxlers, Arnolds, John Shepley, and Adam Everett, all United Empire Loyalists, settled in

1796. Hugh Holmes also arrived in 1796 and his son Abraham was the first white child to be born in the township in 1797. Philip Toll, who came to Harwich in 1804 later became one of the first residents to live near the Ridge. Patrick McGarvin, Solomon Messmare, and Peter Smith settled near Chatham about 1808 but accidents claimed the lives of McGarvin and Messmare, and by 1811 the area was deserted.

A second settlement was begun in the north end of the township in 1816 when Daniel Field took over Philip Toll's land. He was followed by Michael McGarvin, Patrick's son. John Searness arrived in 1820 and Neil McQuarrie in 1822.

The land south of the Ridge was originally the home of the Pottawattomis and Ojibway Indians. Settlers began to establish themselves here 1818-20. The Talbot Road, which was later built across the township, and was known locally as the Old Street, was the main line of advance for incoming families. The early settlement on the Old Street was known as Old or Little Fields. Unfortunately, these pioneers discovered after they had cleared their holdings that the lots had already been granted to non-residents. They were given compensation in the form of land grants elsewhere and soon the area lost most of its inhabitants.

The land around Blenheim was known for a long time as "Ten Mile Bush" because it was unsettled until the 1830's. Richard Chute was one of the first to settle here on the Lower Ridge Road in the early 1830's. Other early inhabitants of the Blenheim area included John Toll, George Maynard, John Ridley, Mungo Samson, and Mr. Gibson, a tavernkeeper. By the late nineteenth century, Blenheim had become an incorporated village.

The western part of the township was one of the last areas to be settled. There were no families living here until 1837. Later, the Raleigh town line was to become one of the most heavily travelled roads in the county. Communities which grew up along this route were Buckhorn (Cedar Springs) and Cook's Corners (Charing Cross).

Arnold's Mill and the surrounding area prospered because a trail which linked the mill with the Talbot Road and Lake Erie provided access to markets. Trade increased when a road was opened from the Thames to Lake Erie. Among the first inhabitants in that area were the Rushtons, John Mills, E. Venecy, and John McBrayne. In 1842 Alexander McKay built a hotel on the heavily travelled road. He donated land to build a crossroad to the new Creek Road, which followed McGregor's Creek, and the community which grew up around his flourishing hotel was known as McKay's Corners. When a post office was established here in 1851, it was called Harwich.

Other settlements in the township included Fairfield or West Troy, a postal village with two stores, a steam sawmill, and a population of 150; Weldon on the Canada Southern Railway, and Louisville Siding on the Great Western Railway. Pikeville was once an important centre as the head of navigation for small vessels on the Thames. Pike and Richardson operated saw and stave mills there. Lumbering was a very important activity in the township in those days and when it declined so did the mills and the communities which depended on them.

The settlement of Guilds was the township's trading centre in the 1880's. It had harness and blacksmith shops, two stores, a church and a schoolhouse.

In 1865 the "Dutch Settlement" was founded by men from Alsace-Lorraine who had come to North America in 1850. Alois Zink and Frank Gerber were the first to buy land here. They were soon joined by Valentine and William Zimmer, George and Louis Blonde, Alois Roesch and Barney Lachine. In the 1870's the town of Shrewsbury was plotted on the proposed route of the Erie and Huron Railway. It was situated on the Rond Eau, an indentation of Lake Erie, which afforded an excellent natural harbour for the county.

In 1850 Alexander R. Robertson was elected as the first reeve of the township. The population which in those days numbered 500 has since grown to over 6,500. In recent years parts of the township have been annexed by the city of Chatham and the town of Blenheim.

H. Belden & Co.: *Historical Atlas of Essex and Kent Counties*, 1880.

Victor Lauriston: *Romantic Kent*, 1952.

HARWICH, community, Harwich Township, Kent County
Position 42° 27′ 82° 00′

Originally known as McKay's Corners after one of its early settlers, this dispersed rural community is situated on the line between Harwich and Howard Townships, about 12 miles east of Chatham.

Settlement in the area began in the 1820's with John Mills and E. Venecy among the pioneers. John McBrayne arrived in 1828 and was followed in the 1830's by the Camerons, Turners, Elijah Newcomb and Alexander McLean. In 1837 the Delmages erected buildings on Lot 19, although they did not settle there. The land was sold to E.A. Unsworth, then to the Burwells, and finally, in 1842, to a Glengarry Scot by the name of Alexander McKay. McKay had learned that the new road between Arnold's Mill and Lake Erie was becoming heavily travelled, and he erected a hotel on the land he had bought. It proved very profitable, although the Creek Road, a new road to Chatham which followed McGregor's Creek and led across Duncan McBrayne's farm a half a mile south of McKay's hotel, threatened to divert business. McKay, however, persuaded McBrayne to close the road. He then donated land for a cross-road to connect the town line with the Creek Road and his hotel thus became the centre of the crossroads in 1846. The community growing up around it became known as McKay's Corners. In 1851 McKay became the first postmaster.

Other early settlers in the community included John Clark, who arrived in 1843, and the Galbraiths in 1847.

By 1881 the community had two stores, a hotel, several shops and a steam sawmill. Its population was about 100. Harwich prospered for many years but with the railways came improved shipping facilities and the establishment of large industries in other centres, resulting in the decline of the community. The 1971 census lists a population of 82.

H. Belden & Co.: *Historical Atlas of Essex and Kent Counties*, 1881.

Victor Lauriston: *Romantic Kent, The Story of a County 1626-1952*, 1952.

HARWOOD, community, Alnwick Township, Northumberland County
Position 44° 08' 78° 11'

Situated on the south shore of Rice Lake, this compact rural community of under three hundred people is a village of summer fishing and vacation camps. At one time it was known as Sully Landing.

Among the first settlers was S.C. Curtis who arrived in 1832. He set up a business as a breeder and dealer in livestock. In the 1850's Harwood developed into a prosperous lumber town with two large sawmills.

The Cobourg and Peterborough Railway built a line via Harwood in the 1850's. Starting at Cobourg, the railway followed an old plank road and from Harwood it headed via Tick Island across the widest part of Rice Lake to Hiawatha and then on to Peterborough. The Rice Lake bridge was severely damaged the winter of 1853 just after it had been completed. No sooner had trains begun to operate after repairs, when ice jams in the lake created a gap in the line of seven feet near the island. Just under three miles in length, the bridge not only was one of the longest railway bridges in North America at the time, but also one of the most ill-fated. Nearly every winter it was damaged and repair cost mounted. When the Prince of Wales visited the area in 1860, he was not permitted to cross Rice Lake on the infamous bridge. During the following winter the bridge disintegrated and floated down the lake. Harwood, thereafter, began to decline.

Today, it is mainly a centre for tourists. Fishing is excellent in summer and the surrounding Northumberland hills offer opportunities for snowmobiling in the winter.

N. & H. Mika: *Railways of Canada,* 1972.

Great Pine Ridge Tourist Council: *Great Pine Ridge Vacation Land,* 1973.

HASSARD, geographic township, Sudbury District
Position 48° 04' 81° 31'

Severed by the Kenogamissi Lake, this township borders the District of Cochrane to the north. Highway 144 runs almost parallel with its western boundary, linking the area with the city of Timmins.

The long, narrow Lower Michegama Lake is situated in the northeast of the township and miscellaneous dry weather roads provide links between lakes.

The townships boundaries were surveyed in 1910 and 1911 and it appears to have been named after a former MP.

HASTINGS, county
Position 44° 45' 77° 40'

Hastings County, the second largest county in Ontario, covers an area of 2,323 square miles. Bordering on the Bay of Quinte in the south, it extends almost 100 miles to the north making it also the second longest county. More than half the population of 103,207 live in the southern part of the county. The county is drained by the Moira,

Trent, Salmon, York and Black Rivers.

It is composed of nineteen municipal townships: Bangor, Wicklow and McClure; Carlow; Dungannon; Elzevir and Grimsthorpe; Faraday; Herschel; Hungerford; Huntingdon; Limerick; Madoc; Marmora and Lake; Mayo; Monteagle; Rawdon; Sidney; Thurlow: Tudor and Cashel; Tyendinaga; and Wollaston.

Until 1980 Belleville remained the only city in Hastings County. At that time, Trenton which straddles the boundary between Hastings and Northumberland counties and which had been a "separated town" for the past hundred years, also achieved city status. The only incorporated town in Hastings County is Deseronto. There are seven villages: Bancroft, Deloro, Frankford, Madoc, Marmora, Stirling and Tweed.

Hastings was named in honour of the family of Francis Rawdon-Hastings (1754-1826), a military leader who had distinguished himself during the American Revolution. His family took its name from the famous town of Hastings in Sussex, England. He himself was created the Marquess of Hastings in 1817.

The naming of the county in honour of a man who fought for the British cause during the American Revolution is indicative of the character of the early settlers of the area. They were mainly Loyalists who had left their American homes to live in a land which remained under the British flag.

The first Loyalists to arrive in Hastings County were members of the Mohawk tribe, named the Fort Hunter Mohawks because their principal village had been Fort Hunter in the Mohawk Valley of New York. These Indians had remained loyal to the British Crown and many had fought on the side of the British during the Revolutionary War. They landed near the present site of Deseronto on May 22, 1784. Following their landing, a religious service of thanks was held and this moving ceremony is reenacted each year by the descendants of the original Mohawk Loyalists.

The Mohawks were soon followed by other Loyalists, mainly from New York State. The first five townships along the Bay of Quinte were surveyed in 1784. As the population of the area grew, the settlers began to demand separation from French-speaking Eastern Canada. This lead to the creation of Upper Canada in 1791. The first lieutenant-governor of the new colony was John Graves Simcoe. Simcoe believed many Loyalists were still in the United States, so he offered free land to any who would take the oath of loyalty, clear land and provide a road past their property.

Simcoe's settlement plan lead to additional land surveys in what is now Hastings County. In 1788 only the concessions of Sidney and Thurlow had been surveyed. However, by the mid-1790's most of the surveys in the southern tier of townships (except Tyendinaga which contained the Mohawk lands) had been completed. In 1793-94, surveyor William Hambly began work on parts of Rawdon and Huntingdon to the north.

Among the first to settle along the front townships of Hastings were Loyalists Alexander Chisholm and Captain George Singleton. Both settled near the mouth of the Moira River and both were involved in trade with the Indians. William Bell, another pioneer, opened a small trading post at the river's mouth in 1787. In 1790 Captain John W. Meyers purchased land in the area from John Taylor and constructed a lumber mill and a grist mill powered by the Moira River in the settlement which is now the City of Belleville. Both the river and the settlement were then known as "Meyers' Creek".

It was in 1792 that Simcoe established the boundaries for the first nineteen counties of Upper Canada. Hastings was one of these early counties set up with its eastern boundary as Lennox County, its western boundary as a line projected northward from the east bank of the Trent River; its northern boundary at that time was the Ottawa River. The county system was created to provide constituencies for the election of members to the provincial legislative assembly. It was not until 50 years later that local government was established along county lines.

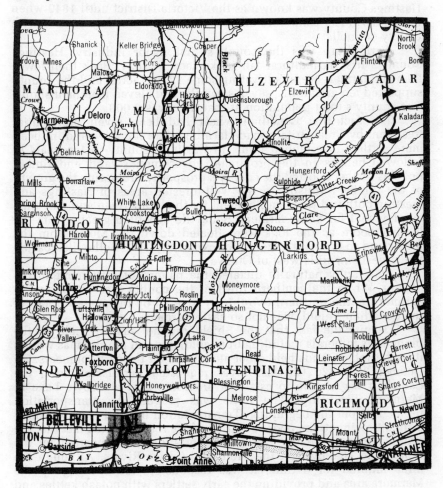

At first Hastings County was part of the Midland District, one of four Districts which at the time comprised the Province of Upper Canada. By the 1830's county inhabitants, particularly those living in the growing community of Belleville, were agitating for separation from the Midland District and were asking for the creation of a new district with Belleville as the district town. At the same time the citizens of Trent Port (Trenton) also petitioned the government for the status of district town, but Belleville won after much heated local debate. The provincial government, in 1837, set up a new district known as the Victoria District after the Queen who had recently come to the throne. Its boundaries were to be those of Hastings County, and a courthouse was to be built in the then Police Village of Belleville. In May of 1838 the cornerstone was laid and the old County Courthouse was to remain a Belleville landmark until 1960, when it was torn down to make way for a new County Administration building. Hastings County was known as the Victoria District until 1849 when the Baldwin Act came into effect and replaced district councils with county councils.

Agriculture was the county's first major industry. Hastings County's first agricultural fair took place in 1821. Back then fewer than 500 farmers were cultivating some 12,000 acres; and the county supported ten grist mills, seven sawmills and eleven merchant shops. The county's total population at that time was 3,000.

The fact that Canadian wheat had been given preferential treatment by Great Britain made farming more lucrative and induced more settlers to establish farms in Hastings County in the years to follow. Changes in the provincial government's land and timber policies further boosted the county's prosperity promoting the growth of the lumber industry in the well-forested areas of Hastings and creating both full-time employment for the lumbermen and part-time employment for many farmers. Belleville benefited greatly from the lumber boom as the logs were floated down the Moira from the hinterland to the river's mouth for export. By 1860 Belleville boasted the largest sawmills west of Ottawa.

Geography naturally dictated the pattern of settlement in the county. While the southern third of the county was conducive to agriculture, the northern two-thirds, covered by the ancient rocks of the Canadian Shield, was not so easily farmed.

Despite the fact that the Shield did not readily yield to the plough, its minerals including iron, gold, talc and uranium, as well as its rich timber stands held other attractions for the early pioneers. On October 26, 1820 Charles Hayes requested permission from the Canadian Legislature to establish an iron works at Crowe Lake in Marmora Township. The mine was plagued by transportation problems from the beginning. Transportation by land was extremely difficult owing to the poor condition of the roads and the fact that the product was so heavy. Water transportation was thwarted by the rapids and shallows on the Trent and Crowe Rivers. Although the mine faltered for a time, it was responsible for opening up the Marmora area and providing the early settlers with potash kettles and bake ovens. Eventually the Marmora mine became the country's leading mineral producer before it was again closed in the late 1970's.

In the 1860's it was the glitter of gold which precipitated a rush to Ontario's first gold mine located near Eldorado, in Madoc Township. Credit for discovering the gold is usually given to Marcus Herbert Posell, a clerk of the division court and a part-time prospector. People flocked to the area, hotels sprang up in Madoc and Eldorado and extra stages were placed on the Belleville-to-Madoc run. Belleville was known as "the golden gate" to this new "Eldorado", prices were inflated and gold was the word on everyone's lips in the county.

Unfortunately this boom turned all too quickly into a bust when it was discovered that the gold was difficult to extract, hard to locate and that the capital backing the venture was insufficient. Operations began in 1866 at the site of the original find on the property of John Richardson only to be closed in 1868 when the return was found to be only about $15 to a ton.

Several other short-lived mines were operating at Deloro, Gilmour, and Cordova. One mine was established by C.J. Gatling, the brother of the inventor of the Gatling Gun, on the shores of the Moira four miles east of Marmora Village. Problems encountered at these mines were due to the fact that the rock which contained the gold was of an arsenical variety making it difficult to extract the precious metal.

When by the 1850's the best land in the southern portion of the county had been settled the Canadian Government decided to open up the northern area. The vehicle for this plan was to be the Hastings Colonization Road. Unfortunately this road, which extended some 75 miles in a northwesterly direction from Madoc Township, passed through inhospitable Canadian Shield country. Three years after it was opened, there were only 299 settlers along its route, and if anything, the number was declining. Thus the attempt to promote agricultural settlement in northern Hastings ended in a "trail of broken dreams".

Roads in the county developed slowly during the first half of the 19th century. Between 1798 and 1801 the Danforth Road had been built to link Kingston and York (Toronto), but the route chosen went through Prince Edward County bypassing Hastings County. When this road fell into disrepair, a second road, the Kingston Road, was built (1815-1816). It differed significantly in that it provided an alternative route from Ernestown to the present site of Trenton thus passing through Belleville in Hastings.

The first regular stage line between Kingston and York passed through the county in 1817 with Belleville being the stage coach stop; but travel was rough and treacherous in those early days, and the roads impassable more often than not. Not until 1850 were roads throughout the county gravelled.

The arrival of the railway in the county heralded economic prosperity. On October 27, 1856 local dignitaries and hundreds of onlookers who had come from the countryside greeted the first train to stop in Belleville. It belonged to the Grand Trunk Railway which ran between Montreal and Toronto. The Grand Junction Railway established a line in 1879 between Belleville and Peterborough and in 1880 the same company inaugurated the Belleville and North Hastings Railway, a narrow-gauge railway which ran north from Madoc Junction on the Grand Junction Railway to Madoc, Eldorado and the Seymour and Moore Iron Works.

Tourism is one of the major sources of income for county residents particularly in the northern regions which offer an abundance of lakes and panoramic scenery. Mining and lumbering also are still being carried on.

The southern section of the county continues to contain the largest part of the county's population. Farming, mostly dairy farming, is being carried on very successfully. Belleville, the industrial centre of Hastings, offers employment to a large number of county residents. Yachting on the Bay of Quinte attracts visitors to Belleville. Here too, the County Museum is located in one of the city's remaining splendid Victorian mansions, known as Glanmore House.

Gerald E. Boyce: Historic Hastings, 1968.

H. Belden & Co.: Illustrated Historic Atlas of the Counties of Hastings and Prince Edward, 1878.

HASTINGS, village, Asphodel Township, Peterborough County and Percy Township, Northumberland County
Position 44° 18′ 77° 57′

The village is located on both banks of the Trent River and on Highway 45, approximately thirty miles northeast of Cobourg and some twenty miles east of the city of Peterborough.

James Crooks was the first settler on the site where Hastings stands today. He built a grist mill on the river's edge in 1827 and in the 1830's he laid out a settlement known as Crooks' Rapids. In 1851 Crooks sold out his holdings to Henry Fowlds. Fowlds renamed the settlement Hastings after the wife of an English nobleman, the Marquis of Hastings. The ruins of Fowlds' mill, which dates back to 1851 remain standing on the south shore of the Trent River into modern times. A post office was established in Hastings in 1852.

The first church in the village was the Presbyterian Church, erected in 1858. Later that same year the Episcopalian Church was built. In 1864 the Methodists erected their house of worship in the village and the Roman Catholics constructed their church in 1865.

Hastings was a part of Peterborough County until its incorporation as a village in 1875. At that time it switched counties in the belief that an association with Northumberland County would be more beneficial. Timothy Coughlin was elected the first reeve of the new village. The Hastings town hall was constructed in 1881.

Only one of Hastings early industries survived into the twentieth century. Today the Breithaupt Leather Company building erected in 1918, stands on the site of the original Hastings Tannery, constructed in the second half of the 1800's.

Hastings village is a popular summer resort. Pickerel, walleye, muskie, and bass in nearby Rice Lake attract fishermen from all across the province, and Hastings' location on the Trent River and the Trent-Severn Waterway makes it a favourite stopping place for boaters. Visitors to Hastings can see the Royal Hotel, an original village hotel that survives from 1857.

The population of Hastings is approximately 950. (1978)

United Counties Centennial Book Committee: *United Counties of Northumberland and Durham*, 1967.

History of Peterborough County.

Hastings, James S. Fawld's Grist Mill

Public Archives Canada, C 27550

HAUGHTON, geographic township, Algoma District
Position 46° 29' 83° 01'

Located north of the town of Thessalon, Haughton was subdivided in 1877 by Silas James. It is possibly named after Samuel Haughton, Fellow of Trinity College, Dublin.

A secondary road connects the area with Thessalon to the south. The Mississagi River wends its way through the township.

HAULTAIN, geographic township, Timiskaming District
Position 47° 43' 80° 43'

Situated to the east of the Montreal River, the boundaries of this township were surveyed in 1900 and 1909. It houses the small community of O'Brien in the southern half. Davidson Lake and Everett Lake water the area.

Highway 560 touches on the southeastern border and links the area with Highway 65.

The township was named after Professor T.E. Hault of the University of Toronto.

HAVELOCK, geographic township, Haliburton County
Position 45° 17' 78° 38'

Situated in the northern area of Haliburton County, Havelock is one of nine townships purchased in 1861 by the Canadian Land and Emigration Company, from the government of Upper Canada for the purpose of settlement. The township, surveyed in 1863, was named in honour of Sir Henry Havelock, a British war hero of the Indian Mutiny.

In 1866 the neighbouring townships of Dysart, Dudley, Guilford and Harburn united to form a joint municipality. Harcourt and Bruton joined the municipal union in 1869 and in 1874 Havelock along with Eyre and Clyde townships also became a part of the municipality. These nine townships have formed a municipal association to this day.

There is very little settlement in Havelock Township. In the 1870's a local lumber king, Mossom Boyd, cleared a farm in the township for a lumber depot. Other than that, Havelock Township over the years was used mainly by lumbermen, hunters, and tourists. Kennisis Lake, the largest lake in the township is noted for its excellent trout fishing.

In 1978 the combined population of Havelock Township and the eight other townships was 3,379.

History of the Provisional County of Haliburton, 1931.

Florence B. Murray, ed.: *Muskoka and Haliburton*, 1963.

HAVELOCK, village, Belmont Township, Peterborough County
Position 44° 26' 77° 53'

The village is situated at the junction of Highways 7 and 30, east of the city of Peterborough. It was named after Sir Henry Havelock, a British war hero of the Indian Mutiny.

In the 1840's Jehiel Breckenridge built a mill on the site where Havelock stands today. The mill was destroyed by fire and P. Pearce constructed a new mill on the same site in the 1850's. When that mill too burned down, Pearce rebuilt it, adding a grist mill. By then a settlement had begun to develop around the mill on land owned by John Mathison. A post office was established in Havelock in 1859 and Mr. Pearce became the first postmaster. By that time Havelock also had a school and two churches, located nearby. A new two-room school opened in 1890 with Andrew Kniewasser as the first principal. Another larger school was built in 1963.

In 1892 Havelock was incorporated as a village. Alex McAuley was elected as the first reeve, and James Bryans was first clerk.

Havelock is a divisional point on the Canadian Pacific Railway which was constructed from Perth via Glen Tay and westward to Havelock and Toronto in 1884. In those days Havelock was a railroad town with shops and a staff of railway men to handle operations, but with the coming of the diesel engines the shops have long since disappeared.

Early street lighting in the village consisted of coal oil lamps on cedar posts. In 1904 the Havelock Electric Light and Power Company was formed and a dam, a flume, a powerhouse, and a house for the operator were constructed on a site on the North River.

An early Methodist church in Havelock became the United Church in 1925 at the time of the church union. The Fellowship Baptist congregation worshipped in the old Mission Hall, until they dedicated their new church in 1963. Our Lady of Mount Carmel Roman Catholic Church was dedicated in 1900 by the Rev. Richard A. O'Connor. Knox Presbyterian Church opened in 1888 and St. John's Anglican in 1889. The Pentecostal Church was dedicated in 1941. For a number of years the Women's Institute operated a library in Havelock. This was replaced by a public library with Mrs. Ada Russell as the first librarian.

Havelock serves as a shopping centre for the surrounding farming community, and local industries include a cheese factory and a fishing tackle plant. The *Havelock Standard* is the village's weekly newspaper.

Belmont Township is well endowed with lakes, rivers and streams and Havelock is the hub of this tourist area. Its population of 1,236 is considerably swelled during the vacationing season.

Historical Atlas Foundation Inc. *Historical Atlas of Peterborough County 1825-1875,* 1975.

HAVERGAL, community, Carlow Township, Hastings County
Position 45° 14′ 77° 37′

This dispersed settlement is located in the northern part of Hastings County. Havergal came into being when the post office was established in John D. Campbell's home in 1886. At that time Mr. Campbell was postmaster and he named the settlement Havergal, in honour of Frances Ridley Havergal, author of several hymns. The Carlow Colonization Road from Combermere to Mayor Township helped settle the lands around Havergal.

Lumbering was an important local industry in the nineteenth century and a lumber depot established on the Lavoy farm in Havergal in east Carlow, contained a store, post office, a boardinghouse and a blacksmith shop.

In 1885 the Havergal school was built. The school that replaced it in 1916 was locally referred to as the "Tin School".

When the lumber industry declined, so did the settlement. The Havergal post office closed in 1929.

Senior Citizens of Carlow Township: *Before the Memories Fade,* 1977.

Gerald E. Boyce: *Historic Hastings,* 1967.

HAVILLAND, geographic township, Algoma District
Position 46° 49′ 84° 25′

Set on the south shore of Batchawana Bay, (Lake Superior) and subdivided in 1865 by Hugh Wilson, this township is Indian Lands except for a part on Batchawana Island.

Highway 17 runs through the eastern half of the area. The township is named for Thomas Heath Havilland, Lieutenant Governor of Prince Edward Island 1879-84.

HAVROT, geographic township, Algoma District
Position 47° 07′ 83° 24′

Formerly designated as Township 6F, the area was named after E.M. Havrot, MPP for Timiskaming.

The West Aubinadong River flows through the southwestern corner of the township, joining the Aubinadong River and ultimately the Mississagi River.

There are no roads in this area, the nearest major town being Thessalon, some 100 miles to the south.

HAWKESBURY, town, West Hawkesbury Township, Prescott County
Position 45° 36′ 74° 37′

Hawkesbury is situated on the Ottawa River, about 60 miles east of Ottawa. It is served by the Canadian National Railways and Highway 17, and is connected with Grenville on the Quebec side of the river by highway and railway bridges. The town was named after Charles Jenkinson, Lord Hawkesbury (1727-1808), a British statesman.

The area was opened up for settlement by Nathaniel Treadwell in the 1790's, and Thomas Mears was the first to take up land near the site of present-day Hawkesbury. In 1804 he bought two islands in the Ottawa River from Treadwell and constructed a dam across the channel to West Hawkesbury where he purchased 1000 acres of land and built a grist mill and a sawmill. The narrow channel was called Chenaille Ecarté (lost channel) by the French Canadian settlers of the area, but the English called the area "Snye Carty", a corruption of the French, and eventually it became known as the Snye. Mears' partner in the mill venture was Dr. David Pattee, the first doctor in the county. Mears also built a distillery, the first paper mill in Canada at St. Andrews, and the ship, *Union*, the first steamboat on the Ottawa River.

During the Napoleonic War, the ports of Europe were closed to Britain which was forced to turn to North America to secure its needed supplies of timber. In 1807 the Hamilton brothers came to Canada from Ireland and set up a business exporting lumber to England. In 1810 they bought Mears' mills and land. The Hamiltons enlarged the sawmill and soon were exporting large quantities of softwood planks to Britain.

As the Hamilton brothers' business grew, the village of Hawkesbury began to expand. The name of the Hawkesbury Mills, then one of the most productive in Upper Canada, was well known and immigrants after the War of 1812 flocked to the area hoping to find work in the mills. Most of the settlement's population depended on the Hamiltons for their livelihood. Among the early settlers were Farquhar Robertson, George Higginson, Alec Hunter, John Fraser, and Douglas Rutherford.

The Hamiltons' enterprises suffered a financial setback in the 1820's, worsened by the destruction of the mill dam which resulted in the loss of the winter's cut of logs in 1822. However, George Hamilton persevered and rebuilt the firm. By the mid-nineteenth century Hamilton Bros., as the company had become known, operated four large sawmills and owned extensive lands on the Gatineau and Des Moines Rivers. It was the largest business of its type in Canada. The mills were owned by the Hamiltons until 1889.

Other industries established in the past century in Hawkesbury, included Thomas White's planing mill and sash-and-door factory. A former axe factory became the carding mill and cloth factory of Hamelin and Ayers, and then a large woollen factory. Mr. Sortais began the commercial growing of garden strawberries. A carriage factory was in operation and Charles Hersey built a tannery. Thomas Mears opened the first store in the community. The Hotel Ouimet catered to visitors. J.G. Higginson also ran a store, and in addition he had the post office, and the telegraph office. By the late nineteenth century Mr. McManus had opened the Bridge Inn and E.P. Rochon the Hawkesbury Hotel. There was also the Royal Hotel and rail passengers were brought to the village from Calumet by the steamer *Glide*. Freight steamers landed at the wharf built by John Higginson.

Hawkesbury was incorporated as a village in 1859. John Hamilton became the first reeve. By 1855 the village's population had reached 2,000. Industries included the pulp and paper mills, lumber mills, a sash and door plant, dress factories, concrete works, a plant producing pre-fabricated houses, and a furniture factory. In 1896 Hawkesbury became a town and Félix Harbic served as its first mayor.

In 1896 the Canada-Atlantic Railway reached Hawkesbury and in 1900 a railway bridge to Quebec was constructed.

The first school was built by John Hamilton in 1846 for the children of his employees. A second school was opened in 1859 and a third one in 1866. In the 1870's these three schools were united in one building constructed by John Higginson. Among the early teachers were Thomas White, Mr. Hamilton, and Mr. Elder. A high school was opened in 1874 with A. Knight as its first principal. There were two classes for the French Canadian students. In 1887 a bilingual separate school was opened, but lasted for only four years. Pupils were then taught by the Soeurs Grises de la Croix d'Ottawa. In 1914 a new separate school was built and classes were held by the Frères de l'Instruction. A regional high school was opened in 1952.

Holy Trinity Church was built by the Anglicans in 1859 on land donated by the Hon. Peter McGill. A Congregational church, erected in 1872, is no longer in existence. The Presbyterian congregation was organized in 1826 by Rev. John McLaurin and a church was built in the late nineteenth century. Rev. H.C. Sutherland served as the first United Church minister in 1925. In 1872 a Roman Catholic chapel was erected by Abbé Brunet, Abbé Elzéar Couture became the first resident priest in 1883 and preached in the first Roman Catholic church when it was completed in 1885. A new church was dedicated in 1913. In 1959 the English Roman Catholic church was built.

A hospital was founded by Dr. Smith and Dr. F.J. Pattee around the turn of the century. In 1925 Father Joseph A. Gascon bought the Lion d'Or Hotel and converted it into a hospital, and in 1927 the Soeurs Grises de la Croix d'Ottawa took over his work.

Increased demand for hydro-electric power resulted in the expropriation of land in the Hawkesbury area by Hydro-Quebec between the years 1950 and 1962. A dam built in the early 1960's caused the flooding of many acres of land and the Snye and all its buildings including Hamilton Hall built by George Hamilton in 1835, disappeared, and is now submerged in the lake behind the dam.

In recent years, however, the town has annexed parts of the surrounding township. Today Hawkesbury has a population of 9,737 (1979) with over ninety percent of French origin. It is headquarters for the provincial health unit for the United Counties of Prescott and Russell. Carillon Provincial Park draws many tourists to the area.

Marie A. Higginson and Mrs. James T. Brock: *The Village of Hawkesbury 1808-1888*, 1961.

HAWKESTONE, police village, Oro Township, Simcoe County
Position 44° 30′ 79° 28′

Situated on Lake Simcoe about 15 miles northeast of Barrie, the village is on the CNR line and can be reached by Highway 11. Originally known as Hodges' Landing after local landowner Richard Hodges, it was named Hawkestone in 1846 by the Hon. James Patton of Barrie after A.B. Hawke, Chief Immigrant Agent for Upper Canada.

The first settlers in the area arrived in 1830. Having sailed up Lake Simcoe, they disembarked at Hawkestone Creek, which remained the site of an Indian settlement for another 40 years. These pioneers were half-pay officers of the British army and included William B. McVity, Johnston B. Allingham, Col. Davis and Col. Carthew. Richard Hodges arrived about the same time and settled on the west side of the creek. He built a wharf in front of his property and the site developed into an important landing-place for incoming settlers. From 1831 to 1832 the land agent for Oro and West Orillia Townships, Wellesley Richey, had his office here and helped immigrants locate their lots while giving them temporary shelter.

A colonization road was built into upper Oro from Hodges' Landing in the 1830's. It joined the Kempenfeldt-Penetanguishene Road at Dalton. The swamp and hills on the Kempenfeldt part of the road made the Hodges' Landing route preferable to travellers and the road became increasingly busy until 1847 when the Kempenfeldt Road was cleared. The village prospered and grew in size in these early years.

A post office was opened about 1846 with Charles Young Bell as postmaster. As traffic north increased, a new wharf for steamers was built in 1856. In 1859 a proposed plan for the village was put forward with the main street being located on the shore. However, this plan was changed with the coming of the railway in 1871 and the village became centred north of the tracks. The railway contributed to the community's growth as Hawkestone was the only regular stop between Barrie and Orillia. It made easier shipping and travelling which had decreased with the decline of the lake steamers.

One of Hawkestone's sawmills was built on the west side of the creek. In 1860 a grist mill was erected by John Williamson on the other side of the stream. Charles Priddle constructed a stone dam in the nineteenth century, as well as a sawmill which also made shingles. Joe Roe built a sawmill in the 1880's. The village also had an early brickyard. The first stores were opened by Hodges and Captain Bell and S.M. Sanford in the 1850's.

In 1900 the government built a new dock and Hawkestone became a regular stop of the Lake Simcoe excursion steamers.

In 1922 the community was incorporated as a police village. Its first trustees were Nathan Butler, Robert Kendall, and Bolton Barnhart. The Orange Lodge, built in 1923, became the Community Hall in 1946. An unsuccessful attempt was made to organize a fire brigade in 1951, but the brigade was finally established in 1967.

Today there is only one store left in the village, and the railway station was removed in 1965. The only recent industry was a basket-making shop which opened in 1957, but closed in the 1960's. Most of the village's 283 residents (1971) commute to work in Barrie or Orillia. Today, Hawkestone's main industry is tourism. The area population doubles in the summer with the advent of cottagers and campers, and a number of facilities have been established for visitors. One of the earliest was Allingham House, a summer guest house on the lake, opened by Fanny Allingham in the 1940's. The Toronto Guides and Brownies bought property here in 1940, including "St. Helen's", the house built by Richard Hodges in 1844. The building has an underground passage from the cellar to the shore constructed to avoid the long climb to the house and, rumour has it, that it once was used to smuggle in illegally-netted fish. In 1962 the Ukrainian National Federation also purchased land here for a children's camp. The Ontario Agricultural Museum was built on Highway 11 in 1965.

The first church in the community was Methodist, and Jonathan Scott was the first to preach to its congregation. A new church was built on the land of R.G. Kendall in 1898. Today this is the Hawkestone United Church. Anglicans worshipped in Metcalf's Hall until a new hall was constructed on the land of Peter Smith. In 1908 the hall was made into the Church of St. Aidan, under the leadership of Rev. Russel McLean.

Andrew F. Hunter: *The History of Simcoe County*, 1948.

Ontario Historical Society Papers, 1905.

Oro Historical Society: *The History of Oro*, 1972.

HAWKESVILLE, community, Regional Municipality of Waterloo
Position 43° 33' 80° 38'

Situated on Highway 86, about 10 miles northwest of Waterloo, this compact rural community is surrounded by rolling hills and is the meeting-place of the Conestogo River and Spring Creek. It was named after John Hawke, one of the early settlers.

The area was first settled about 1848. In 1851 the Hawke family received a land grant here and arrived shortly afterwards. They also bought some land from Mr. Schweitzer, who had squatted on it for a number of years. John Hawke built a grist mill on the Conestogo River. He later erected a sawmill and opened the first store.

Another early settler was John Fry, who arrived in 1857. In 1858 he sold land to George M. Diefenbacher, a wagon-maker and the grandfather of the late John Diefenbaker, former prime minister of Canada.

Hawkesville received a post office in 1852. It grew steadily for a number of years. At its peak it had two hotels, a woollen mill, a feed mill, general stores, blacksmith and wagon shops, a tailor shop, two doctors and a dentist. Its population was about 200 in the 1870's.

Hawkesville, until 1963, was a police village in Wellesley Township. At that time it reverted to the status of a community within the township. Most of the inhabitants are of the Mennonite faith. There are two churches, the Mennonite church and the Hawkesville Bible Chapel. Hawkesville has one public school.

Hamilton Spectator, 1964.

HAWKINS, geographic township, Algoma District
Position 49° 00′ 84° 07′

Named after William Hawkins, an early deputy surveyor in Ontario,
the township is situated to the east of the Kabinakagami Lake and
Cameron Lake. The north, east and west boundaries of the township
were surveyed in 1912.

The area is traversed by the Algoma Central Railway, with a
station point at Langdon. The Oba River flows through the centre of
the township.

HAWLEY, geographic township, Sudbury District
Position 46° 25′ 80° 37′

Located southeast of Sudbury, the township is severed by Nepewassi
Lake, which is its only significant feature.

Subdivided in 1890 but partly annulled in 1953, the township
was named after George D. Hawley, MPP for Lennox 1879-86.

Dry weather roads link the township with Coniston to the
northwest.

HAWTREY, community, South Norwich Township, Oxford County and
within the Regional Municipality of Haldimand-Norfolk
Position 42° 55′ 80° 31′

Situated about 20 miles southeast of Woodstock, the dispersed rural
community of Hawtrey was a thriving village in the nineteenth
century. It is believed to have been named after a poetess.

Settlers began to arrive in the area in the early 1800's. One of the
first local businessmen was George Southwick who built a sawmill,
shingle factory, and planing mill in 1843. A few years later he also
opened two stores. A public hall which he constructed was used for
gospel meetings.

Other businesses included the blacksmith shop owned by Tom
and John Clarke, John Seatter's drug store, and Charles Treffry's
general store, in which the post office, established in 1868, was
housed. Two hotels were run by John Armstrong and Henry
Southwick.

At one time the community was served by two railways, the
Michigan Central and the Grand Trunk. When the Grand Trunk was
sold to the Canadian National Railways in 1932, the trains stopped
running to Hawtrey.

The farmers of the area were mainly involved in dairying in the
last century. About 1930, the dairy farms began to be replaced by
tobacco-growing farms. Today tobacco is the main crop of the district.

Otterville, South Norwich, Sequicentennial 1807-1957, 1957.

HAY, township, Huron County
Position 43° 52′ 81° 36′

Hay Township, which borders in the west on Lake Huron, covers

54,950 acres and has a population of just under 2000 (1979).

Like the rest of Huron County, the township was originally part of the Huron Tract owned by the Canada Company in the early 19th century. It was named in honour of R.W. Hay, then Secretary for the Colonies.

The first settler in Hay Township was William Wilson, who arrived in 1839. The pioneers of the area were mostly of Scottish and Irish origin. In 1846 a German settler named John Orsh landed on the shore of the township, the first of a wave of German settlers who emigrated directly from Germany or from German parts of Switzerland.

In the 1840's a group of French Canadians who had been driven out of Quebec by crop failures, settled in Hay Township around the area known today as St. Joseph. The settlement was originally known as Johnson's Harbour and the settlers chose the site because of the good fishing available there. Among these new arrivals were Claude Gelinas, Abraham Bedard and Baptiste Durand. The St. Pierre du Lac Huron Church, also known as St. Peter's, was erected in 1855 on land donated by the Canada Company. A parish school was operated by the nuns of the St. Ursuline Order.

Prior to 1846, Hay Township was united with Usborne and Stephen Townships. On January 5, 1846 Hay set itself up as a separate independent municipality and the first township meeting was organized. The first wardens were Robert Doig, Chester Willis, and John Kelly.

There are two incorporated villages in Hay Township. The village of Hensall was founded by George and James Petty in 1875. In 1884 the community was incorporated as a police village and in 1896 it achieved full status as a village.

The name of the village of Zurich reflects the German and Swiss heritage of its early settlers. It was founded in 1854 by Frederick K. Knell. In 1898 Zurich was incorporated as a police village, but it was not until 1960 that it achieved full status as a village.

A portion of the township is swamp and the Canada Company found it difficult to sell land in the area. Known as the Hay Swamp, it is today under the control of the Ausable-Bayfield Conservation Authorities and the 2,000 acre site has become a wildlife sanctuary.

Hay Township is a prosperous mixed-farming district. The local economy depends on a trailer factory, grain storage facilities, and bean production. White beans are grown in abundance in the Zurich area, and every year the village celebrates good crops at the Zurich Bean Festival.

Other communities in Hay Township include Dashwood and Hills Green.

James Scott: *The Settlement of Huron County*, 1966.

HAY BAY, community, North Fredericksburgh Township, Lennox and Addington Counties
Position 44° 09′ 77° 01′

Hay Bay north of Adolphustown is a small rural settlement with a rich and colourful past. United Empire Loyalists settled in the area around Hay Bay as early as 1784. The body of water known as "Hay Bay" is a sheltered arm of the Bay of Quinte directly connected to Lake Ontario.

Among the Loyalists who arrived were a large group of Quakers. The first Preparative Meeting of the Society of Friends (Quakers) in Canada was organized in the Hay Bay area in 1798, at the house of a local settler, Philip Dorland. In that year the meeting authorized the construction of a frame meetinghouse. A new meetinghouse, built in 1868, was abandoned after the Monthly Meeting was discontinued in 1871, and, today, only the Quaker cemetery remains at Hay Bay, marked by a historical plaque.

In 1792 a Methodist congregation under the leadership of William Losee, built at Hay Bay the first Methodist Church west of the Maritimes. William Losee was the first regularly appointed Methodist itinerant preacher west of the Maritimes. Thus the Hay Bay settlement was for many years the centre of religious life for Canadian Methodists. Hay Bay Church is the oldest Methodist/United Church building in existence today.

In 1835 the church was reconstructed and enlarged. Later it was abandoned completely and local farmers used the building as a storage shed. In 1910 the Methodists acquired the property and the building and on August 21, 1912 the restored church was officially reopened. Today the church is marked by a historic plaque, and once a year a commemorative service is held in the frame structure.

A post office was established in the Hay Bay settlement in 1875. Hay Bay is surrounded by a serene farming district.

The Rev. Arthur G. Reynolds: *The Story of Hay Bay Church*, 1962.

HAYCOCK, geographic township, Kenora District
Position 49° 37' 94° 17'

Subdivided but partly annulled in 1960, the area was first surveyed in 1895. There are many lakes within its boundaries and the Trans-Canada Highway crosses the southwestern and southeastern corners of the township.

The Canadian Pacific Railway traverses the area, with a station point at Scovil.

The township was named after Joseph T. Hay, MLA, MPP for Frontenac in 1894.

HAYWARD, geographic township, Algoma District
Position 48° 44' 83° 31'

This township is situated north of the Missinaibi Lake Provincial Park and rapids abound in the Missinaibi River, which courses through the area.

The Canadian National Railways travels through the township with station points at Argolis and Fire River.

The origin of the township's name is unknown.

HAZELDEAN, community, Regional Municipality of Ottawa-Carleton
Position 45° 18′ 75° 53′

This small settlement lies less than four miles from the suburbs of the city of Ottawa, on Highways 15 and 7, on the banks of the Carp River. Prior to the formation of regional government in the area, it was part of the Township of Goulbourn in Carleton County.

Hazeldean is a Scottish name that reflects the background of most of its early settlers. The first settlers were a group of disbanded British soldiers who arrived in the area after the War of 1812. Among them were the Hodgins brothers, who were later to become prominent citizens in Hazeldean and Goulbourn Township.

The first church in Hazeldean was a small stone structure built in 1844. At that time, both the Anglican and Methodist congregations worshipped in the one building. In 1874 the Anglicans built their own frame church known as St. Paul's Anglican Church, and it stood opposite the first house of worship. By 1916 the Methodist congregation had dwindled so much that the remaining members joined the Stittsville, Huntley, or Bell's Corners churches. The little stone church was then used as a township hall. In 1935 St. Paul's Anglican Church burned to the ground, but was rebuilt in 1937.

Stittsville Women's Institute: *Country Tales*, 1973.

HAZEN, geographic township, Sudbury District
Position 47° 54′ 81° 37′

Located west of Mattagami Lake, this township houses Tatachikapika Lake, Hazen Lake and Wawongong Lake.

Highway 144 passes through the eastern half of the area, linking it with the city of Timmins to the north.

The northern, southern and eastern boundaries were surveyed in 1911 by H.J. Beatty and the township was named after a former Minister of the Crown.

HEAD, geographic township, Renfrew County
Position 46° 09′ 77° 52′

This township is located in the northern region of Renfrew County, and borders on the Ottawa River in the north, and on Algonquin Provincial Park in the south. It is believed to have been named after Sir Edmund W. Head, Governor-General of Canada 1855-1861. Organized in 1859, the township is united with Clara and Maria Townships for municipal purposes.

Settlement is sparse in the township and today, as in past years, lumbering is the chief industry in the area. The township's only communities are Mackey, located on the Trans-Canada Highway (No. 17), and Stonecliffe, also on Highway 17. Driftwood Provincial Park on the south shore of the Ottawa River is situated southeast of Stonecliffe.

The combined population of the united townships of Head, Clara and Maria is just over 400.

Renfrew County Council: *Notes on the History of Renfrew County*, 1961.

HEAD LAKE, community, Laxton Township, Victoria County
Position 44° 43′ 78° 56′

This small rural community is situated on the southwest shore of Head Lake, approximately thirty miles north of Lindsay and twenty-five miles east of Orillia.

The first settlers arrived in the area in the 1850's. Church services were held in homes as early as 1861 and a school opened in the settlement that same year. In 1862 a post office was established. The Monck Colonization Road passed through Head Lake by the 1870's.

A busy sawmill was once in operation at the locality, and a new school was built in 1884. The old school building was then used as a township hall. A Union Church erected in 1888 was used by inhabitants of the Anglican, Methodist, and Presbyterian faiths.

The community has declined in the twentieth century. The sawmill was gone by the early 1930's and the school was closed in 1945. The church was torn down in the 1950's and the post office was closed in 1957.

Only scattered settlement remains at Head Lake and most of the residences are summer cottages.

Municipal Office.

HEARST, geographic township, Timiskaming District
Position 48° 04′ 79° 42′

This township lies west of the Quebec border. The boundaries were surveyed in 1907 and it was named after Wm. A. Hearst, Prime Minister of Ontario 1914-1919.

Hearst is occupied mainly in the northeastern corner by an arm of Larder Lake. The community of Larder Lake is situated on the northern boundary line. Highway 66 links the area with Kirkland Lake, approximately 16 miles to the west. Highway 624 passes through the centre of the township.

HEARST, town, Kendall Township, Cochrane District
Position 49° 41′ 83° 40′

Hearst, located on the Northern Route of the Trans-Canada Highway (#11), 62 miles west of Kapuskasing, is known as the "Moose Capital of Canada", situated as it is in the heart of the great moose country. Its rivers and lakes yield an abundant variety of fish and offer canoeists extensive routes on the many rivers that course through the Cochrane District and which are set out by the Ontario Ministry of Natural Resources. For hikers and snowmobilers who prefer to take the land routes, trails have also been blazed.

Hearst owes its beginnings in the early 1900's to the "Iron Horse", and its eventual growth to the lumber industry. Originally, it was a transcontinental railway maintenance point and an Algoma Central Railway junction. When the settlement first came into being on the shore of the Mattawishkwia River, it was named Grant. This was later changed to Hearst in honour of a former premier of Ontario (1914-19), Sir William Howard Hearst.

The early settlers of the area were farmers; their heritage has been carried on and in the past fifty years the town has emerged as a major centre of farming in the Great Clay Belt. During its early years of development, Hearst was twice destroyed by fire and twice rebuilt. With the coming of the railway the necessary equipment for operating and repairing trains was installed, and Hearst grew in commerce and population. By the time the railway division was moved southward, the economy of Hearst had been stabilized. In 1922 it became an incorporated town under the leadership of Mayor Gus McManus and his Council.

Hearst has always had a close connection with forest industries, but after World War Two the town experienced a boom when three large lumber companies went into operation. Thus from a population of 995 in 1941, the town has grown to 5,212 in 1979. Lumber, plywood, particle board and pulp are shipped from Hearst to markets in southern and eastern Ontario.

Hearst, the terminus of the Algoma Central Railway running south to Sault Ste Marie, and with secondary Highway 538 and the Trans-Canada Highway, is an excellent centre for trade with other communities. The latter highway (#11) from Hearst to Longlac marked the completion of the first through highway to the west.

The town, predominantly French, is the diocesan seat of the Roman Catholic Bishopric of Hearst. Situated here is Hearst College, affiliated with Laurentian University.

Ontario Ministry of Natural Resources.

HEATH, geographic township, Cochrane District
Position 50° 17' 81° 22'

The township was named after W.H. Heath, Chief Cartographer, Department of Surveys, Ontario, 1923-45. The Little Abitibi River wanders along the western border. Also watering the area is the Bad River.

Some five miles to the southwest is the Ontario Northland railway point of Otter Rapids.

HEATHCOTE, geographic township, Thunder Bay District
Position 50° 17' 90° 21'

Heathcote Lake separates the northwestern part of the township from the rest of Heathcote and a large part of Barrington Lake occupies the southern half. The Canadian National Railways serves the area with a station point at Harvey in the extreme southwestern corner.

The origin of the name is unknown.

HEATHCOTE, community, Collingwood Township, Grey County
Position 44° 30' 80° 29'

Situated on the Beaver River, in northern Grey County, this compact rural community of about 100 inhabitants was originally known as Williamstown after William Fleming, an early settler. When a post office was established in 1859, the name was changed to Heathcote, as there was already a Williamstown post office.

The first settler in Heathcote was Daniel Eaton who built a house on Government Road, one of the first roads to be surveyed in the county. Many township pioneers stopped at his home on their way to claim their lands. In 1847 William Rorke became Eaton's first neighbour. He was soon followed by William Fleming.

Rorke became the first postmaster. The community grew rapidly and, for a short time, was the hub of the township. By 1865 its inhabitants included Luke Bradbury, William Donaldson, Warren Loughead, George and James Wilson, and William C. Hewish.

The growth of the surrounding communities, however, soon robbed Heathcote of its early importance.

E.L. Marsh: *History of the County of Grey*, 1931.

HEBERT, geographic township, Nipissing District
Position 47° 02' 79° 26'

This irregularly shaped township borders the Ottawa River. Its southern and western boundaries were surveyed in 1928 and the northern boundary in 1912. A dry weather road links the area to Highway 11. Owain Lake and parts of Cooper Lake and Maxam Lake lie within the township's boundaries.

It was named after a noted sculptor.

HECKSTON, community, South Gower Township, Grenville County
Position 44° 58' 75° 32'

Situated in the southern part of South Gower Township on County Road 23, this dispersed rural community was named after one of its earliest settlers, John Heck, of the famous Heck family who introduced Methodism in Upper Canada. John was the grandson of Paul and Barbara Heck.

A store was kept here by John Heck. A few years later, Wilson's Inn was built. This former stagecoach stop for travellers on their way from Prescott to Ottawa is still standing and is a village landmark. It is now used as a grocery store.

The Presbyterian congregation in Heckston was organized by Rev. Joseph Anderson in the mid-nineteenth century. Wilson's Inn was used by the Methodists as a meeting-place. About a quarter of a mile from Heckston is the oldest house still standing in the township. It was built some time between 1817 and 1820 by James Egarr.

Ruth McKenzie: *Leeds and Grenville*, 1967.

HECLA, geographic township, Cochrane District
Position 50° 17' 81° 58'

The name origin of this township is unknown. The Mattagami River severs the area at an angle, and the smaller Pike River meanders through the eastern section. The township is situated approximately 8 miles northwest of the Ontario Northland Railway station point of Coral.

HEENAN, geographic township, Sudbury District
Position 47° 48' 82° 24'

This township has three lakes, Gowagamak Lake, Trailbreaker Lake and October Lake. It was named after Hon. Peter K. Heenan, MPP for Kenora and at various times Minister of Lands and Forests, and Minister of Labour.

Secondary roads connect the area ultimately to Highway 124 and the community of Chapleau, approximately 50 miles as the crow flies to the west.

HEIDELBERG, community, Wellesley and Woolwich Townships, Regional Municipality of Waterloo
Position 43° 31' 80° 37'

Situated on the town line between Wellesley and Woolwich Townships, about 6 miles northwest of Waterloo, this compact rural community was named after a city in Germany by either John Meyer or John Kressler, both prominent men in the early days of the settlement.

John Meyer planned the southeast portion of the village and John Kressler, in 1854, became the first postmaster. Most of the inhabitants are of German origin and many are of the Mennonite faith. The community has a Lutheran and a Mennonite church. There is one elementary school.

Today many of Heidelberg's residents commute to work in Kitchener-Waterloo. A number also work in the city for part of the year and work on their farms for the rest of the year. Dairying and poultry-raising are the main agricultural activities.

HEIGHINGTON, geographic township, Cochrane District
Position 49° 15' 80° 35'

Situated northeast of the town of Cochrane, the boundaries of this township were surveyed around 1930. It is linked by a secondary road to the Canadian National Railways station point of Stimson Diamond.

The name of the township is taken from Wilfred Heighington, MLA, MPP for St. David (Toronto) 1929-34.

HELE, geographic township, Thunder Bay District
Position 48° 59′ 88′ 30′

Previously subdivided but annulled in 1956, this township lies north of Black Bay in Lake Superior, and to the east of the towns of Red Rock and Nipigon. It is watered by Black Sturgeon River, which wends its way to Lake Superior.

Dry weather and secondary roads link the area to Highway 11/17.

The township is named after C. Hele, Secretary of the Department of Lands and Forests.

HELLYER, geographic township, Sudbury District
Position 47° 58′ 82° 47′

Located southwest of Ivanhoe Lake Provincial Park, this township is bisected by the Ivanhoe River. Hellyer Creek, interspersed with rapids, cascades through the northern half of the area.

Highway 101 traverses the northern boundary, linking the area with Chapleau to the southwest and Foleyet to the northeast.

The township was named after Albert Hellyer, MPP for Wellington East in 1919.

HEMBRUFF, geographic township, Algoma District
Position 46° 35′ 82° 38′

Formerly designated as Township 151, it is named after Leonard M. Hembruff, R.C.A.F. Sergeant, of Little Current, killed during World War II.

The area houses part of the Mississagi Provincial Park and several small lakes.

A secondary highway links the southwestern corner with the town of Elliott Lake.

HENDERSON, geographic township, Cochrane District
Position 50° 01′ 85° 26′

Named after a former MP by that name, this township borders the district of Thunder Bay on the south. The Canadian National Railways passes through its center, with the nearest station point being a few miles to the east of the township. Various small creeks straggle through the area.

HENDRIE, geographic township, Sudbury District
Position 46° 20′ 80° 38′

Subdivided in 1897, but annulled in 1953, the township was named after Sir John Hendrie, Lieutenant Governor of Ontario 1914-1919. The area is located north of the French River. Lake Nepewassi occupies the northwestern corner and part of Amateewakea Lake points a finger into the southeastern corner of the township. Secondary and dry weather roads connect the area with Highway 535 to the east and the city of Sudbury to the northwest.

HENLEY, geographic township, Cochrane District
Position 49° 00' 80° 13'

Named in honour of the English town Henley on the River Thames, famous for its boat racing, this township is linked by a dry-weather road to the Canadian National Railways line. The township lies just northwest of Lake Abitibi and approximately 45 miles east of the town of Cochrane. The Low Bush River flows through its western half.

HENNESSY, geographic township, Sudbury District
Position 47° 22' 81° 31'

Named after O. Hennessy, a lumberman, all boundaries of this township were surveyed in 1911. It is divided by Hennessy Lake, and the Canadian National Railways passes through the western half of the township with a station point at Stupart.

A dry-weather road leads from Stupart to Donnegana Lake which lies on the western boundary.

HENRY, geographic township, Sudbury District
Position 46° 35' 80° 22'

Located southeast of Wanapitei Lake, this township was subdivided in 1893 by Bolger, but the subdivision was partly annulled in 1964.

The township borders the District of Nipissing on the east, and various secondary roads link the area with Highway 17. Some 25 miles to the west is the city of Sudbury.

Henry township was named after Robert Henry of Brantford.

HENSALL, village, Hay Township, Huron County
Position 43° 26' 81° 30'

Hensall, a village of almost 1000, is located in southern Huron County on Highway 4. The credit for founding Hensall goes back to two brothers, George and James Petty, who arrived in Canada from Hensall in Yorkshire, England in 1851.

These two enterprising men enlarged their original holdings in 1874 just prior to the encroachment of the London, Huron and Bruce Railway into the area, then proceeded to negotiate with the railway company for a station and yard. They offered the company the land if the proposed railway would pass through their property and if the station would be called Hensall. Land being $80 an acre at that time, the company took up their offer, and the London, Huron and Bruce Line was built through the Petty property in the early 1870's.

The Pettys, however, had more to offer than their land for by this time they had established themselves as stock dealers and importers in the area. During the year 1875 they constructed a pork packing plant which was in operation by the time the first train was ready to pass by their door. They worked relentlessly trying to encourage settlement in their would-be community. In 1876 T.J. Wilson established a saw and planing mill at Hensall. The third industry to come to the village was a flour mill, established by Samuel Rennie. The mill was built on a grand scale, three storeys high with four runs of stones operated by a sixty horse-power engine.

The village was laid out into lots in 1877. In 1878 a hotel was added to the cluster of businesses that had grown up, by James Wilson. The same year two small factories opened their doors, a planing mill and sash factory, and a rake and bending factory. Paul D. Bell is credited with building the first grain storage elevator in the village. By 1876 Hensall had a post office with James Sutherland as the first postmaster.

Hensall had mushroomed from one solitary house in 1876 to a population of between 300 and 400 people by 1877. The Petty brothers and T.J. Wilson were building houses as quickly as they possibly could in order to accommodate this boom. In 1878 there were 30 new houses under construction in the little village.

Hensall, famous in the 1880's for its race track, slowed to a more moderate rate of growth following the sudden burst in its infancy. It was incorporated as a police village in 1884. In 1895 Hensall was enlarged beyond its original Hay Township boundaries to include a corner of Tuckersmith Township. This move was in preparation for the day in 1896 when Hensall was incorporated as a village. Its population at that time was 898. The first reeve of the village was G.C. Petty, a nephew of the original settler. William Bell, William Moir, William Hodgins and H. Cook were the first councillors and H.J.D. Cook was elected as the first Clerk of the village. In 1913, G. McEwen willed land to the village of Hensall to build a town hall.

Hensall has remained a prosperous village known in the area for its grain storage facilities. As the crops in the surrounding district changed, Hensall became famous for its production of beans, and the village began to hold annual "bean festivals".

Hensall's industries over the years included a flax mill, a foundry, blacksmith shops, carriage and wagon shops, harnessmakers, an apple evaporator and a corset factory. A trailer factory remains as the only large industry in the village today.

M. Ellis: *Hensall: A Beautiful Place to Live.*

James Scott: *The Settlement of Huron County,* 1966.

HENVEY, geographic township, Parry Sound District
Position 45° 48' 80° 35'

Partly subdivided, this township was surveyed in 1912. It sits on the shores of Georgian Bay and is mainly occupied by a sizeable Indian Reservation. Henvey Inlet penetrates the centre of the Reservation. Grundy Lake Provincial Park lies just to the north.

The Canadian Pacific Railway passes through the area, with a station point at Still River. Also traversing the eastern half of the township is Highway 69.

It was named by Henry Wolsey Bayfield, Admiralty Surveyor in British North America, in honour of Lieutenant Wm. Henvey, R.N., killed in the war of 1812 on the St. Lawrence.

HENWOOD, geographic township, Timiskaming District
Position 47° 38′ 79° 57′

Subdivided in 1889, the township lies east of the border with the Province of Quebec, and northwest of the town of New Liskeard on the Montreal River.

Highway 65 passes through the northern half of the area, and the Ontario Northland Railway serves two station points, Kenabeek and McCool, also in the northern half.

Dry weather and secondary roads are plentiful and the area is watered by a few small creeks.

It was named for a Dr. Henwood, from Brantford.

HEPBURN, geographic township, Cochrane District
Position 49° 01′ 79° 38′

Situated north of Lake Abitibi, this township borders the Province of Quebec to the east. It was named after Hon. Mitchell Frederick Hepburn, Liberal Premier of Ontario during the period 1934-1942.

Secondary roads link the area with the Canadian National Railways station points of Goodwin and Eades.

HEPWORTH, village, Amabel Township, Bruce County
Position 44° 37′ 81° 09′

Situated in Central Bruce County, about 10 miles northwest of Owen Sound, on Highways 6 and 70, the village was named by William Spencer and William Plows after the town of Epworth, England, where they had spent their boyhood years.

The first settler in the area was William Spencer who, in 1862, bought 200 acres 2 miles west of the village. John Paget arrived shortly afterwards. In 1865 Spencer built a hotel at the present site of the village and a settlement grew up around it. With the establishment of a post office in 1866, the community was named Hepworth. William Spencer was the first postmaster.

Among the early inhabitants were William Simpson, William Wilson, William Moffatt, John White, and John Spencer. In 1867 William Plows built a second hotel to serve travellers. The first store was opened by Mr. Briggs and the second one by William Driffil.

In 1882 the railway was built through Hepworth. A second post office was established at Hepworth Station with James Vance as postmaster. The two post offices were later merged. Following the construction of the railway, many new businesses were established in the village, including blacksmith shops, livery stables, butcher shops, grist mills, sawmills, and lumber operations. J.E. Murphy erected a sawmill in 1882. C.H. Witthun's mill later became the site of the Hepworth Manufacturing Company. A stave factory was built by D. Tennant, and E. Brigham set up a wood and timber business. In 1886 Pickard and Rowan constructed a sawmill and the railway put in a siding for them to use in loading poles, posts, and lumber. Other sawmills were run by Reid Bros., E. Todd, and J. Jackson and Son. Frank Campbell was the village doctor and Mr. Sparling edited the *Hepworth Journal*, founded in 1885. It later became *The Hepworth Progress*.

A schoolhouse was erected in the village in 1865. It was replaced by a new building in 1890, which served the community until 1959. The first Hepworth Continuation School was held in Down's Hall in 1919 and a schoolhouse was built in 1921. In 1958 the Continuation School became a public school.

The first Methodist church was dedicated in 1889. This original building is now the church hall. St. Andrew's Presbyterian was erected in 1896. The Anglican Church of the Redeemer was built around the turn of the century. Part of it now houses the public library, established in 1887. The Roman Catholics founded St. Mary's Church in 1906 and the Baptist church opened in 1950.

An interesting feature of the village is an underground river. The source is Skinner's Marsh east of Hepworth. The stream can be heard through several sink holes in the village. It emerges to the west of Spring Creek.

The Bruce County Historical Society Year Book, 1968.

Thomas Johnston, ed.: *The Early Days of Bruce County*, 1936.

HERBERT, geographic township, Thunder Bay District
Position 49° 11' 85° 31'

Situated just to the northeast of the town of Manitouwadge, the township was established in 1955 and named after A. Robert Herbert, MPP for Timiskaming, 1951-55.

Several small lakes are found in the southern part of the area.

HERON BAY, community, Pic Township, Thunder Bay District
Position 48° 49' 86° 17'

Situated on Lake Superior, a few miles east of Marathon, Heron Bay was founded when the construction of the Canadian Pacific Railway was completed in 1885. Two road gangs remained at Heron Bay in order to maintain the track in the area. A post office was established in that year and J.A. Nichol became the first postmaster and stationmaster. Mr. MacDougall opened a store to serve local trappers and Indians. Coal to power the trains was brought to Heron Bay by ship and soon a spur line was built to connect Coal Island, where the product was landed, with the main track.

From about 1900 lumbering became an increasingly important activity in the area. Many of the operations were carried out by small companies. Pigeon Timber, a larger firm, was in business in the district until 1936, when General Timber took over its lease. In 1937 the Ontario Paper Company started operations at Heron Bay, and soon was followed by Marathon Pulp Mills of Canada. A three-and-a-half-mile long flume was built by Ontario Paper from Black River to Heron Bay in order to keep its logs separate from those of Marathon Pulp Mills, which were brought along the Pic River. The Pic and Black Rivers join in the vicinity of Heron Bay a few miles before reaching Lake Superior.

In 1938 Ontario Paper opened a new townsite south of Heron Bay. Known as Heron Bay South, it had an office building, houses for company employees, a warehouse, an infirmary, a machine shop, bunkhouses, and a cookhouse. A combined school and church building was erected, followed by a community club and a curling rink.

The last log drive of Ontario Paper at Heron Bay took place in 1964. After this the community began to decline. The cookhouse, staff house, barking plant, and flume were removed and Heron Bay South almost completely disappeared. Heron Bay, itself, is a dispersed rural community today, numbering about 140 people according to the 1971 census.

Jean Boultbee: *Pic, Pulp, and People*, 1967.

HERRICK, geographic township, Algoma District
Position 46° 56' 84° 38'

An almost triangular area overlooking Pancake Bay in Lake Superior, this township was established in 1866-67 and named after Thomas W. Herrick, a surveyor who did much exploration and survey work in Northern Ontario around 1860.

The Trans-Canada Highway passes through the northern part of the area, and Batchawana Bay Provincial Park lies directly to the east.

HERRON'S MILLS, community, Lanark Township, Lanark County
Position 45° 03' 76° 24'

Situated in central Lanark County, on the Clyde River, this dispersed rural community was named after James and John Herron who operated a sawmill here in the late nineteenth century.

The first settlers arrived in the 1820's and included Henry Glass, James Blackburn, William Morris, and Peter Kerr. In 1842 the Gillies began sawing operations on the Clyde River, and later they also built a carding mill. Hugh McEwen was the community's first blacksmith and James Munro opened an early tannery. "Drummonds" was a nineteenth century grist and shingle mill.

In 1871 the Herron brothers bought the Gillies' sawing operation. A post office was established in John Herron's house in 1891. The Herrons' company dissolved in 1919 but the sawmill continued to operate until 1951.

Claire Thompson, ed.: *Township of Lanark 1820-1970*, 1970.

HERSCHEL, geographic township, Hastings County
Position 45° 09′ 77° 59′

Situated on the western border of Hastings County, Herschel has a population of over 900 (1979). It was named after the distinguished British astronomer, Sir William Herschel.

The boundaries and the eastern part of the township were surveyed in 1856 by J.S. Peterson. The remainder was subdivided by A.B. Perry in 1864. The latter described the township as "considerably broken with lakes, ponds, swamps, marshes and granite hills. . . ."

By then a settlement was flourishing in the northeast corner of the township, although the main portion of it was located in Wicklow Township. Then known as the Doyle Settlement, it was later named Maynooth.

In the southeast, settlements had been started in the Baptiste, York River and Bird's Creek area.

Lumber companies were attracted to the pine forests of the township. One of the first sawmills in Herschel was operating on a bay of Baptiste Lake. The Irondale, Bancroft and Ottawa Railway, built around 1900, carried the township's lumber to market.

Baptiste Lake with its numerous bays is one of the most beautiful lakes in Hastings County. The Hudson's Bay Company is said to have built a fort near Baptiste in the 1700's. Today the district is a tourist's and fishermen's paradise.

Until 1960 Herschel was united with Monteagle, its neighbour to the east. In 1960 Herschel gained separate status. Frank C. Peever was elected as the first reeve.

Gerald E. Boyce: *Historic Hastings,* 1967.

HESPELER, part of the City of Cambridge, Regional Municipality of
Waterloo
Position 43° 26′ 80° 19′

Hespeler, formerly a town in Waterloo County, is situated on both banks of the Speed River, six miles north of Galt and about 10 miles south of Guelph. In 1973 Hespeler became part of the new City of Cambridge.

The beginnings of Hespeler go back to 1818 when Abram Clemens, a Loyalist from Pennsylvania, purchased 515 acres of Indian land in the area from Richard Beasley of Hamilton. In the 1830's, Joseph Oberholtzer acquired land across the river from Clemens' holding. Oberholtzer deeded some of this land to his brother-in-law, Michael Bergey. The Bergey family then built a log cabin, a sawmill, and a small foundry and the settlement became known as Bergeytown. By 1835 the population of the settlement had risen to 100 and the community was renamed New Hope. In 1840 Cornelius Pannebecker and Joseph Oberholtzer, both from Pennsylvania and both of Mennonite stock, built a third sawmill in the settlement. New Hope also had a tannery, a pail factory, two smithies, two tailors, two shoemakers and a tavern.

Jacob Hespeler, originally from Baden-Baden, Germany, moved to New Hope from neighbouring Preston in 1845. Hespeler purchased Clemens' sawmill and replaced it in 1847 with a grist and flour mill. He also operated a distillery and later added a large stone woollen mill — the first woollen industry in the area. In 1848 a post office was established at New Hope and Mr. Hespeler became the first postmaster.

Hespeler's influence was largely responsible for the extension of the Great Western Railway from Galt, through Preston and Hespeler, to Guelph in 1858, and the community of 750 people was booming. In that same year, the settlement was incorporated as a village. In honour of its leading citizen, the village was renamed Hespeler. Mr. Hespeler became the first reeve of the village; other members of the first council included Adam Shaw, Conrad Nahrgang, David Rife, and Charles Karch.

One of the first churches in the area was the Methodist Church of New Hope. The original church building was erected in 1849; in 1868 a larger building replaced it. In 1925 the church became part of the newly-formed United Church. In 1962 St. Luke's United Church was built on Galt Street in Hespeler. The congregation of the Presbyterian Church was organized in 1855. The first church building was erected in 1863 and the present church was built in 1907. The Hespeler United Missionary Church dates back to 1902, and the present church was purchased in 1922. St. James Anglican Church was dedicated in 1893. The original building for St. Mary of the Visitation Church was destroyed by fire; in 1916 the present church was acquired from the Presbyterian Congregation. The first house of worship of the Hespeler Baptist congregation was erected in 1893. St. James Lutheran Church was organized as early as 1854.

The Hespeler Public Library began as the Mechanics' Institute in 1871. In 1901 the Public Library was organized. It was housed in different buildings around the town until the present building was constructed in 1922.

Hespeler was incorporated as a town in 1901. G.D. Forbes was the first mayor; the first town councillors were Dr. R.J. Lockart, J.W. Christman, David Rife, Herman Prestien and August Pabst. Hespeler was one of the first communities in Ontario to enjoy electrical service. Town council, in 1901, took over the electric lighting equipment that had previously been operated by Joseph Shantz in connection with his chopping mill.

Prior to its amalgamation with the new city of Cambridge, Hespeler had a population of about 6,300. C.E. Ware was the last mayor of the town in 1972.

Hespeler is situated in a rich farming district and many small local industries made Hespeler a prosperous town.

Waterloo Historical Society, 1972.

HESSON, community, Mornington Township, Perth County
Position 43° 38′ 80° 48′

Situated about 20 miles northwest of Kitchener-Waterloo, this dispersed rural community was named Hesson by a Member of Parliament of that name who established a mail route to the settlement.

The first settlers who were mostly of German origin, arrived in the 1840's. Among them were George Stemmler, Andrew Beisinger and the Knoblauchs.

A school was opened in 1859 with Mr. Mack as the first teacher. Mack, who also ran a shoe shop, named the community Bethlehem. It was later called Mornington, then became Hesson when the post office was established in 1883.

By the late nineteenth century, Hesson had a hotel, two churches and two schools. Joe Holm ran a sawmill and furniture factory, and Louis Mittleholtz operated a clay tile yard. A barrel and tub shop was established by Romanus Gruff. In the early 1900's, E.C. Knoblauch opened a cement tile yard.

HEYSON, geographic township, Kenora District, P/P.
Position 50° 59′ 93° 51′

Located south of Red Lake and east of Gullrock Lake, the area itself encompasses several small lakes.

Highways 105, 125 and 618 serve the locality and to the southeast is the Pakwash Provincial Park.

The township was named after Charles Thomas Heyes, a metallurgist of Toronto.

HIAWATHA, geographic township, Algoma District
Position 49° 30′ 84° 59′

So named after Henry Wadsworth Longfellow's famous Indian hero, the township lies at the northern part of Nagagami Lake, and east of Nagagamisis Provincial Park. There are no roads within the township's boundaries.

HIAWATHA, community, Otonabee Township, Peterborough County
Position 44° 11′ 78° 13′

Situated on the northern shore of Rice Lake at the mouth of the Otonabee River, this dispersed rural community is part of an Indian Reserve. It was named after Henry Wadsworth Longfellow's famous poem.

The village had started by 1829, but by the 1840's there were only 18 families living in Hiawatha. By 1871 the number of families had increased to 31 and the population was 114. Among the residents were Mozang Paudas, chief of the band, Robert and Henry Crow, Robert and Lorenzo Sopper, William and John Chippeway, Daniel

Cow, and Moses Muskrat. At this time the community had 30 houses, 3 barns, a schoolhouse, a chapel, and a post office opened in 1861. The inhabitants supported themselves by hunting, fishing and gathering wild rice which grew in abundance in the lake. The first resident missionary was the Methodist, George Bissell, who came to the area in 1825. Rev. Peter Jones, believed to have been an Indian or Metis converted to Methodism, was a leader of the community in the 1820's and aided the band in their negotiations with the government. Other early ministers included Wellington Jeffers and Richard Brooking.

Most of Hiawatha's residents work at Canadian General Electric in Peterborough. Others hunt, fish, and trap, or work on projects on the Reserve. Hiawatha Park was developed in 1968 and recently a number of cottages have been built along the shoreline.

D. Gayle Nelson, ed.: *Forest to Farm Early Days in Otonabee*, 1975.

HIBBERT, township, Perth County
Position 43° 27′ 81° 20′

Hibbert is the most westerly of the Perth County townships. The third smallest township with an area of 43,258 acres, it was named after William Hibbert, a director of the Canada Company.

The land is largely undulating, with some high hills, although the northwest corner is more level. Most of the land is suitable for agriculture, and mixed farming predominates. Easy access to two railways, and therefore to markets, encouraged the development of agriculture in the township.

Hibbert was part of the Huron Tract owned by the Canada Company which was greatly involved in the colonization of western Ontario. It was surveyed by John McDonald in the years 1829-1835, but there was little settlement for some time after the survey. The first settler may have been Robert Donkin who opened a tavern on Lot 16, Concession 1. The first settlement in the township was "Irishtown" (St. Columban), founded by Father Schneider. Thomas Fox, Daniel Keenan, and others had taken up land there by 1839. Settlement was later in the eastern part of the township, David Oughton being one of the first pioneers in 1849.

In Ireland from 1845 to 1847 the failure of the potato crop, a staple in the lives of the Irish, created a disastrous famine. Fleeing Ireland for a better life in Canada and the United States, many came to the township of Hibbert increasing the population during that period from 247 to 1,191. They were referred to as the "Famine Irish". The opening of the Centre Road brought further settlement, particularly a number of experienced pioneers from the southern counties who quickly cultivated the land. By 1857 most of the area was settled, mainly by British immigrants and a smaller number of Germans. The population reached 3,394 by 1881, but has since declined to about 1,400.

There was no mill in the township in the early years and this caused much hardship for the settlers who had to travel a long distance to the mill at Mitchell in the neighbouring township. A grist mill was built at Springhill (now Staffa) in 1855 but was not operated for several years. One of the earliest township industries was the manufacture of potash and black salt, which was exported to Montreal by J. & W. Hill of nearby Mitchell. The discovery of salt at Seaforth by Joseph Kidd led to the development of Carronbrook (now Dublin), which became a police village in 1878.

In 1842, Hibbert was united with McKillop and Logan for municipal purposes. Robert Donkin became the first district representative after separation in 1847 and the first reeve of Hibbert in 1850, when the Municipal Act came into effect in Ontario.

Carronbrook's first school opened in the early 1850's. By 1855 there were two schools in the township. In 1887 the first separate school was constructed near St. Columban on land given by Michael O'Connor. There were three separate schools by 1908.

Rev. Mr. Stephens, a Bible Christian, held what was probably the first religious service near Staffa. In 1851 a Presbyterian church was built on land donated by William Roy, and in 1853 another Presbyterian congregation was organized by Rev. Mr. Proudfoot. The first Methodist church was probably begun by Rev. A.A. Smith in 1856 at Staffa School; lessons were held in the church, a reversal of the usual practice. Four more Methodist churches were erected in the township before 1890. In Dublin an imposing new house of worship with Rev. Father Fogarty as priest replaced the old Roman Catholic church in 1899.

Settlements in Hibbert include Dublin, Cromarty, and St. Columban. Staffa was the township seat in the nineteenth century. Municipal offices are now located at Dublin.

W. Stafford Johnston and Hugh J.M. Johnston: *History of Perth County to 1967.*

William Johnston: *History of Perth County, 1825-1902,* 1903.

HICKS, geographic township, Cochrane District
Position 48° 55' 82° 10'

Groundhog River traverses the western half of this township, named either after Andrew Hicks, MPP for Huron South 1919, or for a Mr. Hicks who was a provincial architect in the 1940's. The exact origin of the name is unsure.

A dry weather road to the north links the area to Highway 11 and slightly north of the highway is Remi Lake Provincial Park.

HICKSON, community, East Zorra Township, Oxford County
Position 43° 14' 80° 48'

A dispersed rural community of about 200 inhabitants, Hickson is situated in the northern part of Oxford County, about 9 miles north of Woodstock on Highway 97. It was named after Sir Joseph Hickson, the general manager of the Grand Trunk Railway, 1874-90.

The settlement came into existence after the railway built a station at this point. When a post office was established in 1883 it was given the same name as the railway point.

Ontario Historical Society: *Place and Stream Names of Oxford County, Ontario.*

HIGHGATE, village, Orford Township, Kent County
Position 42° 30′ 81° 49′

Situated 26 miles east of Chatham on Highway 401, Highgate was named in 1865 by postmaster Anthony Atkinson after a small suburb in London, England.

The first settlers in the area were the brothers John, James, and Joseph Gosnell from Ireland. They settled in the vicinity of Middle Road in 1822. Another member of the family, Lawrence Gosnell, arrived in 1832. Other early settlers in what became known as the Gosnell Settlement included John Lee, Finlay and William McKerricher, Thomas Tape, Soloman Teetzel, Richard Baker, and the Demickes.

In the mid-nineteenth century, Anthony Atkinson set up an unofficial post office to which he brought the mail from Duart. He became the official postmaster when the government established a post office in 1865. The community of Highgate developed around this post office.

Already important as a local shopping centre before 1870, Highgate became even more prominent as a shipping point after the construction of the Canada Southern Railway in 1872. The railway opened up new territory and Highgate developed as a market for agricultural goods and timber. The community offered mail, telegraph, and express services as well as steam sawmills, oat, and flouring mills. The building of the Lake Erie and Detroit River Railway across the township in 1894 brought even more business to Highgate.

By 1881 the community's population had reached 300 and in 1884 it became a police village.

A stave factory was built to process timber. Scott and Talson erected a grist mill which was later taken over by the Highgate Milling Company. A Canadian Canners plant was opened and was later turned into a warehouse. By 1915 Murton S. Scott had a flourishing lumber business. "Big John" Lee prospered raising cattle and sheep.

In 1917 Highgate was incorporated as a village and annexed 640 acres to allow for future expansion. D.J. McPhail served as the first reeve. The village became the capital of Orford Township and the centre of the Orford Agricultural Society which built its Agricultural Hall here.

Methodist services were first held in the home of Mary Gosnell, then in a schoolhouse on the farm of W. Milton Attridge. A church was erected in 1849, and a new church was built in 1870. In 1898 Rev. T.T. George was responsible for the construction of a more modern church and when this church burned down in 1917, he was instrumental in the erection of the present church.

Evelyn Beatrice Longman, noted American sculptress, attended Highgate Public School while she lived with her grandparents in the village. In 1916 she designed the symbol for the American Bell Telephone Company.

The village has a population of over 400.

Victor Lauriston: *Romantic Kent*, 1952.

HILL, geographic township, Sudbury District
Position 47° 58' 83° 34'

Located in the Windermere Lakes area and northeast of The Shoals Provincial Park, the township, which is dotted with small lakes, is named after H.P. Hill, formerly MLA, MPP for Ottawa West in 1919. Dry weather and secondary roads link the area with Missinaibi Lake Provincial Park to the north, and the town of Chapleau to the south.

HILLARY, geographic township, Timiskaming District
Position 48° 14' 81° 50'

Bordering on the west with the District of Sudbury, the boundaries of this township were surveyed in 1910 by H.J. Beatty. There are several small lakes in the area, and Highway 101 passes through the northwestern corner, connecting it with Timmins, some 20 miles to the northeast.

It was named after N.T. Hillary.

HILLIARD, township, Timiskaming District
Position 47° 43' 79° 42'

Named after Thomas Hilliard, an Inspector of High Schools and Provincial Member of Parliament, Hilliard was subdivided by Purvis in 1887 and incorporated as a township in 1910.

The first settlers were William Rice, William Kerr, W. Zucker, Neal Edwards, M.R. Edwards, D. Allan, and A. Coutts. They took up land in concessions 2 and 3 and also in an area adjoining the banks of the Blanche River.

The first post offices were established at Ironwood on the Blanche River and Couttsville on the south boundary of the township. The first store was opened in Hilliardton.

The early industries in Hilliard included lumbering, pulpwood, trapping and farming. Today the 318 residents (1978) of the township are engaged in beef and dairy farming and the manufacture of cement products.

The township is situated south of the town of Englehart and the Kap-Kig-iwan Provincial Park. The area is served by Highways 11 and 569.

HILLIER, township, Prince Edward County
Position 44° 00' 77° 25'

The early history of Hillier Township is that of Ameliasburgh Township of which the area was a part until 1824. On the petition of a number of residents, Hillier was established by an Act of Parliament at that time, and the new township was named after Major Hillier, Secretary to Sir Peregrine Maitland, then the Lieutenant Governor of Upper Canada.

Irregularly shaped, Hillier is surrounded by Ameliasburgh,

Sophiasburgh and Hallowell Townships on the northwest, northeast and southeast, while Lake Ontario with its numerous bays and inlets, including part of Weller's Bay and Pleasant Bay, forms the natural boundary in the west and south.

The township, as other parts of Prince Edward County, was largely settled by United Empire Loyalists. Among the early settlers in the Pleasant Bay area were the DeLongs, Beadles, Van Hornes, Bairds, Tripps and Hawleys. On the north side of this bay settled the Youngs, Piersons, Huffmans, Camerons, Careys and Fergusons.

The Williams, Valleans, Hicks, Dorlands, Pearsalls and Mordons were among the first to take up land in the eastern part of Hillier.

In other areas of the township the pioneers included the Clapps, Pettingills, Trumpours, Bowermans, Hutchinsons and Pettits.

The oldest municipal records preserved date back to 1859 when Stephen P. Niles was Reeve. However, it is known that in 1850, the time the Municipal Act reorganizing municipal government in the Province took effect, James T. Lane was elected as the first Reeve of Hillier, by popular vote.

A number of thriving communities grew up in the township, among them Pleasant Valley, on the old Danforth Road, two miles east of Pleasant Bay, where some time in the 1860's a commodious town hall was erected. The hamlet today is known as Hillier. Here the township's first mill was erected at an early date, and subsequently the first potash manufactory in the county.

Wellington, the only incorporated village within the township, was first known as Smokeville. Its pioneer settler Daniel Reynolds, had been given the nickname "Old Smoke" by the Indians among whom he lived for a number of years before other white settlers joined him.

The village, eventually named in honour of Arthur Wellesley, Duke of Wellington, became a separate municipality in 1862.

Consecon, divided by the Consecon River which empties here into Consecon Lake, lies only partly in Hillier as the river forms the boundary between Hillier and Ameliasburgh townships. The area today is a favourite with summer visitors and cottage owners.

Other communities within the township include Allisonville named after the Rev. Cyrus Allison, one of the early Methodist ministers in the area; Melville at the head of Consecon Lake; and Rosehall near the lake shore west of Wellington.

Hillier Township is basically an agricultural district. At one time, hops were a popular crop for local farmers and many a load was shipped from harbours and wharves along the lakeshore to the breweries of the United States. Shipyards were common around the turn of the century and this township, along with the rest of Prince Edward County, turned out some fine vessels. In 1871, a cheese factory was opened in Hillier village but was later moved to Niles Corners where it was known as Cloverdale Cheese Factory. The factory burned down in the 1960's.

A school existed in the township as early as 1804. John Graydon was the first teacher on record. Consecon School was built in 1852.

Pleasant Bay School was opened in 1868, and Niles Corner

School in 1876. All of these schools were closed in the 1960's.

In the 1870's, the railway then being built through the county passed about one-quarter mile east of Hillier village. The Township's main Highway No. 33 is known as the Heritage Highway. It had its beginning in 1798 when Asa Danforth constructed the Danforth military road between Wellington and Consecon as part of a route that was to link York (Toronto) with the Trent River.

The population of Hillier Township numbers 1580 (1979), but is swelled considerably in the summertime when visitors, tourists and cottagers come to the area.

The Historical and Centennial Committee: *Picton's 100 years*, 1937.

H. Belden & Co.: *Historical Atlas of Hastings & Prince Edward Counties*, 1879.

The Trentonian Centennial Edition, 1967.

HILLMER, geographic township, Cochrane District
Position 49° 54′ 82° 45′

This township is located some 25 miles northwest of the town of Kapuskasing and 20 miles west of the Spruce Falls Power and Paper Company Railway. Hillmer Lake straddles the boundary to the west.

The township is named after George Hillman, MPP for Halton 1923-26.

HILLSBOROUGH BEACH, community, Plympton Township, Lambton
County
Position 43° 07′ 82° 05′

Situated in the northwest corner of Plympton Township on a hilly part of the shore of Lake Huron, Hillsborough Beach was named after Thomas Hill, its first postmaster.

A post office was established on Lot 27, Front Concession, in 1853. Known as Hillsborough it remained open until 1901. The settlement which grew up beside it was called Hillsborough Beach.

Among the early residents were Thomas Blain, Eli Cairns, Daniel C. Clark, James Hill, John Jones and Harry M. Scott, all farmers of either British or pioneer Canadian origin. L. Dale opened a store in 1870. William Morrison, who arrived in 1865, served the inhabitants as a miller.

Today, Hillsborough Beach is mainly a summer resort.

A.J. Johnston: *Lambton County Names and Places*, 1925.

Edward Phelps, ed.: *Historical Atlas of County of Lambton*, 1973.

HILLSBURGH, police village, Erin Township, Wellington County
Position 43° 47′ 80° 09′

Situated about 15 miles northeast of Guelph in the northern part of Erin Township, this quiet residential community of just under 700 people serves as the shopping centre for the surrounding area. There are no industries in Hillsburgh today and many of the residents commute elsewhere to work.

The village was founded in the late 1840's and had a schoolhouse before 1851. Among the early settlers in the area were Hugh McMillan, Robert D. Nodwell, D.R. Fielding, Christopher Hamilton and Charles McMurchy.

A Canadian Pacific Railway station was established at Hillsburgh and by 1906 the village had three churches, several stores, two hotels, a flour mill and a tannery. It became known as a resort for trout fishermen and the hatcheries of the Caledon Mountain Trout Club were set up nearby.

The Hamilton Spectator, 1962.

HILLSDALE, police village, Medonte Township, Simcoe County
Position 44° 35′ 79° 45′

Hillsdale, a community with a population of less than 300, is situated in northern Simcoe County on Highway 27.

The village grew up in the early nineteenth century. Patrick Murphy, a retired soldier, became the first settler in the area when he arrived in 1829. Hillsdale developed at the point where the Gloucester Road left the Penetanguishene Road, halfway between Kempenfeldt Bay and Penetanguishene. A post office was established here in 1867.

Andrew F. Hunter: The History of Simcoe County, 1948.

HILLSPORT, community, northwest of Manitouwadge, Thunder Bay District
Position 49° 27′ 85° 33′

Situated on the Canadian National Railways about 35 miles from Manitouwadge, this compact rural community was named after A.J. Hills of Ottawa, General Superintendent of the CNR lines between Hawkesbury and Ottawa.

Hillsport was established by the railway in 1916 as a water stop for its trains. A sectionhouse and bunkhouse were built and 10 men were stationed here. In 1952 Marathon Corporation of Canada Limited set up a depot camp at the site. A branch line south to the copper mines at Manitouwadge was constructed by Canadian National Railways in 1955. In 1960 the railway changed to a block and signal system to control traffic and a maintainer and helper were stationed at Hillsport. New houses were erected at about this time and by 1963 the community's population had risen to about 150. According to the 1971 census, the population had risen to over 200.

Department of Lands and Forests: Geraldton, 1963.

HILTON, township, Algoma District
Position 46° 18′ 85° 53′

The municipality is comprised of the geographic township of Hilton which is on the southeast side of St. Joseph Island. The island lies in Lake Huron southeast of Sault Ste Marie.

Mr. Marks is believed to have been one of the earliest settlers, arriving in the 1870's. The first post office in the area was opened in 1879 at Marksville, now the incorporated village of Hilton Beach. The township of Hilton was incorporated as a township in 1887.

Today Hilton has a permanent population of only 136 (1979). About 80% of the work force commutes to Sault Ste Marie. The Hilton Lumber Company employs some of the residents, but the township's main industries are tourism and farming. There are no hotels or motels in the township, but cottages abound along the shores of the many bays and the township's beaches attract many summer visitors to the area.

Ministry of Natural Resources: *Directory of Statistics and Data*, 1975.

HILTON BEACH, village, Hilton Township, Algoma District
Position 46° 15′ 83° 53′

Hilton Beach is situated on the east side of St. Joseph's Island, less than 30 miles southeast of Sault Ste Marie. It was originally called Marksville after Mr. Marks, an early settler who arrived in the 1870's. The name was changed first to Hilton, and then to Hilton Beach.

A post office was established here in 1878. In 1928 Hilton Beach was incorporated as a village. It now has a population of 217 (1978). About 80% of the work force commutes to Sault Ste Marie. Tourism is the only major industry in the village. The Hilton Beach Hotel provides accommodation for visitors and a marina serves boating enthusiasts. The village is also becoming a retirement area for senior citizens.

Three churches, St. John's Anglican, St. Boniface Roman Catholic, and Grace United, serve the residents of Hilton Beach. The village also has a public library. Children attend school in nearby Richards Landing.

Ministry of Natural Resources: *Directory of Statistics and Data*, 1975.

HINCHINBROOKE, township, Frontenac County
Position 44° 36′ 76° 45′

Situated 20 miles northwest of Kingston, Hinchinbrooke was named for a village in Huntingdonshire, England. Established in 1798, the township was subdivided in 1824.

The first settlers to arrive in the early nineteenth century included John McKnight, James Hickey, Michael Judge, James Hill, Terry Nefcey and James Kennedy who settled in what is now the dispersed rural community of Godfrey, and Solomon Stafford and George Cox. James Hickey Jr. and Ned Judge were the first white children to be born in the township.

Fishing and lumbering were the main occupations of these early inhabitants. Stafford and Cox were both lumbermen. A sawmill was built at Fish Creek by Cale Edmunds and a grist mill by Burnet Andrews.

By 1850 Hinchinbrooke's population was 256. The Frontenac

Road, built through the township and along its eastern boundary, brought more settlers. Mixed farming and dairying were carried on. By 1856 there were seven schools and three sawmills in Hinchinbrooke. By 1878 two villages, Parham and Piccadilly, boasting between them several churches, schools, stores, businesses and a post office, were established on the present-day Highway 38.

Godfrey, also on Highway 38 and a major centre of Hinchinbrooke, was named in 1878 for the donor of the land on which the village is built, Chester Godfrey, who served as reeve and then as warden for Frontenac County. The importance of Godfrey, whose original name had been Deniston, began with the construction of the Kingston and Pembroke Railway in 1870, later to be operated by the Canadian Pacific Railway. Eight trains came daily into the Godfrey Station handling dairy and cheese products from farms and factories. Headquarters for the Felspar Mines, opened up by H. Richardson, Kingston, were established in Godfrey around 1900, and a mica mine was also operated on the Chester Godfrey property.

Parham, on Highway 38 and the CPR, began when the early settlers taking advantage of the lumbering being carried on, built their log cabins along Fish Creek. Logs from trees felled in the vicinity were floated by the river-drivers along the continuous waterways to the early settlement of Perth in Lanark County. Sir Henry Smith, lawyer, owned considerable land along the creek and Parham was first named Smith's Mills, the small mills turning out many wood products from the raw material at hand. An inn for the convenience of the river-drivers was built by an early settler by the name of Mahon (or Mahar). Andrew and George Howes, whose father had come from the United States, and William Bertrim, Peter Neadow, David Goodfellow, Manoah Cronk and Hiram Wagar are other early pioneer names of the Parham area. In 1965 Hinchinbrooke Public School, accommodating the pupils of Hinchinbrooke Township, was built at Parham. An annual Agricultural Fair is held at Parham.

Other communities within the township include Tichborne at the southern tip of Eagle Lake, Oak Flats, Echo Lake and Wilkinson, and on Highway 38, Cole Lake, situated on the lake of the same name. The locality of Wagarville is in the northern part of the township.

Today the excellent fishing in the township's many lakes attracts numerous tourists. United with Portland for municipal purposes in the nineteenth century, Hinchinbrooke is, today, a separate municipality with a population of 1,147 (1978).

J.H. Meacham & Co.: *Illustrated Historical Atlas of Frontenac, Lennox and Addington*, 1878.

Reg Whitty: *Community Spotlight*, 1974.

Mrs. Doreen Howes: *Community Spotlight*, 1974.

HINCKS, geographic township, Timiskaming District
Position 48° 04′ 81° 00′

The northern, southern and eastern boundaries of the township were surveyed in 1910 and 1911, and the western boundary in 1896 and in

1929. The main feature of the area, which borders to the west on the District of Sudbury, is Austen Lake, in the western half. A secondary road in the southwestern corner links the area with Highway 66.

Kirkland Lake lies approximately 50 miles to the east.

The township was probably named after Hon. Sir Francis Hincks, MP for Renfrew and a Cabinet Minister in 1869-73.

HINDON, geographic township, Provisional County of Haliburton
Position 45° 04′ 78° 54′

Hindon Township is located at the northwest corner of Haliburton County. It was surveyed and opened for settlement in 1860 and takes its name from the old town of Hindon in Wiltshire, England. For municipal purposes the township is united with Anson and Minden. The combined population of the three townships is 2,387 (1978).

Some of the pioneer settlers were Alex. Lindsay, William John Walker and James Austin who lived at Brady's Lake. The earliest settler appears to have been James Toye who settled at Hindon Hill in 1869. Hindon Hill is situated some ten miles north of Minden village, and is the only settlement in the township.

The soil in Hindon township is not suitable for farming and the Ontario government in 1927 offered to relocate some of the families in other areas of Northern Ontario. Among those who left were Moses Hewitt, D. Toye, Billy Toye, Abner Trumbull, Malcolm Kent and John Moore. The latter eventually returned to Hindon. Lumbering has been the only important industry in the township.

Nila Reynolds: *In Quest of Yesterday*, 1967.

History of the Provisional County of Haliburton, 1931.

HIPEL, geographic township, Thunder Bay District
Position 49° 47′ 87° 17′

Situated west of the Canadian National Railways station of Longlac, the area contains three lakes, Dumas Lake, Tigerlily Lake and Hipel Lake. Directly to the south is the Canadian National Railways line and Highway 11.

The township was named after Hon. N.O. Hipel, Speaker of the Ontario Legislature during 1935-37, later Minister of Labour and then Minister of Lands and Forests.

HISLOP, geographic township, Cochrane District
Position 48° 30′ 80° 20′

Immediately southeast of the town of Matheson, this area is served by the Ontario Northland Railway, with a station point at Vimy Ridge. Highway 11 connects the township to Kirkland Lake to the south and Iroquois Falls to the north. The area is watered by the Black River.

The main centre of the township is the community of Holtyre. Subdivided in 1905 by V.G. Robertson, the township is named after Archibald Hislop, MPP for the riding of East Huron in 1898-1905.

HOBBS, geographic township, Nipissing District
Position 46° 46′ 80° 06′

Located north of the Sturgeon River and west of Maarten River Provincial Park, Hobbs is watered by a few small lakes and Sinton Creek. Dry weather roads link the area to Highway 64 to the east and Highway 539 to the south.

Its northern boundaries were surveyed in 1881 and it was named for Thomas S. Hobbs, MLA, MPP for London in 1894.

HOBLITZELL, geographic township, Cochrane District
Position 49° 30′ 79° 54′

Approximately 16 miles west of the Quebec border, this area harbors Soucie Lake and East Soucie Lake in the north, and a few miscellaneous small lakes throughout. The Mikwam River wends its way through the northern half of the township.

Established in 1945 by the Deputy Minister of Lands and Forests, the area is named for Fred G. Hoblitzell, MP for Toronto Eglinton until 1945.

HOBSON, geographic township, Cochrane District
Position 50° 25′ 81° 33′

So named after Joseph Hobson, once Chief Engineer of the Grand Trunk Railway, the area is divided by the Abitibi River, at this point active with rapids, and also the Little Abitibi River in the eastern section.

HODGETTS, geographic township, Sudbury District
Position 47° 17′ 81° 19′

Named after Dr. Hodgetts of the Provincial Board of Health, the township's boundaries were surveyed in 1909 and 1910. The area is watered by Esker Lake and a few small creeks.

Dry weather and secondary roads link the township with Sudbury, some 50 miles to the south.

HODGINS, geographic township, Algoma District
Position 46° 45′ 84° 02′

Established in 1878 and formerly part of the Algoma Central and Hudson Bay Railway land grant, the area was named after Thomas Hodgins, KC, MPP for Elgin West in the 1870's.

The Algoma Central Railway passes through the northwestern corner of the township, as does the Goulais River, flowing in a southwesterly direction on its way to Lake Superior.

A secondary road links the area to the city of Sault Ste Marie in the south.

HODGSON, geographic township, Kenora District
Position 49° 30′ 92° 04′

Named after C.W. Hodgson, MP for Victoria in 1945, this township lies southeast of the town of Dryden.

Both the Canadian Pacific Railway and the Trans-Canada Highway pass through the area.

Sandbar Lake Provincial Park is situated 18 miles to the east of the township.

HOEY, geographic township, Sudbury District
Position 47° 47′ 83° 40′

Situated between Chapleau and The Shoals Provincial Park, this township was established in 1945 and was named after Major C.F. Hoey, V.C. from Duncan, B.C. who served with the Imperial Forces in Burma, and was awarded the V.C. for gallantry. He lost his life during the second World War.

Highway 101 crosses the northern part of the township.

HOFFMAN, geographic township, Algoma District
Position 47° 07′ 83° 39′

Known previously as Township 6H, the area was named after P. Hoffman, Chairman of the Temagami Improvement District. It is approximately 25 miles west of Highway 129 and has several small lakes in the southern half.

A dry weather and secondary road connect the township with the Aubinadong River.

HOGARTH, geographic township, Thunder Bay District
Position 49° 10′ 90° 23′

Subdivided in 1911, the township was named after Don Hogarth, MLA, MPP for Port Arthur at that time. The subdivision was annulled in 1958.

The area, located north of Lac des Mille Lacs, is traversed by Canadian National Railways, with a station point at Mack, at an elevation of about 1600 ft.

A dry weather road connects the township with Trans-Canada Highway.

HOGG, geographic township, Cochrane District
Position 50° 25′ 81° 45′

The township was named after T.H. Hogg, a Hydraulic Engineer and head of Ontario Hydro.

The mighty Mattagami River, with numerous rapids, flows in a northeasterly course through the township on its way to joining the Missinaibi and thus forming the great Moose River.

HOLIDAY BEACH PROVINCIAL PARK

This 487 acre Provincial Recreation Park is 28 miles south of Windsor and 2 miles south of the junction of Highways 18 and 18A. A Canada Goose sanctuary is established a half mile east of the park entrance on Highway 18A. From Bog Creek Marsh, in the northwest area of the park, wildlife, waterfowl and aquatic life can be observed.

Lake Erie shoreline provides a sand beach for visitors and there are excellent camp and trailer facilities for vacationers.

Ministry of Natural Resources.

HOLLAND, township, County of Grey
Position 44° 25' 80° 47'

The township is named after Lord Holland, Chancellor of the Duchy of Lancaster, who served in the cabinets of Lord Grey and Lord Melbourne until 1841. It is situated in the northwest central part of Grey County near Owen Sound. It is bordered to the north by Sydenham Township, to the east by Euphrasia, to the south by Glenelg, and to the west by Sullivan.

The township's 73,440 acres consist mostly of fertile clay loam soil, excellent for farming. A large number of small lakes and streams drain the area. Parts are quite hilly, but level areas also exist and encourage farming.

The first settlers arrived after the Garafraxa Road (Highway 6) was laid out along the western boundary in 1840. More concessions were laid out in 1845. The township itself was not surveyed until 1849-50. Early growth was slow, but there were enough settlers by 1851 for Holland to be incorporated as a township with Charles Thorpe as first reeve.

Little is known about the settlers who arrived before 1850, except that most of them were of British descent. More recently, immigrants have come from Holland and Germany. The first known settler was James Hare, who arrived in 1850. His son served as Clerk for 50 years. Other early settlers included the Silverlocks, the Hangers and the Nortons. Alexander Massie gave his name to one of the villages.

The first complete record of a Township Council is that of 1855. George McCauley was reeve that year. The members of the council were John Allan, Stephen H. Breese, and Joshua Faulkener. Another early councillor in Holland was the father of Sir William Hearst, Premier of Ontario during the First World War.

Many early settlers came to the area via the Toronto-Sydenham Road, (Highway 10) which leads diagonally across the township. Originally this road stopped at Arnott, forcing travellers to take sideroads or trails in order to continue to Chatsworth. In 1854 council passed a by-law extending the road to Chatsworth, thus improving transportation within the township. In 1873 the Toronto-Grey and Bruce Railway was built across Holland and contributed to the development of the area. By 1880 the population was 3,429.

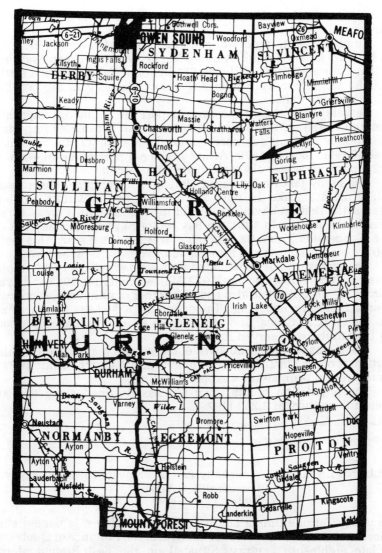

The first school was built in 1852 on Lot 12, Concession 2, with Jack Hyndman as the first teacher. The log schoolhouse was replaced by a frame one in 1868. The number of schools increased rapidly until there were 19 public schools and one separate school. In 1965 many of these schools were replaced by the Holland-Chatsworth Central School.

The Rev. Mr. Mulholland first held Anglican services in the log schoolhouse, which was also used by other denominations. Mr. Williscroft gave land for the Mount Zion Church, the first Methodist church in the area. St. Mark's Anglican Church was built in 1865 on Lot 18, Concession 3. In 1949 it was moved to Holland Centre. Built in the early 1870's Knox Holland Presbyterian Church is now used as a residence.

Lumber was an important resource. The first sawmills included one built at Holland Centre by either Mr. Perry or Mr. Greenaway, and another built at Walter's Falls in 1851 by John Walter, the first settler there. By 1852 there were at least five sawmills, as well as a woollen mill at Walter's Falls.

Berkeley was one of the earliest post offices in the township, opening in 1853. Along with Holland Centre it became an important rail station for shipping lumber. Alexander Massie was first postmaster at Massie, 1864 to 1870. Arnott became a post office in 1868. In 1862 a post office was also established at Glascott.

The many lakes encouraged Holland's development as a resort area. William's Lake is now surrounded by numerous summer cottages, the first lot having been sold in 1947. The hilly areas attract skiers in the winter. In 1961 the Bay Motor Ski Village was built on Lot 5, Concession 3, and the first motel was built that year. Also in the 1960's, a medical clinic and nursing home were built in the township.

The township has contributed four wardens of the county: John Cameron, 1884, Robert Howey, 1922, Wilbert Sutcliffe, 1945 and Lyall McInnis, 1969. There has also been a number of missionaries go from the area, including Rev. Hugh Taylor and his wife; Miss Florence Fee, who did work in China; and Mrs. Horace Braden (Isabel McMullen) and her family, who served in Ethiopia.

The township has 3,000 acres of conservation area, about a third of which is owned by the county which began to buy the land in 1943. Its most recent acquisition was made in 1965.

The population of the township has declined since the late nineteenth century at 2,262 (1979).

H. Belden & Co.: *Historical Atlas of the County of Grey*, 1880.

T. Arthur Davidson: *A New History of Grey County*, 1972.

HOLLAND LANDING, community, East Gwillimbury Township, Regional Municipality of York
Position 44° 06′ 79° 29′

The village, at one time a landing place for Indians, is named after Major Samuel Holland, Surveyor-General of the Province of Quebec in the late eighteenth century. Situated on the East Branch of the Holland River some 30 miles north of Toronto at the head of Yonge Street, the place was the end of the portage leading to Lake Simcoe and the Georgian Bay. To this spot once came the Indians to receive their treaty payments from the government. In 1965 an Indian burial ground was discovered at Holland Landing. It contained forty skeletons and was probably of the Mississauga tribe. It is believed that this was the site of an old Indian village.

A town plot was surveyed by Mr. Wilmot in 1811 near the site of a sawmill built by John Evesin in 1808. Settlers began to arrive in great numbers, many Quakers, Mennonites, and United Empire Loyalists among them. In 1821 Red Mills was erected by Peter

Robinson and soon became the most important mill in the area, with its flour being shipped to Europe.

That same year a post office was established and the community, which had been known as St. Albans, and also as Beverley, officially was named Holland Landing. A daily stage from York (Toronto) which began in 1825 and a steamboat connection set up in 1833, encouraged further settlement. By the 1840's the village was prospering, with industries including a brewery, distillery, two tanneries, a foundry, and Ellerby's carding and fulling mill. The construction of the Plank Road in 1851 facilitated a growing wheat and livestock trade. With cargo boats plying the Holland River, the settlement was a major shipping point between Lake Simcoe and Toronto.

In 1861 the population reached 741 and Holland Landing was incorporated as a village with Richard Titus Wilson as the first reeve. However, the Northern Railway, built in 1853, brought about a considerable decrease in road and lake traffic and the village's importance as a shipping point diminished. In the late nineteenth century, the owner of Tobey Mill moved his business to Collingwood after a dispute with the village over taxes. This action affected many of the other industries which had relied heavily on the mill. Then came a number of disastrous fires which wiped out some of the remaining businesses. By 1921 the population had decreased to 370 and in 1930 council applied to have the village status changed to that of a police village in the Township of East Gwillimbury. The request was granted in 1933. In recent years the village experienced renewed growth and according to the 1971 census, the population has climbed to nearly 900.

In 1842 Chief Justice John Robinson gave land for a Methodist church where the United Church of Holland Landing now stands. The Anglicans built their church in the following year.

Samuel Lount, a native of Pennsylvania, settled near Holland Landing some time after 1811 and became a prosperous farmer, blacksmith and surveyor. As a Reformer and member of the Legislative Assembly for Simcoe, he was involved in William Lyon Mackenzie's uprising and was in joint command of the rebel forces at Montgomery's Tavern on December 7, 1837. A fugitive after the rebels' defeat, he tried to reach the U.S. border, but was captured, convicted of high treason, and hanged at Toronto on April 12, 1838.

The village of Holland Landing is situated near a market gardening area that was largely settled by Dutch immigrants. Known as Holland Marsh, the site comprised some 8,000 acres of black muck. The Dutch, familiar with draining by dykes in their home country, brought their expertise to the project and here built their Dutch village, Ansnorveldt. When the catastrophe of Hurricane Hazel struck southern Ontario in October, 1954, Holland Marsh literally disappeared under 20 to 30 feet of water. Ansnorveldt was submerged, homes swept away or overturned, and losses totalled in the millions. With the retreat of the waters and the loan of huge pumps, the devastation was revealed and the damage appeared irreparable. However, with the aid of County, Provincial and Federal funds, work was begun to restore the land and by the following summer Holland Marsh was once again fully productive.

Jesse Edgar Middleton & Fred Landon: *The Province of Ontario — A History 1616-1927 Vol. II*, 1927.

C. Blackett Robinson: *History of Toronto and County of York, Vol. I*, 1885.

Gladys M. Rolling: *East Gwillimbury in the Nineteenth Century*, 1967.

HOLLINGER, geographic township, Sudbury District
Position 47° 22' 82° 09'

Named in 1974 after Benjamin Hollinger, who discovered gold near Timmins in 1909 and founded the Hollinger Consolidated Gold Mines, this township lies just east of Ramsey Lake. Its main lake is Shanacy Lake.

The Canadian Pacific Railway passes through the southern part of the township, with a station point at Roberts.

HOLLOWAY, geographic township, Cochrane District
Position 48° 30' 79° 42'

South of Lake Abitibi, this township is linked to the town of Matheson to the west, by Highway 101. A small section of the Magusi River straggles through the southern central part of the area, while the northern part is watered by the Mattawasaga.

The township was named after George T. Holloway, Chairman of the Royal Ontario Nickel Commission.

HOLLY PARK, community, King Township, Regional Municipality of York
Position 43° 56' 79° 42'

Holly Park was named after a place in Ireland by Michael O'Neill, one of its first settlers, in 1841. O'Neill bought land on Lot 15, Concession 10, west half, and built a distinctive log house, with each corner constructed in a different way. He also erected a sawmill.

Other early residents included S.A. Hunter, William Smith, John Egan, and Joe Smith, a violin teacher. But it was the O'Neills who dominated the life of the community. Michael's son, Michael Joseph O'Neill, became Holly Park's first postmaster in 1878. Patrick O'Neill, brother of Michael, was another early settler. He built Holly Park House for his son. About 1900 the post office was moved to this home, which was also a popular place for parties and social gatherings. The house, which is still occupied, was featured in the magazine *Canadian Homes and Gardens* in 1939.

Elizabeth McClure Gillham: *Early Settlements of King Township, Ontario*, 1975.

HOLMES, geographic township, Timiskaming District
Position 48° 04' 80° 28'

Holmes lies southwest of Kirkland Lake and just east of an Indian

Reservation. Holmes Lake is situated in the southern part of the township, and Englehart River, together with various creeks, flows through the northeastern corner. A secondary road links the area with Highway 66.

The township was subdivided in 1903 by A. Smith, and boundaries were surveyed in 1889 and re-traced in 1903.

It was named after Joseph W. Holmes, MPP for Haldimand 1898-1902.

HOLMESVILLE, community, Goderich Township, Huron County
Position 43° 39' 81° 36'

Situated in the western part of Huron County, about 8 miles east of Goderich, this dispersed rural community of about 100 (1971) was named after John and Samuel Holmes who were among the early settlers in the area. It was first known as Holmes Villa, but became Holmesville when a post office was established in 1855.

The first settler in the vicinity was James Johnson. In 1832 John and Samuel Holmes from Ireland settled on Lots 34 and 35 of the Maitland Concession, near modern Holmesville, about 9 miles from Goderich and 3 miles from Clinton. The community grew up along the Goderich and Clinton Road and for some time was the only post village in the township, and the only community of any importance, excepting Goderich and Bayfield. Among the early residents were the Potters, Fords, Holmes, Jenkins, Disneys, and Sturdys. Later families including the Dockings, Yeas, Evans, Forsters, and Elfords. John Holmes was the first warden of Huron County and also one of the county's first Members of Parliament. His home community became the "seat of government" for the township.

William Holmes, a relative of John and Samuel, became the first postmaster in 1855. By the 1870's, the community had a tavern, two general stores and three blacksmith shops. Joseph Trewartha set up a business as a carriage-maker. By 1879 a telegraph office had been established. In the late nineteenth century, a cheese factory was opened. By this time, Holmesville's population was about 200.

The community had a school before 1850. Mr. Osbaldesten, who lived near Holmesville, was the teacher in the 1840's. Two churches had been erected by 1879. Another church was built later, so that in time the Anglicans, Methodists, and Bible Christians each had their own houses of worship.

Clinton Women's Institute: *History of Clinton and Surrounding Community*, 1950.

James Scott: *The Settlement of Huron County*, 1966.

HOLSTEIN, police village, Egremont Township, Grey County
Position 44° 03' 80° 45'

The police village of Holstein is located on the southern boundary of the County of Grey. The township was organized in 1850 but Holstein did not become a village until 1855. It soon became the leading village in the township.

In 1864 Prussia marched against Denmark for the control of the duchies of Schleswig and Holstein, and it was at this time that the village of Holstein was named. Chosen by the first postmaster, N.D. McKenzie, former schoolteacher, it was probably based on that event occurring in Europe.

Early sawmills were operated by John Shields and Jake Rawn; grist mills were owned by W.T. Petrie and a Mr. Nicholson. A handle factory was built by Mr. Buller and Mr. Bredner, and a carpentry and wagon-making business opened under the partnership of two early settlers, William Romains and Charles Kerr, the latter the community's first blacksmith. N.D. McKenzie, who had taught school in the 1849 log schoolhouse, changed vocation, built a store and became a storekeeper as well as postmaster.

In 1865 a stone schoolhouse replaced the log structure on the same site. Holstein had three schools until 1964, at which time the first consolidated school in the county was built a half mile north of Holstein.

The first church was also built of logs, later to be replaced by a brick church. Holstein was the birthplace of two noted churchmen, one, Carmen Queen, who became Bishop of Huron, the other Rev. Kenneth McMillan, general secretary of the Canadian Bible Society.

When the Grand Trunk Railway built a line to Durham, Holstein benefited greatly by the station constructed in the village, especially so because of its highly productive agricultural land. In 1922 the Canadian National Railways took over the line and in the middle 1960's the station was demolished.

An annual fair, the Egremont Agricultural Society and the Holstein Creamery further emphasized the early country lifestyle of Holstein. The first bank in Egremont Township was located here. In 1908 Holstein had the distinction of becoming a police village.

In 1967 a new Community Centre, begun in 1965 as a centennial project, opened its doors.

T.A. Davidson: *A New History of the County of Grey*, 1972.

E.L. Marsh: *A History of the County of Grey*, 1931.

HOLTYRE, community, Hislop Township, Cochrane District
Position 48° 28′ 80° 17′

This compact rural community of about 500 is located some 60 miles southeast of Cochrane, on the Ontario Northland Railway and a few miles east of Highway 11. A large percentage of the population is French speaking, and most derive their livelihood from working in the local mines.

The settlement came into existence around 1934. At the time, the Hollinger and McIntyre mines operated in the vicinity, and the name chosen for the new mining community was a combination of these two company names.

HOME, geographic township, Algoma District
Position 47° 16' 84° 25'

Originally part of the Algoma Central and Hudson Bay Railway Land Grant, the township was named after R. Home-Smith of Toronto.

The Montreal River enters the township in the northeastern corner and proceeds southward, emptying into Lake Superior.

Bordering on the southern part of Lake Superior Provincial Park, the area is linked by the Algoma Central Railway to Sault Ste Marie.

HOMER, geographic township, Thunder Bay District
Position 48° 02' 85° 52'

This is a triangular area of land on the shores of Lake Superior, and a section of it forms part of the Pukaskwa National Park. The East Pukaskwa River cascades in rapids through the southern part of the township, thence emptying into Lake Superior.

This picturesque area is named for Homer, famous Greek author and poet.

HOMUTH, geographic township, Cochrane District
Position 49° 38' 81° 34'

The township, located north of the town of Smooth Rock Falls, was named after Karl K. Homuth, MPP for Waterloo South in the 1920's. Highway 807 passes through the eastern half of the township, as does the Ontario Northland Railway.

HONEY HARBOUR, community, Georgian Bay Township, District Municipality of Muskoka
Position 44° 52' 79° 49'

Situated on the east coast of Georgian Bay, about 8 miles north of the town of Midland, this dispersed rural community of just under 300 is a popular summer resort.

The area was first visited by a party of surveyors in 1780 who reached Georgian Bay at the site of Honey Harbour. The community did not develop much until about 1900 when Didace Grisé built the Royal Hotel here. In 1920 he bought the property on which the Delawana Inn, a large resort hotel, now stands.

During World War II, Honey Harbour Boat Works built Fairmiles for the Canadian Navy. Today Honey Harbour's marinas are filled with boats belonging to people with summer cottages on the Georgian Bay islands. The Exhibit and Information Centre of the Georgian Bay Islands National Park is also located here. A winter carnival is held every year.

A large percentage of the community's residents is French-Canadian.

Geraldine Coombe: *Muskoka Past and Present*, 1976.

HONEYWELL, geographic township, Kenora District, P.P.
Position 51° 15′ 92° 34′

Located east of Trout Lake, this township has several lakes, the largest being Okanse Lake, which takes in most of the southeastern portion of the area.

It was named after Albert E. Honeywell, MLA, MPP for Ottawa North in the 1920's.

HONEYWOOD, community, Mulmur Township, Dufferin County
Position 44° 13′ 80° 11′

Situated in the northern part of Dufferin County, about 25 miles south of Barrie, Honeywood is a compact rural community with a population of 133 (1976). It was probably named by the first settlers who discovered the area with its flourishing forest and fertile soil.

One of the first settlers in the area was Mark Mortimer, who arrived in 1826. Other pioneers included the Tuplings, Murdys, Lamonts and Markles. By the late nineteenth century, Honeywood had become a service community for the surrounding area which was one of the best agricultural sections in Ontario. John McConachie ran a general store and Robert Lawrence was proprietor of the drug store. Blacksmithing was done by Joseph Topland and wagon-making by Alexander Coe. Joseph Siddell was the community's tailor.

By the early twentieth century, Honeywood had a school and Anglican and Methodist churches.

Stephen Sawden: *History of Dufferin County.*

HONG KONG, geographic township, Sudbury District
Position 47° 33′ 82° 32′

Named in 1945 after the British Crown Colony of Hong Kong, this township lies just east of Wakami Lake Provincial Park.

It is watered by the Woman River. The Canadian Pacific Railway passes through the area, with a station point in the southwestern corner of the township.

HOOK, geographic township, Algoma District
Position 48° 44′ 83° 43′

Named after Thomas Hook, MLA, MPP for Toronto South East in 1914, the area lies north of Missinaibi Lake Provincial Park.

The township is watered mainly by the Nebotik River and the Fire River. At the far northeastern corner the Canadian National Railways touches the boundary of the township.

HOPE, township, Northumberland County
Position 44° 02' 78° 23'

The Township of Hope is located in the southeast corner of Northumberland County, fronting on Lake Ontario. Surveyed by Augustus Jones in 1791, the township was formed in 1792 when Governor Simcoe issued a proclamation dividing part of Upper Canada into townships. It was named after Colonel Henry Hope, Lieutenant Governor of Quebec 1785-89.

Prior to the Revolutionary War it had been the custom in the American Colonies to grant large tracts of land to individuals on the understanding that they would bring in settlers and develop the land. This practise was tried in the township of Hope. The government was petitioned by Elias Smith, Abraham Walton and Jonathan Walton, who offered to open the township for settlement on condition that they would become the owners of township land, once they had established forty new settlers. The scheme did not work out and the contract expired in 1799. However, settlement was well underway by 1793. The first two families to arrive were those of James Stevens and Nathaniel Ashford, United Empire Loyalists. The first warrants of survey or location tickets had been given to J. Walton, Elias Smith, Johnson, Harris, Stevens, Ashford, Trull and Peck.

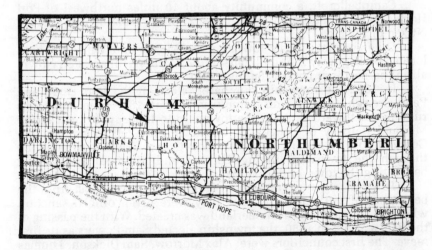

The year 1796 saw considerable immigration from the United States, largely in response to advertisements placed by Governor Simcoe in American newspapers offering land grants in Upper Canada to prospective settlers from the former Colonies. The government, at that time, granted 600 acres to Elias Smith on the condition that he erect a saw and grist mill to accommodate the settlers who had to take their grain a considerable distance to Belleville, Napanee, or even Kingston. The mill was built in 1795 but was less than efficient. In 1799 it was moved to a new site and put in working order. A grist mill was in operation at Port Britain in 1801, at

Canton Mill in 1825, at Port Hope in 1818 and at Britton's Mill on the Duck Pond Stream in 1820. Thus by the early 1800's gristing was no longer a problem for Hope Township residents. The abundance of waterpower in the township was utilised at an early date. There were 38 dams in the township at one time, powering eighteen grist mills and thirty-one sawmills, as well as providing waterpower for wood-working, for woollen mills, and for numerous other enterprises.

The settlement of Port Hope on the shore of Lake Ontario conducted a brisk business exporting local produce in the 1800's. Situated at the mouth of the Ganaraska River, Port Hope was the site of a Cayuga Indian Village in the 17th century. In the 1770's Peter Smith operated a trading post at the location, and the pioneers of the area in the beginning called their settlement Smith's Creek. The first permanent settler of Port Hope, who arrived in 1793, was Myndert Harris, a United Empire Loyalist. Port Hope, long since grown into an incorporated town of industrial importance, has a population of over 10,000 (1979).

Settlement in the Canton area dates back to 1805 when the Harris, Hawkins and Collander families arrived. A Mr. Potter erected a mill here on the Ganaraska River in 1825. "Batterswood", the estate of the late Vincent Massey, Canada's first native governor-general, is situated on the outskirts of this picturesque village.

Campbellcroft, a community about 10 miles northwest of Port Hope, grew up around the mills of Thomas Campbell, a leading citizen of the area.

Other hamlets in the township are Morris and Welcome, both located on Highway 2; and Elizabethville, Garden Hill and Perrytown, all in the northern part of the township.

In 1852 the township purchased stock in the Port Hope and Peterborough Railway, and a line was built in 1857 from Port Hope running northward through the township to Lindsay. Known as the Midland Railway of Canada, it was later extended to Midland on Georgian Bay. Also in the 1850's the Grand Trunk built its line through the township linking Toronto and Montreal and greatly benefitting the town of Port Hope.

Town meetings were held in Hope Township almost from the beginning of settlement. In 1802 they were given official sanction when the District of Northumberland was created. With the passing of the Baldwin Act in 1850, the township elected Sam Powers as its first reeve. The first councillors were: Alex Morrow, Sam Dickson, Thomas Campbell and John McMurtry.

The first school in the township, a private school, is said to have been established in the Smith home at Port Hope in 1797; Mr. Collins was its first teacher. It was not until the early 1800's that public schools were opened in Hope.

The township over the years had its share of notable persons, but William Hunt stands out as one of the most unusual. The son of a schoolteacher, Hunt studied to become a doctor. One day a circus came to town featuring a woman on a tightrope. He was so fascinated by the act that he began to try walking the tightrope. In 1859, so proficient had he become, he was challenging the famous Blondin to better the latter's feats at Niagara Falls. Under the name of Signor Farini, Hunt gained fame as a tightrope walker, performing incredible stunts in South America and on the European Continent. He was the first white man to visit the pygmies, wrote poetry, held 80 patents, and, in his later years, became a very good artist. In 1888 he returned to Hope Township where he bought two farms and operated a sawmill, a chopping mill, and a fish hatchery. Eventually he went to live in the town of Port Hope until his death at the age of 91.

Hope Township, which covers an area of some 66,000 acres, was annexed by the County of Northumberland on January 1, 1974, when the municipalities of the region were reorganized. Prior to this time the township had been part of the United Counties of Northumberland and Durham. The area is served by Highway 401, the CNR and the CPR.

Harold Reeve: *The History of the Township of Hope*, 1967.

HOPE BAY, community, Eastnor Township, Bruce County
Position 44° 55′ 81° 10′

Situated on the western shore of Georgian Bay, about 25 miles northwest of Owen Sound, this dispersed rural community was named after Col. Henry Hope, member of the Legislative Council and Quebec Administrator in 1785.

In 1855 the town plot of Adair was surveyed on the shore of Hope Bay by George Gould. However, it never developed as a town and in 1887 it was resurveyed into farm lots. A community grew up at the site of present Hope Bay during these years, and a post office was established in 1876.

Logging was the community's main industry. The first sawmill was built by W.H. Leonard, and was later bought by Walter Lewis. Many farmers worked part-time in this mill which stood on the shore of the bay. Good shipping facilities aided the industry, which was turning out posts, lumber, barn timbers, and tamarack bark used in the tanning process.

Residents of the community and surrounding area in the 1880's included William Clark, Henry Lemcke, George H. Coram, the Davidsons, Sheffields, Heaths, and Freckeltons. Among the businessmen were William Caldwell, hotel owner; John King, proprietor of the general store; John Dunbar, cooper; F. Guest, shoemaker; and James Muirhead, postmaster and butcher. In 1923 John Dickie established a silver fox farm which prospered for about 25 years until mink became more popular.

Today farming is still carried on, but the most important industry is tourism. Hope Bay's sandy beach and shore lined with limestone cliffs are great attractions for visitors. Above the cliffs are the Indian Wells, pot holes of three to ten feet in diameter and unknown depth. The wells can be reached by the Bruce Trail.

A school built in 1890, is now used as a summer home. There have never been any churches in Hope Bay.

The Bruce County Historical Society: *Year Book*, 1971.

HOPE NESS, community, Eastnor Township, Bruce County
Position 44° 56' 81° 10'

Hope Ness lies in the farming section of Cape Dundas on the Bruce Peninsula, about 25 miles northwest of Owen Sound. The name comes from Hope Bay, on which it is situated, and the Scottish word "ness", meaning point.

Joseph and Francis Waugh were among the first settlers in the vicinity. Other pioneers in the Hope Ness area included Robert Davidson, James Sheffield, A. Strathy, Thomas Schermahorn, and Allan Erwin. Joseph Waugh became the first postmaster in 1882. The post office closed in the early twentieth century when rural mail delivery was introduced.

A school was opened in 1878 on the farm of Francis Waugh. It was the third school in the township and served the children of Hope Bay as well, until 1890. A new school was built in 1893. It is now a community hall.

The Anglicans of Hope Bay held services in the schoolhouse for many years. The Methodists erected a church but it has now been torn down.

East of Hope Ness, on the limestone cliffs by the shore of the bay, is the site of CKCO, Kitchener's 700-foot television tower.

The Bruce County Historical Society: *Year Book*, 1971.

HOPETOWN, community, Lanark Township, Lanark County
Position 45° 05' 76° 27'

Situated in the western part of Lanark Township at the junction of Highways 511 and 44, Hopetown is a small but compact rural community.

Among the pioneers were Samuel Wilson, James Dobbie, Thomas Murphy, Andrew and James Baird, James McInnes, John Cumming, and Fergus Moore. A post office was opened in 1853. By 1858 the community had about 100 residents. Early businessmen included postmaster Robert Cameron, who was also a cooper and tavernkeeper; Peter Kerr, storekeeper; George Ball, wagon maker; and Duncan Stewart, who built a mill combining grist, shingle and carding operations. Stewart arrived in 1849 and bought Robert Curry's land beside "Curry's Creek". He set up his mill here and after his death his wife continued the business. The mill continued to operate until the 1920's.

Other industries included Anderson's, Croft's and Taylor's lumber mills. The Hopetown Cheese Factory, built in 1884, was used by Charles Richardson to manufacture cheese boxes during the 1930's. Moved to the Clyde River in 1937, it burned down ten years later.

Hopetown's first congregation was Methodist. The log building in which they worshipped was later shared by the Congregationalists and Presbyterians of the community. In 1895 a Congregational Church was erected and four years later, in 1899, St. John's Presbyterian Church was dedicated. The two congregations amalgamated at

Church Union in 1925 and used St. John's as their house of worship. St. John's is now known as Trinity Church.

Claire Thompson: *Township of Lanark, 1820-1970*, 1970.

HOPKINS, geographic township, Cochrane District
Position 49° 46′ 82° 10′

Some 20 miles northeast of the town of Kapuskasing, the Spruce Falls Power & Paper Co. Railway passes through the western half of the township, en route to the end of line settlement of Smoky Falls.

Kapuskasing River courses through the central and eastern part of the area, also occupied by Hopkins Lake and a portion of Torrance Lake.

Dry weather and secondary roads connect the township with Kapuskasing.

It was probably named after E.H. Hopkins, candidate for the Ontario Land Survey examinations in 1872.

HORDEN, geographic township, Cochrane District
Position 51° 13′ 80° 46′

Situated on the banks of the Moose River, close to James Bay, this township overlooks Moosonee Provincial Park located on some islands in the Moose River. The Ontario Northland Railway passes through the township, which is named after John Horden, first Anglican Bishop of Moosonee.

HORNE, geographic township, Thunder Bay District
Position 48° 31′ 89° 49′

This township northwest of Thunder Bay was named either after Robert H. Horne or Wm. and Thomas Horne, once prominent citizens of Fort William (now Thunder Bay).

The Shebandowan River with numerous rapids, flows erratically through the centre of the township.

A Canadian National Railways' line follows the river's course.

Highway 11 cuts across the northeastern corner of the township, linking the area with the city of Thunder Bay.

HORNELL, geographic township, Sudbury District
Position 48° 03′ 83° 58′

Situated in the Windermere Lake area and north of The Shoals Provincial Park, Hornell borders to the west on the District of Algoma. The Windermere River, with numerous rapids, flows parallel with the township's western boundary. The eastern half of the area is mainly occupied by Goldie Lake.

The Canadian Pacific Railway touches on the northeastern corner of the township. There are no known roads in the area.

It was named after Flight Lieutenant David E. Hornell, V.C., R.C.A.F., who died at sea after an explosion in a lifeboat while on sub-arctic patrol in 1944.

HORNEPAYNE, community, Wicksteed Township, Algoma District
Position 49° 13' 84° 47'

This northwestern community of about 1800 (1971 census), not far from Thunder Bay District border, was known as Fitzback when the Canadian Northern built its transcontinental line through the area in 1916. It was renamed in 1920 in honour of R.M. Hornepayne, the British financial adviser to Sir William Mackenzie, one of the builders of the line. Today Hornepayne is a divisional point on a Canadian National Railways' line.

Lumbering operations carried out in the district are feeding a large pulp and paper company, giving employment to residents. Hornepayne is the site of a Red Cross outpost which serves the surrounding area.

HORNING'S MILLS, police village, Melancthon Township, Dufferin County
Position 44° 09' 80° 12'

The village, situated on the Pine River, derives its name from Lewis Horning who founded the settlement in 1830. Having arrived in what was then the backwoods of the so-called "Queen's Bush" from Hamilton where he had lived, Horning, with three or four other men, built a cabin, cleared a small lot and planted potatoes, turnips and corn. Some time later the men brought their families from Hamilton, and under Horning's guidance they built a mill. Miles of the finest hardwood forest stretched to the north of Horning's Mills, and the pioneers who by then included the Henry Bates, William Silk and the Vanmear families, had high hopes for a prosperous settlement.

Then tragedy struck the little village. Four children from Horning's Mills, among them nine-year-old Lewis Horning Jr., disappeared in the woods while searching for a lost cow, and when no trace of them could be found, it was supposed that they had been kidnapped by Indians. It was not until a couple of years later that one of the children, Oliver Vanmear, was found, and told the Hornings that their son had been adopted by an Indian Chief.

In failing health, Horning sold his mill and property to William Airth, having returned to Hamilton in 1838. The settlement he founded continued to occupy a prominent place in the township throughout most of the nineteenth century, being noted for its flour mills and serving as a supply centre for the surrounding area.

Among Horning's Mills' leading citizens in the early days were Paul Jarvis who opened the first store; Joseph Rogers who operated the first tavern; and William Airth who ran the mills, was active in township affairs and in later years purchased the village hotel where for a while council meetings were held. Robert McGhee who came to the area in 1848 served as the township's reeve for many years. Dr. John Barr, the first physician in the village, set up his practice in the 1860's.

A post office was opened at Horning's Mills in 1851 with James McGee as the first postmaster.

The police village of Horning's Mills is located on Highway 24, some 20 miles south of the town of Collingwood.

Stephen Sawden: *History of Dufferin County.*

HORTON, township, Renfrew County
Position 45° 30' 76° 38'

Surveyed by Owen Quinn in 1825, the township was established the following year and named after Sir Robert John Horton, member of the British House of Commons and Under-Secretary for War and Colonies at that time. Horton was the initiator of a scheme to assist emigrants from Britain to Canada.

The township borders in the northeast on the Ottawa River where the community of Castleford developed on the south shore of Lac des Chats, one of the many lakes in the Ottawa. Lieutenant Christopher James Bell received a land grant in 1817 in the area southeast of the present hamlet, and here, at the first chute of the Bonnechère River, he built a timber slide and a sawmill in the 1820's. When the Opeongo Colonization Road was built in the early 1850's, Castleford became a stopover for settlers who came up the Ottawa River on their way into the interior of Renfrew County.

Other hamlets in Horton Township include Bonnechère Point, Thompsonhill, Goshen and The Chute.

The site of present-day Renfrew was known as the "Second Chute" (falls) on the Bonnechère River. French Canadian lumbermen searching for timber berths used to stop here before the 1820's, and among the first to settle in this area was Joseph Brunette. He is said to have later built the first farm house at Renfrew. As Scottish families from the neighbouring township of McNab moved into the little settlement, a village began to grow and was incorporated in 1858. Renfrew was to become known as the "Creamery Town" of the Ottawa Valley, when one of the largest creameries and one of the first on the North American continent was established here in 1895.

Horton Township has a population of just over 2,000 (1979). The area is served by Highways 17, 60 and 653, as well as the Canadian Pacific Railway and the Canadian National Railways.

Mrs. Carl Price and Clyde C. Kennedy: *Notes on the History of Renfrew County,* 1961.

HORWOOD, geographic township, Sudbury District
Position 48° 00' 82° 18'

Linked by dry weather and secondary roads to Ivanhoe Lake Provincial Park and Highway 101 and thence to Timmins, some 50 miles to the northeast, as the crow flies, Horwood is occupied mainly by a lake of the same name.

The township was named after E.L. Horwood, an architect from Ottawa.

HOSKIN, geographic township, Sudbury District
Position 46° 14′ 80° 37′

Located north of the French River and southeast of the city of Sudbury, this area was first subdivided in 1899, but the subdivision was partly annulled in 1953. It was named after John Hoskin, K.C. LLD, of Toronto around the turn of the century.

Its main feature is Trout Lake, in the centre of the township. The area is well served by dry weather and secondary roads linking it to Highway 69 to the east and Highway 17 to the north.

HOTTE, geographic township, Algoma District
Position 46° 51′ 82° 00′

Previously identified as Township C, the area borders the District of Sudbury to the east and lies some 50 miles north of the town of Massey. There are various small lakes in the area and a dry weather road links the township with Webbwood in the south. The Canadian Pacific Railway travels past the township some 15 miles to the east.

The name commemorates M. Hotte, Mayor of the Town of Cochrane.

HOUCK, geographic township, Thunder Bay District
Position 49° 47′ 86° 45′

Located east of the Town of Longlac, Houck is severed by the Kenogamisis River. Several small lakes also occupy the township. The Canadian National Railways passes through the southeastern corner of the area, and dry weather and secondary roads link it to Geraldton, east of the township. The MacLeod Provincial Park lies just to the south.

The township was named after Hon. Wm. L. Houck, MPP for Niagara Falls in the 1930's.

HOWARD, township, Kent County
Position 42° 28′ 81° 55′

Howard Township lies between Lake Erie to the south and the Thames River to the north. It was named after Thomas Howard, Earl of Effingham, whose daughter, Lady Mary Howard, was married in 1771 to Sir Guy Carleton, Governor-General of Canada at the time this township was surveyed and named.

A height of land called the Ridge, divides the north and south watersheds of the county. Many small streams flow in both directions from the Ridge, which slopes south to Lake Erie and north to the Thames River. The streams irrigate the clay soil converting it into an easily cultivated loam and Howard Township contains some of the best agricultural land in Kent County. This ridge of land was contained in the tract under the management of Col. Thomas Talbot. He had a survey blazed east and west, some 400 rods from the Erie shore and approximately parallel to it. The Talbot Road, planned to encourage settlers, was lined with 200-acre lots and by 1817 it had been run through the southern part of Howard.

Howard Township was first settled by United Empire Loyalists at the end of the eighteenth century. Scots from Utica, New York and clans direct from Scotland also formed a large portion of the immigration. Among the early settlers was Frederick Arnold on the Thames Front. The original land grants were subdivided and resold, resulting in a considerable settlement called Howard Bridge. In 1815 Joseph and Edward Hackney settled on the shore of Lake Erie and built the first mill in South Kent. Others were Nicholas Cornwall and John Desmond.

Botany, approximately 16 miles northeast of the city of Chatham, was settled about 1830, predominantly by immigrants of Scottish origin. The McBrayne family was followd by Hugh and William Simonton, and then by William McKerrecher, the latter an influential citizen in Howard Township. A post office opened in Botany in 1865.

Morpeth is, today, a compact rural community on Highway 3, the original Talbot Road constructed along the north shore of Lake Erie in 1817. Earlier known as Big Creek, from the deep creek flowing south through the township to Lake Erie, the name was changed to Jamesville in 1842 to honour pioneer James Coll. Shortly after, the Earl of Morpeth while travelling Canada West stopped at Jamesville. In gratitude for his generous donation towards the building of the Anglican Trinity Church, the name was changed to Morpeth.

In 1816 Joseph Woods with his son, James, and his brother Robert Woods, arrived from Nova Scotia and pioneered on the site of present-day Morpeth. Garrett and Edward Lee, storekeepers, active in the founding of Morpeth, built the Red Store, a familiar landmark and supply depot for settlers in more remote areas. Prior to 1832, Edward Garrett had carried mail for the settlers by his own pony express, travelling from Port Stanley on the lakeshore in Elgin County.

By 1847 Morpeth had a diversity of stores, tradesmen and professional men, as well as a Justice of the Peace and a Division Court. Progressing steadily, rivalling the importance of Chatham, its setback came in the middle of the 1870's when the Southern Railway connecting Niagara and Detroit was surveyed and constructed several miles inland. The original plan had been to follow the northern shore of Lake Erie. Deprived of an important transportation system, the communities along the Talbot Road declined, the lakeports now had little trade.

From the Talbot Road through Howard Township to the Thames River, a rough trail was cut through the forest, possibly for military purposes during the War of 1812. In 1822 the area was opened for settlement. Edward Palmer and Alex Marsh chose a spot and settled in 1823, followed by James Watson, Edmund Mitton and Ebenezer Colby. These selected sites later became the site of present-day Ridgetown on Highway 21. Until the first store opened in 1851, the pioneers walked or rode horseback along forest trails to Morpeth for supplies. In the middle 1850's the community had Malcolm McLean's store, James G. Mitton's blacksmith shop, and a log schoolhouse dating from 1830 and taught by an Irishman by the name of Gowdie. In that year, also, the Presbyterians had built the first church. By 1870 the building of the Canada Southern Railway from Niagara Falls to the Detroit River, passing just north of the hamlet, speeded the growth of Ridgetown, so named for its position on the Ridge. It became an incorporated village in 1877 and in 1882 it became a town, with H.D. Cunningham as the first mayor. It was Kent County's most important shipping centre for farm products, having three large elevators, and its canning factory utilized the vegetable and fruit crops grown on the fertile farmlands. George Moody built a mill combining machinery for both flour and wool, because sheep raising was a growing industry. Moody's Mill expanded into a complex of mills until 1889.

The Western Ontario Experimental Farm at Ridgetown was established and expanded. While it closed during the Second World War, it reopened in 1950 and became active in stock breeding and experimentation of new varieties of crops. Many were the business enterprises established in Ridgetown during the busy years following the turn of the century, adding to the strong economy of Howard Township.

Following the construction of the Great Western Railway (now CNR), the Thamesville-Ridgetown stage mail route was established in 1864. One of the last of the old stage routes, it ceased to operate in 1913 with the advent of rural mail delivery.

Howard Township's annual fall fairs became famous throughout western Ontario. The first of these was held in 1854 in Morpeth, considered, then, the centre of activity in the southern part of the township. The permanent site of the fairs was later transferred to the Ridgetown area.

Municipal records show that local self-government was inaugurated as early as 1843 in Howard Township.

The township has an area of 61,260 acres and the population is 2,592.

Victor Lauriston: *Romantic Kent, The Story of a County 1626-1952*, 1952.

HOWE ISLAND, township, Frontenac County
Position 44° 17' 76° 16'

Situated in the St. Lawrence River, about 7 miles east of Kingston, Howe Island is divided from Pittsburgh Township on the mainland by the North Batteau Channel. The island is 12 miles long and 9 miles wide. Originally known as Ka-ou-enesegoan, an Iroquois word meaning "big island", then as Isle Cauchois, it was finally named Howe Island by Lord Simcoe in 1792, after either George Augustus, Lord Howe, Commander-in-Chief in America, or his brother, William Howe, who commanded the Light Infantry under Wolfe at the Siege of Quebec.

The island was first mentioned in the French government's grant of a seigneury to Sieur de la Salle in 1674. In 1682 La Salle gave the deed for the island to Jacque Cauchois. Loyalist leader, Sir John Johnson petitioned the British government for the island in 1791. It was surveyed in 1792 but there were no permanent settlers on the island until the early nineteenth century because of fear of the raiding Iroquois.

The first settler was William Casey who arrived in 1810 and acted as guard of the island for the British government during the War of 1812. Soon after the war, more people came to take up land here. These pioneers were mainly French-Canadians and Irishmen and included the families of Beseau, Lachance, Beaubien, White, Marshall, and Goodfriend. Another wave of Irish immigrants came to the island after the Irish famine in 1845, including the Coxes, Kanes, Melvilles, Quinns, and Mahoneys.

Communication with the mainland was difficult in the early days. At first the only means of transportation to Gananoque, the nearest village, was by rowboat. The first ferry was started at "The Narrows", where the channel is only 426 feet wide, and was operated by John Foley. Later, Joseph Walsh operated a second ferry. At one time there were three ferries, all operated by cables. The cable method was still in use in the late 1940's.

Originally part of the Island County of Ontario, Howe Island was transferred to Frontenac County in 1798. It was part of Pittsburgh Township for much of the nineteenth century, but became an independent municipality in 1871. William Casey was the first reeve.

The first school on Howe Island was built in 1850. Mickey Melville was one of the first schoolteachers. In 1894 the island's predominantly Roman Catholic population opened three separate schools. The last of these schools, St. Mary's, was due to be closed in 1976 but the closing was delayed. A Roman Catholic church was erected in 1848 but was replaced in 1858 by the beautiful St. Philomena Church, built from local limestone, and one of the island's landmarks. The land for the church was given by Joseph Gagneau. Sailors call it the "Star of the Sea" and it is still known as the "Mariner's Church".

Farming was the main occupation of the island's inhabitants in the nineteenth and early twentieth centuries. The number of farmers has been decreasing recently. In 1951 there were 56 farms on Howe Island. There are now less than half that number. The population has dropped from about 250 in 1930 to 214 in 1978. Today many of the island's property owners are summer residents and the number of inhabitants increases greatly during the summer season.

Summer homes began to be built in the township in the early twentieth century. The best-known of these is Nokomis Lodge, built in 1915 by American millionaire, William H. Nicholas. In 1924 it was donated to Kingston General Hospital and was used briefly as a rest home. Later it was used as a boys' camp by Jack Dempsey, the American world heavyweight boxing champion of the Twenties. The most recent owner, René de la Roche, is the stepson of Canadian novelist Mazo de la Roche.

The means of transport to the mainland has been a contentious issue for many years and continues to be so. Island residents have made frequent petitions for a bridge or causeway to replace the ferry service, which is often unreliable in the winter.

J.H. Meacham & Co.: *Illustrated Historical Atlas of Frontenac, Lennox and Addington*, 1878.

Kingston Whig-Standard, 1951, 1973, 1975, 1976.

HOWELLS, geographic township, Cochrane District
Position 49° 55′ 81° 59′

Located approximately 25 miles northeast of Kapuskasing, the origin of the township's name is unknown.

A secondary highway links the area with the Spruce Falls Power & Paper Company Railway station point at Smoky Falls to the northwest, and the Ontario Northland Railway station point of Fraserdale to the southeast.

In the southwestern corner of the township, the Mattagami River is joined by the Kapuskasing River swelling the former to a lake of considerable size.

HOWEY, geographic township, Sudbury District
Position 47° 07′ 80° 52′

Located northwest of Wanapitei Lake, the township is watered by the Wanapitei River.

Dry weather and secondary roads link the area to the town of Capreol in the south.

Boundaries were surveyed in 1909 and the township was named after Dr. W.H. Howey of Sudbury.

HOWICK, township, Huron County
Position 43° 54′ 81° 03′

The most northeasterly township in Huron County, Howick was one of four townships created out of the area known as the Queen's Bush. It was named after Henry George Grey, Lord Howick, who was Under-Secretary of State for the Colonies in the 1830's.

Howick was surveyed in 1847 by Alexander Wilkinson, but no settlers arrived until John Carter built a house on Lot 11, Concession 8, in August 1851. Having established himself on his land, he brought his family and his brother-in-law, Henry Bell, to the area in 1853. In the same year, Jacob Cook settled on Lot 15 Concession 3. Like Carter, he waited some time before bringing his family to their new home. The story is told that when the family did arrive in 1854, the road proved so impassable that they were forced to carry in all their household goods on their backs.

The year 1854 saw the first real influx of settlers into the township. Among the pioneers who took up land at this time were Henry Smith, John Downey, Allan Ireland, the Greer brothers, the Sotherans, W.G. Walker, Arthur Mitchell, and Joel Rogers. Mr. Rogers erected the first frame house in Howick. At about the same time, Nathaniel and James Leech came to the township looking for cheap land on which their family of nine brothers could settle. They chose a site near present-day Gorrie and in 1855 Edward, James, and Nathaniel Leech arrived and built their homesteads.

The first sawmill in the township was built by Hugh Hollinshead and Henry Smith, but the Leech brothers were not far behind and soon their mill at Gorrie, (known at that time as Leechville) became very prosperous. Arthur Mitchell, who became Howick's first postmaster in 1855, also operated the first grist mill and kept the first store. Mr. and Mrs. Joel Rogers opened the first public house.

Settlements developed almost simultaneously all over Howick so there was quite a rapid increase in population. In the 1870's there was large-scale immigration into the township from Waterloo County. By 1871 the population of Howick had reached 5,417, but emigration to the west and to the cities reduced the number of inhabitants to less than half by the 1940's. Recently, however, the population has been increasing. In 1978, 3,080 people lived in the township.

Howick was united with Grey and McKillop Townships for municipal purposes until 1856. This proved inconvenient as legislation was carried out in distant Goderich and in 1856 Henry Smith became the first reeve of the newly independent township. Lack of a town hall meant that council had to alternate the site of its meetings between Fordwich and Gorrie.

The first school in the township was Gough's School, built a mile east of Fordwich in 1857. Miss Waugh was the first teacher.

The Wesleyan Methodist minister, Mr. Clarke, held the first religious services in Howick in the house of Mrs. Greer. When the school was built, the Wesleyans worshipped there until a church was erected in 1862. The first meetings of the New Connection Methodists were held in 1857 in the home of John Gallagher by Rev. Thomas Jackson. This group joined the Wesleyan Methodists in 1874.

The travelling clergyman, Rev. C.H. Drinkwater, was the first to preach to an Anglican congregation in 1858. A church was built in 1869 and Rev. Edward Newman became the first regular minister. Rev. Thomas Muir held services in the new Presbyterian church in Gorrie in 1881. Other early churches include Trinity Anglican at Fordwich (1861), and the Fordwich Presbyterian church (1865). Around the year 1875 a group of families known as Tunkers, among whom was the Rev. John Reichard, emigrated from Waterloo County to Howick Township. Rev. John Reichard, originally from Pennsylvania, conducted services in the different homes of the Tunker group until 1889, when he built a church on his farm known as the Tunkers Church, and now known as Brethren in Christ.

The three main villages in Howick are Wroxeter, Gorrie and Fordwich. Several small post villages were founded in the mid-nineteenth century, including Belmore, Mayne, Newbridge (Spencetown), and Lakelet.

H. Belden & Co.: Historical Atlas of Huron County, 1879.

James Scott: The Settlement of Huron County, 1966.

R.W.N. Wade: Early History of Howick Township in Huron County, 1952.

HOWLAND, township, Manitoulin District
Position 45° 56′ 82° 00′

Situated in the northeast portion of Manitoulin Island, the Indian lands which make up the township were named after the Howland family of Toronto. The Hon. Sir William Howland was Lieutenant-Governor of Ontario, 1868-1872. Howland was subdivided by A. Niven in 1864.

Early industries in the township included a cheese factory, a woollen mill which produced yarn and blankets, a sawmill, and a grist mill. The mills were located at Sheguiandah (place of the grindstone), where they could use the water flowing from Bass Lake into Georgian Bay. There is still a sawmill in Howland today.

The most important industry is now tourism. Two motels and camping facilities provide good accommodation for visitors, and the waters of Bass Lake offer excellent smelt fishing. Three churches attend to the religious needs of the residents.

In recent years the population of the township has been increasing. From 781 in 1971 it has risen to 874 in 1978. The non-native population at Sheguiandah numbers now about 150.

Ministry of Natural Resources: *Directory of Statistics and Data for Incorporated communities in the Northeastern Region*, 1975.

HOYLE, geographic township, Cochrane District
Position 48° 35′ 81° 08′

Subdivided in 1904 by Ontario Land Surveyor G.L. Brown, and named after William H. Hoyle, MPP for the North Riding of Ontario at one time, this township lies close to Timmins and directly north of the town of South Porcupine.

A branch of the Ontario Northland Railway links the area with the station point of Hoyle to the east, and Highway 101 passes through the southeastern corner of the township.

HUBBARD, geographic township, Sudbury District
Position 47° 17′ 82° 32′

Bordering on the District of Algoma, this township lies in the vicinity of Mississagi Wild River Provincial Park. Spanish Lake protrudes into Hubbard's southeastern corner, while Bragh Lake is situated in the northwestern section.

The township is believed to have been named after a one-time alderman of Toronto.

HUDSON, township, Timiskaming District
Position 47° 33′ 79° 49′

The township, which was incorporated as a municipality in 1904, was surveyed in 1888 and named after W.P. Hudson, the MPP for Hastings from 1883 to 1886. The area is located a few miles west of the town of New Liskeard to which it is linked by Highway 65.

Settlement in the township began in the 1890's, when the first settlers arrived from Mattawa via the Ottawa River and Lake Timiskaming, an expansion of the Ottawa. They were attracted by reports that the land in this part of Ontario was extremely fertile. Part of Hudson lies in Ontario's "Little Clay Belt", an area covered with rich topsoil of one million acres, extending northward from New Liskeard.

Several rocky ridges divide the township, running in a northwesterly direction from the southeast corner.

There are several lakes, the largest of which is Hammond in the southwestern section.

Most of the township's population of 430 are living in the community of Hillview, located in the centre of Hudson.

HUDSON, community, Vermilion Additional Township, Kenora District
Position 50° 05′ 92° 10′

Situated on the south shore of Lost Lake, about 13 miles west of Sioux Lookout, this dispersed rural community is known as "The Natural Gateway to the Vermilion and Lac Seul Waterways".

At one time Hudson was a major distribution centre for the Northern Ontario gold-mining areas. A post office was established here in 1932. Hudson's importance declined with the construction of Highway 105 into the Red Lake District, which facilitated the transportation of goods. However, other industries, including commercial fishing, lumbering, and pulp-and-paper making, kept the community alive. By the 1950's tourism was becoming an important source of income for Hudson's residents. Stores supplying provisions, clothing, dry goods, fishing tackle, and camping equipment, hotels and restaurants all cater to the visitors who are attracted by the area's good fishing and hunting. The community is accessible by rail, road (Hwy 116), and air.

Hudson's population numbers about 650 (1979).

HUFFMAN, geographic township, Sudbury District
Position 47° 38′ 82° 09′

The township consists mainly of lakes, the largest being part of Opeepeesway Lake in the southwest of the area.

Lying approximately 12 miles east of Highway 144 and some 30 miles northeast of Wakami Lake Provincial Park, it was named after Karl Huffman, Ontario Land Surveyor.

HUGEL, geographic township, Nipissing District
Position 46° 30′ 80° 15′

Located northwest of Lake Nipissing, this area was subdivided in 1882 and named after a Baron von Hugel. There are two small communities, Hugel and Kipling, within its boundaries.

Deer Lake lies almost central, and a variety of secondary roads link the area with Highway 17.

HUGHES, geographic township, Algoma District
Position 46° 50' 83° 47'

Formerly designated as Township 22, Range 10, it has since been named after Francis Hughes of the Constabulary for the Sault Ste Marie region in the early days of its development.

Situated some 35 miles, as the crow flies, northeast of Sault Ste Marie, it is connected to Highway 17 by secondary roads.

HUGHSON, geographic township, Algoma District
Position 46° 35' 82° 31'

Located 10 miles north of the town of Elliott Lake and just to the east of Mississagi Provincial Park, this area was formerly known as Township 145.

The Boland River flows through the northwestern part of the township, which also incorporates the southern part of Harold Lake.

The township was named after Eric C. Hughes, a Canadian Army Private from the Manitoulin District, who was killed in World War II.

HULLETT, township, Huron County
Position 43° 40' 81° 27'

Situated in the central part of Huron County, Hullett is triangular in shape and is bounded by the following townships: East Wawanosh and Morris on the northeast, McKillop on the southeast, Tuckersmith on the southwest, and Goderich on the west. It was named after John Hullett of the London firm Hullet Brothers & Company. It was to this firm, in the spring of 1824, that John Galt went for consultation concerning the finances for the establishment of the Canada Company. Providing terms were satisfactory, John Hullett, actively interested in Canada, promoted the English firm's financial interest in Galt's promising scheme. On July 30, 1824 they met at London Tavern and successfully negotiated the forming of Canada Company.

A tributary of the Maitland River passing through the fairly flat terrain is the township's main source of drainage. It was probably this very flatness which caused settlement to be slow at first, as the immigrants from England and Scotland were used to a rolling countryside and viewed the stretches of level land with suspicion.

Anthony Van Egmond, one of the first settlers in the county, was the pioneer of Hullett. Thomas Walker, another early immigrant, settled near Clinton in 1833. Most of the early settlement activities in the township were in the area that eventually became the town of Clinton. It was from the Clinton crossroads in 1832 that work was begun in clearing a road through to London, known as the London Road.

By 1844 there were only 195 inhabitants in the township, but in the late 1840's population increased, mostly by English immigrants. Humphrey Snell, one of the first residents, encouraged families to take up land on the road between Clinton and Londesborough. He opened his home as "Travellers' Rest" to assist incoming settlers. To

316

the northwest section of the township came Elijah McFaul, a pioneer arriving in 1847. The Sprung family and E. Elkins took up land in 1848.

The first municipal organization took place in 1848. At a meeting held at Clinton, William Hodgson was elected chairman, Edward Van Egmond town clerk, James Longbottom assessor, and James McMichael collector. In 1850 Hullett and McKillop Townships were united for municipal purposes but they became independent in 1852. Elijah T. McFaul was the township's first reeve. James Allen served as clerk and Jonas Gibbings, James Miller, Thomas McMichael, and James Snell as councillors.

The 1850's saw a number of new settlements established. Londesborough, on the Lake Huron and Buffalo Railway, was the most important of these. The pioneers of the area were R. Wright, William Herrington, and Francis Brown, but it was a later settler, Thomas Hagyard, who laid out the village in 1850. First known as Hagyard's Corners, its name was changed to Londesborough when a post office was established in 1861. John Neelands was the first postmaster.

The first post office in the township had been established at Bandon in 1855, with John Warwick in charge. John Lawson became postmaster at Hullett's second post office, opened at Constance (more commonly known as Kinburn) in 1857. Harlock received a post office in 1872 and Summerhill in 1887.

In 1861 the township's population was 2,704 and by 1880 it had tripled. Since then the number of inhabitants in this largely agricultural area has decreased. Today the population remains fairly stable at just over 1,800 (1979).

James Scott: The Settlement of Huron County, 1966.

Clinton Women's Institute: History of Clinton and Surrounding Community, 1950.

HUMBER BAY, part of Borough of Etobicoke, Municipality of Metropolitan Toronto
Position 43° 38′ 79° 29′

Situated at the mouth of the Humber River, Humber Bay was a boat-building centre in the early days. The first record of the industry was made in 1764 by Alexander Henry who witnessed the construction of canoes here by the Indians who held him captive.

Humber Bay was a port of call throughout the nineteenth century. During the War of 1812 American ships landed here before the attack on York (Toronto). More friendly visitors frequently stopped at the site on their way to the Old Mill upriver. William Gamble, the mill-owner, later built a wharf at the mouth of the Humber. By the late 1800's, small cargo vessels, yachts, tugs, and steam launches all called at the Bay. Among the steamers plying the waters were the Ailsa Craig, Chicoutimi, Jackman, and Watertown. Traffic decreased around the turn of the century and in 1910 the Good News was the last sailing vessel to go through the Humber swing-bridge. Today pleasure motorboats are the most frequent sight. Since the Second World War, Humber Bay boat-builders have made many of these pleasure craft.

The district was also known for its prosperous market-gardeners. Among the early farmers in the area were Francis Daniels, Charles Mason, Charles E. Brown, and Joseph Rush.

In the nineteenth century, Humber Bay had a number of hotels which offered accommodation to travellers. Octavius L. Hicks' Royal Oak Hotel also served as a meeting-place for various groups and had a reading-room for those interested in literary pursuits. Charles Nurse, boatbuilder, carpenter, and fisherman, owned a hotel which was popular for the pleasure grounds behind it. The pleasure grounds of John Duck's Wimbleton House were the site of frequent picnics. Duck also built a wharf to serve travellers arriving by water.

There were many boathouses in the community. The largest and most pretentious was Devin's boathouse which also contained a restaurant and a dance hall.

As there was no township hall, the meeting place of the Etobicoke council changed frequently. In 1912 Humber Bay played host to the councillors who met in Newton's Hotel and the Humber Beach Hotel.

Humber Bay's proximity to Metro Toronto puts it in the enviable position to share in the broad development of Toronto's expanding waterfront.

Robert A. Given: *The Story of Etobicoke*, 1950.

HUMBOLDT, geographic township, Manitoulin District
Position 46° 03′ 81° 07′

The township, which is not subdivided, was named after the Baron von Humboldt, a German explorer. The area lies to the east of Killarney Provincial Park. Part of the southeastern section is Indian Land.

HUMPHRY, township, Parry Sound District
Position 45° 15′ 79° 45′

The township is situated southeast of the town of Parry Sound. Much of the region is covered with lakes, the largest of which are Lake Rosseau and Lake Joseph. Fishermen and tourists come to the area in large numbers, attracted by the scenic beauty and the abundance of fish.

The origin of the township's name is obscure and the spelling is in dispute. The name is officially Humphry but it is spelled as Humphrey by the municipality. Some sources suggest that the name chosen was that of a friend of Sir Alexander Campbell, Commissioner of Crown Lands at the time the township was established in 1866.

There was no settlement in the area before 1861. At about this time, the timber lands of the township were sold, mostly to Cook Brothers, and timber-cutting operations began. Humphry was sub-divided in 1866 and 1867 by Provincial Land Surveyor Gibbs and in 1868 free land grants were made available by the government in exchange for certain settlement duties to encourage settlers to come into the district.

Edward Clifford is considered the first settler in the township. He squatted on the site of present-day Rosseau on the northern tip of Lake Rosseau, in 1864. He later sold some of his land to an American by the name of Pratt. The latter operated the Rosseau House, also known as Pratt's Hotel, which was widely known to tourists as the largest and most comfortable hotel north of Toronto. The enterprising proprietor built a steamboat landing for his guests and annually improved and enlarged his facilities.

Other early settlers included Mr. Sirett, who became Immigration Agent at Rosseau, George Milne, a Mr. Williams, John Lorimer, Richard Irwin and James Ashdown. The latter gave his name to one of the early township villages situated at the junction of the Parry Sound and Nipissing Roads.

Port Cockburn, another pioneer community in the township, was the site of the Summit House, a popular hotel on Lake Joseph which attracted visitors because of its unusually clear waters and picturesque shoreline.

In 1873 the township of Humphry was established as a municipality.

In recent years the population has been expanding, increasing from 563 in 1971 to 800 in 1979. Most of the residents live in small communities scattered throughout the township. Tourism provides a major source of income along with lumbering.

Florence B. Murray: *Muskoka and Haliburton 1615-1875*, 1963.

H.F. Gardiner, *Nothing but Names*, 1899.

HUNGERFORD, township, Hastings County
Position 44° 28' 77° 15'

The region that encompasses Hungerford Township was once a favourite hunting ground of the Mississauga and other Indian tribes. They found an abundance of game and fish in the forests and beautiful lakes and streams of the area. Stoco Lake, in the centre of the township, long since has become a major attraction for tourists and fishermen. The township is drained by the Moira, Clare and Skootamatta Rivers as well as by a number of creeks.

Part of the township was surveyed by Alexander Aitken in 1797. He found the area "one entire continuation of rock and swamp" and did not advocate settlement. A second survey was carried out in 1822 by Samuel N. Benson who received land grants in the township in partial payment for his work.

The township was named after the distinguished military leader in the American Revolution, Sir Francis Rawdon-Hastings, who was a descendant of the Barons of Hungerford.

The first settlers came around 1826 to Sugar Island on the south side of Stoco Lake. They were Owen Dirkin and Martin Donahue. Philip Huffman and Nichol Conlin followed.

Settlement increased when the Canada Company, a group of

British speculators which owned large tracts of land in Upper Canada, began offering reserve lots purchased from the Crown in the area. The village of Tweed, known as Munro in the 1830's, developed on Stoco Lake. A sawmill was operating at Chapman's Corners by 1836, and the population of the township then was 500. Prior to 1837, however the township had neither schools, churches, stores nor taverns.

Around 1850 a town hall was erected at Georgetown, one mile south of Tweed. Felix Gabourie, founder of Georgetown, donated the land. A new town hall was built at Georgetown in 1877. It was renovated and enlarged by township council in 1967.

Around 1853 Abraham L. Bogart of Belleville built a sawmill and a grist mill on the Clare River. The resulting settlement became known as Bogart.

Other settlements which sprang up in the township included Moneymore, Lime Lake and Marlbank. Thomas Clare founded the post village of Thomasburg at the west end of the 4th Concession. The village was named after three pioneer settlers, Clare, Nichols and Graham, all three having Thomas as their first name in common.

Thomas Clare was the first postmaster. Thomas Graham opened a woodworking shop, making carriages and caskets. By the late 1870's the village had several industries, a common school and four churches.

The post village of Stoco by that time had grown into a community of 100. In the 1880's a gold mine went into operation northeast of Tweed. About 1900, sulphide was first produced on the property, and the village of Sulphide was built nearby. The plant at Sulphide was closed in the 1960's.

Hungerford Township's main industry was and remains chiefly agriculture.

Gerald E. Boyce: *Historic Hastings*, 1967.

HUNT, geographic township, Algoma District
Position 48° 35′ 85° 15′

The township is named after Stanley Joseph Hunt, MPP for Renfrew North in 1945. Its main community is White River, a station point served by the Canadian Pacific Railway, and reckoned to be one of the coldest spots in Ontario.

Picnic Lake lies in the northern part of the area.

HUNTER, geographic township, Nipissing District
Position 45° 38′ 78° 48′

This area was surveyed and established in 1881. It is widely dotted with lakes and there is a dam located in the southeastern corner.

Located in the southwestern part of Algonquin Provincial Park, the township is named for James Hill Hunter, MPP for South Grey 1875-90.

HUNTINGDON, township, Hastings County
Position 44° 25′ 77° 28′

Situated in the southern part of Hastings County, about 15 miles north of Belleville, Huntingdon was named after Francis Rawdon-Hastings, a British statesman who was descended from the Earls of Huntingdon.

The land was originally set aside by a group of men who planned to bring in settlers but by 1796 the venture had failed and the township was declared vacant. The lack of roads and nearby stores and mills discouraged potential settlers and by 1817 there were only four families living in the township. These were the Ketchesons and Ostroms and the families of Anthony Denike and Philip Luke. In the 1820's a settlement was begun by the Ashley family near West Huntingdon.

Development of the township was helped in the later 1820's by the Canada Company which bought reserve lots in 1826 and settled much of the land. Early inhabitants of the area included the Vandewaters, Hagermans, Spencers, Thomases and Mortons. Many of these new people were the children of United Empire Loyalists who were used to the pioneering life. By 1835 the township population had risen to 437. Better transportation after 1827 when the government gave money to improve the road north to Madoc Township had helped encourage settlement, as did the building of the Belleville and North Hastings Railway in the latter part of the century.

By the late 1830's Huntingdon had several craftsmen, a store, a tavern, two sawmills and a grist mill. Most of the arable land was settled by 1850 and 2,196 people lived here. The population peaked at about 3,200 in the 1870's, then began to decline so that there were less than 1,500 inhabitants in 1940. Recently the numbers have been rising again and in 1979 the population was 1,726.

The first township meeting appears to have been held in 1836 with Philip Luke as clerk, although records only go back to 1848. These early meetings were rough affairs, with the "west towners" often coming armed with clubs to ensure that they got their own way. In 1850, under the new Municipal Act, Anthony Denike became the first reeve. The village of Moira was made the seat of township government, a position it surrendered to Ivanhoe in 1918.

By 1880 three cheese factories were in operation, including the Moira Cheese Factory established in 1870 and the Ivanhoe Cheese Factory, opened at about the same time by Henry Gavin. Belleville provided an excellent market for their products. Industries at the community of Moira included a wool carpet manufacturer, a fanning mill run by the McTaggarts to clean grain, and Deans' furniture factory. In the late nineteenth century, mining was an important aspect in the township, with talc and fluorspar proving to be very profitable. The Wellington Talc Mine opened in 1899, followed by the Connolly Mine in 1912. It was in this latter year, that the first fluorspar was discovered.

By 1840 the township had six schools. A stone school was constructed at Fuller in 1850 and another school built later brought the total to eight by 1878.

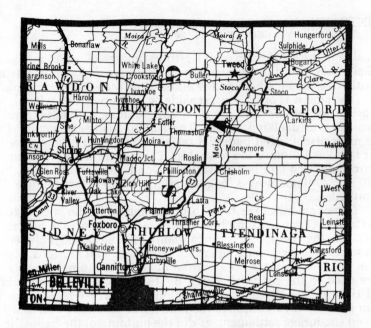

A Quaker meetinghouse which had been erected by 1845 was probably the first house of worship in the township. In 1854 a Methodist Church was opened, on land given by Henry Ketcheson. By 1878 there were three Methodist, one Bible Christian, and one Presbyterian church in Huntingdon. A second Presbyterian Church, St. Andrew's was built in 1882.

Moira was the first post office in the township. Ivanhoe received a post office in 1851. It was originally called St. George but this name was unpopular with the settlers who were mostly of Scottish and Irish descent and in 1857 it was renamed Ivanhoe on the suggestion of Thomas Emo, a schoolteacher. Fuller was named after John Fuller, one of the first settlers there.

Today Huntingdon is a centre of the dairy industry and there still is a cheese factory at Ivanhoe. Lake Moira, the largest lake in the township, offers excellent fishing and a summer cottage settlement has grown up here. A deer hunting area is another major attraction for tourists.

Gerald E. Boyce, *Historic Hastings*, 1967.

HUNTLEY, geographic township, Regional Municipality of Ottawa-Carleton
Position 45° 18′ 76° 04′

Formerly a municipality and a part of the county of Carleton, Huntley, which is situated west of the city of Ottawa, was named after Lord Huntley of Fitzroy, brother of the Duchess of Richmond.

The first settlers in the township were John Cavanagh and

William Mooney who arrived from Ireland about 1819 and built their homes on adjacent lots in the Carp Valley. The fertile soil soon attracted more colonists, including Alexander Workman, William Erskine, William Montgomery, Robert Johnston, Lieut. Campbell, Sergt. Cowie, William Cram, John McEwan, and Joseph Simpson. Most of these early settlers were from Scotland and England. As a result of their hard work, the Carp Valley developed into a prosperous dairy-farming area and Carp village became the centre of the township.

Settlement in the western part of the township began with the 1823 arrival of Peter Robinson and a group of Irish immigrants. The earlier Huntley residents resented the better terms of settlement given to these new arrivals who were known as Ballyghiblins, while the Irish resented the fact that their land was of poorer quality than that of the Scottish and English settlers. The bitter feelings resulted in violence when the local militia was called for a muster parade. Captain Glendinning, who was in charge, allowed his men to drink a toast to the King's birthday, a gesture not appreciated by the Irish. After the parade the soldiers retired to Alexander Morris's tavern, where the Irishmen were not welcome. A fight resulted and a number of men were injured. The next day the Irish set out to find Capt. Glendinning, but he evaded capture by concealing himself in a hidden recess in the fireplace of his home. Finally, the County Magistrates gave warrants of arrest to the deputy sheriff in an attempt to curb the violence. The constables surrounded the Irish settlement. Many of the men fled, but firing broke out and one was killed and three wounded. This ended the troubles and peace has been maintained ever since.

After peace was restored, the settlement of West Huntley increased. Among the new arrivals were the Hunts, Browns, Caseys, Manions, Kennedys, Hogans, O'Learys, and Mahoneys. Small communities began to spring up, including Powell, Manion's Corners, Elm, Clandeboye, and West Huntley (now Corkery). In the 1830's the population was swelled by the addition of labourers on the Rideau Canal, many of whom made their homes here. The area declined somewhat in the 1870's due to extensive emigration to the newly-opened Canadian Northwest.

Early industries in Huntley included sawmills, brickyards, cheese factories, and a woollen mill. Then, as today, the township was mainly agricultural, with dairy and beef farming being the most important activities. In the early twentieth century, many farmers spent their winters in the Ottawa Valley lumber camps.

United with March Township for municipal purposes in the early nineteenth century, Huntley became a separate township before 1840. Robert Johnston was the first District Councillor. In 1850 J.E. Fenton became the first reeve to govern Huntley's 2,500 inhabitants. James Lowery served as clerk and Robert T. Holmes, Wm. E. Bradley, Henry McBride, and David Morehead as councillors. In 1974, the township, with a population of 2,662, was amalgamated with the Townships of Fitzroy and Torbolton as the Township of West Carleton.

The Presbyterian minister, Mr. Glen, of Richmond, was the first to hold public religious services in Huntley. Lowry Presbyterian Church was opened many years later in 1845. Methodism was brought to the township in the 1820's by Rev. George Farr. In 1843 Rev. James Brennan organized a New Connexion Methodist congregation. St. Paul's Methodist Church was built in 1872. The Irish settlers of Peter Robertson's settlement were mostly Roman Catholics, and in 1837 they erected their first church, St. Michael's. The Anglican Christ Church was built on John Cavanagh's land in 1838 and Rev. James Godfrey became the first resident minister in 1853.

Huntley's first school was built on Mr. Mooney's land and Miss Mills was probably the first teacher. Several more schools had been opened by the late nineteenth century, including three Roman Catholic separate schools. In 1965 the modern St. Michael's Separate School replaced the older buildings. At about the same time the Huntley Township School Area was organized and all public school students were transferred to Carp Centennial School.

In 1943 Carp airport was opened as an RCAF Flying Training Centre. Closed as a military installation in 1945, it was reopened as a civilian airport a few years later. The Air Cadet League of Canada has established a glider school here.

Dan Buckley, a counterfeiter who minted false money in Huntley in the 1850's, was one of the township's most colourful characters. John Gourlay, who wrote a well-known history of the Ottawa Valley, lived in Huntley. Other residents have included Dr. Bob Manion, parliamentarian and humanitarian, and Erskine Johnston, Deputy Speaker in the Provincial Parliament, who helped pioneer the development of the 4-H Clubs.

Anne Argue et al: *Beginnings A Brief History of Huntley Township 1819-1930*, 1974.

National Capital Commission: *Early Days in the Ottawa Country*, 1965.

Harry and Olive Walker: *Carleton Saga*, 1968.

HUNTSVILLE, town, District Municipality of Muskoka
Position 45° 20′ 79° 13′

Situated on the Muskoka River, 25 miles north of Bracebridge and 80 miles south of North Bay, this thriving community is known as "the biggest little town" in Ontario. Beautiful scenery and a year-round calendar of activities attract visitors to the "Gateway to the Lake of Bays", which was named after Captain George Hunt, the founder of the town.

The first visitor in the area was William Cann. Cann hunted here in the early 1860's and built a log shanty to serve as a home during the hunting season. The first permanent settler in the district was probably James F. Hanes who erected a house for his family at the east end of Hunter's Bay. Chaffey Township, where Huntsville is located, was surveyed in 1869 by Walter Beatty, and in the same year Captain George Hunt arrived and settled on the north bank of the Muskoka River. In 1873, according to the Crown Lands Report of that year, the settlement was still called Fairy Lake Junction, meaning the junction of the Muskoka and Bobcaygeon Roads at Fairy Lake.

Hunt's home became the central meeting-place for the inhabitants of the surrounding townships and soon a small community began to grow up. William Cann built a hotel about 1870 and Allan Shay who arrived about this time, erected the first substantial house in the community. In the 1870's, Shay had part of his property surveyed into town lots in order to promote settlement.

Huntsville expanded quickly. By 1879 it had two hotels, five general stores, a hardware store, a butcher, shoemaker, tailor, two blacksmiths, seven carpenters, a pump and wagon shop, and two sawmills, one built by Stevenson & Sons. A post office had been established in 1870 with Hunt as postmaster.

Huntsville was incorporated as a village in 1886 when its population was about 400. L.E. Kinton was the first reeve. The councillors were J.F. Hanes, William Proudfoot, J.R. Reece, W. Ecclestone, Robert Scarlett, and F.W. Clearwater.

In the same year the Northern Railway was extended to the village and Huntsville's lumber industry began to flourish, as timber could now be easily shipped out. More sawmills were built including those of the Whaley Lumber Company and the Whiteside Lumber Company. Fred Francis and Duncan McCaffery erected planing mills, and a grist mill and a woollen mill were also constructed. Other industries included L.H. Ware's brickyard and a foundry.

Huntsville suffered a serious setback on April 18, 1894 when a disastrous fire swept through the business section, destroying most of the frame buildings in the area. Many residents lost almost all their possessions in the fire, but through community cooperation villagers soon rebuilt their stores and homes, and Huntsville regained its former prosperity.

In the late nineteenth and early twentieth centuries, the village developed as a tourist resort as steamer cruises became more and more popular. The first steamer to ply the waters near Huntsville was the Northern. Captain G.F. Marsh built and operated the Empress Victoria and the Joe, and C.O. Shaw bought the Sarona and the Dortha. By 1900 the steamers cruised Lake of Bays and Mary, Peninsula, Fairy, and Vernon Lakes.

In 1901 Huntsville, with a population of about 2,000, was incorporated as a town. Dr. J.W. Hart served as the first mayor and George Paget, Thomas Whaley, R.J. Hutcheson, William Turnbull, W.H. Matthews, and J.R. Reece as councillors. The town remained the same size as the village until 1965 when Helstern Subdivision was annexed from Chaffey Township. In 1971 the new town of Huntsville was formed by the amalgamation of the old town, the village of Port Sydney, and the townships of Brunel, Chaffey, Stisted, and Stephenson. The amalgamation increased the population from 3,359 to 8,909. At present (1979) the town has a population of over 11,000.

In the 1890's Hanna & Hutcheson Bros. established a factory to produce flooring, broom handles, etc., in Huntsville. In 1902 they organized the Muskoka Wood Manufacturing Company and built a mill and flooring factory which produced the well-known "Red Deer" brand flooring. The Company became Weldwood of Canada Ltd. in

1955 and has remained one of Huntsville's major industries. The town lost some of its industries during the Depression but the loss was offset by the growing tourist trade. In 1920 C.O. Shaw opened the "Bigwin Inn", which rapidly became a popular summer resort. Rotary Beach (Later Kinsmen Beach) was acquired by the Rotary Club which also established a local museum in 1956 and bought the land for the Huntsville Pioneer Village in 1961. The Lions Club improved the lookout on "the mountain" in the Municipal Park in 1941. An excellent curling rink, opened in 1951, and the Huntsville Ski Club attract sports-minded visitors in the wintertime while fishing and boating are among the many pleasures to be enjoyed by summer tourists.

Since the Second World War many new industries have been established in the town. In the 1950's the International Ceramic Mining Company Ltd. located on one of the biggest deposits of "potter's clay" in the world. In the late 1960's a Kleenex tissue plant was built by Kimberly-Clark. Other industries include Algonquin Metal Products, Canusa Coating Systems Ltd., Huntsville Timber Products Ltd., Husky Carbon Industries Ltd., and Cormack Beverages Ltd.

The first religious services in the community were non-denominational and were held by Rev. Norton Hill in the home of Captain Hunt. Hunt also gave the land on which the first Presbyterian church, St. Andrew's, was erected in the late 1870's.

Huntsville's first church had been a Methodist one, built on William Cann's land in 1875. A second Methodist church, opened in 1879, became Trinity United Church in 1925. An Anglican house of worship was constructed on Cann's land in 1883 and Rev. C.A. French became the first resident minister. A new church was erected in 1895.

The Roman Catholics of Huntsville held most of their early services in the home of John White, later moving to the Municipal Court House. St. Mary's was opened in 1898 with Father Fleming in charge. Father O'Brien became the first resident priest in 1932 and a new church was built in 1960.

The first school was opened by Captain Hunt soon after his arrival. A new building was erected in 1888 and was replaced in 1904 by an institution which also offered some high school work. A private school, Morley College, gave instruction in the 1890's.

A Mechanic's Institute was established in the village in the late nineteenth century. It became the Huntsville Public Library and was at first housed in the Council Chambers, then in the Municipal Building which was erected in 1926. In 1971 it moved to new quarters.

The village's first paper, The Huntsville Liberal, was begun by Dr. F.L. Howland about 1876. It became The Forester in 1878 and still serves Huntsville as a weekly publication today. The latest addition to the media in the town is the new local radio station, CKAR.

Dr. Howland was the community's first doctor. In 1896 he built a hospital to serve the village. It was later closed but in 1950 a new institution, the Huntsville and District Memorial Hospital, was opened.

Baseball leagues were active in Huntsville in the early twentieth century and during the 1930's Huntsville became a major centre for lacrosse. An early curling rink was replaced by a more modern one in 1951. The Memorial Arena and Community Hall was built in 1954. The Huntsville Ski Club was the first in Ontario to provide night skiing. The Muskoka Loppet, held in January, is Canada's largest single day cross-country ski event. The town also has three golf courses.

The Muskoka Cavalcade of Colour, a celebration of the turning of the leaves, and the Muskoka Winter Carnival entertain visitors in the fall and winter while summers see the influx of cottagers and tourists to enjoy the beauty of summer on the lakes. Thus Huntsville is truly a year-round resort.

George W. Boyer: *Early Days in Muskoka*, 1970.

Geraldine Coombe: *Muskoka Past and Present*, 1976.

Capt. L.R. Fraser: *History of Muskoka*, 1942.

George F. Hutcheson: *Head and Tales*, 1972.

Florence B. Murray: *Muskoka and Haliburton, 1615-1875*, 1963.

HUOTARI, geographic township, Algoma District
Position 48° 24' 84° 29'

Originally designated as Township 52, and now named after T. Huotari, a Canadian Army Private from Hearst, killed during World War II, the Township is served by the Algoma Central Railway, with a station point at Wanda.

Two miles north of the township there is the Canadian Pacific Railway and Algoma Central Railway junction of Franz at the tip of Lake Hobon.

HURDMAN, geographic township, Cochrane District
Position 49° 30' 81° 46'

The township was named after George C. Hurdman, MPP for Ottawa West in 1914.

Lying some 10 miles north of the town of Smooth Rock Falls, the area is watered by the Mattagami River.

A few miles to the east is Highway 807 which links with Highway 11 to the south.

HURLBURT, geographic township, Algoma District
Position 46° 46' 83° 39'

Hurlburt is situated northeast of Sault Ste Marie. Originally known as Township 202, and named after Reverend Thomas Hurlburt, a Methodist Minister who served on the north shore of Lake Huron in the 1830's, the township houses Garden Lake in the eastern section.

A dry weather road connects the area to Highway 561 to the south and to the west, ultimately, to Highway 17.

HURON, county
Position 43° 40′ 81° 30′

John Galt, superintendent of the Canada Company, is considered to be the founder of Huron County. The Huron Tract, which contained one million acres on the southeast shore of Lake Huron, was purchased by a group of British speculators incorporated under the name of Canada Company, on August 19, 1826. It was this company that was responsible for opening the area to settlers.

The Huron County of today includes 840,832 acres and has a population of 55,846. There are five incorporated towns within its borders: Clinton, Exeter, Goderich, Seaforth and Wingham as well as five villages: Bayfield, Blyth, Brussels, Hensall and Zurich. The county contains 16 townships: Ashfield, Colborne, East Wawanosh, Goderich, Grey, Hay, Howick, Hullett, McKillop, Morris, Stanley, Stephen, Tuckersmith, Turnberry, Usborne and West Wawanosh.

Galt's first action in the Huron Tract significantly influenced the pattern of settlement for the entire pioneer period. In 1828 he had the Huron Road laid out from Wilmot to Goderich and the site of Goderich cleared for settlement. By 1832 this original trail had, at great expense, been made into a proper road rendering the land accessible to any who would venture there.

In the beginning those adventurers were few, in 1837 there were 385 inhabitants; but in 1838 that figure had jumped to 1,168, in 1842 to 7,190 and by 1848 there were over 20,450 inhabitants.

The majority of the early settlers were from Scotland accompanied by some German families from Pennsylvania. These pioneers proceeded directly to Goderich since it was the only established settlement. The result was that up to 1837 the nucleus of settlement in Huron County was centered in Goderich, extending either to the north into Colborne Township or south into Goderich Township. Small pockets of settlement grew up along or near the Huron Road, the most flourishing of these being Bayfield located twelve miles down the lake from Goderich.

In 1832 work began on the London Road between London and the site of the present town of Clinton where the London Road met the Huron Road. Settlement followed these roads and took shape in those townships created in that section of the county which was originally part of the Huron Tract. These were: Goderich, Tuckersmith, Colborne, Stanley, McKillop, Stephen, Usborne, Hay and Hullet. It is difficult to determine the names of the first settlers as they did not receive clear title to their land for several years so that the records are dated much later than their actual arrival.

The opportunities for water transport were not used effectively to support settlement in the Huron Tract. Although John Galt had planned to develop the port of Goderich in order to supply the pioneers, his successors in the Canada Company did not follow up his ideas. The Company was likewise slow to open the area to rail.

However, by the 1850's railway fever had begun to spread into the county. The Brantford and Buffalo Railway, promoted in 1850, was the first significant line in Huron. It was joined by the Toronto and Guelph Railway which planned to proceed from Stratford to Sarnia. By 1880 Huron County was extremely well supplied with railways.

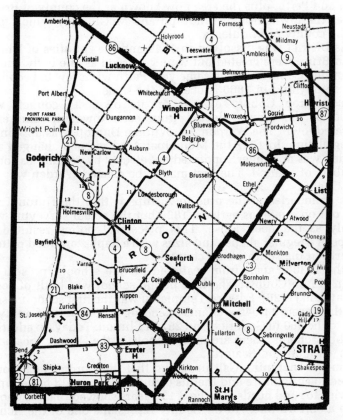

Undoubtedly, railways influenced settlement, for during the period of building up to 1907 no municipality considered itself to have much of a future unless at least one railway line was passing through it. The railways were equally significant to the rural folk who suddenly had access to additional markets for their livestock, cheese, fowl, eggs, lumber, and grain.

Politically, owing to its sparse population, the Huron Tract did not exist as a separate entity until after 1835. This was the result of the fact that in 1788 Upper Canada was divided into districts and the Huron Tract was located in the London district. In 1836, however, it was seen to be worthy of representation in the Legislature of Upper Canada. It thus became known as the District of Huron and held its first elections in that year. Municipal government, however, was carried on by a board of magistrates, appointed by the Crown, who met in London.

An Act of Parliament in 1841 set the county on its way to achieving its political identity municipally when it provided for the establishment of local or municipal authority in several districts. One of the municipal authorities that was set up under this Act was the District of Huron encompassing the territory included in the counties of Huron and Perth, plus the area now known as the county of Bruce, as well as the townships of Biddulph and McGillivray which form part of the county of Middlesex.

This District was dissolved in 1849 and the counties of Huron, Perth and Bruce were created but were governed as one body known as the "United Counties". The same year Perth withdrew to become a separate county and in 1866 Bruce did the same.

Thus Huron County existed on its own, its council was composed of the reeves elected from each township and each incorporated town. The Warden, Dr. William Dunlop, was appointed by the legislature. In 1847 the Municipal Act had been changed and the Warden was no longer appointed but elected by popular ballot by the members of council. The first man to be elected Warden was Dr. William Chalk.

The boundaries of the nine townships within the Huron Tract were set out on a map as early as 1828 but the actual surveying was done only as the need arose. This piecemeal policy resulted in townships of irregular shapes and sizes with a haphazard road pattern particularly in the south of the county.

In the 1830's, apart from scattered private schools, no schools existed in Huron County. The first public school was built of cedar logs in Bayfield (1836). Edward Templeton was the first schoolmaster. By 1861 there were 11,049 students attending school in the County in addition to the 680 in Goderich and 257 in Clinton. Today, in addition to its public schools, there are high schools in the County located at Goderich, Clinton and Seaforth.

From the beginning Galt imagined that the Huron Tract would be devoted to agriculture and that its communities would be set up to be of service to rural needs. The next 150 years showed that his choice had been a shrewd one. Huron County represents one of the richest and best areas for farming in the entire country. This fact no doubt accounts for the success of the early pioneers who struggled with tremendous hardships but were rewarded for their efforts.

By 1850, only two decades after the opening of the Huron Road, 284,037 acres were held. Of these 54,996 were under cultivation; 35,966 acres under crop, 18,688 acres under pasture and 299,000 acres were still in woodland. By the early 1850's the southern townships were becoming filled and new townships were added. East Wawanosh and Morris were created in 1851; Grey in 1852, Howick in 1853 and Turnberry in 1854. This meant increased acreage for cultivation.

The transition from the pioneer period to that phase of agricultural operations which has set the pattern for farming today began in 1858 with the advent of the railway. The Buffalo and Lake Huron which ran between Buffalo and Goderich gave farmers access to the American market. This came at an opportune moment as the advent of the Civil War in the United States produced a need for livestock and drove prices higher. In 1875 the London, Huron and Bruce opened up various markets both foreign and domestic.

By 1870 the County of Huron was able to participate on a large scale in the fruit trade. In that year 109,454 bushels of apples, 8,950 bushels of grapes and 9,501 bushels of other fruit were produced. Evaporators were built and dried apples were exported to Belgium and Holland.

The threshing machine ushered in the final stage of development and "threshing day" became a community event.

Today the farms are larger than in the past and of a more specialized nature. Huron is one of the major egg-producing areas and a source of first class beef and pork products.

Goderich, the first settlement, is the capital of Huron County. It was the focal point for all social, financial, political and commercial activity during the first 25 years of the settlement of Huron. The first County Courthouse was completed at Goderich in 1856. This splendid example of pioneer architecture was destroyed by fire in 1954. The new Courthouse was erected in 1955 and officially opened in 1956. Goderich has not developed into an industrial town but remains a pleasant, thriving town attracting many tourists with its natural charms.

Huron County retains a rural air and is considered by some to be one of the most self-sufficient areas in the nation. It has produced leaders in business, medicine, politics and the church as well as many of the country's best agriculturalists.

James Scott: *The Settlement of Huron County*, 1966.

HURON, township, Bruce County
Position 44° 05′ 81° 35′

Huron Township lies at the southwest corner of Bruce County, fronting on Lake Huron from which it takes its name. It covers an area of 59,462 acres and has a population of 2,676 (1979). Parts of the township were surveyed by A.P. Wilkinson in 1847, the remainder in 1851 by E.R. Jones.

When the Huron lands were offered for sale in 1852, there was a number of squatters already residing there. Most of these people had confined their settlement to the area along the shore of the lake, since transportation was easily afforded by water in summer and on the ice in winter. However, one settlement had been established five miles back from the lake by Malcolm McRae and his son "Big" Duncan, Alex McRae and his two sons, Duncan and Donald-Buie, Findlay McLelland and their families. Louis Bellemore is credited with being the earliest pioneer in the township, having settled at the mouth of the Pine River in 1848.

A sleigh track was cut through the woods of Ashfield, the township to the south, in the winter of 1849-50 and the lakeshore road through Huron was opened in 1853 with a substantial timber bridge being built over the Pine River.

The good agricultural land of the township attracted Scottish and Irish settlers. At one time 75 percent of the population was Scottish following the influx in 1852 of a large group of crofters who had been evicted by their landlord from their homes on the Island of Lewis in Scotland.

Pine River was the name of the first post office established in Huron Township in 1853. J.W. Gamble was postmaster. The first sawmill is said to have been built in 1855, also at Pine River, by William Blair. This mill was purchased by John Hicks who added a grist mill, both mills were destroyed by a flood in 1868.

In 1856 Capt. Henry C. Gamble came to Pine River and decided to establish a business centre on the site of the town plot which had been surveyed in 1855. This survey was known as the Alma Town plot. He proceeded to build a saw and grist mill. The attempt to establish both Alma and another settlement named Lurgen failed.

Until 1853, Huron Township was part of the United Townships of Bruce County. It became a separate municipality in 1854. The first councillors were William Blair, Robert Huston, William Wilson and Samuel Wright. John Hunter presided as reeve with J.W. Gamble as clerk and John Campbell as treasurer.

Huron Township remains an agricultural community with the village of Ripley as its hub. Ripley was first established as a post office in 1856, its postmaster was M. MacLennan. In 1874 the railway was opened and Ripley was made a station. In the same year a number of buildings sprang up and the village boasted a grist and sawmill, six stores and a Presbyterian church. The town hall was built there and three grain storehouses were erected shortly after to serve the surrounding agricultural community.

Norman Robertson: *The History of the County of Bruce.*

HURTUBISE, geographic township, Cochrane District
Position 49° 23′ 79° 47′

Situated to the north of Lake Abitibi, the township was established in 1945 by the Ministry of Lands and Forests, and named after Senator J.R. Hurtubise who was MP for Nipissing until June 1945.

The area, not accessible by road, is watered by the Kabika, the East Kabika and the Burntbush River.

HUTCHEON, geographic township, Sudbury District
Position 47° 27′ 83° 16′

Until 1974 known as Township 10E, Hutcheon is located west of Wakami Lake Provincial Park, and south of Five Mile Lake Provincial Park. It is watered by various small nameless lakes. Highway 129 runs parallel with the township's boundary.

Hutcheon was named after a surveyor of Northern Ontario, Jas. Hutcheon, who, by his reports and speeches, promoted settlement there around the turn of the century.

HUTCHINSON, geographic township, Rainy River District
Position 48° 49′ 91° 18′

Lying to the east of Atikokan and north of Quetico Provincial Park, this township is watered by numerous lakes and rivers. The Sapawe River flowing through the southern half of the area lends its name to a small community in the south.

The Canadian National Railways line jogs into the southwestern corner of the township and secondary roads link the area to Highway 11.

The township was named after Earl Hutchinson, MLA, MPP for Kenora, 1929-34.

HUTT, geographic township, Sudbury District
Position 47° 59′ 81° 06′

Bordering on the District of Timiskaming, Hutt lies approximately 40 miles south of Timmins. It has various small lakes and rivers and is linked by secondary roads to Highway 66 and Kirkland Lake to the east.

First surveyed in 1896 and re-traced in 1929, the survey was partly annulled in 1960.

The township was named after a Professor Hutt.

HUTTON, geographic township, Sudbury District
Position 46° 51′ 81° 00′

Situated northwest of Wanapitei Lake and the town of Capreol, the township was subdivided in 1898 and named after Professor Maurice Hutton of the University of Toronto. It became a part of the newly formed town of Capreol on January 1st 1973.

The Vermilion River flows through the township. Ironside Lake and Hutton Lake are located in the southern half of the township and Moose Mountain rises in this vicinity.

HUTTONVILLE, part of the city of Brampton, Regional Municipality of Peel
Position 43° 38′ 79° 48′

Situated in the western part of the city of Brampton, on the Credit River, this former compact rural community was named after J.P. Hutton, an early mill owner.

Huttonville was founded in 1848 when a man named Brown came to the area known as "Wolf Den" and built a small lumber mill on the bank of the Credit. The mill was taken over by Joseph P. Hutton in 1855. He added more saws and a lath and shingle mill and had soon established a prosperous business. His son, J.O. Hutton, began a woollen mill.

By 1877 the population of the community was about 150. A post office called Huttonville had been established in 1873. Mr. Shawcross kept a general store, Mr. Whiting ran a waggon shop, and Richard Howell served the residents as a blacksmith. There was also a temperance hotel.

Today Huttonville is entirely residential. Many of the inhabitants commute to Toronto or Oakville to work. There is also a fair number of retired people living here.

In 1969 the community became part of Brampton when the city annexed the Township of Chinguacousy, of which Huttonville was a part.

HYDE PARK, community, London Township, Middlesex County
Position 43° 00' 81° 20'

Situated a few miles northwest of the city of London, Hyde Park was named after the famous 341-acre park of that name situated in the heart of London, England, by Thomas Routledge, one of the pioneers of the area.

Duncan MacKenzie from Scotland and Thomas Routledge from England were the first settlers at Hyde Park, arriving about 1818. Other early residents included John Barclay and Truman Hull. These first inhabitants had to travel to St. Thomas to purchase supplies, as it was another eight years before London was founded.

William Lambley opened the first general store in Hyde Park. By 1830 the community had a cabinet shop owned by Alexander Patterson, a tinshop, and a sawmill. Mr. Murch was the first blacksmith. George Tremeer later operated a carriage shop and Mr. McBear offered his services as a weaver. A post office was established in 1859 with Angus Fraser as postmaster.

About 1855 Alexander Forsythe built the first hotel, Hyde Park House. A public dance hall which extended over the hotel sheds became a popular gathering-place until it burned down in 1911. A second hotel, the Old Countryman's Inn, was opened by Charles Woods a few years after Forsythe's establishment was erected.

In 1854 the Great Western Railway was built within a mile of Hyde Park. Rail connections were further improved with the construction of the London, Huron and Bruce line in 1875 and the Canadian Pacific tracks in 1888.

The first sidewalk was laid in the community by Walter C. Reeve in 1905. Largely due to the efforts of Dr. C.C. Ross, a town hall was built in 1906. Hydro power was introduced in 1923. A local library was opened in 1926 and in 1937 it joined the County Library.

Jennie Raycraft Lewis: *Llyndinshire*, 1967.

London Free Press, 1949.

HYMAN, geographic township, Sudbury District
Position 46° 25' 81° 38'

First subdivided in 1887, part of this area was annexed to the Town of Walden on January 1, 1973. It is situated northeast of the town of Espanola.

Agnew Lake is situated in the southern part of the township and at the southeastern end of the lake are two Hydro Electric generating stations, a dam, and the tiny community of High Falls.

The township is named after the Hon. Charles Hyman, a Minister of the Crown.

HYNDMAN, geographic township, Kenora District
Position 49° 36' 92° 04'

Lying to the southeast of Dryden and approximately 20 miles west of Sandbar Lake Provincial Park, this area was named after Harry Hyndman, elected MPP for Toronto — Bracondale, 1945.

The Canadian Pacific Railway crosses the township's southwestern corner, and the Trans-Canada Highway touches the southern boundary line.

HYNES, geographic township, Algoma District
Position 46° 55' 83° 54'

Named after A. Hynes, a constable for the Sault Ste Marie area in its early days, the township lies approximately 40 miles, as the crow flies, northeast of the city of Sault Ste Marie.

Saddle Lake occupies part of the northwestern corner of the township and secondary roads link the area to Highway 17.

I

IDINGTON, geographic township, Cochrane District
Position 49° 30' 82° 45'

Named after Hon. J. Idington, High Court Justice for Ontario, and situated northwest of Kapuskasing, this township was subdivided in 1918 by J. Dobie, and all boundaries were surveyed in 1906. The western half of the township is now part of the Improvement District of Opasatika.

The Opasatika River and a few small creeks water the area.

Highway 11 and the Canadian National Railways pass through the township, which houses the tiny communities of Harty in the southeast and Opasatika in the northwest.

IGNACE, Township, Kenora District
Position 49° 25' 91° 40'

Ignace, about 70 miles southeast of Dryden, is one of Northern Ontario's fastest growing areas due to recent base-metal discoveries in the region. The main community in the township is also called Ignace, first recorded by Sir Sandford Fleming as a station on the proposed route of the Canadian Pacific Railway's transcontinental line; it was named by the railway builder after his guide, Ignace Mentour, who led a cross-Canada surveying expedition in 1872.

The Ignace area, part of an Indian canoe route to the north, was once the home of the Ojibways. There was much fur trading in the district in the early nineteenth century, but no permanent white settlement took place until the coming of the railway.

The first building in Ignace was a surveyor's house constructed by the government about 1875. It became the centre of survey activity in the area, and members of the Ignace Indian Band settled around it to provide services for the surveyors and the construction workers of the CPR. The first white settler in the township was Albert McGillie, who settled along the railway tracks in 1879. The railway had reached Ignace that year and the first train passed through the settlement in 1881. Because of its central position between Kenora and Thunder Bay, Ignace became a divisional point on the CPR.

In 1883 William Henry Cobb moved his hotel from Taché to Ignace and had a town site surveyed. He operated a general store in his hotel and was prominent in the local fur trade. A post office opened at Ignace in 1884 with Cobb as the first postmaster.

The first mining patent in the area was granted in 1889 to Captain S. V. Halstead, who established the Maple Leaf Gold Mining Company and opened the Black Fox Mine. The gold rush of the 1890's brought an influx of prospectors to the area and Ignace became the headquarters for the U.S. Gold Mining Company. W. H. Cobb, who had discovered gold at Sturgeon Lake, built a hotel near the Ignace station in 1899 to accommodate miners on their way to the lake over his newly constructed mining road. Many of these prospectors settled with their families in Ignace.

In 1892 the Canadian Pacific Railway opened a quarry at Ignace and a new station and roundhouse were erected at the settlement in the early 1900's. Housing built for CPR employees, included a boxcar settlement which became known as "Little England" because of its large number of English residents. In 1905 the CPR line was being doubletracked, bringing a renewed influx of workers to Ignace. The railway yards were enlarged and Cobb erected a warehouse. Ignace was now a shipping point for the furs of the Hudson's Bay Company. The township was incorporated in 1908 with W. H. Cobb as the first reeve. The councillors were John Dwyer, Pascal Contini, Dr. Bowen, and David Coates.

In the early twentieth century mining declined, but lumbering took its place as an economic factor. The industry prospered as the demand for railway ties increased with doubletracking. In 1904 J. R. Turnbull built a tie-mill which operated for a number of years. the CPR was also the major customer of the Ignace quarry opened by Bob Bannerman and William Horne in 1912 to supply crushed rock to ballast the railway line.

In 1923 the Keewatin Lumber Company began operations in the Ignace area, providing employment for township residents for the next decade. Charlie Greer who started lumbering near Ignace in 1928, erected a sawmill and built several logging roads to transport ties to the railway. The firm switched to pulpwood production during Word War Two.

Fur trapping continued into the 1920's, although a temporary ban on trapping around 1910 had caused many members of the Ignace Indian Band to leave the area. In 1922 the Great Lakes Fur Trading Company of Fort William opened a branch in Ignace.

In 1921 the Ontario Forest Service began experimenting in the Ignace area with flying forester patrols. A lookout tower was built in 1930 and a number of forestry workers settled in the community of Ignace.

During the Depression of the Thirties employment for area residents was provided by the construction of the Trans-Canada Highway.

The first tourist camp in Ignace was opened in 1932 on Raleigh Lake by Happy Crocker. Others soon followed. White Otter Castle, built by Jimmy McQuat, a colourful early trapper, was a popular attraction. Many of the camps closed during World War Two, but reopened again and today tourism plays an important part in the local economy. During the Second World War, many prisoners of war were employed in the logging camps around Ignace. Lumbering took an upswing in the 1940's with Great Lakes Paper becoming the major company in the district. The industry began to decline in the late 1950's.

When diesel engines replaced the steam locomotives in the 1950's, fewer railway workers were needed. Fortunately, the construction of the Trans-Canada Pipe Line provided employment just as the railway work declined. Pipeline workers settled in Ignace and by 1965 the population had risen to 682.

In 1969 important base-metal discoveries were made in the Sturgeon Lake area. The Mattabi Mine opened in 1972 and the Falconbridge Copper Mine in 1974. The community of Ignace became home for the mine workers, a new subdivision was built and a trailer court was established. A medical clinic, a recreation centre, and a shopping mall were constructed to serve the rapidly growing population. A new mobile home site was opened in 1977. An airport built in 1978 greatly improved communications. Despite a decrease in world demand for lead, copper, and zinc by the late 1970's, the mines continue to operate.

In the early 1890's Miss Isbuster taught the settlers' children in Malcolm Isbuster's hotel dining room. The first schoolhouse was built in 1905. A library was founded by Mr. Hosker for railway workers in 1889. A public library was opened in 1921.

The Presbyterians of the township organized a congregation in the late 1880's and early services were held in a hotel. A Presbyterian church was built on land given by W. H. Cobb about 1912. The Anglican congregation, organized in 1903, erected a church in 1910 under Rev. Arthur Bruce. In 1976 a joint ministry of the United and Anglican congregations, one of the few in Canada, was formed. A Pentecostal congregation was organized in 1956 and Gospel Church erected in 1976. The Faith Lutherans came together in 1974 and opened a house of worship in 1976. The newly-formed Baptist congregation bought land for a church in 1978.

A weekly newspaper, *The Village Tattler*, made its appearance in Ignace in the 1950's. In 1971 Dennis and Jackie Smyk began the *Driftwood* and printed it until 1973. Mattabi Mines put out the *Mattabi Memo* from 1973 to 1976. It was followed by the weekly *Ignace Courier*, founded in 1976. In 1978 radio station CKDR-CKIG opened in Ignace. The township population now numbers about 2,300 (1979).

Elinor Barr and Betty Duck: *Ignace a Saga of the Shield*, 1979.

ILDERTON, police village, London Township, Middlesex County
Position 43° 04′ 81° 24′

Situated about 8 miles northwest of the city of London, on the CNR, Ilderton was named by its first postmaster after his home in England.

The first settlers arrived about 1824 and included William McAndless, Edward Charlton, Mr. McLean, Robert Little, William Lipsett, and Samuel Paisley. Hugh McAndless and the Nixon family took up land in 1827, followed some time later by Richard Porter,

Harvey Hall, William Calvert, Thomas Martin, and J. H. Hughes.

A store was opened by George Ord about 1850. Other businesses established around this time were the shoe shop of Josh Nichol, William Nichol's wagon and blacksmith shop, and Robert Little's wagonmaking establishment. Andrew Little and Herb Aylesworth were the first harnessmakers; H. S. Hudson owned an early butcher shop; and Harry Metcalfe, William West, and William Fuller were among the first carpenters. A tinshop was opened by Harry Storey.

The construction of the London, Huron and Bruce Railway through the community in 1875 greatly improved shipping facilities and stimulated business. T. J. Clatworthy opened a lumber yard, as did William Patrick. The latter also built a grain elevator and a hotel, Lorne House, to accommodate the visitors the new railway would bring. Another grain elevator was erected by John Williams. Tom Cowan, Mr. Scott, and William Kinnear went into business as cattle shippers.

By 1900 Ilderton's population had reached about 300. In 1919 the Ilderton branch of the United Farmers' Club of Ontario organized a Co-operative, bought a grain elevator, opened a mill in 1920, and purchased Fred Clatworthy's lumber and coal business. Alex Stewart was the first President of the Ilderton Co-operative which has proved a very successful enterprise.

In 1928 Ilderton's streets were paved. The following year a skating rink was opened. It was replaced with a new skating and curling arena around 1970. The Ilderton Community Memorial Hall was built in 1950.

Jennie Raycraft Lewis: *Llyndinshire*, 1967

H. R. Page & Co.: *Historical Atlas of Middlesex County*, 1878.

ILSLEY, geographic township, Kenora District
Position 49° 30' 91° 57'

Located approximately 50 miles southeast of the town of Dryden, this township was named after Hon. Jas. L. Ilsley, Minister of Finance, 1940-45.

Mameigwess Lake occupies a large area in the northeastern corner and Crocker Bay encroaches into the southeastern part of the township.

Highway 17 passes through the township, as does the Trans-Canada Highway. There is a station point at Raleigh.

INDIAN RIVER, community, Otonabee Township, Peterborough County
Position 44° 20' 78° 09'

There have been two villages called Indian River in Otonabee Township over the years. The original village was located a mile north and a mile west of the present site. At one time it boasted a stagecoach stop complete with boardinghouse and saloon as well as several houses and a blacksmith's shop. It seems that the village grew up around an early lumber camp.

When the Canadian Pacific Railway built its line south and east of the original village in the 1880's, the residents moved gradually to a new site near the railway depot also known as Indian River. Logs, pulp and fuel wood for the city of Peterborough were shipped over the line from Indian River after the railway went into operation. Later farmers of the district shipped cattle and hogs to the stockyards.

Among the early settlers of Indian River were the Breckenridges, the Evanses, Devlins, Shearers, Sullivans, Tuckers, and the Whibbs. Augustine Whibbs set up a blacksmith shop in 1884.

During the last half of the 1800's and the early 1900's, Indian River flourished. There was a shingle mill and a "Silverwood's" outlet, which pasteurized milk. Butter and casein were also produced in the village. The passenger trains were used a great deal by villagers in those years to make shopping trips to Peterborough or special trips to Toronto. With the advent of the motor car the use of railways declined and the Indian River station was closed in the 1950's. The old railway depot is now merely a flag station.

D. Gayle Nelson: Forest to Farm: Early Days in Otonabee, 1975.

INGERSOLL, town, North Oxford and West Oxford Townships, Oxford County
Position 43° 02′ 80° 53′

Ingersoll, a town of about 8,300, is situated on the Thames River, 9 miles southwest of Woodstock and 20 miles east of London. It was named after Major Thomas Ingersoll, the area's first settler. His son, Charles, is considered the founder of the town which for some years was known first as Oxford and then as Ingersollville.

Major Thomas Ingersoll was a member of a wealthy Massachusetts family who came to the Niagara Peninsula in 1793 where the British government had promised him and his associates 80,000 acres of land. Ingersoll brought many settlers to the area before the government revoked the agreement in the late 1790's. The Major's eldest daughter, Laura, married Loyalist James Secord, a sergeant in the first Lincoln Militia. During the War of 1812, Laura Secord, then living at Queenston, made her way through enemy lines and walked for 20 arduous miles through the bush to warn the British commander of an impending American attack. Her courage and patriotism has secured her a place in history as one of Canada's heroines.

The site chosen by the Major for his new home in Upper Canada was the place where the Indians used to leave the river trail to cross to Brantford when visiting their chief, Joseph Brant. Settlement of the area was slow, although the community had a store and an inn and was self-supporting by 1799. The Major left the area in 1805, but his son, Charles, returned to settle on the old homestead in 1817, moving his family there in 1821. In that year he became postmaster of the first permanent post office in the county. By this time the settlement also had a school, a tavern, mills and a distillery.

In 1831 Charles Ingersoll laid out a town plot. The community, then known as Oxford, remained the centre of Oxford County until

Woodstock became the District Town. Several new stores and mills had been built by 1836. In 1844 the first stagecoach left Ingersoll for Woodstock.

Ingersoll was incorporated as a village in 1852, when its population had reached 1,190. The following year the Great Western Railway arrived at the village, encouraging growth by providing facilities for the shipping of wheat and lumber. At this time, the Crimean War had shut off Britain from European wheat markets, forcing the English to import wheat from North America. Ingersoll became the centre of the area for wheat export to Britain.

In 1856 Noxon Bros. established at Ingersoll an agricultural implement factory and T.D. Miller opened a pork factory in the 1860's.

Ingersoll, Church of the Sacred Heart

In 1857 one of the hoaxes of the century was perpetrated at Ingersoll. It had been rumoured that there was an alligator-like creature in the village pond and 10,000 people came to watch the attempts to capture it. Among them was an eminent scientist from the United States who alienated the local people by keeping aloof. It was much to their delight when the operation supervised by the scientist did turn up a "monster" — the stuffed carcass of a cow.

During the 1850's and 1860's Ingersoll was a "station" on the Underground Railway which brought fugitive slaves from the United States to freedom in Canada. Being halfway on the route between Detroit and Niagara Falls, Ingersoll's Wesleyan Methodist church basement provided a refuge for many a slave. An active anti-slavery organization existed in Ingersoll, with Max and Leonard Bixel, brewers, and Thomas Brown, a tanner, among the leaders. When the negro leader Old John Brown led the raid on the government arsenal at Harper's Ferry, Virginia, in 1858, to try to establish a stronghold for escaped slaves, many of the men who accompanied him had been recruited by him from the people of Ingersoll. There were about 500 blacks in the village at this time.

Over-cropping of the soil which robbed it of its fertility, and the decrease in the demand for wheat after the war, caused the farmers of Oxford County to switch to dairying by the 1860's. In 1864 the first cheese factory in Canada was built in Oxford County, and Ingersoll became the home of cheesemaking in what soon was to be known as Ontario's leading cheese-producing region. In 1866 Ingersoll cheese producers manufactured a 7,300 pound cheese, 21 feet in circumference, which was exhibited at the New York State Fair and in London, England.

In 1865 Ingersoll was incorporated as a town. Adam Oliver, a leading businessman, was the first mayor. Oliver expanded the mills he owned in 1867, and the Adam Oliver Company became the town's third largest industry. He was instrumental in the founding of the Canadian Dairyman's Association at Ingersoll in 1867, and was a leading promoter of the Ingersoll, Tillsonburg and Port Burwell Railway and also of the extension of the Port Credit Railway from Galt.

By 1871, Ingersoll had 4,022 residents and was expanding rapidly. It soon surpassed Woodstock in size, although a serious fire in 1872 had destroyed the business section. A lumber road was built to the south greatly aiding the local lumber trade.

The 1880's saw the growth of two of the town's main industries, meat-packing and cheesemaking. J. L. Grant established a pork-packing factory, later adding cheesemaking. T. D. Miller, in 1888, began the manufacture of soft cheese known as "Miller's Royal Paragon Cheese". When sales of soft cheese dropped, a new formula was developed resulting in the manufacture of Ingersoll Cream Cheese. The Ingersoll Cream Cheese Co. Ltd. was formed and a new plant built with offices, manufacturing plant, cold storage and shipping facilities in the 1920's. Products included different types of pasteurized cheese, such as Ingersoll Loaf Cheese and Old Oxford. The business became the Ingersoll Cheese Company Limited, known throughout Canada for its processed cheese products which include Blue Bonnet Margarine and Fleischman's Golden Corn Oil Margarine.

In 1887 the Evan Bros. opened a piano factory and Hault Manufacturing Co. began a furniture factory at Ingersoll. W. C. Bell & Co.'s planing mill, Sutherland's carriage works, three flour mills and two oatmeal mills also provided employment for the townspeople before the turn of the century. Another industry that had its beginnings back then was the Morrow Screw and Nut Company which became the town's largest industry by the 1960's.

One of the first churches in the community was Presbyterian Knox Church, built in 1842 and known as "the Kirk". Erskine Church was constructed in the 1850's and St. Andrews in 1872. In 1892 the Knox congregation joined St. Andrews, an addition was built, and the church was renamed St. Pauls. Reverend E. R. Hutt was the first minister.

A Roman Catholic church was erected in 1850 on land given by the Presbyterian John Carnegie for that purpose. A new brick building replaced it in 1879. The Anglicans constructed a house of worship on Charles Ingersoll's land in 1852, then built St. James in 1868. A Wesleyan Methodist church was opened in 1854 and an Episcopalian church in 1857. The Wesleyan King Street Church dedicated in 1865 was known as the "two tower church". It became Trinity United in 1925. The Baptists built their first church in 1857, the Bible Christians in 1866. There were also two New Connexion Methodist churches in the town by 1875. The Salvation Army Citadel was erected in 1885. The Pentecostal congregation held their first meetings in 1898; the Jehovah's Witnesses were organized in 1950; and in 1953 a group of Dutch families established the Christian Reformed church in the town.

As for sports, Ingersoll teams have always done well. In 1868 the "Ingersoll Victorias" baseball team won the Canadian championship and in 1930 another Ingersoll team won the Ontario championship. Three Ontario championships were won between 1961 to 1964. In hockey the Ingersoll Reems were victorious at the OHA Junior Championships in 1955 and the Intermediate Marlands reached the Ontario finals in 1960. Softball was popular in the 1930's and 40's. An Ingersoll lacrosse team, the Dufferins, won fame in the 1880's but enthusiasm for the sport died down by the 1920's. In 1966 the IDCI Juniors football team won the Tri-County Eastern Division Conference. A good swimming team has also been formed since the Maude Wilson Memorial swimming pool was opened in the late 1950's. Facilities also exist for golf, curling, lawn bowling and figure skating.

Individuals from Ingersoll have also done well in sports. George Law, a welterweight boxer in the 1930's, was in the Olympic trials in 1936. Harold Wilson, in his Miss Canada speedboats won the world championship in the "225" class in 1934, and the President's Cup in 1939. In 1949 he broke the world speed record at Picton with a speed of 142.8 miles per hour, and although this was not officially recognized as a world record, it was established as the new North American record.

Ingersoll was also the home of Aimee Semple McPherson, a popular evangelist of the 1920's who established the Foursquare Gospel church in the United States. The Hutt family, of which the well known Stratford actor, William Hutt, is a member, comes from Ingersoll. Another famous resident was James McIntyre, a Scotsman who settled at Ingersoll where he became an undertaker and started a furniture business. He became known as the "Cheese Poet" for his published rhymes celebrating the development of the local cheese industry, and as one of Canada's "best bad poets" for the artless form of his rhymes.

Ontario Historical Society: *Papers*, 1976.

Place and Stream Names of Oxford County, Ontario

University of Western Ontario Library: *Western Ontario Historical Notes*, 1970

Upper Thames Valley, 1952

The Ingersoll Tribune, Centennial Edition, 1967

Castle of MacLaren's, Inglewood, Ontario, 1913
Public Archives Canada PA60867

INGLEWOOD, part of the Town of Caledon, Regional Municipality of Peel
Position 43° 47' 79° 56'

Formerly a police village, Inglewood became part of the newly created town of Caledon in 1974. It is situated on the Canadian National Railways less than 20 miles northwest of the city of Brampton.

Although the area was settled in the 1830's, Inglewood does not appear on the map until the railway boom of the 1870's and 80's. The early settlers came from the British Isles by way of the United States. They included the McCall, McCannell, Graham, Martin, White and McGregor families.

In 1843, Thomas Corbett bought lots on the Credit River and erected a small woollen mill. Another settler, John White, made hand looms at his home. The enterprise became known as the Riverdale Woollen Mills, the village in those days being called Riverdale. Twice the mill burned down and twice it was rebuilt. In 1871 it was reconstructed of field stone, about one hundred feet downstream of the original site. David Graham who managed the mill at that time leased it to Ward and Algie of Ancaster in 1875. By 1880 the Riverdale Woollen Mill was a well-known manufactory of full cloth, flannel, blankets, underwear and yard goods.

Outcrops of field stone in the Caledon Hills, which are part of the Niagara Escarpment that lies to the west of the village, became the basis for a prosperous quarrying industry. Joachim Hagerman opened the first quarry here in 1875. The stone was drawn by wagon to Boston Mills, from where it was shipped by train to Toronto on the Credit Valley Railway.

A branch of the Credit Valley Railway was to run through Inglewood in the early 1870's, but because of legal difficulties the line did not materialize until 1879, after the Hamilton and Northwestern Railway had arrived two years earlier. Railway officials, to avoid confusion with another Riverdale village in Ontario, suggested that the name for the station point be changed to Sligo Junction. A post office had been opened under the name of Sligo in 1853 with Isaac Hunter as the first postmaster. The inhabitants did not like the name and the matter was referred to the Honourable Thomas White, the MP for Cardwell in Sir John A. Macdonald's cabinet. He decided on the name Inglewood, after a village of the same name in England.

The arrival of the railway caused a flurry of building and development. William Linfoot built a hotel south of the railway tracks. A livery business was opened and James Graham established a general store, Thomas Ireland a blacksmith shop, and John McCague a wagonmaking business. A glove factory started operations in 1910.

Religious services were held informally in the early days of the settlement. In 1884, the Methodist Church was built. The first schoolhouse was a frame structure; it was replaced by a brick building in 1871.

In 1886 an incorporated company was formed to build a community hall. The Inglewood Mechanics' Institute, forerunner of a public library, was organized in 1891.

In 1974 Inglewood was amalgamated with the villages of Bolton and Caledon East, and the townships of Caledon and Albion to form the town of Caledon in the Regional Municipality of Peel.

William E. Cook: Cook's History of Inglewood, 1975

The Corporation of the County of Peel: A History of Peel Township 1867-1967, 1967

INGLIS, geographic township, Cochrane District
Position 49° 30' 80° 58'

Lying to the north of Cochrane, this township mainly features three lakes, Inglis Lake, Thorning Lake and Big Jawbone Lake. Its northern, southern and eastern boundaries were surveyed in 1900 and 1930 by Speight and Van Nostrand, and the western boundary in 1898 by A. Niven. It was resurveyed by Sutcliff in 1929.

The name origin is unknown.

INGRAM, geographic township, Timiskaming District
Position 47° 49' 79° 42'

Situated east of the town of Englehart and just west of the Quebec border, this township was surveyed in 1886-87 by Niven, and subdivided in 1888 by Purvis. It was named after Andrew B. Ingram, MP, MLA for West Elgin.

The River Pontleroy flows through the southwestern corner of the township and Ingram Creek waters its eastern half. Tomstown, a small community, is situated in the east of the township. Several secondary roads link the area with Highway 11.

INKERMAN, community, Mountain Township, Dundas County
Position 45° 02' 75° 24'

Situated on the Nation River, Inkerman is one of the oldest hamlets in Mountain Township. An abundance of waterpower attracted milling operations around which the settlement sprang up. Transportation privileges being afforded by the river, a flourishing lumber trade developed and accounts for the hamlet's early prominence in the township.

The site on which the village stands was part of a 400-acre land grant made by the government to United Empire Loyalist Robert Parker after the American Revolution. It was Parker who erected the first building in this vicinity. Some time later Robert Thompson arrived and started a grist mill which he eventually sold to Frank Smith. The settlement for a number of years was known as Smith's Mills. Elias Hitchcock operated a sawmill which he sold to Henry and John Merkley. When Joseph Bishop built a substantial stone grist mill in the village, the settlement took on the name of Bishop's Mills. However, when a post office was established in 1858, the name Inkerman was chosen to commemorate the Battle of Inkerman.

The first merchant of Inkerman was A. H. Munroe; Thomas King and Benjamin Little were the early blacksmiths and Charles Storey was the carriagemaker in the hamlet.

Surrounded by fine farming country, Inkerman, with some 400 inhabitants by the late eighteen hundreds, once had two cheese factories and a number of shops, stores and hotels. There were two churches and a public school. Today the population of this once bustling rural centre had dwindled to less than 100.

J. Smyth Carter: The Story of Dundas, 1905

INNERKIP, community, East Zorra Township, Oxford County
Position 43° 13' 80° 42'

Situated a few miles northeast of Woodstock on the Thames River, the village was originally called Melrose. The name was changed because another Melrose already existed. Innerkip was suggested by Mrs. Hugh Barwick who came from a village of the same name in Renfrewshire, Scotland.

A post office was opened in 1853. By the 1870's Stephen Pelton and Son had set up a business as pumpmakers, while the Callan family were engaged in limeburning. Elijah Edwards was the village carpenter, George and James Ronald were millers, and Robert Murray served the community as a physician.

Innerkip's early development was aided by the construction of the Port Credit Railway, which improved transportation facilities. The increase in population became even more rapid in the late 1960's, as the number of residents rose from 417 in 1966 to 584 in 1971. In 1975 Innerkip's former status as a police village was dissolved and the community became part of East Zorra—Tavistock Township.

Place and Stream Names of Oxford County, Ontario

INNES, geographic township, Thunder Bay District
    Position 49° 23' 88° 38'

Situated on the southern shores of Lake Nipigon, this township was surveyed in 1903. It was named after the late James Innes, MP of Guelph, a well-known journalist in the Province in his time.

A small Indian Reserve rests on the shoreline in the northeastern corner. Secondary roads link the township with the community of Nipigon, some 30 miles to the southeast.

INNISFIL, township, Simcoe County
    Position 44° 18' 79° 37'

Innisfil is taken from the poetical name for Ireland, Innisfail. The township, so named by its early settlers, lies on the shore of Lake Simcoe and stretches from West Gwillimbury northward to Kempenfeldt Bay.

The area was surveyed in 1820 and the first settlers to arrive were the Hewson family, who came by way of the Holland River and Lake Simcoe. They took up land at the entrance of Kempenfeldt Bay at what they called Hewson's Point, now Big Bay Point. Francis Hewson later was appointed magistrate and for years he performed all the marriage ceremonies in the township. The first white child born within the boundaries of the township was Anna Hewson. David and James Soules came soon after the Hewsons and were followed by the Clement, Lewis, Perry and Warnica families. James Soules built the first frame house in Innisfil for Lewis J. Clement and it was still standing in the early 1900's. The pioneer in the southeast was Jacob Gill, who located in 1821 in the 2nd Concession, Lot 23, just in from the lakeshore, where he remained for many years alone.

The population grew slowly for the first ten years after the survey, but during that time there had come the Allans, Boyces, Denures, Hattons, Jacks, Longs, Maconchys, Maneers, McConkeys, McCulloughs, Rodgersons, Thompsons, Todds, Wallaces, and Wrights. Tollendal, now called Minet Point, began with the first sawmill erected in Innisfil Township in the 1830's by George McMullen. At one time Tollendal was as large as Barrie, its neighbour

347

across Kempenfeldt Bay, but when Barrie was named as the county seat, Tollendal declined.

The southwestern corner of the township was not settled until after 1840, and the northwest part remained a wilderness for another two years, largely because lands in the area were held by the Canada Company. In 1835 a grist mill was built on Kempenfeldt Bay, near the site of the first sawmill. The site was chosen because it was easily accessible by water for most settlers living along the Lake Simcoe shore. Another reason was the lack of sufficient waterpower elsewhere in the township.

The first census of the township population recorded a count of 762 inhabitants. In 1843 the first school was built in Victoria village and was taught by a Mr. Booth. In 1844 the Innisfil Methodist congregation built the first church in the township. A log building, it too was located in Victoria. The first regular missionary was James Currie.

By 1850 the township population had increased to 1,807 and in that year the first municipal council was established with William Cross as first reeve. In 1856 James Black was elected to the position of the first deputy reeve.

Following the opening of the Northern Railway in 1853 (now CNR), Bell Ewart, today an urban community, became a shipping port and place of lumber manufacturing. Logs were brought in from around the lake and redistributed as finished lumber. Rival shipping points springing up on the shoreline of Lake Simcoe, plus the diminishing forest supply, led to Bell Ewart's deterioration and the wharves and railway branch disappeared.

Allandale, once the principal village of the township, was first settled at the time the Northern Railway was constructed and it was the terminus of the line until 1855 when the railway was extended to Collingwood. Nearby Barrie had refused to grant a bonus to the railway because Allandale was chosen as the station point, whereupon the chief engineer of the line supposedly vowed "to make grass grow in Barrie streets and pave Allandale's streets with gold". Allandale gained further importance with additional rail connections to Orillia and Gravenhurst, to Penetanguishene, and to Beeton. However, Barrie won out in the end and Allandale united with Barrie in 1897.

Lefroy was another station on the Canadian Northern with daily stage connections to Bell Ewart, Churchill and Crown Hill. The hamlet of Craigvale also had a station and a post office in those days, as did Thornton on the Hamilton and Northwestern Railway on the western boundary of the township. Other early post villages in the township were Bramley, Cherry Creek, where a Presbyterian and a Methodist church were located, Fennell, Holly, Innisfil, Killyleagh, Beaumont, Painswick, and Stroud.

Once largely an agricultural township, Innisfil with its many beaches along the Lake Simcoe shore, today attracts large numbers of tourists and cottagers in the summertime. Highway 400 links the area with Metro Toronto some 30 miles to the south. Highway 11, the northern extension of Yonge Street, travels through the entire length of the township. The historic road was built before the end of the 18th century by Colonel John Graves Simcoe from York (Toronto) to the shore of Lake Simcoe.

The 1979 census of Innisfil Township reports its population as 16,178.

Andrew F. Hunter: *The History of Simcoe County*, 1909

INVERARY, community, Storrington Township, Frontenac County
Position 44° 23′ 76° 84′

This compact rural community north of Kingston was formerly known as Storrington. It was renamed in 1860 after the town of Inveraray in Scotland, either by postmaster D. J. Walker or by James Campbell, on whose land much of Inverary was built. The extra "a" shown in the Scottish name was dropped when the Canadian village was named.

The early settlers in the area were attracted by free grants of 200 acres of land. Many such grants were made to officers and soldiers after the War of 1812. Among the pioneers were Isaac Bond, William Duff, George Hunter, Patrick Chrissley, Thomas Conklin, William Lyons, Levi Sills, and Thomas Matthews. Most of these early settlers were Irish.

By 1851 there were 46 families living in the vicinity of Inverary. The first post office in the township was opened here under the township's name of Storrington in 1845. Thomas Conklin was the first postmaster. In 1855 the village was laid out on the lots of James Campbell and D. J. Walker, the first storekeeper and a friend of Sir John A. Macdonald, who was his frequent visitor.

Inverary was a thriving village by the 1870's, benefiting from its location on the Perth Road, the main toll road to Kingston from the northern townships. The toll house in the village became a social gathering place for the young people of the village. At one point Inverary had seven hotels to accommodate travellers. The first tavern, kept by Arthur Campbell, had been opened before 1851. By the early twentieth century, Inverary boasted several blacksmith shops, a general store, two butchers, a cheesemaker, a harnessmaker, a carpenter, a paint shop, and a match factory.

Cheese factories occupied an important place among Inverary's early industries, as dairy farming was the main occupation of the area's residents. Cheesemaking was started in the community by William Duff II, commonly known as "Squire Duff", in 1876. A second cheese factory was opened by Messrs. Thompson and Ferguson and called the Model Cheese Factory. It was replaced by a second Model Cheese Factory in 1913. In 1952 the Inverary Co-operative Cheese Factory was formed by the consolidation of the Model and Duff factories. It continued in operation until 1962.

Inverary's most versatile businessman, undoubtedly was Robert A. Marrison who lived in the community in the late nineteenth century. A carriagemaker and blacksmith, he was also a piano salesman, an apiarist, and an undertaker.

The present United Church was built as a Methodist Episcopal church in 1878. An Anglican church was also built in the nineteenth century, but has since been torn down. The Holiness Movement flourished in Inverary around the turn of the century and a church was built in 1896. It remained open until 1946. Today there is a house of worship for the Jehovah's Witnesses in the community.

The community has doubled in size since 1900, with most of the new construction taking place since the end of World War 2. Dairying is still the main occupation of the area's farmers, but an increasing number of residents commute to work in Kingston. By 1971 Inverary's population was 290.

Frontenac County Directory, 1865

Inverary Women's Institute: Tweedsmuir History, 1978

INVERGARRY, geographic township, Sudbury District
Position 47° 27' 81° 56'

Lying approximately half-way between Timmins in the north and the city of Sudbury in the south, the township is probably named after Invergarry in Scotland. The eastern boundary was surveyed in 1912 and the northern, southern and western boundaries were surveyed in 1921.

Highway 144 runs parallel with the eastern boundary, and a secondary road crosses the northern half of the township.

INVERHURON, community, Bruce Township, Bruce County
Position 44° 17' 81° 35'

Inverhuron, a few miles northwest of Tiverton on the shore of Lake Huron at the south entrance to Inverhuron Provincial Park, was laid out in 1851. William Gunn, one of its pioneer settlers, became the first postmaster when a post office was established there in 1854.

Possessing the advantage of a harbour, docks and warehouses, Inverhuron became a regular calling place for steamers by the 1860's. A lively export trade in grain, bark, cordwood, and lumber was carried on from here. At the time the hamlet had a population of 200.

Inverhuron's prosperity suffered a severe blow when fire destroyed its three grain warehouses with 30,000 bushels of grain on April 13, 1882. The village never recovered.

Today, the population has dwindled to about 50, but the shoreline in the area now is dotted with many cottages.

Nearby, just north of the Provincial Park, is the site of Douglas Point Nuclear Power station started in 1961. Another development on the site is Ontario Hydro's nuclear power station and Atomic Energy of Canada's heavy water plant.

Norman McLeod: The History of the County of Bruce 1907-1969, 1969

INVERMAY, community, Arran Township, Bruce County
Position 44° 28' 81° 09'

Situated just south of the village of Tara on the Sauble River, Invermay was surveyed into village lots in 1855. Soon after Luke Gardner built a sawmill; a grist mill opened in 1857. The name of the post office, which had been opened in 1853 as Arran, was changed to Invermay in 1859.

By 1865, Invermay had a population of 250 and could boast of two stores, two tanneries, one grist mill and two sawmills. There were two churches in the village by then.

The fact that Invermay and Tara were situated only one mile apart caused intense rivalry between the two as to which village would take the lead. Invermay lost out to Tara which was incorporated as a village in 1881.

Norman Robertson: *The History of the County of Bruce,* 1906.

INVERNESS, geographic township, Sudbury District
Position 47° 22' 81° 37'

Named after the largest county in Scotland which houses the famous Loch Ness, this township is located just east of Highway 144 and west of the Canadian National Railways station point of Stupart.

The eastern boundary was surveyed in 1911, the northern boundary in 1912, and the southern and western boundaries in 1921.

Donnegana Lake straddles the entire eastern boundary of the township and South Inverness Lake is located in the southwestern corner.

INWOOD, geographic township, Thunder Bay District
Position 48° 59' 90° 20'

Located just north of Lac des Mille Lacs, the origin of the name is unknown. The Inwood Provincial Park is situated in the northern boundary of the township. Cushing Lake lies in the southern part of the township. Secondary roads connect the area with the Trans-Canada Highway, which passes through the northeastern corner, as does the Canadian Pacific Railway.

INWOOD, police village, Brooke Township, Lambton County
Position 42° 49' 81° 59'

Inwood was founded in the early 1870's when James Courtright, nephew of the president of the Canada Southern Railway, recognized the timber potential of the land through which the railway ran. He formed a partnership with Messrs. Holmes and Moore who were bridge contractors on the new railroad, and together the men bought a 95-acre site which they subdivided into village lots. Three of the village streets commemorate the names of the founding partners. In 1873 the company of Courtright, Holmes and Moore built a stave and sawmill which turned out thousands of feet of board lumber until it closed in 1898.

A settlement which had grown up around the mill was named by C. H. Moore after a town on the Hudson River in New York State. The community in those days was very much under the control of the company. The first store was opened by the company and Courtright became the first postmaster in 1875. The partners also established the first butcher shop. Lumber for the first school, erected in the early 1870's, was donated by the company, as was the land on which the Anglican and Presbyterian churches were erected. The Methodists held their first services in a local boardinghouse.

George Williams opened a second general store about 1880 and Milton Taylor built a third one in 1895. Harry Liddon opened a second butcher shop in 1883. Another sawmill was constructed in the 1890's by George White. Andrew Munro began an implement business about 1900. A Mr. Cooper was Inwood's first blacksmith, William Gordon the first shoemaker, J. Stribe the first tailor, and Frank Carson the first barber. The grain business was started by T. B. Mitchell and came under the control of the Farmers' Cooperative Company in the early twentieth century.

A disastrous fire in 1899 destroyed many businesses and houses in the community, but the people of Inwood rebuilt. The community became a police village in 1920 under the first board of trustees which included: J. P. McVicar, chairman; J. Vance, and S. S. Courtright. Today Inwood with a population of 250, according to the 1971 census, is the centre of an agricultural district.

School was held in a private home in the early 1870's until a schoolhouse was available. Mr. Tullick was the first teacher. An addition to the school was built in 1887 to accommodate the growing number of pupils. The school was closed in 1961 and children are now bussed to Brooke Central School. Inwood has had a public library since the early 1900's.

Sarah L. Campbell: *Brooke Township History, 1833-1933*, 1935

A. J. Johnston: *Lambton County Names and Places*, 1942

INWOOD PROVINCIAL PARK, Inwood Township, Thunder Bay District
Position 49° 01' 90° 27'

Inwood Provincial Park, established in 1958 as a Recreation Park, is situated on the Trans-Canada Highway (#17) and the Canadian Pacific Railway, some eighty miles northwest of the city of Thunder Bay.

This 81-acre park is situated in a northern district noted for its moose population, as well as numerous other wildlife. Northern pike and pickerel are native to its waters. In the early 1800's the Dog and Savanne Rivers were used by the fur traders and between these two waterways, about 20 miles east of the park, is the historic site of their portage.

Tent and trailer sites with picnic tables and fireplaces are there for the use of visitors.

Ontario Ministry of Natural Resources

352

IONA, community, Dunwich Township, Elgin County
Position 42° 41' 81° 24'

Situated about 12 miles southwest of St. Thomas on Highway 3, Iona was named by George Munroe after the Holy Isle of Iona off the west coast of Scotland.

The site was surveyed by Munroe about 1815 and shortly afterwards settlers began to arrive. The Decow brothers were among the pioneers. The community became an important stop for wagons trading between Niagara and Amherstburg. A post office was established in 1852. A number of light industries were begun in the 1860's and by 1870 the population had reached about 600.

The growth of the community was brought to an abrupt halt when the Michigan Central (now the New York Central) Railway built its line two miles north of Iona in 1872. A new settlement grew up at Iona Station as houses, stores, and churches were moved to a new site beside the railway tracks. The railway also ended Iona's wagon trade, while Iona Station benefited from the rail traffic.

Despite the setback to its growth, Iona continued to hold an annual fair for the produce of local farmers until 1895. Today this dispersed rural community of 138 people (1971) serves as a shopping centre for the surrounding area.

H. R. Page & Co.: *Historical Atlas of Elgin County*, 1877.

IONA STATION, community, Southwold Township, Elgin County
Position 42° 43' 81° 25'

Iona Station is a dispersed rural community situated on the New York Central Railway about 12 miles southwest of St. Thomas. It was named after the nearby community of Iona, which, in turn, was named after an island off the west coast of Scotland.

Iona Station grew up as a result of the construction of the Michigan Central (now the New York Central) Railway in 1872. The railway was built two miles north of an existing settlement known as Iona and many of this community's businesses relocated at a new site nearer the railway station. Whole buildings, including stores, houses, and churches were moved to the new community beside the railway tracks. Iona Station benefited from the trade brought by the railway. A post office was opened in 1875.

The community never grew to any great size, although it became a shopping centre for the surrounding area. It still has this function today.

IPPERWASH BEACH, community, Bosanquet Township, Lambton County
Position 43° 13' 81° 58'

This dispersed rural community, about 8 miles north of Forest, is situated on a sandy beach which runs along the shore of Lake Huron from Kettle Point to Stoney Point. The name means "upper wash".

Ipperwash grew up as a summer resort. Most residences are

summer cottages, which house some of the 60,000 people who visit the area each summer. In the 1920's Col. John Ross built the Ipperwash Hotel and a dance hall. He also promoted a casino. The dance hall later became a bowling alley, then a restaurant.

The government established a provincial park at Ipperwash in 1937. The Indians who had lived on Stoney Point Reservation until this time moved to Kettle Point. During the Second World War, a military camp was built on the reservation. Today many of the Kettle Point Indians work at Camp Ipperwash as carpenters, firemen, and general duty men.

In the late 1960's a road was planned from Kettle Point to Port Franks, bypassing the beach and leaving it auto-free. Other plans were also made to upgrade the facilities and enhance the enjoyment of the thousands who visit Ipperwash beach each year.

Forest Free Press, 1967.

A. J. Johnston: *Lambton County Names and Places*, 1942.

IPPERWASH PROVINCIAL PARK, Bosanquet Township, Lambton County
Position 43° 13′ 81° 57′

This 109-acre Recreation Park was established in 1938. It is on Lake Huron, two miles west of Highway 21, and fifteen miles south of Grand Bend. The city of Sarnia is 40 miles to the northeast.

Well supplied with services for tent and trailer sites, it also has an excellent sand beach along Lake Huron with supervised swimming areas.

Ontario Ministry of Natural Resources

IRELAND, geographic township, Cochrane District
Position 49° 30′ 81° 10′

Located northwest of Cochrane, the eastern boundary of this township was surveyed in 1898, the northern boundary in 1900 and the southern and western boundaries in 1922. Re-surveyed in 1929 by Sutcliffe, the township was named after Wm. H. Ireland, MPP for Hastings West during the years 1919—1929.

Trappers Creek and Jawbone Creek water this vicinity and the Ontario Northland Railway travels through the area. There is a station point at Maher.

IRIS, geographic township, Sudbury District
Position 47° 11′ 82° 32′

This township borders the District of Algoma to the west. The Mississagi Wild River Provincial Park occupies part of the township, with the Mississagi River flowing through its centre.

Part of White Owl Lake is located in the southwestern corner of the township and the southern tip of Spanish Lake penetrates the northeastern corner. The origin of the name is unknown.

IRISH, geographic township, Cochrane District
Position 49° 39′ 83° 59′

The Mattawishkwia River flows through the southeastern corner of this township, which is located southwest of the town of Hearst. Irish Creek waters the northeastern corner and the Kabinakagami is the main river in the southwest.

The southern and western boundaries were surveyed between 1915 and 1916, and the township was named after Mark H. Irish, MPP for Toronto northeast around that time.

IRON BRIDGE, village, Gladstone Township, Algoma District
Position 46° 17′ 83° 14′

Iron Bridge, which is situated 70 miles east of Sault Ste. Marie on the Mississagi River, is the gateway to the scenic Laurentian foothills. Originally called Tally-Ho, its name was changed in 1886 shortly after a steel bridge was built to replace the old wooden bridge which stood until 1884.

The first settler in the area was James Tulloch, who located about one mile east of the present village. The community grew slowly, with lumbering and tourism becoming the main industries in the twentieth century. In 1960, Iron Bridge was erected from the Improvement District of Gladstone into a village.

Today Iron Bridge has a population of 813 (1979). Three churches, a public library, a bank, and a primary school serve the residents. A number of hotels and motels provide accommodation for visitors. There are no industries in the village.

Iron Bridge is located on the Trans-Canada Highway and from here Highway 546, known as the Little White River Road, takes the visitor north and thence northwestward along the Little White River through some of the best hunting, fishing, and sightseeing areas in the Algoma District. For rock enthusiasts, the area abounds in unusual rock formations, abandoned mine shafts, and new mine exploration sites. The North Shore Winter Carnival is held in Iron Bridge each February.

Sault Ste. Marie and District Chamber of Commerce: *Algoma Vacationland Visitors' Guide*

IROQUOIS, village, Matilda Township, Dundas County
Position 44° 51′ 75° 19′

Iroquois, a pretty village on the north bank of the St. Lawrence River, east of Prescott, was relocated in its entirety in the late 1950's due to the construction of the St. Lawrence Seaway. Its former site on the mainland, about one mile to the south, across the Galop Canal from Iroquois Point, is now submerged in the new waterway. The village, incorporated in 1857, was named after the tribe of Indians who were the region's original inhabitants. Prior to that time the community was known as Cathcart after Lord Cathcart who had commanded British forces in Canada.

Point Iroquois, converted by the canal construction into a small island, was well known to the early explorers of Upper Canada as it was a favourite Iroquois Indian camping ground. The St. Lawrence once flowing around the point formed a picturesque Bay beside it and it was here that the first white settlers took up their land in 1784. These pioneers were Michael Carman and his son, Captain Martin Walter, Jacob Coons, Captain Ault, and Peter Brouse, all United Empire Loyalists who came to Canada from the United States after the American Revolution.

A mill was built on the river front in 1788 by Messrs. Coons and Shaver and about 1804 George Brouse became the first storekeeper. A small grist mill was erected by Mr. Krause at about this time. Dan Carman constructed a wharf to supply the river steamers with wood and gradually a community began to develop at the site. The British Government erected a fort during the War of 1812, using timber bought from Carman. Another fort was also built on the land of Mr. Shaver, but was never used. It became known as Fort Needless. The last traces of the old building were removed in the 1950's.

The years following the War of 1812 were ones of slow but steady growth. A second store was opened by George Brouse and in

1827 the township post office was moved to this building. In the 1830's Point Iroquois became a regular steamboat landing, with the *Iroquois* being the first ship to provide service to the community.

It was the building of the Point Iroquois Canal from 1842 to 1847 that really stimulated Iroquois' growth. William Elliot, a contractor on the canal, gained water privileges on the new route and erected grist and flouring mills. The community grew up around the mills. Before 1842 much of the settlement had been on Point Iroquois, but now many residents moved north to be beside the new canal. Among the early merchants who established businesses at the new location were Daniel Carman; W. J. Marsh & Son, furniture dealers; Robert Lowery, boot and shoe seller; and Lawrence Burns, baker and grocer.

In 1854 the Grand Trunk Railway was built through the community, establishing a station and telegraph office at Iroquois, further encouraging its growth, as it was the only trade centre between Morrisburg and Edwardsburg.

Iroquois was the first village in the United Counties of Stormont, Dundas, and Glengarry to be incorporated and its status was the result of a municipal dispute rather than its growth in size. In the early 1850's John Laing, the township reeve had detached a portion of land from School Section 3, Iroquois, and attached it to his section, No. 2. The people of Iroquois wished to regain the property and asked that their community be incorporated so that they could include the disputed land within the village limits. Special legislation was necessary as Iroquois did not yet have the required population of 750.

Incorporation was granted in 1857. George Brouse became the first reeve and Rufus Carman the first clerk. On the council were Philip Carman, John S. Ross, William Elliot, and James Grier.

The second half of the nineteenth century saw many municipal improvements and the establishment of several industries in the community, which became known as the "Limestone Village" as the majority of its buildings were made of that material. The main street was macadamized in the 1850's and about 1859 the first public sidewalks were laid. R. H. Buchanan & Co. installed the first waterworks in the county in 1886 and in 1900 the system was purchased by the village. In 1902 a municipal electric light and power plant was built and the construction of granolithic walks begun.

Among the village's early industries were the stave factory of John and William Armstrong, the saw and shingle mills of George Brouse, and John Molson's sawmill. By 1860 Iroquois also had a large number of craftsmen, including watchmakers, carpenters, blacksmiths, cabinetmaker, carriagemaker, tailor, cooper, milliner, and tinsmith.

By 1879 the village's population was about 2,000 and it had become an important shipping centre for the agricultural produce of the surrounding area. In 1883 M. F. Beach's new roller mill replaced the old flouring mill of William Elliot, which had burned in that year. Other industries of that era included the sawmills of A. Patton and L. Cameron, and the carriage manufactory of N. G. Sherman & Son.

In 1897 canal improvements were begun under Messrs. Larkin

and Sangster. A new 800-foot lock was then the longest in Canada. Again canal construction resulted in renewed growth of the village and many new businesses were opened and industries established. In the early 1900's an old shoe factory was taken over by Messrs. Gass and Cardwell, manufacturers and dealers in linen. When it was destroyed by fire, Robert Cardwell built a linen factory. Incorporated as Cardwell Linen Mills Limited in 1923, the industry grew to be Iroquois' largest employer by the 1950's. When the Seaway was built in 1957, Cardwell relocated near the new village.

About 1929 Arnold E. Riddell began to manufacture rubber-tired milk wagons from Model T. Fords. He built about 90 wagons during his years of operation. In 1944 St. Lawrence Valley Co-operative Storage Limited was formed. It was the first company of its kind in Eastern Ontario. J. H. Merkley's plant, which produced concrete and cinder blocks, was established in the 1950's.

There was little growth in the years immediately preceding the building of the Seaway because the eventual oblivion of the village seemed inevitable. Ontario Hydro, in charge of the construction of the Seaway, planned a modern town site one mile to the north, and aided the move to the new site by transporting over 150 homes by machine. Other houses were bought by Hydro on generous terms to ease the purchase of new homes.

The proximity of the village to the mid-river international boundary resulted in Iroquois being chosen as the Canadian terminus of the international dam built to control the water levels of the Seaway. A canal was cut through the headland to bypass the dam, making Iroquois Point an island.

Iroquois' earliest congregation was formed by a Lutheran minister in 1792. A few years later the minister joined the Church of England and much of his congregation followed him. An Anglican church was built in 1857.

The Methodist Church, one of the first in Upper Canada, was built on Point Iroquois in 1823, the result of the work of William Losee, a travelling missionary. The first resident preacher was Joseph Sawyer. In 1825 a larger stone church was built just to the east of the first church. The Reverend Marmaduke L. Pearson was a minister at the new Methodist Church built in 1877. His grandson, Lester B. Pearson, was guest speaker when the church celebrated its 75th anniversary in 1952. He was Foreign Minister in the Ottawa Cabinet at that time and later became a Prime Minister of Canada. The church itself became the United Church in 1925, the year of church union. The first missionary society in Canada was organized in 1832 with Mrs. Waldron, wife of the minister, as president. A Sunday School established in 1839 had Albert Carman, Principal of the Grammar School, as its Superintendent from 1855 to 1857. He later became Principal of Belleville Academy, now Albert College.

Prior to 1846 there was no Roman Catholic clergy in Dundas County. In that year Father Coyle was appointed parish priest and held mass in Iroquois in private homes on a week-day. In 1882 when the Township of Winchester was constituted a separate parish, Iroquois, along with Morrisburg and Matilda, were placed under the care of Father James Connolly. He celebrated mass in a rented room in Iroquois every second Sunday. He was succeeded by Father Morgan O'Brien in 1885 and in that year the Roman Catholic congregation of Iroquois purchased a church from the Episcopalian Methodists. It was then dedicated under the name of St. Cecilia. In 1917 a new church, again dedicated to St. Cecilia, was built on the site of the earlier church, which had been demolished.

After Iroquois was incorporated as a village, ministers of the Canadian Presbyterian Church from nearby areas preached in Iroquois. In 1874 Iroquois built its own Presbyterian church with Rev. Wm. McKibbin as minister. The land, along with a parcel of land on Point Iroquois for a cemetery, was donated by Wm. Elliot.

Sports have always been an important part of Iroquois life. About 1895 Matthew Ryan built the village's first covered rink. In use until 1910, it had the largest ice surface of any rink between Montreal and Toronto. A new metal rink constructed in 1920 caved in in the 1940's, and skating and hockey continued at an open air rink. A Badminton Club was organized in the 1930's and a Ladies' Bowling Club in the 1950's. The new town site included tennis courts, rink, lawn bowling greens, golf course, a lighted baseball diamond, and a municipal beach.

The Dundas County Farmer's Institute was begun in Iroquois in 1886 with John Harkness as president. In 1898 the Matilda Township Agricultural Society held its fair in the village.

Today, Iroquois, a modern planned village has a population of 1200 (1979). A Civic Centre provides facilities for conventions and community activities. The area is a popular site for summer cottages and tourists visit the Carman House Museum with its collection of pioneer artifacts, and the Iroquois Seaway Locks, one of the major locks in the seaway system.

Blue Bell, June 1957.

Nancy Burleigh: *History of Iroquois*, 1965.

J. Smyth Carter: *The Story of Dundas from 1784 to 1904*, 1905.

IROQUOIS FALLS, town, Calvert Township, Cochrane District
Position 48° 46′ 80° 41′

Iroquois Falls on the Abitibi River is situated about 30 miles southeast of Cochrane, on Highway 67 and the Ontario Northland Railway. Known as "Northern Ontario's Original Model Town", it is the home of one of the world's largest pulp and paper companies. Legend has it that the Iroquois Indians at this site attacked a peaceful Huron tribe. Having killed all the Huron braves and captured their squaws, they went to sleep in their canoes tied to the river bank near the falls. During the night the squaws cut the canoes loose and the Iroquois were swept over the falls to their death. The name of the town originates from this legend. Today the 14-foot falls no longer exist, having been replaced by the paper company dam.

The first white men to visit the area of Iroquois Falls were the French soldiers under the command of Chevalier Pierre de Troyes, who, in June 1686, passed through here on their way to attack the Hudson's Bay Company posts at James Bay. Later visitors had more peaceful intentions, being Christian missionaries who held services in Cree for the Indians of the area.

In 1912 a Montreal businessman, Frank Harris Anson, financed two young men in a trip to Northern Ontario to prospect for gold. No gold was found but the men reported to Anson on the great potential of the Iroquois Falls area for a pulp and paper industry. Despite critics who dubbed the venture "Anson's Folly", Anson and Shirley Ogilvie in August 1912 gained the right to cut pulpwood on the Abitibi River. In November of that year backing was gained from Chicago financiers and the Abitibi Pulp and Paper Mills came into being. The first campsite was established beside the falls on Christmas Eve, 1912.

In 1913 seven men from Montreal arrived to begin the building of the first planned town in Northern Ontario. Soon new model homes were replacing the Company "Cookeries", and hotel-size camp-style dormitories which provided accommodation for the construction crews. A groundwood mill was erected in 1914, then sulphite and paper plants were built. Early construction was difficult as there was no road connecting with the railway 6 miles away and materials had to be sent along the river. However, a railway spur line was built, linking the camp with the main line at Iroquois Junction (now Porquis Junction).

From the beginning, Iroquois Falls was a company town. The land was owned by Abitibi, the houses were company-built, the stores were company-owned, and all residents were Abitibi employees. Some of the workers who disliked the idea of a closed town built their homes in nearby Ansonville which became largely a French-Canadian community. However, when the employees formed a union in 1915, the end of the closed town was one of their aims and they asked the company to give the residents control of their own municipality. Abitibi agreed and on June 4, 1915, Iroquois Falls with an area of 271 acres, was incorporated. S. G. McCoubray served as the first mayor, Fred Lyons as clerk, and J. Edgar Patterson as treasurer. The councillors were J. McDonald, R. Stuart, W. J. Tierney, A. C. Robertson, J. Guinn, and E. Thompson.

By 1915 Abitibi was producing its first newsprint and had been incorporated as the Abitibi Power and Paper Co. Ltd. Under the management of R. L. Wilson, the company was well on its way to prosperity and Iroquois Falls was expanding rapidly. Then in late July, 1916, one of the worst fires in Canada's history swept across Northern Ontario, demolishing six towns, 1,000 square miles of farmland and bush, and killing 223 people. The residents of Iroquois Falls were evacuated to the company mill which was spared. Most of the town was destroyed and the company powerhouse was seriously damaged. Both Iroquois Falls and Ansonville became towns of old tents and shabbily constructed temporary buildings until the towns were rebuilt.

In the years following the fire both town and company grew. A post office was opened in Iroquois Falls in 1921. The Hotel Iroquois, which became a well-known place of accommodation, was built in the same year. Abitibi erected a generating station to supply power both to the town and to the company's plant. Three new paper machines were installed so that by the mid-1920's Abitibi had seven machines, three of which were the largest in the world. Production had risen to 500 tons of newsprint per day and the Abitibi operation had become the world's largest mill.

The company suffered a setback in the Depression years, but soon recovered and continued to expand. Today Abitibi has 25 plants and produces about 1000 tons of paper per day. The company remains the main source of employment and revenue for the Iroquois Falls area, employing about 1,000 mill workers and up to 600 lumbermen.

In 1945 a Municipal Office was built in Iroquois Falls and in 1956 the 4,000-seat Community Arena and Curling Club was constructed by voluntary labour. With an ice surface longer and wider than that of Toronto's Maple Leaf Gardens, the arena is the largest volunteer labour project in Canada.

Through its history, the neighbouring township of Calvert, incorporated in 1918, has been closely linked with Iroquois Falls. Residents shared the same hospitals, schools, churches, clubs, and employers, but township residents paid higher taxes as there was no industrial assessment. In 1971 the situation was resolved by the amalgamation of Iroquois Falls, with its population of about 1800, and Calvert Township, including Ansonville, as the Town of Iroquois Falls. By 1979 census the population of Iroquois Falls is 6,307.

The first church services in the area were held by the Anglican missionaries. The mission house was destroyed in the 1916 fire. In 1917 St. Mark's Anglican Church was built. The Roman Catholic Church of St. Ann was erected in the same year, with Reverend Alexandre Pelletier as the first parish priest.

The community's first public school was held in a tarpaper shack in 1915. The Iroquois Falls Public School was built in 1920. Major John Day was the first principal. High school classes were added in 1921 and the school was known as the Iroquois Falls Continuation School. In 1935 it became the Iroquois Falls District High School with G. W. Cushnie as principal. St. Ann's Separate School was opened in 1921.

Today this prosperous bilingual community is known as the "Garden Community of Northern Ontario". The well-planned streets, fine homes, and beautiful lawns make the town one of the loveliest in Ontario. Tourism is becoming increasingly important as Iroquois Falls is an all-season resort area. Four beaches, a golf course, and a public park provide recreational facilities and a number of hotels and motels offer accommodation. As well as road links, the town has daily train service from North Bay and an airfield six miles away at Porquis Junction.

Among the tourist attractions are the Abitibi "Pulp and Paper Path Tours", which take the visitor into the woods to demonstrate the cutting operations, stop at a logging camp for lunch, and then show the various phases of paper production. The Pioneer Museum in the old Ontario Northern Railway building exhibits artifacts of early life in the town.

On January 23, 1935, the lowest measured temperature in Ontario was recorded at Iroquois Falls. It was 73° below zero Fahrenheit.

Olive Mackay Petersen: *The Land of Moosoneek*, 1974.

Rita Proulx: Brief: *Township of Calvert and Town of Iroquois Falls*, 1966.

IROQUOIS BEACH PROVINCIAL PARK

Iroquois Beach Provincial Park, a Recreation Park on the north shore of Lake Erie, is directly accessible by Highway 19. It is adjacent to the commercial fishing village of Port Burwell and is some 16 miles south of Tillsonburg at the junction of Highways 19 and 3. To the northwest, about 40 miles, lies the city of London.

Lake Erie was once a glacial lake created during the retreat of the last continental ice sheet and the upper camping area of the park comprises the Norfolk Sand Plain. Creeks and rivers have cut deep ravines into this sand plain and where the plain reaches Lake Erie, waves and currents have carved steep bluffs. Between the bluffs and the sandy shoreline are wetlands where the Great Blue Heron, the bittern and other marsh birds can be seen. A tribe of Neutral Indians inhabited the Norfolk Sand Plain during the sixteenth century, but were pushed farther west when the Iroquois moved north from the present New York State.

Colonel Mahlon Burwell surveyed the area in 1811 and immigrants from Europe arrived to settle. They harvested timber for export, making use of the natural harbour of the nearby settlement of Port Burwell.

This Ontario provincial park provides excellent camping and recreational facilities. The extensive sand beach has a shallow water area, safe for children.

Ontario Ministry of Natural Resources.

IRVING, geographic township, Algoma District
Position 48° 52′ 84° 07′

Formerly part of the Algoma Central & Hudson Bay Railway Land Grant, the township is named after Sheriff Irving of Sudbury. It is situated to the east of Kaminakagami Lake. The Algoma Central Railway travels through the area with station points at Dana and Akron.

IRWIN, geographic township, Thunder Bay District
Position 49° 42′ 87° 50′

This township lies to the east of Lake Nipigon and is part of Nipigon Provincial Forest. It was named in 1935, however the origin of its name is unknown. There are many lakes within its boundaries, the largest being Windigokan Lake. A secondary road leads to Highway 11, which touches the southeastern corner of the township.

ISAAC, geographic township, Algoma District
Position 48° 05' 84° 20'

Formerly designated Township 26, Range 24, the main feature of this township is the Shikwamkwa River, which flows through its southeastern corner. The township is located northeast of Lake Superior Provincial Park and northeast of the community of Wawa. There are no roads in the area.

It was named after Richard Isaac, a chief of the Six Nation Indians.

ISLAND FALLS, community, Manapia Township, Cochrane District
Position 49° 35' 81° 23'

This dispersed rural community on the Abitibi River, about 70 miles north of Timmins, came into being as a result of a dispute between a gold mining and a power company. In 1923 the Hollinger Gold Mining Company, after a disagreement with the Northern Ontario Power Company, decided to establish a new source of power. The Abitibi Power Company was approached, but all its available power was already being used. However, Abitibi allowed Hollinger to build a plant at Island Falls on the Abitibi River.

By 1925 the new plant was completed. But in the same year Hollinger lost its suit against the Northern Ontario Power Company and was forced to honour its original contract to buy power from that source. Abitibi bought the Island Falls plant from Hollinger and installed two more generators.

The settlement of Island Falls grew up near the power plant to house the men who worked there. It is an isolated community, situated on the Ontario Northern Railway.

Abitibi Golden Anniversary, 1962

ISLINGTON, part of the Borough of Etobicoke, Municipality of Metropolitan Toronto
Position 43° 38' 79° 32'

Today part of Metropolitan Toronto, this urban community was formerly a village in Etobicoke Township, York County. It was originally known as Mimico but the name was changed when Mimico-on-the-Lake asked for a post office called Mimico. At a meeting in Thomas Smith's inn in 1858, held to decide on a new name, Elizabeth Wilson Smith suggested Islington, after her native town in England.

Settlement took place along this part of the Dundas Road in the early nineteenth century. One of the early residents was Mr. Montgomery who bought land here in 1829. He built an inn in the early 1830's, which became a favourite rendezvous for the officers of the York garrison. The inn also had a large ballroom where the old sessions court met and it is said that the first trials of the 1837 rebels were held here.

Thomas Smith's inn was also one of the early buildings in Islington. It served as a post office and general store, as well as offering accommodation. The Islington Hotel began as a grocery store in 1839, becoming Brownridge's Hall in the 1870's. It burned down in 1930 and was rebuilt as Islington House.

Among the community's early businessmen were Edward and Thomas Musson, who bought a mill on Mimico Creek in 1840. They became prominent in township affairs.

In 1881 the Credit Valley Railway passed through Islington, improving communications and aiding the growth of the community. In later years, the suburban railway from Toronto was extended westward and Islington became the western terminus of the line.

Islington United Church is one of the oldest established congregations in the district. The community was part of the Wesleyan Methodist "Toronto Circuit" and Rev. Thomas Demorest held his first services here in 1823. A church was built in 1843, becoming the front part of the Township Municipal Building in 1887. A full-time pastor arrived in 1885 and a new church was erected in 1887. It was replaced by the present building in 1949.

The church of St. George's-on-the-Hill had its beginning in the weekly services held in the 1830's by Rev. Walter Stennett. In 1844 Bishop John Strachan created the parish of St. George's and a church was erected in 1847 on land probably donated by William Gamble. Rev. Dr. Thomas Phillips became the first minister. The church was rebuilt in 1894.

A Temperance Hall, which became known as Jubilee Hall, was erected in 1854.

The first school in Islington was held in a building on Benjamin Johnston's property about 1830. Robert Torritt, a lame shoemaker, was the first teacher and it was reported that he could put his crutch to good use to maintain his authority. The first public school was built on the land of Amasa Wilcox in 1832. Another school on the north side of Dundas Street later became Lambton Kingsway Public School. A new building was opened in 1853, then replaced in 1920. In 1921 continuation classes were begun to provide some secondary education. A high school was built in 1928. In 1948 its name was changed from Etobicoke High School to Etobicoke Collegiate Institute.

In the late nineteenth century, an annual fair was held in Islington. The land of Mrs. R. H. Tier was first used but in 1871 land was leased from Thomas Montgomery. D. L. Streight built a one-storey frame building on the fairgrounds which he named after England's famous exhibition hall, the "Crystal Palace". The last fair in the community was held in 1885.

By the 1950's, one of Islington's major tourist attractions was the James Gardens Museum. Here the visitor could see Indian artifacts, glassware, pioneer articles, and documents, all of which recall the early history of Etobicoke.

Robert A. Given: The Story of Etobicoke, 1950.

Ontario Historical Society, 1954.

IVANHOE, geographic township, Sudbury District
Position 48° 08′ 82° 30′

Situated to the west of Horwood Lake, this township is named after Sir Walter Scott's novel of the same name. Ivanhoe Lake and Ivanhoe Lake Provincial Park occupy a large central area of the township and the Muskego River meanders through its southeastern corner.

A secondary road links the area with Highway 101 which passes through the northwestern corner of the township.

IVANHOE, community, Huntingdon Township, Hastings County
Position 44° 24′ 77° 28′

Ivanhoe is located on Highway 62, about 10 miles south of the village of Madoc. Among Ivanhoe's early settlers were William Mitts (Mitz), Hugh MacMillan, John Wood, and the Carscallen, Burnett and Roy families, most of whom arrived between 1832 and 1837.

A post office opened in 1851 at the locality was called St. George. However, because settlers in the area were of Scottish or Irish descent, the name of England's patron saint was not acceptable for the community. It was, therefore, named Ivanhoe in 1857, the name having been suggested by a young schoolteacher, Thomas Emo, who admired Walter Scott's novel, *Ivanhoe*. Emo served as Reeve of Huntingdon for many years and in 1875 was made Warden of the County of Hastings.

St. John's Presbyterian Church was the first house of worship erected in the Ivanhoe area (1867); it was followed in 1882 by St. Andrew's Church.

Around 1870 a cheese factory was built near Ivanhoe. Milk had previously been taken to the Hallowell Cheese Factory in Thurlow, a long distance when one considers cheese was made twice daily in the days before refrigeration. The first president of the Ivanhoe Cheese Factory was Henry Gauen, a former British sailor who had been a member of the McClure Expedition in the 1850's, unsuccessfully searching for the Arctic explorer Sir John Franklin.

The name of the cheese factory was changed to Beulah in 1889. The industry is still in operation housed in a new building constructed in 1979 to replace the old factory that was destroyed by fire the year before. Beulah is still the name of the co-operative that owns the factory, but it sells its various cheese products under the name of Ivanhoe.

Gerald E. Boyce: *Historic Hastings*, 1967

IVANHOE LAKE PROVINCIAL PARK, Ivanhoe Township, Sudbury
District
Position 48° 09′ 82° 31′

Situated on Ivanhoe Lake, just off Highway 101, 8 miles south of the community of Foleyet, this provincial park of 1,280 acres was established in 1957.

Once the centre of the fur trade, visited by the Ojibway Indians with their packs of furs, the trading post at Ivanhoe Lake was closed in 1892. Logging became the next important industry in the area. During the last ice age glaciers scraped across the landscape leaving long sandy ridges visible in the park. These ancient beds of glacial streams are known as eskers. Huge blocks of glacial ice settled, melted, and left great cavities, known by the geological term as kettles. Some of the park's smaller lakes formed in these kettles. Other unusual features of Ivanhoe are quaking bogs, and several varieties of orchids, flourishing in a former lagoon area. Panne, an unusual formation of plants growing in a uniquely lime-rich soil, is the only known panne in Northern Ontario. The rare osprey can be seen soaring in the skies, then plummeting down into Ivanhoe Lake in search of fish.

Classified as a Natural Environment Park, its reputation for fishing is due to the abundance of yellow pickerel, northern pike, perch, whitefish and trout, the latter stocked in small lakes and streams. The Ivanhoe and Wakami Rivers provide excellent canoe routes.

Ontario Ministry of Natural Resources.

IVY, geographic township, Sudbury District
Position 47° 08′ 82° 17′

Situated to the east of Mississagi Wild River Provincial Park, this township is watered by Phipps Lake in the western part, and a section of Southern Bay in the northeastern corner.

A secondary road links the area ultimately with Highway 144 to the east.

The name origin of the township is unknown.

J

JACK, geographic township, Sudbury District
Position 47° 43′ 81° 50′

The township was named after the Jack family of Sault Ste. Marie. The northern, eastern and western boundaries were surveyed in 1912 by Smith, the southern boundary that same year by Fitzgerald.

The area's only community is Gogama on the Canadian National Railways. It is located in the southeast corner of the township on Minisinakwa Lake. Tourism is the mainstay of the community's economy.

JACKFISH, community, Syine Township, Thunder Bay District
Position 48° 50′ 86° 58′

Situated on the north shore of Lake Superior, east of Thunder Bay, Jackfish was named after a nearby lake and was a fairly busy lake port from 1884 to 1947.

The Jackfish area has a long history. A North West Company fur trading post was operating around 1785, one mile west of the present site of the community. Taken over by the Hudson's Bay Company in 1821, it was closed when the Grand Trunk Railway was built through Longlac in 1916.

In 1871 a prospector named McKellars and two Indians staked a claim near Jackfish Lake and called it the Jackfish Gold Lode. This was the first gold discovery in Northwestern Ontario.

A port was established at Jackfish in 1884 in order to bring in steel and supplies for the construction of the Canadian Pacific Railway. When the line was completed, a coaling plant was installed. Coal, then the fuel for steam locomotives, was brought to the plant by boat and distributed along the shore from Jackfish. When the Canadian Pacific Railway switched to diesel power in the late 1940's, coal was no longer required and the plant's machinery was dismantled.

Commercial fishing began at Jackfish in 1887 with the arrival of Ben Almos and his brothers, John and Fred, and brother-in-law, Pete Dahl. The industry continued until 1955 when the sea lamprey depleted the resources.

In the early twentieth century, Jackfish was an important distribution centre for the surrounding area. Gold and silver from the area's mines were brought by wagon to Jackfish and thence transported by rail in those days. Until 1912 supplies for the construction of the Grand Trunk Railway were shipped from Jackfish.

In 1899 Bill Frazer built the Jackfish Hotel as a stopping place for rafting crews, coal crews, and highway construction gangs. The old hotel burned down in 1961. In the early 1900's the CPR advertised a popular canoe trip from Jackfish up the Steel River into the scenic northern region.

Today the small community of Jackfish is the home mainly of summer cottagers.

Department of Lands and Forests: *Geraldton*, 1963

JACKMAN, geographic township, Kenora District
Position 49° 50′ 94° 06′

Lying northeast of Kenora, this township was named after Harry R. Jackman, Dominion MP for Toronto-Rosedale in 1954. Within its borders are numerous lakes, the largest being Silver Lake, occupying the northwestern corner of the township and straddling the northern and western boundaries.

JACKSON, geographic township, Algoma District
Position 46° 35′ 83° 16′

Formerly designated Township 182, this township was named after A. Y. Jackson, a member of the famous Group of Seven painting school.

Wakomata Lake occupies a substantial part of the western half of the township and extends well across the western boundary line. East Caribou Lake and Skirl Lake are situated in the eastern half. There are no roads in the township.

JACOBSON, geographic township, Algoma District
Position 48° 20′ 84° 20′

Situated in the area of Dog Lake, this township houses a few small lakes, Maskinonge Lake in the northern half, and Godin Lake and Tuff Lake in the south.

The Canadian Pacific Railway passes through the northeastern corner of the township and a secondary road links the area with Highway 17 to the west.

The township was named after Edwin C. Jacobson, Sergeant in the Canadian Army, who was killed in 1944.

JACQUES, geographic township, Thunder Bay District
Position 48° 41′ 89° 20′

Located some 20 miles northwest of the city of Thunder Bay, this area was surveyed in 1914. It was named after Dr. Jacques MLA, MPP for Haldimand at that time. Highway 589 passes through the township, which houses Two Island Lake, Mary Lake and Lottit Lake.

JAFFRAY, geographic township, District of Kenora
Position 49° 47′ 94° 26′

Situated north and east of the town of Kenora, Jaffray was named after either Senator Jaffray or Robert Jafrray, the owner of the Toronto *Globe*.

The first settler in the area was Simon Villeneuve, who arrived in 1891, two years before the township was surveyed. In 1896 gold was discovered and the district opened up for mining claims. By 1908 the population had risen to 200 and the township was incorporated. For municipal purposes, Jaffray is united with Melick Township. The combined population of the two townships in 1979 was 3,533.

There are both rural and residential areas within the township. Most residents work in Kenora, although there are a few lumber industries in Jaffray.

Four elementary schools and Roman Catholic and Mennonite churches serve the inhabitants while motels and resorts accommodate visitors. Recreational facilities include a ski club, a beach, baseball diamonds, the Garrow Park, and an outdoor rink. A meetingplace for social occasions is provided by the Jaffray-Melick Centennial Community Hall.

Jaffray has rail links with southern Ontario in the Canadian Pacific Railway. Kenora Airport is also situated in the township.

Ministry of Natural Resources: *Directory of Statistics and Data,* 1975

JAMES, township, Timiskaming District
Position 47° 43′ 80° 20′

The township was subdivided in 1903 by OLS Baird and was named after M. James, MPP for the East Riding of Nipissing, 1902.

James is situated southwest of the town of Englehart. Highway 65 travels along the Montreal River through the region, which is linked by Highway 560 to the mining district of Gowganda. Most of the township's 600 residents live in the community of Elk Lake on the Montreal River.

The area was settled around 1907 by workers engaged in lumbering and mining activities in the vicinity. Prospectors in search of silver came up the Montreal River to the site of Elk Lake. From here they went westward into the Gowganda region, where they made a number of speculator strikes. Elk Lake's early settlers in summer had to rely on the river as their only means of transportation to Latchford on the Temiskaming and Northern Railway. In winter they were able to use a rough road leading to Charlton and Englehart.

When on February 4, 1913, the railway opened a branch line from Earlton on the main line to Elk Lake, the entire township population turned out to celebrate the event. With the arrival of the Railway, now known as the Ontario Northland, Elk Lake became the supply centre for the region's silver mines.

There are no other communities within the township's boundaries.

JAMIESON, geographic township, Cochrane District
Position 48° 35′ 81° 32′

Named after Hon. David Jamieson, Minister without Portfolio and
Speaker of the Ontario Legislative Assembly, 1926, this township has
been a part of the City of Timmins since 1973. The area was
subdivided in 1907, but the subdivision was partly annulled in 1963.

The main river of the township is the Mattagami which flows
through the eastern half. Secondary roads link the area with Highway
629 and the City of Timmins to the southeast.

JANES, geographic township, Sudbury District
Position 46° 41′ 80° 22′

Located east of Wanapitei Lake, this township was named after S.
Janes of Toronto. Subdivided in 1894, the subdivision was completely
annulled in 1953. The southern and western boundaries were
surveyed in 1881 by A. Niven.

The Sturgeon River flows through the central and southern parts
of the township.

The small community of Glen Afton is situated near the eastern
border of the township. The Canadian National Railways' North-
Bay-Capreol section passes through the southern part of Janes, with a
station point at Chudleigh.

JANETVILLE, community, Manvers Township, Durham County
Position 44° 13′ 78° 43′

This dispersed rural community of 132 people (1971), about 20 miles
southwest of Peterborough, was named after Janet McDermid, the
daughter of local sawmill owner McDermid.

The first to settle at Janetville was Captain John Burn, who, with
Henry Irwin, built a sawmill on the Mill Pond in the early 1800's. The
operation was later enlarged to include a grist mill. In time, two more
sawmills were erected in the same area.

The community began to develop when the first group of settlers
arrived about 1832. Many of them came from Ireland. Among the
pioneers were Richard Johnston, Robert Armstrong, the McGills,
James Marshall, J. K. and Neil McDermid, and Robert McDowell. A
later group included John Madoc, H. Heaslip, Thomas Howe, A.
Bradbull, the Richardsons, McNeils, Syers, Taylors, and Baxters.

Thomas and Robert Timmins opened the first general store in
1854. A second store was opened in the same year by John Burn. A
post office was established in 1862. By 1878 Janetville had a carriage
shop, a harness and shoemaker's shop, a weaver, and a hotel. A cheese
factory was built on the farm of Victor Blatherwick.

Among the community's early merchants were the Cherry

brothers who owned a shoe store, David McGill, proprietor of a general store, and the butcher James Howe. William Arthurs and James Hobbs were blacksmiths. Tommy Hawkins ran an unusual store, locally known as "Tommy Hawkins Ends". All sorts of goods were sold very cheaply but as the articles were not in any kind of order, customers had to search for what they wanted. Prices were not marked. The store became well known for its haphazard form of business and attracted customers from both Canada and United States.

In the 1930's Thomas Richardson, a local blacksmith, became the champion horseshoe pitcher in Canada.

A Presbyterian church was built in 1889, then replaced by a new house of worship on the land of John Burn in 1895. The Reverend Mr. Binnie was the first minister. This church closed in 1955. Seven different churches merged to form Janetville United Church, including a New Connexion Methodist Church, erected in 1861, and the Canada Methodist Brick Church in the Hollow, opened in the 1870's. The present United Church was built in 1896 on land bought from Susanna Armstrong. Reverend C. H. Coon was the first minister.

Janetville has a community park and an indoor skating rink. Burn's Pond, named after the first settler, was used as a swimming hole for many years. Washed out by spring floods in 1948, it was rebuilt in the 1960's.

Violet Carr: *The Rolling Hills*, 1967.

JARRATT, community, Medonte and Oro Townships, Simcoe County
Position 44° 36′ 79° 34′

Situated about 6 miles west of Orillia on the townline between Medonte and Oro Townships, this dispersed rural community was named after its first settler, Charles Jarratt of Kent County, England.

Jarratt arrived in Oro Township in 1831 and took up land on Lot 15, Concession 14. In 1835 he exchanged his land with Rev. Charles Brough and settled on Lot 1, Concession 11, where he opened a store. When a post office was established in 1855, he became the first postmaster. He sold supplies to the early settlers of the community in return for the hardwood ashes from their farms which he sent to Barrie to be made into potash.

By 1870 the Shoepack hall and tavern had been built on the site of the present Community Hall. William Leith ran an early tavern. The Leatherdales operated a blacksmith shop and carriage works and Mr. Heard established a furniture business. The small shop of William Tudhope was the beginning of one of Orillia's major industries, Tudhope Carriage Works. A lumber mill was built on McCallum's Creek by the Clarkes. The Crawford sawmill was in operation around 1900. A brick kiln was run by the Switzers.

Most of the early settlers were Scottish Presbyterians and in 1865 Willis Presbyterian Church was built on land of James Beard. In the early 1870's Jarratt Methodist Church was erected on land given by William Switzer. It became a United church in 1925, but has long since been closed.

Oro Historical Committee: *The Story of Oro*, 1972.

JARVIS, geographic township, Algoma District
Position 46° 40' 84° 10'

Located just northwest of Sault Ste. Marie, this township was subdivided in 1878 by G. B. Abrey. The subdivision was partly annulled in 1951. The township was named after Sheriff Jarvis, who held that office early in the history of Toronto. Upper Island Lake, Reserve Lake and Crooked Lake lie within this area.

JARVIS, part of the City of Nanticoke, Regional Municipality of Haldimand-Norfolk
Position 42° 53' 80° 06'

Situated about 28 miles southwest of Hamilton, on Highway 6, and at a CNR junction, this urban community was formerly a village in Walpole Township, Haldimand County. It was named after Lt. Col. Jarvis, aide-de-camp to Governor Simcoe. Several of the streets are named after Jarvis's daughters.

The community began when the Hamilton and Port Dover Plank Road was constructed in the mid-nineteenth century. James Shearman, the first settler, built a log shanty and a blacksmith shop by the road. He kept a supply of liquor in his shanty to satisfy the thirst of the navvies working on the road and in later years he opened a tavern.

In 1842 W. C. Shannon became the second person to settle in Jarvis. He was the first toll-gate keeper on the Plank Road. A store was opened by John Gowans and soon after this James Sill, John Jones, and Rial Canfield arrived. Canfield established a timber and stave trade and later built a store. He actively promoted the growth of the settlement.

The construction of the Loop Line of the Great Western Railway helped the economy of Jarvis and by 1873 it was a thriving community. A large fire destroyed much of it in the mid-1870's but by 1879 it had been rebuilt with much better homes and businesses. Industries at this time included a steam grist and flouring mill, a steam planing sash-and-door factory, and a steam plough factory. The population was nearing 800.

The community continued to prosper, aided by its position at the junction of the Loop Line and the Hamilton and Lake Erie Railway. By 1903 the population was about 1,000. Jarvis was incorporated as a village in 1910.

By the late 1950's Jarvis's industries included a grist mill, apiaries, and a dairy which produced powdered milk. A newspaper, the *Record*, was published weekly.

In 1966 Jarvis annexed part of the Township of Walpole. In 1974, with a population of just under 1,000, the village amalgamated with the town of Waterford and the town of Port Dover to form the city of Nanticoke.

Rev. Robert Bertram Nelles: *County of Haldimand in the Days of Auld Lang Syne*, 1903

JASPER, geographic township, Sudbury District
Position 47° 01′ 82° 09′

Located east of the Mississagi Wild River Provincial Park, the township borders to the south on the District of Algoma. It is believed to have been named after the North West Trading Company post in charge of Jasper Hawes in 1917.

The area abounds in lakes, rivers and streams. A secondary road passing a few miles west of the township's border links the area to the town of Webbwood in the south.

JASPER, community, Kitley Township, Leeds County and Wolford Township, Grenville County
Position 44° 50′ 75° 56′

This compact rural community was originally known as Olmstead's Mills for the owner of an early grist mill on the site. The name was later changed to Irish Creek after the stream which ran through the settlement. When the railway was built in the late 1850's, railway officials pressed for a new name for the community and Jasper was chosen in the 1870's, although Irish Creek remained in common usage until the beginning of the twentieth century. Straddling the county line of Leeds and Grenville Counties, Jasper is situated on the Canadian Pacific Railway, some 20 miles northwest of Brockville.

About 1806, a grist mill was built on the Wolford Township side of Irish Creek by a Mr. Haskins. The first land grants on the Kitley side were made in 1808 to Reuben Sherwood and in 1811 to Anna Akin. In 1820 Haskins sold his mill to Richard Olmstead and the settlement which grew up at the site became known as Olmstead's Mills. The little community prospered during the 1820's but about 1830 the construction of the Rideau Canal raised the water level in the creek and destroyed the waterfall which supplied power to the mill. Although it continued to be known as Olmstead's Mills for some time, there was no more milling done here, the main activity was the rafting of timber which was floated down from the upper creek.

Renewed prosperity came to the community, at this time still known as Irish Creek, with the advent of the Brockville and Ottawa Railway which was built through the settlement in 1859. Irish Creek became the starting point for crowds that flocked to see the "Witch of Plum Hollow" and learn their future fortunes. She was Mrs. Elizabeth Barnes, born in County Cork, Ireland, a good and kind woman and well respected, who lived at the hamlet of Plum Hollow, southwest of Jasper. Left to raise a family of nine and having a highly developed sense of prophecy, Mother Barnes turned to fortune-telling and her fame spread even to New York State.

The community grew rapidly during the 1860's and by the early 1870's had six stores, a telegraph office, and a population of about 200. During this period of growth Robert Logan built a hotel, and John Marquette began a brickyard. In 1897 William Connerty, proprietor of a general store, branched into the feed business which became one of the largest general businesses in that part of the country. A grandson,

William Connerty, started Connerty Industrial Moulders, engineering and manufacturing of reinforced plastic, and is, today, affiliated with Canadian General Electric.

By 1900 Jasper, as it was now known, had become a sizeable village and in 1910 was incorporated as a police village. On the first board of trustees were N. G. Cross, W. H. Olmstead and A. W. Kendrick.

A major fire struck Jasper in 1939; the importance of the railway began to decline, slowing growth during the 1940's and 50's. Train service to the community ended in 1961.

Jasper relies on its proximity to Smiths Falls for much of its economy today.

Glenn J. Lockwood: *Kitley, 1795-1975*, 1975

JEAN, geographic township, Thunder Bay District
Position 48° 17′ 90° 05′

Established in 1945 by the Deputy Minister of Lands and Forests, this township is located approximately 12 miles north of the Ontario-Minnesota border, and some 40 miles southwest of the city of Thunder Bay.

Whitefish River flows through the township and Highway 588 touches the southeastern corner. The township was named after Hon. Joseph Jean, Solicitor-General of Canada, Dominion Government 1945 (Liberal).

JEFFRIES, geographic township, Sudbury District
Position 47° 33′ 83° 26′

Formerly known as Township 11F, this area was named after Samuel Jeffries, RCAF, from the Sudbury District, killed in action in World War Two, 1942.

The township lies some 25 miles south of Chapleau and just west of Five Mile Lake Provincial Park. It houses a few small lakes and the Pemache River flows through its northern half.

JELLICOE, community, Leduc Township, Thunder Bay District
Position 49° 41′ 87° 31′

This small rural community on the Canadian National Railways, about 120 miles northeast of Thunder Bay, was a thriving community of 1,000 inhabitants prior to the 1930's. Its name commemorates the First Earl Jellicoe, a British naval officer knighted in recognition of his naval victories during World War One.

Jellicoe had its beginnings in 1914 as a Divisional Point on the railway between Hornepayne and Port Arthur (now Thunder Bay). The railway installations included a workshop, roundhouse, coal and water refuelling stations, staffhouses for crew members, station house, and marshalling yard. The village grew up around these railway buildings and soon boasted three hotels, a school, and several small businesses.

When, in the 1930's, gold was discovered in the Hardrock vicinity, prospectors flocked to the area and four mines went into production. Jellicoe had become a boom town by 1934. Once all the highgrade ore had been removed, however, the mines closed one by one and by the late 1930's the goldrush was over. Many of the miners joined the armed forces and went overseas to fight in World War Two. Jellicoe became a railway centre once more.

In 1940 a disastrous fire destroyed two hotels, a restaurant, and a number of small businesses. There was little accommodation left for visitors and the population decreased as many of the businessmen did not rebuild. However, in 1945 the local economy was given a boost when Brampton Pulp and Paper, forerunner to Domtar Newsprint, moved in to harvest the area's timber.

When the railway changed from steam engines to diesel, the shops and buildings in Jellicoe were dismantled and the community ceased to be a railway centre. By 1963 all the railway buildings had been removed except for the original station which served as a bunkhouse for change crews on the CNR.

Today Jellicoe relies on the pulp industry and an expanding tourist trade. A hotel and two outfitting businesses were opened in the 1960's to cater to visitors. Aircraft were made available to fly hunters to outpost camps which cannot be reached by road or by rail.

Department of Lands and Forests: *Geraldton*, 1963

JENNINGS, geographic township, Sudbury District
Position 46° 20' 80° 29'

Located west of Lake Nipissing, the township was originally subdivided in 1897 by Henderson. The subdivision was partly annulled in 1953. The northern boundary was surveyed in 1857, the eastern boundary in 1882, and the southern boundary in 1892. The township is named after W. J. Jennings, a Civil Engineer of Toronto.

For municipal purposes, Jennings is united with Appleby, its neighbour to the north, and Casimir, its eastern neighbour. The combined population of the three townships is about 1200 (1979). There are no communities in the Jennings area. The city of Sudbury is about thirty miles to the northwest.

JERSEYVILLE, community, Regional Municipality of Hamilton-Wentworth
Position 43° 12' 80° 07'

Jerseyville, a dispersed rural community west of Hamilton in the former Township of Ancaster, was probably named by its first settlers after their home in New Jersey.

The settlement was founded in the 1790's by United Empire Loyalists who left the State of New Jersey after the American Revolution. Among these early settlers was Francis Young, whose home, built about 1800, was by the 1960's the oldest frame house in the district.

A wagon works was established in the early nineteenth century. In 1850 it was taken over by John L. Swartz and for a time was used for the manufacture of wooden pumps. It became a feed mill in 1928.

By the late nineteenth century Jerseyville had a sawmill, two grist mills, a cheese factory, two blacksmith shops, two harnessmaker's shops, and three general stores. The Toronto, Hamilton and Buffalo Railway built through the community, was a boon to the local economy. The station, has long since been closed.

Today Jerseyville is a quiet residential community of 165 people (1971). Most of the residents commute to work in Hamilton or Brantford.

A Wesleyan Methodist congregation was organized about 1800 and a church built in 1801. This building was used until 1860 when a new house of worship, the present Jerseyville United Church, was erected. At one time the community also had a Methodist Episcopal church. The congregation united with the Wesleyan Methodists in 1884.

The modern Ancaster Township school was built in Jerseyville to serve the children of the surrounding area.

The *Hamilton Spectator*, 1962.

JESSIMAN, geographic township, Algoma District
Position 47° 08′ 83° 16′

Formerly known as Township 6E, Jessiman was named after James Jessiman, MPP for Fort William. It lies just northwest of Rocky Island Lake. The Aubinadong is the main river of this area. There are no roads in this vicinity. Highway 129 passes some five miles to the east of the township.

JESSOP, geographic township, Cochrane District
Position 48° 35′ 81° 24′

Located north of Timmins, the township was subdivided in 1907 by J. H. Baird. It is named after Elisha Jessop, M.D., MPP for Lincoln from 1898 to 1911, and MPP for St. Catharines in 1914.

Jessop was annexed by the City of Timmins in 1973.

JESSUP'S FALLS, community, North Plantagenet Township, Prescott County
Position 45° 34′ 75° 04′

This dispersed rural community on Highway 17, some 30 miles northeast of Ottawa, was named after Col. Edward Jessup, United Empire Loyalist. Jessup took up arms for the King at the outbreak of the American Revolution. He raised the Loyal Rangers, also known as Jessup's Rangers, and fought under General Burgoyne. For his services he received extensive land grants from the Crown, including the land at the falls on the Nation River. The land was sold to Alexander McDonnell in 1825, and later resold to Alfred Chesser.

Benjamin Anderson who came to Canada from Ireland in 1829, settled beside the Nation River in South Plantagenet Township. A few years later, one of his daughters was drowned and the family left the scene of the tragedy and made a new home for themselves on Lot 16, Concession 6 in North Plantagenet Township. Anderson's son, Alexander, became a blacksmith and settled on Lot 21, Concession 6 where he built a carriage and blacksmith shop, and a sawmill. In 1881 he entered a partnership with Mr. Hagar and in 1883 the two men erected a sawmill at Jessup's Falls. As well as producing sawn lumber, the mill also manufactured laths, shingles, and clapboard.

A small community developed at the site and a telegraph office and grocery store were opened to serve employees of the mill.

C. Thomas: *History of the Counties of Argenteuil, Quebec and Prescott, Ontario*, 1896.

JOAN, geographic township, Nipissing District
Position 47° 02' 80° 05'

Named in 1933 after Miss Joan Parmenter of Toronto, the township is part of a large forest reserve and resort area for sports fishermen and campers. The northern half of Lake Temagami with its various islands and arms covers most of the township, which is accessible by secondary road and waterways from Highway 11 to the east.

JOCELYN, township, Algoma District
Position 46° 10' 83° 58'

Situated on the east end of St. Joseph Island in Lake Huron, Jocelyn was surveyed in 1860 and incorporated as a township in 1886. The township has a population of 133 (1979).

There are no industries within the township. Eighty percent of the work force commutes to work in Sault Ste. Marie. The rest of the residents earn their living from farming and tourism. Major attractions include the recently restored Fort St. Joseph and a Bird Sanctuary.

Jocelyn has two churches, the St. Joseph Island Free Methodist Church and the Holy Trinity Anglican Church. The township hall also provides a place for recreation and entertainment. A trailer park and an inn offer accommodation to visitors.

Ministry of Natural Resources: *Directory of Statistics and Data*, 1975

JOCKO, geographic township, Nipissing District
Position 46° 35' 79° 11'

Lying west of the Ottawa River and northeast of Lake Nipissing, the northern boundary of the township was surveyed in 1822 and the eastern boundary in 1930. The township is named after the Jocko River, which flows through the southern half of the township. Highway 63 passes through the eastern half, and dry weather and secondary roads link the township to the surrounding areas.

JOFFRE, geographic township, Sudbury District
Position 47° 22' 82° 17'

Situated in the Mississagi Wild River Provincial Park area, this

377

township was surveyed in 1915 and is named after Marshall Joffre, Commander-in-Chief of the French Forces in the Great War.

The area's main body of water is Ramsey Lake. Secondary roads link the township with Highway 144 to the east. The Canadian Pacific Railway passes through the township.

JOGUES, geographic township, Algoma District
Position 46° 30′ 82° 53′

Situated to the north of Blind River, this township was named after Isaac Jogues, who founded the mission at Sault Ste. Marie, which was an important rallying point for Indians and thus a centre of the fur trade until about 1840.

There are large bodies of water in the eastern half of the township.

JOHN E. PEARCE PROVINCIAL PARK, Dunwich Township, Elgin County
Position 42° 36′ 81° 26′

This Natural Environment Park is named for John E. Pearce who donated the unique woodlot situated on the 58-acre site overlooking Lake Erie. Some of the trees are over 200 years old. The bluffs rise 100 feet above the lake and an annual hawk migration travelling south each year follow the shoreline, to the great interest of birdwatchers and naturalists.

Located about three miles south of Wallacetown, off Highway No. 3, the park is surrounded by historic country. The Ministry has erected a monument in the park commemorating early settlers and pioneers. Adjoining the park to the east is St. Peter's Anglican Church. The graveyard here is the final resting place of colonizer and instigator of the Talbot Road (Highway 3), Colonel Thomas Talbot.

Ontario Ministry of Natural Resources

JOHNS, geographic township, Algoma District
Position 48° 45′ 85° 15′

Lying to the north of the community of White River, this township borders on the west with the District of Thunder Bay. A few small lakes inhabit the area. There are no roads.

The township was established in 1943 by the Ministry of Lands and Forests and was named after F. V. Johns, K.C., Assistant Provincial Secretary 1943.

JOHNSON, township, Algoma District
Position 46° 23′ 85° 54′

Situated about 30 miles east of Sault Ste. Marie, the township was named after Thomas H. Johnson, Assistant Commissioner of Crown Lands, 1869-88.

Johnson was established in 1877 and was subdivided by E. Stewart that year. It was incorporated as a municipality in 1889. It has a population of about 700 (1979) and tourism is the major industry. There are several tourist camps and resort cabins in the area. At Desbarats on the North Channel of Lake Huron, is the township's main landing dock for the tourist homes and camps on the channel islands. Langstaff Marine boat works and sales is located on the North Channel, and Algoma Packers have a slaughterhouse in the township.

One United Church and one Anglican church serve township residents. There is a primary school with grades 5-8, and a high school, the Central Algoma Secondary School, which is located in Desbarats.

Ministry of Natural Resources: Directory of Statistics and Data, 1975.

JOHNSTOWN, community, Edwardsburgh Township, Grenville County
Position 44° 44′ 75° 28′

Situated about 15 miles northeast of Brockville on the bank of the St. Lawrence River, this compact rural community was originally called Newtown. Its name was changed by its settlers to honour Sir William Johnson, father of Loyalist leader, Sir John Johnson, who had obtained lots in the settlement.

In the seventeenth century the site was an Indian camping ground and a favourite resting-place for French voyageurs. A French post called "La Galette" was established here in the 17th century. It was visited by Governor DeBarre in 1684 and by the Jesuit missionary, Father Charlevoix, in 1720. In 1760, the last stand of the French in Canada took place on Chimney Island (then known as Isle Royale) opposite La Galette. Capt. François Pouchot and 300 men held Fort de Levis against General Jeffery Amherst and 10,000 troops in an effort to delay the British forces and give the French time to travel to Montreal. Pouchot surrendered in late August, 1760 and the British went on to gain control of Canada.

Two decades later, after the American Revolution, Americans who had remained loyal to the British Crown made their way to Canada. The first United Empire Loyalists to come to Grenville County landed at the Johnstown site on the St. Lawrence in 1784. To their surprise, they found already settlers on the land. Chevalier François-Thomas de Verneuil de Lorimier and his brother, Guillaume, members of a distinguished French-Canadian family had received a land grant here and Guillaume had built a house and cleared land around it. The Land Committee allowed him to keep his house and the cleared land when surveyors laid out a townplot on the site for the Loyalists. To compensate the brothers for any land they lost, they were given grants outside the new town's limits.

Survey of the new townplot was completed in 1790. A saw and grist mill was built and Johnstown became the leading centre of the United Counties of Leeds and Grenville when it was made the administrative centre of the Eastern District in 1793. A courthouse and gaol were erected and the court of quarter sessions met alternately here and at Cornwall until 1808 when the courts were moved to

Brockville. This, coupled with the fact that Johnstown's harbour was too shallow, retarded the future growth of the settlement.

Following the War of 1812, there was an influx of British immigrants to Canada. Some of them settled in Johnstown. Mills were built, including Chapman's sawmill and Wharton's shingle and sawmill. The pottery of Mr. Mooney produced crocks, shallow milk pans, flower pots, and bowls for the settlers. Thomas McLatchie was one of the early blacksmiths in the community.

A windmill which stood just west of Johnstown was the scene of fighting in the aftermath of the Upper Canada Rebellion in 1838. A group of Americans, led by Polish immigrant Von Schulz, took control of the windmill holding off the local troops for several days before surrendering in the historic Battle of the Windmill. One hundred and fifty of the invaders were taken prisoners. Their leader was tried and sentenced to death.

Today Johnstown is located at the junction of Highway 16 from Ottawa and Highway 401, the main east-west artery of Southern Ontario. The community is also the terminus of an international bridge from the United States.

Edwardsburg Centennial Committee: *A History of the Township of Edwardsburg,* 1967.

Ruth McKenzie: *Leeds and Grenville: Their First Two Hundred Years,* 1967.

JOLLINEAU, geographic township, Algoma District
Position 46° 51' 83° 39'

Situated just southwest of Ranger Lake, the township was named after E. Jollineau, a constable for the Sault Ste. Marie area in its early days. Secondary roads link the township to Highway 129 in the Rocky Island Lake area.

JOLY, township, Parry Sound District
Position 45° 47' 79° 15'

Joly is situated east of the village of Sundridge and was named after Sir Joly de Lotbinere, KCHG, and Liberal member for Lotbinere Riding in both the Federal and the Quebec Provincial Assemblies.

Subdivided by Thomas O. Bolger in 1878, Joly was organized as a township in 1890. Francis H. Trudgeon was the first reeve, and James Stanacombe the first clerk. On the council were Peter Milne, Matthew Colville, Charles Cunningham and John McGregor.

Among the early settlers of the township were William (Buckskin) Wilson, William Lee, Charles Cunningham, Joe Peacock, George Frost, Tom Winter, Chris Allan, John Bird, Frank Taggart, the Harknesses, the Valentines, and the Smiths. Unfortunately for Joly's inhabitants, the railway was built to the west of Bernard Lake in the neighbouring township of Strong. The resulting isolation combined with the rocky soil of the township ill-suited for agriculture discouraged even the hardiest pioneers. After some years of trying to cultivate the land and make a living, most of the township's settlers left for the prairies.

By 1979, Joly's population has once again grown to 143 inhabitants.

Everett Kirton: *History of Eastern Parry Sound District*, 1964.

JONES, geographic township, Renfrew County
Position 45° 29' 77° 50'

Jones is Renfrew County's westernmost township. Formed in 1863, it was named after Jonas Jones, who was appointed Judge of the Queen's Bench in 1837. The area is located southwest of Golden Lake in the midst of a scenic tourists' paradise.

For municipal purposes Jones is united with Sherwood and Burns Townships. The combined population of these three townships in 1979 was about 1900.

Highway 60 travels through the northern part of the township linking the area with the Algonquin Provincial Park, a wilderness area

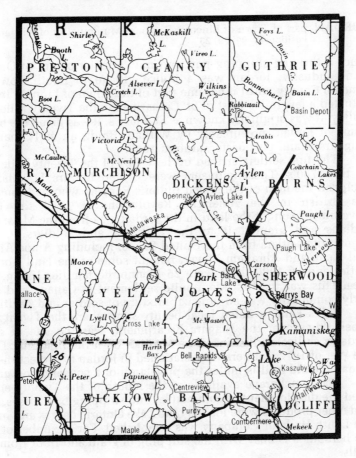

which stretches to the north and west of Jones. The western half of the township is occupied by Bark Lake. In the northeast lies Carson Lake in Carson Lake Provincial Park. The nearest community is the village of Barry's Bay, in neighbouring Sherwood Township. It is the shopping centre for the surrounding tourist region.

Mrs. Carl Price and Clyde Kennedy: *Notes on the History of Renfrew County*, 1961.

JORDAN, geographic township, Kenora District
Position 50° 00′ 92° 04′

Located in the Minnitaki Lake area, this township is watered by several lakes, and houses a large section of the Ojibway Provincial Park.
    Highway 72 links the area with Sioux Lookout.
    The township is named after the River Jordan in Palestine.

JORDAN, part of Town of Lincoln, Regional Municipality of Niagara
Position 43° 09′ 79° 23′

Once a thriving shipping port and now a major centre of Ontario's wine industry, Jordan was a police village in Louth Township, Lincoln County, until it became part of the Town of Lincoln in 1970. Situated a few miles west of St. Catharines in the Twenty Mile Creek Valley, it was originally known as St. Mary's. It was given the biblical name of Jordan, presumably by William Bradt, an early merchant, magistrate, and postmaster, around 1840.
    The first settlers arrived in the valley of the Twenty Mile Creek in the 1780's. These pioneers were United Empire Loyalists and included the men of the famed Butler's Rangers who had fought for the British in the American Revolution. In 1784 the British government bought the land in the Jordan area from the Mississauga Indians and granted it to the Loyalists and soldiers. In 1799 Mennonite settlers from the United States, including Amos Albright and Jacob and Abraham Meyer, bought some of the land from Col. Butler and by 1800 there were 25 Mennonite families living in the area. This was the first Mennonite settlement in Canada and so the early community was an unusual mixture of soldier and pacifist.
    Ball's Falls, a noted local beauty spot where the Twenty Mile Creek flows over the Niagara Escarpment, was the site of one of Jordan's earliest industries. Here Mr. Ball built the first mill. During the War of 1812, soldiers were stationed in Jordan to protect the mill. Today the old mill is under the protection of a conservation group.
    Good anchorage available at the mouth of the Twenty encouraged the development of commercial and shipping businesses. Grain and other products were loaded onto Lake Ontario barges and in 1833 the Louth Harbour Company was established. For a number of years the harbour was busy with the shipping of grain and flour from local mills.

The area was surveyed and laid out in village lots in the 1840's by Jacob Snure. By 1849 Jordan had a carding machine and fulling mill, tannery, ashery, sawmill grist mill and cloth factory. The community of about 200 became the centre of commerce and the religious and social life of the district and retained this position until the construction of the Great Western Railway in 1852.

The railway which gave birth to nearby Jordan Station had an adverse affect on Jordan. The bridge built across the Twenty in 1852 allowed some boats to sail upstream, but when a new stone bridge was constructed in 1855, all traffic to the upper docks ended and Jordan began to decline.

In the 1870's a new industry was born in Jordan when local farmers switched from growing grain to growing fruit. Clark Snure and his son, Eldridge, set up an apple drying plant on the future site of the Jordan winery. Their business became known as the Jordan Vinegar Works. A giant cider press which was used in those days is now preserved in the Jordan Historical Museum. Today, thanks to its climate, the Niagara Peninsula is the only area in Ontario where grapes for wine are successfully grown on a large scale.

In 1921 Jordan's most famous industry was established when Archibald J. Haines began the Jordan winery. The company merged with Danforth Wines in 1964 and is today known across Canada as Jordan Wines Ltd.

Jordan became a police village in 1924. Its first trustees were J. A. Wills, F. Hannigan, and C. S. McIntyre. Jordan has remained a small community. The lack of a suitable water supply has hindered housing development, although by the 1960's council was making plans to rectify the situation. Many of the residents commute to work in nearby St. Catharines.

Today Jordan's major attraction is the Jordan Historical Museum of the Twenty, which draws about 8,000 visitors a year. Philip Torno, vice-president of Jordan Wines, advocated preservation of an old schoolhouse built in 1859. This was the beginning of the museum which was opened in 1973. Today it also includes two other buildings, the Vintage House, erected about 1850, and used by the wine company during the grape harvest, and the Jacob Fry House, an example of a pioneer home. The museum illustrates pioneer life in the area, and its collection is rich in early Ontario textiles and examples of hand-illuminated books.

Lincoln County Council: Lincoln County 1856-1956, 1956.

Ontario Historical Society: Papers, 1954, 1959, 1961.

William F. Rannie: Lincoln, The Story of an Ontario Town, 1974.

The 20th of the Twenty, 1973.

JORDAN STATION, part of the Town of Lincoln, Regional Municipality of Niagara
Position 43° 10′ 79° 22′

Until 1970, when it became part of the town of Lincoln, Jordan Station was a police village in Louth Township, Lincoln County. Originally known as Bridgeport after the Great Western Railway bridge which crossed the Jordan and the harbour at the mouth of the river, its name was changed to Jordan Station in the 1870's when a post office was opened.

The community, situated just west of St. Catharines, owed its birth to the construction of the Great Western Railway in 1852. The line was built north of the nearby settlement of Jordan over the land of Solomon Secord, who sold 6 acres as a right-of-way and used the money to have the adjacent land laid out in village lots. There had been settlement in the area since the first United Empire Loyalists arrived in the 1780's, but it was not until 1852 that a community began to develop.

As it was the only station between St. Catharines and Beamsville, Jordan Station soon became an important shipping centre. About this time, local farmers had switched from grain to fruit-growing and fruit was being shipped in large quantities from Jordan Station.

The early twentieth century saw the beginning of the canning industry in Jordan Station. The first cannery was opened in 1912 by the forerunner of Canadian Canners. Mainly tomatoes were canned at first, but soon the operation expanded to include peaches, strawberries, raspberries, pears, and cherries. A typhoid epidemic in 1918, apparently caused by a carrier in the factory, closed the plant for a four-year period. It reopened in 1922 and continued in operation until 1958.

C. M. Honsberger established the Jordan Station Canning Company. It was later converted into a basket factory and produced both baskets and boxes. A major employer of the community, it was taken over by Canadian Wood Products Ltd.

Three large fruit shipping establishments took advantage of the local rail facilities and started operations in Jordan Station: Jordan Fruit and Supply Ltd., Vineland Growers Co-op, and Southward Fruit Co.

In 1915 Jordan Station became a police village with Alex Troup, John Martin, and H. W. Hunsberry as trustees. The closing of the station after World War Two and the end of the canning operations in 1958 reduced the amount of employment available in the village, and many people at that time moved away.

Lincoln County Council: Lincoln County 1856-1956, 1956.

William F. Rannie: Lincoln the Story of an Ontario Town, 1974.

JOUBIN, geographic township, Algoma District
Position 46° 25' 82° 30'

Previously known as Township 143, Joubin lies to the east of Elliot Lake. It houses several large lakes in the western half. A secondary road links the area with Highway 108 to the west.

The township was named after Franc R. Joubin, a geologist-prospector who was instrumental in the development of uranium at Elliot Lake.

JOYCEVILLE, community, Pittsburgh Township, Frontenac County
Position 44° 22' 76° 20'

This dispersed rural community between Barriefield and Seeley's Bay on Highway 15 was originally known as Birmingham. It was named Joyceville in 1893 after several families of that name who had settled in the area.

The land around Joyceville was once the scene of a number of battles between the different tribes of the Mohawks who fought for its possession.

The first settlers arrived in the vicinity in the early nineteenth century, most being of Scottish and Irish descent. They included the Joyces and the Keyes. The Birmingham Post Office was established in 1817. The first blacksmith in the settlement was R. McIlgorm. Samuel Smythe opened the Joyceville Hotel in 1836. By the late nineteenth century there were two cheese factories in operation, one run by Mike Murphy and W. H. Franklin, the other established in 1886 by Edward Agnew. John Murphy opened Joyceville's second hotel in 1875.

A school was constructed in 1875, with David Robb as its first teacher. A new school was erected in 1958.

Today Joyceville is best known as the site of a minimum security federal prison. Recently it has also become the location of an experimental rural co-operative.

Joyceville Women's Institute: *Tweedsmuir History.*

JOYNT, geographic township, Thunder Bay District
Position 48° 59' 90° 21'

Named after John Joynt, MLA and MPP for Huron North 1919-23, this township lies just north of Lac des Mille Lacs. The Trans-Canada Highway passes through the area, as does the Canadian Pacific Railway line. McKay Creek waters the southwestern corner of the township.

JUILLETTE, geographic township, Algoma District
Position 46° 25' 83° 00'

Formerly identified as Township 167 and located east of Elliot Lake and north of Blind River, this township was named after Mervyn C. Juillette, a Canadian Army gunner, of Blind River, killed in 1944.

Matinenda Lake occupies a large portion of this township and Chiblow Lake is situated at the southwestern boundary.

JUTTEN, geographic township, Thunder Bay District
Position 50° 22' 90° 29'

Named after Thomas W. Jutten, MPP for Hamilton Centre 1926-29, this township is mainly occupied in its western half by Savant Lake. The township lies just north of the Canadian National Railways line and station point of Staunton. Highway 599 passes a few miles west of the township.

K

KAGAWONG, community, Billings Township, Manitoulin District
Position 45° 54′ 82° 15′

This compact rural community of 120 people (1971) is situated on the north shore of Manitoulin Island, near Lake Kagawong. Its name is an Indian word meaning "where mists rise from the falling waters".

Kagawong is the site of an old generating station which used to supply the island's hydro-electric power. The plant used the waters of Lake Kagawong which flowed over a nearby bluff. Today the plant is abandoned and the water goes over the beautiful Bridal Veil Falls and flows through Falls Park. The Falls is a major attraction for visitors.

Kagawong's main industry is tourism. Several resorts and trailer camps, a general store, and a boat repairs and maintenance cater to visitors to this lovely nature area.

Manitoulin Tourist Association: *This is Manitoulin.* 1976.

Kakabeka Falls
Ministry of Industry & Tourism, Toronto

KAKABEKA FALLS PROVINCIAL PARK, Oliver & Conmee Tps.,
Thunder Bay District
Position 48° 24′ 89° 38′

The Kaministiquia River rushing over a rocky cliff of more than one
hundred feet creates the Kakabeka Falls, after which this Natural
Environment Park is named. Over the years the falls have been
eroding the cliff, but this is now controlled by a hydro development
begun in 1904 and which provides the surrounding region with a
source of electricity. The park is located about 11 miles from the city of
Thunder Bay and adjacent to the village of Kakabeka Falls, on the
Trans-Canada Highway. The Kaministiquia River was a voyageur
route for the fur traders canoeing from Montreal to Fort William, the
historic rendezvous of the fur traders, and the falls presented a formidable obstacle, overcome only by a gruelling portage called the
Mountain Portage.

Ontario Ministry of Natural Resources

KALADAR, township, Lennox and Addington County
Position 44° 41′ 77° 09′

Kaladar is situated in the centre of Addington County. There are
several versions as to the origin of the name. One ascribes it to an Irish
place or estate, probably the County of Kildare. Another tradition has
it that the name is a corruption of "kill a deer" as deer was more than
plentiful in the pioneer days of the settlement.

The township was first surveyed by Henry Ewing in the early
1820's. It was later resurveyed by the government to facilitate the
establishment of lumber operations. Cutting and timber licenses were
issued with the stipulation that the applicant first build a sawmill on
the desired land.

The early settlers of the township were mostly French Canadian
lumbermen who came to Kaladar township along the Skootamatta
Indian Trail from the Ottawa River. Charles Brochu, Thomas Dunham, and Trifle Goyette were among the township pioneers. In 1856
the Perry Colonization Road was built north from Erinsville to
Dunham's Place (Northbrook) and soon after a branch road to Flinton
was constructed by Brochu and his neighbours. These roads and a
general survey by A.B. Perry in 1860-61 encouraged settlement and
lumbering operations and Kaladar was growing quite rapidly. Among
the early inhabitants were Francis Desilets, Joseph Dafoe, Matthew
Ruttan, Silas B. Scouten, the Allports, and the Vandebogarts.

One of the first sawmills in Kaladar was built in the early 1850's
near Flinton at the falls on the Skootamatta River. The first lumbering
company in the area was Flint & Holden from Belleville. The company
only lasted a short time and was followed by the Hague Brothers, the
Gilmour Co., Buck & Stewart, and Canniff. Later the Rathbun & Son
Lumber Company and Robert Bryden came in and began their "clean-
up" operations, cutting over old timber limits and buying up patches
of standing timber from settlers. In the 1890's lumbering began to

decline and in 1908 the Rathbun Company made the last log drive down the Skootamatta River.

The early lumbermen were also farmers. Crops included wheat, rye, hill corn, oats, peas, turnips, and some tobacco for home consumption. With the decline of logging and the resulting loss of income, many of the people left for Western Canada. The remaining farmers switched to raising beef cattle. Following World War One there was an even more rapid decline in farming and today much of the township's land has been reforested.

Municipal records for Kaladar go back to 1867 although there was some form of government before this. Kaladar was united with Anglesea Township for municipal purposes in the 1860's. The 1867 reeve of the united townships was Silas B. Scouten. On the council were C. Empey, P.W. Miller, George Fort, and John O'Donnell. The town hall was located in Flinton. Today the two townships are united with Effingham Township. In 1979 the combined population of the three townships was 1204.

Major centres in Kaladar include Flinton, Kaladar, and Northbrook. Highways 7 and 41 serve the township.

Directory of Frontenac, Lennox and Addington, 1865
Lennox and Addington Historical Society: Historical Glimpses of Lennox and Addington, 1964

KALADAR, community, Kaladar Township, Lennox and Addington County
Position 44° 41′ 77° 09′

The community of Kaladar is located at the junction of Highways 41 and 7. Highway 41 contains sections of the "Addington Road," built from 1854 to 1857 to attract settlers to this part of Ontario. The first settlers followed the surveyors and among them were George Forbes and Joe Morton who settled on Lot 14, Concession 7. Joe Morton and Silas Scouten, the Pickerings, Tryon and Hughes families, also were among the early arrivals.

The first hotel was operated by John Lewis on the present site of the old community hall. The village proper was then south of the present Highway 7. In 1882 the railway was built and a small French Village from nearby was moved to Kaladar.

Lumbering was once the main source of income for the inhabitants of Kaladar. Among the early lumber industries in this vicinity was Rathbun Lumber Company which by the late 1800's had expanded into a network of industries in southern Ontario.

The Kaladar United Church was built in 1926 on land donated by Mr. and Mrs. Ezra Weese. Kaladar today provides services to motorists with eating establishments and a hotel.

Gene Brown, Nadine Brunell (eds.): The Oxen and the Axe

KALEN, geographic township, Sudbury District
Position 47° 33′ 83° 18′

Formerly designated Township 11E, Kalen is named in memory of

John Kalen, RCAF, FO, from the Sudbury District, killed in 1945. Five Mile Lake Provincial Park borders the township's northeastern corner and Five Mile Lake extends from here into the heart of the township. Highway 129 passes about one mile east of Kalen's border.

KAMICHISITIT, geographic township, Algoma District
Postion 46° 30' 83° 01'

Formerly designated as Township 168, this township is located north of the town of Blind River. It is named after Kamichisitit, an Ojibwa who was converted by Jesuit missionaries at Sault Ste. Marie and greatly assisted them with work amongst his people. The White River flows through the northwestern corner of the township and the Blind River waters the southern part of the area.

Highway 546 passes through the northwestern corner of the township.

KANE, geographic township, Algoma District
Postion 46° 39' 83° 39'

Formerly known as Township 201, this township was named after Paul Kane, a Canadian artist who depicted Indian life in northwestern Ontario and the Prairies in the mid-1800's. A secondary road connects the area with the community of Bruce Mines, some 25 miles to the south.

KAP-KIG-IWAN PROVINCIAL PARK, Evanturel & Dack Tps., Timiskaming District
Position 47° 48' 79° 54'

This 784-acre Natural Environment Park is situtated on the scenic Englehart River one and a half miles south of the town of Englehart and just off Highway 11. The Indian name means "high falls" from the several waterfalls in the river. This river runs through a 200-foot gorge where the swift waters have eroded an ancient layer of fossil-bearing limestone, a manifestation that warm salt seas once covered the area.

KAPLAN, geographic township, Sudbury District
Position 47° 38' 82° 48'

Formerly designated as Township 22, the township was named after Max Kaplan, a pioneer mining financier and early town councillor of Kirkland Lake.

The area is located southeast of the town of Chapleau and just north of Wakami Lake Provincial Park. The Canadian Pacific Railway passes through the southern half of the township, with the station point of Sultan in the southeastern corner. A dry weather road links the vicinity with Highway 129 to the west.

KAPUSKASING, geographic township, Algoma District
Position 48° 31′ 82° 55′

The township takes its name from the river which flows in a north-easterly direction through the area. Kapuskasing is an Indian word meaning "place where the river bends".

Kapuskasing Lake takes up a large part of the township's central portion. A small Indian Reserve is located on the lake's eastern shore.

Canadian National Railways traverses the mountainous section of the township with station points at Elsas and Agate. Mount Horden rises to a height of 1485 feet in the northwestern corner of the township.

KAPUSKASING, town, District of Cochrane
Position 49° 25′ 82° 26′

Kapuskasing is situated on the Kapuskasing River some 500 miles northwest of Toronto. The name Kapuskasing comes from a Cree Indian word meaning "the place where the river bends".

During the 1800's the area of Kapuskasing was important for the fur trade. Both the Hudson Bay Company and the Old North West Traders operated in the region. In the early 1900's the National Transcontinental Railway (now CNR) from Moncton to Winnipeg was being built through a wilderness of forests, lakes, swamps and rivers of Ontario's hinterland. The station at the point where the railway crossed the Kapuskasing River was known as McPherson until 1917 when it was renamed Kapuskasing.

In 1914, the government acquired 1,280 acres of land west of the Kapuskasing River and south of the Transcontinental Railway tracks for an experimental farm. The area had been chosen because it was part of the fertile Great Clay Belt region of Northern Ontario. Scientists hoped to develop here new hardy breeds of crops that could withstand harsh and severe climate. That same year the government set up an internment camp for aliens and prisoners-of-war. The internees constructed barracks, a hospital, canteen, YMCA, a post office, a bakery and a supply depot, and managed to clear 100 acres of land during their first year at the camp. By the end of 1915 there were 1,200 internees and 250 troops in the camp; 600 acres of the land had been cleared. In 1917 most of the internees were paroled because of labour shortages and four hundred prisoners-of-war took their place at the camp. The camp operated until 1920 when the last prisoner-of-war was repatriated. The graves of thirty-two German prisoners who died while at the camp can be found in a small cemetery across from the present-day public cemetery.

The Canadian government embarked on a land settlement scheme for returned soldiers. One hundred and one settlers arrived in the Kapuskasing area and each was assigned a hundred-acre lot. A training school for these pioneers was established at Monteith and dormitories were built until they could erect their own houses. Farm implements, stock, and seed were available to the settlers on easy terms. On the east bank of Kapuskasing River the government built a sawmill, a planing mill, a blacksmith shop, a steam laundry, a store and a school on the present-day site of the Spruce Falls Power and Paper Company mill. Settlers were organized into groups, each supervised by a foreman, to clear land and start farms. However, many of the men were unhappy with this arrangement and by 1920 most of the settlers had abandoned the settlement project. Only nine remained: the Mairs, McCalls, Yorkes, Wings, MacMinns, Grants, Le Marriers, Goughs and Pooltons.

In 1922 the Spruce Falls Power and Paper Company erected a pulp and paper mill at the site, and a few years later a newsprint mill was constructed to produce newsprint for the *New York Times*. Power for the mills was to come from a new hydro development fifty miles to the north.

Planned and developed for the mill workers by the company, Kapuskasing became a model town. The main business section of the town was set out in a circle, with five streets radiating from it. Some of the town's streets are named after E.C. Drury, then Premier of Ontario, and after members of his cabinet.

The town of Kapuskasing was incorporated in 1921. The town's motto is "Oppidum ex Silvis", meaning, "Town out of the Forest". The first mayor was D.W. Smith, and his councillors were J.P.S. Ballantyne, E.W. Hardman, W.G. MacNaughton, W.M. Mills, A.M. Reid (later replaced by J. Downie), and J.A. Stewart.

In 1945 a new crepe-wadding mill with a daily capacity of 70 tons of cellulose started production at the Spruce Falls company site.

The town of Kapuskasing annexed the suburbs of Val Albert, Brunetville, and West Riverside in 1964. From its unlikely beginnings as a prisoner-of-war camp, and its failed settlement scheme of 1920, Kapuskasing has developed into a prosperous, well-planned town of just under 12,000 people.

M.K. Rukavina: *A Historical Sketch of Kapuskasing*

KARS, geographic township, Algoma District
Position 46° 45′ 84° 32′

Located on a peninsula and bordered on the west by Goulais Bay and on the east by the waters of Lake Superior, Kars was formerly referred to as Goulais Point Township. The present name of the township was probably taken from a Turkish city that during the Crimean War was defended against the Russians by Nova Scotia-born Sir. Wm. Fenwick Williams. The township was established in 1859 and subdivided in 1859-60. The area is Indian Lands. Secondary roads provide a link with Highway 17.

KARS, community, Regional Municipality of Ottawa-Carleton
Position 45° 09′ 75° 39′

Fifteen miles south of Ottawa, picturesquely situated on the west bank of the Rideau and the north shore of Stevens Creek, lies the compact rural community of Kars.

Settlement did not take place until after the American Revolution when the British government opened up the region to provide land for United Empire Loyalists fleeing the United States. North Gower Township, of which Kars was to become a part, was surveyed by John Stegman in 1791-93.

The first settlers at Kars were John and Ellen O'Callaghan who came from Ireland and squatted here in 1815. Some time before 1820 Messrs. Merrick and Stevens explored the area as a potential site for lumbering but the venture ended when Stevens drowned in the creek which now bears his name. Richard L. Garlick arrived about 1821 and began lumbering operations. Garlick and two other lumbermen, Stephen Blanchard and Sebra Beaman, built the first road in the township along Stevens Creek to Richmond. Garlick also launched the first steamer on the Rideau, the *Bytown*, and kept the first tavern.

In 1829 James Lindsay chose the site for a commercial wharf. Returning with his family in 1830, he built a wharfhouse and wharf which became an important dock for freight and passenger boats. Lindsay handled the potash which was exported by local settlers and also bought their wood, reselling it to the river boats for fuel. The wharf became the main entrance to new settlements in the township, as immigration from Britain increased during 1830 to 1850.

John Eastman arrived in 1826 and other early families included the Pollocks, Jamiesons, Callenders, and Wallaces. The improved transportation offered by the Rideau Canal attracted farmers and lumbermen to the area. The Scottish stonemasons who had worked on the Rideau locks between 1826 and 1832 remained and erected the stone houses which contribute so much to the area's appearance.

By 1850 the beginnings of a hamlet were visible around the wharf. Two roads led from a cluster of buildings which included a school, a church, and the houses of James Lindsay and John Eastman. Adam Johnston Eastman gave impetus to the community by erecting a steam sawmill in 1852, providing lumber for the settlers to build their houses and initiating the export of sawn lumber. A tragic explosion destroyed the mill in 1856 and killed four men, but Eastman rebuilt the structure almost immediately. With foresight, he bought the front half of Lot 23, Concession 1, in 1854, and in 1856 he hired Provincial Land Surveyor H.O. Wood to survey a village site which he named Wellington. As there was already a Wellington in Ontario, the name was changed to Kars when a post office was established in 1856 at Lindsay's Wharf, with James Lindsay as the first postmaster. The name was to honour the people of Kars, Turkey, who had defended their city against the Russians in 1855 during the Crimean War.

The first village lot was bought by Peter Dennis Boudry, a French-Canadian blacksmith. A store was opened in 1856 by John Montgomery and in 1857 Eastman erected a grist mill. In the 1860's he added a brewery to his enterprises. The Wellington Hotel, built by Alexander Cryderman, served passengers on the Kars Ferry which operated between North Gower and Osgoode Townships.

In the early 1860's local farmers changed from growing wheat to dairy farming and a number of cheese factories began operating in the township. Cheese joined the other products exported from Lindsay's Wharf. In the 1880's and 90's cruises along the Rideau Canal on luxurious steamers were popular and traffic past the wharf increased. However, in the early twentieth century, the passenger trade diminished and improved roads took away much of the freighting business. Lindsay's Wharf finally closed in 1930.

Today the community of Kars is mainly residential, with many of the residents commuting to work in Ottawa.

Coral Lindsay: *Kars on the Rideau,* 1972
Harry and Olive Walker: *Carleton Saga,* 1968

KATRINE, geographic township, Timiskaming District
Position 48° 14′ 79° 42′

Located northeast of the town of Kirkland Lake and a few miles east of the Quebec border, this township was named after Loch Katrine in Scotland. The Workman Hills are situated in the nothern half of the township. A secondary road connects the township with Highway 66 to the south.

KEARNEY, town, Perry and Bethune Townships, Parry Sound District
Position 45° 33′ 79° 13′

Kearney, situated on the south branch of the Magnetawan River, is one of the smallest towns in Ontario. In 1978 the population numbered 271. It stands now, one year later, at 489. The town, named after Patrick Kearney, one of its earliest settlers, lies some 50 miles east of Parry Sound on a branch line of the CNR.

In 1878-9 the government opened up Perry, Bethune and Proudfoot Townships for agricultural settlement. A depression in Canada at this time caused many unemployed men in cities to move north to make a new life for themselves. The first families to settle in Kearney were the O'Neils, the Kearneys and the Murphys. A.J. O'Neil and William Patrick Kearney, who took up land in the 12th concession on a site known for many years as Old Kearney, had been stonecutters on the Welland Canal. They moved to the Perth-Monteith Colonization Road when it was opened and built Kearney's first store there in 1880. The store was moved to a new location in 1883. A post office was established in 1880 and A.J. O'Neil became the first postmaster.

There had been extensive lumbering in Kearney since the late nineteenth century. The first shingle mill in the community was built by John Lahay. Soon after the Canada Atlantic Railway was constructed and the first freight train to Kearney brought machinery for a chair factory opened by the McGills. They also operated a sawmill. Flatt and Bradley, who carried out timber cutting at Sand Lake, was one of the lumber companies in the area.

By the early twentieth century, Kearney industries included the Booth Lumber Company, the Shortreed Mill, built on the site of the chair factory which had burned in 1907, and Brennan's mill. In the 1920's the Shane brothers erected kilns to produce charcoal and

Tudhope Brothers opened a sawmill. Merrit Brothers, a timber-cutting operation, later became Canada Wood Products and built a veneer plant and a basket bottom factory. In the 1950's a new charcoal plant was established.

In 1908 the Scott Act which allowed local option on the sale of liquor was a matter of lively debates in Perry Township. The businessmen of Kearney, which had two licenced hotels, feared that the township would go dry, and that Kearney's economy would suffer as a result. They therefore petitioned the government for town status and so Kearney became an incorporated town that year. A.J. O'Neil was the first mayor and R.H. Flavelle served as the first clerk.

Kearney, St. Patrick's Roman Catholic Church
Ministry of Industry & Tourism

A church to serve all denominations was built in 1886 on land given by Thomas Mason. It later became a Presbyterian church. A new building, erected in 1898 is now Knox United Church. Early Roman Catholic services were held in the homes of settlers. Father Peter McGuire became the pastor in 1887 and under him a church was opened the following year on land donated by Daniel Thomas, a non-Catholic. A new church, St. Patrick's, was dedicated in 1904 by Father Thomas F. Fleming. In 1901 St. Luke's Anglican was built on the land by Mr. French.

Over the years there have been a number of small mining booms in the Kearney area. A mine on the hill known as "Old Baldy" produced a large amount of mica in the early 1900's. In 1919 William Elliott discovered radioactive ore. Although there was not enough to warrant mining at that time, the mines were reopened after World War Two. A gold rush had occurred in 1932 but little gold was found. Four Kearney men, Bob and Charlie Mann, Bill Ryan, and Pat Murphy, discovered one of the first lodes in the silver rush at Elk Lake. The Kearney district also boasts of a "lost" lead mine. Known to early settlers, Arthur Dodd and James Fry, as far as is known it has not been located to this day.

Tourism is an important industry with many summer cottages on nearby lakes and a number of resorts in the vicinity.

The Town of Kearney 1908-1958, 1959

KEATING, geographic township, Algoma District
Position 48° 14′ 85° 15′

Formerly designated as Township 33, Range 26, this township was named to honour the memory of John J. Keating, a Canadian Army Private from Thunder Bay District killed, April 15, 1943. The township lies south of the town of White River and is not accessible by road.

KEATING ADDITIONAL, geographic township, Algoma District
Position 48° 14′ 85° 19′

Formerly Township 33 Additional, Range 26, this township is a small strip of land bordering in the east on Keating Township, and in the west on Thunder Bay District. It is named after Canadian Army Private John J. Keating, who lost his life in World War Two.

KEEFER geographic township, Cochrane District
Position 48° 20′ 81° 47′

Bordering the Districts of Timiskaming to the south and Sudbury to the west, this township was originally part of the District of Timiskaming, but was transferred to the District of Cochrane in 1974. All boundaries were surveyed in 1910 by H.J. Beatty. The township is named after Francis H. Keefer, MPP for Port Arthur in 1923. The area is served by Highway 101.

KEENANSVILLE, community, Adjala Township, Simcoe County
Position 44° 03′ 79° 52′

This dispersed rural community lies on the north bank of Bailey's Creek, about 25 miles southwest of Barrie. It was named after Robert Keenan, one of its early settlers, prominent in municipal affairs. Harvey Huntley, who settled on the east half of Lot 14, Concession 7, in 1828, is considered the first settler of Keenansville. Other early inhabitants included Keran Egan, Thomas Hollend, and Luke Harcourt.

A post office was opened in 1855 and by the late 1870's, Keenansville had become the most important community in Adjala Township. Businesses included a general store, blacksmith, wagon, and shoe shops, a woolen mill, an undertaking establishment, a printing office, and the Ontario Hotel, owned by James T. Egan. A weekly newspaper, the Cardwell *Sentinel*, was published by George P. Hughes. The Adjala Town Hall was located here and local children were educated at the Keenansville school.

Andrew F. Hunter: *A History of Simcoe County*, 1948.

KEENE, community, Otonabee Township, Peterborough County
Position 44° 15′ 78° 10′

Keene, situated on the Indian River near the north shore of Rice Lake, is a quiet residential community of 334 (1971). In the nineteenth century, however, it was a bustling village and a rival to Peterborough in its bid to become the area's main centre. Known at first as Gilchrist's Mills after its founder, Dr. John Gilchrist, it was later renamed by the doctor after his home town in New Hampshire.

View from the river, Keene, Ontario
Public Archives Canada C29275

The first settlers at Keene were Thomas and Andrew Carr who arrived in 1820, but it was John Gilchrist who started the community's development. In 1819 he had become the first doctor in Ontario to be granted a licence to practise "Physic Surgery and Midwifery". In 1825 Gilchrist built a grist mill on the Indian River and soon after this erected a distillery and houses for his workmen. He opened the first store in Gilchrist's Mills in 1829. Taverns were started up about the same time by Archibald Nelson and a Mrs. Hartley.

Gilchrist became the head of a flourishing export lumber business and the little community became a distribution centre for the lumbering industry. A sawmill and tannery were built and other small industries were established in the community. Growth was especially rapid between 1840 and 1850 when the population rose to about 400. By 1846 Keene had a grist mill, sawmill, tannery, distillery, carding mill, four stores, three taverns, a wagonmaker, and a blacksmith. A post office was opened in 1858. As traffic on the Indian River and Rice Lake increased, so did Keene's prosperity.

A town hall was built at Keene about 1875 and a new municipal building was erected in the twentieth century.

In 1882 the mainline of the Canadian Northern from Toronto to Belleville was laid down about 1½ miles north of Keene. The railway ended the importance of water transport and Keene's industries began to decline.

A Presbyterian congregation had been organized in 1833 by Rev. Archibald Colquhoun and a church was built in 1846 on land bought from Dr. Gilchrist. A new church erected in 1885 later became the United Church. Knox Presbyterian was dedicated in 1927. In 1825-6 a Methodist congregation was established. A church opened in 1860 was replaced in 1875 by a brick building which has since become the Masonic Society Hall and Public Library. Daniel McIntyre built St. John's Roman Catholic Church in 1856 on land given by Thomas Carr.

The community's first school was opened in 1832 with Thomas J. Denehey as teacher. Denehey made the first reliable map of the County of Hastings.

The Keene Curling Club, organized in 1861 by Thomas Miller, is one of the oldest curling clubs in Ontario. Today Keene is largely residential with many residents commuting to work in Peterborough, about 10 miles to the northwest. New homes have been built on the outskirts in the last two decades and Keene is developing into a resort area.

One of Keene's attractions to visitors is the nearby 260-acre Serpent Mounds Provincial Park. Archaeological excavations have revealed that the earth mounds, in the shape of a 200-foot serpent and eggs, were built by the Hopewellians, a tribe of Indians, about 2,000 years ago. Another attraction at Keene is Century Village, a pioneer village of fourteen restored buildings, including a store, shingle mill, smithy, church, inn, and cider barn. There are also two nineteenth century mills which are still in working order, monuments to Keene's earlier prosperity as a centre of water-powered industries.

Central Ontario Travel Association: *Kawartha Lakes*
Ministry of Industry and Tourism: *Traveller's Encyclopaedia of Ontario/Canada*, 1979
D. Gayle Nelson, ed.: *Forest to Farm, Early Days in Otonabee*, 1975

KEESICKQUAYASH, geographic township, Algoma District
Position 48° 03′ 84° 12′

Originally designated as Township 25, Range 24, this township lies east of Wawa, and a few miles north of Highway 101. The area is watered by the Shikwamkwa River and Shikwamkwa Lake. The township was named after Jasper Keesickquayash, head councillor at Cat Lake.

KEEWATIN, town, Pellat Township, Kenora District
Position 49° 46' 94° 34'

Situated on the north shore of Lake of the Woods, three miles west of Kenora, Keewatin is the first Ontario town reached on the Trans-Canada Highway (Highway 17) when entering the province from the west. The name is derived from an Ojibway word meaning "north wind". The town has a population of 1,788 (1979).

One of Keewatin's earliest industries was flour-milling. The second, and at that time the largest, flour mill in Canada was built here soon after the construction of the Canadian Pacific Railway in the early 1880's. A shipment of wheat en route to Great Britain was found to be frozen upon arrival in Keewatin. The quality of the wheat had greatly depreciated and in order to save the reputation of the Canadian product, a group of men led by D.L. Mather formed a flour milling company at Keewatin and milled the wheat before it was exported. The mill prospered and later became part of Ogilvie Flour Mills Limited, producing the famous "Five Roses Flour".

Incorporated as a town in 1901, Keewatin has been the site of many prosperous lumbering and sawmill operations. In the 1950's the local economy was based largely upon flour-milling, lumbering and pulp-and-paper making. Modern industries include Shoal Lake Fisheries and Northern Wood Home Canadian Ltd.

Facilities for sports in Keewatin include an indoor hockey arena and an indoor curling arena, a municipal beach, and two municipal athletic grounds. There is a public library and public and separate schools provide education for the town's children. United, Anglican, and Roman Catholic churches serve the townspeople.

Four hotels and motels offer accommodation to the summer visitors who flock to this vacation area. The Elk Millionaire Days, a summer carnival, draws many tourists. The Keewatin Boat Lift, which lifts boats to the Winnipeg River System, is another major attraction.

Ministry of Industry and Tourism: *Traveller's Encyclopaedia of Ontario/ Canada*, 1979
Ministry of Natural Resources: *Directory of Statistics and Data*, 1975

KEHOE, geographic township, Algoma District
Position 46° 35' 83° 57'

This township, located a short distance northeast of Sault Ste. Marie, is Indian Lands. It was surveyed in 1897 and named after Judge Kehoe of Sudbury. The Garden River courses across the northwestern corner of the township. Echo Lake occupies a fair section of the central portion.

KEITH, geographic township, Sudbury District
Position 48° 08' 82° 18'

Named after William Keith, MPP for York North in 1923, the township houses a portion of Horwood Lake and Groundhog Lake. The Groundhog River flows northward out of the latter lake in the northeast corner of the township.

The Canadian National Railways passes through the area with the station points of Groundhog River, Joburke and Palomar. Highway 101 passes through the northern part of the township.

KELLY, geographic township, Sudbury District
Position 46° 46′ 80° 29′

Formerly known as Township 34, this township is situated east of Wanapitei Lake, and was named after Phillip Kelly of New Durham. The main lakes are Kukagami Lake in the west, and Maskinonge Lake and Gawasi Lake in the east. A secondary road links the township with Highway 17 to the south.

KELSEY, geographic township, Sudbury District
Position 47° 27′ 82° 53′

Originally designated Township 10B, this township houses a large section of Wakami Lake Provincial Park in its eastern half. Wakami Lake and Kebskwasheshi River drain the area.

The township was named after Henry Kelsey, who served with the Hudson Bay Company in the 1700's and made extensive explorations into the interior country.

KELSO, geographic township, Sudbury District
Position 47° 11′ 82° 17′

This township houses part of the Mississagi Wild River Provincial Park with Ramsey Lake occupying much of the eastern half of the township. Swallow Lake takes up a large portion of the western half of the township. A secondary road links the area with the community of Webbwood and Highway 17 to the south. The township is probably named after Mr. Kelso, who was an inspector with the Ontario Provincial Government in 1943.

KELVIN, geographic township, Sudbury District
Position 47° 43′ 81° 19′

This township, located approximately 60 miles south of the city of Timmins, is named after Professor William Thompson Kelvin, 1824-1907, also known as Lord Kelvin. A professor at the University of Glasgow for more than 50 years, Lord Kelvin was recognized as one of the leading physical scientists of his time. The township's boundaries were surveyed in 1910. A secondary road links the area with Highway 144 to the west.

KEMP, geographic township, Sudbury District
Position 47° 49′ 81° 19′

Lying some 50 miles south of Timmins, Kemp was probably named after Hon. A.E. Kemp, Minister of the Crown. All boundaries of the township were surveyed in 1910.

Grassy Lake and Marne Lake inhabit the area. The township is well equipped with dry weather and secondary roads, linking it to surrounding areas.

KEMPTVILLE, town, Oxford Township, Grenville County
Position 45° 01′ 75° 38′

Kemptville on Kemptville Creek, a tributary of the Rideau River, is located on Highway 16 and the CPR, about 38 miles south of Ottawa. The settlement began in 1812 when Lyman Clothier purchased 200 acres of land from John Boyce. Shortly after, Clothier with his four sons began the construction of a dam and a sawmill. In 1821 he erected a grist mill, which was immediately patronized by many local farmers. The next step was the construction of a blacksmith shop. The location of those infant industries attracted new settlers which in turn created more businesses. Levis Church opened a general store and manufactured potash at his ashery on the bank of the river. In 1825 Joel Mack opened a carding mill and started manufacturing cloth. Averell & Hooker constructed a wharf and engaged in shipping, manufacturing potash, and general business.

The locality in the early days was known as the "Branch", Kemptville Creek being the south branch of the Rideau; later the settlement was called "Clothier Mills". As the population increased and the place gained importance, the settlers decided to give it a more dignified name. And so it was named, in 1828, Kemptville, in honour of Sir James Kemp, who was Lieutenant-Governor of Nova Scotia in 1820, and Governor-General of Upper and Lower Canada in 1828.

In 1824 the first physician arrived, a Dr. Fleming. He stayed one year and was succeeded in 1825 by Dr. Cowan. The first school opened in 1823, a small log building on the southwest corner of Reuben and Prescott Streets. Mr. Chase was the teacher. In 1842 a larger stone building was erected on Oxford Street. In 1873 a new commodious school building was opened.

Kemptville, in its early days, was a busy hamlet and marketing point. Mahlon Beach built a small frame hotel in the 1830's. Robert Leslie began tinsmithing; the Blackburns opened a drygoods store; John Stitt erected a blacksmith shop; and James Shaw, a wagon shop on Clothier Street. Stephen Tanny had a foundry and Mr. Bower operated a distillery. A 27-mile plank roadway was laid between Kemptville and Prescott. Steamboats started to ply the river in the 1830's.

The first pioneer church was built by the Anglican congregation in 1827. The building was a plain wooden structure erected near the site of the present church. The Methodist Church was built in 1831 on

Clothier Street between James and Lydia. The present building was erected in 1869. The Church of the Exaltation of the Holy Cross dates back to 1833 when Father Camping built a small stone church.

The first newspaper in Kemptville was the *Kemptville Progressionist*, published by R.W. Kelly in 1855. Its successor is the *Advance*, a weekly which now serves the district.

The Bytown and Prescott Railway reached Kemptville in the summer of 1854. Chartered in 1850 and later renamed the Ottawa and Prescott Railway, this pioneer line into the future capital of Canada had been surveyed by railway engineer Walter Shanley, who walked over four possible routes, a total distance of two hundred miles, before recommending the route via Kemptville. The line was eventually taken over by the CPR and when the latter completed its Montreal-Toronto line in the 1880's, Kemptville became a busy junction.

In January, 1857, Kemptville was incorporated as a village. The first village council met January 26, 1857 and Ambrose Clothier was appointed reeve. The first library, forerunner of the present Public Library, was instituted about 1870 under the auspices of a Mechanics Institute.

On September 22, 1916, the Honourable G. Howard Ferguson, then Ontario Minister of Lands, Forests and Mines, announced the establishment of the Kemptville Agricultural School, to provide agricultural training for the people of Eastern Ontario. Today, the Kemptville College of Agricultural Technology offers training in animal and field husbandry, engineering, home economics, horticulture, poultry farming, dairy farming, and farm management to an ever-growing number of future Ontario farmers.

The Hon. G. Howard Ferguson, a native of Kemptville and the son of a local doctor, became Ontairo's ninth premier from 1923 to 1930.

Kemptville, which was incorporated as a town on January 1, 1963, has a population of about 2,400 (1979).

J. Carr Anderson: *Kemptville, Past and Present*, 1903

KENDAL, part of the town of Newcastle, Regional Municipality of Durham
Position 44° 02′ 78° 32′

At the headwaters of the Ganaraska River, about 18 miles northwest of Cobourg, lies the compact rural community of Kendal. Originally known as Watertown Mills, it was renamed Kendal after the village of Kendall in the Lake District in England, possibly because the picturesque setting of the two communities is very similar.

The area was first settled in the 1830's by John McEuteer who arrived in 1836, Archibald Bawks who came from England in 1837, and the Irish John Carson who built his home here in 1838. Most early Kendal families were of Irish heritage, including the Underwoods, Cathcarts, McMullens, Henrys, Jacksons and Langstaffs.

The hills around Kendal and the nearby Great Pine Ridge were covered with dense pine forest and soon lumbering operations began. A mast road, constructed to haul the trees south, passed near Watertown Mills. Local cedar provided the material for shingle mills. By the mid-1800's there was a number of mills on the Ganaraska River at Kendal and the community was fast becoming the centre of a prosperous lumber trade. Theron Dickey had built the first sawmill in the 1840's and later added a grist mill. Horace LaRue also operated a sawmill by 1848 and two others were in the business near the community, including a mill producing shingles and barrel staves and a cooperage, both run by Timothy Soper. Andrew Howe and Samuel Glass constructed a sawmill in 1856.

By 1857 Kendal had a population of 50. Wm. W. Trull ran a general store and Jeremiah O'Leary was proprietor of the Kendal Hotel. A post office had been opened the year before. The population grew to 150 by 1865. Businesses included 2 general stores, 2 agricultural implement dealers, and 2 shoemakers' shops. The King William Third Hotel, formerly the Kendal Hotel, had been bought from O'Leary in 1859 by William Trull. A second hotel was opened in 1867 by John Carscadden and by 1869 there were four shingle mills in the community. However, Kendal lacked local craftsmen, having no tailor, mason, baker, tinsmith, tanner, or carder.

In the late nineteenth century, the lumber trade decreased as the local forests were denuded. Two sawmills were still operating in the early 1900's, but soon they too went out of business. The sandy soil around Kendal was not well suited for agriculture and as the population dwindled, the community lost its earlier importance. Today a quiet centre with a combined post office-store, a church, a school and an Orange Hall, it is the home of retired farmers and residents who commute to work. According to the 1971 census, the population of Kendal was 144.

Kendal's Presbyterian church built in 1870 served the community until 1917. The New Connexion Methodist Church, erected before 1865, is now the United Church. Kendal's schoolhouse dates back to 1866.

In 1925 a beautiful park was given to Kendal by Mr. and Mrs. Abraham Jackson in memory of their son killed in World War One. Today this community park is adjoined by over 600 acres of Provincial Recreation Area.

Helen Schmid and Sid Rutherford: *Out of the Mists*, 1975

KENDALL, geographic township, Cochrane District
Position 49° 39′ 83° 05′

This township was subdivided in 1912, by Ontario Land Surveyor Dobie, and named by the Ministry of Lands and Forest. The name origin is unknown.

The town of Hearst is situated in the northwestern corner of the township and the community of Hallebourg lies in the northeastern corner. Highway 11 and the Canadian National Railways traverse the area.

KENDREY, geographic township, Cochrane District
Position 49° 15' 81° 34'

The township was probably named after James Kendrey, MPP for Peterborough West, 1900-04. Subdivided in 1907 by Ontario Land Surveyor Fitzgerald, it was first settled by the Tom Moore family who built their home on Lot 22, Concession 8. Lumbering was the main industry in the early years of the township. Today the most important enterprises are paper mills.

In 1954 Kendrey, with the exception of the Smooth Rock Falls area, was erected into an Improvement District. A change of status again occurred in 1960 when Kendrey became a township. In 1975, with a population of about 1,100, the township was amalgamated with Smooth Rock Falls as the town of Smooth Rock Falls.

Kendrey Municipal Office.
Geographic Names Board.

KENILWORTH, community, Arthur Township, Wellington County
Position 43° 53' 80° 38'

Kenilworth is located in the centre of a prosperous farming district. Because of its location on the main thoroughfare of the township, the Owen Sound Road, it was at one time an important shipping point. Midway between Arthur and Mount Forest, it boasted two general stores, a hotel, wagon and blacksmith shops, town hall, schoolhouse and the Sacred Heart Church.

A post office was established in 1848 at Kenilworth, with William Gunn as its first postmaster.

In 1860-61 the Owen Sound Road was gravelled and tolls for its upkeep were charged to anyone using the road. Until the advent of the Toronto, Grey and Bruce Railway in 1871, many a team passed over this road hauling supplies for Mount Forest, Durham and other places. The heavy traffic required accommodation for both men and teams, but Kenilworth's early hostelries have long since disappeared. The community now has a population of less than 100.

A.W. Wright: *Memories of Mount Forest and its Surrounding Townships, 1928*

KENMORE, community, Regional Municipality of Ottawa-Carleton
Position 45° 14' 75° 25'

Named by its first settler and founder, Peter McLarin, after his home in Scotland, this compact rural community is situated about 16 miles southeast of Ottawa.

Peter McLarin arrived in 1832 and the community grew up around the grist mill which he built on the Castor River about 1835. McLarin, a leading member of the settlement, contributed much to its growth and prosperity. The settlement's population was over 100. Local enterprises included three general stores, a steam grist mill and sawmill, a plough factory, a blacksmith shop, a carpenter shop, two shoe shops, and a tailor shop. A school and Presbyterian and Baptist churches served the inhabitants.

Kenmore, once a police village, became part of the township of Osgoode in 1974.

National Capital Commission: *Early Days in the Ottawa Country,* 1967

KENNEBEC, township, Frontenac County
Position 44° 44′ 76° 59′

Situated in the central part of Frontenac County, Kennebec derives its name from an Indian word meaning "serpent" or "long river". The township, traversed by Highway 7, is a fisherman's paradise, its numerous lakes abounding with walleye, trout, pike and bass. The Salmon River rises in one of these lakes and flows southward through the township.

First settled in the 1820's, Kennebec had a population of 429 by 1861. Settlement had been facilitated by the opening of the Addington Road in the late 1850's. Pine forests and fertile soil made lumbering and farming the main occupations of the early inhabitants.

Near the present Highway 7, on the east shore of Big Clear Lake, developed the community of Arden. It was a thriving place by the mid-1800's with a sawmill, grist mill, planing mill, and a sash-and-door factory. Most of its early settlers were United Empire Loyalists; some were of French origin. The Rathbun Lumber Company of Deseronto operating in the area north of Arden gave employment to many of the township's residents. In 1882 the Ontario and Quebec Railway built their line through the township with a station known as Ardendale. The station for many years was a busy shipping point for logs, lumber, livestock and agricultural products from the area. However, when Highway 7 was completed in 1932, the railway's business started to decline. The last train stopped at Arden in April of 1967, and later that year the station house was demolished.

Other communities in the township are Elm Tree, Bordenwood, Henderson, Bakers Valley and Cedarholm. The permanent population of Kennebec numbers 740 (1979). Most inhabitants today rely on the tourist industry. A conservation area of nearly 1000 acres has been preserved in the township.

Frontenac County Directory, 1865
North Frontenac Chamber of Commerce, *North Frontenac Tourist Guide 1974-75*

KENNEDY, geographic township, Cochrane District
Position 49° 07′ 80° 47′

Situated east of the town of Cochrane, this township was subdivided in 1907. The southern and western boundaries were surveyed in 1904.

The township was named after either a Dr. Kennedy, K.C. or a Law Clerk with the Department of Lands and Forests. Dry weather and secondary roads connect the township with the town of Cochrane.

KENNING, geographic township, Cochrane District
Position 49° 15′ 79° 59′

Named after Alfred F. Kenning, MLA, MPP for Cochrane South in 1926-29, Kenning lies approximately 45 miles northwest of the town of Cochrane.

All boundaries were surveyed in 1930 by Angus & Sutcliffe. The Kenning River flows through the area, and Endleman Lake is situated in the southwest corner of the township. There are no roads in the township.

KENNY, geographic township, Nipissing District
Position 46° 46′ 79° 41′

This township, situated northwest of the city of North Bay, was probably named after C.R. Kenny, an Ontario Land Surveyor who did much survey work throughout northern Ontario. The northern boundary was surveyed in 1881 and the eastern boundary in 1961.

Wicksteed Lake separates the township. Secondary roads link the area with Highway 11 to the west.

KENOGAMING, geographic township, Sudbury District
Position 48° 08′ 81° 57′

This township lies southwest of Timmins. Its name is an Indian word meaning "a place with pointed end". The eastern boundary was surveyed in 1910 by H.J. Beatty and the northern and southern boundaries in 1912 by C.H. Low.

Kenogaming Lake empties into the Kamiskotia River, which waters the eastern half of the township. The area is accessible by a dry weather road from Highway 101.

KENORA, district
Position 54° 00′ 88° 00′

The largest district in Ontario, with 153,220 square miles of territory, Kenora is situated in the northwest extremity of the province and is a land of countless lakes and vast forests. To the south lies the Rainy River District, to the west the Province of Manitoba, to the east Thunder Bay and Cochrane Districts, and to the north Hudson Bay. The region north of Thunder Bay and Cochrane is known as the Patricia Portion. The name Kenora was made up of the first two letters of KEewatin, NOrman, and RAt Portage, three communities located on the shore of Lake of the Woods.

The Patricia Portion is drained towards Hudson Bay and James Bay, the main rivers being the Albany, Attawapiskat and Severn. Rivers in the southern part of the District flow towards Lake of the Woods or Lake Winnipeg.

In the early nineteenth century, Kenora was much visited by voyageurs of the two great fur-trading establishments, the Hudson's

Bay and the North West Companies, which amalgamated about 1821. Trading Posts were built, including one near Rat Portage [now the town of Kenora) in 1836. As Kenora lay on the main canoe route to the west, it became a busy and prosperous area for the fur-trading company.

In 1870, the Kenora area was the focus of one of Canada's first boundary disputes. Following Confederation in 1867, Ontario had no clearly defined boundary to separate it from the Hudson's Bay Company lands in the Northwest. In 1869 the Dominion of Canada purchased the land and the question of provincial and federal jurisdiction arose when Ontario laid claim to much of the newly acquired property while the Federal Government supported Manitoba's claim to the territory. The issue was given over to arbitration and in 1878 a decision was made in favour of Ontario. The western boundary was to be the present one, and the northern boundary was to be formed by the English and Albany Rivers. The Federal Government rejected the decision and in 1881 passed an Act making the territory part of Manitoba. However, the British Privy Council in 1884 upheld the 1878 award and Ontario retained the disputed area.

The building of the Canadian Pacific Railway in the years 1879-1884 gave a great boost to Kenora's growth. In 1871 there were few white men in the area but by 1881 the population of the district had risen to 4,564. Many men arrived to work on the railway, during and after its construction, and the town of Rat Portage (Kenora) became a major distributing centre, shipping lumber to the east and supplying provisions to the large lumber camps of the area. The lumbering industry developed largely as a result of the new markets opened up by the railway, both in railway construction and in the building trade as settlement increased in the west. John Mather built the first sawmill in 1880. The discovery of gold in the Kenora District started a gold rush and during the 1890's prospectors arrived in their thousands. By 1901 there were 10,369 people in Kenora. The gold rush lasted only a short time, but lumbering continued to be an important industry, and by 1911 the population of the District had reached 15,490. In the 1920's new mining and lumbering areas were opened in the north resulting in continued growth. Kenora's population had reached nearly 22,000 by the census of 1931.

Today pulp-and-paper making is one of the most important industries in the District. The extensive forests made available large supplies of raw materials for such companies as Ontario Pulp and Paper Co. Ltd. The discovery of uranium, iron, and base metals and the resulting mining operations have also contributed greatly to the district's economy. More recently there has been a renewed interest in gold mining. A number of areas have also been given over to agriculture and hydro-electric developments. The well-known "Five Roses" flour is produced in the town of Keewatin.

Kenora has also become a popular tourist area and offers excellent opportunities for hunters and trappers. Transportation links have greatly improved since the nineteenth century. The district is now traversed by the mainlines of the CNR and the CPR and the

Trans-Canada Highway (Hwy 17). The northern parts of the district can be reached by airplane.

Today Kenora has a population of 36,584 (1979). There are four towns: Kenora, the District Seat; Dryden, Sioux Lookout, and Keewatin. There are also three improvement districts: Balmertown, Pickle Lake, and Sioux Narrows; and six townships: Barclay, Ear Falls, Ignace, Jaffray and Melick, Machin, Red Lake.

Kenora Miner and News: Visitors' Guide, 1973

KENORA, town, Kenora District
Position 49° 47′ 94° 29′

This picturesque town on the northern shore of Lake of the Woods, about 130 miles east of Winnipeg, is the seat of the Kenora District. Formerly known as Rat Portage, it was renamed Kenora in 1899. The name was formed from the first two letters of KEewatin, NOrman, and RAt Portage, three neighbouring communities on Lake of the Woods.

In the late eighteenth and early nineteenth centuries, the area around Kenora was the scene of rivalry between two great fur-trading companies, the Hudson's Bay and the North West Companies. The keen competition ended in 1821 when they amalgamated as the Hudson's Bay Company. By 1836 a post had been set up on Old Fort Island, near present-day Kenora. The post was moved to the mainland in 1861 and around it grew the community of Rat Portage.

Until about 1870 the vicinity was exploited mainly for its fur resources. Rat Portage, so named by the Indians because it was on the road to the country of the Muskrat (the land around the Winnipeg River was full of muskrats), became the chief gathering centre for furs which were then shipped to Hudson's Bay.

In August, 1870, Lt. Col. Wolseley and 1,200 troops arrived at Rat Portage on their way to suppress the Riel uprising at the Red River Settlement in the West. The expedition had demonstrated the need for a railway to the West and in 1876 Canadian Pacific Railway contractors set up camp at Rat Portage. During the construction of the CPR (1879-1884) two post offices were established on the north shore of Lake of the Woods, one called Keewatin Mills, the other Rat Portage.

During the 1870's there arose a boundary dispute between Manitoba and Ontario over the ownership of a large area which included the Kenora District. In 1869 the Hudson's Bay Company had given up this part of its land and both provinces claimed possession of the territory. Much confusion arose from the dispute. In 1878 the Ontario claim was upheld by an arbitration board but the Federal Government refused to recognize the decision and in 1881 passed an Act making the area part of Manitoba. Rat Portage was incorporated as a Manitoba town, and magistrates were appointed. Conflicts in authority arose, however, as magistrates had already been appointed by the Province of Ontario in 1871. In 1883 Rat

Portage held an election, unique in all of Canada. Provincial members were to be elected to the legislatures of both Ontario and Manitoba. In the same year, the citizens of Rat Portage asked that the town become part of Ontario. Their request was granted and the area was incorporated as an Ontario township. The following year the Privy Council put an end to the boundary dispute, awarding the entire Kenora District to the Province of Ontario.

The first Board of Municipal Councillors for Rat Portage was chosen that year and consisted of chairman John McQuarrie and councillors W.L. Baker, Frank Gardner, H.F. Holmes, and F.T. Bulmer. In 1892 Rat Portage was incorporated as a town with A. Campbell as its first mayor.

Kenora
Ministry of Industry & Tourism, Toronto

Men who had taken part in the Wolseley expedition, including Billy Ross, Neil McDougal, and Jack Lepine, were among the earliest settlers of Rat Portage. Development, initially retarded by the boundary dispute, was given impetus by the construction of the CPR in the early 1880's. Soon Rat Portage became a major supply and distributing centre for a bourgeoning lumber industry. The Keewatin Lumber Company was the first and other companies included Western

Lumber, Rat Portage Lumber and Dick & Banning.

Several sawmills operating around Rat Portage served both Canadian lumber companies and Minnesota operations which sent their timber to the town by steamer. The *Lady of the Lake* was the first important steamboat on Lake of the Woods. By the late nineteenth century, freight, lumber and passenger steamers plied the waters of the lake, many of them having their home port in Rat Portage.

By 1891 the construction of the railway and the growth of the lumber industry had boosted the population of Rat Portage to 2,205. About this time several discoveries of gold were made in the area, starting a gold rush and a boom in business. In recent years there has been a revival of gold-mining in the area.

The Ontario-Minnesota Pulp & Paper Co. Ltd. began operations in Kenora in 1923. Its newsprint mill, one of the largest in Canada, became the town's major employer.

Situated on the busy Trans-Canada Highway and at the gateway to both Lake of the Woods and to over 3,000 square miles of recreational country to the north, Kenora today is a bustling tourist centre. Margach Airport, 8 miles northeast of town, provides transportation to the northern areas. Among the attractions for tourists in Kenora are: the Lake of the Woods Museum; LOWISA (Lake of the Woods International Sailing Regatta); seven-day excursions among the islands of the lake; Lake of the Woods International Pow-Wow; Rusking River Provincial Park; and McLeod Park, home of the world's largest Muskie. Built locally from wood, steel and fibreglass and weighing more than two tons, the huge statue of the muskellunge lures the fisherman who may well find a real speciman weighing up to 80 pounds. Other attractions include lake cruises on the *Argyll II*, and the "Nisa-Che-Won" canoe race, a 60-mile canoe trip along the Winnipeg River. Over twenty hotels and motels provide accommodation for Kenora's visitors, who during the summer swell the permanent population of 9,884 (1979) to over 30,000.

The town has eight elementary schools, including two separate schools. The Kenora-Keewatin District High School is one of two high schools in the community.

A library was formed in 1885 under the sponsorship of the CPR. It became a Mechanics' Institute in 1894, then the Rat Portage Public Library in 1895. The present library was opened as a Carnegie Public Library in 1916.

Reverend Albert Lacombe (1827-1916), a missionary renowned for his work among the Prairie Indians and Métis, was among the first to hold services in Rat Portage when he ministered to the CPR construction crews from 1880 to 1882. He built a church here in 1881. By 1896 there were Presbyterian, Anglican, Methodist, Salvation Army, Lutheran, and Roman Catholic houses of worship serving the community. Today Kenora has twenty-one churches.

Kenora's St. Joseph Hospital was founded in 1903. By the 1950's the Kenora General Hospital was in operation. The two institutions later amalgamated as the Lake of the Woods District Hospital. A District Home for the Aged is also located in the town.

Kenora's daily newspaper, the *Kenora Miner and News*, was established in 1894. The town also has its own radio station, CJRL, and had the first Canadian TV Satellite Station.

Kenora became the smallest town ever to win the Stanley Cup in 1907. Winners were the "Kenora Thistles", coached by J.A. Link. The town was also the home of Jack Gaudeur, world champion sculler on a 3½ mile course; and Tommy Phillips, a member of the Hockey Hall of Fame, as well as several Canadian boxing champions. Today residents enjoy a golf course, yacht club, beaches, curling club, skating rinks and a Community Recreation Centre built during 1967, the country's centennial year.

The Colonist, 1896
Kenora Miner and News: Visitors Guide, 1973
Ministry of Industry and Tourism: *Traveller's Encyclopaedia of Ontario/Canada,* 1979

KENT, county
Position 42° 25' 82° 10'

The County of Kent in the southwestern part of Ontario fronts on Lake Erie and contains 613,150 acres sustaining a population of approximately 107,500. There are 22 municipalities within its borders including: the City of Chatham; the Towns of Blenheim, Bothwell, Dresden, Ridgetown, Tilbury and Wallaceburg; the Villages of Erieau, Erie Beach, Highgate, Thamesville and Wheatley, and the Townships of Camden, Chatham, Dover, Harwich, Howard, Orford, Raleigh, Romney, Tilbury East and Zone. Chatham is the county seat.

Kent County is watered by two substantial rivers, the Thames and the Sydenham. It was along the Thames River that the earliest settlements began to appear. The date of these early arrivals, chiefly United Empire Loyalists, has not been exactly ascertained, but it was previous to 1792. Sources indicate that as early as 1790 a man named Parson had taken up a location on the south bank of the Thames, in what is now the Township of Raleigh.

The first concerted influx of settlers to this area of the county took place in 1794. By the end of this year a great many locations were chosen and settled along the Thames. The first grant of land was given in 1794 to Sally Ainse in what is now the Township of Dover.

In 1794 the government established a naval yard on the site of present-day Chatham. Governor Simcoe considered the junction of the Thames River and McGregor Creek a strategic point in the defence of Upper Canada's western frontier. By establishing a fort at this point, Simcoe hoped to divert the Indian trade from Detroit which he feared would eventually be ceded to the Americans. He had a survey made naming the site Chatham, after a place in England, and suggested that it become the future capital of Upper Canada. However, York (Toronto) was chosen as the capital, and the government blockhouse at Chatham was removed in 1798 to Sandwich, where it was to serve as a gaol and courthouse. Meanwhile a town site of 600 acres had been laid out in 1795, but few settlers arrived before about 1802.

The first mill of the county using power furnished by what is now known as McGregor's Creek had been built in 1792 by Thomas Clark just outside Chatham's limits. It proved a great boon to the residents. Clark later lost his mill to John McGregor because of an outstanding debt. Settlers were establishing themselves along the river front in Dover, Chatham, Harwich, Howard and Camden townships around that time.

Many of these early pioneers were former soldiers, generally not suited to the rigors of pioneer life, seldom remaining long on their holdings, and selling them very cheaply. One story is related of how a farm of one hundred acres was sold for a "flitch of bacon".

John Crawford came from Mississippi in the early 1800's to pioneer on the Lake Erie shore within Kent County. There were few other permanent settlers along the lakeshore until the termination of the Anglo-American War of 1812-15, when Col. Thomas Talbot began to colonize the north shore of Lake Erie along the Talbot Road. This road, one of Upper Canada's earliest pioneer highways, was flanked by settlers from the eastern to the western limits of the county by 1818.

Lord Selkirk had colonized a portion of county territory near the mouth of the River Sydenham with more than 100 Scottish Highlanders in August, 1804. Settlements were formed farther up the Syndenham, above Dawn Mills in Camden Township, around 1823 by pioneers who had originally located in Harwich.

Zone was the last township of Kent to be settled. A large portion of this township was occupied by Delaware Indians who ceded their land to the government in 1858 and moved to the Moravian Reserve. Settlements were recorded as early as 1842, but it was at least 1852 before the portion of Zone outside the Indian Reserve was settled.

Kent County played an important role in the War of 1812-14. When in 1813 the British naval force under Barclay was defeated by Commodore Perry, the British commander of the forces in the western part of Upper Canada, Col. Proctor, began to retreat toward Lake Ontario along the Thames River. He was accompanied by 500 Indians under the famous Indian Chief Tecumseh. In October 1813, the British forces were camped on the site of the present village of Thamesville. Tecumseh tried to persuade Proctor to make a stand at "The Forks" of the Thames and McGregor's Creek. The Indian chief feared that his followers would not remain with the British once they retreated beyond their main village at Moraviatown. Proctor, hoping to reach Lake Ontario without a battle, refused. At Moraviatown Tecumseh was forced to put the British commander in the position of choosing between losing his allies or fighting a battle.

The Americans advanced on Chatham on October 3rd. The bridge located there was defended by a party of Indians who temporarily held off the American advance. At Moraviatown the forces met. Col. Proctor, in the face of the American onslaught, gave the signal for retreat. The Indians fought on until their Chief, Tecumseh, was killed. Then they, too, retreated. This was the only major battle fought in the county during the war and it left Western Canada in control of the Americans under Col. Harrison.

The County of Kent originally was comprised of the territory now constituting Kent and Lambton Counties. The area was part of the old Western District which also included Essex County. The boundaries had been set for judicial purposes, but in 1841 the area became a municipality for administrative purposes. The seat of municipal government was located at Sandwich.

As a result of protests against the remoteness of Sandwich, the Western District was divided in 1847 creating the Provisional District of Kent, at that time still including the region of what is now the County of Lambton.

The Councillors of Kent met in Provisional Council for the first time at Chatham on August 17, 1847. One of their first concerns was the construction of a Gaol and Courthouse. The county, at that time, contained the townships of Camden, Chatham, Dover, Harwich, Howard, Orford, Raleigh, Tilbury, Zone and West Tilbury (later annexed to Essex).

On May 30, 1849, an Act was passed abolishing "Districts" in Upper Canada. At that time the present boundaries of Kent County were set. The members of the first Kent County Council meeting in 1850 were: Warden, George Duck, Reeve of Howard; Councillors: James Smith (Camden and Zone); Samuel Arnold (Chatham); Robert Mitchell (Dover); Alex R. Robertson and Alex McKay (Harwich); Daniel Morehouse (Orford); John G. Weir (Raleigh); Thos. Jackson (Romney); Jno. Wilson (Tilbury); Pierre Desjardins (West Tilbury).

Kent County is one of the province's most admirably blessed regions for agricultural or horticultural pursuits. It possesses rich durable clays and loams capable of supporting a wide variety of crops, as well as many fruits of which grapes and peaches are the most suited to it, particularly along the shores of Lake Erie.

In 1828 the county had a population of 3,449. The census of 1851-52, the first in which Kent was independent of Essex and Lambton, indicated a population of 17,469; 64,260 acres were under cultivation; in operation were twelve grist mills, thirty-one sawmills, a carding mill and a woollen mill, two distilleries, a brewery, a tannery, three iron foundries and three asheries. There were twenty churches within county limits.

Chatham on the Thames emerged as the hub of this agricultural county early in its history. By the 1860's it had become the principal shipping port for products from the Thames River area as well as a milling centre for lumber and flour. Today it retains its position as a marketing and distributing centre for the surrounding agricultural area.

Victor Lauriston: *Romantic Kent, 1626-1952*, 1952

KENT BRIDGE, community, Chatham Township, Kent County
Position 42° 31' 82° 04'

This dispersed rural community on the bank of the Thames River, about ten miles northeast of Chatham, was named Kent Bridge when a wooden bridge was built here across the river in 1854.

The first white settler was Frederick Arnold, a United Empire Loyalist, who came to Kent County in the 1790's and built a grist mill on Arnold's Creek, east of the present village. Later a sawmill was erected by his grandson Christopher.

It was at Arnold's Mill that Tecumseh, the great Indian chief, spent his last night. Tecumseh was a friend of Christopher Arnold, son of the mill's builder, and on the day of the Battle of the Thames, October 15, 1813, he stood under a nearby beech tree waiting for Arnold to throw three shovels of earth off the mill dam as a sign that the Americans were approaching. Arnold gave the signal, but the warrior Tecumseh had already seen the enemy and was riding off to join his army. He was killed in battle that same day.

A community grew up around the mill. The main north and south roads met at the spot and in 1826 the first Thames River bridge in Kent was built here. A tavern erected by John Williams became a regular stage stop in 1828. The small settlement at that time was known as Howard Bridge.

In 1834 a bridge was built at nearby Chatham, diverting traffic away from the settlement to the northeast. A few years later the main road to Chatham was straightened and entirely bypassed Howard Bridge.

A government survey placed the county's north-south roads away from the community and with the decreased trade the centre of the settlement moved to Kelley's Corners which had been established in the early nineteenth century.

The settlement grew rapidly in the mid-nineteenth century. About 1843, Frederick Arnold, descendant of the original mill owner, built the first foundry and Thomas Lyons opened the first store. In the mid-1840's Christopher Gee established a brickyard. Gee also ran a ferry and in time the community became known as Gee's Ferry.

Gee's ferry was replaced by a new enclosed wooden bridge in the 1850's. It was named Kent Bridge, thus giving the community its name. The bridge itself was replaced by another structure in 1861. It was a toll bridge, the tolls being removed in 1873. In 1875 an iron bridge was built across the river. The first Canadian Pacific Railway train passed through Kent Bridge in 1890.

The first school and church of Kent Bridge was a long frame structure with a fireplace at each end. Divided in the centre, school was held at one end and church services were conducted at the opposite end. Later, in 1842 a debating school was also held in this building, providing training to many important local speakers. An early 1840's store, the first store in Kent Bridge, was conducted by Thomas Lyons.

Kent Historical Society: *Papers*, 1921
Victor Lauriston: *Romantic Kent*, 1952

KENYON, township, Glengarry County
Position 45° 18′ 74° 44′

Kenyon is situated in the northwest corner of Glengarry County and is bounded on the northeast by Lochiel Township, on the southeast by Stormont County, and on the northwest by Prescott County.

The land is more undulating than that of the other townships in the county. In the southern part lies a large expanse of water known as Loch Garry.

Kenyon was settled in the late eighteenth and early nineteenth centuries. Most of the early inhabitants were immigrants from Scotland. Included among these early families were the McGregors, McDonalds, McLeods, McTavishes, McRaes, McDiarmids, McIntoshes, McNaughtons, McKays and McDougalls. By the 1870's the township was densely populated and several communities had developed including: Dunvegan, Greenfield, Lochgarry and Dominionville.

Dunvegan, settled by Scottish Highlanders, is the site of a pioneer museum housed in the former Star Inn that was built in the 1840's. Dominionville, now a dispersed rural community, was once a thriving place with a carding mill, tanneries and numerous other business enterprises. Its decline began when the Canada Atlantic Railway (now CNR) built its line through Maxville, rather than Dominionville. Tradesmen and labourers moved away, some of them with "lock, stock and barrel", as the saying goes, taking even their buildings with them.

Maxville, in fact, owes its existence to the railway which was built in the early 1880's between Ottawa and Coteau Junction. The village which derives its name from its many Scottish settlers whose names are prefixed by "Mac" was incorporated in 1892. Maxville, which annexed part of Kenyon in 1968, is famous as the site of the Glengarry Highland Games held annually and drawing as many as thirty thousand spectators. The Kenyon Agricultural Society is based in Maxville.

The police village of Apple Hill is located near the CPR line which traverses the southern part of the township. The railway's right-of-way ran through Sandy Kennedy's apple orchard, hence the name.

The township's population numbers approximately 2,900 (1979).

Ministry of Industry and Tourism: *Traveller's Encyclopaedia of Ontario/Canada*, 1979
Standard-Freeholder, 1967

KEPPEL, township, Grey County
Position 44° 40′ 81° 02′

Keppel is the northernmost township of Grey County and is part of the "Indian Peninsula", land retained by the Ojibway Indians until 1855. The city of Owen Sound is situated nearby to the south. The township is bordered to the north by Colpoy's Bay and Georgian Bay, to the east by the waters of Owen Sound, to the south by Derby and to the west by Amabel Township in the County of Bruce. It includes Griffiths and White Cloud Islands off the Georgian Bay shore.

The name, according to some sources, commemorates Sir Henry Keppel, commander of the naval brigade at the destruction of the Chinese war fleet in 1857. Keppel, who later attained the rank of Admiral was a friend of Sir James Brooke, uncle of Viscount Bury, the superintendent of Indian Affairs in Canada.

Even before the Indians had given up possession, settlers, mostly of Scottish and Irish origin, were moving into the area. The earliest known settlers appear to have been Mr. and Mrs. Joseph Davidson, who took up land east of Shallow Lake in 1856. Their son was the first white child to be born in the area. Other early residents included colourful figures such as David Pyette who settled at Pyette's Point in 1856 and was never seen without his constant companions, a sheep and a collie dog.

Settlement increased rapidly after Charles Rankin surveyed the township in 1855. In 1858 Francis Dodds opened an inn in Concession 25 to provide a resting-place for incoming families. William Harvey and James B. Smith built a sawmill in the same year. This was followed in the early 1860's by a grist mill, constructed by John and William Cornish.

In 1859 Keppel and neighbouring Sarawak became a municipal unit. Sarawak, a narrow strip of land along the Owen Sound, had previously been an Indian Reserve. Thomas Ormiston was elected first reeve of the united townships. However, the election was declared illegal because there were too few ratepayers in Keppel and Sarawak. The required number was reached in 1859 and Ormiston was again elected. In 1868 Sarawak separated from the union. Alex Bell was elected reeve of Keppel and was succeeded by Thomas Pettman in 1869.

The 1860's saw the establishment of the first schools in the area. The first teacher was probably Gavin Shaw, whose family has produced a number of members of that profession. A school was built in north Keppel in 1862 with Horace Lymburner as teacher. Miss Seldon was the first instructor at the Cruickshank school which opened in 1863. Wilfred Campbell, the distinguished Canadian poet, was another early teacher in Keppel. He taught at Zion school from 1878 to 1880.

The first church services were Presbyterian and were held in the homes of James Cruickshank, George Wilson, and James Leslie. Reverend Mr. Stevenson came from Owen Sound to hold Communion in the Cruickshank and Butchart barns. A Methodist, the Reverend Mr. Jones, had lived in the township since 1859, but because he had married a Presbyterian, he was not allowed in the Methodist ministry. Nevertheless he held services in a private home. In the western part of the township the earliest preacher was the Reverend Mr. Dribbs, a Congregationalist. Three Presbyterian churches, Kemble, North Keppel and Lake Charles, were constructed in 1874. The Methodists, who had no building of their own at the time, used the Presbyterian church every other Sunday. North Keppel Methodist Church was erected some time later with Mr. Doherty as minister.

Remainders of the past can still be seen in Keppel. A deserted house in the northern part of the township marks the only land in the area which was owned by an Indian chief after 1855. When the time came for him to move to Cape Croker with his people, he felt he had to keep a place of his own to return to. The Government allowed him to retain the house and an acre of land.

In the Oxenden area, Bruce's Cave and Bruce Mines commemorate an early Scottish settler named Bruce who built his cabin near a cave in the rock.

Shallow Lake, an incorporated village, annexed part of the township in 1978. Communities in the township include Cruickshank on Highway 70, a few miles northwest of Owen Sound; Benallen on the Sarawak border; Shouldice and Wolseley in the central part; Kemble near the eastern shore of the Sound; North Kepple on Georgian Bay, and Oxenden, a few miles northeast of Wiarton on the eastern shore of Colpoy's Bay. The population of Keppel now numbers 2,738 (1979).

T. Arthur Davidson: *A New History of the County of Grey,* 1972
E.L. Marsh: *A History of the County of Grey,* 1931

KERNS, township, Timiskaming District
Position 47° 38′ 79° 49′

This township lies a few miles northwest of New Liskeard. The area was once inhabited by Indian Chief Wabi and his band. Wabi Creek which flows eastward through the township still commemorates his name.

The township was surveyed by Ontario Land Surveyor J.B. Speight and was named after MLA Wm. Kerns, MPP for Halton at that time. In 1904, after the government had opened the land at the head of Lake Timiskaming for settlement, Kerns was incorporated as a municipality. The township is part of the fertile Little Clay Belt, which extends from New Liskeard in the south to the vicinity of Englehart in the north. The community of Milberta is located in the central part. Highways 65 and 562 serve the area. The Ontario Northland Railway main line skirts the eastern boundary of the township and the Elk Lake branch of the line passes through the northwestern corner of Kerns. The construction of this railway, once known as the Timiskaming and Northern Ontario, led to the discovery of silver in the Cobalt area to the south.

The township's population in 1979 stood at 466.

KERRS, geographic township, Cochrane District
Position 48° 45′ 80° 13′

Located on the western shore of Lake Abitibi, this township was named after Joseph Kerr, MPP for Stormont in the late 1800's. Subdivided in 1905, the subdivision was partially annulled on July 22, 1963. The western boundary was surveyed in 1902 and 1904 and the southern boundary in 1903.

The Abitibi River leaves Abitibi Lake in this township and flows westward, cascading over the Couchiching Falls. The town of Iroquois Falls lies some 20 miles to the west of the area.

KERWOOD, police village, Adelaide Township, Middlesex County
Position 42° 56′ 81° 45′

Situated about 24 miles west of London on the town line between Adelaide and Metcalfe Townships, Kerwood, with a population of 121 in 1971 is today mainly a residential community, serving as a shopping centre for the district.

The site was first settled in the early nineteenth century by English and Irish officers who were disbanded after the War of 1812 and received land grants as a reward for their services.

A branch of the Grand Trunk Railway was built through the settlement in the second half of the nineteenth century on land belonging to John McKenzie of Hamilton. McKenzie had a village laid out on his property.

By 1878 Kerwood had a popualation of about 200. Businessmen included J.H. Brown, a drover and cattle dealer, and Samuel Foster, a grain dealer. Other area residents were John Morgan, William Dowding, and Joseph Galbraith.

The village's growth reached a peak in the late 1880's when its population was about 300. Among its industries were milling, distilling, blacksmithing, brickmaking, bootmaking, and wagon-making. Richardson's brickyard was opened in 1876.

A Methodist church was built in 1875.

H.R. Page & Co.: *Historical Atlas of Middlesex County*, 1878.

KETTLEBY, community, King Township, Regional Municipality of York
Position 44° 01′ 79° 34′

Kettleby, a small community a few miles west of Aurora, was named after the native Welsh village of Samuel Tyrwhitt, owner of the local mill in 1842.

In 1803 John Bogart from Pennsylvania bought the land granted in 1801 to Dorothy Burger, a United Empire Loyalist. He sold part of this land to Jacob Tool who built a sawmill in 1825. This mill was bought in 1842 by Samuel Tyrwhitt, who also erected a woollen mill, oatmeal mill, cooperage, and distillery. These services attracted many new settlers and in 1851 the post office of Kettleby Mills was established, with James Tipping as postmaster. The name became Kettleby in 1859.

Kettleby, in its heyday, was the hub of the surrounding area. It was the business and shopping centre and supplied lumber to the entire township. Twenty coopers were kept busy making barrels to export flour from Kettleby's mills. A felt hat manufacturer, shoe-makers, a wagon-making shop, and a farm implement factory were among the businesses established in the mid-nineteenth century. Brooks W. Walton from Kettleby invented a combined cultivator and seed drill that was later used by the Massey-Harris Company, noted manufacturers of farm machinery.

The coming of the railway to King Township in 1853 marked the beginning of Kettleby's decline. The timber trade diminished, flour exports decreased, and new factories aided by the railway put many of the local mechanics out of business. Five serious floods, between 1885 and 1934, destroyed many of Kettleby's mill dams. The population decreased until the once bustling village became the small community it is today. According to the 1971 census the population numbered 104.

Mary E. Garbutt: "King Township, York County 1800-1867 A Historical Sketch" in *Ontario Historical Society*, 1960
Elizabeth McClure Gillham: *Early Settlements of King Township Ontario* 1975

KETTLE LAKES PROVINCIAL PARK, German Township, Cochrane District
Position 48° 34′ 80° 52′

This Provincial Recreation Park is located on Highway 67, less than 20 miles west of the town of Matheson, itself situated on Highways 11 and 101. The park's name derives from the many kettle lakes throughout its 2,304 acres. During the last ice age, glaciers settled on the land and formed deep depressions called "kettles". The melting glaciers left small lakes in these kettles. Also a remnant of that era of 10,000 years ago are the "erratic blocks", huge boulders trapped and carried along in mile-high glaciers. These boulders were left behind when the glaciers melted. Artifacts have been found in ancient hunting grounds of some five thousand years ago. In the late 19th century, the first white men came as fur traders, followed by prospectors and lumbermen.

Ontario Ministry of Natural Resources

KIDD, geographic township, Cochrane District
Position 48° 40′ 81° 24′

This township became part of the city of Timmins in 1973. The area was subdivided in 1905 and was named after George Nelson Kidd, MPP for Carleton around the turn of the century. The area is watered by Kidd Creek. Highway 655 links the township with Timmins to the south.

KILBRIDE, community, Nelson Township, Halton County
Position 43° 25′ 79° 56′

This small village, almost joining Cumminsville, is about seven miles from Milton. The first settler was Thomas Simpson, who built a log cabin in this vicinity and cleared the land. Later, he encouraged the erection of the first church. In 1830 the Hunt brothers purchased land near Kilbride.

The village was laid out by Francis Baker and William Panton around 1850. It was named after a village in Ireland. The early settlers were McClure, Corlett, Wilson, Fraser, Agnew, Labourne, Duncan,

Pickett, Clugson, Hewson, Small, Turnbull, Nixon, Harris and Dixon. Lumber was their main source of income. The village had a tin shop, a cooper shop and a drug store owned by Dr. Beattie. A large woollen mill was owned and operated by William Montgomery.

Kilbride Presbyterian Church was founded in 1846 and the Kilbride Methodists built their church in 1850 on land donated by Mr. and Mrs. George Harbottle.

School was held at first in the frame home of John Harris who was the local magistrate. A two-storey stone school was constructed in 1879. The first teacher was W.R. Watson.

In 1958 the village was annexed to the Town of Burlington.

Claire Emery and Barbara Ford: *From Pathway to Skyway*, 1967

KILDARE, geographic township, Algoma District
Position 48° 30′ 83° 31′

A large portion of Kildare is located in the northern part of Missinaibi Lake Provincial Park. The northern tip of Missinaibi Lake occupies the southeastern section of the township. There are no roads in the area. It appears to have been named after the Irish County of Kildare.

KILKENNY, geographic township, Thunder Bay District
Position 49° 27′ 88° 05′

Named after Ontario Land Surveyor, J.M. Kilkenny of Toronto, this township is situated on the southeastern shore of Lake Nipigon. In the northwestern corner of the township is the Blacksand Provincial Park.

The Canadian National Railways pass through the area with a station point at Macdiarmid.

Highway 11 serves the township.

KILLALA, geographic township, Kenora District, P.P.
Position 50° 59′ 94° 06′

Located a few miles southwest of the Red Lake gold mining district, this township was named in 1937 after the town of the same name in Ireland. The township is not accessible by road. The western portion of Red Lake occupies the extreme northern section of the township. There are several other large lakes within Killala.

KILLALOE STATION, village, Hagarty Township, Renfrew County
Position 45° 32′ 77° 25′

Situated on the Canadian National Railways, about 25 miles southwest of Pembroke, Killaloe Station is best known for its weather station, one mile to the east on Highway 60. There is also an emergency airfield here.

The village had its beginnings about 1850 when James Bonfield bought some property on the Brennan River and named the site Killaloe after his home in County Clare, Ireland. William McDonell who arrived in 1857 to work for his uncle in a lumber business was the first to build a house in the vicinity. In 1868 he erected the first water-powered sawmill in the area, about a mile away from Killaloe. He also constructed a boardinghouse for the workers in the mill.

The community that had developed around the mill was known for many years as Fort McDonell because a large rock formation on the east side of the Brennan River gave it the appearance of a fortified town. When the railway came in the 1890's, the hamlet officially became known as Killaloe Station.

An economic boom followed the construction of the Ottawa, Arnprior and Parry Sound Railway in 1893. William McDonell had offered free access to the railway line if it was built over his land and so had brought the railway to Killaloe. The first trains ran through Killaloe in 1893 with supplies for the lumber camps in the area, but the railway was not officially opened until 1896. In the years to follow, thousands of lumbermen disembarked at Killaloe Station on their way to the camps of the McLachlin Lumber Company, the Golden Lake, the J.R. Booth, and the Pembroke lumbering companies. Hotels did a roaring business as did the livery service of William George. Killaloe was a supply depot, providing services and provisions for the large lumber camps on the Bonnechère and Petawawa Rivers.

During the 1890's McDonell sold off much of his property as village lots. Most of the residents at that time were Scottish immigrants, among them were the McMullens, McLeods, McDonalds, Camerons and Stewarts.

A slump came in 1906 when the McLachlin Company closed its operations, but by 1909 the Golden Lake Lumber Company, which had taken the place of McLachlin, had expanded and the community was enjoying a renewed boom. In 1908 Killaloe Station annexed 500 acres from Hagarty Township and was incorporated as a village.

The early Scottish settlers had been followed by a wave of Irish immigrants, after the official opening of the railway in 1896. C.W. Boland who arrived that year built the Beresford House. He was soon followed by many of his fellow Irishmen. The Dennie brothers opened the first sash-and-door factory; Michael Holly became the first postmaster; William Stack established the first liquor store; and Ned Fitzgerald served as the village's first policeman. Today residents of Irish descent make up about one-third of the population.

The Irish settlement was followed by a period of English immigration. These new residents included James Paul, the first machinery agent, Howard Bickles, the first jeweller, and E.A. Bates, the first resident lawyer.

About 1904 a group of settlers began to arrive from Germany. William Hoch built a creamery, C.T. Eckel took over the sash-and-door factory, and others, including Fred Zummach, the Lisks, and Matt Yourth, engaged in the building trade. Polish immigration began about 1908 and there came, among them, the Palubeskie brothers, Anthony Cybulski and P.B. Mask. Between 1894 and 1904 French-Canadian lumbermen were a familiar sight at Killaloe as they stopped on their way to the lumber camps in the area.

Killaloe Station suffered a disastrous fire in the early twentieth century, and just as the community had begun to recover, the lumbering industry, on which the village largely depended, declined and about 1914 many of Killaloe's residents left to seek work elsewhere. Today the population of the village numbers 716 (1979).

Martin Garvey: *The History of Killaloe Station*
Mrs. Carl Price and Clyde C. Kennedy: *Notes on the History of Renfrew County*, 1961

KILLARNEY, geographic township, Manitoulin District
Position 46° 03′ 81° 28′

Formerly known as Timber Berth No. 10, the township was named in 1945 after the village of Killarney in neighbouring Rutherford Township, which in turn took its name from Killarney Lake in Ireland.

The township, traversed by Highway 637, lies entirely within the boundaries of Killarney Provincial Park.

KILLARNEY, community, Rutherford Township, Manitoulin District
Position 45° 58′ 81° 31′

The community of Killarney is situated on the tip of a peninsula on the northern shore of Georgian Bay, opposite George Island. Originally, the site was called Shebanoning, the Indian name for canoe passage. Early explorers, among them La Salle and Etienne Brûlé, passed through the narrow Killarney Channel between the mainland and

George Island. An Indian trading post was located here in 1820.

A post office was opened in the settlement in 1854, and the place probably received its name at that time; but local belief is that the name was bestowed on the village after a visit in 1882 by Lord and Lady Dufferin. Lady Dufferin was said to have remarked that the rugged beauty of the area reminded her of Killarney, Ireland.

The village lies just south of Killarney Provincial Park, a major tourist attraction.

Killarney
Ministry of Industry & Tourism, Toronto

KILLARNEY PROVINCIAL PARK, Goschen, Roosevelt & Stalin Tps., Sudbury District; & Carlyle, Killarney Tps., Manitoulin District Position 46° 05′ 81° 25′

Situated on Highway 637, 38 miles from its junction with Highway 69, this Primitive Provincial Park is in the North Georgian Bay Recreation Reserve. Killarney's 84,990 acres on the northern shores of Georgian Bay attract both campers and naturalists, the latter interested in the Precambrian geology offered by the park's location on the Canadian Shield. Of the several lakes within the park, George and Killarney Lakes are the largest. Killarney village is the largest community. The park encompasses two geological provinces: The Southern and the Grenville Provinces. To the north are the La Cloche

422

Mountains of ancient white quartzite rocks.

Ontario Ministry of Natural Resources

KILLBEAR POINT PROVINCIAL PARK, Carling Township, Parry
Sound District
Position 45° 21′ 80° 11′

This park, a 3,940 Provincial Natural Environment Park, is 22 miles
by road to the northwest of the town of Parry Sound, and about 13
miles west of Highway 69. It projects into the Parry Sound, off
Georgian Bay, and offers the visitor fine sandy beaches and picturesque rock points.

Ontario Ministry of Natural Resources

KILLINS, geographic township, Algoma District
Position 48° 14′ 85° 07′

Formerly designated as Township 32, Range 26, Killins is part of
the Algoma Central & Hudson's Bay Railway Land Grant. The
township is situated northwest of the town of Wawa, and just south
of Obatanga Provincial Park. The township was named after Alfred
E. Killins, a Canadian Army Private from the Thunder Bay District,
killed during World War Two. A secondary road links the area to
Highway 17.

KILLRAINE, geographic township, Thunder Bay District
Position 48° 51′ 87° 22′

Situated on the north shore of Lake Superior, the township was named
after Jack Killraine, a worker with the road gang that built the CPR
along this shoreline. Killraine eventually settled in northwestern
Ontario. Rainbow Falls Provincial Park is located in the eastern part
of the township. Highway 17 serves the area, and the Canadian Pacific
Railway passes through it.

KILMER, geographic township, Cochrane District
Position 50° 17′ 81° 45′

This township, north of Smooth Rock Falls, is located between the
Mattagami River and the Abitibi River.
    Named after Geo. H. Kilmer, K.C. of Toronto, the area is watered
by the winding Onakawana River, Kilmer Creek and Hogg Creek, all
flowing northward to swell the waters of the Abitibi and then the
mighty Moose River.

KILPATRICK, geographic township, Sudbury District
Position 46° 03′ 81° 01′

Located just north of the French River, the origin of this name is unknown.

The northern boundary of the township was surveyed in 1882, the western boundary in 1892, and the southern and eastern boundaries in 1929.

A secondary road links the area with Highway 69 to the east.

KILSYTH, community, Derby Township, Grey County
Position 44° 31′ 81° 01′

Situated about five miles southwest of Owen Sound, this small compact rural community was the earliest village of importance in Derby Township, being located on the well-travelled Owen Sound and Saugeen Stage Road, near the centre of the township.

Many of the early settlers came from Scotland about the middle of the nineteenth century. Among them were Robert Robertson, John Fleming, Andrew Hardie, James Fleming and Alexander Garvie. A post office was opened in 1856.

By 1865 James McCluskie and William Walmsley had established a pottery works which produced both commonly used articles and ornaments. George Smith provided accommodation for travellers in the Sloan Hotel. William Stedman offered his services as a blacksmith; Abraham Finch was the tailor. Stores were run by Thomas Sloan and William Fleming. J. McKenzie Hunt was a carriage and wagonmaker. In 1869 council decided to build the township hall in Kilsyth. The first council meeting in the new hall was held on May 23, 1870.

James Fleming operated a sawmill in the village and it was on the Fleming farm near Kilsyth that the township's first school was opened.

E.L. Marsh: *A History of the County of Grey*, 1931
W.W. Smith: *Gazetteer and Directory of the County of Grey*, 1865

KILWORTH, community, Delaware Township, Middlesex County
Position 42° 58′ 81° 23′

Situated about 6 miles west of London, Kilworth was the site of the first flour mill in the area. Built by the Oliver family on Springer's Creek (now Oxbow Creek), the mill was the nearest place for the settlers to take their wheat during the 1830's.

A post office was established at Kilworth in 1851 and a woollen mill was erected near the flour mill. "Kil-O-Mil", the house built by the Oliver family, still stands today.

Ron Nickles and Ron Davis: *Lobo Township Sketches*, 1976.

KIMBERLEY, geographic township, Timiskaming District
Position 47° 54′ 80° 35′

The township, named after the Earl of Kimberley, became part of the Improvement District of Matachewan as of January 1, 1976.

The mining community of Matachewan lies immediately to the northwest of the township. From here the Montreal River, having joined with the waters of Matachewan Lake, flows in a southeasterly course through the township. Highway 65 follows the river's course in this area.

KIMBERLEY, police village, Euphrasia Township, Grey County
Position 44° 23′ 80° 32′

The village of Kimberley nestles in the picturesque "Cuckoo Valley" of the Beaver River, less than 20 miles south of the town of Meaford.

Many of the early settlers came to Kimberley by the Nottawasaga route which led from the mouth of the Nottawasaga River along the shore of Nottawasaga Bay. They would then cross into Euphrasia Township by trails, or travel up the Beaver River by canoe.

James McGee, Thos. Wickens and Genial Hurd were probably the earliest settlers in the Kimberley district.

In the early 1860's a Mr. Purdy and a Mr. Walling built the first flour mills in the township at Kimberley. Prior to that time area farmers had to take their grain to Meaford. Mr. Purdy was also responsible for opening the township's first store at Kimberley.

E.L. Marsh: *A History of the County of Grey*, 1931

KINBURN, community, West Carleton, Ottawa-Carleton Regional Municipality
Position 45° 23′ 76° 11′

Kinburn, west of Arnprior, is situated in one of the best farming areas in Carleton County. In 1830 Christopher Armstrong built a stage-stop here known as the "Swamp Tavern". The settlement which grew up around it was located on the old stagecoach route from Arnprior to Ottawa.

Some of Kinburn's early settlers were: the Grants, the Frasers, and William Croskey, Wm. Anderson, John Donaldson, and George and Joseph Smith. George Aitkin was the blacksmith; John Fraser, a lumber merchant; George Howard, a carpenter; Robert Johnston, a general merchant; W. Stein, a flour and grist mill proprietor; John Timber was a school teacher; and Mr. Vance was a carriage maker.

A post office was established in 1855 with James Mills as the postmaster. Kinburn was named after a fortress in Turkey, prominent in the Crimean War.

During the Fenian raids of 1866, the Kinburn drill hall was erected and the Kinburn Company of the "Carleton Blazers" drilled under Capt. Fraser. Later it was used as a drill hall during the Riel Rebellion.

Kinburn is the site of the Fitzroy Municipal Hall and a Consolidated School.

Fred Sadler: *Fitzroy Township*, 1967

425

KINCAID, geographic township, Algoma District
Position 47° 06' 84° 40'

Formerly part of the Algoma Central and Hudson's Bay Railway Land Grant, Kincaid is situated on Mica Bay of Lake Superior. Highway 17 passes through the township along the scenic shoreline.

The township may have been named after Robert Kincaid, MPP, for Peterborough West in 1882, or as stated in the Lands and Forest Department's Records of 1905, after a partner in the firm of Steward & Kincaid of Dublin.

KINCARDINE, township, Bruce County
Position 44° 11' 81° 30'

The Township of Kincardine lies on the western shore of Lake Huron. The Bluewater Highway (21) runs along the shore through the township, which was named after the Earl of Elgin and Kincardine, Governor-General of Canada at the time Bruce County was surveyed.

Kincardine Township was surveyed in three stages: Alexander Wilkinson surveyed the Lake Range in 1847; A.P. Brough laid out the Durham Road and three concessions north and south of it in 1848-49; the remainder of the township was surveyed by J.W. Bridgland in 1850.

The first settlers in the township, and probably the first in Bruce County, were Allan Cameron and William Withers. They came in the spring of 1848 and settled at the mouth of the Penetangore River at the site of the present town of Kincardine. Other settlers who arrived in the township later that year included Donald, Alexander and John McCaskill, James and Alexander Munroe, John C. Digman and William Daniel.

A large number of predominantly Scottish settlers came into Kincardine during 1849, squatting on lands along the lake shore and taking up "free grant" lots. The first to settle in the centre of the township was Harvey Wilson who squatted on lot 17, concession 7. Lands were offered for sale in 1851, and the first sale was made to Sam Splan on August 19th of that year.

In the pioneer days Kincardine was the senior township of Bruce County. During 1852 and 1853, the municipality was known as "The United Townships of Kincardine and the Remaining Townships in the County of Bruce". William Rastall presided as reeve over the Council Board in 1852.

On January 1, 1854, the union of the townships was dissolved, and only Bruce and Kinloss remained united with Kincardine. Kinloss separated from this union a year later, and on January 1, 1856, Bruce and Kincardine separated. From then on Kincardine remained a separate municipality. David McKendrick was reeve in 1856.

The first schools and churches, stores and mills in the township were established in the settlement of Penetangore, which later became the town of Kincardine. The public school, opened there in 1851, was the first school in the county. The first post office was established at Kincardine in 1851, with David McKendrick as postmaster. John Riach and Willam Rastall each opened a store at Kincardine as early as 1849.

The first religious service in the county is said to have been held by an Episcopal Methodist preacher at the log house of Anthony Copp, one of the early settlers in Kincardine.

Communities in Kincardine Township include Bervie, a post village dating back to 1853; Armow once known as Reekie's Mills, in the centre of the township, site of the town hall; Millarton on Highway 9; and Kingarf on the Kincardine-Greenock line.

The township lost some of its territory on January 1, 1858, when Kincardine was incorporated as a village. Tiverton in the northwest corner and partly in Bruce Township has been an incorporated village since 1879.

Much of Kincardine Township is suited for farming. Along the lake shore cottagers and tourists contribute to the township's economy.

Norman McLeod: *The History of the County of Bruce 1907-1968.* 1969
Norman Robertson: *The History of Bruce County,* 1906

KINCARDINE, town, Kincardine Township, Bruce County
Position 44° 11′ 81° 38′

Kincardine, located at the mouth of the Penetangore River on Lake Huron at the western terminus of the Durham Road, was the pioneer settlement of Bruce County. Today the town is situated at the junction of Highways 9 and 21, the "Bluewater Highway" along the shore of Lake Huron. Originally known as Penetangore, its name was changed by an Order-in-Council at Ottawa in 1875 at a time when the settlement showed promise of becoming a considerable port. It was named after James Bruce, Earl of Elgin and Kincardine, Governor-General of Canada, 1847-1854.

The first settlers at Kincardine, Allan Cameron and William Withers, were landed at the mouth of the Penetangore River in the spring of 1848 from a schooner owned and sailed by Captain A. Murray MacGregor. They built a log house near where they landed in which Mr. Cameron kept a hotel, and later John Keyworth kept a store.

Mr. Withers, foreseeing the settlers' need for lumber, built a milldam and sawmill which was in operation by 1849.

During the summer of 1848 the small settlement at Kincardine was increased by the arrival of some dozen other settlers who took up land either in the town plot, on the free grants, or on the lake shore to the north of the town. Among these were Donald Alexander and John McCaskill, James and Alexander Munroe, Anthony Copp, Alex. McKay, George McLeod, Wm. Dowell and Patrick Downie.

In 1849 two stores were opened at Kincardine, one by John Riach, the other by William Rastall. The influx of settlers into Bruce County in the early fifties was steady and continuous. Many of these regarded Kincardine as the base from which supplies could be obtained. Storekeepers became increasingly plentiful and in 1851 a post office was opened, manned by storekeeper David MacKendrick.

William Sutton established a grist mill in 1851 to meet the needs of the settlers who had raised their first harvests of grain. However, operation was delayed when the mill stones which had been landed on the beach were washed under the sands and disappeared before they could be removed. Another set was ordered and the mill, the first in the county, began operating in 1852. Settlers came from far away and often, and while waiting for their wheat to be ground, they would heat one of the large boulders near the mill and bake an unleavened cake from their newly ground flour.

During the winters of 1853-54 Malcolm MacPherson came to Kincardine and made arrangements to build both a grist and a sawmill. William Macklem who had settled in the winter of 1849-50 built an oatmeal mill about that time, thus the milling needs of the community were met completely.

James Henry was appointed the first pathmaster in the village in 1851, but it was not until the summer of 1856 that the leading streets and the Market Square were cleared.

Among the first industries in town, other than saw or grist mills, was a furniture factory. George A. Dezeng started it in 1856. Several years earlier George Browne had built a brewery.

The first school was opened in 1851 with Mrs. Jane Nairn presiding over 66 students. The first public religious service was held by the Reverend Mr. Cox of the Episcopal Methodist Church in 1849.

In October, 1857, a census revealed 837 names, a number more than sufficient to allow the village to become a separate municipality. This was made official on January 1, 1858. The first reeve was William Rastall.

Work began as early as 1855 in the effort to establish a harbour at Kincardine. It was not fully completed until 1877. Possessing a harbour, before the advent of the railway, Kincardine developed into a busy grain market. The village was greatly interested in the various railway schemes that agitated the entire county in the 1860's. However, it was not until the 1870's that the Wellington, Grey and Bruce Railway, a line running from Guelph to Palmerston and Southampton, built an extension from Palmerston northward to Kincardine. Leased to the Great Western in 1875, the line was absorbed by the Grand Trunk and eventually by the CNR, which today serves the town.

Large deposits of salt were discovered in 1868 and the Kincardine Salt Prospecting and Manufacturing Company was formed. In order to separate the salt from the water, wood was needed to keep the fires under the brine going, but this was very costly. Thus the company and its rival, the Bruce Salt Company, were forced to close down after a few years.

Kincardine's fishing industry was launched in the late 1850's. It met its demise when eels began to wipe out the trout in Lake Huron.

Kincardine was incorporated as a town in 1875. With a population of 5,481 (1979), it has developed strong industries and good stores catering to the fine agricultural land surrounding it as well as the many tourists who enjoy the natural beauty of the vicinity.

Norman Robertson: The History of the County of Bruce, 1906
Norman McLeod: The History of the County of Bruce 1907-1968, 1969

KINERAS, geographic township, Cochrane District
Position 50° 02′ 81° 23′

Situated some fifty miles northeast of the town of Smooth Rock Falls, the origin of the township's name is unknown.

The southern, eastern and western boundaries of the township were surveyed in 1923. The Little Abitibi River, interspersed with numerous rapids, cascades northward through the area.

KING, township, Regional Municipality of York
Position 43° 58′ 79° 35′

Situated in the northwest corner of the geographic county of York, the township of King is bordered on the north by the Holland River, on the west by the County of Peel, on the south by the Township of Vaughan, and on the east by Yonge Street. It was probably named after John King, British Undersecretary of State in the Portland administration in the late seventeen and early eighteen hundreds.

The area was first surveyed in 1800 by Mr. Stegman, although patents had been granted as early as 1797. An attempt in 1799 to settle French emigrés in the area under French Royalist leader Comte de Puisaye was unsuccessful. The first permanent settlers, a group of Quakers from the United States led by Timothy Rogers, arrived in 1800 and founded the settlement of Armitage.

The Quaker community thrived and a school was organized in 1806 with Timothy Rogers as teacher. In 1810 a meetinghouse was built which still exists. It was from this meetinghouse that David Willson withdrew to found the "Children of Peace" and build a Temple at Sharon.

By 1809, the first year for which municipal records exist, the population of the township was 160. The War of 1812 temporarily halted growth. Furthermore the township was not near the main navigable waterways and the great amount of land set aside for clergy reserves discouraged settlers. However, with the improvement of Yonge Street in the 1820's and the establishment of the Yonge stage in 1825, the influx of settlers increased rapidly. In 1823 the population was 394, but by 1842 it had risen to 2,625 and had more than doubled by 1850. Most of the new settlers were of British descent. The largest number of inhabitants was reached in 1871 when the census recorded 7,482 people living in the township. After this, in common with most other rural townships, the population began to decline until after the Second World War, when Toronto's suburbs began to expand. Today the township has a population of 14,851 (1979).

Forests provided employment in the first years of settlement. By 1851 there were twenty-one sawmills in operation. Deforestation over the years has resulted in the erosion of much of the township's land and floods have taken their toll.

A number of small villages grew up in the township during the 1800's. In 1831 the township's first post office was established at Lloydtown with Joseph Watson as postmaster. The community played an important role in the 1837 Rebellion. The second public meeting in support of William Lyon Mackenzie was held here to organize the local Reformers and advocate Canadian Independence. Many local men joined the rebels. Jesse Lloyd, after whom the village was named, was forced into exile in the United States, where he died. Lloydtown has since declined and is now only a small hamlet.

Gaining importance, Brownsville (now Schomberg) received a post office in 1862. The coming of the railway in 1853 resulted in the rapid growth of Aurora. Situated on Yonge Street, it was founded in 1804 as Machell's Corners and was incorporated as a village in 1863. The village of King also benefited from the railway, although its development never matched that of Aurora. Today King is widely known for Kingcrafts, a craft centre with a worldwide membership. Laskay post office was established in 1884 and Strange post office in 1880.

The first record of a township meeting is that of 1809. William Haines was town clerk and held that position until 1836. In 1850 when Ontario's municipalities were organized, George Hughes became the first reeve. The following year a portion of land from West Gwillimbury was annexed to King, becoming known as North King Township.

The first school was set up by the Quakers in 1806 but with the wave of immigration beginning in the late 1820's, many more were established. By 1843 there were school commissioners to deal with the school administration of the township.

The Quaker meetinghouse was the first house of worship in the township. A Wesleyan Methodist Church was erected in 1844 and two years later the Anglican Street Mary Magdalene parish church was opened for service in Lloydtown under Canon Henry Osler. Eversley Presbyterian Church was established in 1848.

Sir William Mulock, a Liberal politician and Postmaster-General of Canada who became famous for his introduction of the "Penny-Postage" throughout the British Empire in 1898, lived near Armitage. He went on to become Minister of Labour, Chief Justice of Ontario, and Chancellor of the University of Toronto. Sir Henry Pellatt (1859-1939), the builder of Casa Loma in Toronto spent much of his time on his farm in the township near King City.

The area remained largely rural well into the twentieth century. Since 1960, however, the character of the township has been changing as more and more commuters to nearby Toronto are settling in King.

Mary E. Garbutt: "King Township, York County 1800-1867 A Historical Sketch" in *Ontario Historical Society*, 1960
Elizabeth McClure Gillham: *Early Settlements of King Township Ontario*, 1975
Miles & Co.: *Historical Atlas of York County*, 1878

KING CITY, suburban community, King Township, Regional Municipality of York
Position 43° 56′ 79° 32′

Situated southwest of Aurora on the CNR, the village was originally known as Springhill before changing its name to King and finally to King City. The name Springhill probably derived from the many springs in the area.

Patents were granted as early as 1797 to Edward Wright and others, but settlement did not take place until 1836 when a lot was sold to Nathaniel Pearson Crossley. When the railway was built in 1853, Isaac Dennis, owner of a hotel, gave the land for a station, south of the crossroads. The community which grew up here merged with Springhill to form King.

Isaac McBride, who eventually bought the original Dennis hotel, was a grain buyer and provided a valuable service for the local farmers who had earlier been forced to take their produce to Aurora. In 1876 James Stokes became the local agent for machinery and agricultural implements, as well as an auctioneer. Thomas Folliott established a furniture store in 1879. The Crawford Wells Store, in recent times restored as an example of a country store, was built by Benjamin Lloyd in 1863. Stone's Bakery, Charles Hall's harness shop, and Victor Hall's shoe store were all opened around the turn of the century as the village continued to grow. By 1905 the population of King was 200.

In 1890 James Whiting Crossley was elected reeve of King

Township. He asked that 1000 acres be set aside for the incorporated village of King City. In 1898 a survey was made and the streets named. The community became a Police Village in 1934 and a municipality in 1962.

In 1893 J.W. Crossley had organized a Mechanics' Institute Library which was replaced by the Women's Institute book club in 1945. The King Memorial Library opened in 1947.

All Saints Anglican Church appears to have been the first religious building. Dr. Bevan preached the first sermon here in 1857. In 1858, the congregations of Eversley, Strange, and King City amalgamated to form a new Presbyterian church. The earliest records of the Methodist Episcopal congregation date to 1865. George Garrow donated land for a church in 1871, the same year that the Disciple Church was founded. Bethel Baptist Church first opened in 1889.

Since 1947, when a waterworks was built, the population of the village has continued to increase. The Kingcrafts building, a crafthouse with a worldwide membership, attracts many visitors, as does the beautiful Lake Marie estate which once belonged to Sir Henry Pellatt, the builder of Casa Loma in Toronto and a generous benefactor to the village of King City.

Mary E. Garbutt, "King Township, York County, 1800-1867: A Historical Sketch" in *Ontario Historical Society*, 1960.
Elizabeth McClure Gillham, *Early Settlements of King Township Ontario*, 1975

KING CREEK, community, King Township, Regional Municipality of York
Position 43° 54′ 79° 37′

King Creek was once a thriving settlement. Today it is a dispersed rural community about 8 miles west of Richmond Hill, at the entrance to the Humber Trails Conservation Area.

In 1834 Christopher Stokes, a miller from England, recognized the excellent power potential of the east branch of the Humber River and purchased property on Lot 4, Concession 7 in King Township. In 1838 he built a grist mill on his land. Previous to this, Alex McMillan had kept a store on Lot 6 but when Stokes erected his mill McMillan relocated his store nearby and a community grew up around the mill. Known at first as Stoke's Hollow, it became an important centre in the township. Early residents included Archibald Campbell and Dugald McMurchy.

In 1854 Stokes expanded his business and erected a flour mill, hotel and shoe shop. A post office was opened in McMillan's store in 1866 with Alex McMillan as the first postmaster. It remained open until the advent of rural mail delivery in 1913. Robert Simpson, shoemaker, and Jesse Nunn, merchant, were among the community's businessmen in the late nineteenth century.

At one time there were three sawmills near King Creek, one of which boasted the first circular saw in King Township. However, the introduction of steam and electric power rendered the old water-powered mills obsolete and gradually the importance of both the mills and the community declined.

Elizabeth McClure Gillham: *Early Settlements of King Township, Ontario* 1975

KINGHORN, community, King Township, Regional Municipality of York
Position 43° 55′ 79° 34′

The original site of Kinghorn can be found in the present-day inter-section of Jane Street and the King Sideroad. Located in the southern part of King Township, it was a prosperous community in the late nineteenth century. However, it depended almost entirely on the local tanning industry and when the tannery was destroyed by fire the settlement began to decline.

The first settlers were James and Mary Burns who set up a sawmill on their arrival in 1842. In 1847 Elihu Pease bought land on which his son, Edward, built a combined tannery and house. Andrew Davis purchased the tannery in 1856 and his son joined him in the business in 1872. In 1884 a fire destroyed the tannery resulting in heavy losses for the owners. The tannery was rebuilt and production doubled. By 1903 forty-five to fifty men were employed, and markets had greatly increased. However, that year a second disastrous fire again destroyed the tannery. The firm relocated in Newmarket, marking the end of Kinghorn's main industry.

Today the settlement consists mainly of a few spacious homes, including the 1849 Methodist Episcopal Church which became a house in 1890.

Elizabeth McClure Gillham: *Early Settlements of King Township Ontario,* 1975

KING KIRKLAND, community, Lebel Township, Timiskaming District
Position 48° 10′ 79° 57′

Situated 4 miles east of Kirland Lake on Highway 66 and the Ontario Northern Railway, this compact rural community was founded in 1932 by people who wanted to move out of the overcrowded town of Kirkland Lake. At the time most of the people were employed in the Murphy and Morris-Kirkland mines. These mines closed in the 1950's but residents of King Kirkland found employment in the Upper Canada mine and other mines near Kirkland Lake.

In 1971 the population of King Kirkland was 406. The community has one elementary school. High school education and most other services are found in nearby Kirland Lake.

Ministry of Natural Resources: *Directory of Statistics and Data,* 1975.

KINGSFORD, geographic township, Rainy River District
Position 48° 47′ 93° 47′

Located northwest of the town of Fort Frances, and a few miles north of the United States border state of Minnesota, this township was surveyed in 1898, and named after historian William Kingsford.

Secondary roads link the area with Highway 613 to the east and Highway 615 to the west.

KINGSFORD, improvement district, Rainy River District
Position 48° 47′ 94° 00′

Kingsford was named after the historian, William Kingsford. It was surveyed in 1896 and subdivided. In 1944 it was incorporated as an Improvement District. Most of the area's residents are employed in agriculture or in the lumber industry.

There is an elementary school located in Kingsford with secondary schools available in Rainy River and Fort Frances. The hospital, recreational facilities and a library are located in nearby Emo. There are bus connections daily to Kingsford from Rainy River and Fort Frances.

Ministry of Natural Resources: *Directory of Statistics and Data,* 1979

KINGSMILL, geographic township, Cochrane District
Position 48° 56′ 81° 40′

Situated southwest of the town of Cochrane, the township was subdivided in 1908 by T.H. Dunn.

The East Muskego River and the Caribou River water the area. The township was named after Colonel Kingsmill, onetime Sheriff of the Niagara District.

KINGSTON, township, Frontenac County
Position 44° 18′ 76° 34′

Kingston Township is the oldest settled township in Ontario. Here, on October 27, 1783, John Collins, Deputy Surveyor General, planted the first survey post in the province under civil authority in preparation for settlement by United Empire Loyalists. The site, marked by a plaque, is now the City Park of Kingston. The first township to be laid out was called King's Township; it was the forerunner of King's Town, now the City of Kingston, and Kingston Township. In recent years numerous new housing developments and a rapidly expanding population have made the township more urban than rural.

In the summer of 1673 Count Frontenac, the Governor of New France, arrived here at the mouth of the Cataraqui River and built a fort to tap the fur trade of the region. For many years Fort Frontenac (or Cataraqui) remained a French outpost against the Iroquois and the English. It was abandoned in 1689, but rebuilt in 1696. On August 17, 1758, the fort was captured and destroyed by the British under Colonel Bradstreet.

Permanent settlement in the area began in 1783 when Captain Michael Grass, coming by way of the St. Lawrence, led a group of United Empire Loyalists to Cataraqui. Following the War of 1812 many disbanded soldiers took up land in the township. By 1817 the population of the township was about 600. British immigrants began to arrive in increasing numbers and by 1850 the population had reached 4,253.

There were two grist mills, twelve sawmills, four tanneries, two carding and fulling mills, and a shipyard. Portsmouth (now part of the City of Kingston) was once a busy shipbuilding centre. It suffered a setback when the government withdrew from Kingston, which had served briefly as the capital of Canada in the 1840's. By the late 1870's Portsmouth had recovered much of its prosperity and besides its shipyards had a tannery and a brewery. Named after the Deputy Surveyor General, Collinsby (now Collins Bay) had a large harbour and relied on rafting and shipping of timber. Kingston Mills was the site of the first grist mill in Ontario. The construction of the Rideau Canal in the early 1830's made Kingston Mills the terminus of the main route to Ottawa. The Grand Trunk Railway built its line from Montreal to Toronto through the township in the 1850's. Other centres benefitted from their lakefront harbours.

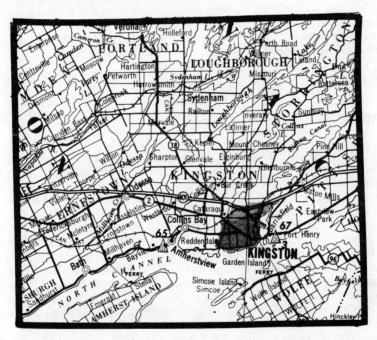

Since 1945 the township has been subject to increasing urbanization. From the early 1960's the encouragement of industry has been a priority. Municipal government's plans called for expanded water services, a sewage treatment plant, the development of light industry, and improved roads. Major industries to locate in Kingston Township immediately after World War Two were Dupont and Alcan. Dupont is still the major industry in the township, but the land on which Alcan stands is now part of the City of Kingston. A number of industrial parks have been proposed and developed. In 1963 ninety acres between Highways 2 and 33 were set aside for industry. In 1978 Cataraqui Industrial Estates was opened near Highway 2. Plans for major shopping centres and the development of 900 acres by Highway 2 as a "downtown core" have also been proposed. In 1972, 110 acres of parkland were set aside for a parks development program. Residential developments, included such as Henderson Place and LaSalle Park. In 1968, 13,760 people lived in the area. The population in 1979 stood at 26,241. About 70% of the population live south of Highway 2 in an almost completely urban area.

The township has also been active in providing opportunities for sports and recreation. Marinas, golf courses, a riding stable, and camping sites are all found in the area. A Community Centre was built despite considerable controversy over its financing. A rollerskating rink and indoor tennis courts are some of the amenities enjoyed by township residents.

Kingston Township, as befits the oldest township in the province, has a number of historic sites, including Cataraqui Village. At Kingston Mills the old blockhouse built to defend the Rideau Canal has recently been restored. Cataraqui Cemetery is the burial place of Sir John A. Macdonald, Canada's first prime minister.

C.W. Cooper: Frontenac, Lennox and Addington, Prize Essay, 1856
Frontenac County Directory, 1865
Kingston Whig-Standard, 1963, 1972, 1977, 1978, 1979

KINGSTON, city, Frontenac County
Position 44° 14' 76° 30'

The historic city of Kingston celebrated its tercentenary in 1973. Originally known as Cataraqui, an Indian word meaning "rocks standing in water", the community was named King's Town, after George III, by United Empire Loyalists who settled here in the 1780's. The name soon became shortened to Kingston.

Situated on Highways 2 and 401, and on the CNR, the city now has a population of nearly 61,000 and is the seat of Frontenac County. It is located on the shore of Lake Ontario at the point where the St. Lawrence River leaves the lake. The historic Rideau Canal, constructed in the 1820's as a military route to Bytown (Ottawa), begins here.

The shore of Lake Ontario was explored by Sieur de la Salle who, in 1671, recommended the building of a fort and fur-trading post at the site of present-day Kingston. On July 12th, 1673 Count Frontenac, Governor of New France, arrived with a flotilla at Cataraqui and the following day met the local Indian chiefs in council to assure them of his peaceful intentions. He then constructed Fort Frontenac and appointed La Salle as its commandant.

In 1674 La Salle was granted the fort and the surrounding lands as a Seigneury. He built a more solid structure to replace the older building and a settlement of 50 French artisans and labourers grew up beside the walls of the fort. A chapel was built for the settlers and a fleet of small ships for the fur traders, the beginning of the area's shipbuilding industry.

While La Salle was away on one of his expeditions, the fort was taken over by Governor de La Barre, Frontenac's successor. The next Governor, the Marquis de Denonville, imprisoned two Indian chiefs and in reprisal the Indians at Cataraqui burned the settlers' homes and crops and besieged the fort for two months. Denonville ordered the destruction of the buildings in 1689 and removed the garrison to Montreal. Later when Count Frontenac again became Governor, the fort at Cataraqui was restored and strengthened and became an important trading post for the French. In 1756 it was used as a base by French commander-in-chief Montcalm to attack the British in the Seven Years War, fought for the control of Canada.

Sixteen hundred British prisoners were brought to the fort after the French victory of Oswego, including Captain Michael Grass, later to become one of the founders of Kingston. In 1758 the fort was captured by the British under Colonel John Bradstreet. The walls were destroyed, the garrison withdrew to Montreal, and French rule of Cataraqui had come to an end.

For twenty-five years the area was nearly deserted. A fort was built on nearby Carleton Island and it was here that many United Empire Loyalists found refuge during the American Revolution. When Carleton Island became part of the United States by the Treaty of Paris, many Loyalists moved to Cataraqui where a post had been established by Major John Ross in 1783. Ross restored the old fort and became the first commandant of the Imperial Garrison. The fort was renamed Tête-de-Pont Barracks, a name which continued in use until the 1930's. In 1783 surveyor John Collins laid out the original town plot of Kingston. In preparation for the settlement of Loyalists, Captain Crawford negotiated with the Mississauga Indians for the purchase of the land along the lakeshore westward from Cataraqui, promising them yearly payments of clothing, blankets, guns, and household articles in return.

In June 1784 Captain Michael Grass arrived with the first group of Loyalists. Housed at first in the fort in temporary shelters, by October, 220 had moved into King's Town. Most of these early settlers were artisans and traders, rather than farmers. By the early 1790's, the community had 50 houses and stores, including the government store at the lower end of Store Street (now Princess Street).

In 1789 the government established a naval dockyard on Point Frederick (now the site of the Royal Military College). This settlement of marines and shipyard workers was connected by ferry to Kingston and stimulated the growing commerce of the community. Because of its position at the mouth of the St. Lawrence, where goods were changed from river to lake boats, Kingston became the most important trading centre between Montreal and the Lakehead area. In the early nineteenth century Kingston merchants owned the largest fleet on Lake Ontario. By 1800 the community was also a regular customs port for American goods.

In 1792 Kingston became the seat of government of Upper Canada. The first Executive Council met here on July 17 under

Lieutenant-Governor John Graves Simcoe. A prominent Kingston citizen, Richard Cartwright, was appointed to the Legislative Council. However, Simcoe did not feel Kingston was a suitable capital and soon after the government moved to Newark, and later to York (Toronto).

This action did not seriously affect the community which, with its trade and export industry, remained the main commercial town in the area. In 1801 there were about 500 inhabitants. A post office was opened and a market established. As one of the few places in Upper Canada where marriage licenses were issued, Kingston became somewhat of a "honeymoon resort". It also became the seat of the Court of Quarter Sessions, with Richard Cartwright as Justice.

The area saw action during the War of 1812. Five wooden blockhouses were built around the town and the first Fort Henry was constructed. From here expeditions against the Americans were led by Sir James Yeo, Commander of the British Naval Forces. Warships were built, including the frigate *St. Lawrence* whose crew of 640 outnumbered the crews of the entire American fleet. Kingston itself was never attacked but the troops and sailors brought prosperity to the town and the population increased to 2,250.

The town continued to grow despite a cholera plague in 1832 which killed ten percent of the population. Kingston became the largest shipbuilding centre in Upper Canada and a new merchant marine replaced the old warships which rotted in Navy Bay. In 1816 the *SS Frontenac* was the first steamship to ply the Great Lakes. Passenger ships and freighters were arriving at the port of Kingston and warehouses were built on the docks to store the merchandise. A wooden bridge constructed across the Cataraqui in 1829 provided easier travel from Point Frederick. In the 1820's the Tête-de-Pont Barracks were enlarged, increasing the business for the town's merchants. The completion of the Rideau Canal in 1832 opened up the hinterland and resulted in the growth of the timber trade. Fort Henry became the most important stronghold west of Quebec, and in 1832 a new fort, named after Henry Hamilton, the Lieutenant-Governor of Quebec, was built to protect Kingston Harbour and the entrance to the canal. The garrison of the fort provided an additional market for Kingston merchants.

Leading citizens of the town were among the first to agitate for responsible government. As early as the 1790's, Richard Cartwright had put forward a plan to make Kingston the first incorporated town in the province, but this status was not achieved until 1838. The first mayor was Thomas Kirkpatrick and the first council included Thomas Smith, James Fraser, Edward Noble and Thomas Greer.

In 1841 Kingston became the capital of United Canada, the title of newly united Upper and Lower Canada. However, Charles Dickens, who visited the area in the 1840's was not much impressed with the town at that particular time. This was possibly due to the appearance of Kingston, whose ruined buildings were still standing from a disastrous fire suffered in 1840. "Alwington House", built before 1830, became the Governor's official residence and the home of three successive Governors, Lord Sydenham, Sir Charles Bagot, and Sir

Charles Metcalfe. New municipal buildings were proposed and under Mayor John Counter the beautiful City Hall designed by the prominent architect, George Browne, was erected in 1843-4. Population of the town increased rapidly and the town experienced a building boom. Many of the beautiful old homes in Kingston date back to the early 1840's. During that period Queen's University was founded.

In 1844 the government abandoned Kingston as the capital of the province in favour of Montreal. The new City Hall, built at escalating cost, was rented out to various tenants, including the post office, customs offices, Mechanics' Institute, a saloon, and a dry goods store. The large hall in the west wing was rented out for social activities. Resourceful Kingston, however, tenaciously overcame this blow and was soon enjoying prosperity once more. In 1846 it was incorporated as a city with John Counter, the town's chief magistrate for several years, becoming the city's first mayor. In 1847 Kingston became one of the first cities in Canada to have gas lights. The last of these gas lamps that once lit the city streets, today is preserved at the corner of King Street East and Lower Union Street.

The Oregon Crisis between Great Britain and the United States which arose in the 1840's caused the British government to look to Kingston's defenses. Four circular towers strategically placed across Kingston's harbour were built, each tower a self-contained stone bastion readied for attack from across the water. However, in 1846 the Oregon Treaty was signed, Britain withdrew to the 49th parallel, and today the famed Martello Towers are reminders of Kingston's past military role as the fortress of Canada West. The Murney Redoubt on Murney Point has become a museum maintained by the Kingston Historical Society. The Fort Frederick Martello Tower, standing on the grounds of the Royal Military College, is also operated as a museum.

Another threat to Kingston in 1847 was a typhus epidemic brought by recently arrived Irish immigrants. Makeshift sheds were erected on the waterfront to isolate the sick. The death toll amounted to 1400.

By the mid-nineteenth century, the population of Kingston was over 10,000. In 1856 the Grand Trunk Railway from Montreal to Toronto passed within two miles of the city, but shortly afterward a branch line was built. Another line, the Kingston-Pembroke Railway, was built in the 1870's. A new Court House was erected in 1855-6, as well as a new customs house and post office.

The threat of invasion in 1866 from the U.S. by the Fenians, Irish patriots from the United States, resulted in recruiting the 14th Battalion to patrol Kingston's streets. From 1855 to 1862 seven Volunteer Militia Rifle Companies had been formed by citizens serving without pay and supplying their own uniforms, but being granted a rifle and bayonet from the government. In 1863 the seven rifle companies united as the 14th Battalion, Volunteer Militia Rifles of Canada. Involved in the celebration of the marriage of the Prince of Wales to Princess Alexandra of Denmark, the 14th Battalion was granted permission to call itself the Princess of Wales Own Rifles.

St. James' Church, Kingston

The character of the city gradually changed in the late nineteenth century. Its importance as a trans-shipping centre decreased as railways opened up the country, although wheat remained an important product and was still shipped by water. As the pine forests were depleted, the timber trade diminished and shipbuilding also declined. With the withdrawal of the Imperial garrisons in the early 1870's, Kingston lost its importance as a military stronghold. The city now developed as an educational centre. This was a period of expansion for Queen's University, founded in 1841. Regiopolis College, established in the 1830's, was given the power to grant degrees in 1866. The Royal Military College was opened in 1876, and in 1844 the Dominion Business College, one of the first in the country, started classes. Kingston had the first grammar school in Upper Canada, opened in 1786 by Reverend John Stuart. Today's Kingston Collegiate and Vocational Institute is the descendant of this first school and can lay claim to being the oldest school in Ontario. In 1800 a private school was opened and Richard Cartwright hired as a teacher John Strachan, who later became the well-known Bishop of Toronto and head of the Anglican Church in Ontario. In 1807 the old Stuart School became the Midland District Grammar School, with John Whitelaw as teacher. In 1850 a Common School Board was appointed which opened its first school, Johnson Street Public in 1859. Sydenham Public School began in 1853. Queen's University Preparatory School which amalgamated with the grammar school in 1872 became known as one of the four best secondary schools in the province. It became a Collegiate Institute and in 1898 initiated the first technical curriculum in Ontario under Principal W.S. Ellis.

440

In 1841 a Royal Charter had been granted for the establishment of Queen's University. Classes began in a rented house in 1842, with Reverend Thomas Liddell as Principal. In 1853 the university acquired its first building, "Summerhill", which today forms the nucleus of the campus. In 1858 the Old Medical Building was erected and in 1880 the Old Arts Building. The university expanding from the late 1870's to the early 1900's under Principal George M. Grant, had ten buildings by 1902. Douglas Library, now containing one million books, was built in 1923, and a new Student Union building was erected in 1947. Queen's most spectacular growth came during the 1950's and 60's when almost 80% of the present buildings were either erected or altered. To the original two faculties of Arts and Divinity have been added Medicine (1854), Mining (1893), Law (1957), and Education (1965). The campus has spread westward to include the MacArthur Faculty of Education. Today there are about 10,000 students attending Queen's, one of Ontario's most respected universities.

Regiopolis College was forced to close because of lack of funds in 1869, only three years after it had become a university. It reopened in 1899 as a boys' high school. In the 1930's it revived its university charter and granted degrees in 1941 and 1942. Today it is the city's separate high school.

The Royal Military College opened in 1876. Lieutenant Colonel E.O. Hewett was the first Commandant. Early cadets saw service in the North West Rebellion in 1885. In 1959 it became the first military college in the Commonwealth to receive university status. In 1947 the Canadian Army Staff College was established at Fort Frontenac, followed in 1948 by the National Defence College.

The city's newest educational institute is the St. Lawrence College of Applied Arts and Technology, which also has a campus in Cornwall. Classes began in 1967.

The earliest religious building was a Roman Catholic chapel built in Fort Frontenac in the 1670's. Reverend John Stuart founded the parish of St. George in 1785 and became the father of the Anglican Church in Upper Canada. St. George's Church was erected in 1791. It was replaced by a new building in 1825 and became a Cathedral in 1862. The first stone church was the Roman Catholic Church of St. Joseph's, dedicated in 1808. It became a Cathedral in the 1820's. The present St. Mary's Cathedral dates from 1848. St. Andrew's Presbyterian Church, built in 1820, was the site of the founding of Queen's University. A Wesleyan Methodist church going back to 1852, is today Sydenham Street United. The first Baptist congregation was organized in 1840. A Jewish House of Worship was established in the nineteenth century. The Salvation Army began services in 1885, a year before its founder, General William Booth, visited Kingston. Today there are about sixty churches in the city, including two Cathedrals.

A hospital has been in operation since 1819 when the women of the Kingston Compassionate Society used the blockhouse on Murney Point (now the site of Murney Tower). In 1832 the town decided to erect a hospital building. It was built in 1835 but there was no money to equip it, so the premises were loaned to the army, then used as the Parliament Buildings when Kingston was the capital of Canada. A grant allowed the furnishing of the hospital in 1845 and in 1849 Kingston General Hospital was incorporated. In recent years KGH has expanded rapidly, building a new Medical Sciences complex along King Street. The hospital is now closely connected with the medical faculty of Queen's University.

Hotel Dieu Hospital was established in 1845 by the Religious Hospitallers of St. Joseph and was the first branch of the Montreal house founded in 1642. Mother Bourbonierre was the hospital's first Superior. The hospital cared for the orphans of the 1847 epidemic. An orphanage was established in 1910 by the Sisters of Providence at St. Mary's of the Lake.

Rockwood House, built in 1842 as a summer home for John Solomon Cartwright, was sold to the government in 1856 and became an insane asylum. This was the beginning of the Kingston Psychiatric Hospital which has recently been greatly expanded and now has facilities to deal with both psychiatric illness and mental retardation.

Kingston Penitentiary was built in the 1830's and received its first five inmates in 1835. The prison was very harshly run in the early years and accusations of cruelty caused the first warden to be replaced. Today there are five penitentiaries in the Kingston area, including a prison for women.

A library had been started in Kingston by 1813, and in 1815 Stephen Miles established a small lending library. By 1819 there was a general library at the Court House with Richard Deverne as chief librarian. A Public Library, the Mechanics' Institute, opened in 1834, the only other one at the time being in Toronto. It grew rapidly and in 1920 became a Free Library. Mrs. Aimee Kennedy, who was librarian from 1909 to 1949, played a large part in building up the excellent collection which exists today. In 1978 a new library was erected as the older building was no longer large enough to house all the books.

Civic improvements continued to be made. City Park, the first public recreation ground in Ontario, was given to the city in 1852. A disastrous fire in 1876 which burned 40 to 50 buildings on Princess Street, led to the construction of a fire hall with Patrick Devlin as Fire Chief. A new company of volunteers, the "Alerts", was formed in 1878, although there was no paid permanent force until after 1886. A street railway was introduced in 1877. In 1880 the Kingston waterworks and gas plant became public utilities. Electricity was installed in 1888. The first telephone exchange was opened in 1881.

Around the turn of the century, the city suffered a decline in the number of manufacturers, from about 400 in 1890 to about 40 in 1910. This was part of a country-wide industrial change to larger enterprises. Following the First World War there was a period of renewed prosperity until the Depression of the 1930's. Kingston was not so hard hit by the Depression as were many other centres because much of its economy was based on military and public institutions rather than on industry. The Penitentiary, hospitals, University, and military establishments provided employment for a large part of the population. Relief camps were set up at Barriefield for the jobless and in 1937 Vimy Barracks was built by these unemployed men.

Kingston again became a shipbuilding centre for a short time during World War II, when modern warships were built. A Flying School was opened, based at Norman Rogers Airport, which was named after the Kingston M.P. and Minister of Defence killed in a plane crash in 1940. At the end of the war, the two major industries of the present day were established, the Aluminum Company of Canada (Alcan) and Canadian Industries Nylon Division.

One of Upper Canada's earliest newspapers was founded in Kingston. In 1810 Stephen Miles began publishing the Kingston *Gazette,* one of the three newspapers in Upper Canada at the time and the only one to continue publication during the War of 1812. In 1818 it was sold to Messrs. Pringle and Macaulay and became the *Kingston Chronicle.* A rival paper, the *Upper Canada Herald,* was founded in 1819 by Hugh C. Thomson. In the 1820's Stephen Miles began the first religious paper in Upper Canada, the *Kingston Gazette and Religious Advocate.* More newspapers appeared on the Kingston scene during the nineteenth century, with one, *The Tourist of the Woods,* even written in Gaelic. In 1834 Dr. Edward Barker founded the *British Whig,* the ancestor of today's Kingston *Whig-Standard.* In 1849 it became the first daily paper west of Montreal. It is now Canada's oldest continuously published daily newspaper.

Walker's Hotel provided the location for entertainment in the early 1800's. About 1812 an amateur theatre group was also active in Kingston. Butler's Theatre was opened in the 1840's. Plays were performed in the "town hall" part of the municipal buildings in the 1850's. Martin's Opera House was established in 1879 and the Barrymores were among the performers who appeared there. The Grand Theatre, recently renovated, first opened in 1902. A number of small theatres have also been established in the twentieth century as amateur dramatic companies continue to flourish. They include the Domino Theatre, Theatre Five, and Queen's University Dramatic Guild.

The Kingston Philharmonic Society was founded in 1846 under Major-General Sir Richard Armstrong. Since that time music has played an important part in Kingston life. Present musical groups include the Pro Arte Singers and the Kingston Symphony. The St. George's Choir has an international reputation for excellence. Oscar Telgmann, a composer, was a native of the city.

Kingston has also made contributions to the field of literature. In 1824 the first novel by a native Canadian, *St. Ursula's Convent* by Julia Catherine Beckwith Hart, was printed here. Pindar Swift's *Poems,* probably the first book of verse in Upper Canada, was also printed in Kingston in the 1820's. Charles Sangster, a well-known Canadian poet, was born in the town in 1822. Major John Richardson, author of *Wacousta,* edited a paper here in the 1840's. In the twentieth century, Robertson Davies and Dennis T. Patrick Sears have both achieved recognition as Canadian authors.

In the nineteenth century Kingston was an important industrial centre. Local entrepreneurs were very involved in merchant shipping and built up the largest fleet on Lake Ontario. In 1836 the Marine Railway Company was formed to build large steamboats. Both the Murneys and the Gildersleeves became well-known names in shipping. Kingston's position as a trading centre encouraged other men to establish industries in the town. In 1857 Neil McNeil opened the Kingston Plumber Works. Other manufacturers included Chown and Cunningham, who made stoves, ploughs, and copper ware; Messrs. Chewitt and Company, iron work; Dillon Company, boots and shoes; the Walker and Berry nail factory; Reid's Furniture Factory (1854), and S. Anglin Co. Ltd. (1866), supplier of building materials. In 1857 James Richardson entered the grain business and built Kingston's first grain elevator in 1882. The first Kingston brewery opened in 1794 and several more went into operation in the next century. This latter industry has now disappeared from Kingston, the last brewery, the Lake Ontario Brewing Company, closing in the 1930's. By 1900 Kingston's industries included Bailey's Broom Factory, Carrington and Ford's tanneries, a cigar factory, piano factory, and a biscuit factory. Shortly after this, the number of manufacturers began to decline. The Second World War brought a new demand for industrial products and Alcan and Dupont were established in the 1940's. Recently industries such as Northern Telecom have begun to operate in the city.

J.B. Cheesman opened the first bookstore. The Bank of Kingston, the first bank in Upper Canada, was established in 1819. At about the same time, the Forsyth brothers operated as agents for the North West Company. Lawrence Herchmer's liquor store and Robert Macaulay's general store were other early businesses. By the 1850's the city had auction rooms, Thos. Glassup's savings bank, a harness shop, hardware store, jeweller, bowling alley, and photographic gallery. Businesses established in the 1800's which still exist today include Smith Bros. Jewelers Ltd. (1840), Cooke's Fine Foods (1868), and Steacy's Department Store, (1881).

Kingston has contributed its share of famous Canadian figures. Its best-known son is Sir John A. Macdonald, Canada's first Prime Minister, who opened a law practice in the town in 1835. His residence, Bellevue House, is maintained as a historic site. Sir Oliver Mowat, Premier of Ontario, 1872-96, was born here, as was Richard John Cartwright, Finance Minister, Minister of Trade and Commerce, and government leader in the Senate in 1909. The famous Mohawk chief, Joseph Brant, and his sister Mollie, lived here in the early United Empire Loyalist days. William Johnston, who burned the British steamer *John Peel* during the 1837 Rebellion, and became a pirate making raids on the Canadian frontier, was a resident of the town. Sir Richard Bonnycastle, author of several books on Canadian history, was active in strengthening Kingston's defence works in the nineteenth century.

In 1952 the city tripled its land area by annexing 5,500 acres

of Kingston Township, including Rideau Heights, Kingscourt, Grenville Park, Hillendale, Valleyview, and Portsmouth village, and
increased its population by 9,000.

In 1976 the city was brought into international prominence when
it became the site of the Olympic yachting events. A beautiful new
harbour complex was constructed at the site of the former Portsmouth
village. In recent years, plans have been made for the development of
the waterfront area and in 1979 these plans have begun to be put into
effect. Fortunately, the city has preserved much of its historic heritage
and has a flourishing Historical Society, founded in 1893. Kingston
continues to live by its Tercentenary motto, "Historic Past, Promising
Future".

Rose Mary Gibson: "An Historical Chronology of Kingston" in *Historic Kingston*, 1969
N. and H. Mika: Mosaic of Kingston, 1969
R.A. Preston: "The History of the Port of Kingston" in *Ontario Historical Society*, 1954
K. Jean Richardson: *Here and There . . . in Kingston*, 1966
Town Watchman, 1930-34

Sir John A. Macdonald's House, Kingston

KINGSTON MILLS, community, Kingston Township, Frontenac County
Position 44° 17′ 76° 27′

Situated about 6 miles from the city of Kingston, this dispersed rural
community was the site of Ontario's first grist mill. In 1784 Robert
Clark supervised the construction of the government-built mill which
was to serve the United Empire Loyalist settlers coming into Kingston
Township. The community which grew up around this mill was
located on the main road linking Upper and Lower Canada (now the
Kingston Mills Road).

The Rideau Canal, built to provide a military route between Upper and Lower Canada, starts at Kingston Mills. Completed in 1832, it traversed 126 miles of then sparsely settled country between Kingston Mills and Bytown (Ottawa). The lock station at Kingston Mills was blasted out of pure granite and several men were accidentally killed during construction.

The community began to decline in the late nineteenth century. A shorter road connection via the LaSalle Causeway at Kingston and the completion of the St. Lawrence Seaway led to a marked decrease in traffic through the community. Competition from other mills closer to Kingston had led to the closing of the local sawmill in 1861. In 1971 there were only 40 people living here.

Today Kingston Mills is a popular place for boat owners travelling up the Rideau Canal. The lockmaster's house, built in 1904, has recently been converted into an interpretive centre explaining the history of the canal. The historic blockhouse, which was constructed for the defence of the waterway, has also been restored.

Frontenac County. Ontario. 1930
Kingston Whig-Standard. 1978, 1979

KINGSVILLE, town, Gosfield South Township, Essex County
Position 42° 02′ 82° 45′

Kingsville was named after Colonel James King, the first man to build a house at this site on the shore of Pigeon Bay, Lake Erie. Some French people had settled in the vicinity during the 1700's because of its proximity to the French post at Detroit. The British government chose the region for the settlement of United Empire Loyalists who came to Canada following the American Revolution.

A few families settled briefly in Gosfield Township during the 1780's, but as no effective method of granting land had been established as yet, they became discouraged and left. In 1788 Upper Canada was divided into four districts and surveys were made. Gosfield Township was surveyed in the late 1780's.

The first recorded settler in the Kingsville area was Thomas Curtis. In the 1790's Andrew Ulch built a grist mill at the site, thus establishing Kingsville's first industry. Abel Augustine erected a grist mill and operated a tile factory in 1815. In 1833 the Pulford family opened the first blacksmith shop in the area.

Until about 1840, however, Kingsville was little more than a cluster of a few shops and mills, but during the next decade a community began to develop on the land of Andrew Stewart and John Herrington. Stewart had offered to name the village after the first settler to build a house on his property, and in 1843 Colonel James King took him up on his proposal. Samuel Rose erected a hotel, and Lewis Jasperson opened a general store and a blacksmith shop. A carding mill was established by Henry Harris. In 1852 a post office was opened with Alexander McDonald as postmaster. By 1867 the community had a population of 500 and had become the lake port for the surrounding township.

A depression in the 1870's halted Kingsville's growth for a few years but in the 1880's the village, which was incorporated in 1878 with J.H. Smart as first reeve, experienced renewed growth. By 1881 the population had doubled and a grist mill, sawmill and a woollen mill were in operation. A slight depression again slowed progress in the mid-1880's, but the later years of the decade saw rapid expansion which was aided by the construction of the Lake Erie and Detroit Railway to Kingsville in 1889. There was much trade in agricultural produce, lumber, railroad ties, and staves. Harris's carding mill was bought by J.E. Brown and J.W. Bird, who became the manufacturers of the famous Ave Saxony blankets for which there was a great demand during the Klondyke Gold Rush days. Two furniture factories were opened by Richard Gregory and Messrs. McDonald and Duggan.

In 1890 Hiram Walker and his son, leading figures in Kingsville's development during the late nineteenth century, drilled wells near the village to tap the natural gas resources of the area. The low cost of natural gas encouraged as a source of power the establishment of industries. An evaporating plant built about 1895 was one of a growing list of Kingsville industries which included a box factory, bicycle factory, broom manufacturer, two carriage works, pump factory, glass factory, and grain elevator.

Around the turn of the century, Kingsville's future prosperity seemed threatened as the harbour gradually filled with sand and the supply of natural gas diminished. Nevertheless, in 1901 Kingsville was incorporated as a town. James H. Sweet was the first mayor.

With the development of specialized intensive agriculture, tobacco became an increasingly important crop in the region. New industries were established in Kingsville to process the product.

In 1900 Messrs. Wilson and Bailey set up a business drying tobacco and manufacturing cigars and tobacco in the old evaporator plant. This industry was the forerunner of Continental Leaf Tobacco Co. Ltd. In 1919 George Jasperson founded the Essex Tobacco Company which later became the Hodge Tobacco Company. The Ross Leaf Tobacco Company was started in 1923.

Kingsville has continued to be an industrial town, with tobacco processing plants, a planing mill, and tile, brick and boat factories. With the improvement of its natural harbour, the town, by the 1950's, developed into the home port for one of the largest commercial fishing fleets on the Great Lakes. A government fish hatchery was in operation as early as 1917.

Today tourism is becoming increasingly important to this town of 5,135 (1979). The potential of the area, with its miles of beaches, was first recognized in the 1890's by the Hiram Walker family who built the Mettawas Hotel in 1891. Since that time, several resorts have developed, attracting visitors both from Canada and the nearby states of Michigan and Ohio.

Kingsville's first house of worship was a Baptist Church, built by Richard Herrington, the earliest preacher in the area. The present Baptist church was erected by Alex Augustine on the land of Charles Stewart, in 1847. In 1806 Rev. Richard Polland held the first Anglican services, and an Anglican church was in existence before 1842. St. John's was opened in 1852 and Epiphany Church in 1891. In 1818 the first Methodist house of worship was built by the Kratz family. Later, new buildings were opened in 1842 and in 1869, the latter being replaced in 1893 by the Epworth Methodist Church. In 1930 a Roman Catholic chapel was constructed on land given by Fred Alice and a church was dedicated in 1945.

Robert McMurray was Kingsville's first teacher, giving lessons in his log cabin. Col. King was another early teacher using Peter Malott's home as a school. A school was built in 1844. It was replaced several times during the nineteenth century. Today the town has a high school and both public and separate schools.

A Mechanics' Institute was established in 1893 and was the forerunner of the present public library which was opened in 1914.

Kingsville's newspaper, the *Reporter*, was founded in 1873 by Dr. S.A. King.

Kingsville today is widely known as the home of Jack Miner, the great naturalist who established a sanctury here for migrating Canada geese and ducks. Miner, a native of Ohio, moved to Kingsville in 1878. He persuaded local hunters to refrain from shooting geese, and eventually 25,000 birds made their home on his property. In 1904 the Ontario Government declared the area around Miner's farm a sanctuary and the Canada goose became Canada's national bird. The first man to band wild fowl on the North American continent, Miner contributed greatly to the world's scientific knowledge of migratory routes. Today an annual Migration Festival is held in October to commemorate the founding of one of the earliest bird sanctuaries in Canada.

Essex Historical Society: *Papers*, 1913
Kingsville Centennial Committee: *Kingsville Through the Years*, 1952
Ministry of Industry and Tourism: *Traveller's Encyclopaedia of Ontario/Canada*, 1979

KINLOSS, township, Bruce County
Position 44° 00′ 81° 27′

The township of Kinloss is shaped like a triangle. It is bounded on the northwest by the townships of Kincardine and Huron; on the southwest by Wawanosh (County of Huron); on the southeast for a short distance by Turnberry (County of Huron); and on the east by Culross and Greenock Townships. The township was named after Lord Elgin, one of whose titles was Baron Bruce of Kinloss. A ridge of hills, known as the Kinloss Mountains, runs through the central portion of the township. Most land in the township is suitable for farming.

The farms on the first concession of Kinloss were the first in Bruce County to be surveyed. The survey was carried out by Alex. Wilkinson in 1847. Two years later the Durham Road and the adjacent "Free Grant" lots were surveyed by A.P. Brough. In 1852 the rest of the township was surveyed by E.R. Jones.

The "Free Grant" lands north and south of the Durham Road were offered for sale in 1849. The remaining portion of the township came on the market at a land sale held on September 27, 1854.

Among the first settlers who established themselves on their grants in 1850 were Joel Eli Stauffer, John and Wm. Shelton, Thomas Hodgins and Mankin Meredith.

During the summer and fall of 1851 most of the township's pioneer settlers were able to earn a little money working at the government job of opening up the Durham Road, an east-west colonization road crossing Grey and Bruce Counties and passing through the northern section of the township. The lack of roads in the early days slowed the growth of the township.

Among the first settlers in the southern part of the township were Norman Nicholson, Duncan and Alexander McKenzie, Martin McInnes, John McDonald, R. Gollan, William, David and James Henderson, Wm. Bryce, Peter Reid, James, John, Thomas and David Falconer, Wm. and J. Tiffin, and Andrew McManus. All these pioneers squatted on their land before it was opened up for sale. Those who purchased land at the time of the 1854 sale included Alex Graham, Thomas Harris, Robert Purves, S.A. Ferrie, Patrick, John and Peter Corrigan.

Kinloss was united for municipal purposes with the township of Kincardine in 1852. In 1854 Kinloss requested separation from Kincardine and after two petitions their request was granted. The first election in 1855 saw Boyer Paul as reeve with councillors Murdoch McKenzie, Murdoch McDonald, Thomas Harris and Wm. Shelton, and Wm. Herndon as clerk.

Because of the absence of water privileges large enough to drive a good grist mill, Kinloss settlers had to journey to Walkerton, Kincardine or Dungannon to have their wheat ground. In 1859 a grist mill was finally built at Lucknow.

The first sawmill was erected by J. Eli Stauffer in the Silver Lake area. It was here that the first efforts were made to develop a village. A post office known as "Kinloss" was opened in 1853-4 with Thomas Hodgins as postmaster. Mr. Hodgins operated the first store. About this time a tavern was opened by Wm. Shelton. It was called the "Black Horse", a name that was also used for the settlement at that time. The first school, a simple log house, was built there and it was at "Black Horse" that the Rev. Thomas Hadwin, a Methodist minister, held his first service in the home of Thomas Hodgins.

The rural communities of Kinloss Township include picturesque Silver Lake, a popular fishing spot; Whitechurch, which has a creamery, a chopping mill and piano-organ business; Holyrood, with its post office dating back to 1856, and the township hall used as a community centre; and Kinlough whose Presbyterian and Anglican churches had their beginnings in the 1860's. The village of Lucknow was once part of Kinloss Township but was incorporated as an independent municipality in 1874.

Kinloss has remained an agricultural community with a Scottish aura retained from its early pioneers.

Norman Robertson: The History of the County of Bruce, 1906
Norman McLeod: The History of the County of Bruce 1907-1968, 1969

KINMOUNT, police village, Sommerville Township, Victoria County
Position 44° 47′ 78° 39′

This village in the Burnt River Valley, on the Canadian National Railways, about 40 miles northeast of the town of Lindsay, is situated in the northeast corner of the county near the borders of Haliburton and Peterborough counties. It lies in the midst of a lumbering district and had its beginning as a mill site.

In 1861 John Hunter built the first mill here on the river's edge. There were several other mills along the river within two miles of the village by the latter part of the 19th century. The railway arrived in 1876.

A disastrous fire on September 26, 1890 almost burned the entire village to the ground. The Lindsay fire brigade, alerted by telegraph arrived within fifty minutes by railway, but needless to say, it was too late to save many buildings in the business section. At least twelve businesses and stores were lost, among them the Victoria Hotel, three general stores, two smithies and the Orange Hall. Another disaster struck on May 24, 1928 when the Burnt River flooded the village. Stores had up to two feet of water and guests at the local hotel were rowed by boat to the railway station.

Kinmount has remained a small community of less than 300 residents.

Watson Kirkconnell: *County of Victoria,* 1967

KINTORE, community, East Nissouri Township, Oxford County
Position 43° 08′ 81° 02′

Situated about 15 miles northeast of London, on Highway 19, this dispersed rural community of 139 (1971) was named by the Hon. George Alexander after a town on the River Don in Aberdeenshire, Scotland.

In the nineteenth century, Kintore was a place of some importance. Among its earliest residents were Mrs. Margaret Pearson who arrived from England in 1829 and Jonathan Graves who began farming in the area in 1835. A post office was opened in 1862. By 1876 the size of the population had grown considerably and included many of Scottish or English descent. Among the businessmen of the community were John T. Crellin who had established himself as a builder and contractor in 1869; Robert Eldon, merchant; David Calvert, painter; Edward Flinn, blacksmith; and William Easson, postmaster. A school and two churches also served the residents of Kintore.

Walker & Miles: *Historical Atlas of Oxford County,* 1876.

KIOSK, community, Pentland Township, Nipissing District
Position 46° 05′ 78° 53′

This picturesque community lies on the shore of Kioshkokwi Lake, a few miles south of the northern boundary of Algonquin Park. A one-industry settlement, Kiosk relies on the operations of the Staniforth

Lumber and Veneer Company, which was established in 1936. The forests of Algonquin Park supply the materials for the company's sawmill, veneer mill, and lumer yard. Products are shipped out by rail.

Most of Kiosk's 332 residents (1971) are bilingual. A general store, church, and school provide services for the people of the community and a logging museum tells the story of the area's lumber industry. Kiosk is accessible by Highway 630 which links the community with Highway 17, about 20 miles to the north.

Hamilton Spectator, 1961

KIPLING, geographic township, Cochrane District
Position 50° 09′ 82° 10′

The township appears to be named after Rudyard Kipling, noted English author, who died in 1936.

Located north of the town of Kapuskasing, Kipling is traversed by the Mattagami River which flows northward through the township. Swelled by several tributaries, the Mattagami supplies power generated at two Hydro Stations within the township.

KIPPEN, community, Stanley Township, Huron County
Position 43° 28′ 81° 31′

Situated some 20 miles southeast of Goderich, this dispersed rural community of about 100 inhabitants was named by pioneer settler Robert Bell after his native parish in Scotland, when a post office was opened in 1855.

The Kippen area was first settled in the early 1830's as immigrants from Britain took up land along the London Road. Robert Doig was probably the earliest to make his home here. Part of the community was later laid out on his lot.

When the London, Huron and Bruce division of the Great Western Railway was built, the residents of Kippen actively encouraged a route through their community. The railway brought increased trade and prosperity and Kippen became a distributing centre for the district.

Kippen's population had reached about 200 by the early 1900's. There were two stores, two blacksmith shops, and a hotel. John McNiven operated a sawmill.

As the railway's importance declined with the advent of the automobile, growth slowed, overshadowed by nearby Clinton, a town located also on Highway 4, a few miles to the north.

Clinton Women's Institute: History of Clinton and surrounding Community, 1950

KIRBY, geographic township, Thunder Bay District
Position 49° 47′ 87° 10′

Located northwest of the town of Geraldton, this township was named after Hon. Harold J. Kirby, MPP for Eglinton (Toronto) 1934-37.

Kirby Lake and Volcan Lake are located in the area.

The Canadian National Railways' line passes immediately to the south of the township.

KIRBY, part of town of Newcastle, Regional Municipality of Durham
Position 44° 01′ 78° 37′

Situated on Highway 35-115 north of Newcastle, this dispersed rural community is today usually associated with the popular Oshawa Ski Club. Known first as Powers Corners after its first settler, then as Jackson's Corners, it was finally named Kirby after a place in Yorkshire by the families who had emigrated to Canada from that English county.

In 1832, Nathaniel Powers, who originally came from the United States, purchased the first lot of land in what is now Kirby on the main road north from Newcastle. The following year Thomas and William Pride and Richard Ruddock arrived as neighbours and with the purchase of land by Calvin Moulton Jr., Powers Corners was established.

The pioneers were soon joined by other families, most of whom came from Yorkshire. These included the Thorntons, Jacksons, Tyermans, Rickabys, Chapmans, and Gilbanks. From Scotland came the Rutherfords, Prides, and Marrs.

Kirby had no stream to provide waterpower and encourage industry, but depended entirely on the farming activities in the area. As a result the community grew slowly. By 1881 there were a few industries in the community, including two sawmills and a shingle mill.

Today Kirby has been divided in half by the highway which runs north from Newcastle. The old stone blacksmith shop of Andrew Morrow, long a local landmark and gathering place, was demolished to provide room for the highway as was the old Powers home. One shop and one church remain in the community.

The Kirby school, built in 1836, was one of the area's first schoolhouses. Henry LaRue Powers was the teacher when it opened. In the 1850's John Gilbank donated some of his land to the Primitive Methodists and on it they erected their church.

Helen Schmid and Sid Rutherford: *Out of the Mists*, 1975.

KIRKFIELD, police village, Eldon Township, Victoria County
Position 44° 34′ 78° 59′

Kirkfield, about 20 miles northwest of Lindsay, on Highway 48, was named by Alexander Munro, the first settler in the area. About two miles north of the small community is the site of a Lift Lock on the Trent-Severn Canal, one of Ontario's major recreational waterways.

Munro came here from Scotland in 1836. His son, John, was the first white child to be born in the vicinity in 1839. A community did not begin to develop until 1859 when Jacob Dixon, Silas Smith, and Jacob Belfry came to Eldon Township and settled to the north of Mr.

Munro. Both Dixon and Smith catered to the men who were building the Victoria Road, Dixon opening a tavern and Smith establishing a general store. Soon more families arrived and Kirkfield began to grow. Most of the early families were Highland Scots, although there were also some Irish and French settlers.

Among the prominent settlers were the McKenzies. Their interests included flour mills, woollen mills, and a sash, door and planing mill. They were also grain buyers and dealers in telegraph poles, posts and railroad ties.

Kirkfield Lift Locks, Trent Valley Canal
Public Archives Canada C21236

A post office was opened in Kirkfield in 1864 with Silas Smith as the first postmaster. By the 1880's the community had four general stores, two wagon shops, a tinshop, a harness shop, a butcher shop, a smithy, and two hotels. The population was about 400. The McKenzie enterprises added to Kirkfield's prosperity for many years, although the gradual denuding of the forests affected the mills' source of cheap water power and the mills disappeared around the turn of the century.

Fortunately, the Trent-Severn Canal from the Bay of Quinte to Lake Simcoe was under construction about this time and the project gave a boost to the local economy. The population rose to about 500.

Kirkfield suffered some severe losses from fires over the years. In 1925 an entire business block and the Kirkland Inn with its valuable furnishings were destroyed, and in 1936 the historic village hall burned to the ground.

By the 1960's, tourism was becoming increasingly important to the area. The Kirkfield Lift Lock, which was for a time the only all-hydraulic and all-steel lift lock in the world, proved to be a major tourist attraction.

Kirkfield's most famous son was Sir William Mackenzie who was born here in 1849 and taught school in the community before going into the lumber business. He contracted to build the Grand Trunk Railway along Lake Simcoe and the mountain section of the CPR. Together with Sir Donald Mann, he built the Canadian Northern transcontinental railway system of which he was the president. Both Lady Mackenzie and he contributed generously to the building of the Kirkfield churches. The noted financier and railway builder died in 1923. His home was left to the Sisters of St. Joseph who made it into a convent and a private school. The house has now become a museum.

The first preacher in the Kirkfield areas was a Presbyterian, Rev. John MacMurchy. In the 1850's the Methodists built the community's first church. By 1962 Kirkfield had Presbyterian and Roman Catholic churches as well as an Anglican church.

Watson Kirkconnell: *County of Victoria Centennial History*, 1967

Ontario Historical Society: *Papers*, 1918

KIRKLAND, geographic township, Cochrane District
Position 48° 56' 81° 48'

Situated southwest of the town of Cochrane, the township was named after the Kirkland family of Toronto. The southern and western boundaries of the township were surveyed between 1905-1908.

The township is linked to Highway 11 to the north by dry weather roads.

KIRKLAND LAKE, town, District of Timiskaming
Position 48° 09' 80° 02'

The town of Kirkland Lake is situated on Highway 66 and on the Noranda (Quebec) — Swastika branch line of the CNR, about 160 miles north of North Bay. The discovery of gold in the area led to the incorporation of the communities of Swastika, Chaput Hughes and Kirkland Lake into the Township of Teck in 1919. In 1972, the township became the Corporation of the Town of Kirkland Lake. For a number of years prior to officially becoming a town, Kirkland Lake had been one of the largest unincorporated towns in Ontario. The population of Kirkland Lake in 1979 numbered 12,460.

The place was named by L.V. Rorke of the Department of Mines. He gave the name to a lake, now filled in, in honour of his secretary in Toronto, Miss Winnie Kirkland.

The first settlers came to the area to work in the mining camps. About half of the population is of British origin and half are of French, Finnish, Yugoslavian, Polish and Ukrainian background. The Little family was one of the first to settle in the Kirkland Lake district; they arrived at Swastika in 1911 and moved to Kirkland Lake in 1928. Mrs. John Murphy was the first white woman to live in Kirkland Lake. The first reeve of the township was W.J. McLeod.

In 1911 a prospector named Bill Wright had staked a claim on the eastern shore of the lake. Gold was discovered, resulting in the opening of the Wright-Hargreaves mine. That same year another prospector, Harry Oakes, staked a claim on the south shore of the lake close to Wright's holdings. He founded the Lake Shore Mines and in partnership with the Tough Brothers, formed the Tough-Oakes Gold Mine, the first producing mine in the area.

Discovery of gold in the north led to an influx of would-be prospectors and miners and with them the tradesmen and businessmen needed to supply services to the growing community. From 1911 to 1930 a number of new mines opened up at Kirkland Lake, among them: Kirkland Lake Gold Mine, Sylvanite Gold Mines (1927), and Teck-Hughes Gold Mine. A strip of land along the shore of the lake had so many mining companies on it that it was named The Golden Mile". The name is more than figurative; the construction crew building the road were instructed to use material from a ballast rock pile — by mistake they took material from the ore storage pile instead. By the time the mistake had been discovered, the ore was covered over by concrete and its recovery was not worth the expense. Ironically, the lake of Kirkland Lake has disappeared. Long ago it was filled with the tailings from ore production of the many mines which lined its shore.

Kirkland Lake
Ministry of Industry & Tourism

St. Peter's Anglican Church in Kirkland Lake was established in 1924. Since then it has been rebuilt twice, in 1940 and again in 1948. Holy Name Parish and The Assumption Roman Catholic Church were established in 1917 and because of their growing congregations, they then were divided in 1932. The Pentecostal Tabernacle was formed in 1936. The present building was erected in 1946. The First Baptist Church was built in 1927 by Mr. W. Morris. In 1933 the Finnish Evangelical Lutheran Church was formed.

Kirkland Lake continued to boom throughout the twenties and thirties. Population in 1928 was 24,000 and the town continued to prosper even when the rest of the country was suffering through the Depression. The decline of Kirkland Lake began during the war years. In the forties many men left the district to mine in base metal fields from which weapons were made. After the war inflation interfered with the value of gold and production dropped. By 1953 the population of Kirkland Lake was under 18,000 people. The residents of the town, refusing to succumb to economic depression, rallied to develop new resources. Since then the lumber industry has grown and expanded and the town now includes a large municipal hospital, a school for nurses, and a campus of the Northern College of Applied Art and Technology. Along with gold and iron ore, Kirkland Lake is famous for another local commodity: it has probably produced more players for the National Hockey League than any other centre.

The tourist industry flourishes in the district because of new hotels, parks and sports facilities. Both hunting and fishing are popular with visiting vacationers. The Museum of Northern History is also located at Kirkland Lake. The town newspaper is the *Northern News*, established in 1922. Macassa Mine, opened in 1933, became the lone survivor of the town's gold rush days.

Ministry of Natural Resources: *Kirkland Lake — The Golden Years*, 1969
Ontario Northland Transportation Commission: *The Quarterly*, 1958
Northern Daily News, 1967.

KIRKPATRICK, geographic township, Nipissing District
Position 46° 25' 80° 15'

Located northwest of Lake Nipissing, this township was named after J.B. Kirkpatrick, a Crown Lands staff surveyor in the 1800's. The township was subdivided in 1882.

The Canadian National Railways and Highway 17 run parallel through the township. The community of Kirk is situated in the northern half of the township.

KIRKTON, community, Usborne Township, Huron County, and Blanshard
Township, Perth County
Position 43° 20' 81° 19'

This urban community lies on the boundary between Huron and Perth Counties, about 17 miles west of Stratford. It was probably named after the Kirk family, who were among the earliest residents of the area.

The Kirkton region was surveyed in the early 1830's by the Canada Company, an organization which promoted the colonization of large areas of Ontario. The first families to settle here following the survey included the Kirks, Hazlewoods, and Hannas. The community of Kirkton eventually occupied part of the land of the Kirks and Hazlewoods.

A post office was opened in Kirkton in 1856 and by 1879 it had become a sizable community. J.G. Shoebottom ran a hotel, a general store was operated by John McCardy, and W. Irving offered his services as physician and surgeon. Robert Porter and John Robinson taught in the local schools.

Today Kirkton serves the local area as a shopping centre. According to the 1971 census its population was 212.

London Free Press, June 11, 1949.

KIRKUP, geographic township, Kenora District
Position 49° 42′ 94° 17′

Located southeast of the town of Kenora, on the eastern shore of Lake of the Woods, the township was named in 1939 after Roy S. Kirkup, Ontario Land Surveyor of Fort William, Ontario.

Longbow Lake and Bigstone Bay (Lake of the Woods) in the western part are accessible by road. Highway 71 passes through the eastern and northern section of the township.

KIRKWALL, geographic township, Algoma District
Position 48° 31′ 83° 07′

Situated on the border of the District of Sudbury and east of Missinaibi Lake Provincial Park, Kirkwall is watered by the Dunrankin River, the East Dunrankin River and the Kirkwall River. The origin of the township's name is unknown.

The Canadian National Railways passes through the mountainous northern half of the township.

KIRKWALL, community, Regional Municipality of Hamilton-Wentworth
Position 43° 21′ 80° 10′

This dispersed rural community west of Hamilton was first settled in the 1830's by families from Scotland. It was probably named after a town in Orkney, Scotland, by one of these early residents.

Settlement took place first along the road to Galt, then along the sideroad which has since become Highway 52. In 1846 a house and blacksmith shop were built by Lemuel Tait and in 1851 the shop became Kirkwall post office. A store was opened by Donald Martin in the early 1850's. Thomas Wheeler, Edward Dayman, and Herb Wise all operated sawmills in the area. Lumber from the district was especially in demand in the early 1900's for the manufacture of hockey sticks.

By 1903 the population of the community was about 100. It never grew much beyond this size and in 1962 the Department of Highways bought many of the old buildings along Highway 52 before widening the road. Recently several new houses have been constructed along the highway.

A Presbyterian congregation was organized by Rev. Thomas Christie in 1833 and in 1835 a church was erected on the land of Robert

Dickson. A new church was built in the 1840's.

School lessons were first held in the church. Early teachers included Mr. Harkness, David Ferris, and R. White. A stone school was opened in 1862 but in recent years has become a Boy Scouts meeting-hall.

Pioneers of Beverly. 1967.

KIRKWOOD, geographic township, Algoma District
Position 46° 20′ 83° 31′

Situated immediately south of the town of Thessalon, this township was established and subdivided in 1877. It is thought to have been named after A. Kirkwood, clerk of the Crown Lands Department at that time.

The Bridgland River flows in a southwesterly course through the area which is linked by Highway 129 to Thessalon on the Trans-Canada Highway.

KITCHENER, geographic township, Sudbury District
Position 46° 51′ 81° 08′

Situated northwest of the City of Sudbury, the township was named after the late Lord Kitchener of Khartoum, GCB, Commander-in-Chief of the British Army during World War I.

The eastern boundary was surveyed in 1888, the southern boundary in 1899 and the northern and western boundaries in 1902.

The township houses Osbourne Lake, Morton Lake and Bigwood Lake.

A dry weather road links the area to Highway 69 to the south.

KITCHENER, city, Regional Municipality of Waterloo
Position 43° 27′ 80° 29′

Kitchener can claim to be one of the fastest-growing municipalities in Ontario. It is situated adjacent to the city of Waterloo, about 60 miles southwest of Toronto, on Highways 7, 8 and 401.

The first settlers named the site Sand Hills because of the large sand dunes they found there. The settlement was next called Ebytown after Mennonite Bishop Benjamin Eby, an early religious and secular leader of the community. Then in the 1820's the name was changed to Berlin to honour the German immigrants who were arriving in large numbers. During World War One, it was felt that the German name of the town might have adverse affects on relations with the rest of Canada and that a more British-sounding name should be chosen. In 1916 the town was named Kitchener in honour of Lord Kitchener of Khartoum, a British war hero who was drowned at sea in that year.

The first settlers were a group of Mennonite families from Lancaster County, Pennsylvania who arrived in 1807. Among them were Daniel and Samuel Eby, Daniel Erb, Joseph Rissor and John and

Frederick Eckert. They were led by Abraham Weber and Benjamin Eby who had purchased land at the site in 1806. Eby built the first house of the settlement. He became a Mennonite minister in 1809 and a bishop of the church in 1812. That year he built the first Mennonite church in Upper Canada. In an annex later added to the church, he opened one of the earliest schools in the area.

Eby was the first leader of the community, but it was Joseph Schneider who is considered the true founder of the city. One of the Lancaster group, he arrived in 1807, built a log house and barn and cut a roadway to the east. In 1816 Schneider constructed a sawmill, the settlement's first enterprise and the beginning of Kitchener's long history of industrial development. A second house erected by Schneider in 1820 is today the city's oldest building.

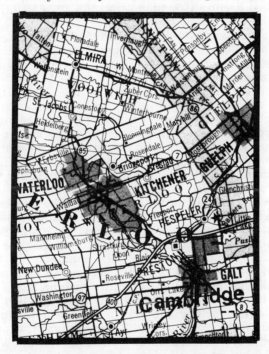

More settlers arrived after the War of 1812-15 and Phineas Varnum set up a blacksmith shop to meet their needs. John Roats operated the first saddlery in the 1820's. In 1830 the Miller brothers, William, David and Frederick, opened a store. Frederick Gaukel erected a hotel in 1833 to accommodate travellers. Simon Bowman became Ebytown's first carpenter and in 1832 Jacob Hailer began to make chairs and spinning wheels in his shop.

Until about 1830 most of the community's settlers were Pennsylvania families of German descent. However, in the 1830's an increasing proportion of the immigrants came directly from Germany. Many of them were skilled craftsmen and they brought a great variety of trades to the place now known as Berlin. By 1837 the community included a potter, bookbinder, printer, windmill maker, shoemaker, carpenter, brewer, weaver, clockmaker, and a wagonmaker, thus establishing the industrial character of the future city.

John Hoffman and Samuel Bowman bought land from Benjamin Eby in 1823 and set up a furniture-making establishment about 1840, the start of one of Kitchener's major industries. Also in 1840, a foundry was built by Messrs. Huber and Ahrens.

In 1840 George Rebscher founded Canada's first lagerbeer brewery and Reingold Lang began operating a tannery in 1849. Louis Breithaupt's tannery, opened in 1857, was the start of the Breithaupt Leather Co. Ltd. which became one of the largest tanning businesses in the country. John Winger's pump factory was established in 1850. J. Maas produced Berlin's first pianos in 1852. In 1856 a tinsmith shop was opened by the Lehnen brothers.

A post office was established in 1841. By 1846 the population of Berlin was about 400. It continued to grow steadily and by 1852, with about 750 residents, the community was considered important enough to be chosen as county seat for the newly-formed County of Waterloo. A Berlin resident, Dr. John Scott, became the county's first Warden.

Berlin was incorporated as a village in 1854. Dr. Scott was elected reeve and presided over councillors Gabriel Bowman, Enoch Ziegler, George Jantz, and Henry Stroh. The first meetings were held in the courthouse which had been built two years before.

Selection as the county seat brought increased prosperity to Berlin with many more German immigrants arriving in the next few years to set up new businesses. In 1856 the first train of the Grand Trunk Railway arrived in the village, boosting the local economy. The next year a second line was built from Galt to Berlin. Although the line closed after a few months, it was reopened in 1870. In 1860 Frederick Rickerman built one of the largest windmills in Canada for Jacob Y. Shantz, a leading businessman in the community. In 1870, with a population of well over 3,000, Berlin became an incorporated town with Dr. William Pipe serving as the first mayor.

Among the many industries established in the 1870's was Jacob Y. Shantz's button factory, the first in Canada to manufacture buttons. By 1900 Jacob Y. Shantz and Company was the largest button manufacturer in North America. In 1912 it became known as Dominion Buttons Manufacturers Ltd.

In 1871 Alexander Miller, one of Berlin's first barristers, founded the Economical Mutual Fire Insurance Company, one of the earliest insurance companies in the county. In 1937 the company became the Economical Mutual Insurance Company.

The 1870's was a period of expansion for the Farmer's Market, established in a building provided in 1869. Famous for the Mennonite foods which the farmers bring to sell, the market has served citizens and visitors alike for over a century and is still one of the city's major attractions.

In 1866, chiefly through the efforts of Jacob Shantz, the Berlin Board of Trade was organized. John Fennell was the first president. It secured many new industries for the town over the years and was responsible for vetoing a Bill which would have allowed Waterloo Township annex a large part of the town. By 1904 it was the largest Board of Trade outside of Toronto and in 1945 it became the Kitchener Chamber of Commerce.

By the late nineteenth century, in the town known as "Busy Berlin", still more industries were established. In 1882 Charles A. Ahrens and Co. took over Thomas Foster's shoe factory. J.M. Schneider, founder of Kitchener's meat-packing business, began to butcher and produce sausages in 1890. In 1895 Williams, Green and Rome opened their shirt-making establishment and C.K. Hagedorn founded the Berlin Suspender and Button Co. The Berlin Rubber Co. begun in 1899 by George Schlee and Jacob Kaufmann, was the start of the Dominion Rubber Co. Ltd.

As well as promoting the industrial development of the town, Berlin's town council was actively involved in introducing the latest civic improvements to the community. In 1898 the first experiment in municipal ownership was begun when the town took over the water-works system established in 1888 by Messrs. Moffat, Hodgins and Clarke. The move was successful and in 1903 the new Berlin Light Commission bought the gas and electric plants of the Breithaupts. The Berlin-Waterloo Street Railway, opened in 1886, became town-owned in 1906. In 1910 an impressive ceremony was held in the town at which Sir James Whitney, the provincial premier, inaugurated the use of publicly-owned power from the Niagara River in Ontario. Berlin was the first municipality at any distance from the Niagara River to bene-fit from the new Ontario Hydro system. It was a Berliner, D.B. Det-weiler, who had first suggested hydro-electric development in Canada and the first meeting to discuss the formation of the provincial com-pany was held in the town in 1903.

By 1900, seventy industries were providing employment for many of the 9,696 residents. The extension of the Galt, Preston, and Hespeler Railway line to Berlin in 1903 encouraged more industrial development. Products manufactured in the town included household and office furniture, boilers and engines, shirts and collars, boots and shoes, trunks, clothing, sugar, doors and window sashes, cigars, clocks, and lager. The American Motor Car Co. Limited became the first in Canada to produce automobiles and the first to manufacture multiple cylinder gas and gasoline engines for general purposes. In 1901 the Ontario Sugar Company built the first beet sugar mill in Canada in the town.

By 1907 Berlin's population had reached 15,000 but it did not apply for city status until 1912 thus becoming the first Canadian town to wait for the statutory 15,000 inhabitants before petitioning for a city charter. W.H. Schmalz was the first mayor.

Berlin felt the effects of the war years more than many cities. The local newspapers were no longer allowed to publish in German, the German language was heard less frequently on the streets and in the stores, and in 1916 there was bitter controversy over the changing of the city's name. However, by the end of the war the new name was generally accepted. An attempt to return to the use of "Berlin" in 1919 was voted down and the city has been known as Kitchener ever since.

A new city hall was built in 1923 to serve Kitchener's 25,000 people. Expanding rapidly, Kitchener was probably the first city in Canada to use an overall city plan which was completed in 1925. In 1927 it was the first municipality in Ontario to appoint a commission under the new Town Planning Act. William H. Breithaupt served as chairman. The only setback to Kitchener's growth occurred during the Depression of the 1930's.

By 1939 with a population of 33,450, Kitchener had 127 factories manufacturing products for the Canadian and international market. By 1954 there were nine major shoe factories in the city. The city was Canada's leader in the manufacture of furniture, shoes, buttons, rubber goods, shirts, and meat-packing and hide-tanning.

Kitchener expanded with the annexation of 3,700 acres in 1958 and another 739 acres in 1963. The city was honoured in the latter year by being named Canada's City of the Year. By 1966 the population had reached 91,321 and by the late 1960's the community was reported to have the greatest organized growth of any city in Canada. Projects undertaken in this decade included the construction of the Conestoga Expressway, the Kitchener Downtown Redevelopment Program, and the building of a Civic Centre.

In 1973 the city annexed Bridgeport, part of the township of Waterloo and part of the city of Waterloo, increasing the population by about 5,000 to 126,162 in 1974. Kitchener was rated as Canada's third fastest growing community in the early 1970's. Among the industries were such well-known names as Dare Foods Ltd., Burns Foods Ltd., Electrohome Limited, J.M. Schneider Limited, Greb Shoes Limited and Silverwood Dairies Limited.

As one of the most industrialized cities in Canada, Kitchener's continued expansion offers many employment opportunities and in 1979 its population reached 136,091.

Benjamin Eby, one of the community's first settlers, was also its first religious leader. Eby became a Mennonite minister in 1809 and a Bishop in 1813. The Mennonites of Ebytown at first worshipped in each other's houses, then in a log cabin which was also used as a schoolhouse in 1809. A log church, the first in the community, was built in 1813. It was replaced by a newer structure in 1834.

In the 1830's a number of congregations of different denominations were organized. The Rev. Frederick Bindemann formed a Lutheran congregation in the years 1833-37. St. Paul's Lutheran Church was dedicated in 1848. An Anglican missionary visited the area in 1835 although an Anglican church was not opened until 1862. In 1836 the first missionaries of the Evangelical Church of Pennsylvania arrived. A church was built in 1839 and in the 1840's Berlin became the heart of the Evangelical Church in Canada. The Swedenborgian Church gained followers in the community in 1833 under the missionary Rev. John Harbin and in 1847 a church was erected.

In the early 1840's a non-denominational church was built by four congregations in the community. Known as the "Free Church", it was later used as a school. The Wesleyan Methodist Church opened in 1842. In 1854 Rev. H. Schneider preached the first sermon at the new Baptist church and Father Laufhuber began the construction of St. Mary's Roman Catholic Church which was finished in 1856. A house of worship was erected by the St. Andrew's Presbyterian congregation in 1856 and Rev. A. Constable Geikie became the first minister in 1857.

By 1940, Kitchener had 35 churches and the major denominations were the Lutherans and the Roman Catholics. The churches included a Catholic building erected in 1903 and the Sacred Heart Church, built by Polish settlers in 1918. By the 1950's, the city, with 47 churches, was the Canadian headquarters for the Mennonite, Lutheran, Evangelical, and Swedenborgian churches. By 1964 there were 73 houses of worship in the community.

The first physician to care for the sick in Berlin was Dr. John Scott, who arrived in 1834 and later became the first reeve of the village. John Eby dispensed drugs from the first drug store and Louis Van Camp served as the community's first dentist, 1869-97. A Board of Health was set up as early as 1854.

St. Mary's General Hospital was opened about 1824. Built in 1895 a hospital owned by both municipalities was known as the Berlin-Waterloo Hospital. In 1952 the new Kitchener-Waterloo Hospital received its first patients. The Freeport Sanatorium, erected about 1912, was used as a convalescent home for soldiers of the First World War and became city-owned in 1920. By 1968 the city had a home for handicapped children and a Crippled Children's Centre.

The first school in the community was held in the log cabin used as a church by the Mennonites in the early nineteenth century. Benjamin Eby was probably the first teacher. He later opened another school in 1836. A Mr. Gravel gave instruction to the children in 1833. Ontario's first kindergarten was opened in Berlin in 1882. In 1840, a secondary school, the Wellington Institute, was started by John F.A.S. Fayette but closed after a few years. The Berlin County Grammar School was opened in 1855 with Rev. Henry McMeekin as headmaster. In 1857 it was replaced by the Central School, which became the Berlin High School in 1871. A new school was built in 1876 and renamed the Berlin Collegiate and Technical Institute in 1903. The old Central School became a Provincial Model School which trained teachers from 1877 to 1907. Jeremiah Suddaby was principal and the school was renamed after him on his death in 1910. In 1914 the High School District was enlarged to include Waterloo, resulting in the two municipalities sharing the cost of their secondary education, an arrangement unique in Ontario. In 1932 the secondary school became the Kitchener and Waterloo Collegiate and Vocational School. The Rockway Mennonite High School was opened in 1943. By 1968 Kitchener had 14 secondary and 91 elementary schools.

In 1864 the Very Rev. Eugene Funcken founded St. Jerome's College in St. Agatha. In 1866 the college moved to Berlin. Taught by the Fathers of the Congregation of the Resurrection, the boys attending the colleges could take a business course, a high school course, or an arts course. About 1960 the college became affiliated with Waterloo University.

In 1900 the Euler Business College opened with the Hon. W.D. Euler as principal. It became one of the largest such institutions in Ontario and was later renamed the Berlin Business College.

The 1960's saw the development of post-secondary education in the Kitchener area. Today the University of Waterloo specializes in Engineering and Science subjects while Wilfrid Laurier University (formerly Waterloo Lutheran University) offers courses in language, business administration, and the arts. Local industries often make use of the universities' facilities for research, teaching, and product development and reap the benefits of the University of Waterloo's co-operative educational program which makes the employment of students in industry part of their course. Kitchener also provides post-secondary education at the Conestoga College of Applied Arts and Technology.

In 1835 Heinrick Wilhelm Peterson began the weekly publication of the *Canada Museum und Allegmeine Zeitung*, probably the first German-language newspaper in Canada. Christian Enslin, a book-store-owner and the first book-binder in Berlin in the 1830's, became the editor of the *Deutsche Canadier* which was published in the 1840's by Henry Eby. In 1859 John Motz and F. Rittinger began publication of the *Berliner Journal* which became the leading German newspaper in Canada. An English-language paper, the *Berlin Weekly Telegraph*, was begun by D. McDougall in the 1860's.

Waterloo County's first daily paper was the *Daily News*, founded in 1877 by Peter E.W. Moyer. In 1897 it amalgamated with the *Daily Record*, first published by W.V. Uttley in 1893, and became the *News Record*. In 1922 it joined the *Daily Telegraph* which was started by D.A. Bear in 1896 and was renamed the *Daily Record*. It became the *Kitchener-Waterloo Record* in 1947.

In 1904 the *Ontario Glocke* of Walkerton joined the *Berliner Journal*. The paper later absorbed the *Stratford Kolonist*, the *Waterloo Bauernfreund*, and the *Deutsche Zeitung* of Berlin. During World War One, Berlin newspapers were forbidden to publish in German. The paper was renamed the *Ontario Journal* and the first English edition was brought out in 1918.

Kitchener also has its share of 20th century media, with a radio station CHYM and a television station.

Berlin produced the first book to be printed in Waterloo County. In 1836 H.W. Peterson printed a song book, the first German book to be published in Canada.

A Mechanics' Institute was opened in the village in 1854. In 1884 it became the Berlin Public Library. With the assistance of a grant from the Carnegie Foundation, the collection of books was housed in a new building in 1904. Three more Carnegie grants helped to expand the library and to renovate it in 1916. In 1908 Dr. B. Mabel Dunham was appointed to the staff. She was the first trained librarian to be put in charge of a library in Ontario. The collection continued to expand and the Waterloo Historical Society opened a museum in the building. In 1962 the new Kitchener Public Library was opened.

German people love music, and the residents of early Berlin were no exception. A band with members from Berlin and Bridgeport was in existence by 1845. In 1856 Mr. Kelk became the bandmaster of the first Berlin Band. A second band was organized in 1859 by Henry Glebe. In 1875 John S. Smith began the Berlin Musical Society Band which became the 29th Battalion Band in 1879. In the 1940's, the city had both a Junior Boys' and a Senior Boys' Band.

In 1853 the United Male Singing Society of Berlin, Bridgeport, and Waterloo was organized. The Male Glee Club began in 1859. In 1875 Berlin hosted an international "Saengerfest", the first of many held in the city. Kitchener and Waterloo have combined to form a number of choirs. In the 1920's the Kitchener-Waterloo Philharmonic Choir was very popular and won a major choral event at the Canadian Music Festival in Toronto. In the 1930's the Kitchener-Waterloo YMCA Chorus was formed. In the 1970's the Twin Cities Operatic Society has been very active.

Theobald Zoellner organized the Berlin Philharmonic and Orchestral Society in the late nineteenth century. In 1926 an orchestra was led by conductor James J. Galloway but it ended when he left in 1929. A new orchestra was formed in 1945 by W. Archie Bernhardt and today entertains the citizens as the Kitchener-Waterloo Symphony Orchestra.

In 1896, Curry Walper built the Berlin Opera House. Earlier, entertainments were held in the Town Hall. The Theatorium, the community's first movie theatre, was opened in 1907. In the 1930's, the Kitchener-Waterloo Centre of Community Arts was started, mainly due to the efforts of Ross Hamilton. When it was disbanded in 1940, the members joined the Kitchener-Waterloo Art Society. The building which housed the Kitchener-Waterloo Little Theatre was located in Waterloo.

Berlin residents were active in sports by the late nineteenth century. Baseball teams were organized in the 1870's. In 1888 the Berlin Rangers' soccer team toured Britain. This was the first time a sports organization from this area had been recognized internationally. Eddie Wettlauffer formed a hockey club in 1890. Since that time, Kitchener has produced many well-known hockey players for the national teams. In 1940 the city's Skating Club became the first in Canada to offer year-round skating.

Kitchener today is a city of parks and flowers. As early as 1872 the town was petitioned to buy the land of Joseph E. Schneider to create a park. This was the start of Woodside Park. Victoria was opened in 1896, Knollwood in 1928, and Kaufman in 1931. Other beauty spots inlcuded Breithaupt and the Homer Watson Memorial Park which became known as Cressman's Woods. In 1872 Alexander Young founded the Kitchener Horticultural Society and the beautiful gardens of Kitchener residents reflected the widespread interest in horticulture and floraculture. In the 1940's a number of areas were reforested.

Kitchener's most famous resident was probably William Lyon Mackenzie King, Canada's tenth prime minister, who spent his boyhood years here. William Wilfred Campbell, well-known Canadian poet, was born in Berlin in 1858. Archbald McKellar Mac-Mechan, scholar, teacher, and author, was born in the town in 1862.

Today this thriving industrial city, along with its twin city of Waterloo, is known continent-wide for its annual 9-day food festival and celebration, Oktoberfest. Kitchener's Oktoberfest is the largest event of its kind in North America and thus is a worthy tribute to the city's German heritage.

A.E. Byerly: *The Beginning of Things*, 1935.
Chronicle-Telegraph: *100 Years of Progress in Waterloo County*, 1906.
Kitchener Centennial, 1854-1954, 1954.
Kitchener Chamber of Commerce: *Kitchener Factual Data*, 1968.
                                The Kitchener Story, 1968.
                                Manufacturers' Index, 1974.
Maclean's Magazine, July 15, 1940.
Bill Moyer: *This Unique Heritage*, 1971.
W.V. Uttley: *A History of Kitchener, Ontario*, 1937.
Waterloo Historical Society Papers, 1922.
                                     1930.
                                     1939.
                                     1966.

KITIGAN, community, O'Brien Township, Cochrane District
    Position 49° 23′ 82° 18′

Situated 5 miles southeast of Kapuskasing on Highway 11, this dispersed rural community was once known as Paquettebourg in honour of Father Paquette who devoted many years' service to the communities of Northern Ontario. Kitigan is an Ojibway word meaning "clearing" or "garden."

Kitigan has a hotel and a store. Facilities for recreation include a hockey rink, baseball and softball field, and tennis courts. There is also a school to serve the children of the community.

Both English and French are spoken in the community. Over half the population is of French origin.

Ministry of Natural Resources: *Directory of Statistics and Data*, 1975.

KITLEY, township, Leeds County
    Position 44° 46′ 75° 59′

One of Leeds County's inland townships, Kitley was named after the Devonshire residence of John Pollexfen Bastard, an English Member of Parliament at the time the township was being surveyed.

The township's first settler, James Finch, made a rough survey in 1795. Following the official survey by Lewis Grant in 1797, settlers began to arrive. Among them were Asa Benjamin, Levi Soper, John Livingstone, Major William Read, Solomon How, Thomas Hubbard, Jabez Eaton, and Jeremiah Day. By 1800 the population of the township was 95 and four years later it had risen to 130.

The policy at the time of reserving certain lands for the Crown and for the Established Church, hindered township settlement and for a number of years growth remained slow. David Kilborn built a mill in 1806 and in the same year Amos Gile began operating a still. By 1814 Duncan Livingstone had erected a grist mill near the site of

Frankville.

The township population decreased during the War of 1812 as many settlers became discouraged by the hardships of pioneer life. Following the war, Kitley experienced renewed growth as more United Empire Loyalists and disbanded soldiers settled in the area. A mill was opened by John Sullivan by 1818 and in 1825 Abel Kilborn was operating both grist and sawmills. The years 1830-50 saw a population boom as Kitley received its share of emigrants who were coming to Canada in large numbers from the British Isles. By 1851 the township had a population of 3,525. Businesses and industries included twenty stores, four inns, a grist mill, four sawmills and three tanneries.

The sudden increase in population bringing with it the need for more agricultural land, resulted in the deforestation of the township. This in turn caused much erosion and, combined with overcrowding in the area, resulted in a low standard of living for many of the inhabitants. In the second half of the nineteenth century, the township's population began to decline as people moved to the cities or into the new farmlands being opened up in Western Canada. By 1901 there were only 2,089 settlers left in the township.

Kitley's population reached an all-time low of 1,445 in 1941. Following the Second World War most of the township's small industries disappeared. Today there is some light industry in the township, including furniture makers, a construction firm, and industrial molders.

The Methodists were one of Kitley's earliest congregations, meeting in the mill of Jonathan Livingstone in 1818. Ezra Healey, an early Methodist leader, conducted the services in the 1820's. In 1834 the Methodists erected Providence Chapel. Other Methodist churches were built in 1857 and 1878.

The first Anglican services were held in township schools. An Anglican congregation was organized in Frankville and in 1859 St. Thomas's Church was opened. Reverend Thomas Bedford Jones became the first resident clergyman in 1862.

A Roman Catholic church was dedicated in 1840 and in 1846 Father O'Reilly was made the first resident priest. In 1906 the Roman Catholics of the township decided to build a city-sized church and St. Philip Neri Church, designed by Henry P. Smith, became the largest house of worship ever erected in Kitley.

The early Presbyterians met in the homes of members in Newbliss. A church was constructed in 1859. In 1960 the United Church at Frankville became the first church in North America to install an infra-red electric radiant heating system.

There were several schools in Kitley in the early 1800's, at least one of which had been built by 1818. Newbliss School was opened in the 1830's, Mahon's School in 1836, and Kinch Street School in the 1840's. By 1900 there were about 20 schools in the township, but during the twentieth century many were closed. In 1961 three new schools were built to replace all the old schoolhouses. Today Kitley children attend Jasper Public School, Frankville Public

School, or St. Joseph's Separate School.

In 1964 the Kitley Historical Association was founded and a museum established near Frankville. In 1973 a log cabin, built in 1825, was declared a historic site and opened to visitors at Kitley Corners.

Kitley has had a number of famous residents. Elizabeth Barnes (1800-91), the Witch of Plum Hollow, became known throughout North America for her fortune-telling ability. Everend L. Bruce (1884-1949), a prominent Canadian geologist, and Rev. Dr. Omar L. Kilborn [1867-1920], the first man to open a Methodist mission in China, were both Kitley natives. Louise Cynthia McKinney, born at Frankville in 1868, was a leader of the movement for female suffrage and in 1917 became the first woman in the British Empire to gain a parliamentary seat.

Kitley's communities include Bellamy's Mills, Jasper, Lehigh's Corners, Newbliss, Shane's Corners, and Toledo. The former police village of Frankville was annexed by the township in 1973.

Glenn J. Lockwood: Kitley 1795-1975, 1974
Ruth McKenzie: Leeds and Grenville Their First Two Hundred Years, 1967

KITTO, geographic township, Thunder Bay District
  Position 49° 32' 88° 06'

This township is situated on the southeastern shore of Lake Nipigon. Blackwater Creek flows through the area, emptying into Lake Nipigon.

The Canadian National Railways and Highway 11 pass through the township.

The area was named in August 1939 after F.H. Kitto, O.L.S. of Brampton, Ontario.

KITTSON, geographic township, Timiskaming District
  Position 47° 22' 79° 57'

The township of Kittson is located on the Montreal River. McLennon Lake, Sonny Lake and Kittson Lake are the main lakes.

The township was named after J.M. Kittson, a member of the Ontario Railway and Municipal Board, Toronto.

KLEINBURG, part of town of Vaughan, Regional Municipality of York
  Position 43° 50' 79° 38'

Situated north of Toronto on Highway 27, a "Sunday afternoon's drive" away from the city, the picturesque compact rural community of Kleinburg is a favourite stopping-place for motorists travelling through Vaughan Township. It was named after its first settler John N. Klein. For many years the name was spelled Klineburg. This was probably due to a clerical error in an agreement which was drawn up when John Nicholas Klein commissioned Ansel D. Melvin to build a sawmill on a branch of the Humber River on the east half of Lot 12,

Concession 8 of Vaughan in 1837. In this handwritten agreement the name is several times misspelled John Nicholas Kline. But the signature affixed thereto is John Nicholas Klein.

The Klein family came to Canada from Germany and settled in Vaughan Township in the 1830's where John N. Klein Sr. operated a grist mill, a sawmill, and a cooper shop. In 1847 John N. Klein Jr. bought some land on the west branch of the Humber River from Andrew Mitchell and erected a flour mill. The mill prospered and Klein was actively involved in promoting the development of the community around it. He advocated bylaws which would open roads through the settlement, and he established a store. However, in 1852 he sold his mill to H.S. and W.P. Howland, and the Klein family disappeared from Vaughan Township. The reason for this sudden departure from a successful business is obscure, but perhaps the Kleins being German Lutherans felt isolated among the other settlers of different faiths and background.

The community which had grown up around the mill at the foot of a hill was known as Kleinsberg. A second small settlement developed on top of the hill and was called Mount Vernon. By 1890 the two centres had grown together and were known by the common name of Kleinburg.

The Klein mill was sold to H.S. and W.P. Howland and under the Howland Brothers the flour mill continued to prosper and was soon expanded until it was the largest mill between Barrie and Toronto. H.S. Howland, who became Kleinburg's first postmaster in 1852, added a sawmill and a store to the operation. A Mr. Gough opened a cooperage to make barrels for the flour. A stave factory and planning mill were then built to supply staves for the barrels. Other local establishments in the 1860's and 70's included two carriage-making shops, two blacksmiths, a tannery, a tinsmith, two cabinet-makers, two shinglemakers, and a saddler.

By 1878 Kleinburg's population was about 350. Three general stores supplied goods to residents and there were three hotels to provide accommodation for travellers as the settlement was a covenient stopping-place for farmers on their way to Toronto. However, by the turn of the century, Kleinburg's period of growth and expansion had come to an end and during the early twentieth century the community declined as most of its small local industries disappeared.

Since World War Two, Kleinburg has developed into a residential area for commuters working in Toronto. Tourism has become increasingly important to the local economy as the community boasts several popular attractions. Probably the best known is the McMichael Art Gallery with its superb setting in a wooded ravine and its excellent collection of paintings by the famous Group of Seven, and its Indian and Eskimo art. The Doctor's House, a gift shop and restaurant in a pioneer home, is a popular stop and the country fair, begun by a local storekeeper and known as the Binder Twine Festival, attracts many more visitors each year.

G. Elmore Reaman: A History of Vaughan Township, 1971
Herb H. Sawdon: The Woodbridge Story

KLOCK, geographic township, Timiskaming District
Position 47° 27' 80° 04'

Located just north of Lady Evelyn Lake and about 20 miles west of the town of Haileybury, this township was named after James B. Klock, a lumber merchant and MP of Ottawa.

The nearest road is Highway 558 which runs from Mowat Landing on the Montreal River in the neighbouring township of Barr.

KLOTZ, geographic township, Thunder Bay District
Position 49° 55' 85° 50'

Located northeast of the community of Longlac, Klotz borders the District of Cochrane to the north. Highway 11 passes by some five miles south of the township. It is named after Dr. Otto Klotz, a German astronomer.

Various lakes are found in the area, the largest being Flint Lake in the southwest. The lake empties into Flint River, a tributary of the Kenogami, flowing northward through the township.

KLOTZ LAKE PROVINCIAL PARK, S. of Klotz Township, Thunder Bay District
Position 49° 48' 85° 55'

This 210-acre Provincial Recreation Park, is situated on the west shore of Klotz Lake, on the northern extension of Highway 11, and 30 miles east of the community of Longlac. Camping facilities, fishing, rock collecting, are some of the diversions offered the visitor. A 30-mile canoe route can be taken from the park along the Flint River.

Ontario Ministry of Natural Resources

KNICELY, geographic township, Algoma District
Position 48° 14' 84° 59'

Located northwest of the town of Wawa, this township is part of the Algoma Central & Hudson's Bay Railway Land Grant. The Obatanga Provincial Park lies just to the north.

Kabenung Lake occupies the northwestern corner and Grayling Lake and Dickenson Lake lie in the eastern part. A secondary road links the vicinity with Highway 17.

The township, formerly No. 26, Range 31, was named in 1974 in honour of William R. Knicely, Canadian Army Private from the Thunder Bay District, killed in 1944.

KNIGHT, geographic township, Timiskaming District
Position 47° 43' 81° 00'

Named after Ayril W. Knight, onetime Assistant Provincial Geologist, the township lies a few miles west of the Gowganda mining district.

The western boundary was surveyed in 1896 and again in 1929. All other boundaries were surveyed in 1909. Secondary roads link the township with Highway 560 just to the south.

KNOTT, geographic township, Kenora District, P.P.
Position 51° 04′ 92° 52′

Located southeast of Trout Lake, the township is watered mainly by the Woman River. Little Bear Lake and Rosen Lake are situated in the southern half of the area. The township was named after Charles Knott, of the Steel Co. of Hamilton. The area is accessible by road from Ear Falls, about 40 miles to the southwest.

KNOWLES, geographic township, Thunder Bay District
Position 48° 35′ 85° 23′

Lying immediately to the west of the community of White River, Knowles is traversed by the White River which cascades with numerous rapids down the mountainous northern section of the township.

The Canadian Pacific Railway line runs for some distance along the river bank. Highway 17 enters and exits at the township's far northeastern corner.

The township was named in September 1945 after Vernon C. Knowles, MPP for Hamilton Centre, 1945.

KNOX, geographic township, Cochrane District
Position 48° 45′ 80° 21′

Situated west of Lake Abitibi and east of the town of Iroquois Falls, this township was named after John Knox (1502-72), Scottish Protestant Reformer.

The township was subdivided in 1904. The boundaries were surveyed between 1902-1904. The Abitibi River flows westward through the central part of the township.

KOHLER, geographic township, Cochrane District
Position 49° 46′ 84° 59′

Named after Jacob Kohler, MPP for Haldimand around 1905, this township lies approximately 35 miles northwest of the community of Hornepayne. Highway 11 runs through the area. The Otasawian River flows northward through the area.

KOHLER, part of town of Haldimand, Regional Municipality of Haldimand-Norfolk
Position 42° 54′ 79° 52′

This dispersed rural community south of Highway 3 was named after the Kohler family who were among the many German immigrants who came to the area in the second half of the nineteenth century.

In 1877 a post office was established in the community's blacksmith shop and Frederick Hoffman became the first postmaster. A school was built on the farm of George M. Findlay and in 1892 Jacob Nablo donated land for the Kohler Zion Evangelican Church.

At the beginning of World War Two, the Department of National Defence bought 387 acres in the Kohler area for use as an auxiliary landing field. After the war it was taken over by the Ontario Department of Agriculture and the first Rural Youth Centre in the province was opened here. The centre also became an Agricultural Centre for the residents of Haldimand.

Cayuga-North Cayuga Centennial History, 1967.

KOMOKA, police village, Lobo Township, Middlesex County
Position 42° 57′ 81° 26′

About eight miles west of London lies the community of Komoka. First called Lobo Station when a post office was opened in 1855, its name was changed in 1856 to Komoka, an Indian word which means "quiet resting place of the dead".

The community was first settled in the 1830's by the McIntyres, the Campbells and other Scottish families. Komoka eventually became the heart of a great Campbell settlement, one of the largest in Ontario. A town site was laid out in 1855 and the Great Western Railway was built through the community. By 1857 the population of Komoka, swelled by the presence of transient railroad construction workers, had reached approximately 700 and several small businesses, including three shoe shops, a general store, and a hotel were opened.

The community's population declined after the 1850's but it remained an important shipping centre for the agricultural produce of the area. About 1860 the Campbell weavers, who became renowned throughout Western Ontario for their bedspreads and blankets, brought their looms to Komoka. The Junction Hotel became a popular social centre for both residents and farmers in the surrounding area. In 1881 the Canadian Pacific Railway opened a line through the community and an elevator was built to store local grain before shipping. By this time businesses included several stores and shoe shops and two hotels. John L. McKellar and Neil Morrison operated mills.

Today Komoka is a quiet residential community. Service on the CPR ended in 1969 and the old station was torn down, but many of the village's other historic buildings have been preserved.

Presbyterian services were first held in a schoolhouse by Reverend J.A. Hay. A church was built in 1873. In 1880 a Methodist house of worship was erected on land donated by George Lofthouse. The Baptist church, dedicated in 1864, became a private school, the Komoka Seminary.

Ron Nickles and Ron Davis: Lobo Township Sketches, 1976

KORAH, geographic township, Algoma District
Position 46° 34' 84° 24'

Surveyed by Ontario Land Surveyor James Johnston in 1859, this township, once a municipality, became part of the city of Sault Ste. Marie as of January 1, 1965. Korah refers to the Indian name for king Korah.

KOSNY, geographic township, Sudbury District
Position 47° 27' 83° 39'

Formerly known as Township 10H, Kosny is situated approximately 25 miles southwest of the town of Chapleau. Cow River flows through the southern half of the township. A dry weather road links the northwestern part of the township ultimately to Highway 101. The township was named after W.M. Kosny, a Reeve of Shuniah Township, Thunder Bay District.

KOWKASH, geographic township, Thunder Bay District
Position 50° 18' 87° 16'

Located northeast of Lake Nipigon, the township derives its name from the Indian name of the river Kowaskagama, which flows through the area.

The Canadian National Railways passes through the southern part of the township. There is a station point at Kowkash. Dry weather and secondary roads connect the area with Highway 643.

L

LABELLE, geographic township, Algoma District
Position 47° 22′ 84° 41′

Formerly designated Township 29, Range 16, this triangular township is located on the eastern shore of Lake Superior and forms part of Lake Superior Provincial Park. Here the Agawa River enters Agawa Bay. Highway 17 follows the shoreline of the township. The origin of the name is unknown.

LABERGE, geographic township, Thunder Bay District
Position 48° 40′ 85° 40′

Formerly designated as Township 71, Laberge was named in 1974 after Daniel J. Laberge, RCAF, Geraldton, Ontario who gave his life in World War Two. The township is situated northwest of White River and is accessible by the Trans-Canada Highway. White River flows eastward through the centre of the township. The Canadian Pacific Trans-Continental line passes through the township along the river. There are two station points on the line, Regan and Mobert.

LABONTE, geographic township, Algoma District
Position 47° 22′ 84° 32′

Formerly designated as Township 28, Range 16, a considerable portion of this township forms part of Lake Superior Provincial Park. The land in the southern half rises to a height of 1,462 feet. The Agawa River, interspersed with rapids and falls, courses through the northern section toward Agawa Bay. The Algoma Central Railway follows the limits of Lake Superior Provincial Park through the township. The station point of Frater is located on the line.

LACKNER, geographic township, Sudbury District
Position 47° 48′ 83° 03′

First surveyed in 1906, this township east of the town of Chapleau was named after Henry J. Lackner, MPP for Waterloo North at that time. The area is drained by the Ivanhoe River.

LADYSMITH, geographic township, Kenora District
Position 50° 01′ 93° 00′

Named after a place of Boer War fame, the township lies northwest of the town of Dryden. Canadian National Railways passes through the centre of the township with the railway junction of Amesdale located just east of the border.

LaFLECHE, geographic township, Sudbury District
Position 47° 02' 81° 54'

Named in 1945 after General Leo Richer LaFleche (1888-1956), soldier, diplomat and co-founder of the Canadian Legion, the township lies northwest of the city of Sudbury. The CPR runs through the northeastern part where the railway point of Forks is located.

LAFONTAINE, community, Tiny Township, Simcoe County
Position 44° 45' 80° 04'

Situated about 32 miles northwest of Orillia on the Penetanguishene Peninsula, this compact rural community of about 200 was first known as St. Croix because of the many crosses erected there by Reverend Father Hennepin, missionary sent from France to Canada in 1675. It was renamed Lafontaine in honour of Louis Hypolite Lafontaine, the leader of the Reform Party in the mid-nineteenth century and, with Robert Baldwin, head of the government from 1848 to 1851.

Lafontaine was first settled in the 1830's, at the time of a French-Canadian migration to Tiny Township. Disbanded soldiers came to take up the grants of land which they had been assigned in Penetanguishene and soon a French-speaking community developed. Louis DesCheneaux built the first house of Lafontaine in 1830 on Lot 16, Concession 16. Charles Cote, John LaCroix, Cyril Pombert, and Joseph Thibeault became his neighbours. By 1836 Colbert Amyot, Louis Desaulnier, and Louis George Labatte had arrived. In 1856 a post office was opened. Lafontaine survived well into the twentieth century as the only settlement of any size where English was not spoken. However, by the 1940's most residents could speak both French and English.

Andrew F. Hunter: *The History of Simcoe County*, 1948.

LAFORME, geographic township, Algoma District
Position 48° 03' 84° 05'

Originally designated as Township 24, Range 24, this township was named after Frank J. Laforme, Chief of the Mississaugas of Credit. The township is located northwest of Windermere Lake and borders to the east on the District of Sudbury. Shikwamkwa Lake occupies the northwestern corner of the township, while Maconner Lake lies near the southern border. Highway 651 serves the area.

LAHONTAN, geographic township, Thunder Bay District
Position 48° 52' 87° 29'

The township, formerly designated as #86, located on the shore of

Lake Superior, west of Terrace Bay, was named after Louis Armand, Baron de Lahontan, 17th century voyageur who travelled in the Upper Great Lakes area. The Trans-Canada Highway passes through the township along the Lake Superior shore, as does the Canadian National Railways. Rainbow Falls Provincial Park is located in the area.

LAIDLAW, geographic township, Cochrane District
Position 49° 00' 81° 48'

The township was first subdivided in 1908, the subdivision to be annulled a half a century later. Named probably after noted Canadian railway contractor, George Laidlaw (1828-1889), the township lies west of Cochrane. Its main river is the north branch of the Muskego.

LAIRD, township, Algoma District
Position 46° 24' 84° 02'

Lying on the shore of the St. Joseph Channel of the St. Mary River, the township is about 20 miles southeast of Sault Ste. Marie. It was named after either J. Laird, a Crown Land Inspector, or the Hon. David Laird, Lieutenant-Governor of the Northwest Territories, 1876-81, and Dominion Cabinet Minister, 1873-76.

Laird was subdivided by W. Beatty in 1875 and named in the same year. The township, which is crossed by Highway 17 East, lies entirely on Indian lands.

Today Laird has a population of approx. 820. The only industry in the township is the Aircraft Maintenance Corp. but plans are being made for future industrial zoning. Farming is the main activity although much of the land available for agriculture is not being used as many of the residents are only part-time farmers who work in industry in Sault Ste. Marie.

For most services, including hospital and shopping, the people of the township must travel to Echo Bay or Sault Ste. Marie. There is one elementary school in Laird. Three churches serve Presbyterians, Jehovah's Witnesses, and United Church congregations. Two trailer parks provide accommodation for tourists, and recreational facilities include two community halls, an outdoor rink, ball diamonds, and Centennial Park on Lake George.

Geographic Names Board.

LAKE, township, Hastings County
Position 44° 43' 79° 45'

Situated in the west central area of Hastings County, Lake is bordered on the north by Wollaston Township, on the east by Tudor, on the south by Marmora, and on the west by Peterborough County. It was named after Viscount Gerard Lake (1744-1808), a British military leader in Ireland and India.

The township was surveyed in 1822 by Henry Ewing but was

476

uninhabited until the 1850's when copper and lead were discovered. By 1860 there were 20 settlers, most of them occupying land along the Hastings Road. Land speculators, poor soil, and bad transport discouraged most pioneers and the township did not develop much after this, although in the late 1800's Kerslewan's and Smith's lead mines were opened in the southeast corner.

For most of its history, Lake has been associated with Marmora Township. In 1979 the combined population of the two townships was 1,507.

Gerald E. Boyce, *Historic Hastings*, 1967.

LAKE DORÉ, community, Wilberforce Township, Renfrew County
Position 45° 38′ 77° 04′

Situated about 14 miles south of Pembroke, this dispersed community lies on the bank of the Snake River and on the shores of Lake Doré. The origin of the name, which comes from the French word for "gilded" is obscure.

Among the first settlers in this area were William Clarke, John Dennison, and Duncan King who arrived in the early 1830's. In 1840 Dennison's son William became the first white child born in the settlement. A post office was established in 1863.

Lake Doré is said to be the largest freshwater lake without an island in the world, a claim supported by Robert Ripley in his famous "Believe It or Not" column.

Mrs. Carl Price and Clyde C. Kennedy: *Notes on the History of Renfrew County*, 1961.

LAKEFIELD, village, Douro Township, Peterborough County
Position 44° 26′ 78° 16′

Known as the "cradle of literary culture in Upper Canada", the picturesque village of Lakefield lies at the head of the Otonabee River just below Katchewanooka Lake, whose Indian name means "sparkling waters running fast". The village was named Lakefield because of its topography.

One of the first settlers of the village was Col. Samuel Strickland, half-pay officer of the British army and a member of the literary Strickland family. Arriving in 1831 with Mr. Rawlinson and the blacksmith Sam Copping, Strickland soon directed the laying out of a road along the Otonabee. He encouraged other young Englishmen to emigrate to Canada and learn agriculture. Many of these men stayed for some years in Strickland's home and brought a cultured element to the settlement, some later to become important in the official life of Upper Canada. Strickland's book *Twenty-Seven Years in Canada* is a valuable record of these times.

Strickland was joined by two sisters, both of whom had married half-pay officers. Catharine Parr Traill and her husband arrived in 1832, and Susanna Moodie followed in 1834. Mrs. Traill proved to be a gifted botanist and became well-known for her book *Backwoods of Canada*. Mrs. Moodie wrote one of the most famous works of nineteenth-century Canadian literature, *Roughing It in the Bush*. Ironically, the two pioneer authors were both unsuccessful in coping with life in the backwoods and eventually both moved to centres of settlement, the Moodies to Belleville, and the Traills to Lakefield village.

In 1833, James Thompson, an early settler, built a mill beside the river. A bridge was built across the Otonabee in the same year. Gradually a community developed, known at first as Nelson's Falls after John Nelson who had settled in the area in 1819, and later named Herriot's Falls after a millowner on the Otonabee.

A town plot was surveyed about 1850 and named Selby. In 1855 John Sherin built the community's first store. A tavern was opened in the same year. When the first sawmill was destroyed by fire, the community declined but new sawmills were built by Strickland and Reid, Shaw and Waite, and John Sherin, and the settlement recovered its former prosperity. Lumbering became an increasingly important activity and the lumber firm of Messrs. R. and G. Strickland became one of the major such firms in Canada. The success of the sawmilling industry was due in large part to the excellent waterpower provided by the Otonabee River.

Another well-known Lakefield industry which was established during these years was boat-building. In 1850 Thomas Gordon started a boatworks which became the Lakefield Canoe Company and gained an international reputation. In the twentieth century, as lumbering declined, boat-building became the village's main industry.

In 1875 a post office was established and named Lakefield. In the same year, the first village council was elected and Major Bolton was chosen reeve. Serving as councillors were R. A. Strickland, J. C.

478

Sherin, John Hull, and Mr. Shields. Mr. Sanders was village clerk.

By 1883 the population of the village, about 1,500, swelled each September by an influx of French-Canadian lumbermen. An extension of the Midland Railway was built to connect Lakefield with Peterborough. Four hotels accommodated visitors who came to the village to enjoy the steamer cruises on the area's lakes.

The construction of the nearby Trent Canal at the turn of the century also benefited the village's trade. In 1903 planing, saw, and flour mills were in operation. Three canoe factories and the Lakefield Portland Cement Company, established in 1900, provided employment. Lakefield became a shipping centre for grain, flour, and lumber. The Lakefield Cheese Company produced the excellent cheddar cheese for which the area was becoming known.

However, in the years to follow the village began to decline as the major lumber companies disappeared. The Cavendish Lumber Company was the last large operation to close in 1913. The Portland Cement Company ended its production in 1912.

Lakefield then turned to new industries. Tourism became increasingly important and the village developed into a supply centre for tourists and cottagers from the surrounding Kawartha Lakes. Lakefield Park provided a camping and picnic site. Natural attractions include the nearby petroglyphs, prehistoric rock carvings, and the Warsaw Caves, tunnels in the limestone bedrock which run for as much as 300 feet.

Today the village has a population of 2,296 (1979). Lakefield Boats Limited now produces mostly outboards instead of canoes and rowboats. The old cement plant has been taken over by Lakefield Research of Canada Limited which carries out extensive mineral processing research. Small arms manufacturing and prefab homes are two other local industries, and the Pine Grove Cheese Factory still produces its award-winning cheese. Lakefield has attracted many retired people, but a good number of the inhabitants commute to work in Peterborough.

One of Lakefield's landmarks is its earliest church, Christ Church Anglican, built in 1853. A Wesleyan Methodist church was erected in 1862 and the following year the Episcopal St. John the Baptist Church was dedicated. By the 1960's the village had 6 houses of worship.

Lakefield is known today for the Lakefield College School, earlier called Grove School, a private school for boys. The school recently brought additional fame to Lakefield when Prince Andrew, of the Royal House of Windsor, took up residence there for a semester. The village's first school was built in 1853. Today there is a district high school, a public school, and separate schools. A public library was in existence by 1903.

A well-known Lakefield resident of the twentieth century was Don McIntyre, champion drummer of Canada, who in 1957 formed the McIntyre Pipes and Drums.

Douro Centennial Committee: *Through the Years in Douro, 1822-1967*, 1967.

History of the County of Peterborough, 1883.

LAKE OF BAYS, township, Muskoka District
Position 45° 15′ 79° 00′

This municipality was formed on January 1, 1971 when the Township of Franklin amalgamated with the Township of Ridout and the geographic Township of Sinclair. The township, a fisherman's paradise and a popular summer resort area, lies southeast of Huntsville. The Lake of Bays, from which it takes its name, empties through the Muskoka River into Lake Muskoka. The lake received its name from Alexander Shirreff, the first man to explore the region in the 1820's.

Settlement in the area did not take place until 1862. One of the best known resort areas is Bigwin Island in the Lake of Bays. During the 1920's and 1930's it was considered one of the most elaborate vacation spots in eastern Canada. Bigwin Inn, built by C.O. Shaw and opened in 1920, was one of the area's attractions.

The former township of Ridout was surveyed in 1862 by a man named Ryckert. It was about this time that the Bobcaygeon Road, begun at Bobcaygeon in 1856 to entice early settlers, reached as far north as Dorset. Here it turned northwesterly to meet the Oxtongue River (then called the Muskoka River) in Franklin Township.

George G. Burwell, who was appointed Free Grant Agent for the lands along the road, noted in 1862 that at the narrows of Lake of Bays a good settlement had commenced. The community referred to was Dorset, which is the largest built-up area of Ridout.

The Bobcaygeon Road was not successful as a settlement road as the countryside through which it passed was not suitable for agricultural purposes. However, during the 1880's and 1890's there was a heavy volume of traffic along it, mostly connected with the lumbering industry.

The logging activities of the area established Dorset as a supply centre; stores, hotels and businesses sprang up making it an attractive village.

The extension of the Bobcaygeon Road, originally intended to proceed northward to Lake Nipissing, was abandoned as it became obvious that the roads running in a westerly direction were more important to the people of the Dorset and Ridout regions.

Franklin Township, the second municipality which helped to form Lake of Bays Township, shares its eastern boundary with Haliburton County. The boundary follows the line of the old Bobcaygeon Road as it was originally constructed in 1863. Settlement of the northern townships of Muskoka began following the passing of the Free Grant Act in 1868, but Franklin was not placed on the market until 1877 when settlers arrived in larger numbers.

It was as a result of the demands of settlers in Franklin and Chaffey that a road was built eastward from the Muskoka Road at Huntsville to connect with the Bobcaygeon Road.

The Portage Road extended westerly from the main Franklin Road. The canal which joined Fairy Lake and Peninsula Lake also meant a great deal to Franklin settlers in the Peninsula Lake area.

Completed in 1888, it allowed steamers to travel the lakes with ease. C.O. Shaw of Huntsville, builder of Bigwin Inn, bought the navigation system which included steamers and a small railway.

Dwight, named after the Toronto businessman and sports enthusiast, H.P. Dwight, is the principal community of Franklin.

Rev. Rowland Hill, a Methodist minister who came from York County in 1869, was the first settler east of Huntsville. He took up 700 acres and established the Hillside settlement. The church at Hillside remains as a monument to Mr. Hill's dedication. The Cunnington family was prominent in the development of the tourist industry at Port Cunnington. Other communities in Franklin include Birkendale, South Portage, Point Ideal and Sea Breeze.

Sinclair Township was settled in the 1860's but never became an organized municipality. The township had only one post office, Antioch, which located in several different places before its discontinuance in 1918.

Andrew Hart is said to have been the first settler in Sinclair. He came when only a path to the vicinity of Bella and Rebecca Lakes existed for the traveller. A small community of settlers was established; their produce was sold to the lumber camps. A school was erected in the 1880's and a church in 1894. Following the turn of the century, when Western Canada was opened up, families moved away and the school and the church were closed.

A road was built in 1876 and improved as resorts were established. But it was not until the Royal Norwegian Air Force training centre at Muskoka Airport was built during World War II, that the Department of Highways took over the road and it became Highway 514.

Sinclair Township is a popular place for summer cottages, and as well has summer resorts and hunters' camps.

The permanent population of the Township of Lake of Bays numbered, in 1979, 2,045.

George W. Boyer: *Early Days in Muskoka*, 1970.

LAKE NIPIGON PROVINCIAL PARK, Kilkenny & Kitto Townships, Thunder Bay District
Position: 49° 29′ 88° 09′

Previously, the name for Lake Nipigon Provincial Park was Blacksand Provincial Park, so called because of the pyroxene granules washed up from Lake Nipigon onto its shores. Diabase, ancient molten rock, contains a great deal of the dark green mineral, pyroxene, and erosion over aeons of time has swept the sand-like particles into Lake Nipigon. The waves have again washed these particles shoreward giving the beach the appearance of black sand. Towering cliffs of diabase can be seen along Highway 11, a direct access to the park.

While Indians camped on the black sands of Lake Nipigon for centuries, leaving buried artifacts of copper, the earliest Europeans may have been Radisson and Groseilliers, voyageurs who crossed the lake on their way to James Bay in 1658. The Hudson's Bay Company fur traders built a trading post on what is now the park beach in the

19th century. A later, but distinguished visitor in the 1920's was the Prince of Wales, heir to the British throne. A retreat lodge was built for him at Orient Bay, just south of the park, where he might enjoy the trout fishing for which the area is noted. Early in the twentieth century rich gold lodes were discovered and Beardmore, five miles to the north on Highway 11 boomed overnight, catering to the needs of the miners. However, the gold did not last and prosperity was short-lived. Along with the wildlife usual to a northern area, can be found the double-crested cormorant, eagles and ospreys. The nearest centre is the town of Nipigon about 20 miles south, at the junction of Highways 11 and 17.

Ontario Ministry of Natural Resources

LAKE OF THE WOODS
PROVINCIAL PARK, Spohn & McCrosson Townships, Rainy River
District
Position 48° 59′ 94° 27′

On the south shore of Lake of the Woods is a Natural Environment Park of some 2,127 acres. From the junction of Highways 11 and 621, at Sleeman, one travels 20 miles north on Highway 621.

During the building of Lake of the Woods Provincial Park for the use of public campsites, workmen uncovered an ancient Indian cooking site consisting of six kilns. Ojibway Indians canoeing along the east shore of the Lake of the Woods on their way to and from the trading post at Rainy River, stopped here to gather wild rice which still grows in abundance. The park area is flat and sandy due to its being under water for hundreds of years. According to the famous 19th century Swiss biologist and naturalist, Louis Agassiz, some thousands of years ago a gigantic glacier, remnant of the ice age, melted and formed a lake which gradually drained away leaving in its stead Lake of the Woods and many smaller lakes nearby. A diversity of plants, trees, and wildlife are to be found in the Lake of the Woods park. White pelicans who nest and breed in a protected sanctuary on the offshore islands are to be seen in the summer months. Each year they migrate between northwest Ontario and the Gulf of Mexico.

Ontario Ministry of Natural Resources.

LAKE-ON-THE-MOUNTAIN
PROVINCIAL PARK, North Marysburgh Township, Prince Edward
County
Position 44° 02′ 77° 04′

Lake-on-the-Mountain, five miles northeast of Picton, along Highway 33, is situated on top of Glenora Hill, some 190 feet above the level of the Bay of Quinte. In circumference the lake is about three miles and its waters are fresh and clear. The level of the lake is constant, despite an outflow over the Glenora escarpment, yet no visible inlet of water can be found. It was thought by settlers that the bottom of the lake was much lower than the Bay of Quinte, or that a subterranean passage connects Lake-on-the-Mountain with Lake Erie, and so replenishes its waters. However, both these conjectures have been disproved.

Where Mohawks once camped is now a Provincial Park of 256 acres, an ideal daytime picnic area. Lake-on-the-Mountain Park, between saucer-shaped Lake-on-the-Mountain and the steeply sloping escarpment to the Bay of Quinte, overlooks Adolphustown, early home of a group of 1784 United Empire Loyalists. The leader of this group, Van Alstine, built two mills, one at the top of the mountain and the other at the bottom. The family of Macdonald operated the mill which was powered by water flowing down a long steep sluice from the Lake-on-the-Mountain. This lower mill still stands today. Sir John A. Macdonald, Canada's first prime minister, was a boy in the Macdonald family who occupied the mill.

N. & H. Mika: *Prince Edward County Heritage*, 1980.

Ontario Ministry of Natural Resources.

LAKESIDE, community, East Nissouri Township, Oxford County
Position 43° 12' 81° 01'

This compact rural community of 122 residents (1971) is situated about 18 miles northeast of London. It was named Lakeside because of its position beside a small lake.

The community was founded about 1837 when Squire Ingersoll built a flour mill at the site. This mill and the sawmill which was erected nearby by George Dalrymple and William Trothem in 1855 continued to operate well into the twentieth century.

A post office was opened at Lakeside in 1856 and, by the late 1870's, the community had become a popular summer resort, known for the excellent recreation available on the lake. In 1876 Lakeside's businessmen and craftsmen included Robert Armstrong, general merchant and conveyancer; Thomas Sparks, doctor; and three blacksmiths.

In the 1870's Lakeside had a number of businesses but few residents. However, with the construction of a railway line between St. Mary's and Woodstock (now the CPR) passing through the settlement, Lakeside grew more quickly. In 1903 its population was about 100. A list of businesses included the hotel of H. W. Kumpf and the general store of F. S. Malcolm. The community has remained stable in size since this time.

London Free Press, 1949.

Walker & Miles: *Historical Atlas of Oxford County*, 1876.

LAKE ST. PETER PROVINCIAL PARK, McClure Township, Hastings County
Position 45° 19' 78° 01'

This small Recreation Park comprises 65 acres only, but the waters are clean and warm and there is an excellent sand beach. The park is easily accessible, just off Highway 127. Logging and forest fires depleted the original forests and, consequently, the new trees are yet quite young. An abandoned trapper's cabin of hand-hewn logs still stands near the park. The park is on the Canadian Shield and a number of abandoned mines in the area attest to the valuable minerals contained in this gigantic bedrock that stretches from southern Ontario to Hudson Bay. Bancroft, the nearest shopping centre is 28 miles to the south on Highway 62.

Ontario Ministry of Natural Resources.

LAKE SUPERIOR PROVINCIAL PARK, Algoma District
Position 47° 25′ 84° 40′

On the east shore of Lake Superior is a Natural Environment Park, one of the largest parks in Ontario. It comprises an area of 520 square miles of rivers, small lakes, public campsites, nature trails and historic vestiges of early Canada. Highway 17 enters the park at its southern boundary and crosses the length of the park, exiting at the extreme north.

Convulsed by earthquakes, gouged by ice-age glaciers, blanketed in parts by volcanic lavas, Lake Superior Provincial Park presents a scenic grandeur of high hills and steep-walled valleys. Old Woman Bay, Agawa Canyon and Agawa Rock are formed by ancient "faults", rock masses sundered by tremendous pressures. Members of the famed Group of Seven early travelled through this northern country and with paintbrush and canvas left a heritage of its natural magnificence. The park and surrounding areas abound with Indian legends, as here, for hundreds of years before the white man, many tribes hunted, fished, camped and left an indelible memorial in Indian pictographs on the face of the Agawa Rock, a vertical cliff face on Lake Superior, just north of Agawa Bay. In the path of the early fur traders, the shore of Lake Superior had many fur trading posts. The clear blue-green waters of Lake Superior is Henry Wadsworth Longfellow's shining "Big-Sea-Water", immortalized in his poem *The Song of Hiawatha*. Gargantua Harbour has been used by commercial fishermen since the 1860's for icing and packing their catches of laketrout and herring. The park is the habitat of wildlife, both birds and animals, native to a northern clime.

Ontario Ministry of Natural Resources.

LALIBERT, geographic township, Algoma District
Position 48° 14′ 84° 51′

This township shown on maps as No. 30, Range 26, was named in memory of Clement J. Lalibert, a Private in the Canadian Army from the Thunder Bay District, killed in 1945, World War Two. The township was formerly part of the Algoma Central & Hudson's Bay Railway Land Grant. Situated north of the community of Wawa, the area is served by Highway 17. Dry weather roads link a number of the lakes within the township and the surrounding area.

LAMARCHE, geographic township, Cochrane District
Position 49° 00′ 81° 00′

Situated just to the south of Cochrane, this township was named after Charles Lamarche, MPP for East Nipissing in 1905. The western boundary was surveyed by Mr. Niven in 1898 and the township was subdivided in 1905 by A. Baird.

Lamarche is served by both the Canadian National and the Ontario Northern railways. The only community of any size in the township is Lamarche. The town of Cochrane annexed part of the township in 1972 and again in 1978.

LAMBERT, geographic township, Cochrane District
Position 50° 25′ 82° 10′

Named after the Rev. Father Lambert of Hearst, this township north of Kapuskasing is not subdivided and is not accessible by road. The Missinaibi River flows through the northwest corner of the township.

LAMBETH, community, Westminster Township, Middlesex County
Position 42° 54′ 81° 18′

Named after a place in England, the police village of Lambeth is about 5 miles south of London. Formerly known as "Junction" because of its position at the meeting of the Longwoods and Talbot Roads (Highways 2 and 4), and also as "Slab Town" because of its sawmills, it was named Lambeth when a post office was opened in 1857.

The early settlers in the Lambeth area bought their land from Colonel Thomas Talbot who actively promoted the colonization of this part of Ontario. Abraham Patrick who built his home here in 1811 was probably the first inhabitant of the district. He was soon followed in 1812 by Jeremiah Schram, John Dingman, and Thomas Poole.

In 1826 Jeremiah Schram died, leaving a will which bequeathed the site of a cemetery to the community providing that an Anglican church be built on the land. Lambeth developed around the cemetery and Trinity Church, which was erected some time before 1863.

By 1878 the community was a thriving centre with a population of about 200. A steam spoke factory and a mill were among the local industries. Businesses included stores, blacksmith shops, wagon shops, and a shoe shop. There were also four churches in the community.

By 1903 the population of Lambeth had increased to 300. A cheese factory and the H. Hamlyn & Son sawmill served the farmers of the district. Two blacksmiths, two painters, a builder, a shoemaker, general merchants, and wagonmakers also offered their services.

Following World War Two, Lambeth experienced a rapid growth in population, although the small local industries disappeared. Today the community is mainly residential, with a number of commercial establishments to serve the 3,056 residents (1971). A large proportion of the population commutes to work in nearby London.

London Free Press, 1949.

H. R. Page & Co.: Historical Atlas of Middlesex County, 1878.

LAMBTON COUNTY

Position 42° 45′ 82° 05′

Lambton County was not settled in great numbers until the 1830's, much later than most of southern Ontario. Anyone looking at this county today with its enviably mild climate, rich soil, abundant natural resources and excellent position on the seaway would surely wonder why its early settlement proceeded at such a modest pace. However, Lambton, then the most westerly county, was heavily forested and because of the prevalence of swamp fever, had acquired· an ominous name among prospective pioneers.

The Crown did not negotiate with the Indians for the bulk of this county until 1827 and for a few years following this only a small number of French settlers had established themselves there.

Many of the early pioneers were from the British Isles, some were first generation Canadians who moved from points east, and some came from Ireland following the potato famines of 1845 and 1847.

In 1834 the population of the county was 1,728, but arrival of the Irish helped to increase this number to 10,815 in 1851.

Lambton originally was part of the District of Hesse which was established in 1788, when the provinces of Upper and Lower Canada were created in 1791.

Upper Canada was divided into 19 counties and Hesse was renamed the Western District, containing Kent and Essex counties. Lambton remained part of Kent for the next 57 years.

Lambton was named in 1849 by the Honourable Malcolm Cameron, local parliamentary representative, in honour of John George Lambton, first Earl of Durham. Durham was named governor-general of British North America in 1838, following the Rebellion of 1837. As a result of his five months tenure in Canada he produced his famous Report which laid the foundation for a union of all British North American provinces under a constitutional government.

Kent withdrew from the Western District in 1851; Lambton remained united with Essex until 1853 when their union was dissolved by order of the Administrator-in-Council. The first meeting of the County Council of Lambton was held in Port Sarnia on October 24, 1853. Archibald Young was the first warden.

Until 1790 the Indians held all of Lambton County. Today they are settled on the St. Clair, Bosanquet, Walpole Island and Kettle Point Reserves. The Indian population on all the Lambton reservations was 1,580 in 1842, in 1965 it had risen to 2,731.

It is believed that the first white settlement in Lambton County was outside its present limits. James Johnston and a man named Fisher, some time before 1804, settled on Bear Creek, now the Sydenham River, on the Chanal Ecarté, the scene of the Baldoon Settlement.

In 1804 the Earl of Selkirk's Highland crofters arrived at the Baldoon tract. Of the original 111 settlers, 42 perished from swamp fever and dysentery during the first winter. The settlement held on and prospered until 1812 when the Americans under General McArthur, raided and carried off most of the sheep and cattle.

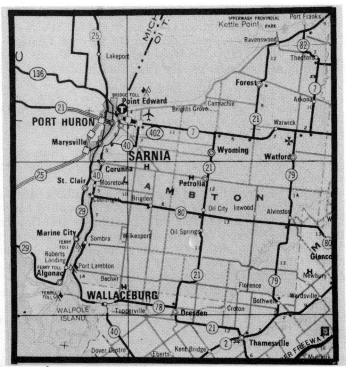

Prior to the establishment of the Selkirk settlement, considerable numbers of French Canadians had settled along the St. Clair River.

Because pioneering depends on the accessibility of the new land, Lambton was settled first along the areas bordering the St. Clair, Lake Huron, and within the reach of the Sydenham River. The central township of Enniskillen was landlocked and also handicapped by large swampy areas. Warwick and Brooke were situated far from navigable waters, but the Egremont or London Road helped to bring in settlers. With the advent of the Great Western and Grand Trunk Railways, new areas of settlement were opened up.

Sarnia, capital of Lambton County, developed slowly. The first English-speaking settler is believed to have been a Lieutenant Vidal who arrived in 1832. Following the Rebellion in 1837, Sarnia began to grow more quickly. In 1853 its population was 800 and it was incorporated as a town. In the same year it was made the county town.

Sarnia's prominence was due to its position as a shipping centre on the Great Lakes waterway. Manufacturing and businesses flourished. With the arrival of the Great Western Railway in 1856 Sarnia's future was assured.

It was just at this point that one of Lambton's most exciting periods began with the discovery of oil. In 1854 or 1855 a man named Charles Tripp, who had recognized the potential of the gumbeds of Enniskillen to produce asphalt, dug a well which yielded oil rather than water. He did not follow up this discovery, selling his holdings to James Miller Williams.

In 1860 the first flowing well was tapped and men rushed to the area. This early success did not last long. However, it was at this point that a man named Shaw struck oil near Oil Springs. Transportation of the oil along the "Plank Road" to Sarnia was difficult. In 1866 the railway finally reached Petrolia near which other oil wells were discovered.

Williams built the first oil refinery at Oil Springs in 1857, the first one built at Petrolia was in 1861. In 1870 the Imperial Oil Company Limited opened a refinery at Petrolia, a year later it moved its head office to Sarnia and built a refinery there.

Oil became the basis for Lambton's chemical industry. Salt, one of Sarnia's oldest industries, also played a supporting role in this development.

During the Second World War a synthetic rubber plant was built at Sarnia. Following the war Dow Chemical expanded the synthetic rubber operations to the production of plastics. In 1947 Dow began the production of Fiberglas. The list of almost 700 chemical products made in the Sarnia area has made Lambton County famous as "Canada's Chemical Valley". The St. Lawrence Seaway has given access to world markets and ensured Lambton's future.

The face of the county has changed throughout the years, where the land was once primarily devoted to farming, towns and villages have sprung up. In 1867, seventy per cent of the population was employed on the farm, whereas today that number has been reduced to less than 20 per cent.

Lambton has an area of 699,539 acres with a population of 118,138. It has one city, Sarnia; two towns, Forest and Petrolia; eight villages: Alviston, Arkona, Grand Bend, Oil Springs, Point Edward, Thedford, Watford and Wyoming; and ten townships: Bosanquet, Brooke, Dawn, Enniskillen, Euphemia, Moore, Plympton, Sarnia, Sombra and Warwick.

Jean Turnbull Elford: A History of Lambton County, 1967.

Victor Lauriston: Lambton's Hundred Years 1849-1949, 1949.

R. M. McPherson & R. M. Ford: A History of the Chemical Industry in Lambton County, 1966.

LAMBTON MILLS, part of the Borough of Etobicoke, Municipality of Metropolitan Toronto
Position 43° 39' 79° 31'

The urban community of Lambton Mills lies on the banks of the Humber River in the western part of Toronto. In the mid-nineteenth century, Lambton Mills and its twin community of Milton on the Humber were often known as Milton Mills but in the 1870's the settlement was renamed in honour of the visit of Lord Lambton to the area.

The first sawmill on the Humber River at the site of Milton Mills was built by the British government about 1793. In 1820 Thomas Fisher took over its operation and in 1834 he built the well-known Milton House on the site of the Home Smith Administration Building. The mill was sold to William Gamble who added a new grist mill in

1837. In 1848 Gamble built the Old Mill. The settlement which developed on the west side of the river during this period took the name of Gamble's Mill and became known as Milton Mills.

William Cooper erected a grist and sawmill in 1806 on the east side of the Humber River. The mill prospered after a bridge was built across the river in 1816 and the community developing around the operation became known as Cooper's Mills. Later a new mill and a distillery were added.

Following the sale of his mill to William Gamble in 1835, Thomas Fisher established another mill nearby, replaced by the Millwood Mill in 1844. In 1888 this operation was taken over by George Smith who converted the structure into a woollen mill. Two of his employees, Mr. Phillips and John R. Berry, formed a partnership and built their own woollen mill and became the exclusive Canadian manufacturers of cutter robes. The business did not prosper and when the mill burned ten years later it was not rebuilt.

In 1892 William Morris's Lambton Mills Woollen Manufactory took over Millwood Mills. The company became a major employer in the community and the destruction of the mill by fire in 1900 was a serious blow to Lambton Mills' development. Many residents moved away and it was a number of years before the community recovered its former prosperity.

In the late nineteenth century, Lambton Mills was a bustling centre with several local industries. A large flour mill built by William Pearce Howland in 1845 provided employment along with the other mills in the area. The community also had a wheelwright, a blacksmith, and a saddle and harness maker. The Lambton Grove Hotel provided accommodation for passengers on the electric railway which ran from Toronto.

A Wesleyan Methodist church was dedicated about 1850 and a new church opened in 1878. In 1881 the Roman Catholics of the community erected a house of worship. Kingsway-Lambton United Church was built in 1937.

The Howland family of Lambton Mills became well-known in Canada in the late nineteenth century. William Howland was a Father of Confederation and the first lieutenant-governor of Ontario after Confederation. He was also Minister of Finance and Postmaster-General. His brother, Henry Stark Howland, became president of both the Imperial Bank of Canada and the Toronto, Grey, and Bruce Railway.

R. A. Given: *The Story of Etobicoke*, 1950.

LAMMING, geographic township, Algoma District
Position 46° 55′ 83° 47′

Formerly Township 22, Range 11, the area is located northeast of the city of Sault Ste Marie. It is watered by the East Goulais River and its tributaries. Secondary roads provide access to Highway 17 to the west. The township was named after T. Lamming, a constable for Korah District in the early days.

LAMPLUGH, geographic township, Cochrane District
Position 48° 35' 79° 50'

The township borders in the north on Lightning and Ghost Bays of Lake Abitibi. The southern part is mountainous, the Ghost Range rising to a height of over 1600 feet. The Ghost River flows northward through the western section. The origin of the township's name is not known.

LAMPMAN, geographic township, Sudbury District
Position 47° 11' 81° 19'

Named after Canadian poet Archibald Lampman, the township lies northwest of Sudbury. Canadian National Railways travels through the southwestern corner and a dry weather road links the area with points north and south.

LAMPORT, geographic township, Thunder Bay District
Position 48° 32' 90° 14'

Located south of the Shebandowan Lake District, the township was named after Allan A. Lamport, MPP for Toronto — St. Davids, in the 1930's. The northwestern and eastern boundaries were surveyed in 1938, the southern boundary remains unsurveyed. The interior of Lamport is accessible only by waterways. Secondary roads link the area in the north to Highway 11.

LANARK, county
Position 45° 05' 76° 20'

Lying north of the Rideau Lake and River, Lanark County is bordered on the west by Frontenac County, on the northwest by Renfrew County, and on the northeast by the Regional Municipality of Ottawa-Carleton. It was named after Lanark in Scotland.

Dotted with many small lakes, the county is drained by the Rideau and Mississippi Rivers. Much of the land is covered with hard rocky soil, but there are also some rich farming areas. The shallow soil has made beef and dairy cattle raising an important agricultural activity.

The settlement of Lanark County began in the early nineteenth century after an 1815 proclamation in Britain offered free passage, as well as provisions and land, to emigrants to Canada. The British Government had decided to encourage the colonization of Upper Canada in order to defend the territory against any further aggression from the United States. The first settlers arrived from Scotland in the autumn of 1815. No preparations had been made for them so they passed the winter in Belleville while the surveyors laid out the lots. The new colonists took up their land in 1816, many of them settling in the Military Settlement of Perth which had been laid out for British soldiers discharged after the War of 1812-15 with the United States.

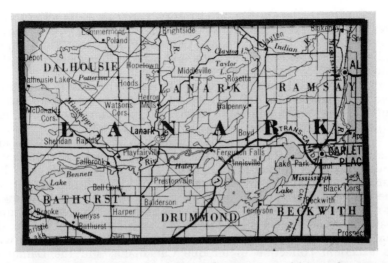

More emigrations soon followed, encouraged by such organizations as the Lesmahago and Transatlantic Societies which sent groups of Scottish settlers to Dalhousie Township in 1820. The southern townships were soon thickly populated. The area along the Rideau was settled by workers on the Rideau Canal in the late 1820's and early 1830's. Continued immigration led to the settlement of the northern townships around the middle of the century.

In 1822 the Bathurst District was set aside from Carleton County and Perth became the district capital. In 1849 Bathurst was divided into Lanark and Renfrew but the two counties remained united for municipal purposes. At the first United County Council held in 1850, Robert Bell was elected warden. Council members from Lanark were Josiah Richey, Jno. Doran, Jr., John Kay, Murdoch McDonnell, Patrick Dowdell, James Shaw, Sr., Andrew Stevenson, R. E. Matheson, William McAdam, and John Robertson. Renfrew was detached from Lanark in 1851.

The county's population increased from 7,928 in 1825 to 9,736 in 1830. The 1830's and 40's were periods of rapid growth. The number of inhabitants rose to 15,198 by 1841 and to 27,317 in 1851. By this time a large number of local industries had been established in the county, including twenty-three grist mills, forty-five sawmills, twelve carding and fulling mills, two woollen mills, a distillery, a brewery, ten tanneries, three iron foundries, and fourteen other factories. Ten years later the population stood at 31,169.

During this period, lumbering had become increasingly important in Lanark. The large number of mills processed the abundant products of the forests. Railways such as the Canada Central were built to connect the lumber regions of the north with the major rail and water routes in the south. However, in the 1860's the depletion of the forests and the resulting decline of the lumber trade led to a decrease in population and by 1871 the number of inhabitants had dropped to 23,020.

During the late nineteenth century, Lanark was important as an area of small local industries. By the 1880's the county with one town, Perth, and four villages, Almonte, Carleton Place, Lanark, and Smiths Falls, had become one of the principal seats of the woollen industry. Lanark is still known today for its fabric industries.

Lanark has remained an area of moderate prosperity during the twentieth century. In 1947-8, the Department of Agriculture carried out a survey of the county to determine the economic, social, and cultural standards of the average home in eastern Ontario.

Lanark has preserved much of its rich historical heritage and these landmarks, along with the beautiful scenery in which the county abounds, attract many visitors and cottagers each year. The Lanark County Byway Tours were developed as sightseeing tours for the motorist, designed to bring to the visitor's attention as many attractions as possible. Among the sites are one of the few remaining water-powered lumber mills in Canada, an old blacksmith shop, the many restored pioneer log homes, the Matheson House Museum, with its excellent collection of antique Canadiana, and the Dalhousie Library Collection which has been in existence since 1828. The Balderson Cheese Factory, and the chocolate and ice cream factories show the continued importance of industry to the county's 45,000 residents. The mill and clearance stores of the fabric industries are also popular attractions.

The county seat of Perth is especially rich in historic landmarks. Here, in 1833, the last fatal duel in Canada was fought. In 1893 the town became the home of the largest cheese in the world. Weighing 11 tons, it was a worldwide sensation. A cement replica was later placed on the CPR station ground.

Smiths Falls is the largest town in the county. However, it has separated town status, which makes it independent municipally from the rest of Lanark. A hospital for mentally-retarded children was built here in 1951.

Lanark has produced a number of well-known Canadian figures. Work of the famous sculptor, Robert Tait McKenzie, is on display in the Mill of Kintail. Local political members have included the Hon. Malcolm Cameron, Minister of Agriculture, Postmaster-General, and Queen's Printer in the 1860's; the Hon. William McDougall, Minister of Public Works in the 1860's; and Alexander Morris, Minister of Internal Revenue in 1869. Capt. A. Roy Brown, D.S.C., the victor over Baron Von Richthofen, the Red Baron, in the first World War, was also a Lanark native.

H. Belden & Co.: *Historical Altas of Lanark & Renfrew Counties*, 1881.

Lanark County Byway Tours (Brochures).

LANARK, township, Lanark County
Position 45° 06′ 76° 24′

Settlement of Lanark Township commenced around and on the site of the present village of Lanark in 1820, Lord Bathurst having organized the emigration of people from Lanark in Scotland. Over 800 prospective pioneers were sent to Canada that year on the ships *Commerce* and *Prompt*. Col. William Marshall was named superintendent of the new settlement.

A government depot had been completed on the Lanark village site to serve as a centre of the settlement, which consisted mainly of unemployed Scottish weavers and discharged soldiers who were to take up land in the newly surveyed township of Lanark, as well as in the townships of Ramsay, North Sherbrooke and Dalhousie. By the spring of 1821 the number of settlers who were established in Lanark Township and vicinity had swelled to 1500. They had received land, tools, farm implements and seeds from the quartermasters-general department.

Among the first of the township's settlers were John Mair, Charles Isdele, John Turreff and Duncan McPherson. Arriving at the present site of Lanark village, they found the government surveyors in the process of completing the survey of the village plot. This first party temporarily returned to Perth and then brought their families back to the banks of the Clyde, where they erected temporary log houses. The majority of the pioneers, however, pushed on and formed a prosperous settlement further north where the community of Middleville now stands. The first settlers there were James Smith, Archibald Rankin, John Mitchell and James Campbell. A schoolhouse was erected here in 1822, and the first teacher was Robt. Mason.

At the present site of Hopetown, Robert Cannon and John Robertson selected land on the second concession. Robert Cannon started a cooperage, opened a tavern, and became postmaster at Hopetown in 1853.

At Galbraith, twenty-six miles from Perth, Robert Affleck, a weaver, settled with his wife and nine children. James Campbell had sold his business in Scotland and purchased land in the centre of Lanark Township. A portion of his land became the site on which Middleville was laid out.

Along the Mississippi River, north of the present village of Ferguson's Falls, many Irish settlers took up land. They were the Braidens, Boyds, Bertrams, Forsyths, Flemings, Francises, Foleys, Grahams, Hopkins, Maloneys and McMannises. The Boyds' location was later called Boyd Settlement.

In the northeast of Lanark Township there were the Sutherlands, Stevensons, Wilsons, Robertsons, Nicholsons, McArtons, Bains, Taylors, Kemps and Dunlops. These settlers had come from Ireland and Scotland.

Lanark and Darling Townships were united for municipal purposes up to 1853. That year Darling withdrew from the union and each of the townships has since then remained independent.

The officials for the united townships during 1850, the first year of Ontario's municipal organization, were: Andrew Ferguson, Reeve; Alex Stewart, Robt. Stead, Robt. Robertson, and John Madden, councillors; J. R. Gemmill, clerk; and Robt. Mason, collector.

Alexander Caldwell, son of William Caldwell, one of the early settlers, became the principal lumber baron of the county. He started in the lumber business when he was twelve years old. In 1846, sixteen years later, he was a well-established man. His fine stone residence in Lanark village was known as "Clyde Hall".

Lanark, long since an incorporated village and known for its textile industry, is also the centre of a prosperous farming district. The township has a population of 982 (1979).

Historical Atlas of Lanark County, 1880.

A Pioneer History of the County of Lanark, 1968.

LANARK, village, Lanark Township, Lanark County
Position 45° 01' 76° 22'

The village is located on the River Clyde about 18 miles north of Perth. The first settlers, immigrants from the Scottish counties of Lanark and Renfrew, arrived here in 1820.

The government had set up a depot on the site of the present village to serve as the centre of a military settlement in the newly-surveyed surrounding townships. By the spring of 1821 about 1500 settlers, mostly unemployed Scottish weavers and discharged soldiers and their dependants were established in the area.

The first log house at what the settlers called "New Lanark" was built by David Bowers. Captain Alex. Ferguson opened a store in his log house and, in 1821, he built the first grist mill on the River Clyde. Other early settlers of Lanark were James Hall, Peter McLaren, William Gordon, John Hall, Henry Glass, and Captain Matthew Leech.

A schoolhouse was erected in 1821 with Robert Mason as teacher. The Rev. John Gemmill arrived in 1823 with his family. His wife died shortly after at Lanark.

In 1824 a post office was opened on Mill Street with postmaster J. Murdock, who was to serve for 28 years. Mail from Brockville and Perth was delivered on horseback. In later years a coach service ran daily between Lanark and Carleton Place.

In 1824, during the ministry of Rev. John Gemmill, the first Presbyterian church, St. Andrew's, was erected. Built of stone, it had a seating capacity of about 300. A new church was built in 1860. St. Paul's Church was built in 1842 on land given by James H. Manahan. The porch, tower and belfry were added in 1906 and 1907. This church is now the oldest church in Lanark. In 1945 fire caused considerable damage to the roof and interior. The Roman Catholic church, Sacred Heart, dates back to 1903.

The Baptist church was organized in 1889, the first church being situated on Princess Street. In 1927 the congregation purchased the Methodist church building on George Street and in 1954 they acquired the Congregational church building. The Methodists, having worshipped in their small church on George Street until 1925, moved into St. Andrew's Church at the time of the Church Union. The old church on George Street was destroyed by fire in 1959. The Zion Congregational Church was organized in 1853. The first frame building, destroyed by fire, was replaced in 1856. Rev. Henry Lancashire was the first pastor.

In 1837 the Caldwell family, John, Alexander and Boyd, arrived from Lochwinnooch, Scotland. For many years they were the lumber kings of the county. Caldwell's woollen mill, famous from coast to coast, was established in 1867. In 1917 the mill fell prey to a disastrous fire and was not rebuilt, but the textile industry has remained Lanark's main employer to this day.

In 1862 the village of Lanark was incorporated and the first council consisted of: Reeve William Robertson; Clerk John Wright; Treasurer Adam Craig, Collector Francis Turner; and Councillors: A. G. Hall, Jas. Drysdale, Peter McLaren, and Thomas Baird. In September 1921 electricity came to the homes and streets of Lanark.

The first town hall built in 1860 at the corner of George and Clarence Streets, was destroyed by fire in June of 1959. A new town hall was built in 1961. In the auditorium of the town hall is a plaque commemorating Charles Mair, poet and dramatist, advocate of Western expansion and original member of the "Canada First" movement. Mair was born at Lanark in 1838.

E. L. Jamieson: *The Story of Lanark*, 1974.

LANCASTER, township, Glengarry County
Position 45° 15' 74° 30'

Lancaster Township was once known as the "sunken township", a name which originated with the French settlers who cleared land up to its eastern limits but did not proceed into it because they considered it too swampy for habitation and cultivation.

It is a tribute to the Highland Scots who pioneered the "swampy township" that it became an agricultural area equal to any in the county.

Few, if any, United Empire Loyalists settled in Lancaster. Highland Scottish immigrants were almost exclusively its pioneers. Among the names of the early colonizers were the McMillans, McDonalds, Macdonells, McLennans, Macdougalls and the McKays.

No villages of any size developed in this primarily agricultural region, other than the village of Lancaster on the Charlottenburgh town line. However, there were many neat hamlets dotting its countryside.

The township covers an area of some 61,894 acres and has a population of 3,092 (1979).

H. Belden & Co.: *Illustrated Historical Atlas of the Counties of Stormont, Dundas & Glengarry*, 1879.

LANCASTER, village, Charlottenburgh and Lancaster Townships, Glengarry County
Position 45° 08' 74° 30'

One mile north of Lake St. Francis at the widening of the St. Lawrence lies the picturesque village of Lancaster. Named after George III of England, who was Duke of Lancaster, the village developed when the Grand Trunk Railway (now the CNR) was built in the mid-nineteenth century.

The original Lancaster settlement was founded in 1787, one mile to the south at the mouth of the Raisin River, by United Empire Loyalists who left the United States after the American Revolution. Before the railway was built the St. Lawrence was the main mode of transportation and the settlement early developed into a thriving business centre. Several piers were built, each handling separate commodities including coal, foods, dry-goods, and passengers. In 1825 the historic Moose Head Inn, which still stands today, was erected on the King's Highway. At the height of its prosperity, the community on the shore of Lake St. Francis had at least three general stores, a tannery, a refinery for lamp oil, a brick factory, a lumber mill, a boat-building industry, and several hotels. It also had the oldest post office in the county, established in 1789.

In 1855 the Grand Trunk Railway was opened between Montreal and Brockville. It was extended to Toronto the following year. The railway which ran one mile north of the lakeshore had a profound effect on the community of Lancaster. A new settlement grew up around the station and gradually the businesses in Lancaster moved north to be near the railway. Known at first as New Lancaster, the railway community soon became simply Lancaster. The original settlement became known as Kirktown and later as South Lancaster, the name it has today.

Almost all agricultural produce from the surrounding townships was shipped out via Lancaster station. Merchants and then hotel operators set up business near the railway. A foundry, a carriage shop, blacksmith shops, and other farm-associated industries were established. Trading firms were set up, including those of McPherson & Alexander, and Duncan and George McBear and Bros., William and David McPherson, and Donald McNaughton ran large general stores.

By the 1870's Lancaster was one of the most important stations between Cornwall and Montreal. Its 500 residents were mostly of Scottish descent, although this was beginning to change as Scottish immigration ended about 1870. Other groups began to arrive from overseas in the 1870's and soon Lancaster's population included people of Irish, English, and German descent. Later, a large number of French-Canadians made the community their home.

Lancaster was incorporated as a village in 1887. By 1903 its population had increased to about 800.

As the railway became a less important form of transportation in the twentieth century, Lancaster's prosperity began to decrease. Today few local industries remain. In recent years the village, which is part of the Seaway Valley Tourist Region, has developed into a popular summer resort. Offering excellent facilities for fishing and hunting as well as many parks and playgrounds, the Lancaster area now attracts nearly a quarter million visitors each summer. Winter recreational facilities are also being developed.

Open air prayer meetings were held on the Lancaster waterfront by the early settlers. In 1796 St. Andrew's, the first Presbyterian church in Upper Canada, was built in what is now South Lancaster. In the mid-nineteenth century, Rev. John Anderson, minister of the Presbyterian Free Church congregation at Lancaster, was one of the leaders of the Great Revival, a wave of religious fervour, which swept the county at this time. St. Andrew's was rebuilt in 1855. A Methodist church was erected in 1890 and in 1904 St. Joseph's opened its doors to the village's Roman Catholic population.

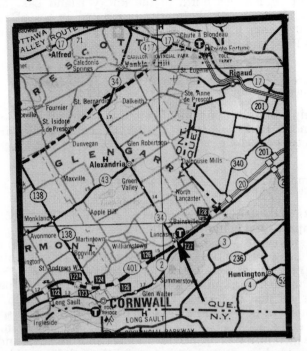

A Lancaster Mechanics Institute was established in the 1890's, the forerunner to a public library built in 1902. In 1971 the village's library became part of the County Library System.

Three large fires during the 1920's virtually wiped out sections of Lancaster's business centre, destroying many of the old buildings. However, visitors today can still see the historic Moose Head Inn, a stagecoach inn erected in 1825. In its early years the inn was used as a courtroom. During later renovation of the basement under the courtroom, a keg of deteriorated gunpowder was discovered. It had been placed directly under the judge's chair.

Lancaster Historical Society: *Historic Moose Head Inn.*

Royce MacGillivray and Ewan Ross: *History of Glengarry,* 1979.

LANDRY, geographic township, Cochrane District
Position 49° 30′ 83° 59′

The township may have been named after Col. P. Landry, Aide-de-camp to the Governor-General of Canada in 1888. The area was formerly part of the Algoma Central and Hudson Bay Railway land grant. The line passes immediately to the east of the township. The town of Hearst lies less than 20 miles to the northeast.

LANE, geographic township, Algoma District
Position 47° 07′ 83° 09′

The township which lies north of the Rocky Island Lake area, is traversed by Highway 129. Formerly designated as No. 6D, it was named in 1974 after John Lane, MPP for Algoma-Manitoulin. The Wenebegon River drains the eastern part of the township.

LANG, geographic township, Sudbury District
Position 48° 14′ 83° 49′

The township which lies immediately to the southwest of Missinaibi Lake Provincial Park, was named after Malcolm Lang, MPP for Cochrane between 1914 and 1923.

LANG, community, Otonabee Township, Peterborough County
Position 44° 16′ 78° 10′

On the banks of the Indian River, about 8 miles east of Peterborough, lies the compact rural community of Lang.

In the survey of Otonabee Township made in 1819, the site of present-day Lang was marked as a mill site. The land on which the community now stands was granted to Robert Weir in 1825. Shortly after this, Thomas Short built a sawmill on the east side of the river and a home on the west side. The Indian River proved to be an excellent source of power and in 1836 William Lang bought some of Weir's land and erected a carding mill, sawmill and shingle mill.

A large grist mill was opened by Thomas Short in 1846, and soon after this he added an oatmeal mill. Around the mill he established a number of industries related to the milling enterprise. A narrow railway linked the mill with a barrel factory which provided barrels for the flour. A sawmill made the staves for the barrels, and a foundry manufactured the castings. Short also established a blacksmith and a carriage shop. The produce of his mills sold widely, but in the 1860's the American Civil War closed the U.S. market and Short went bankrupt.

In 1850 John Huston laid out a village plot which was named Allandale, after a place in Cumberland, England. As there was already an Allandale in the province, the community was renamed Lang in honour of Squire William Lang, when a post office was established in 1872.

In the 1860's and 70's, Lang rivalled nearby Keene with its mills, blacksmith shops, and inns. In 1862 Richard Hope had built a town hall with a cupola on top which became a local landmark. Will Dinsdale and Billy Martin were among the first storekeepers in the community. William Hastie had a carriage, carpenter and repair shop, James Lang ran a shoe shop, and Alexander Connel offered his services as a blacksmith. William Calder operated a tannery.

The mill industries disappeared in the twentieth century, although the old stone grist mill of Thomas Short has been preserved as a historic site. Today the community is a quiet residential centre.

D. Gayle Nelson: *Forest to Farm Early Days in Otonabee*, 1975.

Peterborough Historical Atlas Foundation Inc.: *Illustrated Historical Atlas of Peterborough County 1825-1875*, 1975.

LANGEMARCK, geographic township, Cochrane District
Position 49° 33′ 84° 23′

Langemarck, southwest of the town of Hearst, bears the name of a World War One battlefield in France. The Shekak River, a tributary of the Nagagami, flows first in an easterly and then in a northerly course through the township. The area is linked by road to Highway 11.

LANGFORD, community, Brantford Township, Brant County
Position 43° 10′ 80° 08′

Situated 7 miles east of Brantford on Highway 2, this dispersed rural community was probably named after C. R. Lang, one of its earliest settlers.

Lang came to Canada from Scotland in 1836 and began farming in Brantford Township on the old London and Hamilton Road. Gradually more houses were built along the road and a small community began to take shape. A post office was established in 1867. Alexander Milne, who opened a store about this time, was one of the first postmasters. Other early residents included John and A. G. Ramsay, lumber merchants, and two stock raisers, Alexander Oles and Levi Westbrook.

By the late 1800's, Langford had about 200 residents. A church served the Methodist congregation in the community. The population decreased around the turn of the century.

C. P. Mulvaney: *History of Brant County*.

LANGLOIS, geographic township, Sudbury District
Position 47° 27′ 83° 09′

Named after a miner who bought and developed land in the Algoma and Thunder Bay Districts in the 1860's, the township is designated as No. 10D on old maps. The area, traversed by Highway 29, lies about 40 miles southeast of the town of Chapleau. The northern tip of Wenebegon Lake stretches along much of the township's eastern border.

LANGMUIR, geographic township, Cochrane District
Position 48° 20′ 81° 00′

The area was annexed in 1973 by the city of Timmins. Until 1974 part of Timiskaming District, the township was named after J. W. Langmuir, manager of Toronto General Trust Corporation. Langmuir lies directly south of Night Hawk Lake. The southern part of Carman Bay (Night Hawk Lake) is the area's main body of water.

LANGSTAFF, part of town of Vaughan and part of town of Markham,
Regional Municipality of York
Position 43° 50′ 79° 25′

This compact rural community lying on the townline between
Vaughan and Markham near Thornhill was named after John
Langstaff, one of its earliest settlers.

Langstaff arrived in the area in 1808 and became the first teacher
in the local school. He also erected a pail factory, a store, and an
eavestrough and shingle factory, thus playing a major role in the
development of the community.

By the 1830's a small settlement had grown up along this part of
Yonge Street and when the road was stoned in 1850 a tollgate was set
up here. Robert Thompson operated a stagecoach from 1870 to 1896.
In 1870 a post office was established with John Langstaff, a
descendant of the original Langstaff, as the first postmaster.

In 1903 Edwin Langstaff was a dealer in livestock and Henry
Horne ran the general store to which the post office had been moved
in 1888. An oval half-mile racetrack provided entertainment for the
approximately 50 residents.

Langstaff Baptist Church was built in 1936.

G. Elmore Reaman: *A History of Vaughan Township,* 1971.

LANGTON, geographic township, Kenora District
Position 49° 50′ 93° 25′

Langton, north of Eagle Lake, was subdivided in 1906 and was named
after John Langton, one-time Auditor General of Canada. Vermilion
Bay occupies the southeastern part of the township. Here, on the CPR
and Highway 17 (Trans-Canada Highway) lies the community of
Vermilion Bay.

LANGTON, community, Norfolk Township, Regional Municipality of
Haldimand-Norfolk
Position 42° 45′ 80° 35′

The compact rural community of Langton, which was formerly the
administrative centre of North Walsingham Township, lies in the
middle of a prosperous tobacco-growing area, about 13 miles
southwest of Simcoe.

There was little settlement in this area before 1870, although a
post office was established at Langton as early as 1862. The
community experienced its most rapid growth during the 1870's
when the district's excellent timber stands were first exploited. By
1877 Langton's population was over 150. Businesses and industries
included two stores, a hotel kept by Michael Prue, a cabinet shop, a
shoe shop, a tailor shop, two carriage shops, two blacksmith shops,
two shingle factories, and a sawmill. James Fulton served as
postmaster.

Tobacco growing replaced the lumber industry, once the local
supply of timber was exhausted. Begun in 1926 the industry now

attracts thousands of tobacco workers to the area each summer.

Langton is a pleasant rural community with a population of 478, according to the 1971 census. Township bylaws placing Langton under subdivision control and defining minimum requirements for residents have ensured its attractive development. A large percentage of the population are retired people. About half of the community are New Canadians, mostly from Belgium; but there are also some from Germany, Holland, and Hungary.

Langton had the first central public school in Ontario to be built by a municipality. It was opened in 1945. A separate school was erected in 1936.

The community's Baptist Church was dedicated in 1860. In 1936 the Roman Catholic Sacred Heart Church was built. Plans were made in the 1960's for the erection of a new church which was to be the largest Roman Catholic house of worship in Norfolk County.

The beautiful shrine at Sacred Heart, a replica of the shrine of our Lady of Lourdes in France, attracts many visitors each year. The Belgian Fair, which has been held annually since the late 1930's, is a popular event. A bicycle race course and a baseball diamond are among the recreational facilities available at the community centre grounds and there is excellent trout fishing in the nearby Deer, Venison and Big Creeks.

H. R. Page & Co.: *Historical Atlas of Norfolk County*, 1877.

LANGWORTHY, geographic township, Thunder Bay District
Position 49° 04' 90° 21'

Located north of the Trans-Canada Highway and north of Lac des Milles Lacs, Langworthy was named after a Port Arthur barrister and former member of parliament. The township is watered by the Little Savanne River and its northeastern corner is traversed by the Canadian National Railways.

LANSDOWNE, community, Front of Leeds and Lansdowne Township,
Leeds County
Position 44° 24' 76° 01'

This compact rural community of about 600 people (1973) is situated 10 miles east of Gananoque, and about 4 miles from the Thousand Islands International Bridge. It was named after Major-General William Petty Fitzmaurice, Earl of Shelbourne, who was created Marquis of Lansdowne in 1784. He was born on Lansdowne Road in Dublin, Ireland.

Lansdowne was first settled in the late 1780's by United Empire Loyalists who fled the United States after the American Revolution. Among those to arrive in 1789 were the Findlay family and the family of Oliver Landon. The size of these families contributed much to Lansdowne's early growth. By 1818 Oliver Landon had nine sons and three daughters, and fifty-nine other family members resided in the area.

The community first developed as a stagecoach stop where the Reynolds Road met what is now Highway 2. By 1812 Lansdowne had a church, hotel, post office, and store. When the Grand Trunk was built between Montreal and Toronto in 1856, several buildings at Lansdowne were moved one mile north to be nearer to the tracks.

By 1903 Lansdowne's population was about 500 and the community prospered from the trade brought by the railway. Two hotels accommodated travellers, while five general stores, three blacksmith shops, a furniture shop, and many other businesses served the local residents. A town hall was built in 1890. The sawmills of Blair, McCready and Co., and W. B. Warren cut the lumber of the Rathbun Co. and their products were shipped off to market by rail.

As roads improved in the twentieth century, the railway gradually lost its importance and Lansdowne became a shopping centre for the district rather than a shipping depot. The railway station disappeared in the 1960's when the CNR (successor to the Grand Trunk) discontinued its service to the community. Today Lansdowne is the centre of a milk-producing area and is well-known for its annual fair, established in 1864.

Lansdowne's earliest church was Anglican, originally erected on Highway 2, then moved into the community. The present stone Anglican church was built in 1878. The frame United Church was dedicated in 1876. In 1931 the Presbyterian church opened its doors for worship.

At one time, Lansdowne had its own weekly newspaper, the *Reporter*, which was published from 1948 to the 1950's.

Ruth McKenzie: *Leeds and Grenville Their First Two Hundred Years*, 1967.

LANSING, part of the city of North York, Municipality of Metropolitan Toronto
Position 43° 46′ 79° 25′

An important centre of the Reform Party radicals in the 1837 Rebellion, Lansing today is an urban community situated in the city of North York at Yonge Street and Sheppard Avenue. It was named in 1866 by Saida Shepard, daughter of Joseph Shepard, once a leading member of the community.

Lansing originally developed as a crossroads when Thomas Hill and John Everson opened taverns here in 1802. Hill and Everson had settled in the area in the late 1790's. A third settler was Joseph Shepard who came from the United States and built a house at Lansing in 1798. John Bales settled in 1822 on what is now the site of the York Downs Golf Course.

Thomas Hill's land was bought by Thomas Shepard who erected the Golden Lion Inn in 1824. A sawmill was built by Joseph Shepard and a tannery by Elihu Pease in the 1830's. The Golden Lion was the site of a meeting chaired by Robert Baldwin to choose the Reform Party's York County candidates for the Upper Canada Legislature. Joseph Shepard, Jr., was one of those chosen.

The Shepard mill then became a rendezvous for the radical

members of the Reform Party and on December 4, 1837, William Lyon Mackenzie and David Gibson went there to meet the other insurgents. On their way to Montgomery's Tavern the rebels stopped for a rest at Joseph Shepard's house, where his wife welcomed them. All four of her sons were involved in the Rebellion. After the skirmish at Montgomery's Tavern, Mackenzie was provided with a horse at the Golden Lion. He went first to Shepard's mill and from there fled to the United States. Colonel Van Egmond, another rebel leader, concealed himself in Mrs. Shepard's house but was discovered. Thomas and Michael Shepard were captured and imprisoned at Fort Henry in Kingston. They managed to escape and went to the United States. Joseph and Jacob Shepard were imprisoned for several months.

In 1843 the Shepards returned to Lansing after being pardoned by the Queen. Michael opened a sawmill, while Thomas enlarged the old sawmill and added a grist mill. Joseph Shepard built a large general store about 1860. The store, today known as Dempsey's, soon became a meeting-place of local residents. By this time a small community had developed, much of it on the property of Angus Blue who had opened it up for settlement in 1857.

In 1866 a post office was established in Joseph Shepard's store with R. G. Lambert as the first postmaster. By 1870, the store had been taken over by Shepard's son, Joseph E. Shepard, who also served as postmaster and operated flour and lumber mills. Other businesses in the 1870's included Albert Weed's agricultural implement shop, Robert Bestard's harness shop, and the Morgan's Corners Hotel. Another hotel was operated by Richard Walkinshaw. James Andrews ran a brick and tile manufacturing establishment.

About 1915 Rev. T. W. Pickett took over the Golden Lion Inn as a residence. He held the community's first Methodist services in the barroom of the former hotel. A Sunday School was begun by John Boddy in his home in 1918. Lansing Church was built in 1920. At Church Union in 1925, it became Lansing United Church. With the rapid increase in population after World War Two, the old building became overcrowded and a new church was opened in 1951.

Patricia W. Hart: *Pioneering in North York*, 1968.

Miles & Co.: *Historical Atlas of York County*, 1878.

LAPIERRE, geographic township, Thunder Bay District
Position 49° 47′ 87° 25′

The township is situated north of Highway 11 and west of the town of Geraldton. It was named after E. A. Lapierre, MPP for Sudbury in 1934. Atigogama Lake is along the western border, which is accessible by dry weather road.

LARDER LAKE, township, Timiskaming District
Position 48° 05′ 79° 40′

Situated on the shores of Larder Lake about 18 miles east of Kirkland Lake, the former town of Larder Lake was incorporated as a township in 1946. The area was probably named by early fur traders who discovered that the abundance of fish in the lake provided a natural larder of food for them.

There was no settlement here until 1906 when an Indian staked a claim on a gold find beside the lake. The discovery started a gold rush and by winter four thousand claims had been staked. Gold was discovered on the Harris-Maxwell claim in 1908.

In 1907 a town site was surveyed by C. H. Fullerton on the north shore of the lake and named Larder City. About 1909 the first commercial establishment, the Taylor Hardware Store, was opened. In the same year, a road was cut from Dane, a nearby township. Until this time, the site could only be reached by water routes.

In 1911 Dr. McKay, a Toronto financier, formed Gold Fields Limited to develop the Harris-Maxwell and Kerr-Addison mines. The venture was successful at first and soon a small community began to develop at Larder City. The first settlers arrived from Finland in 1912. The Gold Fields operation was expanded in 1914 but proved unprofitable and soon the company was deep in debt. The resulting loss of jobs led to a decline in the population of Larder City.

The community experienced renewed growth in 1919 when McKay bought the Costello claims and the first successful mine in the area started operations. McKay built a mill near the mine and a post office and general store were opened. In 1921 an electric power generating station was constructed to supply power to the mine and to Larder City. The Ontario Northland Railway passed through the area in the 1920's and a station was built just to the north of the community.

McKay's mine, unfortunately, did not remain profitable and the company went bankrupt. The people who remained at Larder Lake had to depend on lumbering and commercial fishing for their livelihood. The first commercial fishing licence was granted in 1925, but the industry eventually depleted the abundance of trout for which the lake had been named.

The Depression of the 1930's increased the price of gold and mining once again became a profitable venture. The Crown Reserve Mine amalgamated with McKay's mine to rework the Costello claims. In 1935 the operation was taken over by McIntyre Porcupine Gold Mine which enlarged the mine and renamed the business Omega Mine Gold Mines. In 1936 a large gold ore body was found on the Kerr-Addison property. One of the largest gold mines in North America, and still in operation today, the Kerr-Addison mine caused a building boom at Larder Lake and the population increased to 3,000. The town of Larder Lake was incorporated in 1938 with A. A. Howard as its first mayor. In 1946 the town amalgamated with McVittie-Hearst and Skead Townships to form the Township of Larder Lake.

Larder Lake prospered during World War Two as production and demand increased. More shafts were drilled after the war, but the ore grade was not as high and the new properties proved unprofitable. Gold production began to fall off and several older mines closed. In 1938 there had been more than 20 gold mines in the area. By 1955 only the Kerr-Addison and Upper Canada mines were left.

The natural beauty of the area, unspoiled by large commercialized tourist developments, is today one of Larder Lake's greatest attractions. Excellent fishing, swimming, hunting, and skiing provide year-round recreation for visitors. The improvement of roads, including Highway 66, provides easy access to the area. Although gold mining still contributes to the local economy, Larder Lake is developing into an important tourist resort. A large percentage of the population is French-Canadian. Groups of Scandinavians, Dutch, Italians, and English are also part of the community's ethnic make-up.

Micheline Boucher, et al: *Our Timiskaming*, 1977.

LARKIN, geographic township, Algoma District
Position 49° 07′ 84° 42′

Located just to the south of the community of Hornepayne, this township is probably named after the late Hon. Peter C. Larkin, a prominent tea merchant and one-time High Commissioner for Canada in London, England. The township is watered by the Shekak and the Beaton rivers. Highway 631 links the area with Hornepayne to the north and the community of White River to the southwest.

LaRONDE, geographic township, Algoma District
Position 47° 47′ 84° 54′

Township 31, Range 21, as it was first known, was named after Louis Denis, Sieur de La Ronde, the first European to explore the copper deposits of Lake Superior's shore. He established a shipyard at Pointe Aux Pins in 1735 and built there the first decked vessel to sail Lake Superior. The township, watered by the Old Woman River, fronts on Lake Superior, at Old Woman Bay. The Trans-Canada Highway (17) passes through the area which is part of Lake Superior Provincial Park.

LARSON, geographic township, Algoma District
Position 47° 22′ 84° 25′

Named after E. G. Larson, Reeve of McCrosson and Tovell in the Rainy River District, this township was formerly designated Township 27, Range 16, and was part of the Algoma Central and Hudson's Bay Railway Land Grant. Little Agawa and Hubert Lake are the largest lakes in this area. The Montreal River flows through the southeastern corner.

LA SALLE, geographic township, Nipissing District
Position 46° 46′ 79° 27′

The township is situated north of the city of North Bay. It was named after the early French explorer Robert René de La Salle who, together with Father Hennepin, discovered Niagara Falls in 1679. Several lakes occupy the southeastern part of the township which is accessible by road.

LaSALLE, community, Sandwich West Township, Essex County
Position 42° 14′ 83° 06′

Situated 9 miles south of Windsor, on the Detroit River and Highway 18, LaSalle lies in the centre of a farming area which specializes in growing early vegetables. During the prohibition years in the United States, it carried on a prosperous liquor-exporting business. In 1924 it was incorporated as a town.

Following the repeal of prohibition, LaSalle's prosperity declined and its population decreased. By the 1950's it had become largely residential and in 1959 it was annexed by the Township of Sandwich West. Today it is a compact rural community.

LASCELLES, geographic township, Algoma District
Position 49° 07′ 84° 30′

The township is located southeast of Hornepayne and south of the Canadian National Railways line. It was named after Viscount Lascelles, Earl of Harewood and husband of Princess Victoria Alexandra.

LASH, geographic township, Rainy River District
Position 48° 36′ 93° 45′

Surveyed and subdivided in 1876, the township was named after Z. A. Lash, K.C., Deputy Minister of Justice at that time. The area lies west of Fort Frances. The Rainy River flows along the western boundary.

LASKAY, community, King township, Regional Municipality of York
Position 43° 55′ 79° 35′

Located in the southern part of King Township, on the east branch of the Humber River, the settlement was named in the 1830's by settler Joseph Baldwin after his native village of Loskie in Yorkshire, England. In its early days it was nicknamed "Bulltown", either because of a bull which broke loose at a Fall Fair and caused quite a stir, or because of a British army pensioner who sold bull meat here to make a living.

The east and west parts of the settlement developed at different times. Joseph Baldwin settled in the east in 1832 and completed the work on a dam and sawmill which already had been commenced when he arrived. In 1849 he built a grist mill which ground all the wheat in the area and sent most of its produce to Toronto. He also built the first store in 1845 called Laskay Emporium, and which may now be seen in the Black Creek Pioneer Village. A carding and cloth finishing mill was set up by his son Henry.

A post office was established in 1854 with James Bowman as first postmaster. It remained open until 1926.

In 1856 David Reesor settled on the west side on land surveyed by George McPhillips. Industries in this area included a plaster mill, a sawmill, and a mill which produced chairs and beds, and a slaughterhouse. In 1859 Garrett Blough opened an inn on land which later became the site of "The Old Forge" operated by blacksmith Joseph O'Brien. Plans to have Laskay incorporated as a village were never realized as the population declined throughout the twentieth century. In 1971 the population was 164. Recently, however, a number of new houses have been built here as people seek homes outside the city.

Elizabeth McClure Gillham: *Early Settlements of King Township, Ontario* 1975.

LASTHEELS, geographic township, Algoma District
Position 47° 59' 84° 36'

Formerly No. 28, Range 23, the township, just east of Wawa, bears the name of Chief Robert Lastheels. Highway 101 and the Algoma Central Railway travel along the township's eastern border.

LATCHFORD, geographic township, Nipissing District
Position 46° 11' 80° 06'

The township borders in the north on Lake Nipissing's West Bay. The area was first subdivided in 1900 by J. W. Fitzgerald and appears to have been named after the Hon. Francis Robert Latchford, MPP for Renfrew South at that time.

LATCHFORD, town, Coleman Township, Timiskaming District
Position 47° 20' 79° 49'

Eighty-four miles north of North Bay lies the town of Latchford with Bay Lake forming its western boundary and the Montreal River flowing by on the east. This picturesque town which grew up during the days of the Cobalt silver rush was named after the Hon. Francis R. Latchford, Minister of Works, who turned the first sod for the railway from North Bay in 1902 and drove the last spike at Moosonee thirty years later.

The Latchford area was well known to the Ojibwa and Cree Indians who used the Montreal River system as a canoe route. This system later became a major transportation link for the fur traders of the Hudson's Bay Company. In the late 1880's James Mowat and his family arrived to operate the fur-trading post which the company had built on Fiddler's Island. The post burned down in 1905.

Latchford itself did not develop until the construction of the Timiskaming and Northern Ontario Railway which gave access to the Clay Belt farmlands at the head of Lake Timiskaming. In 1903 a railway bridge was built across the Montreal River. In the same year the Legris family opened a store to serve the construction men who formed a small community at the site.

Shortly after Latchford came into existence, silver was discovered at Cobalt and a great silver rush began. Latchford, 9 miles from Cobalt, became a jumping-off place for prospectors travelling along Bay Lake and the Montreal River to Elk Lake. Hotels were quickly built to accommodate the prospectors and stores were opened as the economy of the community boomed. The Upper Ontario Steamship Co. and the Montreal River Navigation Co. ran steamboats along the water routes to the silver mines and did a flourishing business.

The population of Latchford increased to over 1,000 and in 1907 the community was incorporated as a town. Mayor J. J. McNeil presided over the first council of Ira B. Bradley, Arthur Caley, Archibald King, R. H. Burton, Robert Morrison, and Andrew Napier.

The mining boom soon ended, however, and three major fires in 1908, 1910 and 1911 took their toll on the town's prosperity. In 1913 a branch line of the T. & N.O. from Earlton to Elk Lake put the steamboat lines out of business. The end of the transient trade hit the local merchants hard and during World War One the town suffered a depression.

Main Street, Latchford, Ontario, c. 1908

Fortunately for the town, as the mining industry declined, lumbering began to play an increasingly important role. The sawmill erected by Empire Lumber Co. was taken over by A. J. Murphy Lumber Co. about 1916 which operated the mill until 1957 when it burned down. Other sawmills included McNeil's, south of the river, and Donald McLellan's, near the dam, which was sold to A. B. Gordon Co. about 1935.

Latchford's first school was opened near the railway station with Miss Morrison as teacher. Later lessons were held in the present town hall. A new school erected in 1908 was replaced by the present building in 1962. Latchford also had a separate school known as the Tin School in its early years. The school remained closed for a long period and was replaced by a new school in 1956. This building burned in 1960 and soon afterward the present separate school was built.

Father Forget was the first Roman Catholic priest in Latchford. When the Catholic church burned in 1928, a new church was erected. The building was later replaced by a more modern structure. Knox Presbyterian Church was opened under the Rev. R. W. Koffend. Rev. John E. Hunter organized the town's Methodists and Rev. C. G. Longmore ministered to the local Anglicans. The present United Church was built about 1932.

Today tourism is the main industry in this town of 430 (1979). Surrounded by beautiful scenery, lakes, and wildlife, Latchford has become a favourite spot for fishermen and cottagers. Canoeing, pleasure boating, water sports, fishing, hunting, and camping are all available. The February Winter Carnival is a popular attraction, as is the House of Memories with its collection of antiques and memorabilia.

Micheline Boucher et al: *Our Timiskaming*, 1977.

LATIMER, community, Kingston Township, Frontenac County
Position 44° 22′ 76° 31′

This dispersed rural community was named after William Lattimore who owned land nearby. William's brother, Francis, also lived in the area.

One of the first settlers was Captain John Everett, a United Empire Loyalist, who received a land grant in the vicinity of Latimer in the late eighteenth century. Other early settlers included Philander Lyon, Justus Daly, who arrived in 1797, and Samuel Campbell, who took up his land in 1804. Nathaniel Caverley was an early blacksmith in the community. A grist mill was built in 1826 by C. J. McDonald and Co. Until this time, the nearest grist mill had been at Kingston Mills. By 1845 the population had reached 108 and included the families of Orser, Spooner, Snook and Campbell.

The first preacher in the community was William Losee, a Methodist circuit rider who visited the area in 1790. The Latimer Methodist Church was built in 1855.

John Wesley Edwards, Conservative Member of Parliament for Frontenac County, 1908-1921, was born in Latimer in 1865. He became Minister of Health and Immigration. He was also Grand Master of the Orange Lodge in British North America.

Helen Arthur: *Latimer Past and Present 1787-1966*, 1966.

LAUDER, geographic township, Nipissing District
Position 46° 10′ 78° 52′

First surveyed in 1881, this township borders in the south on Algonquin Provincial Park. It was named after Abram William Lauder, MPP for South Grey at that time. The Amable du Fond River flows northward through the township with Highway 630 travelling along the east bank.

LAUGHREN, geographic township, Algoma District
Position 47° 07′ 83° 01′

Named after Floyd Laughren, MPP for the Nickel Belt, Laughren is situated just north of the Rocky Island Lake area. Maskuti Lake is the main body of water. There are no roads in the township, which was formerly known as No. 6C.

LAUGHTON, geographic township, Cochrane District
Position 49° 15′ 80° 48′

Located northeast of Cochrane, the township is named after Frederick S. Laughton, MPP for Middlesex North in the 1920's. The township is watered by the Chin River. Chin Lake lies in the southeastern part.

LANDRIAULT, geographic township, Algoma District
Position 46° 46′ 82° 31′

Originally known as Township R, Landriault lies northeast of the town of Elliot Lake. It was named after J. E. Landriault, Mayor of Massey in 1973. The Boland River and Shoe Creek drain the area. Dry weather and secondary roads connect the township with the towns of Elliot Lake and Massey.

LAURA, geographic township, Sudbury District
Position 46° 14′ 80° 52′

Subdivided in 1892, the township bears the first name of Canadian heroine Laura Secord (1775-1868). The township adjoining to the north is named Secord, thus completing her full name. Laura, which is watered by the Wanapitei River, is located south of the city of Sudbury. In the centre of the township lies Burwash, once a busy community and the site of Ontario's largest medium security prison. The Burwash Industrial Farm was closed in 1974, and the place became all but a ghost town.

LAUREL, community, Amaranth Township, Dufferin County
Position 43° 57′ 80° 13′

This dispersed rural community in central Amaranth Township is situated about 40 miles from Guelph.

By the 1860's there were several families living in the Laurel area. A village site was laid out in 1863. Mr. Morrison opened the first store and Rev. M. S. Gray became the first postmaster. By 1892 businesses and industries in Laurel included P. McGarvey's hotel, the Ewing & Archibald general store, two blacksmith shops, John Hughes' flour mill, the H. and B. Field sawmill, and the Cooney, Johnston, Hamilton & McGowan cheese factory. The township hall was built in the community, which by this time had a population of 195.

The Rev. M. S. Gray, Laurel's first minister, was a leader in Dufferin County's prohibition movement. In Laurel he organized the

Primitive Methodist congregation and built a church in 1863. In 1886 Rev. J. C. Madill erected a Presbyterian church. Laurel was known as the "village of churches" in the late nineteenth century.

Stephen Sawden: *History of Dufferin County.*

LAURIER, geographic township, Parry Sound District
Position 45° 55′ 79° 18′

Subdivided in 1878 by Henry Lillie, the township bears the name of Sir Wilfrid Laurier, Prime Minister of Canada from 1896 to 1911. The area which lies northeast of Sundridge village, is traversed by Canadian National Railways and Highway 11. The incorporated village of South River is situated on the western border. The township is watered by numerous streams, and there are several lakes.

LAURIER, township, Parry-Sound District
Position 45° 55′ 79° 18′

Laurier, northeast of the village of Sundridge, was established in 1878 when it was subdivided by Henry Lillie. It was named after Sir Wilfrid Laurier, a former Prime Minister of Canada.

Lumbering operations were carried out in Laurier for some years before any permanent settlers arrived. The Fraser Lumber Company was the first to locate in the township about 1866. Logs were floated to Lake Nipissing down the South River on which the company built dams and log slides. The first sawmill in Laurier was erected by Charles Byrnes on Lot 1, Concession 2. Another sawmill was constructed by Mr. McAdams and a third by William Erb about 1884. The South River Lumber Company later built a sawmill which was enlarged in 1901 to cut logs for the Turner Lumber Company of Paxton Township. A lath mill was also added. A company store was opened and the men were issued scrip, a written document in lieu of cash entitling the holder to receive something of value. The scrip was taken to the company store and the men would then get groceries, tobacco and clothing.

James Brinen was among the first permanent settlers in the township. He had come to Laurier in 1866 to work for the Fraser Lumber Company. In 1872 he brought his family to join him and settled on Lots 3 and 4, Concession 1. He was the first to grow potatoes in the township.

A few farms on the first concession are still occupied today but the sandy soil made most of the land unsuitable for agriculture. By the early twentieth century many of the farms had been either abandoned or sold to the Standard Chemical Company as Laurier residents joined the great migration to the prairies.

In 1904 Standard Chemical built a sawmill and chemical plant on its newly-acquired territory. Charcoal, wood alcohol, and acetate of lime were produced, and the community of South River in which the plant was located became known as "Charcoal Town". In 1917 the company bought a logging railway to transport timber from Paxton Township. It was converted into a truck road in 1946. The company sold its timber limits and sawmill to Hay & Co. and the chemical plant to Dominion Tar and Chemical Company in 1951.

James Brinen donated the land for the first township school, which was built in 1888. Annie Turnbull was the first teacher. The schoolhouse was also used as a church by different denominations. Rev. Mr. Eaton led the worship of the early Methodists and in 1906 Rev. Mr. Findlay held the first Presbyterian services.

Everett Kirton: *History of Eastern Parry Sound District*, 1964.

LAVAL, geographic township, Kenora District
Position 49° 50′ 92° 29′

Located northeast of Wabigoon Lake, the township bears the name of a noted French family among whose members was Archbishop Laval of Quebec. The township has numerous lakes and is linked by Highway 72 to the Trans-Canada Highway and the nearby town of Dryden.

LA VALLEE, township, Rainy River District
Position 48° 35′ 93° 40′

The township of La Vallee, which lies about ten miles west of Fort Frances, was the trading centre for the local farms before Highway 11 was built. The township was incorporated in 1904 and today it includes the geographic townships of Burriss, Devlin and Woodyat. It was named after the river which drains the area.

Farming is the main industry in the township which has a population of about 920. There are three community halls and two outdoor rinks for recreation. A United Church is located within the township. Most other facilities, including schools, are available in nearby Fort Frances.

The area is served by Canadian National Railways twice weekly, but daily service is available by bus lines.

The dispersed rural community of La Vallee is situated on the CNR line.

Ministry of Natural Resources: *Directory of Statistics and Data*, 1975.

LAVANT, township, Lanark County
Position 45° 06′ 76° 40′

Situated in the northwest corner of Lanark County, Lavant is bounded on the east by Darling Township, on the south by Dalhousie, on the west by Frontenac County, and on the north by Renfrew County. It was named after a prominent officer who served in the French Colonial army when Canada was under French rule.

The township was surveyed by Reuben Sherwood in 1821-2, but as the rocky and swampy land was ill-suited for agriculture there was little settlement for many years. The first to take up land in Lavant was Hercules White, a discharged soldier, who built a home on Lot 1, Concession 8, in 1828. The next settler, John Robertson, did not arrive until 1839. He was followed by John S. Robinson in 1840. David Turnbull, Peter Barr, John Lawson, John Brown, and Archibald

Downing came to the township in the 1840's.

By the 1880's Lavant, with a population of 308, was still a sparsely settled area. It had only two small post offices, Lavant and Ochil. There was a school at each of these centres. The township had no church, religious services being held in the schools. A government road gave access to the area and the Kingston and Pembroke Railway served the lumbering and mining industry of the area. A copper mine on Lot 6, Conc. 7, owned by Archibald Browning, was leased to the Canada Mining Company. An iron mine in the southwest corner of the township had been developed by Boyd Caldwell of Lanark village.

Lavant was governed in conjunction with Dalhousie and North Sherbrooke Townships from its earliest days. Records indicate that some sort of local government had been organized by 1821. In 1850 the Municipal Act officially united the three townships for municipal purposes. On the first council were Reeve John Kay and Councillors Edward Concroy, Donald McNicol, William Purdon, and James Smith. Lavant was governed independently for some years during the twentieth century, but in 1974 when its population had decreased to less than 194, the count by the 1971 census, it was again united with the townships of Dalhousie and North Sherbrooke. In 1979 the combined population of the townships was 1,045.

H. Belden & Co.: *Historical Atlas of Lanark & Renfrew Counties*, 1881.

LaVERENDRYE, geographic township, Algoma District
Position 46° 55′ 84° 02′

The township, located northeast of Sault Ste Marie, was named after explorer Pierre de LaVerendrye, who reached the Sault area on his way west in the 1730's. It was formerly designated as Township 24, Range 11. A secondary road links the area with points south.

LAVIGNE, community, McPherson Township, Nipissing District
Position 46° 20′ 83° 10′

This compact rural community on the western shore of Lake Nipissing, on Highway 64, was founded around the Visitation parish church, built in 1914. It was named after Père Lavigne, the first parish priest.

Today the community is a supply centre for cottagers, many of whom reach Lavigne by the canal which runs through the centre of the settlement. There are camps on either side of the canal, including Au Lys Blanc Camp and Camp Felix.

LAW, geographic township, Nipissing District
Position 46° 56′ 79° 49′

Named after Commander Law, R.N., of Toronto, the township lies south of the community of Temagami and is served by Highway 11. The northern and eastern sections of the township are dotted with lakes.

LAWLOR, geographic township, Algoma District
Position 47° 07' 82° 53'

Named after P. D. Lawlor, MPP of Lakeshore (Toronto), this township is located west of Mississagi Wild River Provincial Park and a few miles north of Rocky Island Lake. The township was formerly known simply as 6B.

LAWRENCE, geographic township, Haliburton County
Position 45° 27' 78° 31'

Lying in the northeast part of Haliburton County, Lawrence is bounded to the east by Nightingale Township, to the south by Eyre, to the west by Livingstone, and to the north by the District of Nipissing. Surveyed in 1877, it was named after Sir John Laird Lawrence, who served the British so well during the Indian Mutiny that he became known as the "Saviour of India".

When the Ontario government designated a vast wilderness region in the northeastern corner of southern Ontario as a conservation area "for the use and enjoyment of the people" in the 1890's, much of the land occupied by Lawrence Township was included in the plan. In the 1930's two-thirds of Lawrence's area was located within the Algonquin Provincial Park. Today the entire township lies within the park's boundaries. As a result, there is no settlement in Lawrence.

History of the Provisional County of Haliburton, 1931.

LAWSON, geographic township, Timiskaming District
Position 47° 38' 80° 35'

The township lies immediately east of the Gowganda silver mining region. It is named after Captain Lawson, a mining engineer. Highway 560 passes through the extreme northern part of the township.

LAXTON, township, Victoria County
Position 44° 22' 78° 55'

This township is located in the northern part of Victoria County. Bounded by Digby on the north, Carden on the west, Bexley on the south and the Gull River and Shadow Lake on the east, Laxton was named after a village in Northamptonshire, England.

The township was surveyed in 1858 by John Roche. However, the first settlers, Augustine Angiers, Albert Courtemanche, William Henry, William Vanmear, and Jesse Hero had arrived in 1855. Alexander A. McLauchlin had built a dam and sawmill at the present site of Norland in 1857. Other early settlers in this area were the Lecraws, a French Huguenot family, the Adairs and the Pearsons.

Schools were established in all sections in Laxton in 1860. Presently there is a consolidated school in Norland to which all children from Laxton as well as Digby and Longford townships come.

The last section school in Laxton was closed in 1965.

The first service of the New Connexion Methodist Church was held at Head Lake in 1861. A church was built one year later.

The township of Digby was surveyed and attached to the municipality of Laxton in 1862. Longford Township was surveyed in 1857 and in 1862 and became part of the municipal union known as Laxton, Digby and Longford in January, 1867. Norland is Laxton's only village and here are located the only churches in the township, one being Baptist, the other United. A library was opened in Norland in 1955 by Premier Leslie M. Frost.

Watson Kirkconnell: *County of Victoria Centennial History*, 1967.

LEADBURY, community, McKillop Township, Huron County
Position 43° 39' 81° 19'

Situated about 20 miles southwest of Goderich, this dispersed rural community was named after the English birthplace of its most prominent citizen, Charles Davis.

Davis came to Canada in 1851. He built a hotel and a store at the site of Leadbury and soon a small community developed. When a post office was established in 1877, Davis became the first postmaster. He also carried out an extensive business in the export of horses and cattle to Europe.

By 1878 residents of the area included William Archibald and Thomas Davidson from Scotland, John Berry from Ireland, and William Pollard and J. H. Swallow from England. Most of these men settled here in the 1850's and 1860's. William P. Bray was the local blacksmith.

In 1903 Leadbury's population was about 100. The hotel proprietor was Thomas Jones; Mrs. M. E. McEwen owned the general store; and A. M. Ross ran the blacksmith shop.

There was a log school at Leadbury by 1863. Thomas Whiteside was the first teacher. A new school was erected in 1907.

Mrs. Joseph Grummett: *A History of McKillop*, 1967.

LEAMINGTON, town, Mersea Township, Essex County
Position 42° 03' 82° 36'

The Talbot Road, laid out by Col. Thomas Talbot to open southwestern Ontario for settlement, was responsible for the beginning of Leamington. Alex Wilkinson started a farm on land bordering both sides of the Mersea Township Sideroad. Two neighbours, John McGaw and Thomas Quick, joined him. A Mr. Ambridge established a store and post office just east of what was known as "Wilkinson's Corners" and three years later Leonard Wigle opened the first tavern, famed for its efficiency and comfort. Trade centred at the spot where the Talbot Road (now Highway 3) and the Mersea Sideroad intersected. Eli Deming built a store and William Gaines erected a grist, saw and carding mill providing employment to many settlers in the area. Caleb Curtis, Martin Truax, James Flood also built stores and

John Avis opened a blacksmith shop. Wilkinson's Corners became a busy spot. A post office was established in 1854 and given the name of Gainesborough. Because another post office already bore this name, a change was made by Mr. Gaines who chose Leamington, after his home town in England. Warren Kimball was Leamington's first postmaster.

By 1858 the population numbered seventy-five. Walter S. Pulford began a carriage factory that year. Because Leamington possessed a fine natural harbour, a dock was built in 1869. A second dock was later sold to Lewis Wigle, a leading citizen in the history of Leamington's early days. Leamington's modern dock can accommodate both lake and ocean freighters.

By 1866 Leamington had a population of 300. There were two hotels, two physicians, a Good Templars Lodge, an Orange Lodge, and a photographic gallery.

The surrounding district is noted for its rich soil and production of fruit, vegetables and tobacco, and the Leamington District Fair is one of the oldest agricultural exhibitions in Western Ontario. First held in 1848 it was known as the Mersea Fair until 1900. Tobacco is no longer cured and packed in Leamington today, though it once was a leading industry in the town.

In 1874 Leamington became an incorporated village and the first council consisted of: George Russell, Reeve; Councillors: William Hazelton, Peter Conover, Charles H. Fox and John Setterington. Council met in the town hall on the southeast corner of the Talbot and Erie Street intersection.

Funds were raised to build a Michigan Central Railway spur line to Leamington in 1887. In 1889 a second railway, the Lake Erie, Essex and Detroit River Railway, linked the village with Walkerville. Walter Stares, William McSween and J. E. Snyder formed an electric light company in 1888; in 1891 a waterworks was installed. Natural gas and oil were discovered in the area, but the wells petered out by 1904.

Leamington was incorporated as a town on January 1, 1890. In 1908 H. J. Heinz Company, one of Canada's largest food processors, came to Leamington. The company's head offices for Canada are located in Leamington.

Close to the settlement in 1835, a union school was built by the Methodists, Episcopalians and Presbyterians on the Malott farm, Concession 1. The first high school was housed in the remodelled Lewis Wigle home on Talbot Street West in 1896. Later schools were constructed under the jurisdiction of the Leamington-Kingsville District High School Board. St. Michael's Separate School was established in 1931 with classes conducted in the basement of the church. The opening of St. Louis Separate School near the town's eastern outskirts accommodated students who had attended classes in the church basement and those from a four-room school built in 1938.

In 1950 the New Leamington District Memorial Hospital opened its doors, replacing the Hopewell Hospital, established in 1932 in a large frame home at 37 Russell Street by two nurses, Miss Mary Dinning and a Miss Humphrey.

Heinz Plant, Leamington, Ontario

Travelling preachers from as far away as the United States brought church services to the settlers of Essex County before the Malott church was erected near the Talbot Road at Leamington. The Anglicans built the first Church of England in 1837 on the William Siddall farm, two miles east of what was then still Wilkinson's Corners. This was followed by the Methodist Episcopals in 1858. In 1883 the Anglicans purchased this church and the Episcopal and Wesleyan congregations united and eventually built their own church in 1890. The first Baptist church was erected in Leamington in 1856 and replaced successively in 1879 and in 1923. The Presbyterians built a frame church on the present site in 1877. Destroyed by fire in 1891, a new brick church was erected the following year. Roman Catholic services were first held in 1874 at the home of William Farren, and the first church was built in 1882. St. Michael's Roman Catholic church built in 1922, since then has undergone many improvements to house its expanding congregation. The Salvation Army came to Leamington in 1886. Mennonites who settled in Leamington in 1925 built their churches by voluntary labour. Located on Highway 3, west of Leamington, now stands their large new church built in 1966. St. Paul's Evangelical Lutheran Church, the Ukrainian Greek Orthodox Church, the Full Gospel Tabernacle, the Christian Science Church and the United Pentecostal Church are all established in Leamington.

A reading room maintained over the years in various downtown buildings with a Miss McIntosh as first librarian, comprised Leamington's first library. By 1912 the Carnegie Public Library, aided by the benevolent Andrew Carnegie, was erected at the corner of Erie and John Streets. In 1959 a new wing was added.

The Sun Parlor Home provides accommodation for about 250

Senior Citizens; another home for the aged is the Leamington Mennonite Home.

In 1874 William McSween published Leamington's first weekly paper, the *Erie Post*. Another early paper was the *Leamington News* of the 1890's. Eventually, it was sold to J. E. Johnson and A. A. Whitwam, publishers of the *Post*, and with the amalgamation of the two papers emerged the present weekly *Post and News*.

Southeastward from Leamington stretches the Pelee Peninsula. The southern part of this peninsula comprises famed Point Pelee National Park, habitat of bird life and resting place for migratory birds in spring and fall. Here, also grow unusual trees and shrubbery not native to the rest of Canada. Leamington is the gateway to the Park.

Leamington's project during Canada's centennial year in 1967 was the construction of a beach building at Seacliffe Park. This 20-acre park had been purchased by the town from Peter Conover in 1907. It was part of 170 acres Conover owned along the Lake Erie shoreline. Known as Sea Cliffe Park Farm, he had developed a park on the site which attracted hundreds of visitors. Seacliffe has since developed into a suburban community.

A. K. Duncan: *Leamington-Mersea History.*

Leamington and District Centennial Board.

LEASIDE, part of Borough of East York, Municipality of Metropolitan Toronto
Position 43° 42' 79° 22'

Situated in the northeast part of Toronto on the CPR, the former town of Leaside is known for the large viaduct built in 1927 to connect it with the township of East York. A post office was established here in 1893. The CPR brought trade and prosperity to the town and by 1959 it was both industrial and a pleasant residential area. A community centre and a public library served the residents. In 1967 the town became part of the Borough of East York.

LEASK, geographic township, Sudbury District
Position 47° 11' 81° 06'

The township's northern, western and southern boundaries were surveyed in 1909. The eastern boundary had been surveyed in 1896. Named after Judge Leask, the township lies north of the city of Sudbury and is accessible by secondary road. The township's main lakes are Barnet, Prune, and Leask.

LEBEL, geographic township, Timiskaming District
Position 48° 09' 79° 57'

Named after the Rev. C. S. Lebel, a missionary of Sudbury, the township was partially annexed to the township of Teck in 1969. The town of Kirkland Lake lies immediately to the west. Highway 66 and the Canadian National Railways travel through the township.

LeCARON, geographic township, Algoma District
Position 46° 41' 83° 01'

The township lies north of the town of Blind River. Formerly known as 1C, it now commemorates the name of Joseph LeCaron, a Recollet missionary who first visited the Huron Indians in 1615. The area is accessible by waterways only. Kirkpatrick is the largest of a number of lakes in the township.

LECKIE, geographic township, Timiskaming District
Position 47° 22' 80° 50'

Leckie's boundaries were surveyed in 1909 and it was named after a Major R. G. Leckie. The township borders in the south on the Sudbury District. The Sturgeon River flows in a southerly direction through the centre of the township.

LECLAIRE, geographic township, Algoma District
Position 48° 14' 84° 43'

Formerly a part of the Algoma Central and Hudson's Bay Railway Land Grant, and known as Township 29, Range 26, the township was named after Eugene J. Leclaire, RCAF, F.O., of the Thunder Bay District, who lost his life during World War Two. The area is located north of Wawa and a few miles to the east of Highway 17, to which it is linked by dry weather road.

LECOURS, geographic township, Thunder Bay District
Position 48° 40' 86° 04'

Shown on current maps as Township #74, Lecours was named in 1974 after the late Joseph Lecours, who worked with the Indians of the Heron Bay area, translating and interpreting letters and official documents for them. The Heron Bay Reserve is just to the west of the township. Both the Trans-Canada Highway and the CPR traverse Lecours.

LEDGER, geographic township, Thunder Bay District
Position 49° 12' 88° 12'

Traversed by Highway 11 and the Canadian National Railways, Ledger is located south of Lake Nipigon. Highway 11 links the area to Nipigon about ten miles to the south. The township was surveyed in 1894 and was named after Alfred Ledger of Burford, Ontario.

LEDUC, geographic township, Thunder Bay District
Position 49° 42' 87° 34'

Much of this township, located west of the town of Geraldton, is covered by lakes, the largest of which are Beatty Lake and Oxaline

Lake. The southern section is traversed by Highway 11 and Canadian National Railways, with the station point of Jellicoe. It is named for the Hon. Paul M. Leduc, MPP for Ottawa East and Attorney General of Ontario in the 1930's.

LEE, geographic township, Timiskaming District
Position 48° 14′ 80° 20′

The township was probably named after John Lee, MPP for Kent East in 1902 at the time some of its boundaries were surveyed. Lee lies northwest of the town of Kirkland Lake.

LEEDS, county
Position 43° 35′ 76° 00′

Fronting on the St. Lawrence River, the county of Leeds is situated between Frontenac County on the west and Grenville County on the east. Rideau Lake and the Rideau River separate the county in the north from the County of Lanark. Leeds was named after Francis Godolphin Osborne, fifth Duke of Leeds, who was Secretary of State for the Home Department in 1783. That year the area was first explored by surveyors to assess its possibilities for settlement by United Empire Loyalists who were fleeing the United States after the American Revolution. A favourable report was made to the government and in 1784 the first Loyalists arrived in batteaux.

Leeds today is composed of ten township municipalities: Bastard and South Burgess, Elizabethtown, Front of Escott, Front of Leeds and Lansdowne, Front of Yonge, Kitley, North Crosby, Rear of Yonge and Escott, South Crosby, and South Elmsley.

The county was one of nineteen counties of Upper Canada created by Governor John Graves Simcoe in 1792. In 1798 it became part of the Johnstown District, and in 1808 Elizabethtown (now Brockville) was made the District capital. Today the counties of Leeds and Grenville are united for municipal purposes, and Brockville is the county seat.

Among the early inhabitants of Leeds were Thomas Sherwood, William Buell, founder of Brockville, Daniel Jones, and Benoni Wiltse. Township 8 (Elizabethtown) was set aside for the soldiers of Edward Jessup's Loyal Rangers, and by the end of 1784 there were 182 settlers in this township.

The land grants were increased in size after 1788 in order to encourage more settlement and soon more Loyalists arrived. One of the earliest communities to develop was Coleman's Corners (Lyn) which grew up around a mill built by Abel Coleman in 1788. Western Leeds was opened for settlement in the same year and colonists were moving into the newly-surveyed townships of Front of Leeds, Lansdowne, and Escott. The earliest residents in this area included Oliver Landon, Enoch Mallory, and William La Rue. In 1790 Nathaniel Mallory established Mallorytown on the Front of Yonge, and in 1792 Col. Joel Stone founded Gananoque on the St. Lawrence in the southwestern corner of the county.

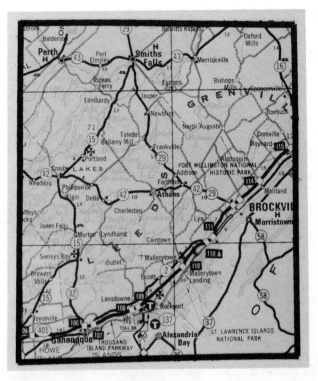

Stone had come to the area in 1787. Impressed by the potential mill power of two falls on the Ganonoque River, he petitioned for a land grant on either side of the river. A conflict arose, however, when Sir John Johnson, leader of a band of Loyalists from New York State, petitioned for the same land. Eventually Johnson received 1000 acres on the east side and Stone 700 acres on the west side. Stone settled on his land in 1792, opened a store and built a grist mill as well as a tavern. A small mill was built on the east side the same year, but no further development took place here for some time to come.

Near Mallorytown, a descendant of the founder established the first glassworks in Ontario. The factory is known to have operated from 1839 to 1849, although it may have been started before that.

The rear townships of Leeds were opened up in the 1790's. Abel Stevens brought a group of Baptists from the United States to Bastard Township in 1794, although the township was not surveyed until two years later. Major William Read, Duncan Livingstone, and Levi Soper were among those who took up land in Kitley Township after it was surveyed in 1796. Truman and Nathan Hickock, Nicholas Sliter, and Justus Seeley settled in Rear of Leeds and Lansdowne about 1800. At Furnace Falls (now Lyndhurst) Wallis Sunderlin opened the first successful iron foundry in Ontario.

One of the first skirmishes of the War of 1812 between Canada and the United States occurred in Leeds County, when an American contingent attacked the settlement at Ganonoque and burned the government stores and depot there. In 1813 a blockhouse was built on the east bank of the Gananoque River to guard against American raids.

The growth of the county's population was fairly slow during the first decade of the nineteenth century, but following the War of 1812-15 there was rapid expansion. Disbanded British soldiers and civilian emigrants from the British Isles were encouraged by the government to settle in Upper Canada in order to strengthen the country's defence against the United States. A large group of settlers, the majority of them from Scotland, arrived in 1816. They were soon joined by more emigrants from both Scotland and Ireland and the county's population continued to expand through the 1820's.

The construction of the Rideau Canal in the late 1820's brought about the settlement of the townships along the Rideau, as many canal workers made their homes in the area. The distinctive stone buildings of the region are largely the work of Scottish stonemasons employed on the canal. At Jones Falls, Leeds boasted the first arched dam in North America.

The Rideau Canal brought prosperity to the county as it provided an improved means of transportation. The lumbering industry, which began to develop about 1817 when the first sawmill was built in North Crosby, had become very important by the 1850's. Lumbermen used both the Gananoque River and the Rideau Canal to raft their logs to markets in the south.

By the second half of the nineteenth century, Brockville and Gananoque had become busy industrial towns. Gananoque was a leader in the manufacture of iron products and was known as the "Birmingham of Canada". Industry also flourished elsewhere in Leeds. There were about 100 manufacturing plants in the county in the late nineteenth century. The construction of the Grand Trunk, the Canada Central, and the Kingston and Pembroke Railways contributed greatly to the development of these industries.

Most of these enterprises have disappeared, and a number of others have taken their place, among them Confederated Foods of Canada Ltd. Founded in 1942 it has become Ontario's largest packer of pure maple products. Today Leeds is largely rural. Tourism has become increasingly important to the county economy. Gananoque is a resort town, catering to the thousands who visit the Thousand Islands in the St. Lawrence River each summer. Parks abound in Leeds and include Charleston Lake Provincial Park. Cottages have been built on the shores of the county's many lakes and the Rideau Canal has become a favourite route for pleasure boats.

The county had a school near Brockville by 1800. Adiel Sherwood was the teacher. Many more schools were built in the nineteenth century. A few separate schools were also opened, although the Roman Catholic population in Leeds has never been very large. Today the county has five secondary schools.

A Baptist church was erected in Delta in 1811 by Abel Stevens' settlers. The first Methodist church in Leeds was built at Lyn before 1817.

The county's first hospital was opened in the early nineteenth century at Delta by Dr. Peter Schofield. St. Vincent de Paul in

Brockville, founded in 1887, was Leeds first permanent hospital. Brockville General was built in 1889.

The *Brockville Recorder and Times*, founded in 1821, is the oldest daily newspaper in Ontario with a continuous record of publication under basically the same name. Chauncey Beach was its first publisher. The *Gananoque Reporter* is the county's oldest weekly paper.

Radio CFJR Brockville, established in Prescott, Grenville County, in 1926, is one of the earliest community stations in Canada. It moved to Brockville in Leeds in 1942.

Many well-known Canadians have been associated with Leeds County. Mazo de la Roche, author of the famous Jalna novels, spent part of her childhood in Athens. Sir Daniel Jones of Brockville became the first native-born Canadian to be knighted in 1836. The Hon. James Morris was Canada's first Postmaster General and was responsible for introducing a flat rate on postage. Sir William Buell Richards became the first Chief Justice of the Supreme Court in 1875. His brother, Albert Norton Richards, was made Lieutenant-Governor of British Columbia in 1876. In 1917 Louise Crummy McKinney became one of the first two women in the British Empire to be elected to a seat in Parliament.

Leeds was also the home of Mother Barnes, the Witch of Plum Hollow, a famous fortune-teller, visited by people from all over North America. Benjamin Chaffey, another Leeds resident, played an important part in the construction of the Victoria Bridge at Montreal (1854-59), the first iron-girder bridge in Canada. Chaffey's son, George, became widely known for his irrigation projects in the desert areas of California and Australia. He also founded the model city of Ontario in California.

Located in Leeds County are the city of Brockville, the separated town of Gananoque, and the incorporated villages of Athens, Newboro, and Westport. In 1979 the combined population of Leeds and Grenville was 80,784. The county is served by Highways 401, 2, 15, 29, 32 and 42, as well as the CNR and the CPR.

Ruth McKenzie: *Leeds and Grenville Their First Two Hundred Years*, 1967.

LEESON, geographic township, Sudbury District
Position 48° 23' 83° 49'

Leeson, named after George M. Leeson, MPP for Grey South around 1919, adjoins Missinaibi Lake Provincial Park to the east. A portion of Baltic Bay (Missinaibi Lake) occupies the township's southeastern corner.

LEFEBVRE, geographic township, Algoma District
Position 46° 46' 82° 23'

Located northeast of Elliot Lake, the township is designated as "N" on current maps. It was named in 1974 after G. L. Lefebvre, then the mayor of the town of Latchford. Lake aux Sables occupies much of the northeastern part of the township which is linked by dry weather road to secondary highways.

LEFROY, geographic township, Algoma District
Position 46° 18' 83° 09'

Situated immediately to the east of the town of Bruce Mines, Lefroy was subdivided in 1860. The township is named after General Sir John Henry Lefroy, soldier and scientist who made a magnetic survey of the Canadian Northwest in the 1840's. The Thessalon River flows in a southeasterly course through the area. Highway 17 and the CPR pass through the township. Communities in Lefroy are Nestorville, Glen Otter and Cloudslee.

LEFROY, community, Innisfil Township, Simcoe County
Position 44° 16' 79° 34'

Lefroy, a station on the Canadian Northern Railway (now CNR) came alive when the railway was built in 1852. It was named after General Sir John Henry Lefroy, who was in charge of the Magnetic Observatory in Toronto. Lefroy once had freight sheds, stock yards, and two elevators. In 1964 the Lefroy station, situated south of Concession 4, was dismantled. Only one elevator and two residences for maintenance men remained.

Probably the first settler in the neighbourhood of Lefroy was Henry Grose who had arrived in Simcoe County in 1832 from Cornwall, England. He operated a sawmill with the help of his two brothers, Richard and Robert, who lived near Lefroy. Henry had over 1,000 acres in the township and his farm was known as The Pines. He was referred to as the Squire and for a time was a member of the Innisfil Township council and a Justice of the Peace. Another early settler was John Cripps who arrived about the same time.

In the early sixties the local hotel, Lefroy Inn, was operated by Mr. Prittie. The general store was kept by Laidlaw and Fraser. Albert Kirkpatrick who also ran a general store, published a monthly leaflet for the farmers which said: "We sell everything Eatons sell and some which they don't." This referred to matches, tobacco and playing cards, which the Eaton store was forbidden to sell by its founder, Timothy Eaton. Later, Kirkpatrick built a grain elevator. Milne and Rogerson operated a sawmill and a lumber yard.

A public library with Mrs. J. T. Sproule as librarian was maintained in Jack Allan's house. Later the library was moved to Churchill, another community in Innisfil Township.

Historical Review of Innisfil, 1950.

LEGARDE, geographic township, Algoma District
Position 48° 09' 85° 15'

Formerly known as Township 33, Range 25, this township, northeast of Wawa, was named in 1974 after Canadian army grenadier Eugene

Legarde of the Thunder Bay District, who gave his life in 1945 during the Second World War. The township is watered by the University River, which flows in a southerly direction through the centre of the township.

LEGAULT, geographic township, Thunder Bay District
Position 49° 42' 87° 25'

Located east of Lake Nipigon, Legault is named after Theo. Legault, MPP for Sturgeon Falls in the 1920's and for Nipissing in the 1930's. Partridge Lake and Vezina Lake take up a large portion of the northern half of the township. The Canadian National Railways passes along the northern shore of Partridge Lake. Highway 11 travels through the township south of this lake.

LEGGE, geographic township, Algoma District
Position 48° 52' 83° 44'

The township which is traversed by Canadian National Railways, lies north of Missinaibi Lake Provincial Park. The name origin is not known. Lower Minnipuka Lake is situated in the northwest corner.

LEGUERRIER, geographic township, Algoma District
Position 48° 24' 84° 20'

Designated as #51, the township is named after the Most Reverend Jules Leguerrier, Bishop of the Diocese of Moosonee. Traversed by the CPR, the township is located immediately to the south of Franz at the junction of the CP and the Algoma Central railways.

LEHMAN, geographic township, Algoma District
Position 46° 30' 82° 23'

Formerly known as Township 138, it was named for Sergeant Leonard W. Lehman, RCAF, of Little Current, Ontario, who was killed during World War Two. The area is located northeast of Elliot Lake. It is accessible by secondary road from Highway 553 to the east.

LEINSTER, geographic township, Sudbury District
Position 46° 51' 81° 23'

The scenic Onaping River cascades in a southerly course through the centre of this township, which bears the name of a county in Ireland. The area lies northwest of the city of Sudbury.

LEITCH, geographic township, Cochrane District
Position 49° 15' 81° 10'

The township which lies east of Smooth Rock Falls, was subdivided in 1907 and was named for Judge Leitch of Toronto. The township is watered by the Frederick House River. Part of the area is now annexed to the town of Glackmeyer.

LEITH, geographic township, Timiskaming District
Position 47° 33' 80° 51'

The township, southwest of the Gowganda mining and tourist area, was probably named after James Leith, one-time chairman of the Ontario Railway and Municipal Board. Hangingstone Lake occupies the township's northeastern corner.

LEITH, community, Sydenham Township, Grey County
Position 44° 37' 80° 53'

On the east shore of Owen Sound, about five miles northwest of the city of Owen Sound, lies the picturesque little community of Leith. In the nineteenth century the natural harbour seemed to promise great growth, but its deterioration as water levels in the Great Lakes dropped hindered the settlement's development. Today Leith is a small but compact rural community.

The first settler in Leith was John Telfer who built a grist mill at the mouth of a stream about 1846. He laid out a village site complete with market-place, although a market would never be held there. A hotel was erected to accommodate the farmers who brought their grain to his mill. A second hotel was eventually opened by William Glen.

In 1853 Mr. Wylie opened Leith's first store and in the same year a post office was established. James Wilson took over the Telfer mill and built a distillery which he operated until 1857 when it was bought by Adam Ainslie. Ainslie constructed a wharf in 1861 and Leith became a fuelling station for steamers in the Sound. Ainslie stored and shipped grain, enlarged the original grist mill and the mill pond, and opened a local telegraph office.

In the 1850's Messrs. James and Allan Ross, builders, established themselves in Leith. Among their projects was a store constructed for Peter Marshall. The Rosses later took over this store. An oatmeal mill and a tannery were built by them in the 1860's. A hotel kept by Mr. Moulton served steamer passengers and mill customers.

The passing of the steamship age led to the community's decline. By 1903 Leith's population stood at about 100. Charles Kemp operated a flour mill and Arthur Cameron ran a general store.

E. L. Marsh: *A History of the County of Grey*, 1931.

LELUK, geographic township, Algoma District
Position 47° 07' 82° 46'

Designated as #6A, this township was named in 1974 after N. G. Leluk, MPP for Humber. Immediately to the east is Mississagi Wild River Provincial Park. Rocky Island Lake District lies nearby to the southwest. The township is accessible by waterway only.

LE MAY, geographic township, Kenora District
Position 49° 41′ 94° 10′

The township which lies east of Lake of the Woods was named in 1939 after Tracy Deavin Le May, Ontario Land Surveyor, city surveyor and town planning commissioner for Toronto. Lakes abound within the township which is linked to nearby Kenora by highway. In the north is Rushing River Provincial Park.

LEMIEUX, community, South Plantagenet Township, Prescott County
Position 45° 24′ 75° 04′

This dispersed rural community on the South Nation River, about 56 miles east of Ottawa, was named after Louis B. Lemieux, who ran a lumber camp in the area and was the first postmaster in 1875.

Among the earliest settlers at Lemieux were Robert Reid, Daniel Harrigan, Alex McInnis, John Macauley, and Henry Bradley. A sawmill was built by Archie Burton about 1850. In the late 1800's the mill was taken over by W. N. Barrie who also owned a store in the community. Lemieux once had a school and a Roman Catholic church.

C. Thomas: *History of the Counties of Argenteuil, Quebec and Prescott, Ontario*, 1896.

LEMOINE, geographic township, Sudbury District
Position 48° 16′ 82° 41′

Lemoine may have been named after L. D. Lemoine, a clerk in the Crown Lands Department during the 1850's. The area is linked by dry weather road to Highway 101 and lies northwest of Ivanhoe Lake Provincial Park.

LENDRUM, geographic township, Algoma District
Position 47° 59′ 84° 51′

The township, known until 1974 as #30, Range 23, was named after Robert W. Lendrum, a surveyor who worked in Northern Ontario during the late 1800's and the early 1900's. It is located immediately to the southwest of Wawa and borders on Michipicoten Bay (Lake Superior). To the west the township adjoins an Indian Reserve.

LENNOX, geographic township, Cochrane District
Position 49° 00′ 81° 24′

The township is linked by roads to Highway 11 and thus to Cochrane less than 20 miles to the east. It was subdivided in 1906 by G. Hutcheon and named after Col. T. H. Lennox, MPP for North York during that period.

LENNOX AND ADDINGTON, county
Position 44° 30′ 77° 00′

Fronting on Lake Ontario and the Bay of Quinte, the County of Lennox and Addington includes Amherst Island across the North Channel of the lake. This island was part of an extensive land grant made in 1675 by Louis XIV of France to explorer Sieur de La Salle, who named it Isle de Tonti after his lieutenant. A ferry today links the island and its communities with the mainland. To the east of Lennox and Addington lies Frontenac County, to the west and southwest are the counties of Hastings and Prince Edward, and to the north borders the County of Renfrew.

Lennox and Addington counties, along with seventeen other counties in Upper Canada, were created on July 16, 1792 by proclamation of Governor Simcoe. Lennox was named after Charles Lennox, the Duke of Richmond, and Addington after Henry Addington, Viscount Sidmouth. Together with Frontenac County, Lennox and Addington then comprised the newly-formed Midland District. Prior to this time the area had been part of the Mecklenburgh District.

Local administration had rested with a Court of Quarter Sessions which met four times a year to levy taxes, authorize the building of bridges and roads, grant licences to tavernkeepers and set ferry tolls. The members of the Court were appointed by the Governor and were not responsible to the people. With the creation of the first nineteen counties in 1792, representative government was inaugurated in the Province, with Governor Simcoe authorizing "Town meetings for the purpose of appointing diverse Parish Officers".

Lennox and Addington counties were "temporarily" joined in 1798, and in 1860 this municipal union was made permanent. Meanwhile, in 1849, Districts had been abolished, but Lennox and Addington County had remained united with the County of Frontenac. By 1863, however, Lennox and Addington had attracted a large enough population to warrant provisional separation from Frontenac, and on January 1, 1865 the separation became permanent.

In 1798 seven townships in southern Lennox and Addington made up the County: Ernestown, Fredericksburgh, Adolphustown, Richmond, Camden, Sheffield and Amherst Island. Timothy Thompson from the "Bay Shore", and Thomas Dorland from Adolphustown, were the county's first representatives. Today the county is comprised of fourteen townships: Adolphustown, Amherst Island, Camden East, Denbigh, Abinger, Ashby, Ernestown, Kaladar, Anglesea, Effingham, North Fredericksburgh, Richmond, Sheffield, and South Fredericksburgh. The population stands at 32,757 as of 1979.

The southern townships were the first to be settled and their progress has been steady over the years. The northern townships, which were opened later, remain sparsely settled even to this day, with only a few small villages. Poor soil conditions may discourage agricultural pursuits, but the untouched beauty of the area attracts visitors in ever-increasing numbers, and with its countless streams and lakes, and a network of roads, the northern part of the county has become a fisherman's and tourist's paradise.

The first permanent settlers in the county, which is often referred to as the "Cradle of Ontario", were United Empire Loyalists who had been forced to leave their homes in the United States of America during the Revolution. The refugees arrived in the spring of 1784 in the area of present-day Kingston, where they remained until the land along Lake Ontario and the Bay of Quinte had been surveyed and distributed. Ernestown in Addington County went to Sir John Johnson and his band of Loyalists; Colonel Rogers chose Fredericksburgh for his people; while Major Van Alstine and his group selected Adolphustown. The townships along the Bay shore were named after the sons and daughters of King George III.

At first the settlers were forced to travel as far as Kingston to have their wheat ground into flour. The government recognized the need for a more convenient mill and in 1786 Robert Clark, the millwright who had built the Kingston Mill, was given the task of supervising the erection of a mill on the Appanee (Napanee) River. Here, where the town of Napanee now stands, the river's falls provided ample waterpower. Until 1788 very little grinding was done there, however, owing to the scarcity of grain following a crop failure, but eventually the mill proved a great boon to the pioneers, since for nearly a decade it remained the only flour mill in the Midland District besides the one in Kingston. The Napanee mills served settlers as far west as the River Trent.

The Honourable Richard Cartwright of Kingston, who bought the Napanee mill in 1792, and seeing that it could no longer cope with the demands of the farmers, had it torn down and he erected a larger structure. Robert Clark was again commissioned to do the work. A sawmill had also been built in 1785 to provide lumber for the settlers. Around these mills grew the community of Clarkville, named after Robert Clark. The settlement flourished and became the manufacturing centre of Napanee.

Following the construction of the Addington Colonization Road from Tamworth to Denbigh, settlers began to move north. In addition to this road, Lennox and Addington was crossed by the Danforth Road which ran from Kingston to Dorland's Point, then crossed the ferry to Lake-on-the-Mountain, from where it went on to York (Toronto).

In 1840 six post offices were reported to be in operation in the County: Adolphustown, Bath, Camden East, Fredericksburgh, Mill Creek (Odessa) and Napanee. Napanee, which had been made the county town in 1863, emerged as the largest centre in the county. The town lies about seven miles up the Napanee River from the Bay of Quinte. Schooners and steamers used to ply the river taking on grain and lumber exported from the county to domestic and foreign markets. At one time Napanee's factories produced goods ranging from boots, hats, soap, yarn, and glass, to barrels, doors and sashes, carriages and sleighs. In 1835 John Gibbard opened business as a cabinetmaker. Later he leased a mill and commenced to manufacture sashes, doors and furniture. This enterprise still flourishes in Napanee and can boast to be the oldest furniture factory in Ontario. Napanee was incorporated as a village in 1855 and became a town in 1864.

There are two incorporated villages in the county today. One of them, Bath, in the early 1800's was a major centre with well over 2000 inhabitants. Today it has a population of just over 1000. The village is located on a snug harbour sheltered by a point jutting out into the Bay of Quinte. The first settlers here were Loyalists, 400 of them led by Col. Jessup arriving in 1784. At Finkle's shipyard in Bath, the *Frontenac*, the first steamboat to ply the waters of Lake Ontario, was built in 1816. At Finkle's Tavern criminal court was held, and the first man to hang in Upper Canada was strung from a tree near the tavern.

When the Grand Trunk Railway built a line between Toronto and Montreal in the 1850's, it bypassed Bath, turning inland at Collins Bay. Bath began to decline. A renewed upsurge in population during the 1960's and 1970's is partly due to the construction of several large industrial plants along Highway 33, which was once known as the "Loyalist Trail".

The second village in the county is Newburgh, home of the Old Newburgh Academy, one of Upper Canada's earliest Grammar Schools. The pioneer school which stands on a hill overlooking the village, closed its doors in 1965, having been in operation for 126 years. Newburgh, like Napanee, owed its existence to the presence of a waterfall on the Napanee River, powerful enough to turn the wheels of a saw and grist mill. The village was first settled in the early 1820's when David Perry, William Van Pelt Detlor, and Benjamin Files arrived. The place was known as "Rogues' Hollow" in its early days. John Thomson, his brother James, and J. W. Rooklidge estabished here the Newburgh Paper Mills in 1872. Thomson had devised a greatly improved method for the chemical manufacture of wood pulp, and in 1864 he had supervised Canada's first commercial production of wood pulp in a Windsor plant. The brothers, in 1880, jointly built the Thomson Mills near Newburgh which remained in operation until the 1930's.

Lumbering was once the county's main industry, the hinterland providing a rich and seemingly inexhaustible source of quality timber. In the winter the trees were felled and hauled to the bank of the Napanee River. With the spring break-up the logs were rounded up, and gangs of riverdrivers steered them downstream through currents and rapids. Communities along the river were booming. The Napanee, Tamworth and Quebec Railway opened up the back townships of the county in the 1880's, and served the lumber interests of the area.

The abundance of waterpower throughout Lennox and Addington was the reason the county's settlements became noted for their numerous mills and factories. But as the timber in the north country dwindled, and large manufacturing centres developed in other parts of Ontario, the county's economy began to rely more and more on agriculture in the south and tourism in the north.

Lennox and Addington Historical Society: Lennox and Addington County, 1964.

Walter S. Herrington: History of the County of Lennox and Addington, 1913.

R. E. Fluke: Old Newburgh Academy 1839-1965, 1977.

LEO, geographic township, Timiskaming District
Position 47° 22′ 80° 13′

Located west of the town of Latchford, Leo's boundaries were surveyed between 1907 and 1909. The name appears to commemorate Pope Leo of the Roman Catholic Church. Nearly half of the township is occupied by Lady Evelyn Lake.

LEONARD, geographic township, Timiskaming District
Position 47° 33′ 81° 00′

The western boundary of this township was surveyed in 1896, all other boundaries were surveyed in 1909. The township is recorded to have been named after R. W. Leonard. The area lies southwest of the Gowganda tourist and mining region.

LEROCHE, geographic township, Nipissing District
Position 47° 07′ 80° 15′

The name origin of this township is not known. LeRoche lies just to the northwest of Lake Temagami. The area is accessible by dry weather road from Highway 11. A portion of Obabika Lake occupies the township's southwestern corner.

LERWICK, geographic township, Algoma District
Position 48° 31′ 83° 20′

The township, which is not subdivided, was named after the capital of the Shetland Islands, Scotland. The Missinaibi River flowing out of Missinaibi Lake in the neighbouring township of Kildare, courses through the southern and central portion of Lerwick in an easterly and northerly direction. In the northern section of the township the river cascades down with numerous rapids which are circumvented by portages.

LESKARD, part of town of Newcastle, Regional Municipality of Durham
Position 44° 02′ 78° 39′

About 32 miles northwest of Cobourg, near the headwaters of Wilmot Creek, lies the dispersed rural community of Leskard. A prosperous mill town in the nineteenth century, today it is a quiet residential community. It was first called Rochester by Samuel Way, an early settler, but the name was changed when a post office was established in 1865 as there was already a Rochester in Ontario. John Davey, who came from Liskeard in Cornwall, England, suggested the name of his native town. The spelling was changed to Leskard.

Among the earliest settlers in the Leskard area was the Brisbin family who arrived in 1832. In 1835 George Wylie and William Nay began farming here. By 1837 their neighbours included Jacob Purdy, William Livingston, John Gibson, Thomas Best, Amos Andrews, and

Foster Hutchison. William Skelding, Alfred Griffin, and Richard and James Bradley came in 1838. Many of the distinctive stone houses of these early settlers were built by Scottish stonemasons.

Three streams flowed near Leskard and the community began to develop around the mills which made use of this waterpower. As early as 1834 Elisha Sabine had constructed a sawmill at the site of the community. It later became known as the Stalker mill. In 1840 Ichabod Richmond, a colourful figure who claimed descent from royalty, built a saw and grist mill. It was taken over by James Elliott in 1848. By 1850 a flour mill and two sawmills had been opened by Samuel Way and his son. The Way flour mill was rebuilt by Richard Ruddock and became one of Ontario's best flour mills by 1890.

The village was laid out in the 1850's, probably by Samuel Way. In 1854 James Bawks sold the first village lots to Thomas Staples, Peter McIntyre, and Roswell Martin. Lots were bought by William Robbins, Joseph Gilfillan, and Samuel Staples in 1855.

The community with a population of about 250 soon prospered. Four carpenters, two blacksmiths, a wagonmaker, two shoemakers, a tinsmith, and a cooper offered their services. Early industries included an axe factory, flour mill, lumber mill, foundry, and sash manufacturer. Samuel Staples was owner of the hotel and McNeil & Bro. ran a general store.

Today Leskard is largely residential, the home of retired people and commuting workers. The old church, school and store stand empty, reminders of a busy past.

Helen Schmid and Sid Rutherford: *Out of the Mists,* 1975.

LESLIE, geographic township, Thunder Bay District
Position 49° 06′ 85° 55′

The township lies immediately to the west of the town of Manitouwadge and is traversed in the eastern part by the Canadian National Railways as well as Highway 614. It was named after John A. Leslie, MPP for York East in the 1940's.

LESSARD, geographic township, Algoma District
Position 49° 15′ 84° 59′

Named after a late member of the General Eastern Division (Militia of Canada), the township is located west of Hornepayne. Canadian National Railways, with the station point of Tondern passes through the northern section of the township.

LETT, geographic township, Thunder Bay District
Position 48° 58′ 87° 58′

Until 1974 the township was known as No. 90. It was named after Charles A. Lett, who surveyed mining claims in northwestern Ontario during the 1880's. Located on the northern shore of Nipigon Bay, Lett, triangular in shape, is one of the smallest townships in Ontario. The

Trans-Canada Highway (#17) and the Canadian Pacific Railway pass through the township along the shoreline.

LEVACK, geographic township, Sudbury District
Position 46° 41' 81° 22'

It is believed that the township, originally subdivided in 1885, was named after Helen Levack, the Scottish-born mother of Sir Oliver Mowat, premier of Ontario from 1872 to 1896. The mining town of Levack, which lies in the southwestern part of the township, amalgamated with the Improvement District of Onaping to form the Town of Onaping Falls on January 1, 1973.

LEVACK, part of town of Onaping Falls, Regional Municipality of Sudbury
Position 46° 38' 81° 23'

Lying on the northern rim of the Sudbury Basin, 24 miles northwest of Sudbury, this compact rural community was probably named after Helen Levack, the Scottish-born mother of former Ontario premier Sir Oliver Mowat.

Levack surrounds the Levack mine of International Nickel Company where most of the community's 2,943 residents (1977) work. In 1973 the town of Levack was amalgamated with the Improvement District of Onaping as the town of Onaping Falls.

LEVESQUE, geographic township, Algoma District
Position 48° 09' 85° 07'

Known as Township #32, Range 25, Levesque was named in 1974 in honour of Alphonse Levesque, Canadian army sapper of Thunder Bay District killed in World War Two. The area is not subdivided. It lies west of Highway 17, approximately ten miles north of the Michipicoten Bay shore of Lake Superior.

LEWERS, geographic township, Cochrane District
Position 50° 17' 81° 10'

Located southwest of Moosonee, the township is named after Richard Lewers of Midland, Ontario. A tributary of the mighty Moose River, the scenic North French River, with its numerous rapids, flows northward through the eastern part of Lewers.

LEWIS, geographic township, Algoma District
Position 46° 14' 82° 30'

The township is located north of the North Channel of Lake Huron. It was first surveyed in 1882 and was named after J. B. Lewis, Ontario Land Surveyor of Ottawa. Effective March 1, 1973 the area was included in the newly created Improvement District of North Shore consisting of the geographic townships of Shedden, Lewis, Spragge, Long and part of Striker. The township borders in the south on a large Indian Reserve. The Trans-Canada Highway passes along the southern border.

LEY, geographic township, Algoma District
Position 46° 48' 84° 30'

Ley lies on the south shore of Batchawana Bay of Lake Superior. Established around 1867, the mainland portion of this township is Indian Lands. It is believed to have been named after Colonel Ley of Sault Ste Marie.

LIFFORD, community, Manvers Township, Victoria County
Position 44° 11' 78° 39'

The dispersed rural community of Lifford is situated about 16 miles southwest of Peterborough. Formerly the council seat of Manvers Township, it was named by early settlers after their home in Ireland.

The first families came to Lifford in the 1830's. Among them were the Staples, Grandys, Vances, Touchburns, Prestons, Wilsons, Neals, Ingrams and Timms. Later the families of Lang, Mills, Cairns, McWatters, Sutton, McGill, McGuire, Rowan, Atchison, Dick and Argue arrived. Most of these settlers came from Ireland, although there were also some Scottish families.

The first general store was opened by Thomas Middleton, who became Lifford's first postmaster in 1854. A township hall was built in 1865. The Wesleyan Methodists of Lifford worshipped first in a building which later became the Temperance Hall. The New Connexion Methodists held their first services in the schoolhouse. Anglican services were held in private homes until 1852 when St. Mary's was built on land donated by Col. Isaac Preston. Reverend William Logan was the first resident minister. St. Mary's is the oldest church in the township.

A survey was made in order to lay out the Midland Railway through Lifford in 1856, but it was found that the hills were too steep and an alternate route was chosen. The community began to decline after this. In later years, many of its buildings were destroyed by fire.

Mrs. Ross N. Carr: *The Rolling Hills,* 1967.

LILLIE, geographic township, Sudbury District
Position 47° 17' 82° 01'

Township No. 9, as it was known, was named after Henry Lillie who surveyed a number of townships along the Serpent River in the 1870's. The area lies immediately to the east of Biscotasing, a community on the Canadian Pacific Railway which travels through Lillie. The southern tip of Biscotasing Lake occupies the northwest.

LIMEBANK, community, Regional Municipality of Ottawa-Carleton
Position 45° 15' 75° 40'

Although it is a dispersed rural community today, Limebank was a bustling settlement in the early 1900's. A post office was established in 1886 and by the first years of the twentieth century, the community had a school, store, carriage plant, cheese factory, and Orange Hall. Among the early residents were the Gambles, Moores, Wilkinsons, Maghers, Gordons, Halpennys, Spratts, Summers, and Larkins. Addie Cuddy, Dewey McKerracher, and Pininnah Sloan were teachers at the Limebank school.

Harry and Olive Walker: *Carleton Saga*, 1968.

LIMEHOUSE, community, Regional Municipality of Halton Hills
Position 42° 38' 79° 58'

Limehouse was once known simply as the "Rock", no doubt because of its topography and its proximity to the Niagara Escarpment. It was also once called "Fountain Green", but when the post office was opened in 1857 it was renamed Limehouse.

As its name implies, the Limehouse area was rich in limestone. As early as the 1850's limekilns were constructed to produce quicklime which was slaked with water for use as mortar, or to manufacture cement. Messrs. Lindsay and Farquhar were responsible for the building of the first limekilns.

Kilns located south of the Grand Trunk Railway line were constructed by Messrs. Bescoby and Worthington. The Bescoby Lime Works at Limehouse was later purchased by Gowdy and Moore who, by the 1880's, employed more than 100 men on three shifts, producing over 75,000 bushels of lime a year from its six kilns. Gowdy and Moore also operated a sawmill capable of turning out 10,000 feet of lumber a day.

The bustling industrial days of Limehouse are now but a memory, but the limekilns and the ruins of the sawmill stand as monuments to its prosperous heyday.

The Credit Valley Conservation Authority has purchased more than 190 acres in the Limehouse area, including the former Gowdy property, and plans to restore the kilns as nearly as possible to their original structure.

John McDonald: *Halton Sketches*, 1976.

LIMERICK, township, Hastings County
Position 44° 54' 77° 40'

Situated in the central area of Hastings County about 50 miles north of Belleville, the township was named after the city and county of Limerick in Ireland.

The area is mountainous and heavily timbered and forms a height of land from which waters flow south to the Trent River and north to the Madawaska River. Farmland is limited among the township's 50,000 acres, and today Limerick's land is mostly private property with over 20,000 acres being owned by one company. The population in 1979 was 313.

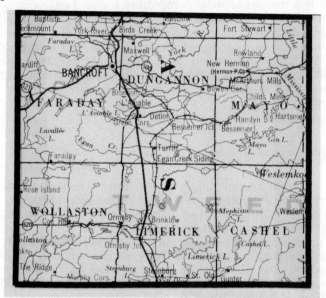

The township grew slowly because the terrain made settlement difficult. In 1854 Peter Chard and Company of Belleville attempted to develop lead and copper ores in the area, but mining played an insignificant role in Limerick's history. Austin Johnston surveyed the land near Salmon (Limerick) Lake in 1857. The survey was completed in 1862-63 by H. A. Macleod, who felt that only one-third of the land was good for agriculture. At this time there were only 12 families living here, mostly along the Hastings Road on the western side of the township. Following the survey, settlement increased somewhat and by 1864 the free grants along the road were all taken up. Other families moved to the southeastern part of the township. By the late 1860's forty-one families lived in the area, including the Murphys and the Nugents.

Lumbering was the main source of income for the settlers, but by 1862 the best timber in the northeast had been taken by lumberjacks from the Ottawa Valley. The Gilmour Company began operating near Salmon Lake in 1863 and, through a series of interconnecting waterways, floated logs to its mill at Trenton. The Rathbun Company also operated in the township, continuing until 1920. The lumber trade still plays a significant role in the township's economy.

Limerick was attached to Hastings County in 1858, but was united to Tudor, Wollaston and Cashel for municipal purposes. Following separation in 1886, Peter P. Clark became the first reeve.

The building of the Central Ontario Railway in 1884 and the advent of a daily stage coach service contributed to the growth of the township's hamlets. The most northerly community was Rathbun (now Ormsby). Early stores here were owned by James Roy and John Bane. Steenburg was named after the owner of four lots in the first concession in the 1880's, operator of the general store and the postmaster, Sidney S. Steenburg. An early school was located at Ham's Corners, which received its name from the township's clerk, James Ham. St. Ola, named in 1869 by Peter Clark after a Scottish church, owed its development to the lumber trade. Canniff's Mill, opened in the 1860's and Timothy Solmes' grist mill were among its early industries. Peter Clark built a dam, a mill, and a chair factory at St. Ola.

Today Limerick has over forty miles of roads and the township is traversed by Highway 62, which brings tourists to the area's many lakes.

Gerald E. Boyce: *Historic Hastings,* 1967.

LINCOLN, geographic township, Sudbury District
Position 48° 16' 82° 53'

The township is situated north of Highway 101 and west of the railway point of Foleyet. The Nemegosenda River, a tributary of the Kapuskasing, flows northward along the township's western border. It was named after the Hon. Lincoln Goldie, Provincial Secretary and MPP for Wellington South in the 1920's.

LINCOLN, town, Regional Municipality of Niagara
Position 43° 10' 79° 29'

Lincoln, a town of 14,296 inhabitants (1979), was formed in 1970 by the amalgamation of the town of Beamsville, the township of Clinton, part of the township of Louth, and the police villages of Campden, Jordan, Jordan Station, and Vineland. It was named after the former county of Lincoln of which it once formed a part.

The Lincoln area was first settled in the late eighteenth century by veterans of the British army, including Butler's Rangers, who had fought in the American Revolution, and by United Empire Loyalists who fled to Upper Canada after the United States gained independence. The Loyalists included Pennsylvania Mennonites, Quakers, French Huguenots, and English. The settlers took up land along the creeks which traverse the Niagara peninsula. These creeks were known as the Twelve, the Twenty, and the Forty because of their approximate distance by miles from the Niagara River. Dominating the area is the Niagara Escarpment, the "Mountain", which divides the land from east to west and makes the lower area especially suited for the orchards and vineyards for which the area has become famous.

Among the early settlers were Aren Bradt, George Ball, who settled at Glen Elgin, the Secord brothers who built one of the first homes in Louth Township, the Beamers, Frys, Tenbroeks, Coles, Bebees, Hares, and Pattersons. Along the Sixteen were the Bertrandes, Books, Hitchcocks, Mingles, and Zimmermans. The Boughners, Fishers, Overholts, and Merrills settled along the Escarpment. Jacob

537

Beam and his family took up land along the Thirty and Jacob became the first blacksmith in the area.

As settlement increased, there began to develop the communities which would one day form the town of Lincoln. The most important of these was Beamsville, situated about 2 miles from Lake Ontario. Jacob Beam, after whom the community was named, arrived in 1788. He later donated the land for what is now the oldest Baptist church in Ontario. In 1790 Beam and William Kitchen built a grist and sawmill and soon a settlement grew up around the enterprise. Small mills, tanneries, blacksmith shops, and a foundry appeared as the local economy prospered. In 1875 Robert L. Gibson established a stone quarry which became a major employer. A basket factory was started by A. W. Reid in 1909 and in 1946 Lincoln Potteries was founded. National Socket Screw Company opened in 1952.

In 1858 Beamsville became a police village. It was incorporated as a village in 1879. It became a town in 1962. By 1970 it had six churches, a new town hall built in 1967, a community centre, a hospital, and a weekly newspaper, *The Beamsville Express*. Its population at the time of amalgamation was just over 4,000.

Clinton Township's first settler was probably William Walker, a Loyalist from Virginia who arrived in 1780. In 1790 Mr. Cohoe built the first grist mill in the township. The first schoolhouse was erected in the same year, on the site of present-day Beamsville. The school also served as a church for the settlers, who were mostly Mennonites from Pennsylvania.

The former police village of Campden was part of Clinton until 1970. Situated about 4 miles from Lake Ontario, it was once known as Moyer's Corners after Jacob Moyer, a prominent early settler. It was named Campden when a post office was established in 1862. Incorporated as a police village in 1905, Campden today is a largely residential community of about 250 people.

Vineland, Clinton's other police village, developed around Franklin W. Moyer's general store on the townline between Clinton and Louth Townships. It was named by Mrs. Moyer in 1894 after the extensive vineyards in the area. The construction of a railway station in 1910 gave farmers direct access to the Grand Trunk and created the community's important fruit-shipping business. Today this largely residential community is best known for its Horticultural Experimental Station, established in 1906, which researches orchard practices and soil management and develops new varieties of fruits and vegetables.

The hamlet of Tintern, now also a part of Lincoln, was named after Tintern Abbey in Monmouthshire, England. In 1856 it became the site of Dean's Mill, the largest flour and feed mill in Lincoln County. Among its early settlers were Andrew Dean, builder of the mill, and Joseph Michener, the ancestor of former Governor-General Roland Michener. The community declined after the mill closed in 1912.

Louth Township, named after the town of Louth in Lincoln County, England, was settled in the late 1700's. Two Secord brothers were among the first settlers. Their log cabin has been preserved. The first recorded township meeting took place in 1793. In 1799 a group of Pennsylvania Mennonites bought 1,100 acres and soon a large number had made Louth their home. In the early 1800's, the mouth of the Twenty became an important harbour and the communities of Jordan and Jordan Station developed into busy shipping centres. Several schooners were built on the Twenty and a number of industries established along the banks.

The construction of the Great Western Railway through the township in 1852 contributed to the prosperity of Louth as farmers switched from the harvesting of grain to the growing of fruit, and the shipping of fresh produce became a major industry in the township. The building of the Queen Elizabeth Way, begun in 1931 and completed in 1939, brought new prosperity to the township's lakeshore communities and today tourism is an important part of the local economy. The Jordan Wine Company is at present the only large industry in the area.

In 1948 Louth lost 50 acres and about 550 residents to Port Dalhousie when that village was incorporated as a town. The community of Vineland became part of Clinton in 1960. In 1970 Louth Township was dissolved. Part was annexed by the town of Lincoln and the rest by the city of St. Catharines.

The former police village of Jordan developed from the first Mennonite settlement in Canada, on the banks of the Twenty. By 1800, 25 Mennonite families were living among the disbanded soldiers of Butler's Rangers. The first mill was built by Mr. Ball at Ball's Falls. During the War of 1812, a regiment of soldiers was assigned to protect the mill. It still stands in the Ball's Falls conservation area.

Jordan developed as an important shipping centre in the early 1800's, loading grain and flour onto Lake Ontario barges. Village lots were laid out in the 1840's by Jacob Snure. Several new industries were established and the community of 200 became the centre of commerce for the surrounding area until the construction of the Great Western Railway bridge in 1852. The bridge prevented ships from reaching Jordan and the community began to decline. However, in the 1870's Clark Snure opened an apple-drying plant in Jordan which, during the twentieth century, became Louth Township's largest industry, Jordan Wines Ltd.

Jordan which became a police village in 1924, is the site of the Jordan Historical Museum of the Twenty which has preserved an old schoolhouse, the Vintage House, and the Jacob Fry House, a pioneer home.

Originally known as Bridgeport after the Great Western Railway bridge, Jordan Station developed as a result of the construction of this bridge, although there had been settlement in the area since the 1780's. As the only station between St. Catharines and Beamsville, the community soon became an important shipping centre for local agricultural products. Fruit-canning was begun in Jordan Station when British Canadian Canners opened a plant in 1912 and rapidly developed into one of the area's major industries.

When the town of Lincoln was incorporated in 1970, Delby J. Bucknall became its first mayor. On the council were Reginald H. Rittenhouse, Cecil E. Bovaird, Elmon Cosby, Charles Fretz, Edward N. Fortune, John Vdoviak, Joseph H. Romagnoli, and Russel High. Its population at this time was 13,661.

H. R. Page: *Historical Atlas of Lincoln & Welland Counties*, 1876.

William F. Rannie: *Lincoln The Story of an Ontario Town*, 1974.

LINDSAY, township, Bruce County
Position 45° 05' 81° 23'

Lindsay Township, which is part of the northern half of the Bruce Peninsula, was named in honour of the Earl of Lindsay. The township was surveyed in 1856.

Abraham West was the pioneer settler of the township. He took up Lot 5, Concession 2, W.B.R., some time prior to the first land sale in Lindsay Township, which did not take place until the year 1870. William Clark, who settled south of Mr. West, became his first neighbour. By 1871 there were only twenty inhabitants in the entire township according to the census taken that year, but by 1879 there were sufficient children in Lindsay Township to warrant the building of a schoolhouse on Alexander McDonald's farm (Lot 4, Concession 1, W.B.R.). A Miss Hurst was the first teacher.

Alexander McDonald who settled in Lindsay in 1877 was one of the township's most prominent men. He was reeve for many years and also county commissioner. In the schoolhouse he established a Sunday School and because there was no resident minister at the time, he conducted weekly prayer meetings. He was also instrumental in the erection of the first church building in the township, the Presbyterian Church in the School Section No. 1 area. The second church building, a Methodist church, was erected somewhat later at Dyer's Bay.

Lindsay Township did not have a post office until 1881. That year the first post office, known as "Stokes Bay", was established with Wm. Lyons as the postmaster. The post office at Dyer's Bay was opened the same year with Thomas Tindall in charge.

In 1873, Lindsay became part of the United Townships of Albemarle, Eastnor, Lindsay and St. Edmunds. On January 1, 1878, Albermarle left the union. Five years later, Lindsay and St. Edmunds were erected into a separate municipality. The first Lindsay and St. Edmunds council after separation consisted of Donald McDonald, Alex. Patch, and John Shute with Peter McVicar as reeve. James Weatherhead held the offices of clerk and treasurer. The two townships remained united until January 1, 1903, at which time each assumed independent municipal status. Peter Alderson was the first reeve of the new Township of Lindsay.

Lumbering was once the area's main industry, and one of the first mills in Lindsay was built in 1880 at Gillies Lake by Hiram Lymburner. By the early 1900's the boom days of the lumbering industry were over. Farming in the township has also declined in recent years. Some commercial fishing is carried on but the mainstay now is the tourist industry. To the nature lover, the Bruce Peninsula is a paradise of unspoiled beauty.

Lake Miller, in the centre of the township is the largest lake. There are no incorporated villages within the boundaries of the township.

Norman Robertson: *The History of the County of Bruce*, 1906.

Norman McLeod: *The History of the County of Bruce, 1907-1969*, 1969.

LINDSAY, town, Ops Township, Victoria County
Position 44° 21' 78° 44'

Twenty-seven miles west of Peterborough on the Scugog River lies Lindsay, county town of Victoria County and a divisional point on the Canadian National Railways.

The Township of Ops, in which Lindsay is situated, was surveyed in 1825 by Colonel Duncan McDonnell and Lots 20 and 21 in the 5th Concession were reserved as a town site. In that same year Patrick Connell, the first settler in the area, arrived, followed by the Bradys, Pynes, Hydes, Murphys, and Hoeys. Rev. Father Crowley, the only Roman Catholic priest in that part of Ontario at the time, was granted land to assist in settlement.

Three Americans, William Purdy and his sons, Jesse and Hazard, are considered the actual founders of Lindsay. Under a government contract the Purdys, about 1827, erected a dam on the Scugog River at the site of present-day Lindsay. The following year they built a sawmill and in 1830 a grist mill was added. A small village which sprang up around the mills was known as Purdy's Mills. Jeremiah Britton and his sons, Charles and Wellington, built a log house and tavern, Thomas Sowden and Major Thomas Murphy operated small stores, and a Mr. Fulford ran a carding mill. Around 1837 William Purdy and his son Jesse moved to Bath leaving Hazard Purdy in charge of the mill. In 1844 the latter sold the mill and a 400-acre tract of land the Purdys had been allotted, to Hiram Bigelow. The Purdy brothers, Hazard and Jesse, moved to Grey County where they became the founders of Meaford and Eugenia Falls.

Meanwhile the designated town site at Lindsay had been plotted into streets and lots by John Houston, Cavan, in 1834. One of the surveyor's assistants, a Mr. Lindsay, was accidentally shot in the leg and died of an infection. Buried on the river's bank, his name and death were entered on the surveyor's plan, and Lindsay remained as the name of the town by government approval. Prior to 1834 settlers on the actual town site were David Ray, Wm. Culbert, and the Edward Murphy family. In 1837 James Hutton moved to what is now Kent Street and opened a store, becoming the first merchant on the original site of Lindsay.

In 1838 the Purdy dam backed the waters of the Scugog River causing much damage over 60,000 surrounding acres. By irate demand of local farmers, Hazard Purdy lowered the level of the dam. At this time plans were being made for a lock at Lindsay to facilitate navigation between Sturgeon and Scugog lakes and by 1844 a new dam and the lock were completed. The year 1851 saw the beginning of navigation on the Scugog River with the steamboats *Woodman*, built at Port Perry, and the *Ogemah* at Fenelon Falls. Lindsay developed into a lumbering and farming centre.

William McDonell had the first tannery, George Colter ran a potashery and William Thornhill an iron-foundry. Hiram Bigelow bought Fulford's carding mill and stores were opened by Thomas Keenan, Jeremiah Britton, Wm. McDonnell and G. M. Roche. By 1851 the population had risen to 300. Brick-making was begun in 1856 by Francis Curtin. The first bank was the Bank of Upper Canada, opened in 1853. The *Metcalfe-Warden*, under the management of Joseph Cooper and Joseph Twell, made its first appearance in 1856. Later the paper's name changed to *Watchman-Warden*. Today's daily paper is the *Lindsay Post*.

A charter had been granted for the construction of a railway from Port Hope to Lindsay. In 1857 steel reached Lindsay coming by way of Millbrook and Reaboro. The railway brought a period of rapid expansion and industrial development. Lindsay, with a population of 1,100, was incorporated as a town on June 19, 1857, and its limits extended to take in three more tracts, one of them the former Purdy tract.

The first town council met in 1857 and included: Mayor Robert Lang; Reeve Foster Cain; Councillors: Wm. Thornhill, David Brown, Jeremiah O'Leary, J. Healey, H.G. Clarke, James Walsh, and J. McCarthy; Clerk and Treasurer, T.A. Hudspetch; and Chief of Police, John Douglas.

In 1861 a fire swept Lindsay destroying four hotels, two mills, the post office and eighty-three other buildings. Four hundred people were left homeless.

A new Town Hall was built in 1863. Thomas E. Bradburn, a few years later, constructed an addition to the Town Hall, the upper floor being set aside as an opera house which over the years attracted many prominent performers from other centres. A new Opera House was built in 1892. Here, at the age of five, Marie Dressler, later to achieve fame as a much-loved character actress, made her first stage appearance. In 1964 the old Opera House was refurbished and re-opened by Lieutenant-Governor Earl Rowe.

Lindsay's first street lights (six coal oil lamps) were put up in 1880. Gas lamps replaced them the following year, and electricity came in 1890. Lindsay remained without adequate fire protection until 1892, when the Lindsay Waterworks Company was formed.

James Ross, a Montreal Millionaire, financed a hospital built in 1901 in memory of his parents, residents of Lindsay for many years. Fred Edmonds was responsible for the establishment of the town's first cinema in 1904.

The first church in Lindsay was Roman Catholic, built of logs in 1841. Father Crowley was the first of the visiting Fathers to conduct worship for the Roman Catholic settlers. A new church opened in 1859 and in 1868 a separate school was erected. The Loretto Convent opened in 1874.

In 1842 a Methodist church was built on Wellington Street, and later a second Methodist church was erected on the corner of Wellington and William Streets. In 1878 another Methodist church was begun on Queen Street. The Presbyterians built a log church in 1845 and in 1887 a new church was constructed. Anglicans first worshipped in the old Town Hall in 1855. In 1859 St. Paul's Anglican Church was built on the site of the present Post Office. A new church was erected in 1885 on Russell Street.

The Baptists worshipped in a private home until a building on Cambridge Street S. was acquired. In the 1860's a church was built on the northwest corner of Wellington and Sussex Streets. About 1886 a church was bought from the Bible Christians and remodelled for use. The Salvation Army began its work in 1883 and built a citadel the following year. A new citadel opened in 1921 on the site of the earlier structure. As well as these churches, the Christian Reformed, the Gospel Hall, Jehovah's Witnesses and Pentecostal are established in Lindsay today.

By 1860 there were two schools in Lindsay, one brick and one frame. High School education was carried on from the 1850's with classes held in the public school. By 1863 the Union School was opened offering instruction for both public and high school students until 1888 when the Collegiate was built.

The CNR and the CPR lines both traverse Lindsay, but do not provide a passenger service. An airport offers plane facilities and includes maintenance services and ground-to-air communication. There is a flying school and charter service.

An influx of immigrants from many countries in the mid-nineteen hundreds meant expansion and Lindsay now boasts a variety of businesses and recreation facilities. Most of the philanthropic societies, lodges, and masonic orders are represented here. The local radio station is CKLY, an affiliate of the CBC. There are two libraries, an arts society, a crafts society, and three music groups: The Kawartha Kavaliers, the Kinsmen Band, and the Lindsay Pipe Band. The Kawartha Summer Theatre entertains with Canada's leading professional summer stock company.

Among the noteworthy personages who have called Lindsay home, was the colourful Sam Hughes (1852-1921). Lieutenant-General the Hon. Sir Sam Hughes, KCB, was Minister of Militia and Defence for Canada in the Borden Cabinet 1911-16. He was created a Knight Commander of the Bath in 1916 for his war services.

In August of 1958 Lindsay was the site of Canada's first bullfight. Protests against the fight had poured in from across the country, but the promoters went ahead and the bulls arrived from Mexico. It was to be a "bloodless" fight, and the matadors had only wooden swords. The first bull refused to fight and was lured out of the arena by a heifer. The other bulls put on a spectacular show, and one enraged bull charged when the town's chief of police strode into the arena after a symbolic "Kill" to lead the animal out. The chief ran to safety in the nick of time! The promoters lost a lot of money as hundreds of spectators had gained entrance without paying admission.

Lindsay, with its proximity to Sturgeon Lake, Pigeon Lake and Scugog Lake, is referred to as the "Gateway to the Kawarthas". The Scugog River which runs through the town is a link in the Trent Waterway System, one of Ontario's great waterways. Resort lodges, modern motels, spacious parks, a nine-hole golf course and a tennis club, both open to visitors, provide enjoyment for vacationers.

Watson Kirkconnell: *County of Victoria*, 1967.

Alan R. Capon: *Historic Lindsay*, 1974.

LINDSLEY, geographic township, Thunder Bay District
Position 49° 42′ 87° 10′

Named after Thayer Lindsley, a prominent mining engineer in the 1930's, the township is located immediately to the west of the town of Geraldton. The Canadian National Railways passes through its northern section, while Highway 11 runs through the centre. Wildgoose Lake occupies the northwest section of Lindsley.

LINWOOD, community, Regional Municipality of Waterloo
Position 43° 35′ 80° 43′

Linwood is located northwest of the city of Waterloo. Thomas Ransom and John Brown were the settlement's pioneers, Ransom having located on the southwest, and Brown on the northeast corner lot, east of the village around 1846.

First to locate on the site of the present-day village was Robert Crooks, joined later by William Owen and Archibald Calder. To the west Wm. G. Woodman and Andrew Case were among the first settlers.

By the 1880's the population of Linwood had grown to 200. The village had two stores and two hotels, as well as other businesses serving the residents of the surrounding agricultural area.

The community, incorporated as a police village, became part of the Township of Wellesley on January 1, 1973.

H. Parsell & Co.: *Illustrated Atlas of the County of Waterloo*, 1881.

LION'S HEAD, village, Eastnor Township, Bruce County
Position 44° 59' 81° 15'

Lion's Head, 22 miles northwest of the town of Wiarton, is situated on Isthmus Bay, a part of Georgian Bay. The village lies two miles east of Highway 6. Wiarton is the nearest railway station. The population is 474 (1979).

Early settlers called the place "Point Hangcliffe" until they discovered a massive rock formation resembling a lion's head on a headland near the village.

George Moore, Richard Tackaberry, and John Richardson were among the first to settle, in 1871, on the site of the present village. Frank Stewart, a lumberman, opened a store and when a post office was established in 1875, he became the first postmaster.

Reverend Leggett, a Methodist, was the first to minister to the spiritual needs of the people of Lion's Head and vicinity, but the Presbyterians were the first to erect a church in the village. It was dedicated in 1881. The Anglicans built their church in 1882 and the Methodists built in 1885.

Back in those days the few existing roads in Eastnor Township were in deplorable condition, and traffic to the area was chiefly by water. To accommodate the vessels calling at Lion's Head, a wharf was constructed in 1883.

The first public school in Lion's Head was a one-room building, moved from the country into the village in 1892. The Continuation School was built in 1932.

In 1917 Lion's Head was incorporated as a village. W.B. Moore was elected as the first reeve. Councillors were Walter Warder, S.F. Warren, Harry Stewart and W.B. Moshier. Johnathan Hill was clerk.

The Lion's Head Women's Institute, formed in 1904, operated a library from 1908 to 1951. The library now forms a unit of the Bruce County Public Library. The Institute assisted in founding a Red Cross hospital in 1924, which became the forerunner to the modern Earl R. Harris Red Cross Hospital erected in 1965.

The excellent harbour on which the village is situated, the famous Bruce Trail which passes through this part of the peninsula, the caves, rock formations and sandy beaches all combine to make Lion's Head a busy tourist centre in the summertime.

Norman Robertson: *The History of the County of Bruce*, 1906.

Norman McLeod: *The History of the County of Bruce 1907-1969*, 1969.

LIPSETT, geographic township, Sudbury District
Position 48° 16′ 83° 17′

The name origin of this township is not known. It lies about 30 miles north of the town of Chapleau to which it is linked by dry weather roads. Lipsett Lake occupies a portion of the township's western half.

LIPTON, geographic township, Algoma District
Position 49° 00′ 84° 30′

This township is located northeast of White River and is named after Sir Thomas Lipton, a noted Irish yacht racing enthusiast and tea merchant of England. The northern tip of Kabinakagami Lake occupies much of the southeastern corner of Lipton. In the northeast lies Kabinakagamisis Lake. The township is accessible by waterways only.

LISGAR, geographic township, Cochrane District
Position 48° 46′ 82° 32′

Lisgar borders in the west on the Algoma District. The township which is accessible by road, was named after Lord Lisgar, Governor General of Canada from 1869 to 1872.

LISLE, community, Tosorontio Township, Simcoe County
Position 44° 16′ 79° 59′

Situated on the CNR about 25 miles south of Barrie, this compact rural community was first named Forestlea by Thomas Crosbie, a local landowner. When the Grand Trunk Railway (now the CNR) was built in 1878, the station was named New Airlie. With the village of Arlie nearby the name proved confusing and so a new name was chosen the following year when Messrs. Wilmott, Harrison, and Hatton, lumbermen, petitioned for a post office. Miss Wilmott suggested Lisle from the popular song "Annie Lisle".

By 1903 the community had a population of 250. Hatton & Son operated a sawmill and a flour mill was owned by J. A. McLean. Local craftsmen included a shoemaker, pumpmaker, and harnessmaker. There were also a dealer in farm implements and three general stores.

Lisle has grown little since this time and today is a pleasant residential community of 254 (1977).

Ontario Historical Society, *Papers*, 1905.

LISMORE, geographic township, Thunder Bay District
Position 48° 12′ 89° 57′

Lismore was named after an estate in England belonging to the Duke of Devonshire. The township lies southwest of the city of Thunder Bay. White Fish Lake takes up much of the northwest corner with Little White Fish River flowing out of this lake in a southerly direction. Highway 593 passes along the eastern border.

LISTER, geographic township, Nipissing District
Position 45° 58′ 78° 33′

The township which is part of the northern region of Algonquin Provincial Park, was established in 1884 and was named after Sir James Frederick Lister, M.P. for West Lambton at that time. The area abounds in rivers and lakes, Cedar, Carl Wilson and Catfish lakes being the largest. There are no roads within the boundaries of Lister.

LISTOWEL, town, Wallace and Elma Townships, Perth County
Position 43° 44′ 80° 57′

Listowel is located on Highways 23 and 86 and on the junction of two CNR lines, about 30 miles north of Stratford. The name, which comes from a town in southwestern Ireland, was chosen by a government official when a post office was established, and it has no connection with the town's history.

The first permanent settler was John Binning, who arrived in 1852. He bought the land belonging to a man named Henry in exchange for a rifle. Several weeks passed before Binning became aware that Peter Twamley, another pioneer, had settled less than two miles away.

In 1853 William Wisner, the Tremain brothers, George Dodd, and James Barber also took up land in the vicinity. In 1855 William H. Hacking bought a parcel of land from John Tremain and erected a store. At a meeting, the inhabitants voted to name their settlement Mapleton. In the same year William Gibson also opened a store not far away and named it Windham. When an application for a post office was approved in 1856, a government decision rejected the rival names and the place was named Listowel.

By 1866 the community's population had grown to 800 and in the following year it became a village with D.D. Hay as first reeve. Incorporation enabled council to raise money to promote the development of railways. In 1871 the Wellington, Grey and Bruce Railway was extended to Listowel and in 1873 the Stratford and Huron Railway began service to the village. Listowel subsequently developed into an important shipping point. The population more than doubled and the village prospered. By 1874 the population stood at 2,054 and in 1875 Listowel became a town. D.D. Campbell was first mayor.

Flour, woollen, saw and planing mills, and the tannery of Messrs. Towner and Campbell were among Listowel's early industries. In 1891 Morris, Field, Rogers Company Limited began the manufacture of Morris pianos and in 1900 the Listowel Furniture Company was founded. Located in the centre of a dairy farming district, Listowel, by 1903, was the second largest manufacturing town in Perth County and the professions were also well represented. The town had five doctors, four lawyers, three dentists, and three banks.

As well as encouraging manufacturing, early town councils did not hesitate to spend money on improvements, going into considerable debt. Schools, gravel roads, a firehall, a jail, and new bridges across the Maitland River were built. Gas lighting was introduced to the town in 1880 and electric lighting began in 1897.

The first log school was used for religious services of all denominations and all types of public meetings. In 1877 the Central School building, noted for the beauty of its architecture, was erected. Benjamin Rothwell was the Principal. James Crozier became Principal of the new High School which was constructed in 1880.

The town has a number of churches dating from the late nineteenth century. Rev. Mr. Snider, a Congregationalist from Stratford, held the first religious service in 1856, and Rev. Mr. McGregor became the first resident minister. The Congregationalists erected the first church in Listowel and made it available for use by other denominations. An Anglican church was established in 1863 under Rev. Canon Newman. Rev. Mr. Sanderson, who arrived in 1865, was the first resident Methodist minister. In 1868 Rev. John Bell began preaching to his Presbyterian congregation and Rev. Philip Winkler organized the Evangelical Association in 1876. Rev. Mr. Dack began the Baptist church in 1886, and in 1887 the Rev. Mr. Love became the United Brethren's first minister.

The *Banner*, founded by Messrs. Ferguson and Elliott in 1865, and one of two weekly papers, still publishes today. The town is served by a public library. Horatio Walker (1858-1938) painter of French-Canadian life and culture, was a native of Listowel, and a plaque at the Public Library commemorates the noted artist.

William Johnston: *History of Perth County, 1825-1902*, 1903.

W. Stafford Johnston and Hugh N.M. Johnston: *History of Perth County to 1967*, 1967.

Main Street, Listowel, Ontario, C. 1924

LITTLE, geographic township, Cochrane District
Position 48° 45' 81° 00'

The township lies west of the town of Iroquois Falls. It was subdivided by J. W. Fitzgerald in 1904 and named after Archibald Little, MPP for North Norfolk just prior to that time. The Frederick House River courses through the eastern part of the township.

LITTLE BRITAIN, police village, Mariposa Township, Victoria County
Position 44° 17' 78° 51'

Little Britain, southwest of the town of Lindsay, was founded by Harrison Haight who settled here in 1834 and three years later built the first mill in the township. The mill was demolished in 1910. The leading merchant in the village in the early days was Robert F. Whiteside. A post office was opened in 1853.

By the 1880's Little Britain was the largest business centre in Mariposa Township and included a carriage and blacksmithing works, a sash, door and planing factory, a shingle mill, a foundry and grocery stores, a tailor and harness shops, and there was a stage to Mariposa Station, just four miles away, where a 30,000-bushel grain elevator was located.

The village, although situated in the most fertile township in Victoria County, declined in importance in later years, having been bypassed by the railway line.

Watson Kirkconnell: *Victoria County Centennial History*, 1967.

LITTLE CURRENT, town, Howland Township, Manitoulin District
Position 45° 58' 81° 56'

The largest centre in the district, Little Current lies at the northeast tip of Manitoulin Island, 100 yards from the mainland. Known by the Indians as Wai-be-je-wung, "where the waters flow back and forth" and by French fur-traders as "La Petit Courant", it was first called Shaftesbury by its English settlers. Little Current is a translation of the French name.

The settlement was originally a Hudson's Bay Company fur-trading post. It also served as a supply centre for the local Indians. In the late nineteenth century, its large natural harbour made it a major shipping-point of the CPR in its transportation of coal to Northern Ontario and it became known as "Port of the North". Today the coalships no longer run but iron ore and other minerals from the north are sent south by ship from Little Current. During the summer the harbour is also full of pleasure craft from all over the Great Lakes.

Incorporated as a town in 1890, Little Current has developed into the most extensive shopping centre on the island. One of the major stores, Turner's Manitoulin, has been in business since 1879. The town of 1,536 (1979) has no industries, relying mainly on tourism resulting from its position as gateway to Manitoulin. A museum reflects life as it was in nineteenth-century Little Current.

The town has a public school and a library, founded in 1931. The library is housed in the former municipal building. Seven churches, St. Joseph's Hospital, and a Home for the Aged also serve the residents. Recreational facilities include an arena, two beaches, a ski hill, a bowling alley, and a curling rink. Hotels and motels provide accommodation for visitors. Local news is reported in the weekly *Expositor*.

Manitoulin Expositor, 1967.

Ministry of Natural Resources: *Directory of Statistics and Data*, 1975.

This is Manitoulin. (brochure)

LIVELY, part of town of Walden, Regional Municipality of Sudbury
Position 46° 26′ 81° 09′

Lively, a few miles west of Sudbury, was built by the International Nickel Co. for the employees of its nearby Creighton Mine. The company named the community in honour of Charles Lively, one of its long-time employees.

Lively was incorporated as a town in 1953. In 1973 it amalgamated with the united townships of Drury, Denison, and Graham, the Township of Waters, and the geographic townships of Dieppe, Lorne and Louise as the Town of Walden.

LIVINGSTONE, geographic township, Haliburton County
Position 45° 24′ 78° 42′

This township is situated in the northern part of Haliburton County and is bounded on the west by McClintock township, on the south by Havelock, on the east by Lawrence (in Algonquin Park), and on the north by the District of Nipissing. It was named after the famous missionary and explorer of Africa, Dr. David Livingstone.

The township was surveyed in 1877. Hollow Lake, which lies partially within its borders, became a popular area for trappers, fishermen, and hunters, but little permanent settlement took place within the township. Among Livingstone's few residents in the late nineteenth century were Arthur Andrews, Charles Baker, H.W. Clark, J.F.W. Ross, and Fred Christensen. The township has remained sparsely settled throughout the twentieth century.

When the Provisional County of Haliburton was formed in 1874, Livingstone was united with McClintock, Sherborne, Nightingale, and Stanhope Townships for municipal purposes. Stanhope became independent in 1898. Today Livingstone, Sherborne and McClintock are united. The combined permanent population of these townships is 466 (1979). Lumbering and tourism are the mainstay of the township's economy.

History of the Provisional County of Haliburton, 1931.

Nila Reynolds: *In Quest of Yesterday*, 1968.

LIVINGSTONE CREEK, community, Thessalon Township, Algoma District
Position 46° 16′ 83° 28′

Located east of the town of Thessalon, this dispersed rural community was named after Captain Livingstone, who abandoned his vessel in distress just offshore in the North Channel of Lake Huron, and travelled up what is now known Livingstone Creek to the site of the present community where he settled. The name has been in use since the turn of the century. The Station Point of Livingstone is located nearby on the Canadian Pacific Transcontinental line.

LIZAR, geographic township, Algoma District
Position 48° 52′ 84° 30′

Lizar is believed to have been named after a Mr. Lizar, K.C. of Belleville, Ontario. The area is located northeast of White River. The eastern half of the township is, to a large extent, occupied by Kabinakagami Lake, with several large and smaller islands.

LLOYD, geographic township, Sudbury District
Position 48° 22′ 83° 16′

Named after noted British statesman, Lloyd George (1863-1945), the township lies north of the town of Chapleau. Dry weather roads link the area to nearby Missinaibi Lake Provincial Park and to Chapleau.

LLOYDTOWN, community, King Township, Regional Municipality of York
Position 43° 59′ 79° 42′

The village was named after Jesse and Phoebe Lloyd, its first settlers. It is situated on the west branch of the Holland River, about a mile west of Schomberg, in the northwestern part of King Township.

Jesse Lloyd was the son of Pennsylvania Quakers who settled in the township in 1812. In 1824 he built a sawmill in Tecumseth Township to provide the lumber for the grist mill which he erected in King in 1826. This was the first such mill in the area and a settlement soon grew up around it. The first post office in the township was opened here in 1831, with Joseph Watson as postmaster.

As the grist mill prospered, Lloydtown grew. By 1851 it had a population of 350. Other businesses included two tanneries, a foundry, two shoe shops, a distillery, a woollen mill and two cooperages. In the mid-nineteenth century, the village was much more prosperous than neighbouring Brownsville (now Schomberg). When the railway was constructed from Aurora to Schomberg, Lloydtown began to decline. Today it is a quiet residential area of about 150 people. The last store closed in 1964.

In the 1830's, the village became a rallying point of the Mackenzie uprising. Jesse Lloyd was a chief associate of Mackenzie.

He held meetings in his house and helped plan the attack on York. Several Lloydtown men participated in the historic march from Montgomery's Tavern. After the failure of the rebellion, Lloyd fled to the United States where he died a year later.

In 1842 the Anglican St. Mary Magdalene Church was opened, with Canon Henry Osler as first rector. Two years later the Wesleyan Methodist Church was built. The congregation moved to Schomberg in 1908 after the building was destroyed by fire.

The date of construction of the first school is not known but records indicate that one existed by 1850. A second school was erected in 1863. It was closed in 1966, but was used as a "historic school" during Canada's Centennial Year.

Mary E. Garbutt: "King Township, York County, 1800-1807: A Historical Sketch" in *Ontario Historical Society*, 1960.

Elizabeth McClure Gillham: *Early Settlements of King Township Ontario*, 1975.

LOACH, geographic township, Algoma District
Position 47° 22' 84° 17'

The area, once known as Township 26, Range 16, was part of the Algoma Central and Hudson Bay Railway Land Grant and lies some 50 miles north of Sault Ste Marie. The township was named in 1974 after L. A. Loach, reeve of Harley township, Timiskaming District. The Montreal River, at times half a mile wide, flows across the southern part of the township.

LOBO, township, Middlesex County
Position 43° 02' 81° 28'

Lying west of the city of London, Lobo was named by Sir Peregrine Maitland, Lieutenant-Governor of Upper Canada 1818-28, who had served in Spain during the Napoleonic Wars. Lobo is the Spanish word for wolf.

The township was surveyed by Col. Mahlon Burwell in 1819-21. There were a few squatters in Lobo before the survey but the first large group arrived in 1819. Among these first settlers were the Campbells, McArthurs, McKellars, Thomas McCall, and John Gray. Soon more immigrants came to take up land in this fertile township. Most of them were Highland Scots. Many of them sailed to Canada from Oban, Scotland on the *Gestian* in 1820, including Duncan McIntyre, Archibald Johnson, Neil McKeith, John McColl, Donald Lamont, and John Sinclair. Agnes McColl became the first white child born in the township in 1820.

After the first wave of settlement in the early 1820's, Lobo's progress was fairly slow until after 1840. The Kilworth flour mill, operated by the Oliver family in the 1830's, was the only one in the township for many years. Swamps, heavy timber growth, and large grants along the Thames River kept the population fairly small for many years. However, after the Great Western Railway was built across the southern end of the township in 1855 and the Grand Trunk nearby, Lobo began to grow rapidly. The railway gave the farmers access to wider markets and also provided shipping facilities for local lumbering operations. At Komoka, the township's major centre, the Sarnia line joined the main railway. In 1881 the CPR also constructed a line through Lobo.

The first town meeting was probably held in 1829 at the house of Donald McArthur. Hugh Carmichael was elected clerk. A township hall was erected in 1842 and replaced by a new building in 1880. In 1853 R. Adamson became Lobo's first reeve.

By 1878 the township was one of the richest in the county. Its population at this time was about 3,500. Several prosperous communities had developed. Industries included the Gold Creek Cheese Factory, the Oliver flour mill, and several sawmills. The main activity in the township was farming.

Today Lobo is still largely agricultural. Many of the nineteenth-century communities have nearly disappeared but others such as Komoka have continued to prosper. In 1979 Lobo's population was 4,783.

A schoolhouse was built as early as 1826 but it was not roofed and therefore never used. The first lessons were held in a blacksmith shop about 1831. A year later, a school was erected on Alexander McKellar's farm. William Matheson was the first teacher. Two more schools were opened during the years 1835-40. In 1864 a Baptist church was built. It became the Komoka Seminary, a short-lived private college which trained students for the medical and legal professions.

A Baptist church was opened in Poplar Hill in 1827 and a Methodist church in Inkerman in the 1830's. In 1849, the Quakers, who formed a distinctive group of pioneers in the township, built a Friends Meeting House.

Today Lobo's rich heritage is preserved in the many historic homes which are still standing. Among these are Oliver Campbell's home built in the 1850's, the Loveless house, the Arrand home erected about 1845 and the farm of Peter McIntyre. Another attraction is the Wishing Well Rock, the site of a cave of petrified rocks, although the original famous rock is now eroded.

Hugh McColl: Some Sketches of the Early Highland Pioneers of the County of Middlesex, 1904.

Ron Nickles and Ron Davis: Lobo Township Sketches, 1976.

LOCHIEL, township, Glengarry County
Position 45° 23' 74° 36'

The most northeasterly of Glengarry's townships, Lochiel was named after the Scottish estate of Chief of Clan Cameron, as many members of the clan had settled in the township.

Lochiel was part of Lancaster Township when Glengarry County was first established, and most of the area's Crown Reserve lands were in the Lochiel area, covering about forty percent of the present township. Although the land could not be sold, it could be leased and therefore the Reserves did not greatly hinder settlement. The land was first taken up by groups of emigrants from the Scottish Highlands in 1786 and 1788. Among the earliest were about thirty families who settled near Lot 26, Concession 6. These included the families of Roderick and Alexander McLeod, John Dewar, John McPhee, and Donald and Archibald McGillivray. They were later followed by the McArthurs, McCuaigs, Campbells, Cains and Frasers.

Lochiel separated from Lancaster Township in 1818. By this time it was well settled and a number of small communities were beginning to develop. Among them Alexandria attained early commercial importance. It was founded in 1819 when the Rev. Alexander Macdonell erected a grist mill here on the Garry River. The settlement was known as Priest's Mill in those early days. Alexandria was part of the township until 1884, when it was incorporated as a village. It became a town in 1903.

Communities in the township today are McCrimmon, Lochinvar, Breadalbane, Laggan, Kirkhill, Dalkeith, Lochiel, McCormick, Glen Sandfield and Glen Robertson.

Royce MacGillivray and Ewan Ross: *A History of Glengarry*, 1979.

LOCHLIN, community, Snowdon Township, Haliburton County
Position 44° 56′ 78° 34′

This settlement is located on Highway 519, on the Burnt River a few miles southeast of Minden. It was first called Egypt; and when the Victoria Railway was built it became known as Ingoldsby Station.

One of the first settlers in this area was Eliazer Yerex who in 1872 chopped a trail from the Haliburton Road to his future homestead. Albert E. Ganvesen from Prince Edward County arrived around the same time. A generous man, he contributed land for the United Church and supplied shingles and building materials. Also from Prince Edward County came Levi Pringle. A post office called Lochlin was established in 1895 and Pringle became postmaster, a post he held for 25 years. Other settlers were Isaah Hicks and his family, Peter Minaker, and John and Louisa Wruth.

Nila Reynolds: *In Quest of Yesterday*, 1967.

LOCKEYER, geographic township, Algoma District
Position 46° 30′ 82° 16′

Named in 1974 in honour of Canadian army grenadier Norman F. Lockeyer of Little Current, killed in 1944, the area was first known as Township 131. It is located north of the town of Massey and is accessible from Highway 553.

LOCKHART, geographic township, Nipissing District
Position 46° 35′ 79° 19′

Located northeast of the city of North Bay, the township was first subdivided in 1890 and was named after Wm. T. Lockhart, MPP for Durham West at that time. Perchfin Lake and Mitchell Lake are the largest of several lakes within the township.

554

LOGAN, township, Perth County
Position 43° 31' 81° 10'

Logan, situated in the west of Perth County, was named after Hart Logan, a director of the Canada Company which sold the land to the settlers.

Survey of the township started in 1830, and was completed by 1835. The first settler was probably John Hicks who took up land at the site of present-day Mitchell on the Huron Road. By 1837 Francis Seibert was established in the south-east corner of the township. Settlement in the early years concentrated mainly in this area. Farther north, a large swampy district made settlement impossible. Extensive drainage projects begun in 1880, however, were successful and all the land in the township became available for agriculture.

In 1844, 134 people lived in Logan, cultivating 49 acres. In 1850, 900 acres were being farmed by 603 settlers. By 1861, the population had increased to 2,257. It continued to grow until the 1880's when it reached about 3,400, largely due to the railway which by then gave access to markets for local farmers. The construction of the Logan Road in 1857-8 also encouraged immigration, mainly from Great Britain and Germany. Today the township's population numbers approximately 2,200.

During the 1840's Logan was represented on the Huron County council but was attached to McKillop for municipal purposes. It became a separate municipality in 1844. Although the people of Logan opposed the division of Huron County, the township became part of the new County of Perth in 1849. By the 1850 Municipal Act, Wallace and Elma, largely unorganized townships to the northeast, were joined to Logan. John Hicks was Reeve. In 1857 Wallace and Elma withdrew and Robert Jones became the first Reeve of Logan in 1858.

The first school was established in 1846 at present-day Mitchell. By 1855 the township had another school and by 1872 the number had increased to eight. However, an 1867 superintendent's report described the schools as being of poor quality. Most schools in the township date from the late nineteenth century. By 1903 there was also one separate school.

The date of the earliest religious service is unknown. In 1858 Rev. J.A. Herenger organized an Evangelical Lutheran congregation and a church was built in 1865. St. Brigid's Roman Catholic Church, the largest in Logan, dates from Father O'Neill's early mission in 1860. In 1862 a Methodist Mission was established by Rev. Mr. Howard. The Willow Grove Methodist Church was built in 1890.

Mitchell, the largest community in the township, was incorporated as a village in 1857 and in 1874 it became a town. Other communities in the township include Willow Grove, Bornholm, Brodhagen, Kennicott and Monkton. The latter is located on the Elma townline and on the CPR. The township is served by Highways 8 and 23.

W. Stafford Johnston and Hugh J.M. Johnston: *History of Perth County to 1967*, 1967.

LOMBARDY, community, South Elmsley Township, Leeds County
Position 44° 49′ 76° 05′

The compact rural community of Lombardy is situated about 30 miles northwest of Brockville on Highway 15. It was originally known as Lombard Corners after Francis Lombard, one of its earliest settlers.

Among the first settlers in the area were Richard Ringer, John McCollum, and Walter Armstrong. Francis Lombard arrived in 1815 and built his home at Lombard Corners. Gradually a community began to develop here. William Cawley opened the first store and Mr. Wilson became the first blacksmith.

In 1873 a post office was established and named South Elmsley. A petition from local residents resulted in the name being changed to Lombardy in 1880.

A bridge built across the Rideau River at Oliver's Ferry in 1878 brought increased trade and prosperity to Lombardy. Charles Lombard opened the community's first hotel. By 1880 there were about 25 families living in the settlement which had two general stores, two blacksmith shops, a cooper shop, a harness shop, and three hotels. A cheese factory was built in 1885.

In 1903 Lombardy's population was about 250. M. Balfe and Peter O'Brien owned the community's two hotels. A sawmill was operated by E. Erratt & Son.

LOMOND, geographic township, Kenora District
Position 50° 01′ 92° 21′

Lomond borders on the western end of Vermilion Lake. The township's name recalls famous Loch Lomond in Scotland. The area is located southwest of Sioux Lookout.

LONDESBOROUGH, community, Hullett Township, Huron County
Position 43° 43′ 81° 29′

Situated about 15 miles southeast of Goderich, this urban community was named by Thomas Hagyard, an early settler who had previously lived on Lord Londesborough's estate in Yorkshire, England.

R. Wright was the first to settle at Londesborough. He was followed by William Herrington and Francis Brown. In 1850 Thomas Hagyard laid out a village at the site which at that time was known as Hagyard's Corners. A post office was opened in 1861.

Many more settlers arrived from Britain after 1850. Among these early residents were Stephen Gray, Elias Lear, Joseph Howson, Thomas Fairservice, Henry Adams, and George Eno. D.S. Huber, who came to Londesborough in 1873, established a business as a miller and a lumber dealer.

By 1880 the community had 2 general stores, 4 carriage and wagon shops, 4 blacksmith shops, 2 shoe stores, 2 merchant tailors, a telegraph office, a private school, and Methodist and Presbyterian churches.

By 1903 Londesborough had become a station on the Lake Huron and Buffalo Railway. Its population was about 300.

Most of Londesborough's small local industries have long since disappeared, although the old grist mill remained as a landmark well into the twentieth century before being replaced by a newer mill. Today this quiet community on Highway 4 has a population of about 200 (1977).

Clinton Women's Institute: *History of Clinton*, 1950.

LONDON, township, Middlesex County
Position 43° 05' 81° 18'

The area which now comprises London Township was once occupied by the Neutral Indians. After this tribe was wiped out by the Iroquois there were no permanent settlements in the region until the early nineteenth century when the first white pioneers arrived. The survey of the 12 mile square township, then one of the largest in Upper Canada, was begun in 1810 by Col. Mahlon Burwell. The War of 1812 interrupted the survey but Burwell resumed his work in 1815 and finished about 1818.

The first settlers arrived before the survey was completed. A land patent was granted to Elizabeth Derenzy as early as 1812 but the first permanent settler, Joshua Applegarth, did not take up his land until 1816. He unsuccessfully attempted the cultivation of hemp. In 1817 he was followed by Duncan McKenzie.

The first wave of settlement took place in 1818. Among these pioneers were Duncan Anderson, Andrew McConnell, Joseph Routledge, Daniel Wood, William Kimball, and John Carmichael. Most of these early settlers were Scottish Highlanders. There were also 25 families from Ireland brought by Richard Talbot. Talbot had applied for government assistance to emigrate and had been told this would be granted if he gathered together a group of people to go to Canada. As London Township was the only large area of Crown Land immediately available in 1818, land was set aside here for the Talbot settlers. Upon arrival in Canada, many of the families went to the Perth Settlement in Lanark County, but a small number accompanied Talbot to London. The Talbot settlers included William Geary, Thomas Brooks, Joseph O'Brien, John Gray, and Charles Sifton. Most of them made their homes in the southeast part of the township.

Robert Telfer arrived from England in 1819. He was joined by Thomas Batie, Thomas White, and Andrew Scott. These men were the pioneers of the English Settlement.

John Matthews came from Wales to London Township. Favourably impressed with the area, he soon persuaded his relatives and friends to join him, and in 1821 the nucleus of Welsh Settlement in Upper Canada was formed. Col. Talbot reserved 1800 acres in the northwestern township for the Welsh settlers, who included David Morgan, John Rosser, and Philip Matthews. Other Welsh families, many of whom had settled first in New York State, were soon attracted to the area and a substantial community developed at what is now

Denfield.

The township's population continued to grow through the 1820's. The founding of the city of London in 1826 gave a great impetus to the area's development. By 1828 the township had about 400 families, stores, mills, and one church under construction. In that year, John Carling (later Sir John) became the first white child born north of the Thames River.

More industries were established in the 1830's. In 1838 Cromwell Wilson built the first woollen mill in the area. The opening of the Proof Line Road in the 1840's greatly enhanced the prosperity of the township. Improved by Freeman Talbot and other local settlers in 1849, it became the main thoroughfare from London, an incorporated town from 1840, to the Lake Huron counties. Several hotels were opened along the road, including William H. Ryan's hotel built at Elginfield in 1855 which was one of the largest rural hotels in Western Ontario.

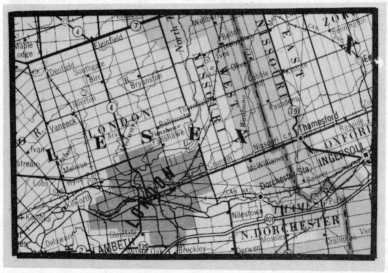

Municipal government in the township dates back to 1819 when the first town meeting was held in the house of Joshua Applegarth. Applegarth was elected clerk. In 1850 Freeman Talbot, who had played an important part in the establishment of the town of London, became the township's first reeve. On the council were Messrs. McMillan, Robson, Walden, and Harrison.

The London, Huron, and Bruce Railway, built in 1875, brought increased prosperity to London Township. The improved shipping facilities led to the establishment of new industries. The Devizes Cheese and Butter Company, founded in 1878, is today one of the oldest co-operatives in the township. Of the mills that were built, the largest were those of John Siddall and Sons which included grist, saw, and carding mills.

Since 1885 the township has been subject to annexation by the constantly-expanding city of London. London Township lost land to the city in 1890, 1912, 1961, and 1967. Today the township covers an area of 85,960 acres and has a population of 5,878 (1979).

Roman Catholic missionaries to the Indians were the first to hold religious services in London Township. Methodist services were held in the early 1820's by Robert Carson in the homes of the Welsh settlers. The first Methodist meetinghouse was built in 1833. The Scottish Presbyterian congregation was one of the earliest to be organized. A Presbyterian church was erected about 1826. Rev. Charles Stewart formed St. John's Anglican Congregation in 1822 and opened a church at Arva in 1823. A religious revival among the Welsh settlers, brought about by the 1830 visit of the Calvinistic Baptist preacher Elder William McDermand, led to the construction of a church in 1834. In the same year the first Roman Catholic church opened its doors to worshippers.

There were private schools in the township from about 1830. Some of the churches such as the Antiburgher Presbyterian in the English Settlement also served as schools. William Donnan was the first teacher and preacher in this church-school.

The *London Sun*, published by Richard Talbot's son, Edward Allen, was the first newspaper west of Niagara and east of Detroit.

Many of the people associated with London Township have become well-known historical figures. Among the earliest were the Tolpuddle Martyrs, a small group of farm labourers in England who were banished when they went on strike. The public outcry which followed brought about their return in 1837 but in 1844 George and James Loveless and Thomas Sandfield emigrated to Canada and settled in London Township.

Thomas Carling was the founder of the Carling Brewery Company. His son, Sir John, became president of the company, and Minister of Agriculture and Public Works in the first Ontario government. He founded the Ontario Agricultural College at Guelph and the Dominion Experimental Station in Ottawa.

The Hon. Hamilton H. Killaly, builder of Killaly Castle, was commissioner of Public Works under Lord Sydenham. Sir Clifford Sifton became Attorney-General of Manitoba and Minister of the Interior for Canada, 1896-1905. He was knighted for his work in encouraging immigration. The Hon. Newton Rowell, Liberal leader of the Opposition in Ontario 1911-17 and Chief Justice for Ontario in 1936, was a noted author. The Hon. William. A. Stewart was Minister of Agriculture and Food in the 1960's and established the Ontario Food Council and the Ontario Agricultural Research Institute.

Dr. Fred T. Rosser, the first bacteriologist to be employed by Swift Canadian, became the president of Algonquin College in 1967. Dr. Edna Guest was awarded an OBE for her services as a surgeon in World War One. Her sister, Emily Guest, was one of the pioneers of Women's Institutes in Canada.

Jeannie Raycraft Lewis: Llyndinshire, 1967.

Hugh McColl: Some Sketches of the Early Highland Pioneers of the County of Middlesex, 1904.

Upper Thames Valley, 1952.

F. T. Rosser: London Township Pioneers, 1975.

LONDON, city, Middlesex County
Position 42° 59′ 81° 14′

London, situated at the forks of the Thames River, is called the "Forest City" because of its wide tree-lined streets and beautiful parklands covering a total of more than 1,400 acres. The city, with a population of 256,789 (1979) is the seat of Middlesex County. In 1792 Col. John Graves Simcoe, Upper Canada's first Governor, chose the site for his future capital and the name, recalling that of the British capital, remains as a reminder of that fact. Simcoe's plan did not materialize and the capital was established at York (Toronto) about 115 miles to the northeast.

No settlement took place in the immediate London area until 1826. That year the government instructed Mahlon Burwell to survey a town plot in London Township. Lots were offered to prospective settlers on condition that they pay $30.00 for the patent and erect a small house on the property. The Thames River formed the western and southern boundaries of the town, which covered about one-third of a square mile; to the east it extended as far as Wellington Street; and on the north it was bounded by North Street (now Queens Ave.). Peter McGregor built the first dwelling in the fall of 1826 on Lot 21, South King Street. A small log shanty, it doubled as a home and a tavern. Whiskey was dispensed to travellers from a jug over the stump of a tree that had stood at the front door. McGregor was joined soon afterward at "The Forks", as the place was called, by Samuel Wood from Long Point, and later by John Yerex. The latter built a log house on the northwest corner of York and Ridout Streets. Levi Merrick constructed the first bridge over the Thames into London. Within a year, Geo. J. Goodhue and Dennis O'Brien followed. Goodhue opened a general store on Ridout Street, while O'Brien took up Lot 13, south side of Dundas Street where he also opened a store.

The judicial centre of the London district was once located at Vittoria, southeast of London, near Lake Erie. When the Vittoria courthouse and gaol burned in 1825, it was decided to transfer the seat of government to London, where a new courthouse was built in the middle of as yet an unsettled wilderness. A frame structure, it was replaced in 1830 by an imposing brick edifice while the original building was converted into a school. The courthouse was a replica of Malahide Castle near Dublin, Ireland, the ancestral home of Col. Thomas Talbot, founder of the Talbot settlement in Western Ontario and owner of close to a 50,000 acre land grant in the London area. Renovated in 1880, the building still stands today, although a new courthouse was opened in August of 1974 across the street from the old structure.

The first appointments made for the Court in 1827 were: Sheriff, Daniel Rappelje; Judge, James Mitchell; Registrar, Mahlon Burwell; Treasurer, John Harris.

As the district's judicial centre, the town was bound to grow, although for the first four or five years of its existence, London remained a small and struggling village, the buildings being mostly of logs. By 1835, however, London had become a place of considerable importance. In that year, with a population of 1,037, separate representation in Parliament was accorded and Col. Mahlon Burwell became London's first member.

Dennis O'Brien built the first brick block on Dundas Street. Here the first barracks were housed. Frame barracks were erected in 1839 on the site of the present Victoria Park for the British troops sent to Canada to guard against border raids following the Rebellion of 1837-38. The presence of the military played an important part in early London society. The troops were withdrawn in 1853 to serve in the Crimean War, but returned to London from 1862 to 1868 because of tension which arose from the outbreak of the American Civil War. The barracks burned in 1873 and this part of the military reserve was dedicated as a Park by Lord Dufferin, Governor-General of Canada the following year. Wolseley Barracks were built in London in 1886 to provide quarters for an Infantry School Corps in the early stages of developing Canada's own permanent forces. The Corps eventually became the Royal Canadian Regiment, and Regimental Headquarters moved to London in 1923.

In 1840 London was incorporated as a police village. A plank and gravel road was built that year to Hamilton. London was well on the way of becoming the trading and industrial centre of the district. In 1848 London achieved the status of a town, and six years later it was incorporated as a city. The Grand Trunk Railway (now CNR) had already reached the city in 1853. The first Provincial Fair was held in September of 1854 and since then has been held in London in regular rotation with other Ontario cities.

Following the discovery of oil in western Ontario, London became the centre of the oil industry and remained thus until the 1880's when the Imperial Oil Company moved its headquarters first to Petrolia and then to Sarnia.

From its infancy, London has enjoyed the status of an important manufacturing town and its early industries included breweries, tanneries, foundries, machine shops, and many other pioneer enterprises that laid the foundation for London to becoming the metropolis of western Ontario. Ideally situated halfway between Toronto and Detroit, surrounded by the most fertile agricultural district in Ontario, and served by a transportation network of rails and roads, London is the distributing and financial hub of the area. Its hundreds of modern industries produce a variety of goods that include cereals, household appliances, steel, hosiery, confectionery, shoes, radios, metal and cardboard products, automotive parts, chemicals, diesel locomotives, electrical apparatus, plumbing and heating equipment and mobile homes. London's breweries are known throughout Canada as is the name of the Carling family, founders of the Carling Brewery and Malting Company in London. Sir John Carling, born in London Township in 1828, the son of a Yorkshire brewer, joined the family business and later entered politics. While Minister of Agriculture for Canada from 1885 to 1892, he established the first Dominion Experimental Farm.

London is not only noted for its diverse industries, but is also called a "microcosm" of Canadian life. It is the headquarters of large life insurance and trust companies; a centre for learning and the site of a great university; the seat of the Anglican Diocese of Huron, and the Roman Catholic Diocese of London.

London's first schoolteacher was Peter VanEvery, who also acted as jailor in the little village. The next teacher was Miss Stinson, daughter of one of London's early physicians. Her first schoolhouse was a one-room log building. In 1835 Miss Mary Proudfoot, daughter of Rev. Wm. Proudfoot, opened a private boarding and dayschool on Bathurst Street. The most notable of the early schools was that of Wm. Taylor, an experienced teacher. In 1842 Robert Wilson opened a school on Ridout Street where he taught not only the "three R's", but also music.

The first meeting of the London School Board took place in January, 1848, when it was decided to build a school on grounds bound by King, Colborne, York and Waterloo Streets. Mr. Nicholas Wilson was appointed as Principal. Until 1857 all children attended the Common School, but in 1858 the first separate school was opened in the city. Modern London has seventy public schools and sixteen secondary schools under the supervision of the London Board of Education, and there are thirty-five separate schools within the city.

In 1863 Huron College was founded by the Rev. Benjamin Cronyn. Its purpose was the training of men for the ministry of the Church of England. Bishop Cronyn Memorial Church, built in 1873 in the Gothic Revival style, commemorates the life and work of the Rt. Rev. Cronyn, first bishop of Huron.

In 1878 Western University was incorporated by an Act of the Legislature. Bishop Hellmuth was named the first chancellor. Born in Poland and educated in Breslau (Germany), Isaac Hellmuth had come to Canada in 1844. Ordained in the Church of England, he assisted Bishop Cronyn in the establishment of Huron College and served as its first principal. He founded Hellmuth College, a fashionable school for young ladies of London. In 1871 he succeeded Cronyn as Bishop of Huron and it was his determination and foresight that led to the founding of the University of Western Ontario, originally known as Western University of London. Located on 550 acres of ground in the north of London, Western is an internationally recognized institution of higher learning and is the city's cultural centre with its several theatres and a concert hall. Composed of ten Faculties, the University also includes Schools of Business Administration and Library and Information Science, and the Althouse College of Education. Huron College became affiliated with the University in 1881. Also affiliated are Brescia College and King's College.

Rev. Alexander McIntosh of the Church of England held the first religious service in London as early as 1826. He was succeeded in 1829 by the Rev. Edward Jukes Boswell, who officiated in this locality until 1831. He was followed by Rev. Benjamin Cronyn who held his first service in the Grammar School. In 1834, on the corner of North and Richmond Streets, a house of worship was erected. Built of wood, it was destroyed by fire ten years later. Upon its ruin rose the fine brick edifice which is now St. Paul's Cathedral.

In 1832 William Proudfoot preached in London. Under him a Presbyterian Church was erected on York Street, and there services were held until 1859 when the church burned down. It was rebuilt of bricks on Park and Dufferin Avenues, and here, in 1872, the first organ was heard in a London Presbyterian Church.

In 1833 a meetinghouse of the Wesleyan Methodist congregation was erected on the corner of Ridout and North Streets. In 1839 the first Methodist church, a frame structure, was built. Here the Wesleyans worshipped until they built a new church on Richmond Street, while their former building passed into the hands of the Baptist congregation.

Rev. James Campian of Niagara, visited London and celebrated mass in Dennis O'Brien's house in 1827. His successor, Rev. John Cullen, increased his visitations to four times a year. He was followed by the Reverend Fathers Mills, O'Flynn and O'Dwyer. In 1834 the Roman Catholics built a little log church on the southwest corner of Richmond and Maple Streets, with Father Downie in charge. After its destruction by fire, they built a brick church on the grounds now occupied by magnificent St. Peter's Cathedral.

In 1835, citizens of London organized the first library service by the establishment of a Mechanics' Institute. Its assets were taken over by the London Public Library, which was located at the corner of Wellington Street and Queens Avenue. To meet increasing demands, a new library, the Elsie Perrin Williams Memorial Building, was erected in 1940. Aside from the library, the building houses an Art Museum, which presents outstanding exhibits of paintings and crafts. In 1962, at the request of City Council, the Public Library Board assumed the operation of two historical museums, Victoria House and Eldon House. The latter is one of the oldest remaining homes in London. Built in 1834 by Captain John Harris, R.N., treasurer of the London District, the house at 481 Ridout Street North was once a social and cultural centre of the garrison town of London. The Harris family gave the historic house and most of its furnishings, along with eleven acres of land, to the City of London for a museum and park. The London and Middlesex Historical Society was founded in 1901 to promote historical research and collect and preserve records and material of historical significance.

The London Free Press, a daily paper, is almost as old as London itself, and plays an important role in Western Ontario. The paper was established in 1849.

Dr. Archibald Chisholm was the first physician to settle in London, arriving here in 1828. At the same time, Dr. Elam Stinson came here from the United States.

The first record of a hospital appears in 1847 when a large number of sick and destitute immigrants arrived from Scotland. A shed was erected for them on the Market Square. In 1855 a building for hospital purposes was erected on the Hamilton Road. It was fired by an incendiary. A new hospital was built in 1874 on South Street. Named Victoria Hospital, it was enlarged in 1898. Dr. Hagarty was the first hospital surgeon. A hospital under Catholic auspices was opened at Mount Hope in 1888 and became the forerunner of the present St. Joseph's Hospital. War Memorial Children's Hospital, Westminster Veterans' Hospital, The Sir Adam Beck Chest Diseases Unit, Parkwood Hospital, and University Hospital, opened in 1972, are other noted London institutions.

In London's Riverside Park stands a historic plaque commemorating the victims of one of Canada's major marine disasters. Near this site, on May 24, 1881, the *Victoria*, a small flat-bottomed stern-wheeler commanded by Capt. Donald Rankin, overturned and sank. The boat had started regular service between London and Springbank Park that day. Overcrowded with more than six hundred passengers on the way back to London, nearly two hundred lives were lost in the incident.

In 1965 Canadian National Railways acquired the property of the London and Port Stanley Railway, a 24-mile line first opened for traffic in 1856. Owned partially by the City of London, the line had never changed its name during its existence, a rare occurrence in railway history. For the return fare of a quarter, Londoners in the good old days were able to indulge in the pleasure of taking a train to Port Stanley and spending a fun-filled day at the Lake Erie Beach. Today, a network of provincial highways, including the nearby Highway 401, link London with the major centres of Ontario. Both the CPR and the CNR serve the city, as does the London Airport.

London, Eldon House

A prosperous city with many magnificent buildings and historic landmarks, including the old Wolseley Barracks, the Grosvenor Lodge dating back to 1853, St. Paul's Cathedral, where the first election of a Canadian bishop took place, the Middlesex County Courthouse, St. Peter's Rectory, and Eldon House, the oldest dwelling, London also has its share of famous sons and citizens.

Headley House was once the home of Sir Adam Beck, founder of Ontario's public hydro-electric system. Beck, who came to the city in 1885, was elected mayor of London in 1902.

The Hon. Edward Blake, born in neighbouring Adelaide Township, was a leading lawyer, legislator, orator, and Premier of Ontario from 1871-2. He was married to Bishop Cronyn's daughter Margaret.

Sir Charles Edward Saunders, born in London in 1867, was a distinguished experimental agriculturist who developed the famous Marquis Wheat and other varieties adapted to prairie conditions, thus bringing untold wealth to Canada. His father, William Saunders, was a manufacturing chemist in London, an authority on horticulture, and one of the founders of the Ontario College of Pharmacy.

Adam Shortt, economist, writer and historian, was born near London in 1859. Professor of political science at Queen's University from 1891-1908, and appointed chairman of the Board of Historical Publications of the Public Archives of Canada, he has been called the "founder of the study of economic history in Canada".

The noted Canadian artist, Paul Peel, born in 1859, was also a native son of London. During the 1870's he had a studio in the marble-works operated by his father on the outskirts of the city. Peel, who died in Paris in 1892, is known throughout Europe and North America for his studies of the human figure. Some of his paintings, including "Devotion", "Mother Love" and "A Venetian Bather" are owned by the National Gallery of Canada.

London's attractions for the visitor include the Storybook Gardens, a 350-acre area site in Springbank Park where colourful displays create a fantasyland from fairy tales and nursery rhymes. Fanshaw Park offers facilities for fishing, yachting, camping, a Pioneer Village and Fanshaw Dam, built in 1952. Victoria Park, site of the first barracks, is located within walking distance from downtown London. Here at the Kiwanis Memorial Bandshell, concerts and other events are staged throughout each spring and summer.

At Richmond and Simcoe Streets stands the Labbatt's Pioneer Brewery, a replica of the 1828 brewery, and featuring authentic brewing equipment of the past.

Theatre London and other Theatre Art Groups, offer live entertainment, including plays, ballet and concerts. The London Gardens is known for its hockey games, Broadway shows, dances, military tattoos, country shows and political meetings. The Western Fair grounds provide a year-round site for exhibitions and other events, and harness-racing meets at the Western Fair Raceway are a major attraction.

The Labbatt Stadium, a spectator park for baseball, soccer and football, seats three thousand and it is one of numerous and varied recreational facilities which Londoners can enjoy.

C.T. Campbell, M.D.: *Pioneer Days in London*, 1921.

F.H. Armstrong and Daniel J. Brook: *Reflections on London's Past*, 1975.

Philip Dodds: *Ontario Agricultural Fairs and Exhibitions*, 1967.

City of London: *The Pioneer Period*, 1897.

W.A. & C.L. Goodspeed Publishers: *History of Middlesex County*, 1889.

W.H. Smith: *Canada, Past, Present and Future*, 1852.

H.R. Page & Co.: *Historic Atlas of Middlesex County*,

LONDONDERRY, geographic township, Sudbury District
Position 47° 33' 81° 31'

The boundaries of this township were surveyed in 1911 and it was named after Londonderry, Ireland. The area lies a few miles southeast of the community of Gogama.

LONG, geographic township, Algoma District
Position 46° 14' 82° 46'

Named after Thomas Long MPP for Simcoe West in the 1870's the township was surveyed in 1881. It is located on the North Channel of Lake Huron and forms part of the North Shore Improvement District created in 1973. Trans-Canada Highway (17) and the CPR pass through the township along the shore line. Lauzon Lake occupies the southeastern corner of Long Township.

LONG BRANCH, part of Borough of Etobicoke, Municipality of Metropolitan Toronto
Position 43° 35' 79° 32'

Lying on the banks of the Etobicoke Creek and along the shore of Lake Ontario, Long Branch was founded as a summer resort and named after a famous resort on Long Island in the United States.

The possibilities of the Long Branch area were first recognized by Lieutenant-Governor John Simcoe in the early nineteenth century. Concerned with the formation of a navy for the defence of Upper Canada, Simcoe inquired into the depth of the water at the mouth of Etobicoke Creek. The ship *Defiance* was built here. About 1837 John Hamilton's Royal Mail Line, the only through service from Hamilton to Montreal, began to stop at Long Branch.

The community developed in the last decade of the nineteenth century. About 1890 Mr. Cornell bought 60 acres along the shore from the Eastwood family to establish a summer resort. Johnny Owe was commissioned to build "Sea Breeze," which was later renamed the Long Branch Park Hotel. The park was subdivided for cottages and soon a summer community began to grow up. A post office was opened in 1891. Many summer visitors lived in tents before the cottages were built.

The park was bought by the Wilkie brothers who brought in a merry-go-round, a roller coaster, ponies, and other attractions for picknickers and campers. A pier was constructed for the excursion steamers which brought holidayers from Toronto. A power-generating plant was installed in the hotel.

With better transportation facilities, many of the holiday homes later became year-round residences. In 1921 Captain Oattes built the first house in the "flats", an area which was frequently damaged when the river overflowed. The community, which was incorporated as a village in 1931, became an influential force in local affairs as the Long Branch Park Cottagers Association led the way in obtaining garbage collection and fire protection for the Etobicoke area. By 1959 the village had a public library and published a weekly newspaper, the *Lakeshore Weekly*.

In 1967 the village of Long Branch, the town of Mimico, and the town of New Toronto amalgamated with the township of Etobicoke to form the Borough of Etobicoke.

Robert A. Given: *The Story of Etobicoke*, 1950.

LONGFORD, township, Victoria County
Position 44° 55' 79° 00'

The most northerly township in Victoria County, Longford is bounded on the north and west by Muskoka District, on the east by Haliburton County, and on the south by Digby Township. It was named after a county in Leinster, Ireland.

The township was first surveyed in 1862 and in 1865 the area was purchased from the Crown by the Canada Land and Emigration Company which auctioned off all pine stands to Thompson and Dodge of Longford Mills in 1866-7. The company stripped the township of its pine forests.

In 1867 Longford was attached to Laxton and Digby as part of Victoria County. It was sold outright to Thompson and Dodge in 1871. The territory passed through the control of several companies, all headed by Thompson, before finally being sold to Longford Reserve Limited, an American-based group of sportsmen and cottagers, in 1928. Since this time Longford, a natural beauty spot dotted with numerous lakes and streams, has been operated as a private summer retreat for well-to-do Americans and Canadians.

Watson Kirkconnell: *County of Victoria Centennial History*, 1967.

LONGLAC, township, Thunder Bay District
Position 49° 48' 86° 31'

Situated at the north end of Long Lake on the CNR transcontinental line and Highway 11, Longlac is about 185 miles northeast of Thunder Bay. It was named after the lake on which it lies.

Although permanent white settlement did not begin to take place in Longlac until after 1900, the natural network of lakes and rivers made the area a centre of commerce as early as 1800. The first white men to explore Longlac were the French coureurs de bois of the fur-trading companies who came via the Pic River from Lake Superior and via the Kenagami River from James Bay. The region was known by 1763.

The large Ojibway and Cree Indian settlements made Longlac a valuable trading area and by 1800 the North West Company had established a trading post. In 1814 the Hudson's Bay Company set up a rival post. There was fierce competition between the two companies until they amalgamated as the Hudson's Bay Company in 1821. Fur-trading remained the main activity in the region for the rest of the nineteenth century. From 1821 to 1885 Long Lake House was a regular station on the winter route from the Red River Settlement in Manitoba to Montreal.

In 1871 the Longlac area was visited by CPR surveyors. In 1906 the former Pic River Route went out of use. Traffic now went from Jackfish on the CPR to the south end of Long Lake and from there to Longlac where the Revillon Frères had built a trading-post in 1905. In 1910 construction began on the Canadian Northern's transcontinental line. Completed in 1914, it was to make Longlac a major railroad outlet for freight.

At that time the Hudson's Bay Company post, the Revillon Frères store, a log cabin, and a church were the only buildings in Longlac. J. E. Mathe opened a store which became the home of the post office in 1919. J. W. Heald erected a store in 1924. In 1931 the Longlac-Nakina branch line of the CNR was built and the following year Maud Gascon arrived and established a restaurant. In 1933 she opened the Longlac Hotel.

Prospecting in the Longlac area attracted many Scandinavians from 1932 to 1938. Lumbering also began to play an important part in the local economy. Pulpwood Supply Company, which began operations in 1937, was the area's first major pulpwood industry. It later became Longlac Pulp and Paper Company, a subsidiary of Kimberly-Clark. At first mainly Scandinavians were employed, but later increasing numbers of French-Canadians were hired. Today French-Canadians and Indians are the two largest groups in the township's rich ethnic mix which also includes Finns, Italians, Germans, Ukrainians, and English.

In 1938 Longlac's white population was about 100 while about 200 Indians lived on the local reserves. The wood company contributed greatly to the community's development, providing both employment and housing. Highway 11, built in 1942, improved transportation to the area. By 1964 the population had increased to 1,215 with 500 Indians living on the two Longlac reserves. Weldwood of Canada opened a plywood plant in 1963 and a chipwood plant in 1973. The CN has also played a part in the local economy and tourism is becoming increasingly important as hunting and fishing attract many visitors. Today Longlac has a population of 2,284 (1979).

In 1952 Longlac became an Improvement District. Municipal government with a council was introduced in 1964 when Longlac was incorporated as a township.

Roman Catholic services have been held in the Longlac area since about 1860 when the first missionaries arrived. In 1884 Fathers Joseph Hebert and Gagnon built a Roman Catholic church. Today there are two Catholic churches in Longlac. Anglican services were first held in the 1920's. An interdenominational Protestant church was erected in 1947.

The first school was built near the lake in 1922. Today Longlac has a bilingual separate school and a public school. High school students are transported to a District High School about 20 miles away from the community.

From 1920 to 1949 Longlac was the site of the apostolate of Father Joseph Couture, Canada's first "flying priest".

Department of Lands and Forests: *Geraldton*, 1963.

LONG POINT PROVINCIAL PARK, S. of Walsingham Township,
Norfolk County
Position 42° 35' 80° 23'

Long Point Provincial Park occupies a portion of a long peninsula, a sand spit which juts out into Lake Erie. Highway 59 is a direct approach from the north, but other highways converging on No. 59 are convenient routes from east and west.

There is a historical plaque marking the spot where, in 1670, Dollier de Casson and Galinee portaged across the peninsula with a party of Frenchmen. Settlement began around 1790 with the arrival of United Empire Loyalists, including Samuel Ryerson. His son, Egerton Ryerson, later a leading Methodist clergyman and founder of Ontario's public school system, was born here.

The park is of great interest to naturalists. It has, on the one side, marsh areas, and on the other side, sand dunes. Great numbers of turtles make an annual journey from the marshes across the park to the sand dunes to lay their eggs. The marshes also provide a habitat for about 300 species of birds and their seasonal migrations delight birdwatchers. The clean waters and sandy beaches attract thousands of summer visitors to this recreation park.

Ontario Ministry of Natural Resources.

LONG SAULT, urban community, Cornwall Township, Stormont County
Position 45° 02' 74° 53'

Long Sault is a new community which was founded after the flooding of the St. Lawrence shore by the Seaway Project in the late 1950's. Situated about 10 miles northwest of Cornwall, on the St. Lawrence shore and the CNR, it was formed by the union of the former communities of Milles Roches and Moulinette which were flooded when the St. Lawrence Seaway was built.

Before the construction of the seaway, Moulinette lay on the shore of the St. Lawrence River and on the Cornwall Canal, 7 miles west of Cornwall. Its name, which means "little mill", referred to the many mills which operated there in earlier days. The former community of Mille Roches lay 5 miles west of Cornwall on Bergin Lake, part of the Cornwall Canal. It was named "Thousand Rocks" because it was situated at the foot of a small rapids in the St. Lawrence where many rocks showed.

Known as New Town No. 2 during the Seaway planning stages, Long Sault is today a pleasant residential community with a population of 963 (1977).

LONGUEUIL, township, Prescott County
Position 45° 35′ 74° 45′

Situated in the northern part of Prescott County, Longueuil is bounded on the east by West Hawkesbury Township, on the south by Caledonia, on the west by Alfred, and on the north by the Ottawa River. It was named after Baron de Longueuil, who became seignior of the territory through his marriage to Geneviève Joybert de Soulanges, heiress to the L'Orignal Seigniory, that had been granted to François Prévost by the Company of New France in 1674. It was one of only two seigniories ever granted in what was to become Upper Canada and for many years, well into the late 1800's, Longueuil was still referred to as "The Seigniory". As the area was remote from the main settlements of the French-Canadians along the St. Lawrence River, no attempt at colonization was made in the 18th century.

When Britain gained control of Canada in 1763, it prohibited the extension of the seigniorial system into Upper Canada and the Baron's grant became virtually worthless to him. In 1796 he sold the territory to an American, Nathaniel Hazard Treadwell. Treadwell built grist and sawmills in the township in the late 1790's and by 1800 the community of L'Orignal began to develop around these mills. Other early settlers included Jacob Marston and Joseph P. Cass who made their homes near Cassburn in 1798.

The Hall family arrived in the township in 1802 and the Pattees in 1804. David Pattee who became a leading figure in the community was a physician, but did not practise his profession. His cousin, Dr. Moses Pattee, who arrived some time later, became the first practising doctor in the area. By 1810 the township was quite heavily settled. Residents included the Kelloggs, Murrays, and Longs. Most of the early settlers came from the New England States, while those arriving during the latter part of the 19th century were of French Canadian descent.

When the Ottawa District was created, L'Orignal became the seat of the District court in 1817, and here a courthouse and jail were built in 1824-25. Designed in the Loyalist Neo-Classic style and constructed by Messrs. Donald McDonald and Walter Beckworth, the courthouse remains today as the oldest such edifice in Ontario. Extensive additions were made to the building in the early 1860's. The lumbering and business centre of the township, the settlement of L'Orignal was incorporated as a village in 1873.

Cassburn was the site of the first schoolhouse erected in the Ottawa District in 1808.

Longueuil is accessible by the Ottawa Valley Route along Highway 17. The population of the township is 1,130 (1979).

C. Thomas: *History of the Counties of Argenteuil, Quebec and Prescott, Ontario,* 1896.

LONSDALE, community, Tyendinaga Township, Hastings County
Position 44° 16′ 77° 08′

The community of Lonsdale had its beginnings in the 1830's when James Lazier built a stone grist mill here on the picturesque Salmon River. The river's excellent waterpower resulted in a woollen mill and a large lumber industry being established later. The village had two hotels, a blacksmith shop, a saddle and harness shop and a general store.

In 1869 the Wesleyan Methodists erected a frame church. The church, standing on a hill, remains complete to this day with the original stoves, pews and door key.

Lonsdale's stone architecture, preserved in some of its old houses, is still admired today because of its very beautiful brownish-coloured stones. The mill still stands, although it is no longer in operation but has been converted into a private residence.

Gerald E. Boyce: *Historic Hastings,* 1967.

L'ORIGNAL, village, Longueuil Township, Prescott County
Position 45° 37′ 74° 42′

The picturesque village of L'Orignal is the oldest settlement in the Ottawa Valley. Situated on the Ottawa River, some 50 miles east of the nation's capital, it overlooks L'Orignal Bay. It was named after Pointe à Orignal, a river crossing for deer. The word "orignal" means "elk" in Canada, although it means "moose" elsewhere.

The history of this area goes back to 1674 when a large tract of land along the Ottawa River was granted as a seigniory to François Prévost, Mayor of the town of Quebec. It became known as the Longueuil seigniory when it passed to Paul Joseph LeMoyne de Longueuil in 1778 through his marriage to the heiress of the seigniory. He granted portions of his land to settlers. In 1796 Longueuil sold the property to an American, Nathaniel Hazard Treadwell.

Settlement of L'Orignal began to take shape around 1798 when Treadwell erected saw and grist mills on Mill Creek and built roads. The mills, unusual in that they lacked iron work in their construction, were in operation by 1800. Initially growth of the settlement was slow, and there were only about a dozen houses and one store owned by Mr. McIntyre by 1812, when Jacob Marston purchased the mills and much of the site of present-day L'Orignal. Treadwell left Canada during the War of 1812 while Marston and his brother Jeremiah became leading figures in the development of the community.

In 1817 L'Orignal was made the seat of the District Court in the newly created Ottawa District, and a courthouse and jail were erected in 1824 on land donated by Jacob Marston. Designed in the Loyalist Neo-Classic style, the building was constructed by Donald McDonald and Walter Beckworth and was completed in the fall of 1825. Extensive additions were made in the early 1860's and today this structure remains as the oldest courthouse in the Province of Ontario. By 1826 William Wait was operating a tannery, John O'Brien had erected a tavern, and a second store had been opened by John G. McIntosh. Charles P. Treadwell, son of the pioneer, re-purchased the mills from Marston.

By 1850 L'Orignal had a population of about 400. The White Inn probably built by William Moody in 1824, had become a well-known stopping-place for travellers. Another hotel was opened by W. Labelle who arrived in 1859.

L'Orignal was incorporated as a village in 1873, with John Millar as first reeve. By 1880 the village had three general stores, three hotels, and several shops. Residents included R.G. Campbell, carpenter; E.P. Johnson, merchant; A. Labelle, carriage maker; Watson Little, printer; and Alfred Cass, nurseryman. The ethnic make-up of the population was beginning to change by this time. Originally most of the inhabitants had been of British descent but by 1880 the majority were of French heritage, and L'Orignal was now the chief centre in Prescott County. A list of businesses and industries by the early 1900's included two general stores, three hotels, a grocery store, two butcher shops, a marble works, a butter factory, a sash and door factory, a sawmill and a flour mill.

The first preacher in the community was the Presbyterian Rev. Mr. McKelkan. A congregation was organized under his successor, Rev. Mr. McLaurin in 1822 and a Presbyterian church built in 1832. Rev. J.H. Macdonough formed a Roman Catholic congregation in 1836 and a church was erected in 1850. A Methodist house of worship was opened before 1880. Rev. E.P. Crawford held the first Anglican services about 1870.

A school was in existence before 1824. It was in this building that court sessions were held before the Court House was erected. A high school was opened in 1877.

The village today (1979) has a population of 1,669.

C. Thomas: History of the Counties of Argenteuil, Quebec and Prescott, Ontario, 1896.

LORING, community, Mills and Wilson Townships, Parry Sound District
Position 45° 56′ 80° 00′

Situated about 60 miles north of Parry Sound, Loring was named by Col. W. E. O'Brien, MP for Parry Sound and Muskoka when petitioners from McConkey Corners asked that a post office be established there. Loring was the maiden name of O'Brien's wife.

The first settlers arrived in the Loring area at the corner of Mills, Hardy, Wilson, and McConkey Townships in the mid-1870's. The community which developed was first known as McConkey Corners. It became Loring when a post office was opened in 1884. Andrew Sinclair was the first postmaster.

Among the early residents of Loring were the Davis and Forsythe families. E.H. Kelcey opened the first store in 1885. William Kirton was the first blacksmith and John Paul the first carpenter. A sawmill was built by Mr. McWhinney in 1890.

A group of settlers arrived from Germany in the 1880's, increasing the size of the community. Transportation was greatly improved by the construction of a road to Trout Creek in 1887. By 1903 Loring's population was about 100. Two general stores, a blacksmith shop, a sawmill, and a hotel were in operation.

The early twentieth century saw great improvement in Loring's communications with the outside world. A road to Salines (now Drocourt) was built in 1908. In 1913 Arthur Walton and Sons began a boat service to Lost Channel. The Schroeder Mills and Timber Company in 1917 laid down the Key Valley Railway from Pakesley on the CPR to Lost Channel. In 1922 the Trout Creek-Loring road was gravelled and it became the community's main transportation route.

Today Loring is a quiet community with a population of 153 (1971).

Everett Kirton: *History of Eastern Parry Sound District*, 1964.

LORNE, geographic township, Sudbury District
Position 46° 20′ 81° 30′

Located southwest of the city of Sudbury, the township was subdivided in 1884 by Ontario Land Surveyor Stewart, and named after the Marquis of Lorne, Governor-General of Canada 1878-83. Lorne became part of the newly created town of Walden on January 1, 1973.

LORNE PARK, part of city of Mississauga, Regional Municipality of Peel
Position 43° 32′ 79° 37′

Lying on the shores of Lake Ontario, 18 miles southeast of Brampton, this urban community was a well-known summer resort in the late nineteenth and early twentieth centuries. It was named after the Marquess of Lorne.

Lorne Park's location, on the Grand Trunk Railway (later the CNR) made it easily accessible to visitors and it was a popular holiday spot for many years. A post office was opened in 1893. A public library was established before 1959. Today the community is a residential area with a population of 540 (1977).

LORRAIN, geographic township, Timiskaming District
Position 47° 18′ 79° 34′

Lorrain, named after the Rt. Rev. Narcisse Z. Lorrain, R. C. Bishop of Pontiac, borders in the east on Lake Timiskaming. The towns of Latchford, Cobalt and Haileybury are situated nearby.

LOTUS, community, Manvers Township, Victoria County
Position 44° 07' 78° 42'

Situated 35 miles northwest of Cobourg, this dispersed rural community was originally known as Frogpond. It was named Lotus after the lotus flowers which grew on the local ponds.

In 1854 a large tract of land in Manvers Township, including the present site of Lotus, was granted to Bishop Mountain, the Anglican Bishop of Quebec. Two years later the property was transferred to Henry McQuaid who deeded it to Robert McQuaid in 1860. The community of Lotus developed on Lots 3 and 4 on Concessions 5 and 6.

Most of the early residents in the Lotus area came from Ireland. They included Thomas and Agnes Ney, William McCabe, William Myers, and Rev. William C. Windell. Adam Scott erected the first saw and grist mills in the community. The mills were taken over by William McCabe and inherited by Samuel McCabe who also ran a dry-goods store, a carding mill, and a tannery. By the 1870's Lotus was a bustling little community with a tavern owned by Thomas Somerville, Gen. John Hughes' (the father of Sir Sam Hughes) general store, several blacksmiths, a tailor shop, and a shoeshop.

A post office was opened in 1873 in the store of David Bingham. In 1877 Thomas H. McNelly established himself as a woollen manufacturer. Tinsmiths included George Purdue and William Gilders. The McGill Hotel accommodated visitors.

A school was erected on land donated by Henry McQuaid in 1876. The building which is now in use was opened in 1904.

Rev. William C. Windell was the first clergyman in Lotus. A Presbyterian church was built under his leadership in 1856. It is now closed. Early Methodist services were held in the Temperance Hall. In 1913 the Methodist church was moved from Ballyduff to Lotus and rebuilt. It closed in the 1950's.

Mrs. Ross N. Carr: *The Rolling Hills,* 1967.

LOUDON, geographic township, Nipissing District
Position 46° 14' 80° 16'

Located at the west end of Lake Nipissing, the township was surveyed in 1897 by D. Beatty. It is named after James Loudon, noted educationist and one-time President of the University of Toronto. Highway 64 passes along the township's western border.

LOUGHBOROUGH, township, Frontenac County
Position 44° 26' 76° 32'

Situated in the southwestern part of Frontenac County, the township was named after Lord Loughborough, Lord Chancellor of Britain in the last decade of the eighteenth century. Part of the township is covered with lakes, the principal one being Loughborough Lake.

The township was formed in the 1790's. The first recorded

settlers were Michael Sloat and Captain Peter Ruttan, who arrived in 1807, although there were probably some pioneers in the area by the 1790's. Other early inhabitants were Lawrence Raile, John Amey, Horsea Perdy, Henry Wood and Ben Boyce. By 1851 the township's population had risen to 2,003 and its main village, Sydenham, had been laid out.

In 1836 George W. Yarker built a saw and grist mill and shortly afterwards another one was constructed on Millhaven Creek. By 1856 Loughborough had a grist mill, six sawmills, four churches, ten schools and several productive mines. The late nineteenth century saw the establishment of a brick factory, two distilleries, a brewery, a tannery, a turning lathe, a fulling and carding mill, and several asheries. The Lacey Mine, opened in 1880, had become the largest producer of amber mica in Canada by 1912. The mica mines have closed but new industries were established in the township, one, a rubber manufacturing plant, was opened here in 1963.

The first school in Loughborough was opened in 1819 by George Rutledge who was also the first teacher. A school was built in Sydenham in 1858. The township had a large number of free schools long before legislation calling for their establishment was passed in 1870. A high school was constructed in Sydenham in 1873 with Rev. Francis Checkley as the first headmaster.

A Methodist Chapel on Lot 5, Concession 5, was the township's first church. It served Wesleyan, Episcopal and Primitive Methodists, as well as Anglicans and Mormons. There was a large number of Mormons in early Loughborough, partly as a result of the visit of the Mormon leader, Brigham Young, in 1833. St. Paul's Anglican Church was built in 1837, followed by the Roman Catholic church of St. Patrick soon afterwards. An Episcopal Methodist church was erected in 1861 and a Holiness Church in 1897.

Today Loughborough is mainly rural. The Gould Lake Conservation Area and the Frontenac Provincial Park are attracting tourists. The Rideau Trail, which walkers can follow to the nation's capital, winds through the township. There is a ski hill outside Sydenham. The many lakes in the northern part of Loughborough offer opportunities for recreation. A large number of summer cottages have been built in the area.

The limited agricultural potential of the southern part of the township has led to suggestions that the area could be used for residential development. However, so far this has not happened. Many of Loughborough's residents commute to work in Kingston, but are farmers as well. The township has a population of 3,244 (1979).

C. W. Cooper: Frontenac, Lennox and Addington Prize Essay, 1856.

J. H. Meacham & Co.: 1819 Census of Loughborough, Frontenac County, 1970.

Hugh S. De Schmid: Mica, Its Occurrences, Exploitation, and Uses.

LOUGHEED, geographic township, Algoma District
Position 48° 31′ 82° 44′

The township, which is not subdivided, was named after Senator

Lougheed. The Canadian National Railways, with the Station Point of Oatland, passes through the southwestern corner of the township. Not accessible by road, Lougheed is located northeast of the town of Chapleau and east of Missinaibi Lake Provincial Park.

LOUGHRIN, geographic township, Sudbury District
Position 46° 35′ 80° 29′

Loughrin is situated southeast of Wanapitei Lake and less than 20 miles northeast of the city of Sudbury. The township was first subdivided in 1893 and was named after John Loughrin, MPP for Nipissing at that time.

LOUISE, geographic township, Sudbury District
Position 46° 20′ 81° 22′

Located southwest of Sudbury, the township was subdivided by E. Stewart in 1884 and was named after the Marchioness of Lorne, wife of the Marquis of Lorne, Governor-General of Canada from 1878 to 1883. The area forms part of the town of Walden since January 1, 1973.

LOUISVILLE, community, Chatham Township, Kent County
Position 42° 28′ 82° 07′

Lying on the banks of the Thames River, 6 miles northeast of Chatham, this dispersed rural community was named after Lewis Arnold, a pioneer settler in the area.

The first families arrived at Louisville in the early nineteenth century. The Everett family began farming here some time before 1815. John Traxler built his home in 1821. In the 1830's the site was seen as the head of schooner navigation on the Thames and its potential as a port for the surrounding townships was recognized. The extensive timber in the area also made it an ideal place for shipyards. In 1835 John Sharp surveyed Lot 15, Front Concession into village lots and the community of Louisville began to develop.

Lewis Arnold opened the first tavern in 1836. A second tavern was built by John Traxler in 1840. Bought by George Simpson in 1842, it was renamed the Buck's Head. In 1841 Crowe & Sterling established their grocery store and by 1849 Robert Bedford had erected the Louisville stage house. A post office was opened in 1842 with John Crowe as postmaster.

Sailing vessels coming to Louisville were loaded with grain and other produce from the surrounding farms. Timber, floated down from the upper reaches of the Thames, was transferred to ships at the port. Louisville became a bustling community, with its population increasing from 75 in 1845 to 200 in 1857. Shipbuilding became an important industry and for some years Louisville was a rival of Chatham in its prosperity.

By the 1870's the community's importance began to decline as nearby Chatham continued to grow. In 1881 its population was about 100 and it had 2 stores, 2 hotels, some mechanics' shops, a school and 2 churches. Louisville never regained its former prosperity and has remained about the same size to the present day.

Victor Lauriston: *Romantic Kent*, 1952.

Ontario Gazetteer and Directory, 1903.

LOUNT, geographic township, Parry Sound District
Position 45° 50' 79° 39'

Established in 1874, the township was named after Wm. Lount, Q.C., of Toronto, then the MPP for Simcoe North. The area lies west of Highway 11 and the Village of South River. Most of its numerous lakes are accessible by road.

LOUTH, geographic township, Regional Municipality of Niagara
Position 43° 09' 79° 20'

Cut by three deep ravines, the Twenty, Sixteen, and Fifteen Mile Creeks, Louth Township stretches southward from Lake Ontario for about 8 miles. It was named after the town of Louth in Lincoln County, England.

Formerly a part of Lincoln County, Louth was first settled in the late 1700's by soldiers of Butler's Rangers and United Empire Loyalists. Among the earliest settlers were the two Secord brothers who had been scouts for Butler's Rangers and who had fled to Niagara after the 1777 raids on American settlers in Cherry Valley, New York, by Loyalist troops and Indians. The log cabin which they built was one of the first dwellings in Louth. It has been preserved by W.E. Troup to house his collection of early Canadiana.

Much of the land in the township was granted to Butler's Rangers but soon a substantial number of other United Empire Loyalists came to Louth. Among these early families, many of whom were from New Jersey, were the Pattersons, Smiths, Haynes, Prices, Beamers, Futneys, and Coles.

In 1799 Amos Albright and Abram Moyer visited Louth to assess its potential as a settlement for a group of Mennonite families from Pennsylvania. They bought 1100 acres and brought a party of Mennonites to the township in the same year. As more Mennonite families arrived in the following years they made a distinct economic and cultural impression on the area.

The communities of Jordan and Jordan Station developed into busy shipping centres on the Twenty (also known as the Jordan River). Early exports included logs, tan bark, hides, and ashes. Later agricultural produce became increasingly important. Several schooners were built on the Twenty, including William Bradt's *Sweet Home* and Moses Overholt's *Flying Dutchman* and *Mayflower*. By 1850 several industries had been established along the banks of the Twenty to serve Louth's 1,786 residents. Among them were a tannery, sawmills, a brick yard, a grist mill, and a woollen mill. The township also had 3 other grist mills, including the one built by George and John Ball at Glen Elgin in 1807. This mill was considered so essential that a regiment of soldiers was assigned to guard it during the War of 1812.

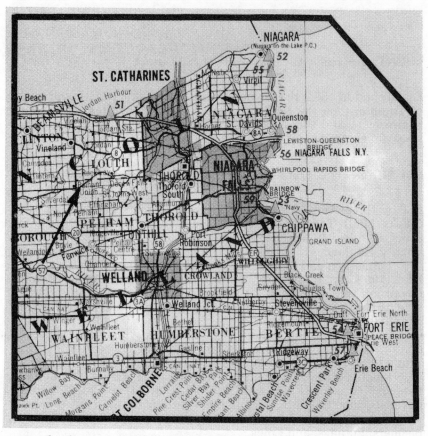

The first recorded township meeting took place in 1793 when Adin Bebee was elected clerk. With the advent of the municipal system of government in 1850, John Adams became the first reeve. Early meetings were held in the Jordan taverns. Louth did not have a separate town hall until 1950.

With the construction of the Great Western Railway bridge across the Twenty in 1852, the site lost its importance as a harbour, but Jordan Station continued to grow, and eventually the shipping of fruit became a major industry in the township. Construction of the Queen Elizabeth Way in the mid-1900's brought new business to the lakeshore communities and by the 1950's Prudhomme's Garden Centre Hotel and Motel had become one of the largest and best-equipped country hotels in North America.

Today Louth is mainly agricultural. The Jordan Wine Company is the only large industry in the township. The products and tools of the small local industries of the 1800's are preserved in the Jordan Historical Museum of the Twenty.

The township's first church was probably the Presbyterian one in Rockway, organized by Rev. Daviel Ward Eastman in 1809. A new church built in 1824 served both Presbyterians and Episcopalians. The present building was erected in 1892.

By 1850 Louth had 9 schools. The support of these schools was a contentious issue which caused many disputes in the municipal government during the 1800's.

In 1948 Louth lost 50 acres and about 550 residents to Port Dalhousie when that village was incorporated as a town. The community of Vineland became part of Clinton in 1960. In 1970 the municipality of Louth Township was dissolved. Part of it was annexed by the town of Lincoln and the rest became part of the city of St. Catharines.

George A. Carefoot: *History and Geography of Lincoln County.*

Lincoln County Council: *Lincoln County, 1856-1956,* 1956.

William F. Rannie: *Lincoln, the Story of an Ontario Town,* 1974.

LOVELAND, geographic township, Cochrane District
Position 48° 40′ 81° 40′

Since January 1, 1973 this township has been part of the city of Timmins. The area, watered by Enid Creek, lies less than 20 miles to the northwest of Timmins. It was named after an early lumberman of northern Ontario.

LOW, geographic township, Thunder Bay District
Position 49° 55′ 85° 38′

Named after E.P. Low, an explorer and geologist, the township lies north of Highway 11 and east of Long Lac Station. The area is accessible by dry weather road and waterway from Highway 11.

LOWBANKS, part of town of Dunnville, Regional Municipality of Haldimand-Norfolk
Position 42° 52′ 79° 27′

Stretching along the shore of Lake Erie for about two miles, the dispersed rural community of Lowbanks, twelve miles west of Port Colborne, is a popular summer resort for cottagers from Buffalo and Hamilton.

During the summer, many cottagers commute to work in Hamilton each day, leaving their families to enjoy the resort. A large number of permanent residents work in Port Maitland, Dunnville, Port Colborne and Welland.

First settled in the early 1800's, by the 1860's Lowbanks had a rope factory, a wagon shop, blacksmith shops, and several other small businesses. A post office was opened in 1864.

A school was opened in Lowbanks in 1866. It was replaced by a new building about 1960. The community has two churches, a United Church and a Reorganized Church of Jesus Christ of the Latter Day Saints.

The historic Furry Tavern, built about 1822, still stands in the community. Another interesting building is a stone castle erected on the lakefront by Charles Moebius, a summer resident from Buffalo.

At one time two telephone companies, the Dunnville Consolidated and the Bell Telephone, existed in Lowbanks, a fact which resulted in long distance charges being imposed on calls between certain neighbouring buildings.

Hamilton Spectator, 1964.

LOWTHER, geographic township, Cochrane District
Position 49° 30′ 83° 46′

Subdivided in 1913 by Beatty, the township was named after Major Lowther. The area, traversed by the Algoma Central and Hudson Bay Railway, lies just southwest of the town of Hearst. The railway points of Mead and Coppel are located within the township.

LUCAN, village, Biddulph Township, Middlesex County
Position 43° 11′ 81° 24′

This village of 1,589 people (1979) is situated in a farming and fruit-growing district about 17 miles north of the city of London. Originally known as Marysville after the sheriff's wife, Mary Macdonald, it was renamed Lucan when a post office was established in 1857.

An early settlement on the site of Lucan was comprised of Negroes. In 1829 a group of fugitive slaves in Cincinnati, Ohio purchased 800 acres of land in the Lucan area with the help of Ohio Quakers. They established one of the earliest Negro settlements in Upper Canada. Soon other groups from the New England and New York States joined them. They named their new home after William Wilberforce, the great British abolitionist. By 1833 there were thirty-two families in Wilberforce. Among the early residents were Peter Butler and Messrs. Wyatt, Whitehead, and Pinkham. A school was founded by the Quakers and a sawmill was built. However, a series of bizarre murders and the suicide of Mrs. Wyatt, who was a religious fanatic, caused the Quakers to leave in the 1840's and the settlement declined.

By 1855 Peter Butler owned most of the western part of the present village, while the eastern part belonged jointly to the Hon. Donald MacDonald and John MacDonald. The first village lots were sold in 1855 in anticipation of the construction of the Grand Trunk Railway to Sarnia. With the completion of the railway (now the CNR) in 1857, Lucan began to prosper and soon became an important centre in South Huron, of which Biddulph then formed a part. A post office was opened in the same year with William Porte as the first postmaster.

In 1865 Biddulph Township and Lucan became a part of Middlesex County. The village was incorporated in 1871. Robert O'Neil served as first reeve. The councillors were: D. McRobert, William Porte, H.B. Quarry, and A. Goodacre.

By the late 1870's Lucan had a prosperous grain business and a number of local industries. The Lucan Foundry, which produced agricultural implements, was established in 1861. Two steam grist mills, a flax mill, and a sawmill also provided employment for the village's 1,100 people.

Near Lucan was the homestead of the infamous Donnellys, who for decades carried on a feud which climaxed in 1880 with the murder of five members of the family.

By the early twentieth century, Lucan had developed into an important manufacturing centre. Local industries included a planing mill, a flax mill, a sawmill, flour and oatmeal mills, and a cheese factory. The village had three blacksmiths, three carriage makers, a gunsmith, and four farm implement dealers. Five grocers, five general merchants, two jewellers, and a book merchant also served the residents. Three hotels provided accommodation for railway passengers.

London Free Press: June 1949.

LUCAS, geographic township, Cochrane District
Position 48° 50' 81° 16'

Situated southwest of the town of Cochrane, the township was named for the Hon. I.B. Lucas, MPP for Centre Grey from 1898 to 1914, and Attorney General from 1914 to 1919. The township is watered by the West Branch of the Buskegau River.

LUCKNOW, village, Kinloss Township, Bruce County
Position 43° 57' 81° 31'

Situated on Highway 86, on the Lucknow River, about 12 miles southwest of Teeswater, Lucknow has a population of about 1,100 (1979). The pioneer settler was Eli Stauffer, a German from Waterloo County who arrived in the area in 1849 and erected a sawmill on the Nine Mile River (now the Lucknow River) in 1856-57. However, James Somerville, who came to Wawanosh in Huron County in 1851, is considered the actual founder of Lucknow. He purchased Mr. Stauffer's property in 1858 and had the south halves of Lots 57, 58, 59 and 60 on the first Concession of Kinloss surveyed into village lots. The lots were offered for sale on September 1, 1858. The place was named Lucknow after a city in India much on everyone's mind in the days of the "Indian Mutiny". The settlers celebrated the christening by setting off twenty-one charges of gunpowder placed in auger holes bored into trees.

The Wawanosh and Ashfield portion of Lucknow, where Daniel Webster and James Henderson had settled in 1854, was not surveyed into village lots until 1861. This area at the time was part of Huron

County.

Malcolm Campbell opened the first store in the village in 1859. That year a post office was established and he was appointed postmaster.

The village, populated largely by Scottish immigrants, grew rapidly. By the middle 1860's there were already more than four hundred residents. However, it was the railway, built in 1873, which brought prosperity to Lucknow making it a shipping point for farm produce and inducing merchants and manufacturers to settle there.

Lucknow was incorporated as a village on June 7, 1873. A number of villagers at the time favoured annexation to Huron County, while Council of Huron and the County Council of Bruce passed a by-law on the same day, annexing the village to their respective county. Excitement ran high over the dual annexation and the heated dispute was not solved until June 11, 1874, when the Lieut.-Governor of the Province issued a proclamation annexing the village of Lucknow to the County of Bruce.

The first village council elected in January 1874, was composed of Reeve M. Campbell and Councillors Thomas Lawrence, Charles Mooney, Alex. McIntyre, and Walter Treleaven. George T. Burgess was the first Clerk and Treasurer.

In January, 1874, the *Lucknow Sentinel*, a weekly newspaper then owned by Messrs. Bowers and Hunt, published its first issue.

The first modest Public School building was erected in 1862. It was replaced by a more commodious school house in 1878. Secondary school subjects were also taught at this school and by 1908 there was a distinction made between the Public and Continuation School. The latter became a High School in 1935. In 1953 district High School students moved into a new building in Lucknow.

Lucknow's Wesleyan Methodist Church dates back to 1885. The Presbyterians attended services in a church just outside the village until Knox Presbyterian Church, a frame building, was erected in Lucknow around 1869. St. Andrew's Presbyterian Church, a stone edifice, was built soon after that. This building was later sold to the Baptists and then to the Roman Catholics. The two Presbyterian congregations eventually united and in 1888 built a large brick church in Lucknow.

The Anglicans built St. Peter's Church in 1878, and St. Mary's Roman Catholic Church had its beginnings as a mission in 1898. Today, Lucknow also has a Dutch Reformed Church, the congregation of which started out in the basement of the Presbyterian Church.

A public library, established in the early 1900's, is located in the Town Hall.

The thriving village, situated in the midst of fine farming country, has a number of industries making wood products and bag pipes and processing butter, flax, barley and oats.

Norman Robertson: *The History of the County of Bruce*, 1906.

Norman McLeod: *The History of the County of Bruce 1907-1969*, 1969.

LUMSDEN, geographic township, Sudbury District
Position 46° 41′ 81° 07′

Lumsden, west of Wanapitei Lake, is traversed by the Vermilion River. The area was first surveyed in 1887 and is believed to have been named in later years after Alex Lumsden, MPP for Ottawa in the 1890's. Since January 1973, Lumsden is part of the newly established town of Valley East.

LUNDY, geographic township, Timiskaming District
Position 47° 33′ 79° 57′

Located west of the town of New Liskeard, the township was surveyed by Code in 1903 and was probably named after Lundy's Lane, near Niagara Falls, site of the bloodiest battle of the War of 1812.

LUNKIE, geographic township, Algoma District
Position 47° 07′ 82° 46′

Until 1974 the township was known as No. 23, Range 12. It was named after A. Lunkie, RCAF of the Algoma District, killed during World War Two. Lunkie is located northeast of Sault Ste Marie and is linked by dry weather road to secondary roads and Highway 556 to the south.

LURGAN, community, Huron Township, Bruce County
Position 44° 05′ 81° 44′

This hamlet is located on the shore of Lake Huron and at the mouth of the Pine River, about 10 miles southwest of the town of Kincardine.

In the 1850's Captain Henry C. Gamble, a well-to-do Irishman, endeavoured to develop the area into a business centre. He was instrumental in getting a post office established at Pine Point in 1860. It was named Lurgan after a town in northern Ireland, said to be his birthplace. About that time, the government erected a lighthouse at "The Point".

The Captain's efforts to expand his enterprises were unsuccessful, and after sinking a great deal of money into various ventures he became discouraged and returned to Ireland.

Not far from Lurgan, extending from the 6th to the 10th Concession of Huron Township, is well-known Bruce Beach. This fine resort area had its beginning in the late 1890's when tents were first pitched there during the summer and the first cottages were being built. Today the visitor finds a golf course, several tennis courts and a baseball diamond among the recreational facilities at Bruce Beach.

Norman Robertson: *The History of the County of Bruce*, 1905.

Norman McLeod: *The History of the County of Bruce 1907-1969*, 1969.

LUTTERWORTH, township, Haliburton County
Position 44° 50′ 78° 47′

This township, located at the southwestern corner of the County of Haliburton, was surveyed in 1858-1859 and was named for a market town on the River Swift in Leicestershire, England. Gull Lake, a tourist attraction since the 1880's, occupies a large section in the township centre. The land east of the Gull River is of good quality for farming in contrast to the area west of Gull Lake, which is unsuited to settlement. The area has large deposits of iron ore, molybdenum, and marble.

Among the first settlers were John Hillier, Wm. Hartle and Solomon Eastman. Other early homesteaders in the township were Thomas Ranson, the Schraders, Mortimers, Robinsons and Harrisons.

Buller Settlement which was located on Lot 16, Concession 3, had an early post office operated by Charles Hearstwood. Also there, on the road between Miner's Bay and Buller, was a Catholic Church, the first in the county. The settlers of this district were Julius Bradamore, the Gillespies, the Brohms and the Porters. The Greers, Trotters and Grozelles lived at Miner's Bay and the Tracey family operated Miner's Bay Lodge. A nearby stone Baptist church was erected in 1906.

Stephen, Nancy and Dennis Wessel and a man named Van-Louven were the early settlers in the Moore Lake area. Other residents there were the Martin family and Ned Bell, who settled south of the lake on the Gull River. The physician looking after these pioneers was Wm. Ellis. At Deep Bay were the Pogue family, Andrew Cree Soutar, and Fred Sawyer. On the east side of Denny's Lake were Alfred Carpenter and his son John, who settled there in 1869. Others included Anthony and John Bowron, John Pomeroy, George Wyatt and Arthur C. Lindop.

Frank Pearce, a Minden merchant, operated a steamboat to Moore's Falls near the southern end of Gull Lake. It was discontinued when the Victoria Railway reached Kinmount in the southeastern corner of the township. John Hulbig was, for 53 years, the clerk of the Township of Lutterworth. He was also for many years treasurer and a school trustee.

On the shores of Gull Lake, John Hounsell, with his sons, operated a sawmill, shingle mill and planer. In the early years most of Haliburton's settled townships were part of Victoria and Peterborough Counties. Haliburton became a county in 1874 and Lutterworth was one of twenty townships that made up the new county.

William Hartle was Lutterworth's first reeve. His family came from Cornwall and he encouraged settlers to come to Lutterworth from the Stormont and Glengarry areas. Among these settlers were the Barnhardts, Calverts, Hamiltons, Johnstons, and Fetterlys.

Nila Reynolds: *In Quest of Yesterday*, 1967.

LYBSTER, geographic township, Thunder Bay District
Position 48° 16′ 89° 49′

Lybster is named after a village in Caithness, Scotland. Located southwest of the city of Thunder Bay, the township was surveyed in 1885. The community of Nolalu is located on White Fish River, which waters the area. Lybster is well served by roads.

LYELL, geographic township, Nipissing District
Position 45° 26′ 78° 58′

The township is situated south of Algonquin Provincial Park and the Madawaska River. It was established around 1861 and was sub-divided by Thomas A. Bolger in 1872-3. Sir Charles Lyell (1797-1875), a noted geologist, is commemorated in the naming of the township. Highway 523 traverses Lyell. The largest of its many lakes are Moore, Cross and McKenzie lakes. The community of Cross Lake is located on Highway 523. The hamlet of McKenzie Lake lies in the southwestern corner of the township.

LYMAN, geographic township, Nipissing District
Position 46° 35′ 79° 41′

Lyman, north of Lake Nipissing, was originally subdivided by T. Bolger in 1890 and was named after Major Henry H. Lyman, manufacturing druggist and chemist of Toronto and Montreal. Highway 11 passes via the community of Tilden Lake through the northeastern part of the township.

LYN, police village, Elizabethtown Township, Leeds County
Position 44° 35′ 75° 47′

Situated 6 miles west of Brockville, this village was originally called Coleman's Corners after its founder, Abel Coleman. In 1839 its name was changed to Lowell in memory of the Massachusetts home of many of the early settlers. However, as there was already a Lowell in Upper Canada, the community was renamed Lyn from the descriptive Scottish word "linn", meaning waterfall.

In 1788 Abel Coleman and a small group of fellow United Empire Loyalists who were seeking a new home after the American Revolution found an excellent mill site at what was to become Lyn. The early history of the mill is obscure but by 1805 Coleman had built a grist mill on the site. The area's potential was recognized by others and by 1815 Coleman's mill had been joined by Stuart's grist mill and sawmill, and, at the nearby falls, Joseph Jessup's sawmill, grist mill, and carding and fulling mill.

By the 1830's a community had developed around the mills. Lyn post office was established in 1851. The Coleman family continued to expand their operations during this period. They erected a sawmill and two leather factories, rebuilt the old grist mill, and in 1856 constructed one of the largest flour mills in Eastern Ontario. Extensive waterpower was needed for the mills and the Colemans provided this by building dams and canals, diverting water from Temperance and Graham Lakes to form Centre Lake and storing water in Lees Pond. The resulting lawsuits bankrupted R. Coleman and Company. In 1880 James Cumming bought the mills, and modernized the flour mill which continued to operate as a successful business until 1933.

By 1871 Lyn was a busy manufacturing centre. Factories produced shoe lasts, farm implements, hubs and spokes, woollen goods, medicinal syrups, and cheese. The Brockville-Westport Railway contributed to the community's prosperity, providing excellent transportation facilities for its manufactured goods.

Lyn's importance as a manufacturing centre ceased when the railway branch line was closed. Today Lyn is a pleasant residential community of some 500 people, with lovely old stone and brick houses set in beautiful natural surroundings. Many of the residents commute to work in nearby Brockville.

The first Methodist church in Leeds County was built in Lyn where the Anglican church stands today.

Ruth McKenzie: *Leeds and Grenville Their First Two Hundred Years*, 1967.

LYNCH, geographic township, Sudbury District
Position 47° 27′ 83° 02′

Known as No. 10C until 1974, the township was named after F.H. Lynch-Staunton, a surveyor who worked in northern Ontario in the 1880's. The area lies east of Highway 129. It is linked by dry weather roads to nearby Wakami Lake Provincial Park, a few miles to the east.

LYNDEN, community, Flamborough Township, Regional Municipality of Hamilton-Wentworth
Position 43° 14′ 80° 09′

This pretty community, situated 17 miles east of Hamilton was originally known as VanSickle after an early pioneer family. When a post office was established in 1851 Jeremiah Bishop suggested the name Lynden after a town in Vermont in the United States.

Barnabus Howard was among the earliest to build his home in the Lynden area some time before 1835. Isaac Blasdell was another early resident. In the 1840's Benony VanSickle erected the first sawmill in the community.

With the construction of the Great Western Railway in 1855, Lynden's prosperity greatly increased. A second sawmill was opened by Mr. McRae and a hotel built by Francis Hore. Rufus Dodge ran a tavern; John Howard was owner of a general store; and Peter Hathaway was the local blacksmith. William Clement built a large woollen factory, which later burned. The Jas. E. Orre Co. oil refinery suffered the same fate.

The lumber industry became an important part of Lynden's economy in the second half of the nineteenth century. Robert

Thompson established a mill to supply the Great Western with fuel. He also produced shingles and later added a cooper shop. By 1889 there were sixteen sawmills in the Lynden area.

In 1879 Peter Hathaway and Darius Mulholland had opened a flour and chopping mill, which was purchased by Robert Thompson the following year. Thompson's son, R.A. Thompson, became a pioneer in the export of turnips to the eastern United States. The Lynden pottery was opened by Joseph and Edward Bradwin. Lynden, in these days, had five lodges of benevolent institutions, an unusually large number for a community of just under 500 people.

Lynden was incorporated as a police village in 1905. The first trustees were Amos Dyment, Dr. J.L. Gibson, and Albert VanSickle.

As the forests were exhausted, the lumbering industry declined. In 1941 Mr. and Mrs. Harry Wald started an apple-packing plant in Lynden. By the 1960's Ella-Riva Farms had become the community's major industry, enjoying international markets. In 1959 the Lynden and District Co-operative took over the old Thompson flour mill.

In 1974 Lynden lost its police village status and became part of the township of Flamborough and part of the Town of Ancaster.

Silas Bishop, a Lynden native who measured 7' 6'', became the Barnum Circus 5-foot Giant. Steve Ihnot, a well-known movie actor, lived in the community for a number of years. Edgar Krouse of Lynden became one of Canada's champion trap-shooters.

John A. Cornell: *Pioneers of Beverly*, 1889.

LYNDHURST, community, Rear of Leeds and Lansdowne Township, Leeds County
Position 44° 33' 76° 08'

This picturesque community on the shore of Lyndhurst Lake, 36 miles northwest of Kingston, was originally known as Furnace Falls because of the falls here on the expansion of the upper reaches of the Gananoque River, and an iron works established there in 1801. By 1851 when a post office was opened, the name had been changed to Lyndhurst in honour of John Singleton Copley, Baron Lyndhurst, who served as Lord Chancellor of England.

When iron ore was discovered in Leeds County, several men petitioned the government for the right to build a foundry near the present site of Lyndhurst. The land was given to Wallis Sunderlin who in 1801 erected the first successful iron furnace in Upper Canada. The Lansdowne Iron Works continued to operate until 1811 at which time a settlement began to develop around the enterprise.

Shortly after 1816 Charles and Jonas Jones acquired the falls and rapids and erected mills which served the local farmers until 1853. A village plot was laid out by the two men and the community prospered. A woollen mill was built at the lower rapids in 1853 and Henry Green installed the first spinner in this part of Canada. A dye house, store, and salesroom were added to the mill.

In 1868 the Jones property was bought by John Roddick and Henry Green. The mills of these two men, one on each side of the river, were Lyndhurst's main industries for many years. It was Roddick who designed the triple-arch stone bridge, built in 1857, which is one of the community's main attractions today. Green constructed the first cheese factory in eastern Ontario. He also opened a general store and acted as postmaster.

In the second half of the nineteenth century, Lyndhurst was a prosperous commercial centre. There were five cheese factories within five miles and two flour mills, three sawmills and a woollen mill in the community itself. A brickyard opened by John B. Wiltse in the 1850's provided the materials for most of the brick buildings in Lyndhurst. William Patterson began a furniture manufacturing establishment. There were also two milliners, a tailor, and two blacksmiths.

The sawmills produced a wide variety of lumber products, including cedar shingles and cheese boxes. In 1911 George Roddick installed a dynamo in the Roddick mills, providing the area with its first electric power. The mills ended production in 1959.

The community's first house of worship was the Methodist Episcopal church, built in 1843 under the Rev. James Smith. A new church was erected in 1881 on land bought from Henry Green. Presbyterian services were first held in the Orange Hall. The Presbyterian church was bought by the Methodists in 1920 and for many years served Lyndhurst as a United Church. Anglican services were conducted in the schoolhouse by Rev. A.H. Coleman from 1872 to 1878. St. Luke's Anglican was opened in 1882. Pentecostal services were held in the Orange Hall in the early 1930's. The Pentecostal Tabernacle was constructed in 1958.

The children of Lyndhurst attended lessons in the Methodist Church until 1851 when an old house was purchased and became Lyndhurst's first school. John Irving Scott was the teacher. In 1860 Thomas Webster became the first teacher in the new school erected in that year. This building was replaced in 1892. A continuation school opened in 1928 and in 1937 a combination public and continuation school was built. It functioned as a public school from 1960 and was closed in the 1970's.

With the coming of the automobile, Lyndhurst developed into a tourist and camping resort. Camp Hyanto, opened in 1946, serves many young people from all over eastern Ontario. Other visitors, such as the late painter Manly MacDonald, were attracted by the picturesque community itself. Today Lyndhurst has a population of about two hundred.

Kingston Whig-Standard, February 1973.

Ruth McKenzie: Leeds and Grenville Their First Two Hundred Years, 1967.

LYNDOCH, township, Renfrew County
Position 45° 18′ 77° 20′

Situated in southwestern Renfrew County, Lyndoch is traversed by the scenic Madawaska River which flows eastward through the township.

Organized in 1862, the township was named after the distinguished soldier Thomas Graham, Baron Lynedoch (1750-1843), who was in command of the forces which captured the French fortress of Malta in 1800. Despite the incorrect spelling, the name Lyndoch has continued to be used.

Lyndoch is united with Brudenell Township for municipal purposes. In 1979 the combined population of the townships was 827.

Highway 515 traverses the northern part of the township where the communities of Quadeville and Wolfe are situated.

Mrs. Carl Price and Clyde C. Kennedy: *Notes on the History of Renfrew County*, 1961.

LYON, geographic township, Thunder Bay District
Position 48° 52' 88° 21'

The township of Lyon surveyed in the 1870's, 1890's and in 1911, covers a large area south of Red Rock. In the east it is bordered by Nipigon Bay, and in the southwest by Black Bay (Lake Superior). The Sturgeon River flowing southward through the centre of the township empties into Black Bay. The Trans-Canada Highway passes through the northwestern section of the township, as do the Canadian National Railways and the Canadian Pacific Railway. Lyon was named after Robert A. Lyon, MPP for Algoma in the 1870's and 1880's.

LYONS, community, South Dorchester Township, Elgin County
Position 42° 51' 80° 59'

Lyons is located on Highway 73, a few miles north of the town of Aylmer. Until 1860 it was called Hale's Corners after William Hale who had established a wayside inn at the site.

The first store was erected by Messrs. Winder and Baker; P.J. Putnam opened a factory producing pumps which were sold throughout the district. A Methodist church built in 1866 has long since been closed.

Lyons can claim to have been one of the first communities in Ontario to have organized a Historical Society.

A Capsule History of East Elgin, ed. by Giles A. Hume.

M

MABEE, geographic township, Cochrane District
Position 49° 00' 81° 40'

In 1908, Ontario Land Surveyor J. Dunn surveyed the entire township. It is situated west of the town of Cochrane and south of Smooth Rock Falls. The township is named after a Judge Mabee of the High Court of Justice, Ontario.

MACASKILL, geographic township, Algoma District
Position 48° 09' 84° 59'

Initially a part of the Algoma Central and Hudson Bay Railways land grant, Macaskill Township, situated northwest of Wawa, was named after John Macaskill, a Canadian Army Sapper from the Thunder Bay District, who died in 1942 in World War II.

MACDONALD, geographic township, Algoma District
Position 46° 29' 84° 02'

Macdonald is part of the municipality of Macdonald, Meredith and Aberdeen Additional. The township was established in 1860 and was surveyed the following year by Ontario Land Surveyor Miles. It was named after the Hon. John Sandfield Macdonald, joint Premier of United Canada, 1862-64, and the first Premier of Ontario, 1867-71.

The area which is Indian Land, borders in the west on Lake George. The main community is Echo Bay on the Trans-Canada Highway about 15 miles east of the city of Sault Ste. Marie. In the early days an important trading post was located here on the shore of Lake George.

The township's economy depends largely on agriculture and tourism.

MacFIE, geographic township, Kenora District
Position 49° 46' 92° 21'

Named for C.M. MacFie, MPP for Middlesex South, 1934-37, MacFie Township lies southwest of Sioux Lookout. The southern portion of Sandybeach Lake occupies the northern end of the township, which is accessible by road.

MacGREGOR, geographic township, Thunder Bay District
Position 48° 33′ 89° 00′

The area was probably named for James Patrick MacGregor, solicitor for Latchford and police magistrate for Gowganda in 1909. MacGregor Township includes the communities of Beck, MacKenzie, Navilus, Wild Goose, and Silver and Amethyst Harbours.

MacGREGOR POINT PROVINCIAL PARK, Saugeen Township, Bruce County
Position 44° 26′ 81° 24′

This Recreation Park, opened in 1976, borders the east shore of Lake Huron. The town of Port Elgin, some 2 miles to the north on the Blue Water Highway (Highway 21), is the nearest centre.

Algonquin Lake, an ancient glacial lake of over 10,000 years ago, once covered today's Lake Huron and the Georgian Bay waters as well as farther inland areas. To the east of the park is the prominent bluff of vanished Algonquin Lake. The land between this old beach and the present shoreline of Lake Huron is known as the Huron Fringe. The scattered ponds and wetlands within the Huron Fringe are the homes of a variety of nesting and migratory waterfowl.

Ontario Ministry of Natural Resources.

MACHAR, township, Parry Sound District
Position 45° 52′ 79° 29′

The township was established in 1875 and was named by Sir Oliver Mowat, the premier of Ontario at that time, in memory of his friend, the Rev. John Machar, D.D. Rev. Machar, a leading figure in the early days of the Presbyterian church in Canada, served for many years as minister of St. Andrew's Church in Kingston where Mowat was born and educated.

Prior to the arrival of settlers, Machar and the adjoining township, Laurier, were being logged by several companies who floated their logs down the South River.

Many settlers came into Machar Township via the Nipissing Road. Practically all the land east of the Nipissing Road was claimed before 1900 and some as early as 1860. Large farms were cleared but after a few years the shallow soil would no longer produce the original bumper crops and had to be abandoned.

The first store and post office in Machar was built in 1878 by Peter Shaughnessy. Known as Uplands, the site was located four miles west of the present town of South river. Shaughnessy, who was also Justice of the Peace, brought supplies to his store from Rousseau using a team and wagon.

The first log school in the township was built at Uplands, about a mile north of Shaughnessy's store. Jack Armstrong established a cheese factory south of Uplands which he operated for many years. Farmers drew their milk by horse or oxen to the factory. Today, this area is deserted; the school and the cheese factory have disappeared; the farms are now commons or have grown up with trees.

Muskoka Road, another colonization road, ran north from Bracebridge, reaching Huntsville in 1880, proceeding on to Burk's Falls, Sundridge and Uplands. Later it was extended north to join the Commanda-Trout Creek Road at Granite Hill. The Jerusalem Road, also a colonization road, joined the Muskoka Road and the Nipissing Road and ran through the northern parts of Lount and Machar Townships.

The second post office to open in Machar was Bray Lake; it was kept in "Red" John Taylor's shanty. Mrs. Taylor was the postmistress and mail carrier. The third post office, kept by William Smyth in his cabin, was at Midford Bay at the north end of Eagle Lake.

Among the names of early settlers of this area were "Black" John Taylor, Joseph McGirr and James Hawthorne; the latter bought the first deeded farm in 1884.

The northern parts of Machar were settled by Angus McLaren, John Bumstead, the Baumann's, Fred Kuehni, Chris Nixon, Bob Walters, and others.

The Township of Machar comprises an area of 46,278 acres with a population of 549 (1979).

Everett Kirton: *History of Eastern Parry Sound District.*

MACHIN, geographic township, Cochrane District
Position 49° 23′ 81° 58′

This township is located midway between Smooth Rock Falls and Kapuskasing, north of Highway 11 and the CNR.

For municipal purposes, Machin is united with Shackleton, its neighbour to the south. Most of the municipality's 890 residents live in the Shackleton area. The township is drained by the Groundhog River and Shackleton Creek.

The name origin is unknown, but it is possible that it was named for Col. H.A. Machin, MPP for Kenora in the early 1900's.

MACHIN, township, Kenora District
Position 49° 47′ 93° 25′

The name of this township commemorates Col. H.A. Machin, MPP for Kenora prior to World War One, at the time boundaries were being surveyed.

The township municipality of Machin comprises the geographic townships of Langton, Temple, Sanford, and the west half of Aubrey. Vermilion Bay on Highway 17 (Trans-Canada) and the CPR, is the township seat. The area lies west of Dryden. The population of the township stands at 1,112 in 1979.

Vermilion Bay is the gateway to nearby Blue Lake Provincial Park and to the gold mining and tourist areas of Red Lake and Balmertown to the north, accessible from here via Highway 105.

MACK, geographic township, Algoma District
Position 46° 19′ 82° 53′

First surveyed in 1881, Mack Township is located approximately ten miles north of Blind River by way of Highway 557. It was named for William Mack, MPP for Cornwall in 1879 and for Stormont in 1890.

MACKELCAN, geographic township, Sudbury District
Position 46° 51′ 80° 37′

Located northeast of Sudbury, Mackelcan Township was named for F. McKelcan, Q.C., of Hamilton, Ontario. The area is extensively covered with water, including the Chiniguchi River and the North Arm of Matagamasi Lake.

MacLEOD PROVINCIAL PARK, Ashmore Township, Thunder Bay
District
Position 49° 41′ 86° 51′

MacLeod is a Recreation Park of some 200 acres on Highway 11 near Kenogamisis Lake, 6 miles southeast of the town of Geraldton. This campsite provides excellent fishing in the Kenogamisis Lake waters and rock hunters will find, at the eastern tip of the campground, the same rock formation as in the gold-bearing rock of the Geraldton area.

Ontario Ministry of Natural Resources.

MacNICOL, geographic township, Kenora District
Position 49° 50′ 93° 57′

This township, located northeast of Kenora, was named after John Richie MacNicol, MP for Toronto-Davenport, in 1945. The area is extensively covered by small lakes, and includes the CPR station point of Hawk Lake and the community of Willard Lake.

MACPHERSON, geographic township, Nipissing District
Position 46° 20′ 80° 16′

The township was named for the Honourable David Lewis MacPherson, Cabinet Minister from 1880-83. It is situated to the west of Lake Nipissing, whose western shore forms the southern part of the eastern boundary. The community of Notre Dame du Lac lies within the township, on Highway 64, and Lavigne is situated near the eastern boundary.

MacQUARRIE, geographic township, Kenora District
Position 49° 30′ 94° 10′

Situated to the east of Lake of the Woods, the township was named in 1939 for Edison Malcolm MacQuarrie, an Ontario Land Surveyor of Sault Ste. Marie, Ontario. Long Bay, part of Lake of the Woods, extends across the southern part of the township and the western half is occupied by an Indian Reserve.

MACVICAR, geographic township, Cochrane District
Position 49° 07′ 82° 10′

Situated southeast of Kapuskasing, Macvicar Township was named either for Malcolm McVicar, MPP for Elgin East in 1919, or Milton D. MacVicar, MPP for Lambton East, 1934-37.

The Groundhog and Wakusimi Rivers flow northeast through the township, which is accessible by road.

MADOC, township, Hastings County
Position 44° 35′ 77° 30′

This township, north of Belleville, was named after Madoc Ad Owaiin Gwynedd, a legendary Welsh prince reputed to have discovered America about 1170.

The township was opened for settlement in 1821 and was joined to Hastings County that year. The first pioneers included Michael Zerim, James O'Hara, Cyrus Riggs, and Barnabas Vankleek. Settlement was slow at first, only 37 people living in the area in 1834, but increased after the road from Huntingdon Township was improved.

The village of Madoc began to grow up around the mill and store built by Donald MacKenzie on Deer Creek and by 1830 the population of the township was 139. The establishment of an iron works by Uriah Seymour of Madoc village in 1835 also aided the development of the township. By 1837 the population stood at 600. Madoc prospered in the following years, particularly following the construction of the Hastings Road in the 1840's. It suffered a temporary setback when the Iron Works closed, and the demand for potash, at one time one of the township's main export commodities, dwindled. However, a new source of employment was provided by a growing lumber industry. The Gilmour Company of Trenton and the Rathbun Company of Deseronto both operated in the area.

At first Madoc was united with Tudor and Elzevir for municipal purposes but separated before 1850. John R. Ketcheson was the first Reeve of Madoc. At that time Eldorado was the heart of the area and the township hall was located there.

In 1866 the Powell brothers and Nicholus Schneider were prospecting for copper on John Richardson's farm, Lot 18, Concession 5, when they discovered gold-bearing rock and set off Canada's first gold rush. Prospectors poured into the area; property prices soared, and restaurants, boardinghouses, and hotels seemed to spring up overnight. The population quickly rose to 5,000 and Eldorado and Madoc village grew rapidly. Mounted police had to be sent in to maintain order. However, fortunes were made by very few. Two men named Carr and Johnson took an option on the Richardson mine, then disappeared after taking away the gold. Several farmers "salted" their property with gold fragments to encourage buyers. The operators of a crushing mill for the Richardson mine underpriced the ore, then left the area. This led to disagreement between the Belleville owners of the mine and their Chicago counterparts who insisted that in the future the ore be sent to New York. When the Belleville men objected, the Americans sold their stock and the mine closed shortly after. Other seemingly rich strikes produced only low-grade ore. There was a lack of the proper equipment to separate the gold from the quartz. Within a couple of years, the excitement of the gold rush ended and the population of the township began to decline. By 1878 none of the quartz mills in the area was operating fully.

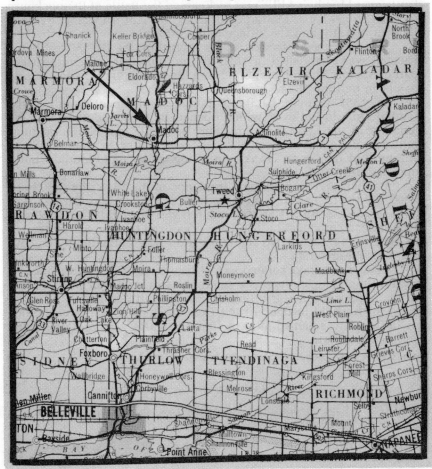

Other minerals were also discovered in the township, including large deposits of copper, lead, and lithographic stone. In the late nineteenth century a hematite iron mine provided employment for local miners. In 1889 a rich gold vein was discovered resulting in another small gold rush. A talc mill was established by George H. Gillespie in 1906. Today's Canada Talc Industries is one of three in

Canada and the only one to produce pure white talc. From 1910 to 1913 American iron and copper mines operated in the area. Stoklosar Marble Quarries was also opened.

Next to lumbering, agriculture played an important role in Madoc's development. The first mill in the township was built at MacKenzie's Mills in 1836. James O'Hara's mill, built in 1846 near Madoc village, has been restored and is now a historic site, one of two muley-type mills still operating in Ontario. Other mills included A.F. Wood's flouring mill built in Madoc in 1862. The name of the village of Bannockburn was the result of a lawsuit over one mill. A legal battle over Mumby's Mills was nicknamed the Battle of Bannockburn by hotel owner James Maitland, recalling the Scottish victory over the English in 1314, and the village took the name.

The first cheese factory in the township, the Bay State Cheese Factory, was established in 1870 by Jim Tanner in the southeastern part of Madoc. Three more, including the Alexandra Cheese Factory, had been built by 1874.

In 1882 many inhabitants found employment building the Central Ontario Railway, which opened in 1884. Eldorado was the junction of the Central Ontario and Belleville and North Hastings railways. Bannockburn was also a railway centre. In 1890 a railway was built by the Grand Trunk connecting Madoc and Eldorado, but it operated only until 1897.

Baptist services were held in Madoc in the 1820's by Rev. Isaac Reed, but the first church, a Methodist one in Hazzard's Corners, was built in 1857. A Bible Christian church was erected before 1860 and an Anglican congregation had been organized by Rev. A. Whitmarsh by 1862. In 1878 over half the population was Methodist with about one-fifth Presbyterian.

Madoc was incorporated as a village in 1878. Eldorado, once its rival in importance, remains a small community. Other post villages in the nineteenth century included Kellar's Bridge named after the man who built the bridge in 1840; Cooper which became a post office in 1861 and was named after its first postmaster; Hazzard's Corners, and Bannockburn.

H. Belden & Co.: *Historical Atlas of the Counties of Hastings and Prince Edward*, 1878.

Gerald E. Boyce: *Historic Hastings*, 1967.

MADOC, village, Madoc and Huntingdon Townships, Hastings County
Position 44° 30′ 77° 28′

Situated on the southern boundary of Madoc Township, about 25 miles north of Belleville, Madoc is on the junction of Highways 62 and 7 and on the direct route from Highway 401 to Algonquin Park. The name comes from Madoc ad Owaiin Gwynedd, a legendary Welsh prince said to have discovered America in 1170.

Indian legend tells of an important battle that took place on the site of the present village between the Mohawks and the Mississaugas. Signs of Indian encampments were found at the centre of the village.

Donald MacKenzie was the founder of the settlement, building a saw and grist mill on Deer Creek. The O'Haras were among the first settlers. The settlement was called MacKenzie's Mills for twenty years, before the name was changed to Hastings, and finally to Madoc. MacKenzie prospered and made additions to his mill in 1835. In the same year, Uriah Seymour and John G. Pendergast opened an iron works, employing up to 100 people. The works was profitable at first but the difficulties of transportation and the lack of proper fuel forced it to close down in 1845. The reopening of the iron mines in 1851 brought a renewed period of growth and the population increased from 200 in 1851 to 500 in 1855, when the community became a police village. At this time, proposals were also put forward suggesting the village as a possible government centre for North Hastings in the event that it separated from Hastings County.

The village continued to grow in the boom years of the 1860's. It became an important trade centre on the Hastings Road. A.F. Wood set up a new grist mill in 1862 and Charles Kirk opened a flouring mill. The village boasted four carriage shops, five blacksmith shops, two cabinet shops, a tannery, watchmaker, and an organ company. It had its own newspaper the *Mercury and North Riding News*, edited by Albert Smallfield from 1862 to 1871. By 1865 the population was almost 900.

In 1866 gold was discovered in Madoc Township. The effect of Canada's first gold rush on the village was dramatic. The hotels overflowed with prospective "millionaires". Madoc's population rose to 1700 almost overnight. Twenty-five mounted police had to be stationed in the village to keep order. Although most of the gold mines failed, due to the difficulty and expense of extracting the gold, other mineral deposits were discovered including copper, lead, marble, talc, and lithographic stone. A quartz mill, owned by the Merchants' Union Mining Company, opened in the village in 1869 providing employment for residents.

Although many left after the excitement of the gold rush was over, Madoc continued to grow, aided by the construction of the Belleville and North Hastings Railway and a gravel road south to Belleville. A fire destroyed much of the village in 1873, but it was quickly rebuilt. In 1878, with a population of 1,000, Madoc became an incorporated village. By 1880 the population was nearing 1,500. Soon after this, however, the village began to decline. The closing of the iron mines, the decrease in the lumber trade, and the routing of the Toronto and Ottawa Railway through Ivanhoe instead of Madoc caused many people to leave the area. Recently the population has begun to increase again. In the 1930's, Highway 7 gave the village an east-west link and its central position on the main road south to Belleville has encouraged its growth. By 1979, the population had reached 1,274.

A private school was opened in 1838 by Mrs. Olmstead. In 1853 a district grammar school was erected and in 1880 a new model school took in its first students. By 1865 the village also had a township library.

The first Baptist preaching was heard in Madoc in the 1820's in the home of the O'Haras. Presbyterian missionaries were active by 1843 and a Presbyterian congregation was organized by 1853. In 1857 a Methodist Episcopal church was built and in 1864 the Anglican Church of St. John the Baptist opened its doors to worshippers. By 1878 there were five churches in Madoc, including the Roman Catholic and Canada Methodist churches. The Rev. Mr. Wishart contributed much to the development of the village, building two churches and being largely responsible for the construction of St. Peter's.

William Archibald Mackintosh, well-known educator, economist, and administrator, and Principal of Queen's University (1951-61), was born in Madoc in 1895.

H. Belden & Co.: *Historical Atlas of the Counties of Hastings and Prince Edward*, 1878.

Gerald E. Boyce: *Historic Hastings*, 1967.

Garnet Pigden and Ardith McKinnon: *Way Back When. . . .* 1975.

St. John's Anglican Church (Madoc)

Drawing by Robert Hudson

MAFEKING, geographic township, Kenora District
Position 49° 56' 93° 08'

Located between Kenora and Sioux Lookout, the area is named after a place in Africa connected with the Boer War, 1899-1901.

MAGLADERY, geographic township, Cochrane District
Position 49° 23' 83° 20'

Magladery Township, situated southeast of Hearst, was named for Thomas Magladery, MPP for Timiskaming, 1914-19 and was originally part of the Algoma East Railway land grant.

MAGNETAWAN, village, Chapman Township, Parry Sound District
Position 45° 40' 79° 39'

Magnetawan derives its name from the river on which it is situated. The original spelling was "Maganetawan", an Indian name which means "swiftly flowing water", an apt name for a river whose source is in Algonquin Park, and which flows westerly through Parry Sound District, emptying into Georgian Bay at Byng Inlet after an 800-foot drop.

The numerous rapids of this river were a source of constant danger to the early log drivers who at spring break-up guided the logs downstream.

Lieutenant F.H. Baddeley, of the Royal Engineers, was the first to explore the area in 1835. Alexander Murray, Assistant Provincial Geologist, inspected it in 1854 and reported that the Magnetawan watershed contained good agricultural land.

Settlement did not get underway until after the Nipissing Road was cut out by the Dodge Lumber Company from Rousseau to Magnetawan in 1873. That year the town plot was marked out by Robert Sparks as squatters had already begun to move into the area.

By 1879 there were two licensed hotels, four general stores, a tin shop, baker's shop, a watchmaker, flour and feed store, schoolhouse, and three churches (either built or under construction). There were a grist mill and a sawmill, a Crown Lands Office, a post office and a temperance hotel. A steamboat ran daily from Magnetawan east to Burk's Falls, a distance of 25 miles through country well settled on both sides of the river. A second steamboat plied between Magnetawan and the foot of Ahmic Lake to the west. These routes were joined by a lock in 1885-86.

In 1878 John Kennedy built the first water-powered sawmill and grist mill in Magnetawan. The grist mill eventually became an electric power plant supplying power to the surrounding area. The same company that owned the power plant also operated a grist mill, a small sawmill and a planer and shingle mill.

Lumbering was the main industry in an area where pine, hemlock and hardwood grew in abundance. Men worked in logging camps in the winter and on log-drives in the spring. The soil, although rich, was not deep enough to support agriculture to any extent. When in 1885 the CPR completed its transcontinental railroad and glowing reports of the vast areas of fertile land in the prairies began to filter back, many settlers left the Magnetawan area to seek their fortunes in the west.

The inhabitants of Magnetawan petitioned the government to be incorporated as a village in 1918. It was at this time that the spelling of the original name Maganetawan was changed to Magnetawan. The first reeve was George McKnight; the first councillors were: John Schade, Louis V. Smith, Alfred Paget, and Thomas Langford.

Previous to 1885 when steamboats were the popular mode of transportation, Magnetawan was the "metropolis of the north". But with the advant of the railway which passed through Burk's Falls, Magnetawan lost its former importance.

Everett Kirton: *History of Eastern Parry Sound District.*

MAGONE, geographic township, Algoma District
Position 48° 52′ 85° 16′

Established in 1943 by the Ministry of Lands and Forests, Magone Township was named for C.R. Magone, K.C., a solicitor in the attorney general's Department at that time. It is located north of the White River CPR station.

MAHAFFY, geographic township, Cochrane District
Position 48° 50′ 81° 32′

The Mattagami River flows through the township, providing power for a hydro electric generating station, located in the southeastern corner. Named for A.A. Mahaffy, MPP for Muskoka from 1904-11, the township is situated north and slightly west of Timmins.

MAHER, geographic township, Cochrane District
Position 51° 04′ 81° 11′

The area is drained by numerous tributaries of the Moose River, traversing the township in a southeasterly direction. The township was named for "Pete" Maher, locating engineering for the Timiskaming and Northern Ontario Railway in the Cochrane District. The Ontario Northland Railway passes through the southeastern corner of the township, which is situated southwest of Moosonee.

MAHONEY, geographic township, Cochrane District
Position 50° 25′ 82° 22′

Watered by the Missinaibi River and its tributaries, Mahoney Township lies north of Kapuskasing. The area was named for T.G. Mahoney, MLA, MPP for Wentworth South from 1923-29.

MAIDSTONE, township, Essex County
Position 42° 15′ 82° 48′

Maidstone Township took its name from Maidstone, the county town of Kent, England.

This township was not settled as early as those in the southern part of Essex County. However, owing to its northern boundary being

Lake St. Clair, French fishermen and trappers had visited the area long before the first homesteaders arrived.

It was not until 1828, when the Middle Road from Charing Cross, Kent County, to the River St. Clair had been surveyed along with its adjoining lands, that the area was thrown open to settlement.

It was mainly Irish Roman Catholics who settled on the Middle Road. They came in poor circumstances, but through their industry and the fertility of the land were able to become very successful. The first family to settle along this road were the O'Connors followed by the Kavanaghs. As late as the Rebellion of 1837 the township was still sparsely settled. Farther east, other Irish families settled including the Scullys, O'Callaghans and Costigans (who kept the first tavern in this area as early as 1838).

John Moran, who pioneered in the centre of the township north of the Middle Road, arrived in 1837. He was joined by the Laydon family and Michael and John Gallagher.

Only a few settlers located along the Tecumseh Road before the Rebellion. There, a man named Woods operated the first sawmill in the township.

A Scotch Settlement formed in the northwestern extremity of Maidstone. Among its pioneers were: Duncan Grant, Alex. Malcolm, Daniel Halloway, the Martindales, Patullos, and the Wallaces.

No settlement took place south of the Middle Road and between it and Gosfield until the latter part of the 1800's, when Thomas Small, and the Ewart and Baxter families located there. In the 1830's Talbot Street, which crosses the southwestern corner of the township, was settled by Alex Taylor, Robert McEwen and the Dewhursts.

H. Belden & Co.: *Illustrated Historical Atlas of the Counties of Essex and Kent*, 1881.

Essex Historical Society: *Papers and Addresses Vol. 1,*, 1913.

MALAHIDE, township, Elgin County
Position 42° 45′ 80° 26′

The township of Malahide was named by Col. Thomas Talbot, the founder of the Talbot Settlement in southwestern Ontario, in remembrance of the baronial Castle of Malahide, Ireland, where he was born.

The earliest settlers of Malahide were the brothers William, Andrus, Daniel, Simeon and Joseph Davis, who came from New York State around 1810. They were joined by Stephen Leek, Henry House, Isaac Crane, Daniel McKinney, Isaac and Thaddeus Ostrander, Onesimus, G. and Thaddeus Bradley, Wm. Teeple, and John Vanpatter, before the outbreak of the War of 1812.

William Davis settled on the north side of Talbot Street where he built a log house and a "mill". It was a simple stump mill, hollowed from a standing tree stump and powered by human muscle. A crude device, but it ground the flour and meal for home consumption. The nearest mills were at Long Point and Port Talbot. William Davis who lived on his farm until the age of eighty, was responsible for organizing the first Baptist Church in Elgin County.

The first saw and grist mills in the settlement were built in 1817 on Catfish Creek by Andrus Davis and John D. Brown. Simeon Davis erected the first frame house which also served as a wayside inn.

Although Malahide fronts on Lake Erie, the opportunities it offers were not readily grasped in the early years. Colonel Backhouse, then living at Port Rowan, purchased a lot along the lake at Silver Creek, building a sawmill in 1814 and a grist mill in 1816. Within ten years the mills were closed. Henry Dalley attempted to found a village called Davenport in this area. Some lots were sold, a hotel and a few businesses were established, and a railway line was built connecting Davenport to London. But the dream faltered and slowly died, leaving the buildings to decay.

Port Bruce on Lake Erie, a mile west of Davenport, was a village and shipping port of considerable importance from 1840 to 1860. In 1855 the Aylmer and Port Bruce Gravel road was built and eventually the prosperity of Port Bruce was absorbed by Aylmer.

The schooner, *Nettie Davis*, which was built there, ceased to stop at Port Bruce with the end of the stave and lumber trade and the railway began taking over, transporting grain produced in the area.

The first school in Elgin county was established at Rodger's Corners in Malahide, which prided itself on raising more money for educational purposes than any of its sister townships.

Aylmer had emerged as the most thriving community in the township by 1851, possessing several sawmills and flour mills on Catfish Creek.

Other post offices included Luton, in the centre of the township, and Mount Salem on the Stage Road between Aylmer and Gravesend. Springfield, situated on the line between Malahide and South Dorchester, was the second largest community and an important station on the Canada Southern Railway.

Malahide Township has an area of 64,819 acres and a population of 5,168 (1979).

H.R. Page & Co.: *Illustrated Historical Atlas of the County of Elgin*, 1877.

MALCOLM, community, Brant Township, Bruce County
Position 44° 14′ 81° 06′

The small community of Malcolm lies two and a half miles west of Elmwood. It was of considerable importance in the rural community in earlier years being at that time composed of two hotels, a store, a church, a school and a post office. It gained greater prominence in 1914 when the first Farmers' Buying Club in Ontario was formed there. This organization carried on until 1940 when it merged with a Consumers Co-Op in Grey County to become the Grey-Bruce Co-Operative Association. Still later it merged with The United Co-Operatives of Ontario.

In 1968 the local Women's Institute erected a cairn on the site of the old Buying Club to commemorate the pioneers of the community. In the cairn hangs the bell from the old village school, long since closed.

The pioneer Presbyterian Church erected on Concession 10 in the late 1850's was replaced by a brick church in 1873. Closed in 1925, the building has been taken down but the cemetery is still kept. Rev. Daniel Duff served from 1868 to 1899 in this church.

Norman McLeod: *The History of the County of Bruce 1907-1968*, 1969.

MALDEN, township, Essex County
Position 42° 05' 83° 03'

Malden Township is located in the southwestern part of the County of Essex and borders in the west on the Detroit River and in the south on Lake Erie. It contains 21,715 acres and has a population of 5,293 (1979).

Although it appears that the first settlers in the area were United Empire Loyalists, there is evidence that several French settlers had located a short distance below Elliotts' Point in Malden a considerable time prior to the Revolutionary War and the arrival of Loyalist refugees from that war. The Reaume family was among these early French pioneers.

In 1796, under the Jay Treaty, the British military post at Detroit was turned over to the Americans, and the British chose the site of present-day Amherstburg on the east bank of the Detroit River near its junction with Lake Erie to erect a new fort the following year. A portion of the military reserve was laid out into the town site of Amherstburg and settled by Loyalists from Detroit. Fort Malden, or Fort Amherstburg as it was also called, was strengthened during the War of 1812. Here General Brock made his plans that led to the capture of Detroit in August of 1812, and near the fort ships were being built for the British naval force. In 1813 the fort was captured by the Americans, but at the end of the war it was restored to the British.

Amherstburg, today the site of Fort Malden National Historic Park, remained a part of Malden Township until 1851 when it was incorporated as a village with town powers.

The township's economy greatly benefitted by the Canada Southern Railway (leased to the Michigan Central) which constructed a branch line from Amherstburg to Essex.

Amherstburg remains the hub of this primarily agricultural township. Holiday Beach Provincial Park and other beach resorts on the Lake Erie shore are popular attractions, and easily accessible from Windsor via Highway 18.

H. Belden Co.: *Illustrated Historical Atlas of the Counties of Essex and Kent*, 1880.

Essex Historical Society Papers, 1913.

MALLORYTOWN, police village, Front of Yonge Township, Leeds County
Position: 44° 29' 75° 53'

Located on Highway 2, about 15 miles southwest of Brockville, Mallorytown was founded by Nathaniel Mallory, a native of Vermont and a United Empire Loyalist.

Nathaniel, who came to Canada in 1790, had thirteen children and the Mallorys became one of the township's most prominent families. His eldest son, Daniel, and another son, Lemuel, owned land on the broken front along the lake shore and on the first concession of Yonge. His second son, Andrew, operated a glass factory where glass was blown into beautiful blue-green flasks, pitchers, bowls and paper-weights. The factory, the first of its kind in Upper Canada, existed for a year (1839-1840) and then closed down. Its site, just west of the village, was excavated in 1953. David Mallory, another of Nathaniel's sons, ran a store in Mallorytown and a brickyard outside the village. The large three-storey red brick Mallory house at the western edge of the village was probably built of the bricks made in David's yard.

In 1852 a post office was established; five years later the Masonic Lodge was organized. A cheese factory was erected in the village in 1870 and was operated by Amasa W. Mallory.

The Mallory United Church was built in 1876 and the Presbyterians erected their church in 1888. The Oddfellows Lodge was instituted in 1885 and in 1891 a spacious lodge hall was built. In 1908 the Northern Crown Bank opened a branch bank in Mallorytown. It was taken over in 1918 by the Royal Bank of Canada. In September 1920 a Consolidated School was opened in the village.

A Century and a Half of Progress, Mallorytown, 1934.

MANCHESTER, community, East Wawanosh, West Wawanosh and Hullett
Townships, Huron County
Position 43° 46' 81° 32'

Manchester, which touches on four townships — East and West Wawanosh, Colborne and Hullett, became a police village on January 6, 1895. The village post office was named Auburn, but for municipal purposes the place is known as Manchester.

More than one hopeful pioneer had visions of this area becoming an important town site. The first was Eneas Elkin, an Irish immigrant who had landed first in the Maritimes before coming to Upper Canada in 1851. He bought property on the Hullett side and in 1852 subdivided and sold enough land to allow him to build a grist mill on the remainder. He built a clay dam to contain the water needed to power his four-storey grist mill which was built under the supervision of Stewart Plummer. The mill's waterwheel is on exhibit today in the yard of the present chopping mill.

Just when Elkin was about to commence operation another pioneer, named Vanstone, began to excavate on the east side of the river to create a mill race for another dam. When Elkin's dam flooded the Vanstone property he was sued for $3,000. By the time Elkin and his sons had worked that debt off the Maitland River's spring flood washed away his clay dam. He was forced to sell out to John Cullis in 1869.

Cullis built a stone and timber dam which remains, but for an added concrete top, the same today. A sawmill was added to the gristmill and for many years it was a successful business.

Other early settlers on the Hullett side were John McDonald and Samuel Caldwell, a carpenter who built many of the buildings in the village.

George Fulton also had plans for Manchester when he bought property in 1854. He had a second survey of town lots registered in 1858. He was not a patient man and when the village did not develop as quickly as he had anticipated, he sold his land and moved to the United States.

The next person to draw up plans for the development of Manchester was Mac MacDonald, a surveyor who had blazed a trail through to Goderich in 1827. His plans, too, were unsuccessful and in 1867 he sold his holdings to Robert Downs.

A post office was established in 1854 with William Garrett as postmaster.

By the 1860's there was a hotel, a shoemaker, a wagon shop, two blacksmiths, two general stores, two churches, an Orange Lodge, and a school.

James Scott: *The Settlement of Huron County*, 1966.

MANDAMIN, geographic township, Algoma District
Position 46° 30′ 82° 08′

This township, east of Elliot Lake, was named in 1974 for Henry E. Mandamin, Canadian Army Rifleman, Manitoulin District, who was killed in 1944, during World War II. Its former designation was Township 124.

MANESS, geographic township, Algoma District
Position 47° 59′ 84° 28′

This township (formerly Township 27, Range 23) is situated twenty miles east of Wawa. The Algoma Central Railway travels through the township which was named for General Maness, Chief of the Chippewas of Sarnia.

MANION, geographic township, Thunder Bay District
Position 50° 12′ 90° 21′

This remote area, accessible by water and by Canadian National Railways, is situated northwest of Thunder Bay. It is covered by small, interconnected lakes, including Sunray and Savoyard Lakes. The area was named for the Honourable R.J. Manion, Minister of Railways and Canals, Ottawa.

MANITOULIN, district
Position 45° 45′ 82° 30′

The District of Manitoulin, one of Ontario's most picturesque vacation lands, covers an area of 1,588 square miles and includes the islands of

Manitoulin, Cockburn, Fitzwilliam, Great Cloche, and some lesser islands, as well as a portion of the mainland. The district is situated between the major portion of Lake Huron and the North Channel, to the south of the Algoma District. Georgian Bay lies to the southeast and Drummond Island, U.S.A., to the west.

The series of islands is an extension of the Niagara Cuesta, and, were it not for a few low areas, the scarp would divide Lake Huron in two and would be a part of an extensive land formation stretching from the Bruce Peninsula to northern Michigan. The land is deeply scored and Manitoulin Island alone has more than 100 lakes, each with at least one island of its own. The three largest lakes are Kagawong, Mindemoya, and Manitou, with a combined surface area of more than 65 square miles.

Manitoulin Island, which comprises the largest portion of the district, is about 100 miles long, and from two to forty miles in width, making it the largest freshwater island in the world. Its topography features flat rock plains, long perpendicular cliffs and the previously mentioned great inland lakes.

The story of the Manitoulin District is, essentially, the story of Manitoulin Island.

Due to its proximity to the big waters of Lake Huron and Georgian Bay, the climate of the district is reasonably temperate, both in summer and winter. Rainfall is moderate, snow is heavy. Spring comes late in this region and the nights are cool, even in summer.

The original inhabitants of the district were the Ottawa (adawhe-trader) Indians who, in 1615 met Samuel de Champlain on the mainland and told him of their island home, the home of the great Indian god, Manitou. Thereafter the natives were visited occasionally by Jesuit missionaries who, in 1648, established a mission under the directorship of Father Joseph Antoine Poncet. The mission was short-lived, however, as the Iroquois ravaged it in 1650.

Very little information is available regarding the period following this attack or, in fact, for the next 150 years. A legend reports a huge fire which devastated the island and made settlement there impossible.

Following the War of 1812, a band of Ottawa and Potawatomi Indians settled at Wikwemikong, on the eastern end of Manitoulin Island. A treaty of 1836 promised the entire island to the Indians, a proposal which, it was hoped, would remove the natives from the mainland to accommodate the expansion of European settlement. When, 16 years later, the government felt pressure from white groups wanting to settle the island, a new treaty was proposed whereby the Indians would relinquish their claim to the land. Most of the natives complied, but those in the eastern section of the island prevailed in their resolution to hold their land. As a result of their determination, the Manitoulin Unceded Reserve, Wikwemikong, exists today.

In 1838 surveys were begun and European settlement on the island commenced. Manitowaning was the first white settlement in the district. It was established in 1838 by a Captain Anderson, whose original intention was to establish an Anglican mission. St. Paul's

Anglican Church, built in 1845-49 by its Indian congregation, still stands in Manitowaning.

The vast acreages of evergreen and hardwood forest gave rise to a profitable lumber industry, which, along with fishing, farming, and the production of maple sugar, provided a livelihood for the earliest settlers. There was also an early Makinaw boat building concern.

Farming is still practiced extensively in this largely rural district. Market crops are grown in the lush areas and range cattle graze the scrubbier land. Turkeys are raised and marketed in great numbers and fur farms produce mink and fox pelts. Once the location of a booming commercial fishing industry, the district is now more noted for its excellent sport fishing.

In 1869 the Provincial Judicial District of Manitoulin was created by the Ontario Legislature and Gore Bay was chosen as the judicial seat. In 1902 part of the mainland was included and the Electoral District of Manitoulin was born. A further change was effected in 1935 when the district became known as Algoma East-Manitoulin. Since then it has become, simply, Manitoulin District.

The 1891 population figure of 10,000 has actually decreased. The 1979 figures place the permanent population at 7,144, about one-fifth of it Indian.

The district is largely rural, the exceptions being Little Current (pop. 1536) and Gore Bay, the District City, with a population of 791. In addition, there are several small settlements, including Manitowaning, Mindemoya, Sheguiandah, Providence Bay, Kagawong, the Indian village of Wikwemikong, McGregor Bay and Killarney.

The townships include Assiginack, Barrie Island, Billings, Burpee, Carnarvon, Cockburn Island, Gordon and Allan, Howland, Rutherford and George Island, Sandfield, and Tehkummah, and several geographic townships.

Highway 68 runs south from Highway 17, entering Manitoulin Island over a bridge at Little Current. The highway continues south along the eastern end of the island, west of the Indian lands, ending at South Baymouth. Canadian Pacific Railway also serves the district, running parallel to Highway 68, as far as Little Current, its termination point.

The 110-car ferry, Chi-Cheemaun (Big Canoe) provides access to Manitoulin Island from the south, running between Tobermory, at the tip of the Bruce Peninsula, and South Baymouth, on the island.

Little Current, originally designated Shaftesbury, is an important lake port and yacht harbour, and boasts a small airport. The Department of Transport operates a bigger airport, capable of handling larger aircraft and jets, at Gore Bay.

The major industry in the district today is tourism. Sport fish abound in the waters of Lake Huron and the North Channel, and in the sparkling clear inland lakes. Boating is a natural activity in this watery paradise and many impressive boats berth at Little Current each summer. Many visitors to the area come solely to bask in the natural scenic loveliness, or to enjoy the natural and man-made recreational facilities in the district.

On the mainland, Killarney Provincial Park assures the maintenance of the unspoiled beauty of that area, and provides its more rugged visitors with camping facilities.

The founder of Killarney, Etienne Augustin de la Morandière, established a trading post here after the War of 1812. He raised crops and brought cattle to Killarney, then accessible by water only. At one time the small settlement was an active commercial fishing centre. With the opening of Highway 637 in the 1970's, the once remote village is now within reach of tourists.

Manitoulin Expositor, 1967.

Ministry of Culture and Recreation: *Ontario Historic Sites.*

MANITOUWADGE, township, District of Thunder Bay
Position 49° 10′ 85° 55′

Incorporated as an Improvement District in 1954, Manitouwadge became a township in 1975. The area, covering 144 square miles, is comprised of four geographic townships and lies some 30 miles north of the Trans Canada Highway. The population is concentrated in the community of Manitouwadge, about 250 miles equidistant between the cities of Sault Ste Marie and Thunder Bay.

The word Manitouwadge means "Cave of the Great Spirit" in the Ojibway language. These nomadic people were, until recent times, the only ones to venture into this region.

In 1931 James Edgar Thompson, a student working for the Ontario Department of Mines (later the Department's chief geologist), entered the Manitouwadge area to make an assessment of its mineral resources. He reported the discovery of sulphides, and an aerial map of the area was made in 1932.

Several prospectors showed interest, but it was not until 1953 that serious attention was focussed on the area by two Geraldton residents. Roy Baker and William Dawd, who have been described as "members of the fraternity of weekend prospectors", found themselves a third partner, Jack Forster. Forster owned a plane and the three formed an agreement they never regretted.

Flying to the spot James Edgar Thompson had labelled "Sulphides", they were dismayed to find someone had been there before them. However, no claim had been recorded, so they staked and recorded their own claims.

Two months later these prospectors were able to interest a company in their find, and Geco Mines Limited was incorporated to develop the copper-zinc-silver ore body. The enterprising trio eventually received a cash payment and a royalty on every ton of ore mined from their four staked claims.

The results of the test drilling touched off one of the biggest staking rushes in the history of Canadian mining, consisting of more than 10,000 claims. As these claims were staked in the winter, the hopeful prospectors had to wait until spring to find out if their stakes would pay off. Unfortunately, for most, they did not.

However, several discoveries were made near the Geco property. One held by the Willroy Mines Limited (named after William Dawd

and Roy Barker) was particularly promising. Underground development was started in 1957 and also in that year a mill with a capacity of
1000 tons a day began production several weeks before the Geco mill
opened.

In 1954 the Department of Mines had built an access road to
Manitouwadge to connect with Highway 17. Railways put branch
lines into the areas. A town sprang into existence on the shores of
Manitouwadge Lake. The well-planned town has six churches of
various denomination, one public school, one high school and one
separate school. It also has a library and a hospital.

The population is dependent for its employment mainly on the
area's base metal mines and on the Ontario Paper Company.

L. Carson Brown: *Manitouwadge: Cave of the Great Spirit*, 1963.

MANN, geographic township, Cochrane District
Position 48° 50′ 81° 00′

Located northeast of Timmins, Mann Township was named for Sir
Donald Mann, of the firm Mackenzie and Mann Limited, of Toronto. It
is accessible by dry weather roads or by the Frederick House River.

MANOTICK, community, Regional Municipality of Ottawa-Carleton
Position 45° 13′ 75° 41′

This community on the Rideau River and on the CPR and Highway 16,
is a suburban centre for the greater capital region.

Manotick is an Indian name meaning "long island"; part of the
community is located on an island in the Rideau. The settlement dates
back to 1860 when Moss Kent Dickinson and Joseph Currier jointly
began operation of a flour mill, around which formed an industrial
complex which two years later included a sawmill as well as a textile
mill. The old Long Island Mill, with some of its original machinery,
still in working order, is now a historic site.

MANROSS, geographic township, Kenora District
Position 49° 36′ 94° 18′

Established in 1945 by the Ministry of Lands and Forests, the region
was named for Park Manross, MP for London, Ontario, at that time. It
is situated on the east shore of Lake of the Woods, and southeast of
Kenora. Pipestone Park Reserve occupies the northern section.

MANVERS, township, Victoria County
Position 44° 08′ 78° 40′

Manvers Township was part of Durham County until January 1, 1974
when it was annexed by Victoria County. The township was surveyed
in 1816-17 by Samuel S. Wilmot, and was named in honour of Charles
Pierrepoint, Duke of Kingston and Earl of Manvers.

The early settlers were nearly all farmers and predominantly

Irish. Shortly after the survey, lands were taken by Robert McNaughton, John P. McKee, Duncan McDonald, Ronald McDonald, George Gillinger, Josiah Hawley and others. A large part of the township was granted to Bishop Mountain, the first Anglican bishop of Quebec, who had jurisdiction over both Lower and Upper Canada.

In the early 1800's James Preston built a grist mill not far from Bethany on Pigeon Creek. A few years later his brother, Porter Preston, installed a mill for grinding grain and flour about two miles farther up on Pigeon Creek.

The first township council of 1850 met under Reeve William Hunter. Thomas Sommerville, Joseph Porter and Harry Sanderson were the councillors. Bethany is the seat of township government. The present Town Hall was completed in 1912.

Manvers has many fine old churches. Two miles northwest of Bethany there is St. Mary's Church constructed of wood in 1852. Alexander Preston and his young wife, Mary, helped to build this church.

Communities in Manvers include Bethany, Franklin, Ballyduff, Lotus, Yelverton, Janetville, Pontypool, and Fleetwood. Ballyduff was named by pioneer settler Joseph Porter after the Irish town. Here the first Manvers post office was opened in 1858. Bethany owed its development to the Midland Railway built from Port Hope to Lindsay in the 1850's.

The township today is served by Highways 35 and 7A and the CPR.

H. Belden & Co.: *Historical Atlas, Northumberland & Durham*, 1878.

Two Centuries of Change, United counties of Northumberland & Durham, 1967.

MAPLE, part of the Town of Vaughan, Regional Municipality of York
Position 43° 51' 79° 31'

Maple was first called Noble's Corners or Nobleville, after Joseph Noble, the local postmaster.

Until the Ontario, Huron and Simcoe Railway built its line through the settlement, Maple was overshadowed by the more prosperous villages of Sherwood and Teston. The road south from the community (now Keele Street) covered boggy territory and alternate routes were taken by most travellers. This situation was changed by the railway, and Maple began to grow.

A hotel was built in the 1850's to accommodate the increasing number of travellers passing through the community. By the late nineteenth century, businesses included a sawmill, rope factory, creamery, hardware store, shoemaker, and harness shop. Maple became a police village in 1928. Since the 1930's, the number of businesses has decreased but the village remained fairly large, with a population of over 1000 when it became part of the town of Vaughan in 1971.

The first church was that of the Presbyterians, established in the 1830's. Methodist meetings were held from 1835, although a church was not built until 1870. St. Stephen's Anglican Church was organized in 1838.

Maple's most famous native was William Maxwell Aitken, Lord Beaverbrook, a publisher and philanthropist, who also served on the British Cabinet during the Second World War. Dr. Fred Routley, General Commissioner for the International Red Cross Society, in the 1930's, practised here.

Historic institutions in the village include the Masonic Lodge, one of the oldest in Upper Canada, founded in 1854, and the Maple Women's Institute, which was the third one in the world when it began in 1899.

Pennsylvania Folklore Society of Ontario: *Canadian German Folklore*, Vol. 6, 1977.

MAPLEDORAM, geographic township, Thunder Bay District
Position 49° 10′ 85° 55′

Established in 1955, this township, northwest of White River, was named for the Honourable Clare E. Mapledoram, Minister of Lands and Forests, 1954. Nama Creek flows in a southwesterly direction through the area. One secondary road links the area to Manitouwadge, to the southeast.

MARA, township, Simcoe County
Position 44° 35′ 79° 11′

This township on the eastern shore of Lake Simcoe was part of Ontario County until January 1, 1974 when it was annexed by the County of Simcoe.

A survey of the township was begun by J.G. Chewitt in 1821 and completed by Robert Ross in 1836. The name Mara appears to have been derived from the Spanish language.

Patrick Corrigan, an Irishman, was the first settler in Mara taking up Lot 15, Concession 7 in 1823. He was followed three years later by Arthur Kelly. In time came the Camerons, McDonaghs, McDermotts, Doyles, Boyles, Flynns, Duffys, McNultys, and others. The Irish Catholics settled mainly in the central part of the township while Highland Scots were predominant in the northern and southern sections.

From 1850 to 1868 Mara and its northern neighbour Rama were joined in a municipal union. Michael McDonagh served as the first reeve. The first reeve of Mara after its separation from Rama was Philip McRae.

The first bridge across the Narrows (between Lakes Simcoe and Couchiching) to Orillia was built at Atherley in 1853. Atherley, which became a post village in 1851 had grown up around a saw and grist mill opened by Alexander Kennedy. The pioneer of Brechin now a police village on Highway 12, was J.P. Foley.

Several early railways constructed lines through Mara. One of them was the Midland Railway, now a part of Canadian National Railways.

Mara's permanent population stands at close to 3700 (1979), a figure which is swelled considerably in the summer by cottage owners and visitors.

J.H. Beers & Co.: *Atlas of the County of Ontario*, 1877.

MARA PROVINCIAL PARK, Mara Township, Simcoe County
Position 44° 35′ 79° 22′

Just off Highway 12, four miles from the city of Orillia and less than a mile from the community of Atherley on Highway 12, is the Recreation Park of Mara. The Huron Indians once lived here setting up fishing weirs at the Narrows, a channel between Lake Simcoe and Lake Couchiching. Some 350 years later when archaeologists were digging in the channel, these Indian fishing weirs were found. With the beginning of the fur trade, competition between the Hurons and the Iroquois became rife. Samuel de Champlain, French explorer, colonizer and founder of Quebec, who had formed an alliance with the Hurons and the Algonkins against the warlike Iroquois, supplied the Hurons with musketry and aided them in an attack against the Iroquois. However, the Hurons were defeated and vanquished and the Iroquois took over their land around the Orillia area, the Narrows providing them with a fur trading route to other waterways via the Trent River system.

Ontario Ministry of Natural Resources.

MARATHON, geographic township, Cochrane District
Position 48° 56′ 80° 21′

This township was named after the plain of Marathon near Athens, Greece, the site of the battle of Marathon in 400 B.C. and the Olympic Games in 1906. It is located northeast of Iroquois Falls and is served by Canadian National Railways at the station point of Bingle.

MARATHON, township, District of Thunder Bay
Position 49° 46′ 86° 26′

Marathon lies about 200 miles east of the city of Thunder Bay. The area, an Improvement District since 1946, was erected into a township on January 1, 1970. It has a population of 2,323 and covers some 40,128 acres. Most of the population is concentrated in the community of Marathon at Peninsula Harbour on the north shore of Lake Superior. Three miles to the north passes the Trans-Canada Highway (No. 17).

It was the lucrative fur trade that once enticed the white man to Peninsula Harbour. Gabriel Cotté is said to have been the first to build a trading post at the mouth of the Pic River between 1790 and 1792. Around 1800 the post was taken over by the Northwest Company, which brought their supplies from Montreal via the Great Lakes. In 1821 the Hudson's Bay Company absorbed the Pic post along with the rest of the properties of the Northwest Company. Supplies were now brought to the post overland from James Bay. When the American locks at the Sault were opened in 1850, it became possible for steamers to stop regularly at the Pic post on their run from Collingwood to Fort William.

The importance of the post began to decline after 1870 when the Hudson's Bay Company sold most of their territory to the Government of Canada. In 1888 the Company moved the post to Montizambert (Mobert). The land at the mouth of the Pic was sold to a Port Arthur resident who, in turn, sold it to the Marathon Paper Mills.

Peninsula Harbour (now Marathon) was a significant link in the construction of the Canadian Pacific Railway, being the base of operations for one of the most difficult and costly phases of the entire construction program. The charter for rail construction through the area was granted in 1881 and work began in the spring of 1883.

At the peak of construction, an estimated 12,000 men using 5,000 horses worked out of Peninsula Harbour on the railway project. The crew transformed the Peninsula Harbour into a bustling, brawling, transitory frontier town. The last spike joining Ontario and the prairies was driven at Noslo, near Jackfish, on May 16, 1885.

After that peace again descended on Peninsula Harbour, disturbed only by the occasional tourist. The station, section houses and outbuildings were all that were left of the former temporary community. Along the waterfront, weeds and brush once more encroached on the all but deserted town site.

The first permanent store at Peninsula was built following the turn of the century by a man named McCoy. Another store was opened by Mr. McDonnell. A post office was established in 1935 when the population numbered twenty-eight.

In 1936 the General Timber Company of Port Arthur, a subsidiary of the Marathon Paper Mills of Rothschild, Wisconsin, built a warehouse and office at Peninsula Harbour. In the spring of 1944 the company decided to build a pulp mill at Peninsula and by July there were 560 men in the camp. As soon as an adequate dining hall was available 60 to 70 women were brought in as waitresses.

During the six months of development in 1944, the name of the community was changed to Everest. Postal authorities, however, felt that this could easily be confused with Everett, Ontario, and thus, later that year, Marathon, the name of the parent company of the mill was bestowed on the expanding community. The mill remains Marathon's main industry.

The community has a hospital, a public library, a weekly newspaper, two public schools and one secondary school, and there are four churches (United, Anglican, Roman Catholic and Lutheran). Recreational facilities include, among others, a Community Centre, a golf course, an artificial hockey rink and a race track. There are numerous snowmobile and hiking trails in the area.

Jean Boultbee: *History of the Marathon District*, 1967.

MARCEAU, geographic township, Cochrane District
Position 49° 46' 81° 47'

This isolated township is located north of Smooth Rock Falls. It is accessible only by water, notably the Marceau River, which meanders northward, then eastward across the township. The name commemorates Joseph H. Marceau, MPP for Nipissing, 1919.

MARCONI, geographic township, Sudbury District
Position 47° 07' 80° 45'

The area, north of Sudbury, was named for the inventor of the wireless and radio. It is accessible by water, as the Sturgeon River flows through the northeastern section. The boundaries were surveyed in 1909 and 1910.

MARGARET, geographic township, Sudbury District
Position 47° 17' 82° 09'

Formerly designated Township 10, Margaret Township is situated northwest of the City of Sudbury. It was named in 1945 for Princess Margaret Rose, second daughter of King George VI, and sister of the present Queen, Elizabeth II.

MARIA, township, Renfrew County
Position 46° 10' 78° 04'

Maria Township lies in the northwestern part of the county and on the northern edge of Algonquin Provincial Park. In the north it borders on Holden Lake, an expanse of the Ottawa River.

The township is joined with Head Township and Clara Township to form a municipal unit. Together they encompass an area of 197,702 acres with a total permanent population of 372 (1979).

Maria, which was organized in 1859, is presumed to have been named in honour of Anna Maria Yorke, the wife of Sir Edmund Head, Governor-General of Canada 1855-61.

The township is dotted with lakes and rivers. The Trans-Canada Highway travels through the extreme northern part, as does the CPR. Bissett Creek, located here, had its beginnings in 1841 when William Stewart and Alexander Grant constructed dams and slides here at Holden Lake. Adelard is the only other community of note. It is located just to the east of Bissett Creek.

Clyde C. Kennedy: *Notes on the History of Renfrew County*, 1961.

MARIPOSA, township, Victoria County
Position 44° 18' 78° 52'

This township was surveyed in 1820 and attached at that time to Durham County the following year. The name is the Spanish word for "butterfly", but there are no records to indicate why it was chosen.

Despite the fertility of Mariposa's soil, the township was not settled until 1827. The Canada Company had large holdings in the township as did a prominent member of the Family Compact, the ruling class of the day. Finally, in 1827 S. Patterson of Markham, Ontario, settled near the present site of Manilla. Other early settlers in the Manilla area were the Ewings, McLeods, Houghs, McPhersons, Pillings and Winters.

Around 1831 a large group of Scottish settlers, mostly from Argyllshire, came into northern Mariposa Township. By this time speculators had become so numerous that the Land Office refused to grant further land without the promise of actual settlement. For the next three years, a steady stream of pioneers, mostly Canadian-born, came and settled in the central part of the township. Prominent settlers in the eastern portion included Wm. Brown, Wm. Bowes, and John Cruse.

By 1850 the township had a population of 1863. The first Township Council taking office that year included the following: John Jacobs, Reeve; Samuel Davidson, Obadiah Rogers, Robert Whiteside, and William Ramsey, Councillors. A.A. McLaughlin, Clerk; James Thorndyke, Treasurer.

Communities which developed in Mariposa include Manilla, which grew up around the township's first post office opened in 1837 in Jacob Ham's store. The settlement had a steam-powered flour mill and a rake factory by the 1880's. Oakwood had its beginnings in the early 1830's when James Tift settled at the site. The first Township Hall was built here in 1845. A new Hall was erected in 1875. It was replaced in 1924.

Another of the small villages in Mariposa is Little Britain on Mariposa Brook. Harrison Haight settled here in 1834, and built the first mill in the township. By the late 1880's Little Britain was the business centre of Mariposa. It had a carriage works, a shingle mill and a sash, door and planing factory, a foundry and two flour mills.

Watson Kirkconnell: *County of Victoria Centennial History*, 1967.

MARKDALE, village, Glenelg Township, Grey County
Position 44° 19' 80° 39'

Markdale is situated in the northeast corner of Glenelg Township on Highway 10.

The first settlers were George Walker and Joseph Price who took up land along the Toronto-Sydenham Road (Hwy. 10) in 1846. They were followed by John and Lily Atkinson in 1849, George Walker in 1850, and the Armstrongs in 1852.

With the establishment of a post office under John Atkinson around 1851, the community became known as East Glenelg. When Atkinson was killed, his wife became postmistress. Her brother, Donald McDuff, became next postmaster and changed the name to Cornabus, after his home town in Scotland. Finally in 1873, the community became known as Markdale when Mark Armstrong sold land to the Toronto, Grey and Bruce Railway on condition that the town be renamed.

Markdale was a police village from 1877 until it was incorporated as a village in 1888. The first reeve was W.J. McFarland.

By 1880 Markdale had a population of 800. It had express and telegraph facilities and a weekly newspaper, the *Expositor* (now *The Standard*). It also had three hotels, a school, three churches, twelve stores, three flour mills, and a number of factories. The first store had been opened by Tom Lawler in 1858. Shortly after this, Solomon Hill and W.J. McFarland opened general stores. McFarland became involved in the grain trade and in 1883 established the McFarland and Hull Stove Factory. Another large store was run by the Mercer family.

The Armstrong Brothers of Markdale built a sawmill veneer plant, a furniture factory, a cheese box factory, and a foundry. In the 1890's Thos. L. Moffat and Sons established a machine shop. The company developed into one of Canada's foremost heating and cooking equipment manufacturers.

A branch of the Saugeen River, the Rocky Saugeen, running through the town, provided water power for the many mills which were established. The four-storey Barrhead Mill was built by Matthew Irving in 1855. Another early flour mill was that built by J.W. Ford.

With the coming of the railway in 1873, Markdale developed into an important market centre for farm produce and stock.

George Walker gave the land for an Anglican church in 1857. A Methodist church was built in the vicinity in 1869, followed by a larger church built in Markdale itself on land donated by Mark Armstrong. The second church was destroyed by fire. An Anglican church was built in 1880, a Presbyterian church in 1882, and St. John's Roman Catholic Church was opened in 1893.

Dr. R.L. Carefoot, one of Markdale's doctors, turned a former hotel into a private hospital in 1930. In 1949 it became the Centre Grey Hospital. It was replaced by a modern hospital in 1959. Markdale, with a population of just over 1300, has a district high school and a public library.

T. Arthur Davidson: *A New History of Grey County*, 1972.

E.L. Marsh: *A History of the County of Grey*, 1931.

MARKHAM, town, Regional Municipality of York
Position 43° 52' 79° 16'

Situated north of Scarborough and east of Yonge Street, on Highway 48, Markham is a fast growing community on the Rouge River. Formerly a village, Markham became a town effective January 1, 1969. In 1971 when Regional government was established for the area, part of the Township of Markham was annexed by the town, and with that its population jumped from 9,124 in 1969 to 34,113 in 1971. The Town of Markham also includes the former villages of Milliken, Buttonville, and Unionville. Markham's population in 1979 stood at more than 67,000.

The area's first settlers arrived about 1790, before the township had been surveyed. At this time York was still a hamlet and Yonge Street did not yet exist, although its line had been marked out. The first known group of pioneers, 64 German families from Genessee, New York, who were led by William Berczy to the area in 1794, cut a wagon track through the forest from York to Markham. This track was the beginning of Yonge Street. The immigrants settled on the Rouge River and here Berczy built the first saw and grist mills in York County. They were known as the German Mills and, despite frequent change of ownership, they formed the nucleus of the early settlement in the area.

More settlers soon arrived and added to the township's cultural mosaic. Governor Simcoe encouraged United Empire Loyalists to take up land here. English immigrants came in increasing numbers. They were followed by a group of French emigrés, so that found among the early land patents are such names as René Augustin Comte de Chalus, Jean Louis Vicomte de Chalus, and the Comte de Puisaye. Conditions proved too hard for most of these French aristocrats and the majority returned to Europe. In 1794 Nicholas Miller built a grist mill on the Rouge River and the settlement around the mill was then known as Markham Mills.

Joseph Reesor, a Mennonite from Pennsylvania, bought land from Mary McIntyre and in 1826 he laid out a plot for the village of Reesorville. The name was not a popular one and the other settlers first called the community Mannheim, and then Markham after the township. The Right Reverend William Markham had been Archbishop of York until his death in 1803 and the township was named after him. Markham was the name chosen for the post office which was opened in 1828 with James Johnston as postmaster.

Speight Wagon Works, begun in 1830, at one time employed 125 men. T. and G. Morgan, an implement manufacturer, produced the well-known Morgan cultivator. By 1851, with the village's population at 650, there were two grist mills, a woollen factory, an oatmeal mill, a distillery, a foundry, two tanneries, and a brewery. The rich agricultural land in the surrounding township greatly contributed to Markham's development as a centre of trade, and the village prospered. The building of the Toronto and Nipissing Railway in 1870 gave an added boost to its growth and eighteen months later, with its population standing at 954, it was incorporated as a village.

By the late 1920's new industries had been established in Markham including a manufacturer of overalls and a factory producing prepared cereals. Markham's population began to grow after the Second World War, as more people moved outside Toronto.

One of the earliest newspapers outside of York (Toronto) was started in Markham in 1829 by Mr. H.W. Peterson, although it lasted only a short time. In 1856 David Reesor, a native of the village, began to print the *Markham Economist*. George J. Chauncey founded a rival paper, the *Markham Sun*, in 1881. Both papers continued publication until 1915 when the *Economist* took over the *Sun* and brought out the *Markham Economist Sun*.

A hotel was erected in Markham in 1830 by Capt. William Armstrong. The Nipissing Hotel, the White Star Inn, and the Tremont Hotel provided accommodation to travellers by the 1870's. A town hall and meeting-place was built in 1882. A fire department, known as the Markham Hook and Ladder Company was in existence by the 1840's. In 1874 the Bank of St. Lawrence was established in Markham with F.A. Reesor as manager.

There was a school in the village as early as 1830. A frame school was built in the 1850's. The Markham Grammar School, which became Markham District High School, was begun in 1857, with the backing of David Reesor.

The first church in the village was probably the Presbyterian Church which was dedicated in 1840. A second building, opened in 1873, is now the Veteran's Hall. The Congregational Church, now the Orange Hall, was organized about 1850 and was followed six years later by St. Patrick's Roman Catholic Church. The Mennonites constructed their church in 1877.

Well-known residents of early Markham have included David Reesor, who began a chain of cheese factories in the township and was elected to the Senate in 1867; and Colonel Moodie, who was shot at Montgomery's tavern during the Rebellion of 1837. The history of the township is illustrated in the Markham District Museum which is located here.

Jesse Edgar Middleton and Fred Landon: *The Province of Ontario — A History 1615-1927*, Vol. II, 1927.

Pennsylvania Folklore Society of Ontario: *Canadian German Folklore*, Vol. 6, 1977.

C. Blackett Robinson: *History of Toronto and County of York*, Vol. I, 1885.

MARKS, geographic township, Thunder Bay District
Position 48° 22′ 89° 49′

The township is situated west of Thunder Bay and is linked to that city by Highway 590. The Marks, Whitewood and Pitch Creeks flow eastward across the area, which was named after G.T. Marks, of Port Arthur, Reeve of Prince Arthur's Landing (later Fort William), in 1878.

MARKSTAY, community, Hagar Township, Sudbury District
Position 46° 29′ 80° 32′

This compact rural community of some 500 people is a railway station on the CPR. Supposedly a man named Marks was once a telegraph operator at this station. When he applied for a transfer to another CPR point, he received a wire message stating, "Mark stay where you are." Hence the name of Markstay was given to the community.

MARMORA, township, Hastings County
Position 44° 32′ 77° 40′

Situated in the west central part of Hastings County, Marmora is bordered on the north by Lake Township, on the east by Madoc Township, on the south by Rawdon Township, and on the west by the County of Peterborough. The name is the Latin plural for marble, and comes from a huge marble rock on Crowe Lake.

The region was originally inhabited by members of the Ojibway tribe, but in 1820 Charles Hayes discovered iron ore here and asked the government to open up the area for settlement. Marmora

Township was subsequently established in 1821 and attached to Hastings County. A 15-mile-long road was constructed from Sidney Township to Marmora, and by 1824 the population of the township had reached 400. However, there was little settlement outside the mining village as the area seemed remote to most potential immigrants and the poor soil made farming difficult. The prosperity of the township depended almost entirely on the iron works built by Hayes on the Crowe River, and when lack of capital and a decline in markets caused the works to close in the late 1820's, the population fell to 202 by 1830 and remained below 300 for the next decade.

By 1837 the manufacture and export of potash had become the township's main industry. That year, a commission was appointed by the government to inquire into purchasing some property in order to move the penitentiary from Kingston to Marmora. The plan was to have convicts work in the mines and the iron works. However, the difficulty of transporting the ore caused the project to be abandoned.

After 1850, agriculture expanded in the township. A lumbering boom in the 1860's also contributed to the township's prosperity. James Cummins was one of the first to set up a lumbering business in 1862-63. He was followed by A.S. Page, the Pearce Company, the Rathbun Company and Michael O'Brien. The gold rush in neighbouring Madoc in 1866-67 led to the mining of gold and silver in 1870, but the difficulty of separating the gold prevented most mines from being profitable. The iron works, too, were re-established, but the opening of canals on the St. Lawrence and the convenience of the Great Lakes for rival Michigan companies put an end to the venture by 1873. The lands were bought by T.P. Pearce in 1883 for lumbering.

In the twentieth century the mining of iron ore regained its importance and Marmoraton Mines (part of the American Bethlehem Steel Corporation) went into operation near Marmora village. Millions of tons of limestone had to be stripped from the top of large magnetic beds to permit open pit mining. A sintering plant was set up in the 1950's to reduce the ore to a concentrate which was shipped to the company's mills in New York State. Up to 1500 tons of the concentrate were produced daily at the height of the plant's activity. Mining operations were closed in the late 1970's, and the township's economy now depends to a large extent on lumbering, mixed farming, and tourism.

Marmora has been associated with Lake Township for most of its history. In 1978 the population of the combined townships, which cover an area of 137,837 acres, was 1,538. The area is accessible to tourists by Highways 7 and 14 and Crowe Lake has proved especially popular.

Gerald E. Boyce: Historic Hastings, 1967.

W.R. Freeman: A Short History of Marmora, 1946.

Anita Wisti and Jim Airhart: Glimpses of Marmora, 1975.

MARMORA, village, Marmora Township, Hastings County
Position 44° 29′ 77° 41′

The village is situated on the Crowe River in the southern part of Marmora Township, about 30 miles north of the city of Belleville, on the CNR and the junction of Highways 7 and 14. A huge marble rock on Crowe Lake gave the township and the village their name, which is the Latin plural for marble.

Marmora grew up around the iron works opened up in the early 1820's by Irish immigrant Charles Hayes. The subsequent closing of the iron works stunted the village's growth for a number of years but it began to grow again in the late 1830's when lumbering and farming had become the mainstay of its economy. The discovery of gold in the vicinity resulted in increased business activities for Marmora's merchants in the 1860's and 1870's.

Although Hayes' operation had closed in the late 1820's, other companies periodically tried to revive mining activities. The Marmora Iron Works was responsible for a rail link to the village when the mining company amalgamated with the Cobourg and Peterborough Railway in 1866. The following year a spur line was opened from the Trent River to the Marmora Iron Mines.

From 1873 to 1880 gold mining was carried out by the Gatling Gold and Silver Mining Company, but its property was later sold when the operations proved too expensive. Cobalt was also mined in the vicinity for a world-wide market until 1915. A new era for Marmora's mining began in the early 1950's with the formation of the Marmoraton Mining Company (Bethlehem Steel Corporation). Millions of tons of limestone were stripped from the top of ore beds near the village and a huge open pit mine began operations. A sintering plant at the site converted the crude ore into concentrate before shipping it by rail to Picton, where Canadian National Railways had built special docks to handle the export of the ore to the company's New York State mills. Bethlehem Steel closed the Marmora mine in the late 1970's.

By 1878 the population stood at 400. A sawmill and a carding and woollen factory had been set up, as well as the new grist mill of Messrs. Pearce and Son. Another early businessman was B.C. Hubbell who, in 1888, dealt in drygoods, groceries, footwear, furniture, and undertaking. The *Marmora Herald* was begun by Zed LaFontaine in 1893. The Marmora Flour Mills of W.H. Hubbell had gained a widespread reputation by 1898.

A disastrous fire in 1900 destroyed the main business district and forced the relocation of many businesses. Pearce and Co. grew to be the main employer of the village in the early 20th century. The company's enterprises included a grist mill, sawmill, planing factory, dry kiln, sash and door factory, and woollen mills.

In 1901 Marmora was incorporated as a village with Joseph Warren as the first reeve.

The first church in Marmora was erected in 1825 by the Roman Catholics. It was replaced by a new one in 1876. The first resident priest was Rev. Thomas Murtagh, who arrived in 1894. The present Roman Catholic church dates back to 1904. Rev. John Dowler organized the Wesleyan Methodist Church in 1874. In the same year Rev. Charles Mountain Harris became the first resident Anglican rector at St. Paul's. The "Common Cemetery", formerly an Indian burial ground and now the Protestant Cemetery, was the resting place for the early settlers of the village, including Royal Keys, an Irish immigrant who lived to be 107.

Gerald E. Boyce: *Historic Hastings*, 1967.

W.R. Freeman: *A Short History of Marmora*, 1946.

Anita Wisti and Jim Airhart: *Glimpses of Marmora*, 1975.

MARNE, geographic township, Algoma District
Position 46° 55′ 84° 10′

Marne Township north of Sault Ste Marie and formerly a part of the Algoma Central and Hudson Bay Railways land grant, was surveyed in 1901. It was named after a World War I battlefield in France.

MARQUETTE, geographic township, Sudbury District
Position 47° 11′ 81° 49′

Surveyed by Ontario Land Surveyor Gallagher in 1921, this township was probably named after Jacques Marquette, Jesuit missionary to the Huron Indians, 1666-1675.

MARQUIS, geographic township Timiskaming District
Position 47° 59′ 80° 04′

Located south of Kirkland Lake, Marquis Township was named for a Dr. Marquis of Brantford. The community of Tarzwell is situated in the extreme northeastern corner, on the shore of Round Lake.

MARRIOTT, geographic township, Cochrane District
Position 48° 30′ 79° 35′

Marriott Township was named for Hugh F. Marriott, one time president of the Institute of Mining and Metallurgy. Highway 101 traverses the northern end of the township.

MARSH, geographic township, Sudbury District
Position 48° 14′ 83° 57′

Formerly designated Township 44, the area is named for John Marsh, a governor of the Hudson Bay Company in the 1600's. He commanded the expedition to recover Fort Albany, which had been captured by the French.

MARSHALL, geographic township, Sudbury District
Position 47° 58′ 83° 26′

Named for Thomas Marshall, MLA, MPP for Monck, 1911 and MPP

for Lincoln, 1914-19, Marshall Township is situated north of Chapleau.

MARSHAY, geographic township, Sudbury District
Position 47° 11' 81° 25'

Situated northwest of Sudbury, the township takes its name from a Colonel A. Marsh Hay. The dispersed rural community of Appelo is situated near the centre of the township, on the CNR line.

MARTEL, geographic township, Algoma District
Position 47° 01' 83° 09'

Formerly designated Township 5D, Martel Township is located northwest of Elliot Lake. It was named for E.W. Martel, MPP for Sudbury East.

MARTEN RIVER PROVINCIAL PARK, Sisk Township, Nipissing District
Position 46° 43' 79° 49'

Situated in what was once a massive pine forest, this Recreation Park is at the junction of Highways 64 and 11 between the city of North Bay, about 40 miles to the south, and the community of Temagami, some 30 miles north.

A logging museum and blacksmith shop in the park record the history of the early logging days when the huge pines were cut and transported downriver to sawmills to meet the building demand of the cities to the south. Some of the remaining white pines are over 300 years old.

Ontario Ministry of Natural Resources.

MARTER, geographic township, Timiskaming District
Position 47° 54' 79° 49'

Named for George F. Marter, MPP for Toronto North, 1894-98, Marter Township is located southeast of Kirkland Lake. The communities of Marter and Wendigo Lake lie within the township.

MARTIN, geographic township, Algoma District
Position 48° 44' 84° 06'

Originally a part of the Algoma Central and Hudson Bay Railways land grant, Martin Township is located east of White River. It was named in 1912 by the Ministry of Lands and Forests, for John S. Martin, MLA, MPP for Norfolk South during the 1920's.

MARTINTOWN, community, Charlottenburgh Township, Glengarry County
Position 45° 09′ 74° 42′

Located on the banks of the Raisin River in southeastern Glengarry County, Martintown was first known as MacMartin's Mills after the mills erected by Lieutenant Malcolm MacMartin. Among the names of the early Loyalist pioneers of the Martintown area are: John Grant, John Byrne, Hugh McGregor, John Haggart, Donald McBanc, Robert Smith, James Mulloy, Alexander Ross, Sgt. Duncan Murchison, Donald McArthur, Peter Smith and Ebenezar Ears.

Malcolm MacMartin was an enterprising man. Within the short span of three years, 1801 to 1803, he erected a sawmill, a planing mill, a carding mill and an ashery on the west side of the river, and a flour and grist mill on the east side. Later he also built a store.

The forests of Glengarry and the Ottawa Valley to the north were the main source of income for the early inhabitants of the little settlement. But when lumbering came to an end in those areas, many young men of Martintown moved on to lumber camps in the United States. Some families moved to Montreal.

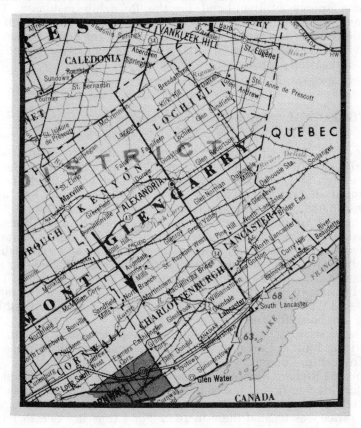

A cheese factory was built in Martintown around the turn of the century by D.M. MacPherson. This brought about a change in the rural scene as large barns went up to accommodate increased dairy herds.

Today, small settlements such as Martintown no longer enjoy the prominence they once had as the hub of the rural community, but they are still remembered in the annals of local history books.

R.C.M. Grant: *The Story of Martintown: A Pioneer Village*, 1974.

MARTLAND, township, Sudbury District
Position 46° 09' 80° 22'

Martland was incorporated as a township in 1905. It was named for Prof. John Martland, Classical Master at Upper Canada College. In 1951 the township merged with two of its western neighbours to form the municipal township of Cosby, Mason and Martland.

The first settlers in this region were four lumbermen who had come from across Lake Nipissing in 1895 to work in a lumber camp. Attracted by the area's rich soil, they decided to settle in this vicinity.

During the last two decades, tourism has replaced agriculture as the main source of livelihood for the township residents. The combined population of the municipality is just over 1600 (1979).

Highway 64 serves the area which contains the communities of Monetville, Chartrand Corners and Noelville. The Wolsely River flows southeasterly through the township.

Ministry of Natural Resources: *Directory of Statistics and Data*, 1975.

MARYBOROUGH, township, Wellington County
Position 43° 45' 80° 45'

Maryborough Township, primarily an agricultural township, was originally a Clergy Reserve. It was named after the Baron Maryborough of Queens County, Ireland, a brother of the Duke of Wellington. It was surveyed by Patrick Callaghan in 1849 and contains 56,986 acres. The population numbers 2,262 (1979).

The first patent was given to John Wells for Lot 6, in the fifteenth concession. The township's pioneer settlers, the Rolls, Bonds, Porters, Greenwoods, Dicksons, and Booths came in 1848 and established themselves on the fourth line. Richard Rolls is said to have been the first man to cross the Conestoga River to settle in Maryborough. The Mitchells came in July, 1849, and the Welshes in February of the same year. David Welsh brought in the first team of horses to the township, trading one horse for 100 acres of land.

The first store in the township was kept by John Dickson. A sawmill was built at Hollin in 1853 by a man named Hollingshead of King Township. The next year he opened a grist mill.

In 1852 Richard Moore settled with his family of ten children. It was after this family that the community of Moorefield was named.

Huston was named for John Huston, the first settler in that area. A post office was located there in 1855. For a time it was a thriving

624

spot with a blacksmith's shop and a hotel.

The first schoolhouse in the township stood on Lot 5, Concession 9, a Miss Tate being the teacher.

Maryborough was first mentioned in 1850 in the records of the United Counties of Wellington, Waterloo and Grey as being joined with the Township of Peel. In 1854 Wellington County had a council of its own and Maryborough elected Samuel Robertson as its representative.

Historical Atlas Publishing Co.: *Historical Atlas of the County of Wellington Ontario,* 1906.

MASON, township, Sudbury District
Position 46° 03' 80° 29'

The French River forms the southern boundary of the township, part of the township municipality of Cosby, Mason and Martland. The western boundary is the shore of Eighteen Mile Bay. The North Channel of the French River crosses the northern half of the township. The area was named for Robt. M. Mason, MLA, MPP for Victoria East in 1910-11 and Victoria North in 1914. Highway 64 follows the northern boundary and provides access into the township.

The pioneers of the area were four lumbermen. Working in a nearby lumber camp, they explored the region with the aid of an Indian friend, and finding the soil suitable for agriculture, they decided to settle. Other families joined them later.

In 1907 Mason was incorporated as part of the township municipality of Cosby and Mason, merging with the township of Martland in 1951.

Prior to 1922, when a road was completed into the region from Noelville, the settlers' only access to other communities was by water. Until the 1960's, agriculture was the mainstay of the township's economy, but since then its importance has greatly diminished and tourism has become the main source of income.

Ministry of Natural Resources: *Directory of Statistics and Data,* 1975.

MASSEY, geographic township, Cochrane District
Position 48° 30' 81° 47'

Named for the Massey family of Toronto, the township lies west of Timmins. Unimproved roads traverse the township from south to north; otherwise it is accessible only by water.

MASSEY, town, Salter Township, Sudbury District
Position 46° 12' 82° 05'

Massey, a scenic town of some 1300 people, is located on the Spanish River, the Trans-Canada Highway (No. 17), and the CPR, about 60 miles west of Sudbury. The town, incorporated in 1904, serves the farmers and lumbermen of the nearby Spanish River Indian Reserve. To the north lies popular Chutes Provincial Park which draws increasing numbers of tourists each year.

The Massey Agricultural Fair which had its beginnings in 1907 when the once bustling lumber centre began to turn to farming, attracts thousands of visitors each year. The fair used to be held in September, but early frost often damaged crops and the time was changed to late August.

Part of the old Town Hall, one of Massey's landmarks, had once served as a livery stable. At the time of incorporation, the building became the municipal headquarters. Consisting of three stories, the ground level served as fire hall and entrance to the municipal offices and council chamber upstairs. The basement area, accessible from the outside, since the building stood on sloping land, housed police headquarters, two jail cells, and a dog kennel built onto the back. A bell on top of the building summoned the volunteer fire brigade in case of fire. The Town Hall was replaced with new municipal headquarters in 1968.

Massey has a public library, two public and a Roman Catholic separate school. The town's houses of worship include United, French Roman Catholic, English Roman Catholic, Anglican, Lutheran, Presbyterian, and Wesleyan Methodist churches.

Corporation of the Town of Massey; Office of Clerk and Treasurer.

MASTER, geographic township, Nipissing District
Position 45° 48′ 77° 38′

Established in 1892, the township was named for Isaac Master, MPP for South Waterloo, 1878-86. Canadian National Railways follows the course of the Indian River across the area, linking it to Pembroke, to the east. The station points of Kathmore and Dahlia are located on the CNR line within the township.

MATACHEWAN, Improvement District, District of Timiskaming
Position 47° 56′ 80° 39′

The Improvement District of Matachewan was incorporated on January 1, 1975 and is made up of the geographic townships of Kimberley, Yarrow, Cairo, Doon, Midlothian and Powell.

The area covers a total of 267,130 acres and has a population of about 520. It lies to the north of the Gowganda mining and tourist region and is served by Highways 65 and 66. The latter provides a link with the Kirkland Lake area to the northeast, while the former connects the district with New Liskeard to the southeast.

MATAWATCHAN, township, Renfrew County
Position 45° 11′ 77° 05′

This township which is part of the municipality of Griffith and Matawatchan, is sparsely populated except for the summertime when tourists come to enjoy the scenic beauty of the area. Centennial Lake, a large body of water in the southern half of the township is the main attraction. Near its shores are located the communities of Matawatchan and Camel Chute. The latter lies on the bank of the Madawaska River where the river enters Centennial Lake.

The township was surveyed in 1859 and its name is thought to be another form of Madawaska, the name of the river which has its source among the lakes of Algonquin Park and flows through the township in a southeasterly direction on its way to the Ottawa River.

MATCHEDASH, township, Simcoe County
Position 44° 48′ 79° 34′

Matchedash occupies the northeastern extremity of Simcoe County, bordering in the west on Midland Bay (Georgian Bay), and in the north on the Severn River.

It is uncertain how the township received its name. Official papers, prepared in 1818 by the Crown Lands Department, spelled the name "Mattuhidah", obviously an Indian name of which it seems "Matchedash" is a corruption. The government of the day appears to have intended the area as an Indian Reserve as it, along with its southern neighbour, Orillia Township, was one of the last townships in the county to be settled.

The Matchedash Road from Coldwater northward along the east side of the bay was surveyed and cut by James Hamilton Jr. in 1830. Captain Hamilton and his family drew 800 acres in the township and settled around 1831 on a clearing near the North River. When the rising waters of Georgian Bay flooded their land a few years later, the family left and moved to Penetanguishene.

As late as 1845 there was only one settler living in the township, but by 1850 there were about seven. Among them were Joseph Gill and his wife who had taken over the Hamilton farm, and the Lovering family.

Until 1888 Matchedash was united with Orillia for municipal purposes. Effective January 1st that year, it became an independent township with Oliver Burrows as its first reeve. In the years immediately following, roads were built to open up the interior and a bridge was built across the Black River. The CPR which traverses the township, was opened for traffic in 1907. Having established the stations of Lovering and Buckskin, the railway played an important part in the gradual expansion of settlement.

The township today (1979) has a permanent population of just over 500.

Andrew F. Hunter: The History of Simcoe County, 1948.

MATHER, geographic township, Rainy River District
Position 48° 47′ 93° 55′

Situated northwest of Fort Frances, Mather Township was named for John Mather, Esq., President of Keewatin Lumber and Mining Company.

MATHESON, township, Cochrane District
Position 48° 35′ 81° 00′

Located between Timmins and Matheson, Matheson Township is part of the municipal township of Black River-Matheson. It was surveyed in 1903 by Ontario Land Surveyor Fairchild and named for Arthur James Matheson, MPP for Lanark South at that time. The area is served by Highways 101 and 610 and by the Ontario Northland Railway, whose station points, Dugwal and Kidd, are located within the township.

MATHIEU, geographic township, Rainy River District
Position 49° 03′ 94° 10′

The northern boundary of the township lies along the south shore of Sabaskong Bay, Lake of the Woods. The township was named in 1912 by the Department of Lands and Forests, after James A. Mathieu, MLA for Rainy River, 1911-26.

MATILDA, township, Dundas County
Position 44° 55′ 75° 22′

This township was named in 1787 in honour of the Princess Royal, Charlotte Augusta Matilda, oldest daughter of George III. Matilda fronts on the St. Lawrence River and lies in the southwest corner of the United Counties of Stormont, Dundas and Glengarry.

Along with all the other townships of Upper Canada bordering the northern shore of the St. Lawrence, Matilda was colonized by United Empire Loyalists. Among the early settlers, largely from the Mohawk Valley, were the Coons, Aults, Dorans, Brouses, Shavers, Merckleys, and Casselmans. These families settled in the front of the township and it was not until after 1812 that later pioneers began to work their way towards the rear of the developing township. The Lockes formed a settlement on the fifth concession in 1815, later joined by the Wholehans and the Doyles.

The first school in Dundas county was built in Matilda in 1788, only four years after the arrival of the Loyalists. A Scotsman named Clark was its original teacher.

The first township council was elected in 1850 and its first meeting held on January 21st of that year. Jacob Brouse served as the first reeve; Philip Carman as the first clerk.

Matilda farmers prospered, particularly in dairy farming. In 1894 the Iroquois Board of Trade was established which bought most of the dairy products produced in the area.

Several small communities and post offices sprang up in the township including Brinston's Corners, Dixon's Corners, Dundela, Glen Stewart, Haddo, Hainsville, Hulbert, Irena, New Ross, Pleasant Valley, Rowena and Toye's Hill.

Brinston's Corners grew around a sawmill built by Messrs. McDonell and Brouse to supply plank for the Matilda plank road. The pioneer merchant and hotel owner here was George Barton. In its heyday the hamlet had two public halls, a cheese factory and a Methodist church.

Dixon's Corners, too, was a lively place in the early days. The first house was built by William Stevens. J.A. Dixon opened a store and erected a large brick hotel in the village. By the late 1800's there were three churches in Dixon's Corners. A post office was opened in 1852.

Dundela received a post office in 1865 with Thomas Wharton as postmaster. Originally the place had been known as McIntosh's Corners. Two general stores were owned by members of the McIntosh family.

Pioneer William Stewart became the first postmaster at Glen Stewart in 1874. Haddo post office opened in 1894 under G.E. McKnight; and Hainsville which had an early grist and sawmill, became a post village in 1887. Richard Hanes, after whom Hainsville is named, was the most prominent of the early businessmen in the hamlet.

Hulbert, Pleasent Valley, Irena, and Toye's Hill, like most villages in Matilda, had cheese factories and at one time were busy postal villages.

Matilda covers 64,486 acres, sustaining a population of 3,178 (1979). The Macdonald-Cartier Freeway and Highway 2, as well as Canadian National Railways, travel through the southern part of the township.

H. Belden and Co.: *Illustrated Historical Atlas of the Counties of Stormont, Dundas and Glengarry*, 1879.

MATTAGAMI, geographic township, Sudbury District
Position 47° 49′ 81° 31′

Mattagami Lake and the Missinaibi River meet in Mattagami, a word which means, appropriately, "where the waters meet". Much of the northern and central sections is occupied by the southern portions of Mattagami Lake, and by an Indian Reserve on the shore of the lake.

MATTAWA, town, Papineau Township, Nipissing District
Position 46° 19′ 78° 42′

Mattawa is the oldest settlement in the Nipissing District and its recorded history goes back to the 17th century. This town of some 2,600 people is located at the junction of the Mattawa and Ottawa Rivers. The site had been named by the Indians long before the white man arrived. In their language "Mattawa" meant "meeting of the waters". Here the great Canadian explorers, missionaries and fur traders, coming up the mighty Ottawa from Quebec in centuries past, turned up the Mattawa River to Lake Nipissing and the Great Lakes watershed.

Through Mattawa passed Brûlé, discoverer of Lake Huron; Champlain, the Father of New France; the Jesuit martyrs, Brébeuf and Lalemant; La Vérendrye, explorer of the prairies, and Thompson, the noted explorer and cartographer. Radisson, instead of turning westward on the Mattawa had continued from here northward on the Ottawa when he explored James Bay, which led to the founding of the Hudson's Bay Company.

Later, to Mattawa, came the lumbermen searching for tall timber suitable for the navy's ships' masts. Those were the days of giant log drives down the Ottawa River. A settlement sprang up, then land was cleared and crops were planted to supply food for the lumbermen. By the turn of the 19th century Mattawa had become a major logging centre and a supply point for incoming settlers.

The CPR reached Mattawa in 1881. Today the Trans-Canada Highway brings tourists into this area which is an outdoorsman's paradise.

In its colourful history this crossroads town has experienced periods of boom including a mining rush and a flourishing lumber trade, as well as days of great poverty when depression dried up the markets in the world. In the 1950's the town once again began to thrive owing to the development of the hydro-electric resources.

Lumbering is still a major factor in this town "in the Pines", but smokestacks of modern industry, shopping centres and commercial establishments tell of great strides in recent years.

The town's population is predominantly of French-Canadian origin.

The North Bay Nugget, September 1968.

Ministry of Natural Resources: *Directory of Statistics and Data*, 1975.

MATTAWAN, township, Nipissing District
Position 46° 22′ 78° 50′

This township borders in the east on the Ottawa River. Logging and farming are the mainstay of this municipality which has a population of about 100, mostly of Anglo-Saxon origin. The nearest centre is the town of Mattawa in the southeast corner at the junction of the Mattawa and Ottawa Rivers.

Both the Samuel de Champlain and Antoine Provincial Parks are located within the township's boundaries. The Mont Antoine Ski area opened in the mid-1970's features one of the finest ski hills in Ontario.

Ministry of Natural Resources: *Directory of Statistics and Data*, 1975.

MATTHEWS, geographic township, Algoma District
Position 49° 00′ 75° 06′

Established in 1943 by the Ministry of Lands and Forests, Matthews Township is located north of White River. It was named for the Honourable Albert Matthews, LLD, of Toronto, Lieutenant Governor of Ontario from 1937-46.

MAUDE, goegraphic township, Algoma District
Position 48° 55′ 82° 55′

Maude Township was named after the British general who was in charge of forces in Mesopotamia during World War II. It is located north and slightly east of Chapleau, and is accessible by dry weather roads.

MAUND, geographic township, Cochrane District
Position 49° 55' 81° 10'

Maund Township was named for Treasurer Maund, of the Timiskaming and Northern Ontario Railway. It is situated north of Cochrane and is drained by the Abitibi and several lesser rivers.

MAXVILLE, village, Kenyon Township, Glengarry County
Position 45° 17' 74° 51'

The village of Maxville some 40 miles east of Ottawa was originally called Macsville, because of the great many people in the area whose names began with the prefix "Mac". The name was later simplified to Maxville. Many of the early inhabitants came from Perthshire, Scotland, where from 1810 to 1815 almost continuous crop failures had plunged them into severe poverty.

The first building in the settlement is said to have been erected by Duncan P. MacDougall in 1869 who, that same winter, built a sawmill. Five years later the mill was destroyed by fire.

Peter McEwen opened the first store in the area in 1870. A blacksmith shop was established by Hugh McEwen two years later.

At that time all the land east of what is now Main Street was owned by John McEwen; Donald MacDougall owned all the land to the west. The present site of the village was still thickly wooded, except for the east side which was partly cleared. Among the fallen trees red and black raspberry canes grew in profusion, a popular place at berrypicking time.

The Campbells of Athol were the mail carriers who brought the mail three times a week on horseback. Since it was often after midnight when the mailman passed through Maxville, it was necessary that someone watch for him because his habit of falling asleep while riding often resulted in his passing on through the village without stopping. The inhabitants of the area did not find this satisfactory and agitated for a post office. It was opened in the store of Peter McEwen; his father, John, was the first postmaster.

The community of Maxville as such did not come into existence until a railroad was built between Ottawa and Coteau Junction via the Maxville area, about 1881. Local trains used this track before the line was completed to Ottawa. Known as the Canada Atlantic Railway, it was later purchased by the Grand Trunk Railway and is now part of the Canadian National's system. In September of 1882 the first express from Montreal to Ottawa pulled into Maxville.

The village was incorporated in 1891. The first council, composed of Reeve A.D. MacRae, and councillors J.P. McDougall, D.A. McKinnon, James Burton and M.L. Stewart, met in 1892.

At one time Maxville had a sawmill, sash and door factory, a carding and cloth-dressing mill, a foundry, a tannery, a grist mill, a pump manufacturer, and a furniture and woodturning shop, as well as several other shops. The Borden's Farm Products company built a plant there which was replaced in 1957 when the original building was destroyed by fire.

Maxville took part in an experiment in street lighting in the early 20th century. Solidified acetylene was shipped from an Ottawa carbide plant to Maxville where it was successfully used to light village streets until electric lighting was introduced.

The village is the home of the annual Glengarry Highland Games which draw crowds of up to 30,000 to the area.

Maxville Women's Institute: *History of Maxville and the community.*

MAYO, township, Hastings County
Position 45° 05′ 77° 36′

Situated in the northeast of Hastings County, Mayo is named after County Mayo in western Ireland and the sixth Earl of Mayo, an important figure in the British government in the 1850's.

When the first settlers came to the area, mostly by canoe from the Ottawa Valley, they found Indian families already living there. The Indians traded with the white pioneers and helped them as they established themselves. One of the best known of the local Indians was White Duck, who lived in the northeast corner and sold canoes.

The township was joined to the County of Hastings in 1858 after the Hastings Colonization Road had been built north from Madoc. Branch roads were constructed in the 1860's, including the east-west Mississippi Road in 1866-67, and the north-running Carlow and Mayo Road.

Archie McArthur erected a mill on the Little Mississippi River in the 1860's, but settlers did not arrive in any numbers in the township until after 1869 when H.O. Wood surveyed lots along the Hastings Road. Among these early settlers were the Kerry, Vandusen and Douglas families. Thomas Dobbs was one of the pioneers at the site of "Old Hermon", while John Hannah became the first settler at Hartsmere, once known as Deer Corner. Despite a report of M.J. Butler, who surveyed the area in 1880, that the stony soil would not be conducive to settlement, by 1890 there were more than 100 resident landholders. Mayo separated from Carlow, to which it had been joined in 1870, and in 1891 William McMunn became the first Reeve of the township.

Lumbering, the mainstay of the township's economy in the early development, was hindered by the fact that the western third of the township was repeatedly burned over and second-class trees grew up. By the early 20th century the forests had been stripped, depriving many inhabitants of their main source of income. Lumbering on a limited scale is still carried on today.

Mining gained importance in the early 20th century. In 1906 the Bessemer Iron Mines opened, providing employment for about fifty men until 1914. The Childs and Rankin Mines also operated during this period, but closed with the advent of World War One.

A school was opened on the Mayo boundary before 1875 and another one was established at Hartsmere by 1879. Mary Wadsworth was the first teacher at a school built at McArthur's Mills in 1896.

The Presbyterians of the area were organized in 1880 by Reverend D. Beattie, although a church was not built until 1910. A Methodist Church opened in 1897 and the Anglicans erected a house of worship after 1912. A number of Mennonites moved into the township in the 1960's.

The first post office was opened at "Old Hermon" in 1875, with Thomas Dobbs as postmaster. Present-day Hermon was originally called Stringer's Corners. In 1881 William Brenner, who also owned a store and a mill, became the first postmaster of Hartsmere. A post office was established at McArthur's Mills in 1895.

In 1979 the permanent population of the township stood at about 378. There are three stores, two churches, two schools and a hall. The area's game and fish resources encourages tourism and cottage settlements are growing. The Toronto YMCA has established Camp Wangoma on Wanamaker Lake.

The township is served by a network of roads and Highway 500.

Gerald E. Boyce: *Historic Hastings*, 1967.

McALLISTER, geographic township, Thunder Bay District
Position 48° 57' 87° 53'

Formerly Township 89, McAllister is located on the north shore of Nipigon Bay, in Lake Superior. It was named after J. McAllister, the constable for Fort William and District during the late 1800's.

McALPINE, geographic township, Cochrane District
Position 49° 46' 81° 10'

The township is situated north of Cochrane. The Little Abitibi River flows in a northwesterly direction through the northeastern section. The township was named after Donald McAlpine, MPP for Brockville, 1919.

McAREE, geographic township, Kenora District
Position 49° 50' 92° 21'

Highway 72 links the area with Sioux Lookout, some thirty-five miles to the northeast. The township gets its name from John McAree, a pioneer Provincial Land Surveyor who surveyed townships along the CP Railway and the Timber Berths.

McAUGHEY, geographic township, Algoma District
Position 47° 22' 84° 10'

The most notable geographic feature of this township, north of Sault Ste. Marie, is the broad Montreal River, which passes through the southern end of the township. The township was named for E. McAughey, a Reeve of McMurrich Township. It was formerly known as Township 25, Range 16.

McAUSLAN, geographic township, Nipissing District
Position 46 ° 46 ′ 79 ° 19 ′

McAuslan Township, named for H.J. McAuslan, a surveyor from North Bay, is situated north of North Bay and east of the southern end of Lake Timiskaming.

McBRIEN, geographic township, Cochrane District
Position 50° 09′ 82° 58′

Located north and slightly east of Hearst, McBrien Township was named after F.G. McBrien, K.C. MLA, MPP for Toronto, 1923. The Missinaibi River flows northeasterly across the township.

McCANN, geographic township, Cochrane District
Position 48° 25′ 80° 29′

Named for the Very Reverend J.J. McCann, Vicar General of Toronto, McCann Township is located northwest of Kirkland Lake. The area includes Wildgoose, Turkey and Turtle Lakes.

McCART, geographic township, Cochrane District
Position 48° 45′ 80° 52′

Situated west of Iroquois Falls, McCart Township was named for William J. McCart, MPP for Stormont, 1902-08.

McCARTHY, geographic township, Sudbury District
Position 46° 51′ 80° 29′

This township, northeast of Sudbury, was named for D'Alton McCarthy, Q.C., of the firm of McCarthy, Hoskin and Creelman, Toronto.

McCAUL, geographic township, Rainy River District
Position 48° 49′ 91° 25′

Named for a Dr. McCaul, of the University of Toronto, McCaul Township is located northeast of Atikokan. Canadian National Railways enters the township at its southern boundary, and unimproved roads provide access into the township.

McCAUSLAND, geographic township, Cochrane District
Position 50° 17′ 82° 22′

Situated north of Kapuskasing, the township was named for James A.

McCausland, MLA, MPP for Toronto Southwest in 1923. Only the western boundary has been surveyed.

McCLINTOCK, geographic township, Haliburton County
Position 45° 21' 78° 50'

The township, situated in the northwest corner of Haliburton, is part of the municipal union of Sherborne, McClintock and Livingstone. The three townships combined have a population of 466 (1979). The area is a land of lakes, streams and forests popular with fishermen, hunters and tourists.

McClintock was surveyed in 1876 and was named in honour of Sir Francis Leopold McClintock, an Arctic explorer who lead the expedition in search of Sir John Franklin. Although he did not succeed in finding Franklin, he did discover Franklin's fate and that of his crew. On his return he was knighted and had the freedom of London conferred upon him. He was made an admiral in 1884.

The voters' list of the township in 1890 included Emmerson and Joseph Allen, Albert Rackstone, Jeremiah Clayton Sr., Jeremiah Clayton Jr., James and Joseph Carlton, Joseph and John Dart, Charles Dawson, Jacob Eeler, Robert Harbottle, Erastus Lockman, J.W.F. Ross and George Tutt, the first reeve of the municipality.

History of the Provisional County of Haliburton, 1931.

Nila Reynolds: In Quest of Yesterday, 1968.

McCLURE, geographic township, Hastings County
Position 45° 17' 78° 03'

McClure is part of the municipal union of Bangor, Wicklow and McClure, the three townships forming the northern boundary of Hastings County. The township's name honours Sir Robert John McClure, the British Arctic explorer who proved the existence of the Northwest Passage.

The area was first surveyed by J.S. Peterson in 1856, who laid out some lots for settlement in the southern concessions. Peterson reported the best lands to be in the southeastern part in the vicinity of the present community of Maynooth. For a number of years Bangor and Wicklow were considered better suited for settlement and not until the winter of 1870 was the rest of McClure laid out into lots. The government surveyors at that time were Messrs. Forneri and Kennedy who had to contend with heavy snow, poor transportation and labour shortages, the latter being caused by lumber companies operating in the area offering higher wages than the government. The surveyors reported numerous swamps and beaver ponds and found that the central part of the township had been devastated by a recent tornado.

At the time, only one small settlement existed in the interior of the township. Located north of the village of Maynooth, it was known as the Scotch Settlement. Maynooth which had grown up on the intersection of the Hastings and Peterson Roads on the four corners of McClure, Herschel, Monteagle and Wicklow was already a flourishing centre with a schoolhouse, four stores and several pioneer industries.

Among the early settlers of McClure were the Doyle, Dillon, Bennett and Lynch families who had come via the Hastings Road from the south. Other township pioneers were the MacLarens, Barrs and Cannons from the Perth area, and the Baragars, Gannons, Hewitts and Hamiltons. In the southeast corner of the township, Michael Doyle opened the first store, and the settlement in this vicinity was known as Doyle's Corners. Here a post office was established in 1861 under the name of Tara. The name was changed two years later, first to Oxonden and then to Maynooth. The township's first schoolhouse which stood on Lot 11 of the Hastings Road was built prior to 1870.

Lumbering from the beginning an important part of the area's economy, received a boost with the arrival of the Central Ontario Railway in the early 1900's.

Lake St. Peter, a settlement in the northern part of the township, was first known as Porterville. It was given its present name when the Central Ontario Railway extended its line northward to Whitney and built a station at Porterville around 1910. Today Highway 127 provides access to the village and nearby Lake St. Peter Provincial Park.

From 1871 to 1874 McClure was part of the municipal unit of Bangor, Herschel, McClure, Monteagle and Wicklow. Michael Doyle served as the first reeve. Monteagle and Herschel withdrew from the union in 1874. The population of the remaining three townships in 1979 stood at just under 900.

Gerald E. Boyce: *Historic Hastings*, 1967.

McCOIG, geographic township, Cochrane District
Position 49° 46' 84° 48'

Situated about sixty miles from Hearst by way of Highway 11, McCoig Township was named for A. Blake McCoig, MPP for West Kent, 1905. It is drained by the Pitopiko and Fraser Rivers.

McCONNELL, geographic township, Sudbury District
Position 46° 56' 80° 37'

Situated northeast of Sudbury, this heavily watered area was named for either Renaldo McConnell, an explorer and pioneer in the area, or his son, Rinaldo, a well known nickel prospector and nickel industry promoter.

McCOWAN, geographic township, Cochrane District
Position 49° 38' 82° 58'

McCowan Township is situated east of Hearst. It was subdivided in 1907 by J.L. Moore. The area was named after Alex. McCowan, MPP for East York in 1905-11.

McCOY, geographic township, Thunder Bay District
Position 48° 47' 86° 26'

The township was named for the McCoy family, who built the first permanent store at Peninsula, about 1900. It is situated on the north shore of Lake Superior, west of White River. Highway 17 traverses the area, as does Canadian Pacific Railway, which follows the shoreline, south of the highway.

McCRANEY, geographic township, Nipissing District
Position 45° 36' 78° 58'

The northwestern half of the township, located north of Huntsville, lies within Algonquin Provincial Park. Established in 1879, the area was named for Daniel McCraney, MPP for East Kent, 1875-1885.

McCRON, geographic township, Thunder Bay District
Position 48° 40' 85° 31'

Highway 17 links this area to White River, some fifteen miles to the southeast. Previously Township 70, it was named for Sergeant Samuel L.W. McCron, RCAF, of Geraldton, who was killed in 1944 during World War II.

McCROSSON, township, Rainy River District
Position 48° 57' 94° 26'

Part of the township municipality of McCrosson-Lovell, this township is located on the southeastern shore of Lake of the Woods. Lake of the Woods Provincial Park lies in the northwestern corner of the township, while Highways 600 and 621 intersect in the southwestern section. The community of Bergland lies to the east of Highway 621. Two small rivers flow north, then westward, to drain the area.
    The township was named for Thomas McCrosson, onetime superintendent of the Mental Health Centre at Penetanguishene.
    The municipality was incorporated as a farming community in January 1929. The population numbers 224 (1979).
    The township has a Lutheran and a Mormon church. Schools and other facilities are available at Fort Frances or Rainy River.

McCUAIG, geographic township, Cochrane District
Position 50° 41' 82° 00'

Numerous tributaries of the Missinaibi River water this isolated township, situated north of Kapuskasing. It takes its name from a prominent Glengarry family.

McCUBBIN, geographic township, Thunder Bay District
Position 50° 27' 90° 37'

Highway 599 runs through the township, located northwest of

Thunder Bay. The name is for Ontario Land Surveyor George Albert McCubbin, of Chatham, Ontario.

McCULLAGH, geographic township, Kenora District, Patricia Portion
Position 51° 30′ 89° 57′

Named for a Mr. McCullagh, managing editor of the Toronto *Globe and Mail*, the township is located north of Thunder Bay. It is drained by McCullagh Creek and the Kawinogans River.

McDONOUGH, geographic township, Kenora District, Patricia Portion
Position 51° 10′ 93° 51′

Red Lake occupies part of the southern and eastern sections of the township. Located northeast of Kenora, the township was named for a prominent mining prospector.

McDOUGALL, township, Parry Sound District
Position 45 ° 25 ′ 80 ° 01 ′

The municipality of McDougall is situated on the Parry Sound, Georgian Bay. The town of Parry Sound is located in the southwestern corner, on the shore of the Sound, on Highway 69.

Canadian Pacific and Canadian National Railways both run through the west side of the township. The community of Nobel lies on Highway 69, north of the town of Parry Sound; and Waubamik, Bell Lake and Badger Corners lie on Highway 124, which meets Highway 69 north of the town of Parry Sound. Trout and Mill Lakes occupy much of the central portion.

The township was surveyed and named in 1866 for the Hon. Wm. McDougall, one of the Fathers of Confederation.

The first settlers of McDougall Township included Wm. Beatty, Alfred Burritt, Wm. Bowers, Thos. R. Caton, Frank Strain and D.F. Macdonald.

The harbour at Parry Sound was known to the Jesuit missionaries who visited the Georgian Bay in the 17th century. The first sawmill was built here in 1857 by Messrs. J. & W. Gibson of Willowdale. A few years later the mill and timber rights were sold to J. & W. Beatty & Co., and a settlement began to grow. By the 1880's about 25 million feet of lumber were shipped annually from this port, and the area with its scenic beauty was beginning to attract summer tourists.

The township today (1979) has a resident population of 1587.

H.R. Page & Co.: *Guide Book & Atlas of Muskoka and Parry Sound Districts,* 1879.

McDOWELL, geographic township, Algoma District
Position 48° 30′ 85° 15′

The township was named after James McDowell, RCAF, from Geraldton, who died in World War II in 1943.

McELROY, geographic township, Timiskaming District
Position 48° 04' 79° 49'

First surveyed in 1907, the township was named for Robt. H. McElroy, MPP for Carleton, 1908-11. It is situated about 20 miles southeast of Kirkland Lake, south of Highway 66.

McEWING, geographic township, Algoma District
Position 49° 30' 84° 35'

Established in 1943 by the Ministry of Lands of Forests, McEwing Township is situated some twenty miles north of Hornepayne, by way of Highway 631.

Most of Nagagamisis Provincial Park is located within the township and shares a common southern boundary. A large part of the park is occupied by Nagagamisis Lake.

The township was named in 1943 after Ross A. McEwing, MPP for Wellington North, 1937-43.

McFARLAN, geographic township, Algoma District
Position 49° 23' 84° 12'

McFarlan Township is located northeast of Hornepayne. Its eastern boundary was surveyed in 1912 by Sutcliffe, its western boundary in 1915 by Lang and Ross. It was named for John McFarlan, MLA, MPP for Middlesex East in 1914.

McGARRY, township, Timiskaming District
Position 48° 09' 79° 38'

The township is situated at the Quebec border and east of Kirkland Lake.

Incorporated as an Improvement District in 1946, McGarry Township was erected into a township in 1962. Highway 66 and Canadian National Railways serve the area, which is also accessible by secondary roads. The area includes the communities of Virginiatown and Kearns and the station point of Cheminis. The northern arm of Larder Lake covers part of the southwestern section.

The township is named after the Hon. Thos. W. McGarry, MPP for Renfrew South in 1905.

The population which slightly exceeds 1300 (1979) is mainly concentrated in the communities of Virginiatown and Kearns on Larder Lake. The area was the scene of a gold rush in the early 1900's. Hugh Kerr and his friend, a Mr. Addison, staked a mine, later known as the Kerr-Addison Gold Mine. A closed company town site was established in 1937.

McGEE, geographic township, Sudbury District
Position 47° 58' 83° 11'

McGee Township, along with its neighbour to the west, D'Arcy

Township, was named for D'Arcy McGee, one-time chairman of the Committee on Immigration. The township, lying northeast of Chapleau, is approached by Highway 101.

McGEORGE, geographic township, Kenora District
Position 49° 25′ 94° 10′

Most of this township, located east of Lake of the Woods, lies under Whitefish Bay. It is part of the Sioux Narrows Improvement District, and the community of Sioux Narrows lies near the eastern boundary, on Highway 17. The township was named for William G. McGeorge, an Ontario Land Surveyor of Chatham, Ontario.

McGIFFIN, geographic township, Timiskaming District
Position 47° 22′ 80° 28′

First surveyed in 1907-08, the township was named after C. Allen McGiffin, *Mail and Empire* Legislative Reporter, Toronto, Ontario. It is located west of Cobalt and north of Sudbury.

McGILLIS, geographic township, Thunder Bay District
Position 50° 27′ 90° 21′

Situated northwest of Thunder Bay, the west boundary of the township is the eastern shore of Savant Lake. No roads or railways approach this remote area, which was named for Angus McGillis, MPP for Glengarry, 1926.

McGILLIVRAY, township, Middlesex County
Position 42° 12′ 81° 35′

The township of McGillivray is named after Simon McGillivray who was a Director of the Canada Land Company in the early 1800's. McGillivray was once the property of the Canada Company, along with the neighbouring township of Biddulph. Both these townships were part of Huron County, but owing to their distance from the county town of Goderich, the inhabitants decided in 1852 to petition for annexation to the County of Middlesex. Annexation to Middlesex County finally became a reality on January 1, 1863.

The extreme western end of McGillivray was known as "the Canada Company's drowned lands", as the area was prone to inundation by the Ausable River. The eastern section of the township is watered by the Little Ausable and other tributaries of the main stream.

Among the early settlers of McGillivray were Patrick Flanagan, Richard Shoults, James Barber, William Carter and James C. Priestly.

The first recorded town meeting was held in 1843 at Robert Hodgins' house. William Carter was chosen clerk; Lawrence Barry, assessor; John Hodgins, collector; Thomas Laughlin, pound-keeper; Wm. Henry, R. Long and Isaac Moody, Wardens. Five others were appointed as school commissioners.

In 1850 when the township was organized under the new Municipal Act, five freeholders were to be elected to form the council. At the time there were only six such landowners in the township. The first reeve was William Fisher; John Flanagan was appointed clerk; Thomas Richardson, collector; James Simpson, assessor; and Thomas Hodgins, treasurer.

By the 1880's several small post villages had formed, among them West McGillivray, Lieury, Corbett, Moray and Brinsley. Ailsa Craig, a railway station on the Grand Trunk (now CNR) since 1858, had been incorporated as a village in 1875. David Craig had been the first to settle on the village site in 1835.

A Wesleyan congregation was organized in the Ailsa Craig area in 1862. The Presbyterians of Lieury built a brick church in 1880. St. Mary's Anglican congregation dates back to the 1860's. In the 1840's the Rev. H.C. Cooper ministered to an Anglican congregation of eighty in what was known as the Devonshire settlement. Father Kirwan served the early members of the Catholic church back in the 1840's.

McGillivray Township covers an area of 69,658 acres and is the second largest township in the county. Sparsely populated, it has a count of approximately 1900 inhabitants.

W.A. & C.L. Goodspeed: *History of the County of Middlesex*, 1889.

McGIVERIN, geographic township, Algoma District
Position 46° 19′ 82° 46′

Located just south of Elliot Lake, McGiverin Township was named for Colonel McGiverin, a former Member of Parliament. It is accessible by dry weather road, and contains within its boundaries McGiverin and Rossmere Lakes.

McGOWAN, geographic township, Algoma District
Position 48° 30′ 85° 00′

McGowan Township is located sixteen miles southeast of White River, by Canadian Pacific Railway.

The township was named for Tom McGowan, an early forest ranger who made the first fire patrol in the Geraldton District in 1913-14, using a railway car on the main CNR line from Gogama to Geraldton, a distance of over 300 miles.

McILVEEN, geographic township, Algoma District
Position 47° 01′ 83° 31′

Formerly known as Township 5G, McIlveen Township lies northeast of Sault Ste. Marie. It was named for C.E. McIlveen, MPP for Ottawa.

McKAY, geographic township, Renfrew County
Position 45° 52′ 77° 28′

This township is united for municipal purposes with Rolph, Buchanan and Wylie.

Established in 1855, it was named after the Hon. Thomas McKay of Ottawa, onetime MP for Russell County and at the time of his death in 1855, a member of the Legislative Council.

Situated west of Pembroke, the township borders in the east on Algonquin Provincial Park. The area is drained by several streams, the largest of which are the Petawawa, Barton and McKay rivers. Lumbering has been carried on in this township since the early days. The scenic area is accessible by secondary roads from Highway 17 to the east.

Ross Cumming: *Historical Atlas of Lanark & Renfrew*, 1972.

McKELLAR, township, Parry Sound District
Position 45° 30′ 79° 50′

Situated northeast of Parry Sound, the township contains the communities of McKellar, on Highway 124, and Inholmes, Broadbent and Hurdville. Manitouwabing Lake occupies much of the western section. The township was named for the Hon. Arch. McKellar, MPP for Bothwell, 1867-74.

McKellar Village was the second stop on the route from Parry Sound to the northern townships of the District. Here the early travellers and incoming new settlers found welcome and rest at the McKellar House run by Wm. Thompson.

The township was surveyed into farm lots in 1869 by J.W. Fitzgerald. The first settler was Peter Leach, a trapper who had come to this vicinity the year before. He was followed by David Patterson who settled near the present McKellar village. Samuel and John Armstrong became the leading figures in the township establishing the first store, post office, saw, grist and shingle and lath mills, as well as a blacksmith shop. Other pioneers were John Henley, Peter Leach, James Brownlee, James Buchner, Samuel Armstrong, Henry Moffatt and Alex. Hardy.

The township was incorporated in 1873. Samuel Armstrong was the first reeve. As the first councillors, there were: Wm. A. Hurd, James McKeown, George B. Lee and Samuel E. Oldfield.

H.R. Page & Co.: *Guide Book & Atlas of Muskoka and Parry Sound Districts*, 1879.

McKELVIE, geographic township, Thunder Bay District
Position 49° 37′ 86° 52′

Named in 1939 for A. McKelvie, a prominent citizen of the Timiskaming District, McKelvie Township is situated south of Geraldton. Its northwestern corner is occupied by a southern arm of Kenogamisis Lake, and McKelvie and the Triplet Lakes lie within the township.

McKENZIE, geographic township, Parry Sound District
Position 45° 44' 80° 00'

This township was named for the Honourable Alexander Mackenzie, Prime Minister of Canada from 1873-78. It is situated north of the town of Parry Sound, and incorporates the communities of Wahwashkesh, Maple Island and Whitestone.

McKEOUGH, geographic township, Algoma District
Position 47° 07' 82° 38'

McKeough Township (previously known as Townships Z and 6Z) lies north of Elliot Lake. It is named for W.D. McKeough, MPP for Chatham-Kent, 1973.

McKEOWN, geographic township, Timiskaming District
Position 48° 14' 81° 31'

Kenogamissi Lake divides the township, east from west. Located West of Kirkland Lake, it is traversed by Highway 144 running north to south on the western side. Surveyed in 1910, it was named after Charles R. McKeown, MPP for Dufferin in 1908.

McKILLOP, township, Huron County
Position 43° 36' 81° 20'

This township derives its name from one of the first directors, and later the Deputy-Governor of the Canada Company, James McKillop. The section of McKillop which immediately adjoins the Huron Road is flat with comparatively light soil, but farther north the township becomes more rolling and hilly and in several places provides an excellent supply of first quality gravel. The township is watered by a branch of the Maitland River and by Silver Creek, a tributary of the Bayfield River.

The nucleus of settlement was centred around two areas known as "the Irish settlement" and "the Scotch settlement". Of the two the Irish settlement was probably established first for records show that at least two Irish families had secured deeds for their land as early as 1827 and 1828. These were the families of Michael Hawley and P. Carlin. The first settlers in the Scottish settlement arrived in 1832. They were the Scotts and the Dickinsons. Other early names were, in the Irishtown area; Dennis, Downie, O'Sullivan, Fox and O'Neill; in the Scottish settlement; Govenlock, Grieve, Hays and Kerr.

The third largest group among the early settlers were the English, but they accounted for only about one-third of either the Irish or Scottish population. In addition, there was a light sprinkling of German settlers.

By the 1860's more than 10,000 acres had been cleared and were under cultivation. Major crops were wheat, potatoes, turnips, peas and hay.

Except for Seaforth, partly in Tuckersmith Township, no major villages or towns developed in the township. Some crossroad settlements developed to the point of acquiring post office status, but the two that reached any size were located outside the township boundaries. They are Dublin (originally Carronbrook) and Walton. Only the northwest corner of the town site of Dublin is located in McKillop Township, the remainder is in the county of Perth.

The earliest settlement in McKillop to acquire a post office was Roxborough. The nucleus of this settlement was a grist mill established by James Scott, driven part of the year by water power from the south branch of the Maitland River and during the dry season by steam.

McKillop's municipal organization in 1842 included the townships of Hibbert and Logan in Perth County. Two years later Logan withdrew to become a township in its own right and a year later Hibbert did the same. From this point until 1856 McKillop was affiliated with one or more neighbouring townships, such as, Hullett, Morris, Grey or Howick.

Until the twentieth century, McKillop had a rather unique system of financing which eventually resulted in the Treasurer of McKillop being left without money. Under this system the township was divided into wards, with representatives from each ward empowered to let contracts and control all township work done in their territory. McKillop, today, uses a system similar to those of other townships.

James Scott: *The Settlement of Huron County*, 1966.

McKINNON, geographic township, Sudbury District
Position 46° 09′ 81° 53′

Situated on the north shore of Lake Huron, the township was named for S.F. McKinnon, a wholesale merchant. Evangeline and Maple Lakes lie within the township, which is located southwest of the town of Espanola.

McLAREN, geographic township, Nipissing District
Position 46° 41′ 79° 49′

Highway 11 cuts across the northeastern corner of the township, linking it with North Bay, about forty miles to the southeast. It was named for Alex. McLaren, MPP for Hastings East, 1894.

McLARTY, geographic township, Rainy River District
Position 49° 03′ 93° 48′

The township was established in 1945 by the Department of Lands and Forests, and named after Norman A. McLarty, MP for Essex West at one time. It is located northeast of Rainy River.

McLAUGHLIN, geographic township, Nipissing District
Position 45° 42′ 78° 37′

The township lies completely within Algonquin Provincial Park and is extensively covered by water. Originally established in 1883, it was named after Dr. James Wellington McLaughlin, MPP for West Durham, 1879-83.

McLAURIN, geographic township, Thunder Bay District
Position 50° 12′ 90° 13′

Kawaweogama Lake occupies most of the eastern half of this township, located northwest of Thunder Bay. It was named after an early settler in the Fort William District.

McMURRAY, geographic township, Algoma District
Position 47° 59′ 84° 43′

Within this township lies the town of Wawa, at the junction of Highways 101 and 17. The Algoma Central Railway traverses the extreme northwestern corner, and Wawa Lake occupies a large part of the northern half of the township. The area is named for William McMurray, a missionary to the Ojibway Indians in the Algoma area during the 1830's.

McMURRICH, township, Parry Sound District
Position 45° 28′ 79° 27′

Located northwest of the town of Huntsville, McMurrich Township was named after the Hon. John McMurrich, MPP for York North, 1867. It incorporates the communities of Whitehall and Sprucedale, on Highway 518, which crosses the northwestern end of the township. Haldane Hill lies within the township and Fern Glen and Bourdeau are situated on the northeastern and the northwestern boundaries, respectively.

The township is watered by numerous small streams running into Round and Buck lakes.

The pioneer resident and founder of the township community was A. Begg, a native of northern Scotland. He had come to Canada in the 1840's and by the 1870's began actively to promote emigration from Scotland. He selected McMurrich Township in 1874 as the site for a settlement for a group of temperance people and built roads, a sawmill, a shingle mill and a grist mill over the next couple of years. His plan to reserve the entire township for temperance people only did not materialize as the government threw open the township to anyone willing to settle there.

H.R. Page & Co.: *Guide Book & Atlas of Muskoka and Parry Sound Districts*, 1879.

McNAB, township, Renfrew county
Position 45° 25' 76° 30'

The town of Arnprior is situated within the boundaries of this township.

The township was named after Allan McNab, chief of a Highland clan to whom the government had granted the land within the township's borders on condition that he pay a nominal price for arable land and bring in settlers within a stipulated time.

McNab arrived with the first contingent of his settlers in the Arnprior area in the summer of 1823. Among the party were Peter and Duncan Campbell, several McDonalds, James Carmichael, James Brown and Alex. McNab. Some of these settlers took up land in the vicinity of Sand Point and at Roddy's Bay.

A second contingent of settlers arrived soon after including the Robertsons, McCoys, Stuarts, Stevensons, Andersons, and Wallaces. James Morris who came with his family in 1830 was to take a prominent place in the life of the township.

Allan McNab, unfortunately, tried to establish the patriarchal rule of a Scottish chief, compelling his settlers to pay illegal fees for their land. A government investigation resulted in McNab being deprived of his rights in 1840. He later returned to Scotland.

The pioneer preacher in the township appears to have been Richard McConnell, a Methodist. The Rev. Dr. Mann of Pakenham was the first Presbyterian minister, and Alex. McNab became the first school teacher.

The township, with a population of over 4,200 occupies the eastern extreme of Renfrew County, being bounded in the northeast by the Ottawa River.

Communities within McNab include: Waba, White Lake, Robertson Corners, Clay Bank, Clay Valley, Stewartville, Dochart,

Braeside, Dewars, Sandy Hook, Sand Point, Goshen and Glasgow Station on the CNR.

Ross Cumming: *Historical Atlas of Lanark & Renfrew*, 1972.

McNAMARA, geographic township, Sudbury District
Position 47° 07' 81° 08'

The township is largely inaccessible by road or rail, although one road traverses the northwestern tip. Named for either John M. McNamara, K.C., or Joseph McNamara, MPP for Riverdale, 1919, it is located north of Sudbury.

McNAUGHT, geographic township, Sudbury District
Position 47° 48' 83° 11'

Situated east of Chapleau, the township was named for Wm. K. McNaught, MPP for North Toronto, 1908-11. The south section of the township is accessible by secondary road and the area is drained by the Nemegosenda River.

McNEVIN, geographic township, Kenora District
Position 49° 15' 91° 10'

Highway 17 and Canadian Pacific Railway lines run across the township and link it with the town of Dryden, about eighty miles to the northwest. The community of Martin lies on the CPR line within the township, and McNevin, Cloven and Lower Scotch Lakes water the area. The township was named after B. McNevin, MP for Victoria, 1940-45.

McNIE, geographic township, Algoma District
Position 47° 01' 83° 24'

Situated northeast of Sault Ste. Marie, McNie Township was named for the Honourable Jack McNie, MPP for Hamilton West. The area is drained by the Aubinadong and West Aubinadong Rivers.

McNISH, geographic township, Sudbury District
Position 46° 46' 80° 22'

The name commemorates former MLA Donald McNish, MPP for Elgin West in 1894. The area is approached by Highway 805.

McOWEN, geographic township, Sudbury District
Position 47° 54' 82° 09'

Originally a part of the Algoma Eastern Railway Land Grant, the area takes its name from a former director of the Algoma East Railway Company. Located southwest of Timmins, it is inaccessible by road or railway.

McPARLAND, geographic township, Algoma District
Position 47° 22′ 84° 02′

The Montreal River flows southwesterly through the centre of this township, situated north of Sault Ste. Marie. The area was originally part of the Algoma Central and Hudson Bay Railways land grant and is presently accessible only by water. The name is after H.J. McParland, a Reeve of Schreiber.

McPHAIL, geographic township, Sudbury District
Position 47° 11′ 82° 09′

Extensively covered by water, and located northeast of Elliot Lake, the township was named for Agnes McPhail, MP for South Grey, 1921-40, and MPP for York East in 1948. Part of Mississagi Wild River Provincial Park lies within the township, on Ramsey Lake.

McQUESTEN, geographic township, Thunder Bay District
Position 49° 47′ 86° 52′

Highway 584 connects the township to Geraldton, just to the south. The Burrows River flows northeasterly across the township, which was named for the Honourable Thomas B. McQuesten, Minister of Highways, MPP for Hamilton Wentworth, 1934-37.

McQUIBBAN, geographic township, Cochrane District
Position 49° 30′ 80° 35′

Named after George A. McQuibban, MLA, MPP for Wellington Northeast in 1926-29, McQuibban Township is situated northeast of Cochrane.

McRae Point Provincial Park, Mara Township, Ontario County
Position 44° 34′ 79° 20′

Situated on a peninsula jutting out into Lake Simcoe from its eastern shore, this Recreation Park can be reached by Highway 12. The city of Orillia is some 12 miles to the north.

Lake Simcoe was an important link in the ancient canoe route that connected Lake Ontario with the upper lakes and used by Indians and settlers alike. The Ojibways lived here, and still do at the nearby Rama Reserve. A physical feature of the peninsula is a "drumlin", a long hill composed of sand and gravel deposited by a glacier from the ice age, on the south side of the peninsula.

Ontario Ministry of Natural Resources.

McTAVISH, geographic township, Thunder Bay District
Position 48° 40′ 88° 41′

Established in 1869-70, the area was named in 1869 after a Donald

McTavish, of the Hudson Bay Company. It is situated on the western shore of Black Bay, in Lake Superior, about twenty-five miles northeast of the City of Thunder Bay.

McVITTIE, geographic township, Timiskaming District
Position 48° 09' 79° 42'

Surveyed in 1907, the area was named for a William McVittie, of Sudbury, Ontario.

Situated some 25 miles east of Kirkland Lake, the township is served by Canadian National Railways and by Highways 66 and 59. The communities of Diamond Lake and Larder Lake are situated within the township on the CNR line.

McWILLIAMS, geographic township, Nipissing District
Position 46° 41' 80° 06'

The Temagami River flows through the southern half of the township, located northwest of North Bay. The township was named after J.B. McWilliams, a Crown Land Agent.

MEAFORD, town, St. Vincent Township, Grey County
Position 44° 36' 80° 35'

This town of over 4,100 lies at the mouth of Big Head River which empties into Nottawasaga Bay (Georgian Bay). It was once known as Stephenson's Landing after William Stephenson who built the first tavern at the site in the 1840's.

Prior to this, the place had been called Peggy's Landing for Peggy Miller, wife of the first settler, David Miller. The Millers arrived in 1838 and their pioneer cabin on the river bank served as a stopping place for early travellers. Miller's son, David Jr., built the first grist mill on a nearby creek, but not being an experienced millwright, he was not successful in his venture. The Miller property eventually was sold to Jesse T. Purdy who built a large mill and became a prominent businessman in the settlement.

A village was laid out in 1845 and was named for Meaford Hall, the English estate of Admiral Sir John Jervis, Earl of St. Vincent. The township of St. Vincent in which Meaford is situated also commemorates the Earl's name.

Hassard Purdy, Jesse's brother, was the first to build a sawmill in the village and Meaford soon began to expand. A school was opened in 1848 with Harriet Ann Purdy as teacher.

In the 1850's Jesse Purdy erected a woollen mill and laid out a new village site on his land. Known as Purdytown it became for a while a fierce rival of neighbouring Meaford.

In 1855 the Northern Railway was opened to Collingwood to which Meaford was linked by steamers and road. New industries flourished and ten years later Meaford had a population of 1000.

Inhabitants began to agitate for incorporation as a village, supported by the editor of Meaford's first newspaper, the *Monitor*. Meaford never did become a village, instead it was incorporated as a town in 1874 with W.D. Pollard as the first mayor. James Stewart was elected reeve, and the councillors of the day were: Thomas Harris, John Hill, J.J. Johnston, Frank Law, David Layton, Lorenzo Londry, John D. McGee, Elliot Thompson and Chas. Watt.

The Meaford public library dates back to a Mechanics' Institute, organized around 1869 by Hugh Watt, the editor of the *Monitor*. In 1967 the Library moved into the former post office building.

A modern General Hospital was opened in 1952, replacing the Meaford Cottage Hospital that had served residents for a number of years.

Over the years Meaford has been the home of numerous industries producing a variety of goods. There were tragic fires and some disastrous floods causing temporary setbacks to the town's prosperity. One of the most spectacular fires occurred in the summer of 1913 when a grain elevator was destroyed in the harbour. For a time the whole town seemed threatened by the blaze that lit the sky for miles around.

Nineteen hundred and twelve had gone down in the town's history as the year of the "big flood". The power dam, a flour mill, a bridge, a woollen mill, a tannery, a dwelling, and the railway embankment all were swept away.

The hero of one of Canada's most favourite dog stories lies buried in "Beautiful Joe" Park at Meaford. Margaret Marshall Saunders who wrote the novel *Beautiful Joe*, had visited Meaford where she was inspired by the story of a dog rescued by a local miller from a brutal master. First published in 1894, the book was translated into at least ten languages, and by 1939 had sold seven million copies. Miss Saunders, a Nova Scotian who later settled in Toronto, was awarded the C.B.E. for her contribution toward securing humane treatment for animals.

T. Arthur Davidson: *A New History of the County of Grey*, 1972.

MEDONTE, township, Simcoe County
Position 44° 38' 79° 49'

It was along the Penetanguishene Road constructed in 1814 from Kempenfeldt Bay as a supply route to the garrison at Penetanguishene, that the first survey was made in what was to become Medonte Township. Thomas Craig (from whom Craighurst took its name) was the first settler along the Road in Medonte, arriving in 1818. The township itself was not surveyed until 1820.

There was very little early settlement in Medonte beyond the Craigs and a few others who came soon after. The area was heavily forested and far from the nearest mill. Stories are recounted of Mrs. Craig who made the trip to Holland Landing and back (some 80 to 100 miles) on foot with her load of wheat on her shoulder.

Another reason the Penetanguishene Road in Medonte did not

attract settlers was the fact that the original route to the military post
had been changed by way of Orillia and Coldwater. Supplies landed
at Orillia were carried over a newly cut portage road to Coldwater
where they were again loaded onto boats and transported down the
river and round the bay to the military post at Penetanguishene. This
road, known as the Coldwater Road, was later extended to the shore of
Sturgeon Bay.

The government set up a mill, store and school, and houses were
built at every mile along the Coldwater Road for Indian families. No
white settlers, unless connected with the Indian Agency, were
allowed on the Coldwater Reserve until the 1830's. Among the early
white settlers of Coldwater were John Borland, who had distinguished
himself during the War of 1812-14, William Rawson and Joseph
Craddock.

Lumbering and shipbuilding were the early industries and the
village grew in size and importance, reaching its zenith in the
mid-1800's. Early prosperity declined when the pine timber of the
area was depleted. Coldwater was incorporated as a village in 1908
and today is mainly a residential community, its businesses catering
to tourists and area farmers.

The first immigrant settlers in Medonte were two Irishmen,
Ferris and McClure, who had set out for Canada in 1831. Ferris died of
cholera at the quarantine station in the St. Lawrence, but his family
came on with the McClures and located on the Oro town line where
Coulson's mills were later built. Captain Steele, R.N., settled with his

family on a grant of 1,000 acres in 1832. The population of the township in 1842 was only 548, mostly settled in the eastern portion, or the extreme west of the township.

The first school was located at Jarratt's Corners on the Medonte side of the Oro-Medonte line. Duncan Clark was its teacher. In 1842 William Lovering settled on the Sturgeon Bay Road in the northeastern corner of the township. A man named Lobb started the first tavern in this area.

George Wilson was the elected representative to the District Council of Simcoe in 1843. When municipal government was instituted in 1850, George Bell was elected Reeve.

In addition to coldwater, Hillsdale and Craighurst were thriving villages. Other early post villages were: Coulson, Creighton, Fair Valley, Hobart, Medonte, Mount St. Louis, Warminster, Price's Corners, and Waverley, the latter being located on the Tiny town line.

H. Belden & Co.: *Illustrated Atlas of the County of Simcoe*, 1881.

MEEN, geographic township, Algoma District
Position 47° 01′ 83° 01′

Meen Township, named for A.K. Meen, MPP for York East, is located north of Elliot Lake. Its most notable feature is Seven Mile Bay, an arm of Rocky Island Lake, which traverses the entire township from north to south.

MEINZINGER, geographic township, Thunder Bay District
Position 49° 09′ 90° 36′

Established in 1945 by the Ministry of Lands and Forests, the area was named after Joseph Meinzinger, MPP for Waterloo North at the time. The area is drained by the Firesteel River.

MELANCTHON, township, Dufferin County
Position 44° 10′ 80° 17′

Melancthon Township, the largest of the six townships of Dufferin County, contains 77,254 acres and is located in the northwest corner of the county. It is divided into the "Old and New Surveys". The former, comprising the first four concessions and approximately one-third of the area of the township, was surveyed in the 1820's by Charles Rankin. The "New Survey" was started when the "Toronto Line" was surveyed from Hall's Corner to Owen Sound in 1848. Known as the Toronto and Sydenham Road, this route traverses the township diagonally from south to the northwest. The following year lots were surveyed parallel to the road amounting to a total breadth of four miles.

The other concessions of the New Survey were made shortly after and were also diagonal to the township lines. Thus, Melancthon has the distinction of having been the only township in Upper Canada whose concession lines were not laid out parallel to one or more sides of the township. David Gibson was the surveyor of these concessions which were an extension of the ranges made in the Old Survey of neighbouring Proton and Artemesia.

The township derives its name from Philip Melanchthon, a German leader of the Protestant Reformation and a contemporary of Martin Luther. His actual name was "Schwarzerd" (black earth), but his family preferred the Greek translation: Melanchthon. The township's name dropped the first "h" in the spelling.

The eastern side of Melancthon is rolling and hilly with deep ravines between ridges. The soil is fertile and suitable for raising wheat, corn and other cereals. The eastern part was once heavily timbered with swampy land in the low areas.

The first person to try to establish a settlement in Melancthon is said to have been Lewis Horning. He came in the 1830's after the Old Survey had been made. He built a saw and grist mill on the Pine River around which the community of Horning's Mills grew.

The community of Corbetton on Highway 10 and the CPR had its beginnings in the 1840's when James Corbett built a log tavern on the Toronto-Sydenham Road near the present-day site of the village. It was here at the tavern that township council met in the early days.

Stephen Sawden: *History of Dufferin County.*

MELGUND, geographic township, Kenora District
Position 49° 36′ 92° 21′

Highway 17 traverses the township and links it to Dryden, about forty miles to the northwest. The township was named after Lord Melgund, Earl of Minto, and Governor General of Canada from 1898-1904.

MELICK, geographic township, Kenora District
Position 49° 51′ 94° 26′

The township lies north and east of the town of Kenora. Incorporated in 1908 as the municipal township of Jaffrey and Melick, the area has a population of approximately 3,500 and encompasses both rural and residential parts. Many of the residents are employed in Kenora, a lumbering, mining and tourist centre. Most services and amenities are found in Kenora. The Kenora airport is located in the township.

MELROSE, geographic township, Sudbury District
Position 48° 22′ 82° 04′

The Groundhog River runs northward through the eastern section of the township, located southwest of Timmins. The name comes from Melrose Abbey, in Scotland.

MEMASKWOSH, geographic township, Algoma District
Position 48° 24′ 85° 15′

Formerly designated Township 33, Range 28, Memaskwosh Township lies northwest of Wawa. In 1974 it was named for Louis Memaskwosh, the Indian Chief who was the first fire ranger in the Pays Plat District and a guide for surveyors and railway exploration teams in that area.

MENAPIA, geographic township, Cochrane District
Position 49° 30' 81° 23'

Menapia Township is located approxiamtely twenty miles northeast of Smooth Rock Falls. It is served by the Ontario Northland Railway, and is also accessible by road. The community of Island Falls and the station points of Island Falls and McInnis lie in the northeastern quarter of the township.

MENARD, geographic township, Algoma District
Position 46° 56' 83° 39'

Menard Township was named in 1974 for Rene Menard, a Jesuit missionary who, in 1660, travelled up the Ottawa River, through Lake Huron and the Sault, and said the first Mass heard on the "Northern Sea".

MENARY, geographic township, Rainy River District
Position 48° 57' 93° 54'

Established in 1945, the township was named for Lewis Menary, MP for Wellington North at that time. It is located to the northeast of Rainy River and is accessible by Highway 71.

MENZIES, geographic township, Algoma District
Position 48° 09' 84° 51'

Formerly Township 30, Range 25, Menzies Township was named in 1974 after Edison Menzies, a Canadian Army Sergeant killed in 1945 in World War II. It is situated about twelve miles north of Wawa.

MERCER, geographic township, Algoma District
Position 49° 38' 84° 59'

Named for C.G. Mercer, MPP for Durham from 1937-43, Mercer Township located north of Hornepayne, was established in 1943.

MEREDITH, geographic township, Algoma District
Position 46° 29' 83° 55'

This township is Indian Lands. Surveyed in 1875, it was named after the Hon. Sir William Meredith, elected to the Legislative Assembly in 1872, and appointed Chief Justice of Ontario in 1912.

Located east of Sault Ste Marie, the township is part of the municipal union of Macdonald, Meredith and Aberdeen Additional.

MERLIN, police village, Raleigh & Tilbury East Townships, Kent County
Position 42° 14' 82° 14'

The village is located on the Chesapeake and Ohio Railway southeast of Windsor, about three miles inland from the Lake Erie shore. Formerly known as Smith's Corners, Merlin became a police village in 1917.

Although there were a few farm settlements in this largely agricultural area by the early 1820's, the first settlers on the site of the present village did not arrive until 1830. They were a Mr. Smith and his five sons, and John Powell. William Hickey came in 1833. Powell had settled on Lot 2, Middle Road South; Hickey took up Lot 2, Middle Road North.

A hamlet of sorts gradually developed at the intersection of the Raleigh-Tilbury East town line and the Middle Road. In the late 1840's the Rev. William King settled nearby with a number of freed slaves from the United States forming the nucleus of a small negro community.

A post office was opened on the southeast corner of the intersection in 1855 with Patric Sullivan as postmaster. As there was another Smith's Corners in Ontario, the name was changed in the 1860's to Merlin. A merlin is a small European falcon, but it is not known why or by whom the name was chosen.

In 1877 George C. Marshall built a saw and grist mill as well as a mercantile establishment at Merlin giving the settlement its first economic boost and thus laying the foundation for its future growth.

By the 1880's there were several stores and shops and a temperance hotel. A Methodist Church was built at the cost of $5,000. in 1898.

Merlin's subsequent development was aided by the construction of the Lake Erie and Detroit River Railway (now Chesapeake and Ohio) in 1894.

Victor Lauriston: *Romantic Kent: The Story of a County, 1626-1952*, 1952.

Municipal Office.

MERRICK, geographic township, Nipissing District
Position 46° 30' 79° 27'

Merrick Township is located about fifteen miles north of North Bay on Highway 11. The name of the township is in honour of Henry Merrick, MPP for Leeds and Grenville North, 1871-75.

MERRICKVILLE, village, Montague Township, Lanark County and Wolford Township, Grenville County
Position 44° 55' 75° 50'

The first white man to settle in the area of Merrickville some 40 miles south of Ottawa, was William Merrick, a Loyalist of Welsh descent from Massachusetts. He had been a millwright, so he brought his family to settle by the falls on the Rideau River, 25 miles from the nearest settlement, in order to re-establish himself in his trade. John

Chester was operating a store and Samual Dow a blacksmith shop near the falls before the turn of the 18th century.

By 1800 Merrick had dammed the river and had built a sawmill followed in 1803 by a grist mill. Other units were added as more settlers arrived. The McCreas, Staffords, Chesters, and Dows were among the early pioneers of the community, known as Merrick's Mills. The War of 1812 had made it apparent that a supply route other than the St. Lawrence River was needed along the Canada-United States border between Montreal and Kingston. Consequently, in 1826 Lt. Col. John By of the Royal Engineers began the building of the Rideau Canal which would go through all-Canadian territory. Thousands of skilled workmen were brought from the British Isles to work on the waterway. Many remained and built the fine stone houses and buildings that still grace the Rideau area.

Merrickville Blockhouse   Mika Collection

A blockhouse to defend the canal should the need arise was erected at Merrickville to accommodate some fifty men. Restored and preserved to this day, it never saw military action, but over the years has served as lockmaster's quarters and canal maintenance building, and even as a church.

Construction of the canal which was completed in 1832 greatly helped to stimulate the growth of the village. A post office had been opened in 1829 under the name of Merrickville. By 1850 the community had a population of about 700. There were two flour mills, a cloth factory and various other industries. In 1859 M.W.H. Magee and William Pearson formed a partnership and established a company to make farm implements, stoves and small items. After the death of Mr. Magee in 1887, the business was sold to Roger C. Percival, the founder of the Percival Plow and Stove Co., who put Merrickville on the map with his products which were sold across the country. The firm was eventually divided into two parts, one remains as a foundry the other is a boat works. With the increase in population, Wm. Merrick and his sons expanded their operations. They had a sawmill, two grinding mills, a shingle mill, an inn, a store and a woollen mill which operated from 1848 to 1954.

The canal brought a great deal of traffic through Merrickville until 1880 as goods passed between Kingston and Montreal. With the opening of the St. Lawrence River Canals and the coming of the railways, the Rideau Canal's role as a commercial artery ended.

In 1884 the Ontario and Quebec Railway which passed through Merrickville was leased by the Canadian Pacific Railway and became part of the main line between Montreal and Toronto.

The first nursery and seed farm in Ontario was located just east of the village, and it was at Merrickville that the Rev. Ernest Thomas organized in 1908 one of Canada's first Boy Scout troops.

Max and Virginia Martyn: The Story of the Lower Rideau Settlement: Merrickville, Burrit's Rapids and District, 1976.

MERRITT, geographic township, Sudbury District
Position 46° 14' 81° 45'

The town of Espanola is situated within this township, about sixty miles southwest of Sudbury. The township was named in 1873 for Thos. H. Merritt, President of the Imperial Bank.

MERRITTON, part of the city of St. Catharines, Regional Municipality of Niagara
Position 43° 10' 79° 15'

Merritton, once a town in Lincoln County, is now part of St. Catharines. The town had evolved from a group of settlements which grew into one. They included Centreville, Westport, Protestant Hill and Slabtown.

The chief industry of Centreville was Towers' Gristmill. The names of some of the first settlers in the area who arrived in 1783 or 1784 are George Hartsell, Philip Shaven, Ball and Newkirk, followed shortly after 1800 by Thomas Ker and Robert and David Bessey.

The completion of the first Welland Canal in 1829 gave the early impetus to the growth of the settlement. About 1850 the Welland Canal Loan Co. was formed under the management of the Hon. Jas. R. Benson and the Hon. W.H. Merritt. In 1851 this company bought up a large part of Merritton to found an industrial area and to develop the water power. At this time the community was called Welland City. It was in 1858 that it became known as Merritton.

Following the formation of the Loan Co., Merritton flourished; sawmills, grist mills, cotton mills, paper mills and various other businesses sprang up.

The village was well supplied with rail facilities as early as 1852 with three lines running past its door. The first electric railway on the

North American continent was built in 1887 to connect Merritton and St. Catharines. By 1918 the population was 2,358 and the village became a town.

Frequently spoken of as "The Factory Town", Merritton has continued to attract industries to its gate and its population is still growing.

The name of Merritton did not die with the town's annexation in 1961, for this area is still known as the Merritton Ward, a reminder of its proud past.

The Hamilton Spectator, 1961.

A.E. Coombs: Niagara Peninsula and the New Welland Canal, 1930.

MERSEA, township, Essex County
Position 42° 08′ 82° 34′

Mersea Township occupies the southeastern corner of Essex County where a peninsula with Point Pelee National Park at its tip juts into Lake Erie. Point Pelee forms the southern mainland extremity of Canadian territory, and is noted as a resting place of migratory birds.

Mersea was named after an island in the North Sea off the coast of Essex County, England and was surveyed in 1818 by Col. Burwell. At the time Talbot Street was being extended to the site of present-day Leamington. The first settlers located on the Talbot Road. Among them were the Fox and Wigle families. The latter's name is perpetuated in the community of Wigle, north of Leamington. Other pioneer settlers were William Coultis, Charles Hairsine, Francis Wilkinson, John Lemarsh, John Richardson, and Alexander Wilkinson. The first store in the township was opened by William Emridge around 1824, just east of Leamington.

The first township council session under the new Municipal Act of Ontario was held on January 21, 1850. Ralph Foster was elected reeve. Fred Ambridge and George Dresser became auditors. Joseph D. Otter was appointed clerk, F.A. Wilkinson, assessor, and Ralph Foster Jr., tax collector. A post office under the name of Mersea was opened in 1851.

Leamington, surrounded by a prosperous agricultural region, grew into an incorporated village by 1875 and became a town in 1890. It is located at the junction of the Michigan Central and the Chesapeake & Ohio Railways.

The village of Wheatley developed on the Kent county line. The first Methodist church in the township was the Derbyshire church, built about 1854. It was located two miles west of Wheatley. Mersea's first Church of England had been constructed in 1837 on the William Siddall farm two miles east of Leamington. It was the first church built in Mersea Township.

Baptists built the Gosfield and Mersea Temple at Olinda in the 1830's. A church at Blytheswood was established by the Presbyterians in the late 1860's. The first Roman Catholic Church was erected at the end of 1882.

The area is noted for its rich soil suited for the production of fruit and vegetables. Mersea agricultural exhibitions were first held in 1848. Today known as the Leamington District Fair, it is one of the oldest such fairs in Western Ontario.

H. Belden & Co.: *Historical Atlas of Essex County*, 1881.

METCALFE, township, Middlesex County
Position 42° 53' 81° 44'

The township of Metcalfe did not exist prior to 1846, at which time portions of the adjoining townships of Ekfrid and Adelaide were detached and set off to form a new township. The newly created township was named Metcalfe, in honour of Lord Metcalfe, the Governor-General of Canada, 1844-45. Lord Metcalfe died in 1846.

The first settlement in the area was formed when a number of retired officers established a small colony in the northern section of the township around 1832. Among them were Captain Beear who obtained a large tract on Sydenham Creek, and Captains Johnston and Hughes. Several other of the "commuted pensioners", as they were called, who came at that time were unable to cope with the privations of life in the backwoods. The township in those days was an unbroken forest.

David Brown was the first to settle in the Ekfrid side of the township in 1834. He lived only two years after his arrival but his son, Robert, carried on and later served as reeve. John Lemon and George Mortimer arrived in this area about the same time. The western portion of Metcalfe was settled mostly by Scotsmen. Among them were the Walkers, the Mitchells, and the McCallums.

A large number of settlers arrived shortly after these pioneers and by 1838 the township was fairly settled. At this time the nearest markets were London, 30 miles away, and Port Stanley, 50 miles distant. To reach the nearest grist mill, the early pioneers had to travel 20 miles south to the River Thames.

Napier, on the Sydenham River, emerged as the principal village of Metcalfe. Here a Mr. Keefer, originally from Strathroy, in partnership wth Col. Arthur built a sawmill in 1852 to utilize the walnut timber of the area. They also opened a store, and Mr. Keefer acted as the first postmaster. Only a few years later, Napier had a population of 150, and its industries included Sutherland & Co.'s grist, saw, and woollen mills, and the steam grist and sawmills owned by Henry Sifton.

Another early village was Katesville, which in the mid-nineteenth century had a population of 150.

The population of Metcalfe, which comprises an area of 37,523 acres, is said to have been about 3,000 in 1878; this figure has declined to less than 900 (1979).

W.A. and C.L. Goodspeed: *The History of the County of Middlesex*, 1889.

METHUEN, township, Peterborough County
Position 44° 40' 77° 58'

This township commemorates the name of the Duke of Richmond,

Baron of Methuen. (Near the village of Methuen and historic Methuen Castle in Scotland, Robert Bruce was defeated by the English in the early 14th century.)

Methuen Township was joined, very early on in its history, to its neighbouring Township of Belmont. These two townships are located in the southeast corner of Peterborough County. They lie astride the Crowe River Valley with Methuen north of Belmont. Their economy depends mainly upon lumbering, mining, farming and tourism.

The two townships were surveyed in 1823 by Henry Ewing, but it was not until 1857 that the first settler, John Vansickles, moved into Methuen Township. The settlement did not increase at a rapid pace, the number of ratepayers in 1866 was only 22.

By 1870 lumbering was providing the townships with a heyday which has not been matched since. It is said that some of the finest pine in Canada was taken out of this area. The population then was perhaps three times what it is today.

Belmont has faired better than its more remote partner in respect to mining, but the northern part of Methuen Township contains enormous deposits of Lepheline Syenite. This material is used in the glass industry and in the glazing of tile and plumbing goods. These unique deposits are expanding their markets every year and have reserves for the next hundred years.

The combined population of Belmont and Methuen today is 2,120 (1979).

Peterborough Historical Atlas Foundation Inc.: *Illustrated Historical Atlas of Peterborough County 1825-1875*, 1975.

Donald Kelloway, Clerk-Treasurer of Belmont and Methuen.

MICHANO, geographic township, Algoma District
Position 47° 59′ 84° 20′

Originally a part of the Algoma Central and Hudson Bay Railways land grant, Michano Township was named in 1974 for Toussant Michano, an Indian Chief from Pic Township (Heron Bay). It lies approximately 30 miles east of the town of Wawa by way of Highway 101.

MICHAUD, geographic township, Cochrane District
Position 48° 30′ 80° 05′

Named after J. Michaud, MPP for the West Riding of Nipissing, in 1902, Michaud Township lies north of Kirkland Lake and east of Matheson. Highway 101 passes through the northeastern corner.

MICHENER, geographic township, Thunder Bay District
Position 48° 49′ 89° 49′

Named for Roland Michener, former Governor General of Canada, the township is located northwest of Thunder Bay. The community of Horne lies just north of the southern boundary, on the CNR line. The Oshkondaga River flows southward through the township.

MICHIPICOTEN, township, Algoma District
Position 48° 00′ 84° 45′

The township is a sportsman's and tourist's paradise and embraces the community of Wawa. The latter is noted for its huge monument of a Canada Goose which stands at the entrance to the little town.

Michipicoten Township was created on January 1, 1952. The name is Indian for "great bluff". The area was opened up in 1960 when the final link was completed in the Trans-Canada Highway (17). A mining and sintering operation is carried out in the township.

Ministry of Natural Resources.

Directory of Statistics and Data.

MICKLE, geographic township, Timiskaming District
Position 47° 43′ 80° 28′

The township is located southwest of Kirkland Lake and its southern half is traversed by Highway 560. It was named for George R. Mickle, a mining assessor of Toronto.

MIDDLEBORO, geographic township, Sudbury District
Position 47° 54′ 81° 50′

Surveyed in 1911 by H.J. Beatty, the area was named for an unidentified former member of Parliament. It is located northwest of Sudbury and is accessible by road.

MIDDLE FALLS PROVINCIAL PARK, Stuart Location Township, Thunder Bay District
Position 48° 01′ 89° 37′

About 36 miles south of the city of Thunder Bay, this small Recreation Park, is on the Pigeon River and is five miles north of the Pigeon River International Bridge border-crossing to the United States. There are three waterfalls on the lower 21-mile stretch of the Pigeon River and the park is located at the middle waterfall. Highways 61 and 593 both give access to the park.

Ontario Ministry of Natural Resources.

MIDDLESEX, county
Position 43° 00′ 81° 25′

Prior to 1794, the county was an unbroken wilderness. Governor Simcoe, on his way to visit the fort at Detroit, passed through Middlesex in February 1793. Major Littlehales, who accompanied him on the journey, tells in his journal, that the party breakfasted at the Delaware Indian village on the high bank of the Thames River. On their way they came across the occasional fur trader, Chippewas making maple sugar, but no white settlers.

The first permanent settlement was established in the Township of Delaware, near the Thames River. Delaware Village, just north of the present village, was the first to be called a village. Here the pioneering families of the Springers and Tiffanys settled and a mill was erected at the beginning of the 1800's.

Middlesex County was named after the County of Middlesex, England. At the time the area was opened up for settlement, Middlesex was known as Suffolk County. It was part of the Western District, the seat of which was Turkey Point (in present-day Norfolk County) until 1816 when it was transferred to Vittoria (also in Norfolk). In 1827 the District seat was moved once again, this time to London in Middlesex County.

Until 1852 Middlesex County also included the Townships of Bayham, Malahide, South Dorchester, Dunwich, Southwold, Aldborough and Yarmouth. These southern townships were separated from Middlesex that year to form the new county of Elgin. In 1865 the townships of McGillivray and Biddulph, formerly part of Huron County to the north, were added to the County of Middlesex.

A road was opened up in the county very early, from Delaware Village westward to Chatham. Longwoods road, as it was called, was little more than an Indian trail back then. During the War of 1812-14 the road was continued eastward to Burlington Heights. Built under the direction of commissioners appointed by the government, it was known as Commissioners' Road, part of which later became the Hamilton Road. Another road, the North Talbot Road, was opened under the direction of Col. Talbot. Along these early roads settlement proceeded. About 1832 the Egremont Road through Lobo and Adelaide Townships was opened; the Canada Company built the Goderich Road through London, and on through the townships of Biddulph, McGillivray, and a part of the County of Huron to Goderich. This colonization road assisted in the opening up of East and West Williams, Biddulph and McGillivray for settlement. These latter townships were part of the tract of land owned by the Canada Company.

During the War of 1812-14 the Battle of the Thames took place in Middlesex on October 5, 1813, about three miles west of the Moravian Village. The British under General Proctor were greatly outnumbered by the Americans and were quickly routed. Tecumseh, the Chief of the Shawnees, was killed during the battle, a great loss to his tribe and to the British. Middlesex men took part in other smaller skirmishes during the course of this war. Their numbers were not large since the only settlements at the time were at Delaware and Westminster with a few families scattered along the Longwoods Road.

There were only two post offices in the County of Middlesex in 1831. One was at London with the Hon. G.J. Goodhue as postmaster; the other at Delaware under postmaster B.B. Brigham.

It was not until 1842 that records are available of a Municipal Council having control of the expenditure of money raised through municipal taxation. John Wilson, Q.C., was the Warden of the county that year.

London at the forks of the Thames River became a police village in 1840. Its name recalls the fact that Governor Simcoe had once chosen its site as the place where Upper Canada's capital should be built. His plans did not materialize, but the name of England's capital was attached first to London Township and later to the district capital. London received its first impetus when it became the judicial centre of the Western District in 1827. Later it grew into the trading and industrial capital of the county. In 1848 it was incorporated as a town, and in 1855, only two years after the Great Western Railway had built its line through London, it became a city. Since then London, the seat of Middlesex County and now a city of nearly 257,000, has developed into the metropolis of western Ontario. With its vastly diversified industries, its large financial and educational institutions, its location at the hub of a modern transportation network that includes highway, rail and air facilities, and its importance as an ecclesiastical centre and military headquarters, London ranks among the great cities of the country.

From the 1860's to the 1880's the development of the petroleum trade boosted the fortunes of the county and inflicted many with "oil fever". Oil refineries were built in London adding to the growing prosperity of this community. New industries sprang up in the years to follow with breweries emerging as the most important. Railways were encouraged to enter the county and in return fostered the development of the area. The main line of the Great Western built in 1853 entered the western side of the county, just north of the Thames, in North Dorchester, crossing that township, and traversed the townships of London, Lobo, Caradoc, Ekfrid and Mosa. Along this line many villages sprang up including Mount Bridges, Glencoe and Newbury. In 1858 the Grand Trunk Railway was opened. About 1865 the Sarnia Branch of the Great Western was built from Komoko, near London, to Sarnia; Glencoe and Buffalo were joined in 1870 by the Canada Air Line Railway. In 1876 the London, Huron, Bruce Railway was opened.

Much of Middlesex County is comprised of rich agricultural land, which is drained by the Thames River and its tributaries. The landscape is gently rolling with fertile valleys between the ridges.

There are two incorporated towns within the county: Parkhill and Strathroy. The county's five villages are Ailsa Craig, Glencoe, Lucan, Newbury and Wardsville.

Ailsa Craig in McGillivray Township had its beginnings in 1835 when David Craig settled on the site.

Glencoe, which lies midway between London and Chatham on the CNR, is the largest village in the county. The area where it stands was still a swamp in 1860 when A.P. McDonald and Ross made the first plan of the village.

Lucan, second largest village in the county, was founded in anticipation of the Grand Trunk constructing a line through Biddulph Township westward to Sarnia. Its early settlers were members of the Wilberforce Settlement, a Negro colony founded by fugitive slaves from the United States with the help of Quakers in the area, around 1830.

Newbury was once known as Wardsville Station. The first house here was built in 1851 by Robert Thompson south of the railway. A post office was opened here in 1853.

Wardsville, a short distance to the southeast of Newbury, was first settled in 1810 by George Ward who purchased the land from the Indians.

Parkhill, a town of 1300, is located in a cattle farming district on the CNR halfway between Stratford and Sarnia and is the gateway to the Lake Huron resort areas.

The town of Strathroy on the Sydenham River has a population of about 8,400. It grew around an early sawmill, but a townsite was not laid out until 1850. It was incorporated as a village soon after the railway's arrival in 1856, and became a town in 1870.

The townships within its borders include: Adelaide, Biddulph, Delaware, East Williams, Ekfrid, Lobo, London, McGillivray, Metcalfe, Mosa, North Dorchester, Westminster, West Nissouri and West Williams. Most of the townships are rural in nature with the exception of London and Westminster, both of which derive their urban character from the proximity of the city of London.

H.R. Page & Co.: *Illustrated Historical Atlas of Middlesex Ontario*, 1878.

MIDLAND, town, Tay Township, Simcoe County
Position 44° 45′ 79° 53′

The town is located about 90 miles northwest of Toronto on Georgian Bay, in the heart of historic Huronia. The Midland region was once populated by members of the Huron Indian tribe. Near the site of the present town, French Jesuit missionaries established the mission of Sainte-Marie-among-the-Hurons in 1639, at the time the most westerly outpost of white civilization. Here the first hospital was established in what is now Ontario. A fortified centre, it was a place of refuge for the Huron Indian converts, and the site of Ontario's first church. Housing more than fifty Frenchmen, the well-run community was what amounts to the first organized municipality in the province.

Following the destruction of the Huron nation by the Iroquois, the outpost was burned by the missionaries and abandoned on June 14, 1649. Fathers Gabriel Lalemant and Jean de Brébeuf were captured and tortured to death by the Iroquois.

Reconstruction of the historic site was begun in 1964 and Sainte-Marie and its museum now attract thousands of visitors each year. From the hill above the internationally known Jesuit Martyrs' Shrine immediately to the southeast of the town on Highway 12, may be seen the bay which, in those early days, was the western terminus of an 800-mile canoe route which connected New France with the Huron settlements.

The region remained sparsely settled as late as the 1870's. One of the early white settlers who came in the 19th century was Asher Mundy. It was after him that Mundy's Bay, an arm of Georgian Bay, had been named. Other early settlers were Michael MacDonnell, Thomas Murphy, Thomas Hartley and Samuel Fraser.

The town site of Midland was laid out in 1872-73 following the decision of the principal shareholders of the Midland Railway of Canada to locate the northern terminus of their line on Munday's Bay. The line at that time ran from Port Hope to Beaverton. The extension to Georgian Bay was completed in 1879 with the first train steaming into the new station of Midland on July 1st. The settlement which owed its existence to the railway grew rapidly into a shipping centre deriving its early prosperity mainly from the trade in lumber and grain.

Midland, which had been incorporated as a village in 1878, became a town in 1887. J.B. Horrell served as the town's first mayor.

H.H. Cook opened the first mill, which was followed by that of the Chew brothers. Soon the harbour shoreline was lined with mills. In 1913 the Midland Planing Mills Ltd. was opened, producing sashes, doors and other wood products for the home. The company was closed in 1935 but local citizens backed the Fine Silk Mills venture which later started to make automobile seat belts under a different name. Another forest-related industry in Midland is the manufacture of wallboard.

As well as tapping the natural resources of the surrounding forests, Midland residents also looked to the waters for a living. Frank Bonter who came from Prince Edward County was one of the commercial fishermen. In the 1880's John and Harry Yates from Peterborough also started a commercial fish business. Today commercial fishing is no longer possible and even sport fishing is being threatened by the pollution and contamination of the lake waters.

Grain elevators were first built at Midland in 1881 to accommodate grain arriving from the Lakehead and today the grain business is still thriving.

In the early 1900's James Playfair and D.L. White began a partnership that contributed greatly to Midland's economy. They started out in lumbering but soon became involved in shipbuilding. At first they did only repairs, but eventually they acquired a fleet of freight boats. Their first super-lake freighter was launched in 1926. That year Canada Steamship Co. took over the Midland Shipbuilding Co. and Midland Dry Dock Co.

Many other industries have grown up in Midland which today (1979) has a population of 11,822.

Among the wide variety of products made in Midland are cameras and optical equipment, textiles, flour, tools, fibreglass and wood specialties. Tourism plays an ever-increasing part in the town's economy as it is the centre of one of the largest recreation areas in Ontario.

Midland has a hospital, a public library and a district high school. The *Midland Free Press* which dates back to 1881, publishes twice weekly. The town is served by the CNR and by Highways 12 and 27.

Rena Bell: *A Peek into the Past 100 Years,* 1978.

Andrew F. Hunter: *The History of Simcoe County,* 1909.

MIKISEW PROVINCIAL PARK, Machar Township, Parry Sound District
Position 45° 50′ 79° 30′

A 300-acre Recreation Park on the west shore of Eagle Lake it takes its name from the Ojibway word for eagle, mikisew. Sand left behind by waters of the ancient Glacial Lake Algonquin, which receded some 10,000 years ago, is a physical feature of the park terrain. The villages of South River and Sundridge, to the east on Highway 11, are the park's closest centres. Some four miles to the west the Rosseau-Nipissing colonization road opened in 1874 and the first settlers of the narrows of Eagle Lake arrived in 1876.

Ontario Ministry of Natural Resources.

MILDMAY, village, Carrick Township, Bruce County
Position 44° 03′ 81° 07′

Mildmay is situated on Otter Creek about six miles south of Walkerton, on Highway 9 and the CNR. Population: 985 (1979).

The village had its beginnings in 1867 when Samuel Merner had a survey made of part of Lot 26, Concession "C". The place was known as Mernersville for several years thereafter, despite the fact that a post office established here in 1868 was officially called Mildmay. Donald McLean, pioneer merchant of Mildmay, was the first postmaster. Among the early settlers were Ignatz Bitchey, Adam Johnston, and Joseph Weiler.

William Murray operated a grist mill in those days; John Lenhardt had a blacksmith shop and Charles Schiel ran a hotel.

In the early 1870's the Wellington, Grey and Bruce Railway, then being constructed between Guelph and Kincardine, reached Mildmay and the hamlet soon began to thrive. William Carnegie was a prominent businessman of that period and his enterprises helped the village to prosper.

By the 1880's the manufacturing industries of Mildmay included brickyards, a steam flax mill, a steam sawmill, a steam planing mill, two large flour mills, three wagon and four blacksmith shops, a cooperage and a pump factory. There were four churches, a fine school with three teachers, four hotels and a new Town Hall.

Although the population at the time had already climbed to about 800, the village was not incorporated until 1918. Mildmay's first reeve was John M. Fischer. The first councillors were: Peter D. Lisemer, Henry B. Miller, Ernest Witter and Urban Schmidt. Charles Schurter became the first Clerk-Treasurer.

Today, Mildmay's citizens are served by four churches. Elementary students from Mildmay and Carrick Township attend the Central Public School built on the outskirts of the village. Sacred Heart Separate School at Mildmay, dating back to 1928, has since doubled in size. High School students are bused to Walkerton.

Among Mildmay's industries is the Lobsinger Brothers Foundry, which made a name for itself in Western Ontario as the manufacturer of the famous "Lion Thresher". The company which also produces "Mildmay Brand" Apple Butter, was started in the 1890's by Jonas Hergott who operated a foundry, an apple butter factory, a cider mill and a repair shop for steam engines.

A number of other business establishments in Mildmay can boast of a history going back to the late nineteenth century. Some are still operated by members of the founding families. To name a few, there is the Liesemer Hardware Store established by Conrad Liesemer in 1871; Schwalm's Sawmill and Building Supplies started by George Schwalm in 1880; Wendt's Jeweller and Watch Repairs opened by Charles Wendt in 1885; and Schurter's Book Store established in 1885 by Charles Schurter.

One of the beauty spots of Bruce County is Mildmay's Coronation Park on the outskirts of the village. Started by public-spirited citizens in the late 1930's, the project of converting acres of marsh land along the winding Otter Creek into a park was taken over by the Mildmay Rotary Club in 1945. Assisted by the people of Mildmay, Rotarians cleared a 12-acre site. In 1954 the park was leased to the Saugeen Valley Authority which has since developed it into a major tourist attraction.

Norman Robertson: *The History of the County of Bruce*, 1906.

Norman McLeod: *The History of the County of Bruce 1907-1969*, 1969.

MILFORD, community, South Marysburgh Township, Prince Edward
    County
    Position 43° 56′ 77° 05′

Milford on the Black River derives its name from the many mills once located there.

At one time the village was the "lumber capital" of Prince Edward County.

Among the first settlers was Joseph Clapp, a United Empire Loyalist who arrived in 1808 and with his five sons erected a large saw and grist mill. Around this mill grew the village. Expanding rapidly, Milford boasted two grist mills, a sawmill, a carding and fulling mill, two churches, stores and several hotels and taverns and shipping wharves by the 1850's. When the lumber trade declined, shipbuilding at nearby Port Milford, fishing and farming kept the village thriving during much of the second half of the century. Barley grown in the county and shipped in large quantities to the United States brought prosperity.

When the "barley days" came to an end by the 1890's and shipbuilding had all but ceased, the village taverns and hotels closed their doors for lack of customers. Clapp had sold his mill to William B. Scott and various members of the Scott family continued to operate it until the 1940's. The last owner, Carson Scott, sold the property consisting of the mill, mill pond and a parcel of land to the Prince Edward Region Conservation Authority. The latter now maintains the mill as a reminder of early rural life in the county.

N. & H. Mika: *Prince Edward County Heritage*, 1980.

MILLBROOK, village, Cavan Township, Peterborough County
Position 44° 09′ 78° 27′

Surrounded by hills, trees and sparkling streams, Millbrook lies about twenty miles northwest of Port Hope and fifteen miles southwest of Peterborough. In 1816 John Dyell came from Ireland and cleared a farm in the eastern part of Cavan Township. Beside a brook he built a grist mill and the mill by the brook gave Millbrook its name.

One of the earliest settlers in Millbrook was John Thorn. He made bricks and burned limestone for lime in order to build his house. He also constructed the first mill run by hand to grind corn.

In its early days, Millbrook was a prosperous village with many stores in all lines of business. There was Needler's three-storey flour mill and McIvor's mill where oatmeal was ground. Paddy Latimer had a cooper shop, and Walter Green a pump factory.

The first newspaper in the village was the *Millbrook Messenger* published in 1862 by Alfred E. Hayter. When Charles Richards and Son took over the paper the name was changed to *Mirror*. In 1936 Mr. Richards sold the paper to the Barringer brothers of Peterborough and the paper was then called *Millbrook Mirror-Reporter*.

The first church was the New Connexion Church which stood on the hill, west of the present high school. The Anglican Parish of Cavan was organized in 1819 and is represented today by St. Thomas Church. In July, 1881, the cornerstone of the present Methodist church, now United Church, was laid by George A. Cox of Peterborough. The pastor at that time was Rev. Newton Hill.

Millbrook's first school was a single-room building. For a while, the old Town Hall was used until the red brick school was built on Union Street. This school was burned in 1887. A larger white brick school was opened in 1890.

Millbrook Town Hall was built in 1877 and was owned jointly by the Township of Cavan and the Municipality of Millbrook. The present township hall was built in 1880, replacing the original hall which was destroyed by fire.

There have been a number of disastrous fires in the village over the years. The worst one occurred in 1876 when all the buildings on the north side of King Street were destroyed.

Millbrook was incorporated as a village in 1880. The first reeve was Richard Howden. Millbrook's population then was 1,500, but migration to the newly opening western provinces greatly reduced the number of people in the village in the years to come.

In 1894 David Hampton organized the local library, under the auspices of the Mechanics' Institute. In 1895 it became a free Public Library. The first librarian was Bruce White.

The first mounted band in Canada was organized in Millbrook in 1875. Known as the Light Cavalry Band, it was connected with the Prince of Wales Dragoons. Millbrook Community Band was organized in 1935 by Bandmaster Martin Chenhall.

The Millbrook Annual Fair, one of the oldest in Ontario, was founded in 1849 as the East Durham Fair, and every year since then it has attracted young and old alike.

The population of the village numbers 922 (1979).

M. Sloane Eakins: *The Village of Millbrook*, 1937.

United Counties of Northumberland and Durham, 1967.

MILLER, township, Frontenac County
Position 45° 04' 77° 00'

Situated in the northern part of Frontenac County, the area was known to lumbermen as the Frontenac Hills.

Originally home of the Algonquin Indians, the township was surveyed in the years 1857-1862 by I.S. Harper. Thomas Gibbs, who surveyed the Frontenac Road which passed through Miller, felt that the township's best agricultural land lay in its northern part. The Snow Road gave access to the northwest corner.

Timber cutting started in the 1840's, but permanent settlement did not begin until the late 1850's. The communities which grew up, included Wensley, founded in 1861, and Gore Mountain, founded in 1863. By the late 1860's Wensley had a store, a cooper, a furniture maker, a blacksmith, and a plasterer. A school was open in the settlement by 1869, with Fred Wensley as teacher. A cheese factory was also built.

The early settlers of the township were all farmers, although many men supplemented their income by working in the lumber camps. The population peaked in 1919. Since then it has decreased steadily and today the township has mainly a summer population of cottagers or part-time homeowners.

Miller is in the heart of the Land O' Lakes tourist area and tourism is the township's main industry. Among its many lakes are Fortune, Schooner, Mosquito, and Mackie, all of which provide excellent fishing and boating opportunities.

Miller, once a separate municipality, was united with Clarendon in 1867. Bramwell Watkins served as first reeve. The combined population of the two townships in 1979 was 418.

C.A. Armstrong: *Away Back in Clarendon and Miller*, 1976.

North Frontenac Chamber of Commerce: *North Frontenac Tourist Guide 1974-75*.

MILLHAVEN, community, Lennox and Addington County
Position 44° 12' 76° 45'

Millhaven, located on the North Channel of Lake Ontario and at the mouth of Millhaven Creek, came into being as a port of entry for Ernestown. It was the site of the county's first registry office and a large grist mill, which also served the settlers on Amherst Island opposite the village.

The area was first settled by United Empire Loyalists in the 1780's, but Millhaven was not laid out until 1840 when Isaac Fraser did the survey. A post office was opened in 1845 with Jeremiah Amey as the first postmaster.

The community lies 15 miles west of Kingston on Highway 33. Attracted by its ready access to water and shipping facilities, Canadian Industries chose the site for a large textile plant in the 1950's. An ammonia plant was built a short time later. In 1964 the Canadian government erected near Millhaven a maximum security prison.

Lennox and Addington Historical Society: *Historical Glimpses of Lennox and Addington*, 1964.

MILLIGAN, geographic township, Cochrane District
Position 48° 40′ 80° 05′

First surveyed in 1903, this township, north of Kirkland Lake, was named for the Reverend George Milligan, DD, Toronto. It is accessible by dry weather roads and is drained by Low Creek.

MILLS, geographic township, Manitoulin District
Position 45° 46′ 82° 29′

Established in 1878, the township is situated on the southern edge of Manitoulin Island, and is Indian land. Named after the Honourable David Mills, the area includes the community of Poplar.

MILTON, town, Regional Municipality of Halton
Position 43° 31′ 79° 53′

Halton County, in the centre of which Milton is situated, was unsettled prior to the purchase of the Mississauga Tract from the Mississauga Indians in 1806. The purchase of this land, from which Halton was carved, and the construction of the "York Road" (now Highway 5) from York (Toronto) to London sparked the settlement of the lands west of Toronto. By 1817 the population of Halton County was 668.

In a short period of time "grist mill" communities sprang up, Milton being the first, in the early 1820's. Jasper Martin and his wife, Sarah, established the first grist mill here on the Sixteen Mile Creek in 1822. Soon Martin expanded his business to include a sawmill, an ashery and a small store. By 1830 a small community known as "Martin's Mills" had sprung up around these enterprises.

Early pioneer families in the Milton area included the Whitefields, Martins, Fosters, Greeniases and Huffmans. They were attracted by the rich soil, the forests and the fast-flowing rivers which provided the ingredients necessary for agricultural and industrial development.

By 1837 Martin's Mills had grown to more than 100 people and George Brown's general store and Foster's cooper shop had been added to its businesses. A log schoolhouse was built in 1837.

At a meeting held that year, it was decided to rename the town. Jasper Martin by then had passed away but his four sons maintained his businesses and the family's prominent position in the community. They were partial to the English poet John Milton and upon their suggestion Milton became the new name of Martin's Mills. Some sources say that Milton may have been a corruption of Milltown, as the place was referred to in the early days.

By the 1850's the population of Milton had risen to well over 300 people including blacksmiths, shoemakers, masons, wagonmakers, cabinetmakers, and coopers. Three hotels were in operation and churches had been established. Sawmilling was now the main industry, the number of sawmills having grown to nineteen. A growing overseas market demanding lumber for shipbuilding kept Milton's sawmills humming.

When in 1853 the united counties of Halton and Wentworth were separated, Milton was made the county seat of Halton. The county buildings and gaol were completed in 1855. Milton's new status meant a further boost to its development and for the next two decades rapid residential and industrial growth took place.

In 1857 Milton was incorporated as a town. The first mayor, George Brown, and his council initiated the construction of a suitable town hall which was officially opened in 1863.

Despite the fact that Milton lacked railway connections, the number of its small businesses and manufacturing enterprises continued to grow between 1857 and 1877. Robertson's Steam Sash Door and Blind Factory; Rodler and Huff's Tannery; Socrates Center's Ashery; Ramshaw's Quality Buggies and MacKenzie's Blacksmith and Carriage works, all were established during this period.

A threshing machine, invented by the Joseph Brothers of Milton in the 1870's, was one of the most important improvements in the agricultural practises of the day as it cut down the time it took to separate the chaff from the grain. The Milton area has always been, and remains so, a progressive agricultural community.

Old grist mill in Milton, Ontario C. 1925

Public Archives Canada PA 87034

The railway finally came to Milton in 1877 when the Hamilton and Northwestern pushed through the town, followed in 1879 by the Credit Valley Railway.

The railways encouraged further industrial development. One of the enterprises established after 1877 was the Robertson Lime Kiln. This company was taken over by Domtar Chemical Ltd. in 1927, but closed in the early 1930's. The local brick industry was very important around the turn of the century. Robertson's Screw Company, home of the "sockethead screw", is another Milton success story. At one time this company employed nearly 20 per cent of the total work force of the town.

Between 1930 and 1950 Milton's population hovered around 2,000 but the fifties brought an upsurge in population largely due to the construction of Highway 401. Today this bustling town on the CNR and the CPR is a combination of both the old and the new. It has a population of 24,163 (1979) and its business establishments serve a large farming district. There are also a number of small industries.

William E. Cook: Milton: Welcome to Our Town, 1977.

MILVERTON, village, Mornington Township, Perth County
Position 43° 34′ 80° 55′

The village of Milverton is located on Highway 19 and on the CNR and the CPR, about 15 miles north of Stratford. The first settler was Andrew West, a shoemaker from New York State. He arrived in 1848 and bought Lot 6 in the 4th Concession from Joseph Hamilton in exchange, so the story goes, for a pair of boots. West opened a shoe shop and a tavern which became the nucleus of the settlement of West's Corners.

A post office was established in 1854 and mail in the early days was brought by horseback from Stratford along a trail blazed by the settlers. The first postmaster of West's Corners was Daniel Matthews, although Andrew West appears to have handled the mail at his hotel for the first little while as a convenience to his patrons. Andrew West died in 1858. His grave may be found in the old Methodist cemetery of the village.

In 1871 the post office was renamed Milverton after a village in Somersetshire, England at the suggestion of the local Presbyterian minister, the Rev. Peter Musgrave who had been born in that English village.

By the 1870's, Milverton had a population of about 500. Local industries included a flour mill, a sash and door factory, a planing mill, a sawmill and a brickyard. There were four general stores, a hardware store, a drug store, two jewellery stores, and a photographic studio.

Both Milverton and nearby Millbank, which was of equal size, vied for the Stratford and Huron Railway line (now CNR) to pass through its village. When the line was completed in 1877, it ran within one half mile of Milverton bypassing the village of Millbank, a fact which resulted in Milverton continuing to grow at the expense of its neighbour.

On June 17, 1880 a by-law was passed by Perth County Council incorporating the Village of Milverton. The first reeve of the new municipality was businessman J.D. Pierson. Councillors elected were:

Jacob Karn, Henry Hasenpflug, Walter J. Passmore and J.G. Grosch.

The first issue of the *Milverton Sun* came off the press in 1891 under the management of Thomas Whalley. The village which has a district high school and a public library, is the business centre for a large Mennonite community in the district. It has a population of 1443 (1979).

William Johnston: *History of Perth County 1825-1902, 1903.*

Milverton Old Boys & Girls Reunion: A Century of Progress: *Mornington Centennial*, 1957.

MIMICO, community, Borough of Etobicoke, Municipality of Metropolitan Toronto
Position 43° 37′ 79° 30′

Located on Highway 2 and fronting on Lake Ontario, the urban community of Mimico, formerly a town, became a part of the Borough of Etobicoke on January 1, 1967.

The township of Etobicoke, of which early Mimico was a part, was established in 1792, but the area remained Indian lands for several years thereafter. Surveying continued at intervals until 1838, and most lots were taken up by the 1840's. Mimico on the Lake Shore Road received a post office in 1857.

The name Mimico is believed to have been derived from the Mississauga Indian word "Omimeca" for "place of wild pigeons". In the early days great flocks of passenger pigeons used to feed in the fields along Mimico Creek.

What is thought to have been the first organized Anglican congregation between the Humber and Etobicoke rivers was Mimico's Christ Church parish dating back to the 1820's. John William Gamble donated the site where a small frame church was erected around 1832. The Rev. Dr. Thomas Phillips was the first preacher at Christ Church.

The first Mimico schoolhouse stood on the south shore of the Lake Shore Road near the foot of Church Street. Attention focussed on the settlement during the 1850's when a group of Toronto businessmen purchased land here along the new railway line. Visualizing the start of a model town, they divided the land into lots which were auctioned off. A recession in the wake of the Crimean War, however, put a stop to their plans. Most of the land continued to be farmed for some time to come.

In 1897 Mimico was incorporated as a police village with a Board of Trustees, and in 1911 it became a village. The first reeve of the village was Robert Skelton; Austin Werden, John Harrison, Geo. E. Bryer, and Dr. W. Woods served as councillors.

In 1917 Mimico gained the status of a town. John Harrison was elected mayor; Geo. E. Bryer was reeve, and George Stubbs deputy reeve. Councillors were Edwin Eland, James Harlock and Alex Johnson.

In September of 1917 the first edition of the local weekly newspaper was published under the name of *Mimico and New Toronto Advertiser*. In 1918 a Fire Brigade was organized and fire-fighting equipment was purchased for the town. In 1922 the

Mimico Public Utilities Commission purchased the old Methodist church building on Church Street and converted it into offices.

Mimico at one time was noted for its brickyards and its thriving market gardens. Hotels and picnic grounds catered to visitors and Torontonians built their spacious summer houses here.

Edwin Eland: *The Story of Mimico*, 1935.

Robert A. Given: *The Story of Etobicoke*, 1950.

MINDEN, geographic township, Haliburton County
Position 45° 00′ 78° 40′

The township which is part of the municipal union of Anson, Hinden, and Minden, was surveyed in 1858 by J.W. Fitzgerald. It was named after the ancient and historic town of Minden in Westphalia, Germany.

The sale of lots in the township did not get underway until August 24, 1859. Some homesteaders, however, had already cleared part of their farms by 1858. Among them was Francis Kent who had settled northeast of the present community of Minden. Frederick Shove had built a cabin and cleared a few acres at the foot of Mountain Lake. Other early settlers in the township included Samuel Whittaker, George Hilton and John Norce.

The community of Minden grew up where the Bobcaygeon Road crosses the Gull River. The site was once an Indian camping ground, as the Gull River watershed was the hunting ground of the Indians living along the shore of Lake Simcoe. Before white settlers came to the area, lumbering companies harvested here large quantities of white pine. Lumbering continued to be a source of income for the inhabitants. A building erected in Minden, probably by a lumber company in 1870, was later acquired by the Anglican Diocese of Toronto and during the early 1900's it served as headquarters for itinerant missionaries travelling throughout the district.

Early post offices in the township, aside from Minden, were: Ingoldsby, Allsaw, Blairhampton, Elsie and Carnarvon. Minden Township's first hotel was opened by Benjamin Sawyer in 1863. A large portion of the township is covered with lakes; among them are Mountain Lake, Horseshoe Lake, Twelve Mile Lake, Canning Lake, and the largest, Kashagawigamog Lake.

Nila Reynolds: *In Quest of Yesterday*, 1967.

MINTO, township, Wellington County
Position 43° 55′ 80° 53′

Minto Township, the most northwesterly township of Wellington County, was named in honour of Sir Gilbert Elliott, the first Earl of Minto. It was surveyed by Charles Rankin of Owen Sound in 1853. Settlers began arriving around that time, however, the first patent was not obtained until January 1856 by Augustus C. Fyfe.

William Reynolds was one of the first settlers in the township followed by George Lyons who located between Minto and Arthur in 1851. In 1853 the Wilkins family, the Harrisons and Fergusons, along with Robert and George Bell, came to settle. A large influx entered from the southern part of the county just prior to the land sale of September 1854.

Minto was originally part of the Township of Arthur for municipal purposes, but was officially separated in 1856. The first township meeting was held in January 1857. Archibald Harrison was the first reeve, and William Yeo the first clerk.

In 1862 the gravel road from Elora to Saugeen was completed, and in November, 1870, the Wellington, Grey and Bruce Railway was opened to Harriston, improving communications greatly.

The township has good soil with sandy and clay loams predominating. Primarily an agricultural area, with Harriston as its hub, the population of Minto is 2,086 (1979).

The village of Clifford on the northwestern corner of the township, being on both the main road and the railway, is also catering to a prosperous farming community. Several other communities which once flourished in Minto have faded with the passage of time. The village of Drew, once famous for brickmaking, is now but a memory. Teviotdale, which at one time boasted a hotel, a store and a blacksmith ship, has lost its heyday. Cotswold, where once were a blacksmith shop, a store, a pump factory and a cheese factory has only a church to mark its site.

A.W. Wright: *Memories of Mount Forest and Surrounding Townships*, 1928.

Historical Atlas Publishing Co.: *Historical Atlas of the County of Wellington, Ontario*, 1906.

MISCAMPBELL, geographic township, Rainy River District
Position 48° 42′ 93° 32′

This L-shaped township is situated northwest of Fort Frances. The name commemorates Andrew Miscampbell, MPP for East Simcoe, 1890-94, and for Sault Ste. Marie in 1902.

MISKOKOMON, geographic township, Algoma District
Position 47° 59′ 84° 12′

Formerly Township 25, Range 23, Miskokomon was named after Harry Miskokomon, Chief of the Chippewas of the Thames. The township lies east of Wawa. Highway 101 traverses its southern end, and the turbulent Jackpine River drains the area.

MISSINAIBI, geographic township, Sudbury District
Position 48° 20′ 83° 41′

There are several interpretations of the Indian word Missinaibi. The translation "pictures on the water" refers to old Indian pictures painted on cliffs above the water and reflected in the waters of Missinaibi Lake. Most of the Township of Missinaibi lies within Missinaibi Lake Provincial Park.

MISSINAIBI LAKE PROVINCIAL PARK, Missinaibi Township & part of Calais Township, Sudbury District, & Kildare Township, Algoma District
Position 48° 24' 83° 36'

This Natural Environment Park comprises some 111,782 acres and is situated in the heart of the Chapleau Game Preserve, the largest game preserve in the Western Hemisphere. It is reached by a private logging road beginning at the town of Chapleau to the south on Highway 101 and travelling about 55 miles north to the park. The road belongs to a period when logging was carried on by the Missinaibi Logging Co. from the early 1900's to the late 1950's.

The 20,000 acre Missinaibi Lake, where voyageurs and Indians alike camped on their way to Moosonee, was a link on that ancient fur trading route between Lake Superior and James Bay. Brunswick House, a Hudson Bay fur trading post, formerly stood on the northeast shore of the lake. Indian pictographs on the rock cliffs at Fairy Point on Missinaibi Lake tell of a great battle once fought between the tribes.

Ontario Ministry of Natural Resources.

MISSISSAGI PROVINCIAL PARK, Townships 155, 156, 161, 162 (Bolger, Beange, Timmermans, Jogues) Algoma District
Position 46° 35' 82° 45'

Formerly known as Elliot Lake Provincial Park, this Natural Environmental Park is situated about 16 miles north of Elliot Lake on Highway 108. Highway 639 traverses the park and within it are several lakes including Semiwite Lake. Parts of Flack Lake and Helenbar Lake also enter the park's boundaries. The park itself is surrounded by the wilderness of an extensive Park Reserve.

Ontario Ministry of Natural Resources.

MISSISSAUGA, city, Regional Municipality of Peel
Position 43° 35' 79° 39'

What was once the Township of Toronto, became the Corporation of the Town of Mississauga at midnight, December 31, 1967. There were ceremonies and fireworks to celebrate the event, and among the special guests were the Chief of the Mississaugas and his wife. The name of the new town had been chosen by popular vote in the municipal elections that December.

The land at one time had belonged to the Mississauga Indians. On August 2, 1805, four Chieftains of the Mississaugas met with the Hon. William Claus, Deputy Superintendent of Indian Affairs, at Government House, located at the mouth of the Credit River. Here they signed a treaty under which the Mississaugas agreed to sell to the Crown the southerly part of the Mississauga Tract for the sum of one thousand pounds. The lands comprising 70,784 acres covered an area starting at Etobicoke Creek, stretching westward to the outlet of Burlington Bay, and reaching back from the lakeshore for five or six miles. This area became the Township of Toronto in 1805.

The new township was surveyed in 1806 and 1807 by the Deputy Surveyor of Upper Canada, Samuel Wilmot. Shortly thereafter settlers began to arrive. The first is said to have been Philip Cody who opened an inn in Sydenham, a place later known as Fonthill and eventually as Dixie. One of the first guests at the Cody inn was wealthy Joseph Silverthorn, who lived at the inn while a cabin was being built for him. In 1822 Silverthorn built "Cherry Hill", a mansion which still stands near the northwest corner of Cawthra Road and Dundas Street.

Other early settlers in the township were Daniel Harris, Allan Robinette, William Berber and Absolom Wilcox. Some of those who took up land in the township following the completion of the survey were Loyalists from New Brunswick where they had sought refuge after the Revolutionary War. The lands bordering Lake Ontario had been claimed before the outbreak of the War of 1812. While the war slowed down immigration from the United States and Britain to a trickle, the rest of the township was quickly filled following the Treaty of Ghent that ended it in 1815. In 1818 further lands were acquired for settlement when the government purchased the balance of the Mississauga Tract consisting of 648,000 acres.

The flow of settlers into the township soon swelled to a flood. A survey was made of the northern part of the township by Timothy Street, for whom Streetsville was named. His work was completed 1818-19 and lands were quickly swallowed up. The availability of water made it possible to establish saw and grist mills. At this time twenty-six families, Irish Loyalists, came to settle in Toronto Township. Among them were millwrights, tradesmen, and artisans who built and ran the mills along the Credit River. It was not long before communities began to emerge in the township, usually along the river or at crossroads, among them Streetsville, Meadowvale, Churchville, Derry West, Dixie, Springfield, Britannia, Palestine, Cooksville and Summerville. In 1821 the township had a population of 803 with less than 3,000 acres of its land cleared. By 1851 over 7,500 people lived in the township and more than 36,000 acres were under cultivation, producing barley, wheat, oats, vegetables and fruit. Many of the farmers were raising sheep.

Throughout the township small industries were busy manufacturing anything from hosiery to ploughshares.

The boom turned to "bust" during the second half of the nineteenth century. Railways entered the picture and markets shifted. The old waterpowered industries in the rural areas no longer could compete with those run by electricity in larger centres. By 1901 the township's population had dropped drastically to 4,690. Not until the 1950's did the area's economy recover. Industries moved into the township and the resulting growth was nothing less than phenomenal. Streetsville which had been incorporated as a village in 1858, became a town in 1962. Port Credit, Mississauga's neighbour to the south, had achieved town status the year before.

When Mississauga, itself, became a town in 1968, it had a population of 107,000, and covered an area of 70,598 acres. What was once a quiet agricultural community had become one of the most thriving towns in Canada, growing at the rate of 12% a year. By the 1970's more than 1,200 industries had made Mississauga their home. Recreational facilities, modern homes, apartment buildings, townhouses, expressways, new hospitals, schools and shopping centres had replaced the rural scene.

On January 1, 1974 the towns of Port Credit, Streetsville and Mississauga joined together to become the City of Mississauga, encompassing 117 square miles. Now Canada's twelfth largest city, it has a population of 283,429 (1979) and a growth rate that leads planners and developers to predict that in 30 years it will be a city of one million people.

In the heart of Mississauga stands the new City Centre which houses the administrative body. Sheridan Park, the world's largest industrial research and development centre, is located in the city, as is Canada's largest air freight terminal. Major expressways, and rail lines link the city with U.S. and Canadian centres. Harbour and nearby deep sea facilities provide access to ports the world over. Mississauga is the site of the world's largest steam generating station. Strategically located in the centre of one of the richest market area's in the country, Mississauga is a city on the move.

On November 10, 1979 at 11:53 p.m. a train derailment occurred within the city limits that caused a flurry of excitement throughout the country. Dangerous chemicals were leaking from overturned tank cars spelling potential disaster. While the rest of Canada anxiously awaited news on the accident, more than a quarter million people were evacuated from the Mississauga area in what was the largest peace time evacuation of a city ever attempted. Several days were to pass before all of the residents were allowed to return to their homes. During that time most of the usually bustling city had turned into a ghost town. The only vehicles on the streets were police cars checking deserted properties and vans of the Ontario Humane Society, whose officers worked around the clock to feed thousands of dogs, cats, birds and other pets left behind by their owners. No loss of life occurred, and there were no incidents to mar what amounted to a gigantic effort on the part of Mississauga's authorities.

Arthur Lowe: *Mississauga News Annual Industrial Supplement*, 1968.

Mississauga Jaycees: *Mississauga as a City*, 1974.

Corporation of the Town of Mississauga.

MITCHELL, town, Fullarton and Logan Townships, Perth County
Position 43° 28′ 81° 12′

This small but thriving Ontario town of some 2,700 people is situated on the North Thames River, at the intersection of Highways 8 and 23 and on the CNR, less than 20 miles northwest of Stratford.

The founders of the town were William Hicks and his son, John, who opened a tavern here on the Huron Road in 1837. The settlement grew very slowly at first but in 1843 settlers began to arrive in larger numbers, including James McClacherty, Daniel Kerr, and the Campbells. W.E. McCullock opened the first store in 1844. A mill was built by Mr. Small, with financial assistance from the Canada Company which tried to encourage settlers to buy land it owned in this region. Thomas Matheson, who arrived in 1844, carried out the duties of postmaster.

Post Office and War Memorial, Mitchell, C. 1924

Public Archives Canada PA 31378

The arrival of the Bruce and Lake Huron Railway in 1857 greatly influenced the community's development. Mitchell became a significant trade centre, and its population increased rapidly. Incorporated as a village in 1857, it became a town in 1873, with Thomas Matheson as first Mayor.

Five years after the building of the railway, Robert Thomson and Co. started to manufacture agricultural implements. Other industries followed and at one time Mitchell had more factories than any other centre in Perth County. Messrs. Tucker and Beer's wagons and carriages were sold in both Ontario and Manitoba. The A.M. Gibson Manufacturing Company which began in 1877, made iron and woodworking machinery and safes. A woollen mill, plough factories, and planing, flouring, and oatmeal mills also contributed to the town's prosperity.

Unfortunately, the boom did not last. Both the A.M. Gibson Company and Tucker and Beer failed; Thomson and Williams, the largest manufacturer in the county, left Mitchell and moved to Stratford. The timber resources of Logan and Elma Townships were exhausted, resulting in the closure of the sawmills and the end of the lumber trade. Today, Mitchell's main function is to act as a market for the produce of the surrounding countryside. Of the old industries, Messrs. Dufton and Waterhouse, the woollen mill, and Buritt and Son, hosiery manufacturers, were among the few to survive into the twentieth century.

An 1872 school superintendent reported that the education provided by Mitchell's schools was the best in the county. The high school, built the following year, continued this tradition. In 1946 Mitchell organized the first high school district in Ontario.

The *Mitchell Advocate*, begun in 1860 by W.R. and John E. Davis, was the town's first paper. It preached Conservative politics, while Reform doctrines were advanced by the *Mitchell Recorder*, founded by Thomas H. Race in 1877. A public library was set up in the late nineteenth century.

The first religious services were probably held by the Presbyterian Rev. Dr. Burns in 1846. Irregular services were held in a blacksmith shop in 1847 and 1848. Rev. Thomas McPherson organized the Knox Presbyterian congregation in 1849. A church was built in 1856 and Rev. James Findlay became the first resident minister. The English church was organized in 1861. Rev. Mr. Ralley was the first minister at Old Trinity Church, erected in 1862. In 1858 a Roman Catholic church was constructed and was replaced by a new brick edifice in 1882. The Methodist congregation was established in 1852, although regular services were not held until a church was opened in 1855. Rev. J.A. Herenger began to minister to the first Evangelical Lutheran Grace congregation in 1858.

W. Stafford Johnston and Hugh J.M. Johnston: *History of Perth County to 1967*, 1967.

William Johnston: *History of Perth County, 1825-1902*, 1903.

MOGGY, geographic township, Sudbury District
Position 47° 22' 83° 47'

Previously known as Township 22, Range 16, the township was named in 1974 after H. Moggy, a Reeve of Assiginack in the Manitoulin District. The area is located north of Sault Ste. Marie.

MOIRA, community, Huntingdon Township, Hastings County
Position 44° 21' 77° 24'

The village of Moira, north of Belleville, was named after Sir John Rawdon, Earl of Moira, County Down, Ireland. Early settlers in this vicinity included Anthony Denike, Philip Luke and Hugh Daly. The latter bought Lot 15, Concession 3 in 1827.

The Quakers were the first to erect a house of worship in Moira, probably before 1845. They were followed in the 1850's by the Methodists who built a church on land donated to the Moira congregation by Henry Ketcheson. The Methodist church was destroyed by fire in 1872, but was rebuilt soon after.

From 1850 to 1918 Moira was the seat of government for Huntingdon Township. A stone building was erected in 1851 to serve as a town hall and division court. Lectures and temperance meetings were also held here. The township's first post office which opened in 1841 was located at Moira.

Among Moira's industries in the 1800's were a fanning mill, a furniture factory, and a carriage works, which was operated by Ira Hoskins. A cheese factory was opened in 1868; it remained in production until the 1930's.

Gerald E. Boyce: *Historic Hastings*, 1967.

E. Thompson & E.M. Welsh: *Moira Past and Present*, 1976.

MONCRIEFF, geographic township, Sudbury District
Position 46° 46′ 81° 38′

Approximately fifty miles northwest of Sudbury, the area was named for George Moncrieff, K.C., MP for Lambton East, 1887-96. The CPR station point of Benny, the only community in the township, is located in the central northern section.

MONESTIME, geographic township, Algoma District
Position 46° 46′ 82° 16′

Located northeast of Elliot Lake, Monestime was named in 1973 for Dr. S.F. Monestime, who was mayor of Mattawa at that time. The township is interspersed with lakes, including Lac Aux Sables, and the smaller Russian, Richie and Gibson Lakes.

MONKLAND, police village, Roxborough Township, Stormont County
Position 45° 12′ 74° 52′

Monkland, northwest of Cornwall, is situated on the CPR and at the junction of Highways 43 and 138. The village is said to have been named after a small place outside Glasgow, Scotland. The first family to remain in the area were the Kenneys who settled on the first concession of Roxborough township.

The original village of Monkland eventually disappeared when in the 1870's the railway passed it by. But a new community grew up around the nearby "Monkland Station" and it is this place that is now known as Monkland Village. The railway station was demolished in 1972.

The first post office was situated at the west end of the present village. The first postmaster was Lanieul Waldroff.

Shortly after the building of the railroad station, the village became a "going concern" with coal shutes, a water pumping station, cattle yards, two lumber mills, a cheese box factory, a shingle mill, a feed mill, a general store, a shoe and harness making shop, a blacksmith shop, a wheelwright shop, a hotel, boardinghouse, and two churches.

Today Monkland Village retains only a grist mill, a grocery store, an egg grading station and various service industries.

Information supplied by local residents.

MONMOUTH, township, Haliburton County
Position 44° 58′ 78° 17′

This is one of the eastern townships of Haliburton. Surveyed in 1862, it was named after the County of Monmouth which is situated on the border between England and Wales and is famous for its ancient castles.

Settlement of the township was greatly facilitated by the construction of the Monck and Burleigh colonization roads. Free land grants were offered along the routes of these colonization roads to persons willing to fulfill certain settlement requirements.

Most of the early settlers in Monmouth were farmers, although some came for the timber, and some were construction workers on the Irondale, Bancroft and Ottawa Railway. Mossom Boyd, R.C. Smith, J.C. Hughson, and John R. Rogers held the first timber licences within the township.

The southern section was settled early by Isaac Ritchie and his sons. S.S. Ritchie kept a store and Robert Ritchie operated a sawmill. Another mill owner in this area was William Hadley.

The first school in the township was a log cabin located in Wilberforce in the northeast corner of the township, which is Monmouth's largest settlement. A post office was opened here in 1880. Tom Rowe ran a blacksmith shop, Mr. Dillman kept a store and R. Couckell & Sons are believed to have operated a cheese factory.

One of the oldest churches in the county originally built in 1858 at Kidd's Corners, Cardiff Township, was moved to Wilberforce, and later was replaced by a frame structure in 1899. The United Church cemetery at Wilberforce has the graves of early settlers like Patterson, Thomson, Ritchie, Austin, Burton, McCrae, Johnston, and Madill. The Anglican Church was built around 1890 and is still in use.

Essonville, four miles north of Tory Hill, counts among its pioneer settlers Foster Gibson, John Roscoe, George Hammel, Jeremiah McGuire and Fred Bradley. A post office was established here in 1882. At Tory Hill, John Anderson operated a post office by 1893.

The permanent population of the township numbers 736 (1979). The area is served by Highway 121.

Nila Reynolds: *In Quest of Yesterday*, 1967.

MONO, geographic township, Dufferin County
Position 44° 02′ 80° 04′

There are conflicting versions as to the origin of the township's name. It may have been chosen by Sir Peregrine Maitland, Lieutenant Governor of Upper Canada from 1818-1828, who appears to have favoured Spanish words when suggesting names. He named the townships of Oso, Zorra and Lobo, meaning, respectively, "bear", "she fox", and "wolf". In Spanish, Mona means "monkey". Local residents prefer to believe that the name comes from Mona, the name of Chief Tecumseth's daughter. However, there is some doubt that Tecumseth had a daughter.

The first survey was made in 1823, east of the Centre Road, by David Gibson, and west of the road by Surveyor Black. The first settler was George McManus who took up Lot 2, Concession 8 in 1823. Adam Raven came in 1824 and settled on Lot 3, Conc. 3 west. He was followed by Robert Henry a year later. Other early settlers' names were: Allan, Brady, Lundy, Hutchinson, McCutcheon, McMaster, Montgomery, Perry, Smith, Wright, Turnbull and Williamson. Most of the early settlers entered the township from the southeast corner at Mono Mills. The majority of those who settled in the eastern part were Irish or Scottish.

Native Mississauga Indians lived on either side of the Credit River which rises in Mono Township. Gradually, however, the government acquired the land from the Indian chiefs and sold lots to incoming settlers. By 1850 the township had a population of close to 2300.

Mono Mills in the southeast corner of the township rivalled Orangeville on the headwaters of the Credit to the west, as the fastest growing community of the township. Both places had mills, stores, industries, hotels, churches and schools. The opening up of the Prince of Wales and the Victoria roads, both of which linked the Centre Road with the Toronto Line, put Orangeville in a more favourable position, as it was the main stage stop between Owen Sound and Brampton. When, in 1873, the Toronto, Grey and Bruce Railway (now CPR) completed its line from Toronto to Owen Sound via Orangeville, the latter's dominance was assured. Today Orangeville is a town of 13,000 and the seat of Dufferin County.

Among the villages that sprang up in the township are Mono Centre, so named because it is situated in the centre. Camilla, Hockley, Glen Cross, Blount, Lucille, Elba, Elder, Granger, Relessey and Sheldon.

The township covers 69,805 acres and has a population of 4,122. The eastern section with its hills and dales is part of the Niagara escarpment and is considered one of the most scenic areas in Ontario.

Stephen Sawden: *History of Dufferin County.*

MONS, geographic township, Algoma District
Position 48° 47′ 83° 07′

Mons is named for the Belgian town where British forces entered action in World War I in 1914, and which was recaptured by the Canadians on the last day of warfare in 1918. The township is located northeast of Wawa.

MONTAGUE, township, Lanark County
Position 44° 58′ 75° 58′

The township, named after the Irish Earl of Montague, lies in the southeastern corner of Lanark County where it borders on the Rideau River.

William Fortune began a survey of the township in 1774.

However, the survey was interrupted when it was proposed that the forest of Montague be thrown open to children of United Empire Loyalists. Under an agreement with the British Government, these children, upon reaching the age of twenty-one, were to receive free grants of 100 acres of land each. The plan, however, was not followed in Montague, and in 1797 a Mr. Stegman completed the survey.

William Merrick was the first to cross the Rideau into the township in 1798, locating on the northern bank at a spot which became known as North Merrickville. North Merrickville later became a part of Merrickville Village, the major part of which is located on the south bank of the Rideau River in Grenville County.

Merrick was followed by the McCraes, the Chesters, Bartons, McIntyres and Vandusens. By 1802 there were 90 inhabitants in the township.

The first school in the township was established as a private enterprise by Jesse McIntyre in his own house in 1804.

No public religious services were held in Montague until Ezra Healy conducted services in the schoolhouse in 1815.

Montague was united with Wolford, Oxford and Marlborough Townships for municipal purposes until 1845 and was part of the Johnstown District. In that year it became a part of the Bathurst District and elected its own representatives, Knapp and Loucks, in 1846.

When the present system of municipal government came into effect in 1850, R.E. Matheson was elected as the first reeve.

Smiths Falls, an incorporated village since 1854 and a town since 1882, emerged as the largest centre in Montague, as a result of the building of the Rideau Canal. Two other smaller communities, Montague, on the second concession, and Andrewsville in the southeast corner of the township, developed to serve the needs of the settlers in the township.

Montague is an agricultural area possessing soil of varying depth and fertility. It has a population of 3,710 (1979).

H. Belden & Co.: *Illustrated Atlas of Lanark County*, 1880.

MONTEAGLE, township, Hastings County
Position 45° 13' 77° 50'

Situated in the northern part of Hastings County, the township was named after the Rt. Hon. Thomas Spring-Rice, Lord Monteagle (1790-1866), Secretary of State for the colonies.

Monteagle was first surveyed by Publius V. Elmore, who laid out the Hastings Colonization Road along the western boundary in 1853. Settlers arrived in the area soon after this. The survey was continued in 1856 by J.S. Peterson who mapped out Monteagle's boundaries. He felt that the soil in the southern part was too sandy and light for agriculture, but that the land in the interior showed more promise. John J. Haslett completed the survey in 1861 but found no settlers in the central part of the township.

The first inhabitant of Monteagle may have been Jerard Welsh, who arrived in 1835. He married an Indian girl and spent his life trapping in the area. George Bartlett arrived sometime after 1861 and James McAlpine and his sons settled along the northern boundary in 1863. Other settlers who came before 1865 included John Daly, Patrick Ward, Martin Hughes, and the Musclow family who founded the community of Musclow.

Monteagle was added to Hastings County in 1858. It was joined to Herschel Township for municipal purposes from 1874 to 1960. John Fitzgerald was the first reeve of the united townships.

Lumbering was the mainstay of the township's early economy. The E.B. Eddy Company was later followed by the Whitney, Rathbun, and Valley lumber enterprises. Industries in the township included a tannery run by Mr. Bell at Bell's Creek. Mr. Bell also made shoes, harness, and moccasins. A number of cheese factories provided a market for local farmers.

Mining played a part in Monteagle's development in the early twentieth century. Graphite mines were opened in 1911 and 1916 and feldspar was found near Hybla in the 1920's. The MacDonald Mine was the largest feldspar concern, but many other smaller mines were established near it. Feldspar mining continued until 1950.

A Protestant church, built in 1882 on the northern boundary and used by Anglicans, Methodists and Lutherans, was probably the first house of worship in the township. It was later called Emmanuel or White Church. Zion Church (1886), Maynooth Methodist Church (1896), Christ Anglican Church (1901), and the Lutheran Church (1901) followed.

Today soil depletion, a decline in the lumber trade, and the closing of the nearby Bancroft uranium mines have caused many people to leave Monteagle. However, deer hunting and fishing in the area is an attraction for visitors.

Gerald E. Boyce: *Historic Hastings*, 1967.

MONTEITH, geographic township, Parry Sound District
Position 45° 25' 79° 37'

Situated east of Parry Sound, Monteith Township was established in 1870 and named after Andrew Monteith, MPP for Perth North, 1867-74. The community of Bear Lake is situated on Highway 11.

MOONBEAM, community, Fauquier Township, Cochrane District
Position 49° 21' 82° 09'

This farming community of some 900 people west of the town of Cochrane, on Highway 11 and the CNR, dates back to 1913 when the first settlers arrived. Flashing lights in the sky falling down like "moonbeams" into a little creek, so the oldtimers of the area say, gave the creek its name. Later the settlement took its name from Moonbeam Creek.

The population is predominantly French-Canadian.

686

MOORE, township, Lambton County
Position 42° 50′ 82° 20′

As a result of its easy accessibility, located as it is on the St. Clair River, Moore Township was one of the first areas in Lambton County to be settled. When Surveyor Mahlon Burwell interviewed the inhabitants of the township in 1826 to establish the land claims which they had worked out with the Indians, he found that there were 15 French-speaking and 5 English-speaking families, all located on the waterfront. John Courtney, one of the Englishmen, claimed to have been on his lot since 1804 which would make him the original English-speaking settler both in Moore Township and in Lambton County.

The Indians gave up their rights to Moore in 1827; a reserve was set up for them along the Sombra border, but it was purchased by the Crown in 1843. All the settlement in Moore remained along the river until 1836, when the "Bear Creek Settlement" was established in the neighbourhood of Brigden. Those involved in the founding of this community were Robert Brown, John Grant, John Coutts, John McKenzie, John Galloway, Ira Sturtevant and Charles Duncan.

The Township of Moore was named by Sir John Colborne in 1829 in honour of Sir John Moore, the celebrated British General who was killed in Spain in 1809 at the Battle of Corunna. Moore had previously been a part of St. Clair Township, which also included at that time, Sombra, Walpole Island and the Gore of Chatham.

The survey of the township was completed in 1829 by Roswell Mount who squeezed as many lots along the St. Clair River front as possible. Many of these lots were given to veterans of the Napoleonic Wars.

In 1836 there were 573 inhabitants in the township and by 1846 this number had risen only to 780. During the succeeding 20 years, however, the population quadrupled, reaching 3,999 in 1871. The advent of the Canada Southern Railway in 1872 provided a further boost and in 1881 the population had risen to 5,146.

Among the early villages of importance in Moore were Froomfield, Corunna, Mooretown and Courtright on the St. Clair River; Brigden near the west boundary; and Sutherland.

Froomfield, south of the Moore-Sarnia town line, was founded in 1835. Its name was a combination of the Christian names of two brothers, Froom and Field Talfourd. It centred around a grist mill built on what was later called Talfourd Creek.

The oldest settlement in the township, Mooretown, was once a large village, the bustling centre of trade relating to forest products. It was the headquarters for the Mooretown Mounted Infantry which saw action along the St. Clair River front during the Fenian Raids from 1866 to 1870.

Sutherland was the home of the township's first schoolhouse, which opened its doors in 1835 with James Pullman as the teacher.

Although some measure of self-government was granted to Moore settlers in 1840, it was not until the Municipal Act came into effect in the Province in 1850 that the first township council was elected. The first officers were: Reeve, Thomas Fisher; Councillors, James Baby, William Featherstone, John Galloway and Froom Talfourd.

Most of the 74,777 acres of the township is still in farmland, its principal products being corn, wheat, beans, livestock and poultry. The population of Moore in 1979 stood at 9,735.

Jean Turnball Elford: *A History of Lambton County*, 1967.

A.J. Johnston: *Lambton County, Names and Places*, 1925.

MOOREFIELD, police village, Maryborough Township, Wellington County
Position 43° 46′ 80° 45′

In 1852 Richard Moore and his family of ten purchased and settled on the east half of Lot 9, Concession 9 of Maryborough Township. The village of Moorefield derives its name from this same family, for it was Richard Moore who laid out its plan.

Situated in a flourishing agricultural section and on the railway, which was built through the township in 1869, Moorefield became, essentially, an important shipping point.

A thriving village in the last half of the nineteenth century, it contained at one time a number of churches, a schoolhouse, a bank, three hotels, stores, blacksmith shops, a wagon works and a stove factory.

The decline in the importance of the railway cast a shadow over Moorefield's hopes of expansion. However, it does remain a social and trade centre for the surrounding rural population.

Historical Atlas Publishing Company: *Historical Atlas of the County of Wellington*, 1906.

MOOSE CREEK police village, Roxborough Township, Stormont, Dundas and Glengarry County
Position 45° 15′ 74° 58′

Moose Creek, a little stream, flows through this community situated on the CNR, about 20 miles north of Cornwall. Near the village is a small waterfall which rarely freezes over. Moose used to come to this drinking hole, having followed the creek from some distance. While the moose were there lesser animals would stay out of the way, and, therefore, local hunters referred to the stream as Moose Creek. Subsequently, the settlement which first developed on a ridge of land on the west side of the creek, was named by the inhabitants after the creek.

Early settlers were mostly of Scottish origin. Today, both English and French-speaking people live in Moose Creek, which is the centre of a dairy-farming area, and was incorporated as a police village.

The first house was built by a Mr. McFall; two early general stores were operated by Mr. Steinburg and Mr. Vineburg; and a sawmill was erected on the bank of the creek. Most of the young men of the village farmed in the summer and in the winter worked in nearby lumber camps. The construction of the Canada Atlantic

688

Railway between Montreal and Ottawa in 1881 through Moose Creek contributed greatly to the early development of the village.

H. Belden & Co.: *Illustrated Historical Atlas of the Counties of Stormont, Dundas and Glengarry*, 1879.

Moose Factory, Ontario, Photo by J.V.S. Sproat

Public Archives Canada C. 37472

MOOSONEE, Development Area, Cochrane District
Position 51° 17' 80° 39'

This area which stretches over 141,120 acres has a population of 1400. Situated on the west bank of the mighty Moose River near its mouth at James Bay, is the fishing community of Moosonee, northern terminus of the Ontario Northland Railway which was completed in 1932 under the name of Temiskaming and Northern Ontario Railway. Moosonee had its beginning as a fur trading post, operated by the Revillon Frères and located on the site of the present Moosonee Lodge. The French called the post Moosonee, "home of the moose".

The community is the seat of the Roman Catholic diocese of Moosonee, and the predominantly Indian population is served by a modern Roman Catholic hospital.

Opposite Moosonee, on Moose Island, lies Moose Factory. Here the Hudson's Bay Company established its second trading post, built in 1673 by Governor Charles Bayly. The fortified post, known then as Ste. Anne, was captured by a French expedition from Montreal in 1686 and renamed St. Louis. It was later restored to Britain but was not reopened until 1730. Destroyed by fire in 1735, it was rebuilt and became the Hudson's Bay Company's principal post in the James Bay Region. An Anglican mission was established here in 1850.

Twice weekly in the summer months, the so-called "Polar Bear Express" comes to Moosonee bringing tourists and sightseers over the only land transportation route to Ontario's arctic tidewater. In the winter, preceded by a snow plough, the train provides a vital line into this northern region.

The Moosonee Development Area Board.

MOREL, geographic township, Timiskaming District
Position 47° 49′ 80° 43′

Surveyed in 1908-09 by Ontario Land Surveyor Rorke, the township was named for Henry Morel, MPP for Nipissing in 1908. The area, accessible only by its waterways, is situated southwest of Kirkland Lake.

MOREWOOD, police village, Winchester Township, Dundas County
Position 45° 11′ 75° 17′

Located in the northeast corner of the county, Morewood received a post office in 1862 with Alex. McKay as the first postmaster. Messrs. Carlyle built a sawmill here in the late 1860's followed by a grist mill constructed by Thomas Moffat. Early merchants were W. Wallace and Joseph McKay. T. Dupuis was the first blacksmith.

J. Smyth Carter: The Story of Dundas, 1861.

MORLEY, township, Rainy River District
Position 48° 42′ 94° 11′

First surveyed in 1876, this township, today, is a farming community of some 500 people. It was incorporated in 1903 and was named after John Morley, a British statesman.

The mainstay of the area's economy is beef production, and the District cattle auction yard is located in Morley.

The population is served by churches of the United, Roman Catholic and Mennonite denominations.

The township is situated to the north of the Rainy River and across the international boundary from the State of Minnesota. Highway 11 and Canadian National Railways provide transportation routes across the township, while other roads run throughout. The station point of Stratton lies on the CNR line. Tributaries of the Rainy River drain the area.

Formerly Township 55, Range 25E, Morley Additional is situated to the east of Morley Township.

MORNINGSTAR, geographic township, Algoma District
Position 47° 01′ 82° 53′

Formerly Township 5B, Morningstar was named for E.P. Morningstar,

MPP for Welland. The township lies north of Elliot Lake, and is not accessible by road or rail.

MORNINGTON, township, Perth County
Position 43° 35' 80° 53'

Located in the northeast of Perth County, the township is named after Lord Mornington, a member of the British government in the early nineteenth century. Mixed farming predominates in the area which once formed part of the "Queen's Bush", as the district north of the lands owned by the Canada Company was known. Settlement was generally later here than in the southern portion of the county. The earliest settlers of the township were John Chalmers and his sons who came from Scotland in 1843 and cleared land in the east. They were followed by many others throughout the 1840's, including Andrew Harron, the ancestor of actor and author, Don Harron.

After the 1848 survey, settlement increased rapidly and by 1861 3,040 inhabitants lived in Mornington. Although a large number were of German and British descent, over half of the residents came from other parts of Canada or the Atlantic provinces. In the 1860's Mennonites arrived from Waterloo County, helping to enlarge the German element in the township.

When under the Municipal Act of 1850 Perth County became independent, organization of local government in the north resulted in the creation of Mornington, Elma, and Wallace Townships. Mornington became a municipality in 1854, having been annexed to Ellice for municipal purposes until then. The first Reeve was James Whaley, with council consisting of Adam Chalmers, William Rutherford, John Nicklin, and John Hamilton.

Road construction was difficult in the township as there were few deposits of gravel. The settlers were, therefore, anxious to have a railway to take their produce to market and in 1869 helped to fund the construction of the Wellington, Grey, and Bruce Railway, which linked them with Hamilton. However, the lack of a north-south railway linking the township with Stratford, resulted in a movement in the 1870's in which northern townships wished to separate from Perth County. In 1882 the amalgamation of the Grand Trunk and Great Western Railways led to the building of a line to Stratford and helped to reunite the county.

The first mill in the township was established in 1847 by John Freeborn, with another one being set up about the same time by John Nicklin. In 1848 William Rutherford opened the first store. Small communities grew quickly with Millbank and West's Corners (now Milverton) rivalling for the commercial business of the township. Millbank became very prosperous, with several mills and an agricultural machinery works. However, commercial supremacy passed to the other community when the Stratford and Huron Railway was built 2½ miles away from Millbank, but with a station at Milverton. By 1880 Milverton was large enough to be incorporated as a municipality and it separated from Mornington in the same year.

Most of the inhabitants were either Presbyterian, Methodist, or

Anglican, although a large number of Lutherans and Mennonites had arrived after 1860. The oldest records are those of an Anglican congregation in Millbank in 1850, led by the Rev. William Clotworthy. The Methodists under the Rev. Mr. Robinson were established in Milverton from 1855 and the first Presbyterian service was held in 1856. The Roman Catholic parish of St. Mary's at Hesson in the north end of the township, founded about 1855 by Andrew Biesinger and George Stemmler, was probably the first German congregation. Rev. Mr. Staebler organized the Evangelical church in 1872 and Rev. Mr. Shumbach, the Lutheran church in 1873.

In 1879 Mornington was noted for the large number of its post offices. Millbank became a post office in 1848 with William Rutherford as postmaster. Milverton developed from a shoe shop and tavern opened in 1848 by Andrew J. West, and called West's Corners. In 1854 David Matthews became the first postmaster there. It was renamed Milverton in 1871. Poole was an unincorporated "town", which was planned but not built up. Topping and Brunner were small post offices. Other areas of settlement included Morningdale, Burns, Carthage, Tralee, and Musselburg.

H. Belden & Co.: *Historical Atlas of Perth County*, 1879.

W. Stafford Johnston and Hugh J.M. Johnston: *History of Perth County of 1967*, 1967.

William Johnston: *History of Perth County*, *1825-1902*, 1903.

MORRIS, township, Huron County
Position 43° 47′ 81° 17′

Located in northern Huron County, Morris Township derived its name from the Honourable William Morris, a Cabinet Minister in the Legislature of Upper Canada at the time the township was being surveyed.

Morris was laid out in the shape of a parallelogram, bounded on the north by Turnberry, on the south by Hullett and McKillop, on the east by Grey, and on the west by Wawanosh. It is watered by the south branch of the Maitland River which enters the township at Brussels and winds through it in irregular fashion to Wingham. With the exception of the areas along the river, the land is even and of good quality.

The township was surveyed under the direction of Alexander Wilkinson who had a map completed by 1849. The first public Crown Land sale in Morris was held in 1852, followed by another in 1853. Prior to this time there were hardly any settlers in the township.

The first clearings in the township are believed to have been made between 1849 and 1850 by Kenneth McBean and William McConnell, both of whom eventually settled near the present village of Blyth. The only other settlers known to have come into the township before the land sale of 1852 were a group which settled in the Belgrave area. This party included John McRae, Christopher Corbett, John Brandon and Robert Armstrong. All four were Irish from the County Fermanagh.

In the latter part of 1852, after the sale, settlers took up land in various sections of the township. Charles Parker was the first of these to arrive. Other early settlers were Joseph England, William, John and David Geddes, Hector McLean, Abraham Proctor and Joseph Stubbs. John Kelly, William Wilson and the Laidlaw brothers purchased their land in the 1853 sale. Settlement proceeded at a rapid pace in the ensuing years, the settlers being primarily of English and Scottish origin with a good sprinkling of Irishmen. The result was that in 1861 the township had a population of 2,333 with more than 7,000 acres under cultivation in crops such as wheat, peas, oats, potatoes and turnips. In terms of livestock the settlers of Morris concentrated on cattle and pigs and produced large quantities of butter by 1861.

The two main settlements which are partly located in Morris are Blyth and Brussels, both incorporated villages. Blyth was once known as Drummondville after John Drummond who operated the local hotel and a shoe shop. Brussels had its beginning in 1852 when William Ainley arrived and cleared some land. In 1855 he laid out a town plot and named it Ainleyville. The settlement took on the name of Brussels in 1872 when it was incorporated as a village.

The first school in the township was on Lot 11 of Concession 6, and the first teacher was Rebecca Vance from Brucefield in Tuckersmith.

The New Connexion Methodist itinerant preacher, Rev. Mr. Atkins began his rounds as early as 1853, travelling by snowshoes and carrying his provisions and clothing in a pack on his back.

Along with Grey, Morris was united with the Township of McKillop until 1856 when it became an independent municipal unit. Charles Parker was the first reeve with Christopher Corbett, William Wilson, John McRae and Charles Forrest serving as councillors. The first township clerk was J.B. Taylor and the first assessor, John Laidlaw. Donald Scott was collector.

The township continued to prosper and by 1875 over half of it, 28,372 acres, was cleared. Cattle had doubled and sheep had become important in the agricultural economy.

Besides Brussels and Blyth, there were several small crossroads post offices established in the township. Morrisdale was the earliest, with Donald Scott as its postmaster (1854). In 1855 the settlement of Bodmin became a post village with William Harris as postmaster. The only other settlement of any size was Belgrave which received a post office in 1864 with Simon Armstrong as postmaster. This village, on a tributary of the Maitland River, developed out of the early settlement of the Irish pioneers who had come from Simcoe County. In time it became a thriving community, largely due to the fact that the London, Huron and Bruce Railway passed through it and established a station there.

James Scott: *The Settlement of Huron County*, 1966.

MORRISBURG, village, Williamsburgh Township, Dundas County
Position 44° 54' 75° 11'

Morrisburg, prior to incorporation known as West Williamsburg, owes its birth to the construction of the St. Lawrence Canals, in particular to the Rapid du Plat Canal, at the foot of which the village developed. Among those who first settled here were the Roses, Merckleys and Casselmans.

Morrisburg was but a crude settlement in 1813 when an American force of more than 7000 men marched down the shores of the St. Lawrence towards Crysler's farm near the site of the present village. Here in a decisive battle of the War the Americans were defeated. The actual battle site was flooded by the St. Lawrence River when the canals were built, but a short distance to the east of Morrisburg, at Upper Canada Village, this epic battle is commemorated. Upper Canada Village was created by the government as a museum pioneer village in order to save some of the historic buildings of the area that would otherwise have been submerged by the St. Lawrence Seaway Development in 1958.

The visitor entering the village is carried back 100 years and more, to the time of the early settlers. Upper Canada Village is filled with the artifacts of their daily lives; the village shops and businesses carry on pioneer activities. There are early homes, a school and a church, a woollen mill, a bakery, a blacksmithy, a cabinetmaker's shop, an inn and a printing office.

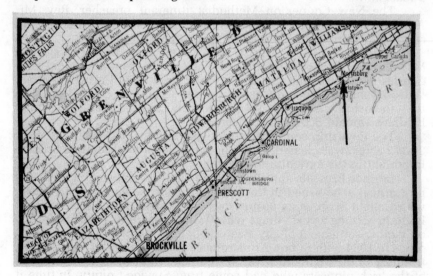

A local historian tells us that the land on which Morrisburg stands was once traded for a bottle of rum. But the deal was not quite as paltry as it would seem; in those days a "bottle" was much larger, holding more than one gallon. With the building of the Rapid du Plat Canal in 1844, the little settlement of Morrisburg became the centre of Dundas County commerce.

Between 1850 and 1860 the village grew rapidly aided by the construction of the Grand Trunk Railway which passed nearby in 1855. By 1860 Morrisburg was large enough to be incorporated as a village. The first council was elected in 1861 consisting of the following members: James H. Casselman, Isaac N. Rose, James W. Miller, Fred Bradfield and Alexander G. Macdonell. Macdonell was elected reeve.

At the time of its incorporation the village received its present name of Morrisburg in honour of the Hon. James Morris, Canada's Postmaster General, and a resident of Brockville.

In 1867 Morrisburg had a population of 1,400. There were three hotels, a schoolhouse, a Roman Catholic church and thriving mercantile and industrial shops.

Today Morrisburg has a new face. During the construction of the Seaway, about two-thirds of the old village including Main Street, the river front, the Music Hall, and many residences, disappeared beneath the St. Lawrence River. They were replaced by new developments, a modern shopping centre, and new subdivisions.

Modern Morrisburg, located at the junction of Highways 2 and 31, and on the CNR's Toronto-Montreal line, about 25 miles west of Cornwall, has a number of manufacturing plants and is the business centre for the surrounding agricultural and tourist area.

Cornwall Standard-Freeholder, 1967.

The St. Lawrence Parks Commission: Ontario's Living Heritage: Upper Canada Village.

MORRISTON, police village, Puslinch Township, Wellington County
Position 43° 27' 80° 07'

In 1844 Donald Campbell kept a small store in a log building in this vicinity; James McIntosh operated a tailoring business and John McEdwards had a blacksmith shop. At that time there were no other houses in the place.

R.B. Morrison who came in 1847, opened a store at one end of the blacksmith shop. Shortly after this, work of improving the Brock Road, also known as Dundas Road, commenced in the township.

In 1849 Mr. Morrison built a frame store on the east side of the road, and about that time the settlement was named.

A post office was established in 1854. Archibald Little opened a hotel, and in 1856 Messrs. McLean and Clark erected a sawmill, followed by oatmeal and grist mills. Known as the Puslinch Mills, they were destroyed by fire in 1861. At the turn of the century, Morriston had a hotel, flour and planing mills, and a carriage factory.

The village lost one of its old landmarks in 1965 when the CPR station was demolished to make way for the reconstruction of Highway 6.

Puslinch Historical Committee: Annals of Puslinch 1950-67, 1967.

Historical Atlas Publishing Co.: Historical Atlas of the County of Wellington, Ontario, 1906.

MORSE, geographic township, Sudbury District
Position 46° 56' 81° 46'

Situated northwest of Sudbury, Morse Township was named after

John M. Morse, patentee of mining lands north of Thunder Bay. The township was surveyed in 1888 and 1911.

MORSON, township, Rainy River District
Position 49° 03' 94° 18'

Morson was established in 1928 and incorporated in 1956. Nine families — the Kanutsons, Bergs, Swensons, Donaldsons, Rodeyards, Holzes, Walkers, Morrissons, Sundeans — were the early settlers of Morson Township. They located at the head of Big Grassy River at the Rapids. It was here that a post office was established.

The township was named after the Morrisson family. However, the spelling was changed to "Morson" because at the time another Morrison Township existed in Ontario.

Logging, commercial fishing, trapping and tourism are the present-day industries in the township which has a population of 177 (1979). In the summer months the population is swelled by a large influx of visitors, particularly from the United States.

Township of Morson.

MORTIMER, geographic township, Cochrane District
Position 48° 56' 80° 38'

Mortimer Township was named after the Honourable Sir Wm. Mortimer, Lieutenant Governor of Ontario from 1902-08. Canadian National Railways provides access to the northern end of the township.

MOSA, township, Middlesex County
Position 44° 43' 81° 46'

This township was established in 1821. Mosa is the Latin name for the River Meuse in Belgium. On the banks of this river the Prussian army had been drawn up just before the epic Battle of Waterloo on June 18, 1815. The township, triangular in shape, occupies the southwestern corner of the county. In the south it is bounded by the Thames River which divides it from Elgin County.

The first settlers were Talbot St. John Ward, Big John Ward, Alex. Ward, John D. Anderson, John Coyne, Andrew and George Fleming and James Allgeo. Alex. Ward opened a tavern west of Strathburn. Talbot St. John Ward, who had been christened by Colonel Talbot, colonizer of southwestern Ontario, owned part of the land on which Wardsville now stands. As late as 1849, Wardsville on the Thames was the only large settlement in the township with a population of about 200. There were two grist mills, two sawmills, one fulling and one carding mill in operation back then.

The northern part of the township, where the soil was of hard clay, was settled by Highland Scots. Among the early settlers there were the Campbells, McClarktys, and McCalluns.

One story related by Duncan Campbell who came to Mosa in

1831 is typical of the problems facing the early pioneers in Mosa as well as other townships. After two years of hard work the Campbells and several of the neighbours had managed to raise some pigs. They were looking forward to enjoying a good supply of pork when they realized they didn't have any salt to preserve the meat. Port Stanley, a distance of 50 miles, was the nearest source. Mr. Campbell yoked his oxen and journeyed to Port Stanley where he bought a barrel of salt. Using the crotch of a tree as a sled, he tied the barrel to it and completed the round trip of 100 miles home. Back in Mosa he was received with rejoicing, the salt barrel remaining a neighbourhood treasure for many a day.

Mosa Township's first Reeve was pioneer settler William Neal. He took office in 1850 as a result of the new Municipal Act organizing municipal government in the Province.

Mosa today (1979) has a population of 1370. Communities include Strathburn, Woodgreen and Kilmartin. Newbury and Wardsville are incorporated villages, as is Glencoe on the Ekfrid town line. The area is served by the CNR and the CPR and Highways 2 and 80.

MOSCOW, community, Camden Township, Lennox and Addington County
Position 44° 26′ 76° 48′

The dispersed rural community of Moscow is located about 20 miles northwest of Kingston and fifteen miles northeast of Napanee.

Jacob Huffman who formerly lived in Richmond Township was the first to take up land in the vicinity in the early 1820's. He was later joined by his brother, Elijah, and the place was known for many years as the Huffman Settlement. Elijah was noted in these parts of the county for his hunting skills and with the bounty he received from the government for the wolves he shot, he was able to build a road to the settlement which stood up well enough to be incorporated in a highway of more recent vintage.

Other early settlers in the area included Joseph Foster, a farmer and a staunch supporter of temperance who, from time to time, visited other settlements to lecture on this subject; and Joseph, Lyman and John Amey, three brothers, who had come from Bath near Kingston.

A school was opened around the middle of the century with Zara VanLuven as the first teacher. A Mr. Cromer operated a store and served as the first postmaster. He later sold the store to VanLuven. The post office had been established in 1854 under the name of Springfield, but the inhabitants soon found out that their mail frequently went astray as there were several other Springfields in the country. At a meeting in the VanLuven's house, the name Moscow was suggested to commemorate Napoleon's retreat from that city in the winter of 1812. Russian history was a much discussed subject in the days of the Crimean War which raged from 1853 to 1856 between Turkey and the Russian Empire.

In the 1870's a cheese factory was opened in Moscow by George Garrison. It was later purchased by the VanLuven brothers. Struck by lightning in 1906, it was rebuilt, but was once again destroyed by fire a few years later. Rebuilt for the third time, the operation was finally discontinued in 1957 when yet another fire levelled the building.

Walter S. Herrington: *History of the County of Lennox and Addington*, 1913.

MOSES, geographic township, Sudbury District
Position 46° 35' 82° 00'

The area is named for Elliott Moses, one of the most outstanding Indians on the Six Nations Reserve. Situated northwest of Espanola, the area is accessible by road and drained by the Wakonassin River and Alces Creek.

MOUNTAIN, township, Stormont, Dundas and Glengarry County
Position 45° 03' 75° 26'

Mountain Township was named in 1798 after the Rev. Dr. Mountain, first Protestant Bishop of Canada. The first settlers in Mountain were of Loyalist stock and included David Brown, Jas. Jackson, Daniel Garnsey and his son Samuel. They located along the banks of the Nation River. By 1815 the township reported an assessment roll of twenty-eight persons. Arriving in 1819 were the McIntyres, and in 1826 came John Hyndman. The area they settled was later referred to as "the Old Settlement".

Land in this township was reasonably fertile and agriculture prospered. Several early communities grew up to supply the outlying farm areas. Inkerman was the most important village in Mountain during the 1800's. It is situated on the Nation River near the centre of the township.

The site was originally part of a 400-acre grant owned by United Empire Loyalist Robert Parker. He erected the first building where the village now stands. Saw and grist mills powered by the Nation River formed the nucleus of the settlement which was known for many years first as Smith's Mills and then as Bishop's Mills. The place was christened Inkerman to commemorate a famous battle during the Crimean War when a post office was opened in 1855. A flourishing lumber trade was once carried on in the village which boasted a population of about 400 by the late 1870's.

Boyd's Bridge was the earliest settlement in the township. Here the pioneer traveller could rest at the hotel, have his horses shod and buy supplies at the store. When in 1835 Samuel Guernsey built a grist mill on the Nation River a few miles to the west of Boyd's Bridge, a new community developed there known as South Mountain. In time it grew into a flourishing village of 450 with industries, shops, stores, hotels, and five churches. It was incorporated as a police village in 1901.

Another early community of the township was Hallville with 300 inhabitants.

The village of Mountain a few miles to the south of Hallville owes its existence to the Canadian Pacific Railway. The railway station became the nucleus of a settlement in the late 19th century. A grist mill and a sawmill, as well as elevators, were erected. Albert Brinston opened a planing mill, L. Richardson built the CPR hotel, and a temperance house was built by A.J. Stewart.

Mountain Township, today, has a population of just over 2900. The area is served by Highway 43.

H. Belden & Co.: *Illustrated Historical Atlas of the Counties of Stormont, Dundas and Glengarry*, 1879.

J. Smyth Carter: *The Story of Dundas*, 1905.

MOUNTAIN GROVE, community, Olden Township, Frontenac County
Position 44° 44' 76° 51'

This hamlet just south of Highway 7 is the main settlement in Olden Township. It was named for a large grove of pine trees still standing near the village cemetery.

A post office was opened at Edmund Godfrey's homestead in the mid-nineteenth century. The house also served as a stopping place for travellers. In the early years the manufacture of potash and the production of maple sugar were the main industries in this vicinity. In the winter many men supplemented their income by lumbering. A schoolhouse, built in 1862, served also as a town hall and on Sundays as a church.

The CPR building a line through the township in the early 1880's provided construction work. The first train arrived at the Mountain Grove station in 1883, and with the railway came an era of prosperity. Mountain Grove became the shipping point and supply centre for the surrounding area. Dairy farming was carried out in Olden Township and tons of cheese and butter, as well as large quantities of cream, were shipped to market from the Mountain Grove Station.

Alex MacDonald opened a new general store, and four generations of MacDonalds since then have served the area in this line. Another store was built across the road by Gilbert Flynn. Alfred Lardley operated a boardinghouse and a store, and Bill Crawford erected a hotel near the station. About that time a Methodist church, an Orange Hall and a new town hall were added to the village. In 1900 Sam Abbott opened a cheese factory which continued in production until 1940.

The community began to decline in the 1920's. The effects of the Depression of the '30's were somewhat alleviated when Highway 7 was built north of Mountain Grove in 1932, providing employment in construction work. In 1962 the CPR line between Tweed and Glen Tay was closed and the old Mountain Grove station dismantled. Today there are few farms left and dairying has all but disappeared. Many of the inhabitants commute to work in Kingston, Verona, or Perth.

Kingston-Whig Standard.

Marjorie Euns: *Community Spotlight*, 1974.

MOUNT BRYDGES, police village, Caradoc Township, Middlesex County
Position 42° 54' 81° 29'

Mount Brydges was one of those communities brought to life by the railroad. Situated on Highway 81, southwest of London, in a thriving agricultural district, it became an important shipping point when the Great Western Railway (later Grand Trunk and now the CNR) arrived in 1854. Part of the name is derived from the fact that the village stands on the highest point in the area, hence the prefix "Mount". Brydges commemorates C.J. Brydges, one time general manager of the Grand Trunk Railway. Originally the settlement was known as Hartford.

In the 1850's the place had a population of 180. There were two saloons, a steam sawmill, a cabinet and a harnessmaker, and a number of the inhabitants were lumbermen.

The Caradoc Township Hall was erected at Mount Brydges in 1870 and remodelled in 1920. In 1906 Mount Brydges was incorporated as a police village.

H.R. Page & Co.: *Illustrated Historical Atlas of the County of Middlesex*, 1878.

MOUNT FOREST, town, Arthur Township, Wellington County
Position 43° 59′ 80° 44′

Mount Forest is located in the centre of a rich agricultural section of Western Ontario, on the south branch of the Saugeen River which was at one time thought to be part of the Maitland River. As a result of this geographical error, the community was originally named "Maitland Hills", and "Maitland Woods". A blending of these two names supposedly produced the new name, Mount Forest, in 1853 when Francis Kerr surveyed and laid out the town plot.

The location of the town is the result of the original survey for the Garafraxa Road made by Charles Rankin between the Fergus settlement and Owen Sound. Rankin, in order to avoid the swamps of Luther Township, jogged to the west, crossing the Saugeen River near the future site of Mount Forest. The survey was carried out between 1837 and 1841, being interrupted by the Mackenzie Rebellion of 1837.

John Foster is believed to have been the first settler of Mount Forest north of the Saugeen. He arrived probably before 1840.

Pressure was being applied on the government by the pioneers as early as 1843 for the establishment of a mill in the central part of the road to Owen Sound. The result was the construction of a sawmill in 1850 and a flour mill in 1851 at a site on the Saugeen River half a mile from the Garafraxa Road. No settlers lived at the present site of the town when these mills were built. The customers were the people who had settled along the Garafraxa Road.

Richard Chaloner is said to have built the first log house on the actual site of Mount Forest and to have established the first blacksmith's shop.

The Mount Forest Post Office was opened in 1847 with Thomas Adam Young as postmaster. This post office was located on the north side of the Saugeen and lots were also laid out on this side of the river. In 1855 a considerable number of settlers came in.

By 1864, the population had grown to 1,185 and Mount Forest was incorporated as a village. Both the Counties of Grey and

Wellington claimed the Village of Mount Forest. A Royal Proclamation of November 23, 1865, settled the dispute annexing the village to the County of Wellington.

During the middle of the nineteenth century, Mount Forest experienced a growth in industries. There were saw and grist mills, an oatmeal mill, a shingle and planing mill, and a cooperage and stave mill, making barrels for flour. The town also had a woollen mill, a furniture factory, a tannery, a sash and door factory, a pump factory, a potash and soap factory, a brewery, a foundry, and a wagon and carriage factory.

On November 13, 1871, Mount Forest welcomed its first train on the Toronto, Grey and Bruce Railway. Mount Forest's growth rate accelerated rapidly after the coming of the railway, and in 1878 it was incorporated as a town. The population today is 3,453 (1979).

The town is served by the CNR and CPR and Highway 6, which runs through the centre.

William J. Edwards: Mount Forest: The Way We Were, 1979.

A.W. Wright: Memories of Mount Forest and Surrounding Townships, 1928.

MOUNT HOREB, community, Manvers Township, Victoria County
Position 44° 15′ 78° 39′

Located eight miles southeast of Lindsay on the boundary of Manvers and Ops Townships, Mount Horeb derives its name both from its height affording a magnificent view of the countryside, and from the ancient Bible name Horeb, the mountain where, according to the Bible, the Law was given to Moses.

The early settlers came from County Cork, Ireland, in 1840. They included the Reynolds, Pogue, Skuce, Southam and Beamish families. Two small stores were owned by Lees and McGills from 1840-70. There were also in 1858 two hotels owned by William Reynolds, and William Rea and James Lindsay.

The first log school was built in 1850 and the Methodist Church was erected in 1861.

The post office was established in 1863 and William Reynolds was the first postmaster.

Mrs. Ross N. Carr: The Rolling Hills, 1967.

MOWAT, geographic township, Parry Sound District
Position 45° 55′ 80° 26′

Situated south of the French River, the area was established in 1866 and named after Sir Oliver Mowat, Lieutenant Governor of Ontario, 1897-1902. The township includes two Indian Reserves in the northern region, and Grundy Lake Provincial Park in the central portion. Pickerel River flows westward across the northern section and the Key River across the centre. Canadian National and Canadian Pacific Railways and Highway 69 serve the area, which contains several communities, including French River, Bon Air, Pickerel, Pakesley, Ludgate and Mowat.

MULLOY, geographic township, Cochrane District
Position 49° 54' 84° 48'

Mulloy Township, the location of numerous dams on the Otasawian River, is situated west of Hearst. The name is for a Trooper Mulloy who lost his eyesight fighting in the Boer War, 1899-1901.

MULMUR, geographic township, Dufferin County
Position 44° 12' 80° 06'

The rural township of Mulmur occupies the northeast corner of the County of Dufferin.

Locally it is said that the township was named after a son of Tecumseh, the famous Shawnee Indian Chief who was killed fighting on the side of the British at the Battle of Moraviantown in the War of 1812. Although Tecumseh had a son, it is not known what his name was.

The first survey of Mulmur was made in 1823 and the first settlement grew up in the area of present-day Stanton. The Hands and the Walkers were among the early settlers, along with the members of the Gallaugher family who located around Mansfield. A few years later the settlement of Whitfield developed in the centre of the township with the names of Whitley, Lloyd, Graham and Holmes appearing. In the northwest corner of the township, where Honeywood sprang up, settled the families, Tupling, Murdy, Lamont, Markela and Mortimer.

Mulmur elected its own council in the year 1851 as follows: Reeve, Paul Gallaugher; Councillors, David McCutcheon, William Hand, James Mitchell, and John Cooper.

In 1881 the population of the township was 3,505. The main communities, each with its own small industries and mills, included Mansfield, Honeywood, Rosemont, Stanton and Primrose. With the decline in the use of waterpower, the industries of these communities faded, being attracted to larger centres.

There are no incorporated villages in the township which depends largely on agriculture. The population has dwindled to just over 1800 (1979).

Stephen Sawden: *History of Dufferin County.*

MULOCK, geographic township, Nipissing District
Position 46° 30' 79° 19'

The Ontario Northland Railway cuts across the extreme southwestern corner of the township situated northeast of North Bay. The station point of Mulock is located in the southwestern section, on the railway line. The name commemorates Sir Wm. Mulock, Toronto Member of the King's Privy Council.

MULVEY, geographic township, Cochrane District
Position 49° 54′ 83° 22′

Partially surveyed in 1907, this township takes its name from Thomas Mulvey, K.C., one time Assistant Provincial Secretary for Ontario. Located northeast of Hearst, the area is watered by the Missinaibi River and several smaller creeks.

MUNRO, geographic township, Cochrane District
Position 48° 35′ 80° 12′

Located about twelve miles east of Matheson by Highway 101, Munro Township was first subdivided in 1904 by Ontario Land Surveyor S. Dobie. It was named for G.P. Munro, MP for Renfrew North, circa 1903.

MURCHISON, geographic township, Nipissing District
Position 45° 34′ 78° 02′

Established in 1872, the township was named after Sir Roderick Impey Murchison, the famous geologist from Scotland. The area is situated southwest of Pembroke and includes Victoria Lake in the northern corner.

MURDOCK, geographic township, Sudbury District
Position 48° 03′ 82° 56′

Murdock Township is located northeast of Chapleau, just north of Highway 101. It was named for James Murdock, a former MLA. The Shawmere River flows through the eastern section, and Murdock Lake lies just south of the Northern boundary.

MURPHY, geographic township, Cochrane District
Position 48° 35′ 81° 16′

First surveyed in 1904, Murphy Township takes its name from G.G. Murphy, a chief clerk in the government Sales Branch Department during the 1860's. Located just north of Timmins, it is accessible via Highway 655, and the Ontario Northland Railway.

MURPHYS POINT PROVINCIAL PARK, North Burgess Township,
Lanark County
Position 44° 47′ 76° 13′

Opened in 1977, this Natural Environment Park is on the Big Rideau Lake portion of the Rideau Canal about equidistant from Kingston and Ottawa.

Murphys Point is situated on an extension of the Canadian Shield known as the Frontenac Axis and is a park of rocky outcrops and forest, with access to other lakes. Mica, feldspar and apatite native

703

to the rock formation were once mined here. The park was probably named for John Murphy who built a log house there in 1856 and whose family continued to live on the point until the 1930's.

The Rideau Canal, constructed between 1826 and 1832 under the direction of Colonel John By as a safe water route from Montreal to Kingston, was defended by blockhouses against American invasion. One of the blockhouses remains at the Narrows Lock, three miles upriver from the park. County roads leading from the town of Perth, about 6 miles to the north on Highway 7, and from Highway 15, out of the city of Kingston to the South, reach Murphys Point Provincial Park.

Ontario Ministry of Natural Resources.

MURRAY, township, Northumberland County
Position 44° 09′ 77° 39′

Murray Township, bordered in the north by Percy Reach of the Trent River and in the south by Wellers Bay of Lake Ontario, was surveyed first in 1791 and again in 1796. It was named after James Murray, a distinguished British soldier who took part in the siege of Quebec in 1759 and became Governor of Quebec the following year.

The township was settled early by United Empire Loyalists, some of whom had moved in from the townships along the Bay of Quinte. Among those who received grants along the broken front of the township after the first survey was made, were Hugh McQuaid, Capt. Bullock, Thos. Potts, Thos. Smith, Rolph Bell, Jas. Powers, Samuel Sherwood, Asa Weller and many others.

Asa Weller opened a tavern at Carrying Place. He also kept a sled and oxen to convey passengers up the lake shore. Peter Maybee settled in the north of the township along with the Wessel family. An English family by the name of Flendall were also among the early settlers. George and Stephen Flendall operated farms and ran a brewery in Trenton.

On the second concession developed the so-called English Settlement. Here the Pilkey, Lovatt and Power families resided. Wooler village, located on the fifth concession, became the township seat and here the town hall was built. In the early days the village was known as Smith's Corners after settler Thomas Smith. Smith's wife had beautiful long red hair and, so the story goes, she had quite a temper that resulted in frequent arguments with her husband. The latter supposedly, one day, dragged her through the street by the hair. "Wool her, Wool 'er!" shouted an onlooker, and, according to local legend, the village from then on was known as Wooler.

Once heavily wooded with pine and other hardwood, the township today is primarily a farming district producing fruit and vegetables, as well as providing excellent pasture for dairy herds.

One of the township's most important establishments is the Dominion Experimental Farm at Smithfield. The station occupies 300 acres and has a processing lab, cold storage, greenhouse, and pole barn. Here research is carried out related to the fruits and vegetables native to this area.

H. Belden & Co.: *Illustrated Historical Atlas of the Counties of Northumberland and Durham*, 1878.

Leona M. Austin: *Wooler 100 Years*, 1975.

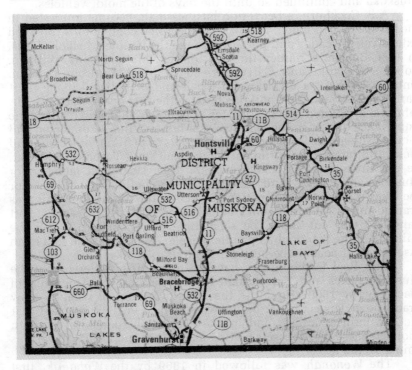

MUSKOKA DISTRICT Municipality
Position 44° 37' 79° 22'

The District Municipality of Muskoka covers an area of 987,283.2 acres. It is 60 miles at its widest point and 42 miles at its longest, and is bounded by Georgian Bay on the west and the Severn River on the south.

Muskoka, one of Ontario's most popular resort areas both in summer and in winter, owes its beauty to the rock formations of the Precambrian Shield with its many lakes carved by the ice-sheets of the last glacial period.

The name Muskoka is said to have derived from the Chippawa chief Nesqua Ukee, whose Indian name meant "Not easily turned back in battle".

Algonquin Indians were the first recorded inhabitants of what is now known as Muskoka. They were nomadic, trading meat and furs with the Hurons for agricultural products. In 1649 the Hurons were annihilated by the Iroquois; gradually the Algonquins moved southward and by 1763 when the British took over, an Ojibway band was located in the Muskoka District. A treaty made in 1850 with the Ojibway ceded an ill-defined area in Muskoka to the Crown.

The district is drained by a maze of lakes and rivers which ultimately empty via the Muskoka River into Georgian Bay.

Navigation played an important part in the development of Muskoka and continued so until the days of the motor vehicles.

A.P. Cockburn, a Beaverton businessman, became interested in the Muskoka area when, in 1865, he and some companions travelled extensively by canoe and portage through the various Muskoka lakes. In 1866 Benjamin Hardcastle Johnston and his four sons, William, Robert, Benjamin and Garry, arrived in Muskoka from London, Ontario. He built a dwelling on the island of Indian Village (Port Carling) near the rapids, and this became the first post office with Mr. Johnston appointed first postmaster in 1868. Mr. Johnston realized the importance of having the waterways at Indian Village connected and secured signatures from most of the settlers to petition for a canal and locks. But he received little encouragement from Toronto. However, he did interest A.P. Cockburn, at the time Dominion member for Muskoka and Parry Sound, who promised to build a line of boats for the lakes if government sanctioned work on the waterways. This was granted and in 1869 the canal and locks were started. The canal at Port Sandfield was cut about the same time. Mr. Cockburn began the building of the *Wenonah*, a paddle wheeler, which was the first of an assortment of boats to be built for the Muskoka lakes.

John Beal is thought to have been the first settler to ply the Muskoka Lakes and Bracebridge River, reaching the Township of Macaulay in 1860. He built the first dwelling at what is now Bracebridge. James Cooper built a wooden boat in 1862; the next year McCabe built a sailboat and in 1864 James Sharper followed with another. These three vessels carried passengers and freight to various points on the lakes.

The *Wenonah* was followed in 1869 by the *Wabamik*, first propeller boat on Muskoka waters. The fleet was increased by the *Nipissing*, a paddle wheel boat in 1871. The *Simcoe* was brought by rail to Gravenhurst in 1875, this tug was used mainly for towing logs. The *Muskoka* was built to replace the *Simcoe*. The *Kenozha* (Indian for pickerel) built at Gravenhurst in 1883, was one of the most popular of the lake steamers.

There were many other steamers which were part of The Muskoka and Nipissing Navigation Co. fleet. The company changed its name several times, finally known as the Muskoka Lakes Line. Many people lamented the passing of the steamers, claiming that with them disappeared some of the summertime glamour of the Muskokas.

At one time it was advocated that the area should be made into a large Indian reservation. However, in 1859 R.J. Oliver was appointed land agent and applications for settlement at Severn Bridge were received and 17 location tickets were issued for land adjoining the road. In 1861 the Townships of Morrison, Muskoka, Draper and Macaulay were offered for settlement and the remaining townships of Muskoka and Parry Sound were surveyed and laid out into lots.

The land was made available under the Public Lands Act of 1860 which was amended in 1868 by the Free Grants Act. The Muskoka townships opened for location after the passing of the 1868 Act were:

Cardwell, Macaulay, Watt, Brunel, Draper, McLean, Muskoka and Stephenson.

The Muskoka district was annexed to Simcoe County in 1851. The Parliamentary Representation Act of 1853 divided Simcoe into two ridings. The north riding, which included Muskoka, elected Angus Morrison to represent it in 1854.

Emigration societies in England played a role in the settlement of Muskoka. By 1869 a dozen such organizations in London alone were helping families emigrate.

Settlement did not proceed quickly until the clearing of the Muskoka Road. In 1861 the only post office in Muskoka was at Severn Bridge, the mail being carried there on foot from Orillia once a week. In 1864 a post office was established at Bracebridge, the first postmaster was a man named Bailey.

Rev. Gillman Willson was the first stationed minister in Muskoka. He ceased active ministry in 1865 and went into the manufacturing of lumber, shingles and siding in Bracebridge with his son-in-law.

Much of the Muskoka District was not suited to settlement. After several years the humus built up by the forests was depleted and farms were abandoned. Many areas are covered today with natural new forest and reforestation plantings, the abundant virgin forest having long been cut by pioneer families and lumbermen.

In addition to the 36,665 permanent population (1979), the transient summer population occupying vacation homes in the resort areas is estimated at another 70,000 to 75,000.

In 1970 the District, formerly consisting of four towns, three villages and eighteen municipal townships, was reorganized into three towns, namely, Gravenhurst, Bracebridge and Huntsville, and three large townships: Georgian Bay, Lake of Bays and Muskoka Lakes.

George W. Boyer: *Early Days in Muskoka*, 1970.

Geraldine Coombe: *Muskoka: past and present*, 1976.

MUSKOKA LAKES, township, District Municipality of Muskoka
Position 45° 01' 79° 37'

Formed in 1971 by the amalgamation of the Town of Bala, the Village of Port Carling, the Village of Windermere and the Townships of Cardwell and Watt, and parts of Medora and Wood Township, and Monck Township, Muskoka Lakes Township has an area of 205,292.8 acres with a total of 7,706 households, including summer cottages, and a permanent population of 4,712 (1979).

Port Carling (once known as Indian Village) was the first settlement in the Township of Medora and Wood. The Bailey family were the first permanent residents arriving in 1865. In 1868 Mr. Johnston became the first postmaster. He was responsible for naming the village in honour of his friend, Sir John Carling of London, who was Minister of Public Works when the locks were built at Port Carling. This village and the township in which it was situated were and are dependent on the tourist trade, a business plied most successfully.

Bala, a summer resort and one of Muskoka's tourist attractions, was once the site of a sawmill built by Thomas Burgess who came to the area in 1868. Among other pioneers in this vicinity were the Tobins, Norrises, Pensons, Stephensons, Giles, Stubbs and the Masseys.

Watt Township was named after James Watt of Greenock, Scotland, inventor of the steam engine. It is one of the best agricultural areas in Muskoka. The first settlement appears to have taken place in the Ufford area. The earliest permanent settlers were the Sheas, who arrived in 1861 or 1862. They were joined by the Bogarts, Morleys, Sufferns, Gotts and Pickerings. The first teacher in the area was H.W. Gill.

Watt and Cardwell townships were united in 1871 with Anthony Suffern as the first reeve of this municipal union. Seven years later Cardwell separated from Watt and became an independent municipality with Charles Robertson as reeve.

Windermere, named after the famous lake of that name in England, was one of the communities that developed in Watt Township. The earliest settlers at Windermere were Thomas Aitken, Francis Forge and David Fife. In 1924 Windermere was incorporated as a village with Henry Longhurst as its first reeve.

Thomas Aitken pioneered the tourist business in this region erecting Windermere House, one of the first tourist resorts in Muskoka. Mr. Fife, too, was in the resort business, erecting a large building which is still operated by members of his family. Mr. Forge became a successful farmer. A memorial window in the United Church has been installed in honour of these three men by the people of Windermere.

Raymond, Ullswater, Beatrice and Bent River are communities which were established early in the history of Watt Township. There was also a great deal of settlement along the Muskoka Road between Bracebridge and Parry Sound.

The Muskoka Lakes area is a thriving tourist region today, but it was no less popular as a resort in the days of the luxury steamers that plied its waters at the turn of the century.

George W. Boyer: *Early Days in Muskoka*, 1970.

MUSQUASH, geographic township, Algoma District
Position 48° 09′ 84° 43′

Formerly designated Township 29, Range 25, Musquash Township was part of the Algoma Central and Hudson Bay Railways land grant. It was named in 1974 after Peter Musquash, a Canadian army private from the Thunder Bay District, killed in 1945 in the second Word War.

INDEX